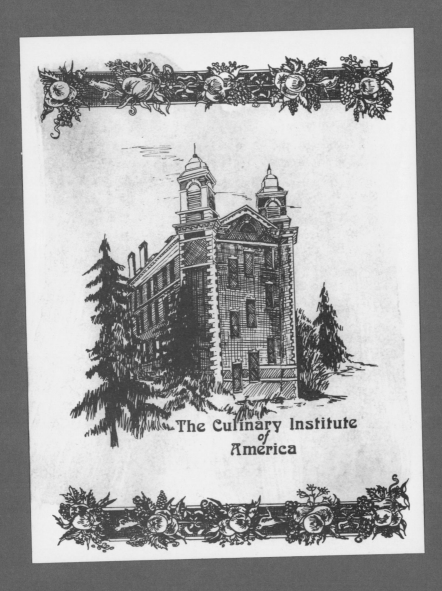

The Culinary Institute
of
America

The Professional Food Buyer

STANDARDS, PRINCIPLES, and PROCEDURES

M. C. Warfel

James Madison University, Harrisonburg, Virginia;
formerly a vice-president, Sheraton Corporation of America

AND

Frank H. Waskey

California State University, Chico

McCutchan Publishing Corporation

2526 Grove Street, Berkeley, California 94704

©1979 by McCutchan Publishing Corporation

Library of Congress Catalog Card Number: 75-46108
ISBN: 0-8211-2254-1

Printed in the United States of America

Cover design and illustration by
Terry Down, Griffin Graphics

Preface

Any person who makes a good living and at the same time derives pleasure and satisfaction from his job owes that profession something in return. Certainly, if trades, professions, and industries are to continue to progress, it is the responsibility of the members to contribute to the education, training, and direction of those who will assume responsibility in the future.

We are both educators. Our careers, though varied, do, when taken together, span sixty-five years in the purchasing area of the food service and hospitality industry. In spite of the many excellent publications in the field, we felt that no single work fully explained how the food market, the food buyer, and the industry interact. The industry being what it is—complex, often controversial and frustrating, sometimes employing questionable practices—problems arise primarily because there is a lack of understanding of the system itself. All of those involved, from board members, administrators, owners, general managers, food service managers, production managers, chefs, and controllers to those on every step of

the ladder, need to understand the whole as well as the parts that affect their work. From experience we know that many of the problems that arise in the industry result from lack of personal communication caused by limited knowledge of how the system works and limited experience in a system that often varies from week to week and is constantly changing.

In addition to its possible use as a textbook, we hope that this book will provide a better understanding of the problems of the food buyer within the larger context of the industry. However capable and honest the buyer may be, he needs the support of management and others in the industry to do his job well. What is contained in these pages may well profit others who participate in the industry if it provides a greater understanding of the problems the food purchaser faces.

Much is heard today about the "bottom line." In the food industry the bottom line is many things. It can be well-fed students and patients, happy employees, satisfied guests, healthy school students, minimum costs, budgets that are met. None of these goals can be reached, however, if the process does not begin well, and purchasing is frequently the first step.

We thank the many companies, organizations, and individuals that have helped us put together this textbook. We have tried to mention all of them in the Selected Bibliography, but it is necessary to make special mention of: Jack D. Ninemeier, Ph.D., owner, New Orleans Chart House and Toulouse Street Wharf, Madison, Wisconsin, and formerly Assistant Professor at the University of New Orleans; Myron W. Hedlin, Ph.D., San Francisco; and H. Kenneth Johnson, Mark W. Thomas, and Jayne Hager, National Live Stock and Meat Board, Chicago.

Finally, we express appreciation to John McCutchan, who made it possible for this book to be published, and to Rita Howe, the editor of the volume, who did an outstanding job in coordinating the project.

M. C. Warfel
Frank H. Waskey

Contents

Preface   v

1   *History and Traditions in Purchasing*   1
2   *The Food Market*   15
3   *Market Regulation*   33
4   *The Purchasing Department in the Food Service Industry*   47
5   *The Food Buyer and His Job*   59
6   *The Mechanics of Buying Food*   71
7   *Specifications and Testing*   105
8   *Receiving: A Hidden Hard Spot*   125
9   *The Storeroom: A Place to Make Money*   143
10   *Controls and Checklists*   167
11   *Common Market Practices: Ethical Considerations*   191
12   *The Face of Things to Come*   211
13   *Convenience Foods: An Alternative*   223
14   *The World's Food Supply: Today and Tomorrow*   241
15   *Food as Commodities: Sources of Information*   253

Appendix I   Guides to Purchasing Food   277

Table 1   Portion and Yield Factors for Meats, Poultry, Fish, and Shellfish   277
Table 2   Amounts of Foods for 50 Servings   281
Table 3   Summary of Federal Standards for Grading meats, Poultry, Fish and Shellfish, Eggs, Dairy Products, Fruits, and Vegetables   288
Table 4   Approximate Quantities Required for Some Common Fruits and Vegetables   293
Table 5   Egg Equivalency Table   297
Table 6   Milk Conversion Table   298
Table 7   Dipper Equivalency Table   298
Table 8   Common Container Sizes   299
Table 9   Food Servings per Container   300
Table 10   Substituting One Can Size for Another   304
Table 11   Guide to Cost per Serving for Canned Foods   305
Table 12   Food Serving Chart   307

Appendix II   Calcumetric: Anglo-Metric Converter   319
Appendix III   Canadian Food-Grading System   325
Selected Bibliography   333
Index   351

Exhibits

1-1 Bill of fare for a supper served at a ball held at a Boston hotel, 1865   10

2-1 Produce life cycle curve where skimming takes place   19

2-2 Flow of products through middlemen   28

3-1 Special stamp used for acceptance inspection by the United States Department of Agriculture   37

3-2 Inspection certificate of the United States Department of Agriculture, supplied to buyer upon request   38

3-3 Hypothetical crop harvesting curve for a representative seasonal commodity   39

3-4 Recommended daily allowances as they would appear on the label of a food can   45

4-1 Chart showing management responsibilities in the general organization plan often used in the food service industry   49

4-2 Chart showing an organization plan for the dietary department in a hospital   50

4-3 Chart showing an organization plan for a hotel   51

4-4 Chart showing an organization plan for the food and beverage department in a franchised motor inn   52

6-1 Form used to requisition food, items not listed   78

6-2 Form used to requisition food, items listed   79

6-3 Inventory and quotation list for fresh and refrigerated items   80

6-4 Examples of market reports   84

6-5 Form used by all state agencies in Florida to request bids, with name of agency appearing in the top, left corner   90

6-6 Form used to order merchandise   101

7-1 Butcher test card: (*a*) Front, uncooked item; (*b*) Back, cooked item   118

7-2 Score sheet for taste test   119

7-3 Table showing food purchasing and receiving specifications, by item   120

8-1 Examples of scales used in the receiving department   128

8-2 Form for receiving clerk's daily report   133

8-3 Form for beverage receiving clerk's daily report   134

8-4 Form for recording merchandise received   135

8-5 Form used for correcting an invoice   136

8-6 Form indicating goods received without an invoice   137

9-1 Sketched layout for refrigerated storage area   146

9-2 Various types of shelving for storage   147, 148

9-3 Pallets or dunnage racks used to keep stored items off the floor   150

9-4 Motorized vehicles for storeroom work   151

9-5 Three-deck hand truck for storeroom deliveries   152

9-6 Working out the formula for space requirements in a food service facility   154

9-7 Allocation of storage area in a food service facility   154

9-8 Perpetual inventory stock record   161

9-9 Typical storeroom requisition form   163

10-1 Pages from typical storeroom inventory books   170

10-2 Checklist for purchasing food and beverages   173

10-3 Checklist for inspecting food and beverages received   175

10-4 Checklist for issuing food and beverages stored   177

10-5 Checklist for securing food and beverages stored   179

10-6 Checklist used in establishing cost controls for food and beverages   181

10-7 Example of a report on food service sanitation   188

12-1 Typical Universal Product Code symbol (*a*), as used on a corrugated shipping carton (*b*), and on an invoice (*c*)   217

13-1 The location of sample food items on a raw-to-ready scale   225

13-2 Fiscal implications of convenience foods use on prime costs   233

13-3 Example of a cost analysis to determine whether to make or buy twelve pecan pies   235

13-4 Example of a cost analysis to determine whether to make spaghetti sauce or to buy and modify a prepared product   235

1 *History and Traditions in Purchasing*

THE EGYPTIANS

Innkeeping—that is, catering to the felt and real needs of people away from home—is both an art and a science as old as history itself. The first recorded instances of innkeeping, with the attendant food service catering, date back to ancient times. The Egyptians even raised altars to their god of gastronomy.

Egyptian inns of the day were generally small "mom and pop" operations, and most of the foods served were from the innkeeper's own gardens and flocks. The meals consisted mostly of dates, figs, apricots, grapes, bread, fish, chicken, duck, onions, red cabbage, and shat cake, and the cooking media were largely olive oil, milk, and wine. Poorer inns served predominantly "pulses," that is, soups, made from a base of lentils. It is curious that red cabbage seems to have been the most aristocratic of foods.

Items, such as fish, that were not raised on the premises were bartered for by the host, who traded with fishermen from the nearby Nile River or the Mediterranean. One can be sure that the inn-

keeper quickly learned that "food well bought is well sold." If he did not, he probably soon went broke.

Other items not normally produced on the premises, therefore purchased, were wines and beer. Wine from the famed grapes of Mareotis, pressed by local vintners, was served in upper-class homes and inns as early as 4500 B.C. Beer did not come into being until some fifteen hundred years later, and the beer of Pelusium seemed to be most popular. Around 3000 B.C. there was strict market regulation in the form of fees paid for inspection of breweries, on which depended permission to continue operation. These controls constitute the first recorded evidence of governmental intervention into food production and marketing, and they are the forerunner of many similar controls today.

When the Israelites left Egypt after more than four hundred years of bondage, they took many local customs into the desert with them. There are many biblical references to Hebrews and Israelites vacillating between the worship of God, mammon, and other deities, with

1

consequent turmoil over the eating of "unclean" and "clean" food. Little, unfortunately, is known about innkeeping in the promised land.

THE GREEKS

The next people who left written and pictorial records of eating, drinking, and sleeping away from home were the ancient Greeks, and the culinary world owes much of its knowledge to them. Almost all of the foods purchased and prepared today, as well as many types of beverages, both nonalcoholic and alcoholic, were used during middle and late Grecian times. The Greeks were the first to clarify wines, and the first to use amphorae, earthen wine jars later immortalized by the Romans. The oldest cookbook preserved today is that of Apicius, written sometime between 400 B.C. and 100 A.D., depending upon the historical source. This book, seemingly written by a Roman from Greek recipes, contains not only detailed instructions for preparing the cuisine of that day but also rigid specifications for purchasing food. Here, then, is the first recorded instance of purchasing for intended use.

The town of Sybaris was the seat of emerging classical Greek cuisine and, perhaps following the work of Apicius, many of the local chefs learned, prospered, and became famous. The art of cookery and its prerequisite, the purchasing of food, thence spread to Rome, Syracuse, Leucadia, Rhodes, Chios, and Athens through the accomplishments of Thimacedis, Arcusteatus, Philoxenus, Aegis, Nereus, and Charides. This is only a partial list of the many worldwide disciples of the great Apicius. Chefs of that day were negatively as well as positively motivated to learn the art of purchasing and preparing food. For instance, Galara usually began eating before dawn and demanded meals so expensive that many hungry families could have been fed for the price. At whatever hour of the day or night Galara wanted to eat, he was promptly served to his exact specification. If not, the chef in charge was summarily executed. The chefs and the whole kitchen retinue were slaves in every sense of the word. If, however, they could learn the art and practice it with great aplomb, even under threat of death, they were raised to high rank and held in great esteem.

The first indication of sexism in the culinary arts appeared in Greece. Page and Kingsford, in their definitive book, *The Master Chefs*, note: "Although the women were seldom allowed to cook, they were frequently employed to make sweetmeats. . . ." Men, again according to Page and Kingsford, acted as the purchasing agents: "the men slaves, apart from the cooks, worked as *buyers, fire stokers, waiters* and *wine waiters*" (emphasis added). All of these positions entailed apprenticeships, and a young boy might well become a practicing purchasing steward and cook after two years of hard training, as did the most famous of all Greek chefs, Cadmus, who served the King of Sidon.

Finally, the Greeks must be credited with developing the first comprehensive set of kitchen utensils and equipment. Many tools designed during the heyday of Grecian cuisine are still in use today, including the cauldron (cooking stockpot), frying pan, gridiron (broiler), colander, dripping pan, bain-marie, saucepan, sauté pan, cleaver, and butcher knife, as well as earthenware containers for storing cooking wines.

THE ROMANS

It was at about this time that the Romans sent a group of scholars to Greece to study literature and the arts, including the culinary arts. Not only did they study Grecian food purchasing and preparation techniques, but they also lured away many of the finest Greek chefs. In Rome these men were treated as professionals, worthy of the highest respect and esteem; they were not treated as slaves. In turn, they brought the best of the Greek culinary achievements to Rome and integrated them into the Roman culture.

It did not take long for the Romans to begin radically changing the cuisines of Greece and of all other countries they conquered. Rome learned from those she conquered, cross-fertilizing culinary concepts the world over in her role as world ruler. The Romans developed a passion for disguising both the form and the taste of food, and it appeared, at serving time, as masses of seasoned carbohydrates, proteins, and fats in as many forms as the purse would allow. The final product, liberally laced with a marinade, retained none of the individuality of the basic foods. Probably the most popular of the sauces was called garum. The principal ingredient was fish entrails, which were salted, fermented, and then pureed and to which were added spices and perhaps a dash of wine, vinegar, seawater, or other ingredients.

Why, then, were Roman chef-stewards such good buyers? It seems that only the soups and the main dishes were disguised in this manner. The Romans loved vegetables, either raw, in salads, or boiled, and fruits and nuts were highly prized— both local produce (apples, beans, figs, walnuts, almonds, and chestnuts) and imported delicacies (pomegranates and dates). Whatever one may think of the combination of sow's udder and garum as an entree, the Romans did develop excellent purchasing habits, whether in their inns or in the private homes of the wealthy. Page (Page and Kingsford, 1971) talks about a typical day in the home of a rich man as follows:

First thing in the morning, the slaves under the charge of the obsonator [the purchasing steward], went to the markets in Rome, which specialized in different kinds of food, at the Triqemagate, the Metasudante, the Suburdway, and the Sacred Way. The obsonator was required not only to recognize quality in food but also to know the personal likes and dislikes of his master and all of the guests to be entertained that day. When the goods arrived at the house they were examined for quality and they were stored in the larder under the supervision of the storekeeper [the structor].

Centuries passed, and, by the mid-sixteenth century, the tastes of the Romans and their cuisine had slowly evolved into the Italian cuisine that we know and enjoy in the Western world today. The dishes of southern Italy, as well as the wines of those regions, remain on the robust side, but, as one travels north, the cuisine becomes more subtle. Sauces become lighter, and the dry heat cooking medium changes from the ubiquitous olive oil to sweet, fresh butter.

Although the two main classical cuisines are considered unique to France and China (before Communism), French cuisine actually had its main roots planted firmly in northern Italian cuisine as described briefly above. And it is in the middle of the French heritage that we find another strong forerunner of the feminist tradition.

THE FRENCH

In October 1553 Catherine de' Medicis married a young Frenchman destined to become King Henry II. Although the bride was only fourteen years old at the time of the marriage, her appreciation of the finer things in life led her to insist upon bringing a whole battery of Florentine cooks with her. The slabs of meat served in medieval France were thus supplanted by more subtle fare. Her choices of delicately flavored foods matched her taste in the arts, and soon her court "was a veritable earthly paradise and a school for all the chivalry and flower of France. Ladies shone there like stars in the sky on a fine night." From Catherine's time to the present, dining etiquette in France has changed, but firm grounding in the principles of basic stewardship has preserved the principles of purchasing intact, as two illustrations spanning nearly three hundred years show.

Vatel, chef or maitre d' to King Louis XIV, is the first example. In 1671 Louis planned a round of festivals in honor of an impending visit by his cousin, Charles II. On the very night the monarch arrived, Vatel ran out of roasts for the table. He locked himself in his room, declaring that his bad stewardship had cost him his honor, and, as he said, "I cannot stand such an affront." Early the next morning he was walking in the garden when a fishmonger commissioned to deliver an order appeared. Vatel asked him if the relatively small amount of fish to be seen were all the vendor had brought, and the fishmonger answered in the affirmative. Not knowing that this was but one of several vendors who would be delivering that day, Vatel went back to his rooms, unsheathed his sword, placed the hilt against the door, and, on the third try, succeeded in running himself through, thereby in some small manner compensating for his lost honor. Although written accounts of Vatel's work indicate that he was a chef, rather than a maitre d'hôtel, French chefs have been trying to disown him ever since because of the lack of follow-through in his kitchen stewardship.

Phileas Gilbert (1852-1934), writing in *Larousse Gastronomique*, noted that Vatel "did not have the character of a cook, because he did not know how to make the best of a bad job. He could not rise above difficult circumstances." One might well take note that, had Vatel ordered properly in the case of the roasts, and, having delegated the authority for ordering the fish, had he checked with his subordinate regarding the quantity and quality ordered, he might have saved both his honor and his life, at least temporarily.

In the early 1960's, again in France, a well-known restaurant on Paris' Left Bank, which will remain anonymous, enjoyed the second highest rating (two stars) in the *Guide Michelin* and had done so for some time. When the founder of the restaurant retired, the quality of the food slipped ever so little—and *voilà!*—the two-star appellation was summarily rescinded. When the chef, who also did the buying, got the devastating news, he promptly shot himself.

THE ENGLISH

The student of cookery in England soon finds that the daily fare of poor, rich, and royalty alike was somewhat less elaborate than that of other Western European countries. A look at the "Fairfax inventories" of kitchen equipment and utensils in use during the seventeenth century indicates that contemporary requisite technologies were probably present for the purchasing and production of all known foods. The English, however, just seemed content with less elaborate fare—and perhaps a little more of it.

It was in the area of purchasing that the English excelled, which once more tends to point out that the type and amounts of food served have little to do with sound purchasing practices; all food purchasing requires the same precise care. The duties of the English purchasing steward, although they were much the same as those of contemporaries from other lands, were assigned to a functionary called the "butler," who acted as curator of the wine cellar, domestic steward, and storekeeper. It was his business to purchase, to the cook's specifications, all necessary items for the pantry and the kitchen. If the inn or lord's manor were in the suburbs or an even more remote area, the butler might have to go great distances in order to fill the chef's orders.

Feudal prototypes of today's purchasing steward had a much wider span of control than their present-day successors. This is primarily because transportation was difficult and lack of refrigeration greatly limited the ability to store foods.

MESSRS. SOYER AND ESCOFFIER

Although the eighteenth and nineteenth centuries are liberally sprinkled with the names of such famous chefs as Boulanger, Montagne, Gilbert, Nignon, Careme, Sailand, Point, Dumaine, Diat, Soyer, and Escoffier, only the last two have left much in the way of historical accounts that demonstrate their prowess in purchasing. Of Soyer's many culinary feats, his organization and maintenance of the purchasing and preparation of food for the hospital kitchens at Scutari and at Balaklava during the Crimean War in the late 1850's stand out as heroic. This work, which was monotonous, voluntary,

and nonremunerative and in which he worked hand in hand with Florence Nightingale, must be considered one of the great humanitarian endeavors of all time. Working under almost impossible field conditions, Soyer performed feats that, along with those of the "lady of the lamp," were credited with saving literally thousands of lives. It was the long hours and the poor conditions he endured at this time that eventually cost him his life.

Escoffier, the legendary "Chef of Kings and King of Chefs," is best known for introducing many different foods and methods for preparing them. He brought the white asparagus above the ground so that it would turn green and thereby be more palatable to the English, and he introduced frog's legs in that country, calling them "nymph's thighs at dawn." Escoffier also served in wartime, but as a conscripted mess sergeant. In times of stress and under fire, both of which are poor purchasing situations, he performed prodigious feats with whatever he could beg, borrow, or steal. Although he is better known for organizing the kitchen into straight-line and functional-flow patterns for optimum food production, he was equally adept in carrying out the purchasing function.

THE MELTING POT

In a country where the Puritan ethic had demanded an austere posture at the dinner table, people needed the Italians' unabashed Dionysian camaraderie to urge them on to the joyous realization that man ought to mind his belly very carefully and very studiously at least once a day.

Pellegrini (1971), in lyrical if somewhat chauvinistic prose, was speaking, of course, about the pleasures of the table enjoyed by those who live in the United

States, pleasures different from those of any other land on earth and yet much the same. The image of America as the melting pot of the world is reflected in the eclectic cuisine and the purchasing for it.

Until the 1880's, most of the people who came to the New World were from Northern and Western Europe. Thus, the basic cuisine and the purchasing for it stem from there. The British settled the Atlantic seaboard. The French, who inhabited the lower Mississippi River area and Louisiana, influenced Creole cooking, and, because of the trapping and trading capabilities of the French, their influence spread along the entire Missouri-Mississippi watershed, all the way to the headwaters. The Spanish influence is found in the Southwest, and Germans developed a Pennsylvania Dutch (*Deutsch*) cuisine and provided other influences. Scandinavians settled in the Northwest, and soon local denizens of the sea, the fields, the forest, and the air were being either purchased or raised and prepared to satisfy hearty appetites. And, in every part of America where the black man came to live, whether as a slave or as a free man, his influence was manifested in the food of that region. Much of what is called "southern" cooking today could more accurately be called "black," or, in even more contemporary language, "soul food."

Food Buying prior to 1825—Beginnings

In the early part of this country's history, traveling was done by horseback, coach, and often by foot on land and by coastal steamer, flatboat, and canoe on inland waterways. Travelers depended on the hospitality of residents of the countryside or on shooting their dinner, but, in case this failed, most, like the Indians, carried a supply of food. Jerky, pemmican,

parched corn, hoecake, and dried soup were certainly better than nothing.

Some renowned early travelers, such as John Bartram, a botanist employed by King George III, and Thomas Jefferson, testify to the inconvenience of travel in colonial times. There were taverns and inns throughout the country, but most of them were small, with modest dining and drinking facilities. Because they were social and political meeting places as well, travelers brought both news and rumors from distant parts of the colonies, and local residents depended on the inns for their "outside hustings."

Early taverns and inns depended primarily on their own and neighbors' gardens, and, in many instances, the innkeeper kept a few head of cattle, swine, and chickens to supply his table. Marketing during that period was largely restricted to the purchase of local products at the crossroads store, often using a barter system with whiskey as a popular exchange medium. Hard money, usually Spanish dollars, was scarce, and colonists were reluctant to part with it.

Then, as now, families consumed most of the food. The army, schools, jails, and travelers followed, in the order given. Practically all supplies of fresh meats, poultry, dairy products, fish, and fruits and vegetables, purchased either daily or when available, were consumed before spoilage.

Fresh food was stored in icehouses where ice, cut in winter, was stored in sawdust beneath the ground for use during hot weather. Some homes had their own icehouses, but fruits and vegetables were largely stored in root cellars. Meats were smoked or "put down in lard." The first meat packer in the United States was Captain John Pynchon of Springfield, Massachusetts. He is reported to have cured with salt and packed away pork, beef, veal, and venison as early as 1641. The French invented the process of canning about 1794, and the first successful canning business in the United States was established in 1820.

Because bartering was the primary means of exchange during this period, prices varied tremendously, but some records of price quotations have been kept. Passenger pigeons were six for 1 cent, but two whole three-quarter-inch nutmegs cost 35 cents in hard cash. Tea was 25 cents to 35 cents a pound, but mutton was $1.50 for twelve pounds, and a hindquarter of veal weighing twenty to twenty-five pounds could be had for $3.00. Porgies were 5 cents a pound, "pick them up yourself." Sweet potatoes were 5 cents for a half peck, and the cobbler potato, when available, averaged about a half cent a pound. Whiskey was about $1.00 a quart until inflation raised the price to $1.00 a pint, and for a long time this was one of the standards of exchange for supplies.

After the hard times that marked early colonial history, food became plentiful, and the quality was excellent. Exports to Europe became the biggest single source of revenue, and, in turn, as people became wealthier, the New World became a market for fine wines, whiskeys, and other potables from Europe—an important factor in the European economy.

A cookbook written by William Parks of Williamsburg, Virginia, in 1742, basically a revision of *The Compleat Housewife* published in England in 1727, listed the variety of foods available in the American colonies:

Fish—brill, carp, cod, crabs, crayfish, dace, eels, flounder, haddock, herring, lamprey, lobster, mussels, oysters, perch, pike, plaice, prawns, shrimps, skates, smelts, sole, sprat, sturgeons, tench, thornback, turbot, and whitings.

Meat—beef, lamb, mutton, pork, veal, and venison.

Poultry—capons, fowl, tame pigeons, pullets, rabbits, and turkeys.

Game—grouse, hares, partridges, pheasants, snipes, wild fowl, and woodcocks.

Vegetables—beets, broccoli, cabbage, carrots, celery, chervil, watercress, cucumbers, endive, lettuce, parsnips, potatoes, savoy cabbages, spinach, turnips, and herbs. For summer use: mushrooms, fresh peas, string beans, and just about everything available today.

Fruits—apples, grapes, medlars, nuts, oranges, pears, shaddocks (grapefruit), walnuts, preserves, dried fruits, raisins, French and Spanish plums, prunes, figs, and dates. For summer use: melons, nectarines, pineapples, plums, raspberries, strawberries, and, again, just about everything available today.

Although there is some question about the quality of some of the foods of those days, there was a great variety, and it was plentiful for those who had the means to procure it. But then, as now, many a meal consisted of mush and milk, corn bread and apple butter.

Food Buying, 1825 to 1900—Years of Change

People were on the move in this country, and the transportation system, consisting mostly of stagecoaches, river barges, and horses, proved inadequate. There were some horse-drawn railroad cars, but not until 1831 was a successful railroad operating. Production of food continued to soar, and clipper ships (later steamboats) sailed the seas, maintaining a favorable balance of trade and bringing back exotic foods from all over the world.

As mass production in Europe put thousands of people out of work, immigration to the United States began in earnest. In the 1880's new groups of people came to America, and, by the mid-1920's, over 14 million people had crossed the Atlantic from homes in South, Central, and Eastern Europe, bringing new methods for use in the "recruiting," selecting, and cooking of foodstuffs. Whether these peoples arrived at a time in history when people in general were more aware and more sophisticated is a matter of conjecture. Or perhaps it was an emerging Old World chauvinism that prompted these new Americans to cling more tenaciously to old customs and food habits than their predecessors did. Whatever the cause, Italians, Czechs, Poles, Ukrainians, Jews, Hungarians, Rumanians, Slovaks, Slovenes, Croats, and Serbs came and brought a new mélange of religions and cuisines. People came from Turkey, Prussia, Lithuania, Greece, Portugal, and Armenia; Basques came from the Pyrenees along the French-Spanish border. People, though relatively few in number, came from other Mediterranean countries, as well as from the Lowlands, Africa, and the East, including the South Pacific and various islands. Of the Eastern countries, China and Japan have certainly had the greatest influence on American cuisine, with India perhaps ranking next. Hawaii has also had a tremendous impact, particularly since the Second World War and since it has become a state.

Alaska, too, has been an influence, particularly in regard to seafood. Apart from the traditions of Old Mexico, the culinary impact of other South American countries has been small because of the relatively few immigrants, but these countries have, nonetheless, affected the eating and drinking habits of their northern neighbors. Chilean wines, for instance, are becoming highly respected the world over.

Each of these lands, as well as others not specifically mentioned, has influenced and is still influencing food buying, preparation, and service in the United States. In terms of food purchasing, it is fortunate that the many positive contributions have been made throughout recorded history. Even had this not been the case, however, it would still be worthwhile to study one's culinary heritage, for the many cuisines and customs create opportunities for the food buyer in terms of both variety and quality.

Some famous restaurants and hotels started in the early part of this period. Delmonico's restaurant was started in New York City in 1827, and the Tremont House, probably the first modern hotel in the United States, was opened in Boston in 1829. Each room had a key and was rented to an individual or a group of individuals who wanted their own room and privacy. Twenty rooms even had private baths.

Not until the period of prosperity following the Civil War, however, did the number of restaurants and hotels multiply to accommodate the increase in travel. By the late 1860's famous "watering places," such as the resorts at Saratoga Springs, New York, White Sulphur Springs, West Virginia, Newport, Rhode Island, and seacoast towns in New Jersey were popular. The Palmer House (Chicago), the Waldorf Astoria and the Astor (New York), the Palace (San Francisco), the

Ritz-Carlton (Boston), the Bellevue-Stratford (Philadelphia), the St. Charles (New Orleans), and the Willard (Washington, D.C.) were planned and built during these years. And, in addition to sumptuous hotels, there were the riverboats, the railroads, and restaurants. This was truly the time of the "deluxe restaurant."

To list all of the outstanding restaurants of the late 1800's would be an impossible task, but some are noteworthy: Rectors', the Knickerbocker Grill, and Delmonico's (New York); Antoine's and Brennan's (New Orleans); Bookbinder's (Philadelphia). The very mention of these names conjures up visions of delicious foods, as exemplified by the bill of fare for a supper served at a ball held in a Boston hotel in 1865 (see Exhibit 1-1). At these and other places like them, dining became a way of life. Nor should we forget the Poodle Dog, the Pup, and the Louvre (San Francisco), all of which had the indiscreet atmosphere of Playboy clubs today.

The supermarket also came into being during this period. George Huntington Hartford and his partner, George Gilman, started the Great American Tea Company in 1859. The original company dealt primarily in coffee and tea and a few spices. Ninety-five profitable stores in the East and the Midwest did not, however, satisfy the ambitious young Hartfords, who made it into the company it is today. By manufacturing some of their own products, they found they could sell items at a better profit than they would have made if they had bought them from others.

There were still charge accounts, store deliveries, orders, premiums, and credits, but around the turn of the century they hit upon an idea that blossomed into the modern supermarket. John Hartford gambled that people would pick up their own merchandise, carry it home, and pay cash for it if they could buy it cheaper. "Keep the volume large, the profit small, and the prices low" was his creed. He started the first store in Jersey City in 1912, and, within five years, there were over three thousand A&P stores in the United States.

Others tried to duplicate his success. This led to specialized buying of foods and the development of markets to satisfy the needs of the housewife, who was then, and is still, the biggest buyer of food supplies.

The importance of the army and the navy in the food business became increasingly evident during this period. A wave of prison reform also swept the country, and the proper feeding of "guests of the state," as prisoners were called then, became important. The institutional food business was expanded to include hospitals and schools, and some large manufacturing firms fed their employees a hot meal at noon when they found that this improved production.

In 1880 a more modern food supply and distribution system became possible with the introduction of the refrigerated railroad car. The brine system for making ice had been developed in 1851, and, with mechanical refrigeration, food supply houses could hold fresh foods. At about this same time ice refrigerators were introduced into the home.

Other inventions affected the food service industry. Alexander Graham Bell patented the telephone in 1876, and three years later Thomas Edison developed the carbon filament light. Both inventions, which facilitated travel and eating away from home, changed the whole mode of life throughout the world.

Dish of Lobster, cut up.

Tongue.
Ribs of Lamb.
Two Roast Fowls.
Mayonnaise of Salmon.

Veal-and-Ham Pie.

3 Compotes of Fruit. *3 Dishes of Small Pastry.* *3 English Pines.*

4 Blancmanges, to be placed down the table.

Charlotte Russe a la Vanille.

Lobster Salad.

Epergne, with Flowers.

Lobster Salad.

Savoy Cake.

4 Blancmanges, to be placed down the table.

3 Cheesecakes. *3 Fruit Tarts.* *20 Small Dishes of Various Summer Fruits.*

Pigeon Pie.

Mayonnaise of Trout.
Tongue, garnished.
Boiled Fowls and Bechamel Sauce.
Collared Eel.
Ham.
Raised Pie.
Two Roast Fowls.
Shoulder of Lamb, stuffed.
Mayonnaise of Salmon.

Dish of Lobster, cut up.

Dish of Lobster, cut up.

Larded Capon.

Epergne, with Flowers.

Boar's Head

Pigeon Pie.

Mayonnaise of Trout.
Tongue.
Boiled Fowls and Bechamel Sauce.
Raised Pie.
Ham, decorated.
Shoulder of Lamb, stuffed.
Two Roast Fowls.
Mayonnaise of Salmon.

Pigeon Pie.

Dish of Lobster, cut up.

Savoy Cake.

Lobster Salad.

Epergne, with Flowers.

Lobster Salad.

Dish of Lobster, cut up.

Char- lotte Russe a la Vanille.

Veal and Ham Pie.

4 Jellies, to be placed down the table.

3 Dishes of Small Pastry. *3 English Pines.*

4 Jellies, to be placed down the table. *3 Cheesecakes.* *20 Small Dishes of Various Summer Fruits.*

3 Fruit Tarts.

3 Compotes of Fruit.

Mayonnaise of Trout.
Tongue, garnished.
Boiled Fowls and Bechamel Sauce.
Mayonnaise of Trout.
Tongue, garnished.
Boiled Fowls and Bechamel Sauce.
Collared Eel.

Dish of Lobster, cut up.

Exhibit 1-1. Bill of fare for a supper served at a ball held at a Boston hotel, 1865

The development of mass transportation and mass food distribution increased the possibility of food poisoning epidemics and created a need for sanitary regulation by the government in order to protect the eating public. This need became so urgent that the Meat Inspection Act of June 30, 1906, initiated control of the care of perishable foods and canned goods in the United States (Chapter 3 traces government control over the food industry).

Food Buying since 1900—Period of Growth

If the 1800's was a period of change, the 1900's proved to be one of growth. The basic groundwork was completed by the late 1800's, and the last seventy-five years have witnessed specialization, expansion, and concentration of purchasing power in the food industry.

After 1922 the country's economy was good, and there was a spectacular growth in the number of large hotels and gourmet restaurants, stimulated by a rapid rise in the amount of traveling and in the number of travelers. More luxury liners were bound for Europe and the Orient. Buses were starting to carry thousands of people, and railroads added new, larger luxury trains to their schedules almost every month. The automobile industry was selling cars by the millions each year, and the road system was expanding as fast as money could be found to build the roads. A few hardy and venturesome souls were even tackling a new means of travel, the airplane, but there were still only a few nonpressurized airplanes that were cruising at about 150 miles an hour and had a total range of about 300 miles to 400 miles.

Universities were growing rapidly in both size and number. New hospitals were being built, and, of course, the needs of the army and the navy grew along with everything else. This period of expansion put tremendous pressure on the food industry both in the United States and elsewhere in the world.

Stockbreeders developed new crossbreeds of cattle, larger and better steers that needed less food. Mortality rates were cut because cattle, swine, and other meat animals had better care. The amount of milk per cow was increased by about 25 percent. New varieties of fruits and vegetables that were disease and insect resistant were developed through hybridization, and farmers soon found that it was possible to have almost a complete line of fresh fruits and vegetables delivered anywhere in the United States on a year-round basis.

Expansion slowed greatly during the Great Depression of the 1930's, but World War II came along about a decade later. The pressure on the food industry was greater than ever.

Packers had been freezing surplus supplies of meats and poultry since about 1915, when a good compressor was developed. In the late 1920's the U.S. Department of Agriculture was sponsoring experimental laboratories in a search for the best method of quick freezing tender fruits and vegetables and better ways to freeze meats and poultry. About 1932 a man named Birdseye introduced a line of frozen fresh vegetables that he had developed at a government experiment station in Geneva, New York. This process was quickly adopted by many other companies, and the race was on to see who would make the most money and be the biggest in the field. General Foods, the company that controlled the Birdseye patent and name, created the largest single line of frozen products yet available in the food industry.

In the middle 1930's trade papers of the food industry began reporting on the progress of companies experimenting with the preparation and freezing of certain entrees that could be used by merely reheating. This started what has been termed the biggest rip-off or breakthrough (depending on one's point of view) in the history of the food industry. Storms of protest, volumes of rhetoric, lawsuits and counterlawsuits, and increased government regulation followed. Convenience foods have, in the opinion of many, affected the general level of the quality of food in the United States and lowered the chef's profession in the eyes of many. Despite opposition, the frozen food industry has developed to a point where, at present, it is producing at least 25 percent of the food consumed in the United States today, and, regardless of the arguments over convenience foods, the institutional food service business in this country would be in a turmoil without them. Most of the frozen products and other convenience foods are consumed in average households and in institutions. As quality has improved, however, the better white-tablecloth restaurants have begun to use them.

The airline business expanded at a phenomenal rate during the second half of the twentieth century. At the same time, the railroad passenger business and steamship passenger business declined at an almost equally phenomenal rate. The net result, however, was that there were still more travelers. It was the demand for convenience foods by the airlines that provided an unprecedented stimulus for the convenience food industry.

Chain food operators were just getting started in the 1940's. After World War II, the tremendous progress that had been made in developing convenience foods caused this business to explode. Today, "fast foods" are a way of life.

As the size of the food business grew, the importance of the food buyer also grew. When the hotel and restaurant business was small in scale, food and supplies were generally purchased by the proprietor. As the operation grew, the proprietor no longer had time to take care of purchasing, and this responsibility fell to the chef, who acted as chef-steward.

The chef was absolute king of kitchen and commissary, not only buying all of the foods but purchasing wines, liquors, and other supplies as well. There were practically no quotations offered; cash was paid on a daily and weekly basis. With almost no accounting control of bills and payments, it was natural that some bad practices got started. With the advent of large, modern hotels, supermarkets, large military installations, large schools, and an ever-increasing prison population, the demand for a good cost control system led to the development of modern, computerized accounting systems.

As the need for constant supervision on the part of the chef in the kitchen increased, it became necessary to free him from the duties of steward. The duties of the steward included the purchasing of foods and liquor, but, about 1900, liquor purchasing was separated from the responsibilities of the steward in many operations. The wine steward's position became increasingly important in the industry. This arrangement continued until the advent of Prohibition in 1919, and it was during the period when stewards controlled procurement that questionable practices such as accepting kickbacks became common. Few people considered such practices to be outright thievery, and little was done to stop them.

Prohibition made it necessary for food departments in the hotel and restaurant business to start making a profit. The advent of food and beverage control greatly influenced the whole food procurement and distribution system, for control required daily quotations, competitive buying, specifications, independent receiving, independent inventories, perpetual inventories, testing, portion control, and complete internal control of all assets by an accounting department. Because food service operations had become large and cumbersome, someone was needed to coordinate the activities of the various departments and their supervisors on an hour-to-hour basis. The position of food and beverage manager or director evolved naturally.

About 1935, when the country was in the depths of the Great Depression, a basic organization for managing hotels, institutions, restaurants, and other public food services began to emerge. The positions of food and beverage manager, chef, kitchen steward, banquet manager, restaurant manager, food and beverage controller, and independent purchasing agent were established, and the responsibilities of each were outlined.

This organization and the division of responsibilities seemed also to adapt itself in the hospital field, where the food and beverage manager became known as the food service manager. Regardless of what business was involved, it seemed best to separate purchasing from day-to-day operations, making it an independent arm of management, usually under the control of the accounting department. This is the organizational pattern that is in common use today.

From meager beginnings, the food business in the United States has grown to colossal proportions. Approximately 300 million meals are eaten at home daily, while another 50 million are consumed elsewhere. There are no estimates of how many snacks, hot dogs, pizzas, or hamburgers are eaten by people "on the run." The raising of foodstuffs and the shipping, processing, selling, and consuming of food has become the largest and most important industry in the world.

Because billions of dollars are spent each year on food in the United States, large operators have learned that food buying is not just a matter of "making a phone call" and that millions of dollars are lost through inept purchasing. The demand for trained and competent food buyers has grown with the size of the industry. Good food buyers, like good dietitians, chefs, and food and beverage managers and controllers, are trained. That is the purpose of this book. A food buyer in upstate New York may not have much opportunity to buy jicama or tomatillos from the Mexican Southwest. The food buyer in Yuma, Arizona, may wait years before he has a request for bagels and blintzes. But in the mobile catering society of today, especially if the young food buyer is employed in an interstate chain operation, promotion often means a move across the continent. If the young food service-lodging worker restricts himself geographically, he automatically restricts himself to the limited opportunities in that area as well. It behooves all food buyers, as well as those who participate in the education and training of food buyers, to learn as much about every facet of their chosen specialty as possible.

2 *The Food Market*

CLASSIFICATION

The food buyer should be acquainted with available markets, most of which can be classified, first, by type of food sold. A second aspect that must be considered is the individual representing the market and determining the channels through which food must pass. Finally, the location of the marketplace is important.

Type of Food

The food market has been divided, historically, into the main areas of meats, fish and poultry, dairy products, fresh fruits and vegetables, groceries, and dry stores. Frozen foods and convenience lines have more recently come into their own as legitimate market divisions. The normal practice has been for buyers to select several different purveyors to fill various needs, but there have been efforts at the national level (John Sexton and Company and Foodco Corporation) and at the regional level (S. E. Rykoff and Company, with its home office in the southwestern part of the United States) to provide one-stop shopping for food service establishments. The capital outlay required to fund the plant, equipment, delivery systems, and inventories needed for such an extensive enterprise, as well as the need for specialized personnel to program, plan, budget, operate, and evaluate such an endeavor makes it prohibitive in most cases. There is also potential danger that quality will be uneven when a buyer consistently relies upon a single firm, or a group of related firms, for every buying need. One-stop buying as a means of purchasing is discussed again in Chapter 6. The so-called "free market" system is, in truth, a set of differentiated oligopolies that attempts to fill food needs under less than free market conditions. In professional football, defensive players attack the opposing quarterback not just to stop him, but to eliminate him from the competition. It is precisely this same tradition of fierce, clean competition working in the market place that should provide the best goods for the best prices consistent with need. Anytime a buyer relies on a single purveyor regularly, some element in the "carrot and stick" combination, which works in the buyer's favor even under a less-than-pure competitive system, is likely to be omitted, or some specification is less likely to be met. It should be recognized, however, that the increasing costs of transportation may force a reassessment of one-stop shopping. It may well be the coming thing, and so the buyer must be cognizant of an increased need for vigilance in the marketplace.

Individuals and Channels

Buyers can often choose whether they will buy directly from a producer, from a wholesale jobber who, in turn, buys from larger food brokers or wholesalers, or, in certain instances, from a salesman who represents a food manufacturer directly. At the end of this chapter, where marketing is examined "as a business enterprise," the roles of the individuals involved are described more fully.

Location

There are primary, secondary, and tertiary (or local) markets. The primary ones exist in areas surrounded by a good transportation network that is used to deliver the vast quantities of goods sold there, and the commodities are usually either extracted or produced in the locale of the primary market. The Boston fish market and the Chicago grain market, examples of primary markets, have survived the many changes that have occurred within the transportation network since World War II. Wherever such markets still exist, all subordinate levels in the marketing structure are affected. Buyers should learn to utilize information concerning activities at the various levels, for such activities govern the availability and the price of commodities purchased at the local level. The U.S. Department of Agriculture (USDA) publishes many *Agricultural Marketing Reports* at both the primary and secondary levels. These reports, available upon request, are use-

ful sources of information that can help an establishment make decisions in areas of precost and precontrol. For example, a purchasing agent for a chain hotel in Fresno, California, can read the market reports for poultry and eggs published by the USDA Agricultural Marketing Service in Los Angeles and, by adding standard markups and transportation costs, can accurately predict what these items should cost in Fresno the next day. Another buyer in another hotel within the same chain but hundreds of miles away in the Scottsdale-Phoenix area can also add on standard charges, allow another day of lead time, and be as well informed as his colleague across the Colorado River. If the price of eggs differs by as much as a penny per dozen, these buyers have enough information to question local egg and poultry purveyors.

Secondary markets traditionally received goods from the primary markets and distributed them to local markets. Since few of the original primary markets have survived, the functions of secondary markets are changing. Beef used to be brought to the stockyards in Chicago as "feeder stock." Now the feeders' agents purchase mainly in the lowland country during the winter season and in the high, cool country during the summer season, and cattle are shipped directly to feedlots in what were once secondary markets in Phoenix, Kansas City, Omaha, and other cities. Such changes often favor the buyer and his consuming guests in that they eliminate one or all of the middlemen, all of whom must take a legitimate markup on goods passing through their hands. Other forces for change are also at work.

Supermarkets have had much to do with the changing market structure. The supermarket has been glorified, not because it is the only possible method of merchandising certain types of goods to the ultimate consumer, but because direct purchasing works so well. Growers and packers can easily service them, packaging foods in ultimate consumer-type sales units. Because supermarkets buy more goods than food service establishments, they influence packaging. For example, it is difficult to buy hundred-pound sacks of carrots anymore because most carrots are packaged in small plastic bags for sale to supermarkets. Food service personnel are forced, on occasion, to use company time and payroll dollars to remove useless, costly plastic bags that were not needed in the first place. Most chains and their co-op rivals have, through direct purchasing, helped revolutionize these and many other aspects of the traditional marketing picture.

Large chains in the hospitality industry, likewise, spend enough in the marketplace to make direct buying not only feasible but mandatory on a cost-effectiveness basis. One such chain had a combined volume of between $60 million and $70 million in revenue in 1960. At that volume of business, which is not large by modern standards, the meat-purchasing agent of the chain was buying hams directly from the Hormel curing plant in Chicago in carload lots. As reported in *Institutions 400*, this same chain increased its volume by more than a thousand percent by 1973, and just one year earlier the same magazine reported the first billion-dollar hospitality area corporation. It is obvious that the top four hundred corporations covered in the magazine, because they do a large percentage of the total volume of food service-lodging business today, alter the patterns of the marketplace.

Also, individual hospitality businesses have consolidated their efforts over the past two decades. The referral system was set up to fight the chains. It seems that individual motels were unable to com-

pete successfully for reservation business with, say, the Sheraton Corporation, where one hotel referred departing guests to another hotel in the same chain. As a result, referral systems, such as Best Western, were set up. After such systems had been in use for a time, it became apparent that there were other benefits to be gained from consolidation. In order for a referral system to work, there has to be some control over quality and ways to inform guests what they might expect from each of the establishments in the system. This information could be supplied and kept up to date only through the use of computers. The most time-consuming part of any computerized system is the input-output phase, and so there is free time when machines can be used to perform a prodigious amount of routine arithmetical work ("massage" data) for individual members of the system. Machines perform such tasks more rapidly and efficiently than they could ever have been done before, and they are the same machines already being used to maintain the referral system. By processing data from individual units through a centralized system, centralized purchasing and advertising plans could be developed and savings could be realized. Individual operators found themselves in a position to make direct purchases, thereby having their own effect on the market.

FUNCTIONS

After determining the kinds of markets that are available, the buyer should learn what is done there. Four functions—exchange, information, physical supply, and general business—are generally performed.

Exchange

As the term implies, exchange has to

do with the actual workings of the market-place. Transfer of ownership, which requires buying and selling, merchandising, commodity pricing, and sales effort, is the most obvious accomplishment. The role of sales in moving specific products from the warehouse to the receiving dock is growing in importance, according to Kenneth Runyon. He argues that, on the basis of the total marketing concept, "the agency is in a position to make a major contribution—to provide the touch of magic that spells the difference between product success or failure, and, for him, 'the touch of magic' depends on 'product positioning,' that is, 'the creation and implementation of a selling concept that will be appealing to consumers'" (Mc-Laughlin and Mallowe, 1971:262).

It is the sales force that continuously endeavors to promote one product over all others, and knowledge of the positive effects of various sales efforts allows the buyer to negotiate for price according to his specifications, as well as for delivery times that best fill his needs. The last considerations in the function of exchange are delivery, inspection, and either acceptance or rejection of the product. And, last though they may be, they are as important as the purchase.

Information

The USDA Agricultural Marketing Service fills an information need as well as aiding in the exchange of goods. The buyer, the seller, and all intermediaries need to know the who, what, when, where, and why of the marketplace: What commodities are in or out of season? What is the price of a commodity in relation to possible substitutes? Are there any substitutes available? What are the price trends, if any, or is the market fairly static? Are new innovations imminent? Which firms are testing the new products? How can one avoid paying an exorbitant price for a new product?

Competitive firms rely on the information function to carry on successful "industrial espionage" activities. Once a new food product has been discovered in a competitor's laboratories, it takes most major food corporations less than twenty-four hours to run quantitive and qualitative analyses on the product and duplicate it. *Dun's* magazine mentioned several cases of industrial espionage. One case in particular seems germane to this discussion:

A short time ago, Lever Brothers Co. came up with what it thought was a marketing coup. After spending a great deal of time and money on research and development, the company developed a new table syrup called "Mrs. Butterworth's," which featured the addition of butter. Smacking its lips over an anticipated major breakthrough, Lever Brothers put the product on the test market. Result: "Mrs. Butterworth's" caught the eye of a major rival and by the time Lever Brothers was ready to go national, so was the competitor.

Dun's concluded that:

Lurking in the path of the test market are all the booby traps that ingenious rivals can rig up. "It is," says one insider, "the most dangerous game in marketing" (reprinted in McLaughlin and Mallowe, 1971:255, 256).

Test marketing may be dangerous, but it is necessary. Without such tests, many products would have to enter the national market without sufficient knowledge of the product's market potential (see Exhibit 2-1). Whereas an unsuccessful test-marketing effort might cost $1 million or $2 million, an unsuccessful national sales effort might cost a minimum of $10 million. The risk is that another company may, through industrial espionage, steal a product before the firm that developed it has had a chance to recover the research and development costs, a process known as "skimming" (as cream from new milk). If one firm's tests enable it to go national ahead of other firms, they can ask, and usually get, an exorbitant price for the new product, at least during the exponential growth phase.

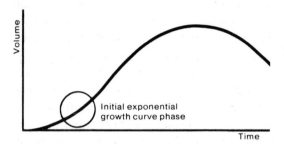

Exhibit 2-1. Produce life cycle curve where skimming takes place

An astute buyer, in a case like that of Mrs. Butterworth's syrup, may decide to wait a while before buying. If he has been correctly reading the market, he knows that two or more companies are rushing to introduce a similar product, and it is less expensive to buy a nonexclusive product.

Many buyers do not take advantage of legitimate information available through those from whom they buy. They think, incorrectly, that all information flowing from the seller is "trade puffing." The advertising media are, it is true, replete with windy phrases and filled with descriptive adjectives. As Ernest Dichter puts it, man is thought to be "in the eyes of the organization man . . . socially secure, adventurous, conservative, timid, a hypochondriac, gadget-minded, or as fitting one of the numerous other profile descriptions."

Dichter further argues that American man is in the process of changing his buying pattern from one where he sets

out "to keep up with the Jones's" to one where he decides to keep up with his own needs:

Instead of saying that thousands of people are buying a particular product, the advertiser may want to stress the uniqueness of his product and the satisfaction which his particular brand provides. [Advertising] displays of the future will be arranged *not* on the basis of technological classifications, but more along psychological lines [emphasis added; McLaughlin and Mallowe, 1971:289, 290, 291].

Dichter and the advertising men he is talking about are concerned, however, with appealing to the *ultimate consumer*—the homemaker and those for whom the homemaker buys. To differentiate between such supposedly gullible buyers and those who buy food and other goods and services for industries, the trade buyer is called the *industrial consumer*. Industrial consumers should train themselves to think logically. They must be able to tell the difference between trade puffing—or, even worse, misleading information—and legitimate advertising. Legitimate advertising can help the buyer.

Advertising a substandard product may actually serve to shorten a product's life by acquainting more buyers with it in a shorter time span, thereby increasing initial sales. Subsequent word-of-mouth advertising kills the product in the marketplace. Even though the sellers receive their just dues sooner than would otherwise have been the case, this practice is illegitimate and should be condemned. It is fortunate that most of those selling to industrial consumers realize that, in the long run, honesty is the only sure measure for success.

The many trade associations formed in the food field serve the buyer through their efforts to upgrade products and practices within their respective fields. This effort goes beyond their major function, which is to secure exposure for their products—exposure that helps the buyer in his continuous search for products. The terms "U.S. Choice Grade" and "Swift's Premium" immediately bring a set of standards to the mind of the experienced buyer. "Swift's Premium," "Armour Star," "Rath Blackhawk," and similar labels appearing on meats might more accurately be called "brand names," and the desire to protect this "packer grade" or brand name causes firms to patrol their own products carefully. Firms endeavoring to finance purchases find that trade acceptances, loans, purchase contracts, and other means of acquiring capital can be more readily obtained by virtue of the extra security accruing to food that bears a recognized grade.

Descriptive labeling is another source of information when it accurately describes the contents of the package. Federal regulations do not usually apply to products that are not a part of interstate commerce. But they do apply in the case of food packaged in closed containers. Whether or not canners and other packaging firms are sure that their products will eventually cross a state line, most of them still follow government regulations. Almost all of the labeled foodstuffs in closed containers packaged in this country meet federal regulations, which means that the buyer can believe what he reads on the label. Here again, however, the buyer must know the parameters of the law. There is nothing illegal in printing "of the highest quality" on a can of peas. This merely means that the appellation, as such, conforms to some person's idea of "highest quality," whether that person is a genius or a simpleton. If, however, the label reads "fancy," the buyer can assume that the contents meet the requirements of the federal grade "U.S. Fancy."

If they do not, the buyer can take action against the can labeler. The term "can labeler" is used advisedly; the canner may or may not be the person applying the label.

In the Nushagak Bay salmon cannery area in Alaska many companies are or have been engaged in salmon canning. Only one (Libby, McNeill, and Libby) consistently added its own label, which was applied at the Clark's Point Cannery. The salmon was then loaded onto a Libby steamer at anchor in the bay, and, at the end of the canning season, the ship carried the salmon to a stateside Libby warehouse. Libby's growth was so phenomenal that the company could afford its own marketing system by the early part of the twentieth century, which meant that their marketing strategy would move the salmon through the system to ultimate and industrial consumers using the product. Salmon was just one of the many foods packed and marketed by Libby. By the 1920's "Libby's" had become a household word. The other canners were in the business of canning only. Their salmon was cased without labels and shipped, via Alaska Steamship Lines, to Seattle and sold to various food companies that then placed their own brand labels upon the can.

The Stokely-Van Camp Corporation cannery in Oroville, California, has a similar history. Among the several things canned there in the proper season are cling peaches. Within a radius of twenty miles of the cannery there are several hundred thousand acres of peach groves, and all of the peaches "come ripe" within a few short weeks. Because the stones "cling" to the flesh of the peaches, as well as for other technical reasons, they are not used in their fresh form, and all must be canned. The Oroville plant, as well as similar canneries up and down the Sacramento Valley, is on twenty-four-hour duty until the last peach has been processed. If a person walks into the Oroville plant at any time during the peak period, he can observe USDA inspectors, there by invitation, and a dozen or more private inspectors on the premises at any one time. Each private inspector is there as the paid representative of one or more of several companies who sell canned peaches, and he selects the peaches for each of his company's brands (private labels). It is, therefore, entirely possible that a canned goods distributor might have on hand assorted brands of yellow cling peaches, all canned by Stokely's. The packages may look different, but, besides having been canned by the same cannery, it is possible that the peaches were picked by the same men (or a mechanical picker) from the same orchard, perhaps even from the same tree. The parameters of information available to the buyer in such cases are the minimum assurances made possible through continuous federal inspection and grading, the expertise of the brand name inspector, and the integrity of both the inspectors and the corporation owning the brand—no more and no less.

If a food service establishment has the kind of business that warrants the level of food cost involved, consistent quality can be maintained by buying according to brand, descriptive label, and federal grade, each of which costs money. As with food cost control in the restaurant proper, each control applied to a commodity before it reaches the receiving platform is costly. The cannery must pay for continuous inspection by federal inspectors in order to meet interstate commerce and federal grading qualifications, and the company that puts its label on the can must

pay dearly to maintain a high level of expertise and integrity among its inspectors. These expenses are passed along to the consumer, for the seller would not pay to maintain high standards if the buyer did not demand them.

Many restaurateurs automatically think "low" when standards are mentioned, but this is not necessarily so. Standards can be set anywhere on an ordinal scale. In terms of a successful food service operation, standards of quality are initially determined during the first feasibility study, and they are set at necessary and sufficient levels to meet expectations identified during formative stages of the operation. Once standards are set and conformity has been rigorously and consistently enforced, they become habit, needing only intermittent supervision. Of course, this "habit" implies work practices that, for consistently high cost-effectiveness food purchasing, reflect specifications for purchase determined by the needs of the menu and are continuously followed by those who order and receive the food.

Supply

Supply deals with physically moving food through the market, from either extraction or production to the industrial or ultimate consumer. Innovations in techniques of *transportation*, such as piggyback hauling of truck trailers on railway flatcars and other forms of packing and shipping, have improved performance. Recent advances in cooling and refrigeration techniques have made it possible to increase market offerings, and faster transportation schedules have opened distant markets, far from the growing source. The war against perishability is constantly being fought. It is interesting to note how much of this new, highly profitable transportation business has been lost for all time by the railroads. Theodore Levitt shows how the "marketing myopia" of the railroads worked against the innovative and visionary thought that would have altered this outcome. Levitt contends that, from the beginnings of the railroad, the so-called leaders of the industry knew that they were in the railroad business. If they had not been so shortsighted, they would have realized that they were in the transportation business, which would have allowed them to expand their holdings to include trucking and air passenger-air freight methods as they evolved. The present condition of the railroads might have been much healthier had they been able to capitalize on their hindsight.

There is another situation that tends to illustrate what clear, unimpeded marketing vision can do. Some thirty years ago, both Continental and American Can Companies made nothing but cans. Apparently they both had either prescient leadership or long-range innovative technologists working toward new ways of increasing their market shares in the field. Whatever the source, they developed an outlook that allowed for expansion and change. They never felt that they were just in the can business. Instead, they thought of themselves as being in the packaging business, which allowed them to invent different packing materials, such as new kinds of cardboard, high molecular weight hydrocarbon polymers, urethane foams with various packing specificities, and so on. These new materials increased storage and shelf life, made handling easier, shortened freezing time, made possible lower or higher container temperatures, and did much more. All aided the supply function in one way or another, and, consequently, brought these two corporations much "found money."

Although the yellow cling peaches mentioned earlier are all canned within a few weeks, they must be stored and distributed to the market in an even flow throughout the entire year. If the flow is erratic, then the price of canned peaches also fluctuates, often bearing little relation to the true value of the aggregate crop. Many commodities must be stored for varying lengths of time, and storage costs money, which makes *storage* another important part of the supply function.

Bourbon whiskeys provide what must be almost a classic example of a costly storage situation. To bear the "bottled in bond" appellation on a green strip stamp, the whiskey must be 100 proof, it must have been distilled in one year by one distillery, it must be stored in wooden barrels for at least four years, and the owner may only enter the warehouse under the supervision of federal officials, who keep the keys. The owner cannot remove any of the spirits without official permission (records are kept by the federal agent in charge on all who enter the storage area and on all movements of spirits). Finally, the whiskey must be bottled under federal supervision.

A second type of bond used for security and finance purposes is a fidelity bond. It is intended to ensure the honesty of employees and officers of various corporations having access to the warehouse as a means of ensuring the integrity of the commodities stored therein. The threat of almost inevitable apprehension through the tenacity of detectives employed by a bonding company and the broad jurisdiction allowed them, as well as the threat to an employee's career if he is declared unbondable, reduces the chance of theft from a bonded warehouse and makes the contents of a bonded warehouse easier to finance. All such bonding activities cost money, and these costs are passed on to the buyer.

As there have been innovations in transportation systems, there have been equally beneficial advances in storage. One of the older innovations is that of altering the conditions within the storage area. One example is the addition of ethylene gas or partially oxidized kerosene to warm, humid air and introducing it into citrus fruit storage areas to remove "greening" that occurs in various varieties. The green color has no effect on either the caloric or the nutritive value of the fruit, but it interferes with the mental set of the buying public and, thereby, its willingness to buy.

In a similar vein, air can be exhausted from the chilled space used to store eggs, and carbon dioxide gas can be added to replace it, thereby lengthening the time eggs in storage will hold their initially applied grade. This method seems much better than older ones where eggs were flash heated or oiled. The principle is fairly simple. As eggs age, the pH goes up, primarily because a chemical breakdown "throws off" carbon dioxide gas. The carbon dioxide is normally respired through the shell into the surrounding area. By replacing air in the storage room with carbon dioxide, levels inside and outside the shell are equalized, which slows the degenerative reaction.

Such practices are generally regarded as being completely harmless, both to the food and to those who eat it, but opposition is growing. Since Rachel Carson's *The Silent Spring* was published and since Naderism has become a word in the consumer's vocabulary, much unwarranted criticism has been directed toward food production and storage practices. Scientists who have dedicated their lives to enhancing the well-being of man, as well as those who apply scientific

findings, are coming under increasing attack from laymen. The conflict that has invaded the marketplace has grown in volume and intensity to the point of swaying the U.S. Congress. Much of the legislation that reform groups have succeeded in introducing before Congress has either been passed or is under study by congressional committees. Far from enhancing the commonweal, the stated evangelical goal, such measures inhibit forces engaged in the life-and-death struggle to produce adequate food for the human race. As Edward Gross, a sociologist, puts it, a group lobbying for such things as "organic" or "natural" foods, ecological integrity, or some other initially legitimate goal may eventually begin to "claim for itself a mandate to tell society what is good for it." Because of such Darwinistic changes in societal awareness, the professional in every facet of the hospitality business must be alert to the attendant problems and must seize every opportunity to combat the more irrational attitudes. It goes without saying that such "combat" should be in the form of honest public relations.

Another change affecting the storage function is that an increasing share of the fresh fruit and vegetable crops are being frozen or held in cold storage. "Cold storage" by definition occurs when these foods are held at temperatures between 30° and 45°F. for thirty days or more. Companies that freeze and pack such foods as peas have greatly speeded up the process. It is not uncommon to see such commodities as peas arrive at the packing shed already sized, graded, washed, blanched, and partially frozen. This means that "fresh frozen" fruits and vegetables may actually be "fresher" than some of those sold in their "fresh" state. And the color fixation caused by flash heating when blanching foods that are about to be frozen (to kill heat-specific enzymes, as well as other microbial hitchhikers) provides the restaurateur with an attractive product.

A few areas, such as the Imperial Valley in southeastern California, south central Arizona, and the growing areas of Old Mexico, raise the market several greengrocer crops per year. The norm, however, is still one crop per year. Whatever the status of local laws on the storage time allowable for cold storage and frozen products, the buyer should be aware that the maximum time food may be held by a commercial storage facility is also one year. Storage spaces must be emptied to receive the new year's crop.

Knowledge of this practice and of the approximate harvest times of the various crops forewarns a buyer against seemingly "windfall" prices offered by salesmen, whether in thousand-case or one-case lots. If he is offered fresh frozen peas at a drastically lowered price in mid-June, he can be assured that he is being offered last year's crop, possible "freezer burn" and all.

This is not to imply that such a sale should never be accepted. If a new banquet has been booked with an "open menu," if the supplier guarantees delivery of the entire amount of food "subject to approval" on the loading dock, and if the available discounted food meets the menu requirements of color, flavor, and texture contrasts, it may be a good buy. The yardsticks applied before taking advantage of any such deal should be stringent. Buying any product just because the price is "right" (meaning significantly lower than normal) is bad business.

A restaurant is not a warehouse. Food service establishments usually have a very high facility cost per square foot. It is un-

realistic to tie up any more expensive square footage for storage than is necessary for day-to-day operations, given the constraints of volume and availability of deliveries. When the now defunct Forum of the Twelve Caesars in New York City was being designed in the mid-1950's, it was one of the first ultraluxurious operations to open in brand-new facilities. The corporation had to plan to seat the maximum number of guests at one time in order to make the project feasible. Because of this need, because of the volume of business that provided "buying clout," and because of the restaurant's prime location in Manhattan, where deliveries could be made several times per day, the smallest proportion of total square and cubic footage in the history of innkeeping was allotted to storage. In fact, the only dry storage area of any size was on top of the special oven designed to roast chickens baked in clay at 750°, one of the main entrées.

General Business

Business functions have to do with *money* as a means of exchange. In the marketplace, when goods change hands, money or the promise of money also flows from buyer to seller, and the exchange takes into account the cost of doing business, which involves credit, interest, insurance, taxes, and foreign exchange differentials. To compete in the marketplace for the money needed to do business, a food service establishment must maximize its operation in every way possible. If storage space costs money, food held in inventory in storage spaces costs even more. A chalet restaurant in either Vail or Purgatory, Colorado, may need storage space to allow for an immobilizing blizzard. Real estate is not nearly so expensive there as it was at the Forum, and the extra food must be considered part of the business' operating expenses and must, therefore, be reflected in the menu-pricing structure. Food inventories cost money through initial purchase price, waste, interest and other carrying charges, depreciation, occupation of space, spoilage, possible vermin infestation, and other factors. Excess inventories cost more—prohibitively more. According to most experts in the field, the overall inventory turnover rate, the hypothetical rate at which all the food in the house is consumed and replaced, should be somewhere in the neighborhood of thirty-six times per year. This turnover is "mixed out," which means that the dollar amount and the ratio to the total cost are figured in each of the food categories (meats, poultry and eggs, fish, dairy products, fruits and vegetables, groceries, and dry stores). An arithmetical mean or average is struck for the accounting period, and the average yearly turnover is extrapolated from these figures. In the case of the Forum, the produce probably turned over more than 300 times per year; restaurants in more remote locations (and, indeed, all locations during fuel crises such as those experienced during the winter of 1973-74) may have a lower turnover rate. Meats are often received on Monday, Wednesday, or Friday, for a turnover rate of about 165 times per year. Bread and dairy products, normally sold on a "cash truck" basis, are delivered daily or even more often.

If an establishment enjoys good *credit*, and, indeed, few survive that do not, the usual method of purchasing food at wholesale is to buy on credit from the first of the current month and for the entire month, and pay by the tenth of the follow-

ing month, thereby taking advantage of any discount if one is offered by the seller. An invoice used in such a buying arrangement usually bears a notation similar to: "2/10; N/30, meaning 2% discount, if postmarked and paid by the 10th of the following month—but net due by the 30th at the latest." It is not unusual to hear a buyer who is not well informed say that one might as well buy a certain quantity in order to take advantage of discount savings as a credit to food cost. There are no savings in discounts. The discounted price is the lowest price the seller can legitimately offer. This point may seem to be rather technical at first glance; it gains relevance if one considers the philosophy of the wholesale grocery trade. Wholesalers, as sellers to wholesale accounts, owe those accounts service during the month. According to the "going concern" concept, the wholesaler assumes that the buyer will continue to operate his business for an indefinite time, that is, liquidation of the firm is not anticipated in the future. Deliveries made to the buyer during the month are, therefore, part of an overall monthly order represented by a monthly statement compiled and sent out on the first of the following month or shortly thereafter. The buyer is given a reasonable time to price, extend, cross-foot, and balance individual invoices representing individual receipt of goods and to reconcile the total of all invoices with totals on the monthly statement. Traditionally, these accounting measures can be finished by both parties, following commonly accepted methods of accounting, by the tenth, and so that is the day on which the money for the prior month's goods is due and payable. Although the 2/10; N/30 notation on invoices is becoming a thing of the past (most discounts for prompt payment are now negotiated on an individual basis), the main ideas mentioned above still apply and probably will continue to apply in the forseeable future.

The grocery purveyor, too, has to meet his bills. If he handles produce, he may have to pay for it every ten days, regardless of his excellent credit position, while receiving payment from his customers only once per month. And so the grocer incurs expenses in following the tradition of payment the following month, whether he gives a discount or not. If the buyer does pay by the tenth of the month and takes an offered discount, he is availing himself of the lowest price offered by the seller because, in the selling and the collecting, minimum expenses have been incurred. Customers who do not meet the discount date and pay the full fee are actually paying a penalty to cover the additional expense incurred through delinquency. Wholesale grocers who have been in business for some time can almost always predict credit problems, and often the eventual demise of a food service establishment, by whether or not the firm takes advantage of discounts offered. Some negotiated discounts may run as high as 5 percent. In a business where the manufacturing cost of food sold is generally hovering at or above 40 percent in a tight market, a savings of 2 percent to 5 percent, or even less, on part of a 40 percent cost can be crucial. The restaurateur who is not taking advantage of discounts is probably also discounting his own accounts receivable (for instance, the unpaid bill for a large banquet) at the bank to meet his payroll. These and similar desperate measures usually sound the death knell for a food service establishment.

A buyer should always remember that his legitimate purveyors are competing as cleanly as possible for his business by rendering optimum service at the optimum price. The buyer, in turn, must be honest and fair with the seller.

INDIVIDUAL FUNCTIONARIES FROM EXTRACTION TO CONSUMPTION

Various persons or positions involved with the food market have been mentioned in passing. Now each position will be examined more carefully.

According to Kotchevar (1961):

Producers are those who create form and substance in a commodity. They may be a canner, a meat packer or a miller. A cook who takes foods and makes a meal is a producer. Similarly, the farmer, the fisherman or the cattle raiser is a producer. A produce house that purchases spinach in bulk, stems, washes and packages it is functioning as a producer.

The term "extractive" relates to those who collect or husband the raw materials that form the first part of the food chain as it relates to the marketplace. It connotes the physical removal or extraction of the food from its original matrix—fish from the sea, carrots from the ground, and so on. If we allude to the first part of the food chain in this way, it is necessary to add a further delimiting statement for reasons of accuracy. It seems that, by the time the crew of the tuna clipper "horses" a "three-pole tuna" on board, its weight of perhaps three-hundred pounds represents a part of the food chain that started with some small denizens of the deep that matured on a diet of microscopic organisms. The three hundred pounds of tuna represent possibly several thousand pounds of protein consumed by fish of ascending sizes, of which the tuna is the last in line. Because of the ever-increasing population of the earth and the proportionately decreasing amount of resources available to supply food and other forms of energy, today's food buyer should have at least a rudimentary grounding in ecology so that he can understand, appreciate, and perform in accord with his responsibility to society. The world is not the never-ending source of supply it was once thought to be. On the other hand, the industrial consumer who buys raw-to-ready food for preparation or service has an obligation to maximize potential contributions to the overhead and profit of the food service facility. This means, among other things, that a buyer should understand the problems and functions of both individuals and institutions in the marketplace that stand between tuna and table. Those in the chain between production and consumption do not add anything to the physical properties of the commodities that they buy and sell. There is no change in form or substance. Economists hold that such middlemen contribute to the food chain only what has been called "the creation of time and place utility" within the commodity. "Utility," as a Malthusian term, is less than two hundred years old. For the food buyer, time and place utility might be explained as follows: if the purchasing agent had to go to the source of supply to buy commodities at the time they were needed to conform to menu needs, he would spend all his time running around. Even in the jet age he could not begin to collect the various items needed for today's relatively complex recipes. The buyer must look to others to move commodities through the market so that they arrive on the receiving dock in the right amounts at the right times, and he must pay for the added worth or utility so accruing to the food.

Indeed, as has been pointed out, this is the only way the food buyer can function with the efficiency and effectiveness needed to meet the constraints of a reasonable profit potential in the processing and sale of the food purchased. The ecological doctrine of "mutual dependency" has erased for all time whatever truth and efficacy there might ever have been in the old bromide: "In God we trust; all others help themselves." Because we are forced to put our faith and trust in middlemen who directly or indirectly serve us, we should understand at least the basis of their operational principles and practices.

BUYING AS A BUSINESS ENTERPRISE

Direct Purchase

Most buyers in metropolitan areas have an opportunity to deal with "truck hucksters," who run individual operations by buying food (usually produce) from any source available and selling it from a truck bed at the back door of the food service facility. In many instances, there is no provision for refrigeration or sanitation. Because of the mobility and the ephemeral nature of such a business, it can easily escape the watchful eye of county health authorities. There is another consideration. Transfer of ownership to the food buyer in this manner usually entails paying cash. This is a bother to the busy buyer, for it requires much necessary paperwork to account for the cost and to allocate it to the proper food cost category. Also, by paying cash the buyer uses money that normally would be utilized during the month in other ways. These are just a few of the reasons why this type of buying is considered unwise by many professional quantity food personnel.

It is true that large companies find it profitable to buy direct, but in these instances the firm employs totally qualified personnel. It must be recognized, however, that buyers with the knowledge and the skill to purchase processed meat products directly from a processing plant are rare, and they command salaries commensurate with their unique combination of skill and judgmental capabilities.

A food buyer who is also the general purchasing agent for a food service firm may have an opportunity to buy other types of merchandise—beer, detergents, cleaning supplies, kitchen equipment—direct.

Indirect Purchase

The part of marketing that has to do with the workings of middlemen is called "place strategy." It has as its primary thrust the functions of moving and storing commodities so that they will have

the right product,
at the right place,
at the right price,
at the right time for
maximum customer
satisfaction.

It costs money to implant time and place utility in a product. When more people are involved, there is more red tape, and it costs more money. Another basic point to be made here is that the fewer the qualified professionals involved in the place strategy, the lower the price to the buyer. The word "qualified" is used advisedly, for expertise is required in dealing with the vast and complex food chain. Many unqualified persons decide to eliminate a link from the chain, thereby saving on the markup by eliminating some middlemen.

In one instance a large multifaceted food corporation hired a new director of

purchasing in the late 1950's. When the new purchasing agent saw the total bill for dishwashing detergent for the roughly one hundred food service establishments comprising the corporation, he decided the corporation should manufacture its own detergent. He asked a chemical firm to analyze the leading detergent used in dishwashing machines. When the analysis, which was expensive, was completed, the director of purchasing obtained the raw materials and had the detergent made. There was only one problem; it did not wash dishes.

The flow of products from either manufacturer or extractor provides an excellent basis for listing the various types of middlemen. Exhibit 2-2 shows both the flow and the four types of middlemen encountered in the marketplace.

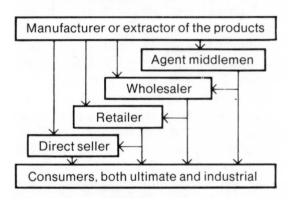

Exhibit 2-2. Flow of products through middlemen

The arrows pointing both down and to the left indicate that each of the four levels may deliver to the buyer directly from the source of original supply. All but the supplier, who acts as terminal seller to the consumer, are served by middlemen.

Agent Middlemen

Manufacturers that do not employ their own sales force must rely on agent middlemen. There are four types of agents under this category: brokers, commission men, manufacturer's agents, and sales agents.

Brokers. The broker is in business for himself, and his business is usually limited to a standard statistical marketing area or certainly falls within a rather limited metropolitan area. The distinguishing characteristic of the broker is that he does not take title to the goods he sells. And, as with any middleman who does not buy goods for resale, his markup is proportionately smaller. The broker hires his own salesmen and clerks as he sees fit for the proper conduct of his business. Brokers call regularly on their customers, which are usually food service establishments, supermarkets, and chain stores. Their commission usually runs from 3 percent to 5 percent of sales. Brokers may do some "missionary selling" but usually only when one of the members of the producing company's sales force is present to provide the particular expertise necessary to display the product to the potential buyer. The major broker handles so many lines of merchandise that he could never become intimately acquainted with all of the products on hand, and there is a need to understand a product to sell it.

When a quantity food purchasing class makes a field trip to a food plant, the students usually want to see the latest convenience foods available. Often the plant acts as broker for a large company that owns such a line. The student tour can be scheduled to coincide with a visit from a company representative, who demonstrates and lectures on the latest innovations. He does not directly sell anything; he just spreads the "good word" about his company's products to students of institutional management, who are excellent potential buyers. This, then, is an example of missionary selling. Another instance where companies develop or cement relations with buyers or potential buyers occurs at conventions. Company representatives express appreciation by "treating" those attending the convention, or they sponsor what are known as "dog and pony shows," that is, they have cocktail parties for those in the trade.

Commission men or commission houses. These agent middlemen are like brokers in all respects except one: they take title to the merchandise they pass on down the chain. Physical possession and title are necessary so that the commission man can control prices. These functionaries, or "facilitating intermediaries" according to Kotler, purchase and sell mainly produce, which is highly perishable. They rely on their unique expertise to search the market, select the quality necessary to satisfy their customers' needs, and speed the commodities on their way. For their services they extract a commission or percentage fee in return for expertise and service.

Manufacturer's agents. Like the broker (indeed, the agent is a special kind of broker), the manufacturer's agent does not take title, bill, or set prices. Agents differ from regular brokers, however, in that they function as account executives for the parent company. Their lines are specialized, and they carry fewer of them, which means they can concentrate their product expertise and sales efforts on fewer products. In some respects, everyone concerned profits by such specialization. Agents work on commission, which may fluctuate greatly—from, say, 2 percent to 20 percent.

Sales agents. These agents, too, are selling agents for manufacturers, but usually for "boutique-type" operations. They take over the sales effort for the entire inventory of a "small" manufacturer, such as Loma Linda or Worthington foods. These two manufacturers specialize in nonmeat complete protein products for vegetarians, and they were two of the earliest companies to utilize TVP (texturized vegetable protein), which is also used as a breakfast meat substitute and has been marketed by Morningstar Farms since early 1974.

Wholesalers. The American colonies imported all manufactured goods from England. Often raw materials were sent from the colonies, and then the finished products were shipped back to be handled and sold by men who performed the functions of today's wholesaler. It is interesting that 1776, the year the colonists rebelled against these and other practices limiting manufacturing, was also the year in which the Reverend Adam Smith published his definitive work defending mercantilism.

The main idea behind the wholesale business is that wholesalers function primarily as buyers for those who subsequently sell to the ultimate consumer, whether it is the retailer, the U.S. government, or the food service company. The wholesaler has the same problems of "inventory drawdowns" as the buyer. Wholesalers were among the first businessmen to experiment with linear programming, using the digital computer, in their efforts to eliminate these problems. The following discussion is limited to wholesalers involved exclusively or in part with the food service establishment.

Full-service wholesalers have relatively large lines of stock. They give credit to deserving customers and may endeavor to offer a full line of services to the buyer. These are the companies that are getting into one-stop shopping. They offer everything from frozen foods and regular institutional pack groceries to china,

glassware, silver, linen, cleansing compounds, paper goods, kitchen equipment, office machines, shared computer time, and other commodities.

Limited-function wholesalers sell bakery goods, potato chips, dairy products, and similar commodities on a "cash truck" basis. "Wagon jobbers" fall into this category. This does not necessarily mean that they sell for cash. It indicates that the truck driver is personally charged with the value of the truck's contents in terms of sale price. When he begins his day's business, the driver is held accountable for the merchandise as follows:

Opening Inventory	$A
Less: Sales, accounted for by either cash or authorized signed sales slips	−B
Closing Inventory Turn-in	$C

Petty larceny can be a problem where cash truck sales are involved, and a receiving steward who does not verify the quality and quantity of merchandise delivered before he pays or signs the invoice falls easy victim. (He soon becomes known in the trade as a "loose receiver.") It is relatively simple for a driver to short the count on goods delivered. He then has extra merchandise, paid or signed for, to sell for himself, and he can pocket the money. Costs are still correct for the wholesaler, but the food cost percentage creeps up in the food service establishment. The tradition of motion economy brought into the food service business some years ago, specifically, the concept of "store at point of first use," makes the unwary buyer susceptible to such illegitimate practices. Translated into terms of milk and bread deliveries, one example works as follows: the truck driver is instructed to rotate the stock FIFO (first-in, first-out) as he delivers it to a rack or reefer close to point of use. It is assumed that the driver can perform these tasks with less effort than anyone else, and the practice is so commonly accepted that the cost has been worked into the selling price to the food service establishment. Such a practice, if not supervised by someone in receiving, could well mean that the restaurant keeps less money for the effort. *Slippages in these and in all other cases, without exception, occur when an establishment does not properly receive a delivery.*

Drop shipment wholesalers make large shipments on a "drop" basis. These are potentially useful to a firm with fairly predictable month-to-month volume. There are other types of wholesalers (limited line, rack jobbers, and cash and carry, among others). They do not usually concern the food buyer. If a restaurateur catering to the young set puts in a line of the latest phonograph records or tapes for sale to those waiting for a table, he would probably utilize a rack jobber who would carefully husband the selection, pricing, and other sales efforts of items completely out of the normal realm of the restaurateur's expertise. This and similar ideas are not as preposterous as they might seem, and they should possibly enter into the marketing potential study of a food service establishment.

Jobbers. This position does not appear in the middleman picture illustrated by Exhibit 2-2. Pure jobbers do not customarily do business with food service customers. They are mentioned here because "old salts" will expect younger buyers to be familiar with the term. Actually, the term "jobber" is often mistaken for "wholesaler." The jobber was, historically, an additional middleman between the wholesaler and the food buyer, and so the position is still vital in other lines of food purchasing.

Before the energy crisis in 1973-74, the Arab oil embargo, and the subsequent increase in gasoline prices, almost any trainee in any food service program that was not completely structured could and did tell what were perhaps exaggerated stories of money made the previous week in mileage. The boasting was usually based on the "cents per mile" paid the trainee for driving to a local retail grocery store for emergency food items, an expense usually paid out of petty cash. While this is not a text in food service management, it seems well to point out that the practice of buying food on an emergency basis, even when blessed by the usually unallocated labor costs of trainees on the premises, is bad business. It is costly to use petty cash, and such measures, if tolerated, become habit at the expense of logistical planning. These practices violate the principle of specificity of tasks. A trainee is there to learn the principles and practices of the firm; he is not an errand boy.

The theory behind specificity of tasks also suggests, in terms of buying, that those accustomed to purchasing food can do it with greater ease and at less expense than others in the firm. Knowledge of the principles and practices of middlemen enables the buyer to evaluate services rendered and prices charged.

3 *Market Regulation*

The federal role in market regulation is a controversial one. While a news broadcaster comments that "the velvet glove of federal aid masks the iron fist of federal control," the commissioner of the Food and Drug Administration (FDA) contends that their most important task is "to protect consumers against harmful, unsanitary, and falsely labeled foods, drugs, cosmetics, therapeutic devices, and the like. The beneficent influence of the law does not, however, extend only to the ultimate consumer. It adds to the assurance of those who use or deal in foods, drugs, and cosmetics that these products are safe and above suspicion." At the same time a recognized authority on business regulation contends that the Sherman Act is "one of the best laws ever written." Specific arguments opposing federal regulation are just as strong:

We have not had free enterprise since the Sherman Act. Private enterprise under government regulations is called a "mixed economy." I call it "mixed up." Why? Because government regulates both for and *against* private enterprise.

In ruling in the Electric Companies case that nolo contendere could be taken as guilt admission, the federal court made an unannounced change in the ground rules, and that's not kosher.

Privity (the basis of "reasonable care" in civil negligence suits) is a concept even lawyers find hard to define.

The Federal Trade Commission has broadcast powers, but the bumbling bureaucracy therein has not used them. We have had to create the SEC, FCC, FAA, and so on; this is Mickey Mouse; the FTC could have done it.

If one reads the literature on federal legislation as it pertains to the business enterprise, it is hard to keep score, but one thing is certain. Whether the entrepreneur of today is for or against and whatever his political or other persuasion, he will be faced with governmental regulations.

There is an old saying: "If we seem to see farther than our fathers, it is because we are standing on their shoulders." It applies here. We may be able to see farther than those who initially had to deal with regulatory legislation, but it would be impossible to provide a complete history of federal regulation, given the space available here. The goal of this chapter is to provide an understanding of the end result, which will perhaps prompt further study.

It should, in any case, make one thing clear. Without an overall understanding of federal regulation, the buyer is not adequately prepared to engage in the activities of the marketplace.

There has been an attempt to approach each important act historically and treat it chronologically in instances where the laws have been amended (if the amendments seem relevant to you as a food buyer) and randomly in instances where the laws have remained fairly static. Many federal, state, semipublic, and private business associations are beyond the realm of congressional mandate. These are listed and discussed when they are deemed important.

FEDERAL REGULATION OF BUSINESS

The Sherman Antitrust Act of 1890

The objective of the Sherman Act, a landmark in federal regulatory legislation, seemed to be control of the "robber barons." After the Civil War, businesses flourished. Bigness and power became a kind of golden calf—a postbiblical god to be worshiped for its own sake. The act, which was broad, constituted an almost zealous effort on the part of Congress to prevent restraint of trade through monopolies or attempts to monopolize.

The Clayton and FTC Acts of 1914

The Sherman Act was considerably strengthened by the Clayton Act of 1914, and the Clayton Act was followed, in the same year, by the Federal Trade Commission Act. Corporations were still able, under the Sherman Act, to buy out competition. The two newer acts forbade such monopolistic practices as tying contracts, exclusive dealings, price discrimination, intercorporate stock acquisitions to lessen competition, interlocking directorates of competing firms, and the making of extravagant and false claims.

These acts, which affected interstate commerce, were clarified, amended, or strengthened by subsequent legislation: the *Robinson-Patman Act of 1936* (forbade unfair methods of competition); the *Tydings-Miller Act of 1937* (concerned with price fixing and the exemption of interstate fair-trade items); the *Wheeling-Lea Act of 1938* (altered the FTC regulations to include "unfair or deceptive acts or practices" in relation to methods of competition); the *Antimerger (Celler-Kefauver) Act of 1950* (increased the power of regulatory agencies to investigate and prosecute in situations that might adversely affect competition); the *McGuire Act of 1952* (strengthened the fair-trade regulations by binding all dealers to an agreement signed by one). This act was later repealed, effective as of 1976. Further amendment now allows states to set up their own regulatory agencies to control the marketing of milk, fruits, vegetables, and other foods.

Court tests for monopoly seem to revolve around answers to the following questions: Does the defendant have the power to take a big market share? Could he have avoided it? The most notorious and far-reaching decision that has been handed down in such cases was against not only electrical companies but against corporate officers as well. For the first time a plea of nolo contendere—literally, "no contest" (a plea historically used to wind up the case without a fight against substantively unfavorable evidence, but without any implication of guilt)—was construed as admission of guilt. For the first time in history corporate officers went to jail. Early in 1974 a case against five baking companies in the Phoenix area was decided in a similar fashion. The court, citing the electrical case and subsequent ones, again found both the companies and the officers guilty.

FEDERAL REGULATION OF FOOD AND DRUGS, SANITATION, AND SAFETY

The Meat Inspection Act of 1906

The first meat act, funded for just one year, resulted from the activities of a single individual. Upton Sinclair wrote a disturbing book called *The Jungle*, which was based on conditions that prevailed in the Chicago stockyards. The Meat Inspection Act, which was a direct result, provided for the enforcement of sanitary regulations in packing plants and for federal inspection of all companies selling meats in interstate commerce. This act, refunded in 1907, then provided for the labeling of inspected meats. It was to be enforced by the USDA. Specifically, the act contained provisions intended to detect and destroy diseased and otherwise unfit meat, to regulate the sanitation practices at meat plants, to require that all inspected meat be stamped, to prevent the addition of harmful substances in foods containing meats, and to prevent false or deceptive labeling. Probably the first of these provisions is most important in terms of the health of the nation.

The Meat Inspection Act was amended by the *Wholesome Meat Act of 1967*, which extends federal meat inspection requirements to plants not covered in the earlier act. The act requires inspection, at least as stringent as federal inspection, of all meat, whether it moves within or between states. It also provides assistance to plants in order to improve their meat inspection procedures. In addition, this act provides for inspection of foreign plants exporting meats to the United States. This means that the buyer can have the same confidence in the wholesomeness of foreign and intrastate meats that he could previously have had only in meats transported interstate.

In April 1972 the inspection duties were assumed by the Animal and Plant Health Inspection Service (APHIS) division of the USDA. By 1974 APHIS had completely revised all aspects of the provisions of the 1906 and 1967 acts, and today the Meat and Poultry Inspection Program is administered by APHIS, as well as two others: Veterinary Services and Plant Protection and Quarantine.

The Poultry Products Inspection Act of 1957

The provisions of the poultry act, originally administered by the USDA, but now under APHIS, required inspection of all poultry moving in interstate commerce. The act was amended in 1968 and was called the *Wholesome Poultry Products Act*. As is the case with meat, the act requires inspection, at least as good as federal inspection, of all poultry, whether or not it moves in interstate commerce, and it provides assistance to the states to improve their poultry inspection procedures. Inspectors insist on high standards of cleanliness and on the maintaining of equipment. They approve the labels used on poultry and on poultry parts and remove adulterated products from the market. They also run tests on poultry to guard against contamination. The act provides monetary and technical assistance to plants in an effort to help them meet federal requirements.

The Pure Food and Drug Act of 1906

At almost the same time that the first Meat Inspection Act was being considered,

Harvey W. Wiley, chief chemist for the Department of Agriculture, was laboring for the enactment of legislation that, among other things, was intended to curb the adulteration and false labeling of foods. His efforts resulted in the Pure Food and Drug Act of 1906, which was later revised and became known as the *Food, Drug, and Cosmetic Act of 1938.*

There were further revisions and amendments in 1954 (additives introduced by pesticides), 1958 (required "just cause" for introducing any additive), and 1960 (concerned with color additives). Probably the best-known controversy over the use of additives stems from a provision of the 1958 amendment that "producers may not use any additives found to induce cancer in man or animals, *in any amount and under any conditions*" (emphasis added). It was this provision, called the "Delaney clause," that stirred the tremendous controversy over the use of cyclamates, as in artificial sweeteners. By 1960, at least, the legislation did permit a manufacturer who held a different opinion concerning the safe use of an additive to request review by a panel of experts appointed by the National Academy of Sciences.

The food and drug acts, as amended, have affected the market. If a product is deemed unsafe, the Consumer Product Safety Act Commission calls, through the *Federal Register*, for volunteers to help work out new standards. If qualified volunteers come forward, they can be paid; if they do not, the commissioners set the regulation. This opens the way for a new trend in governmental-corporate cooperation.

As for names of foods or technical names on labels, these are scrutinized carefully to ascertain whether they are understandable before they can be used on cans or other packages. And, in terms of packages and all other sealed containers (bulk and open containers are exempt), food and drug regulations provide that the container must:

1. list the common name or names of the food item.
2. give the name and address of the manufacturer, packer, or distributor.
3. list the net contents either by count or by fluid or avoirdupois measure.
4. be sufficiently prominent to be easily comprehended and must contain no foreign language that might circumvent label requirements.
5. bear the specific names and not a collective name for ingredients unless the product is a commonly known food, but the group words spice, flavoring, coloring, and so on may be used.
6. list, in order of greatest proportion down to least, the names of all ingredients.
7. bear exact definition of dietary properties if dietary value is claimed.
8. bear the term "artificial" if artificial coloring or flavoring is used, or "chemical preservative" if chemicals are used.

National Marine Fisheries Service. The National Oceanographic and Atmosphere Administration (NOAA) was established on October 3, 1970. Under the auspices of the U.S. Department of Commerce, it was intended, among other things, to create a civilian center to expand effective and rational use of ocean resources. The National Marine Fisheries Service (NMFS), one of eight components under NOAA, assumed duties formerly the responsibility of the Bureau of Commercial Fisheries of the U.S. Department of the Interior. The NMFS provides for three types of inspection of seafood: contract, lot, and miscellaneous. NMFS works with representatives of the FDA in areas involving food plant sanitation and product wholesomeness (see Chapter 20).

The Agricultural Marketing Services Act of 1953 (revised 1957)

There has been legislative provision for strict inspection based on quality in order to establish grading procedures for various foods. It is administered by the USDA. The various commodities are divided into several logical inspection categories that are determined by type of procedure.

Grain inspection has as its main thrust the verification of standards for raw cereals about to enter the market chain. Dairy inspectors are responsible for examining milk, milk products, and margarine. Another division checks the quality and fitness for use of fresh fruits and vegetables, as well as commodities processed and marketed in containers, such as fresh and cooked frozen foods; dried, freeze-dried, or otherwise processed and preserved foods, including meats, poultry, poultry products, and eggs in all market forms.

The commodities inspected bear an easily recognized stamp, either on the product (in the case of meats, for instance, one on each "primal" or commercial cut) or on the container, so that a buyer of any unit or part can readily see and can depend on the inspection thereby represented. The agencies are usually located at main points in the marketing chain, such as shipping areas, or at incoming points, such as the Mexico-Arizona corridor located at Nogales, Arizona-Sonora, or at other way stations in areas through which relatively large amounts of food enter or are passed along the chain.

In certain instances (always if the com- modities are involved in interstate commerce) the federal inspector will inspect and certify using USDA quality grade standards. In other instances the individual standards of the establishment, the purveyor, or both may be used. Federal standards are rather broad. They were primarily established for fitness, but they can be and sometimes are used to aid aggregate producers in the sale of their commodities.

Often an establishment will have specifications that are rigid by government standards. They were, perhaps, set up by the organization to meet some unique need or needs of the menu. In such a case, if the establishment does not have either the qualified personnel or is too far from the market source, federal agents inspect and pass commodities to the establishment's specification. When the specifications of the buyer are used by the Agricultural Marketing Services (AMS) agent, it is called an acceptance inspection, and a special stamp (see Exhibit 3-1) is affixed by the federal agent.

Exhibit 3-1. Special stamp used for acceptance inspection by the United States Department of Agriculture (Courtesy: USDA)

An inspector will, upon request, supply the buyer with an inspection certificate (see Exhibit 3-2). This is not necessarily a part of acceptance inspection, which is paid for by the institution requesting it.

F. P. I. 20

ORIGINAL

UNITED STATES DEPARTMENT OF AGRICULTURE

VIRGINIA DEPARTMENT OF AGRICULTURE AND IMMIGRATION

Nº 4377

INSPECTION CERTIFICATE

This certificate is issued in compliance with the regulations of the Secretary of Agriculture governing the inspection of various products pursuant to the Act making appropriations for the United States Department of Agriculture, the Acts of Virginia Assembly, and is admissible as prima facie evidence in all courts of the United States and of Virginia. This certificate does not excuse failure to comply with any of the regulatory laws enforced by the United States Department of Agriculture, or by the Virginia Department of Agriculture and Immigration.

Inspection point __Winchester, Va.__ *Billing point* __Winchester, Va.__ *Date* __Oct. 4, 1945__

Applicant __Winchester Packing Co.__ *Address* __Winchester, Va.__

Shipper __Same__ *Address* __Same__

I, the undersigned, on the date above specified made personal inspection of samples of the lot of produce herein described, and do hereby certify that the quality and condition, at the said time and on said date, pertaining to such products, as shown by said samples, were as stated below:

Car initial and number __FGEX 5 1 8 1 3__ *Kind of car* __Refrigerator__

Inspection begun __1:30 P. M. Oct. 4, 1945__ *Inspection completed* __6:15 P. M. Oct. 4, 1945__
   (Hour, date)   (Hour, date)

Car equipment and condition at completion of inspection:

Products: York Imperial APPLES - in tub type bushel baskets labeled "W Brand, Winchester Packing Co., Winchester, Va." and stamped "U. S. No. 1, 2¼ inches up, York." Loader's count 516 baskets.

Loading: Through load, end to end offset, 3x3 rows, 4 layers.

Pack: Tight. Ring faced. Paper pads under lids. Good amount of oiled paper distributed uniformly through baskets.

Size: Generally 2¼ to 3, mostly 2¼ to 2½ inches in diameter.

Quality and condition: Mostly well formed, some fairly well formed, clean, 15% to full red, mostly 25% to 50% good red color. Grade defects within tolerance. Generally hard. No decay.

Grade: As marked, U. S. No. 1, 2¼ inches up.

Fee __$5.16__
Expenses
Total __5.16__

__L. F. Laney__

Inspector.

U. S. GOVERNMENT PRINTING OFFICE 8—7124 A   PLEASE REFER TO THIS CERTIFICATE BY NUMBER

Exhibit 3-2. Inspection certificate of the United States Department of Agriculture, supplied to buyer upon request (Courtesy: USDA)

If the purveyor has sold to an institution on the basis of special grading instructions and is including this cost in his selling price to the firm, he is responsible for paying the AMS representative. If the buyer is picking up the commodities and paying the producer directly, then the buyer pays the inspection fee. The buyer in the first instance would also pay for inspection if he were to send samples of commodities for a spot check of specification adherence or if he were to claim that commodities inspected and paid for by a purveyor did not meet the specifications and subsequent reinspection and certification proved the claim to be false.

A federal standard, when first published by the AMS, is called "tentative." After it has been market tested at a representative number of inspection stations in the area where the food is raised or marketed, the standard may be rejected, revised, or accepted. The AMS is extremely thorough in testing new standards. Crops for which new standards have been written are tested over a long period, sometimes years, until the AMS is sure that the test represents most possible sets of weather conditions or whatever else the test is based on. If it meets the requirements of the marketplace in such representative tests, it then becomes permanent.

The inspection divisions establish the standards of quality in their respective areas. This gives the inspectors the opportunity to amass more experience in a narrower band of the market spectrum and makes them more efficient and effective in their tasks. Various trade associations are liberally consulted for revision of present standards, suggestions for future standards, and short-term help to the market in general. Although it might be difficult to find such duties formally stated in the job description of a federal inspector, the standards applied by inspectors appear to be not only broad but rather elastic. One example of this involves the growing season for crops.

Crop Supply. The growing season of a particular crop is plotted as shown in Exhibit 3-3. Both the beginning and the end of the growing season are illustrated by the letter A. The normal part of the growing season, between the short-supply situations that occur at the beginning and the end of the season (not necessarily in the percentage quantities of the total crop as depicted above), is indicated by the

letter B. The peak of the season, when the greatest amount of the commodity is on the market on a daily basis, is indicated by the letter C. Products that represent

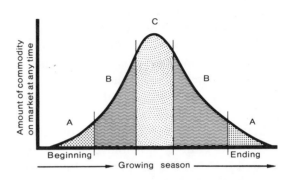

Exhibit 3-3. Hypothetical crop harvesting curve for a representative seasonal commodity

the "normal" characteristics found in regularly high-quality foodstuffs during the "normal" part of the crop season are generally identified as U.S. No. 1 grade.

During the beginnings and endings of seasons, the average quality of the commodity is generally below that of the "normal" part of the season. This is because the varying combinations of sun, soil, humidity, temperature, and other elements are less than optimum for achieving the best results. Consequently, the inspector will grade a larger part of the available crop as being U.S. No. 1 at the beginning and end of a season. During the peak of the season a smaller percentage of the day-to-day crop meets the tightened standards set for the U.S. No. 1 grade than at any other time of the year.

Because of the laws of supply and demand, each unit of a given quality brings a higher price when the crop is in short supply. At the season's peak, however, it is possible that there is a greater supply than the producers can readily sell on a day-to-day basis, which means that each unit would bring a lower price.

Price Stabilization. If the secondary thrust of the AMS Act is to aid all concerned in moving the entire crop through the marketplace, it stands to reason that, in times of fluctuating prices, government agents would try to help stabilize the market, which is what they appear to do in their grading practices. By grading more loosely when the supply is short, the price is held in check, and demand keeps the price at a profitable level. During the peak of the season, conversely, the price is kept higher by tightening grading standards. It is entirely possible that produce graded U.S. No. 2 at the peak of the season may be of a higher quality than that given the same grade at the beginning and end of the growing season.

The federal government works toward price stabilization in other ways as well. The practice of paying farmers not to plant all of their land is a well-known means, but there are other ones that are more important for the food buyer. The government purchases commodities to feed the armed forces, it administers child nutrition programs including school lunches, and it provides food for the consumption of its own employees, as well as providing for increased consumption through such means as the food stamp program.

One reason that gratuitous commodities (so-called "donated foods") available for school lunch programs fluctuate so much per year is that the government buys selectively. A classic instance when government practices greatly affected the market occurred during the fall and early winter of 1965-66. A combination of poor calf yield on the breeding ranges, poor rain for forage, and other factors reduced the number of steers and heifers needed for top USDA grades. In the fall, federal purchasing agents bought thousands of full loins of beef for the armed forces

food service establishments. All of these factors combined to create a shortage of the primal cuts that produce the best steaks. The price of such cuts, particularly on the West Coast, was so prohibitive that most restaurants either had to price steaks much higher or serve a lower grade of meat. In a time of long supply, cattlemen and middlemen would have welcomed government intervention; in this case, it caused everyone concerned much unnecessary grief.

Fish and Shellfish. Since its inception, the AMS Act has been amended to include fish and shellfish. The Fish and Wildlife Service has been given responsibility for establishing regulations, standards, and inspection procedures for denizens of shallow and deep waters within and around America and for imported foreign products as well. At present these services are performed by the National Marine Fisheries Service. Another agency, the United States Public Health Service (USPHS), is active where bivalves are concerned. Because the areas where oysters, mussels, and clams thrive are often polluted, because of the things that they eat, and because such animals, if dead, make a particularly good medium for the growth of pathogenic organisms, they are subject to special consideration. The sacks or barrels in which they are packed and shipped are marked with the date and place of origin. The packer must keep an accurate record of the names of the fishermen from whom he procured the shellfish. The person who unpacks the container, either for use on the premises or for repacking and further distribution, must keep the tag for six weeks. If an illness such as diphtheria or typhoid originated with shellfish, such measures make it fairly simple to check all the way back through the marketing chain to the beds, which can be closed down if the finding is affirmative. Cooked crab meat, such as lump, special, regular, and claw meat from blue crabs sold in pound cans along the Delmarva Peninsula and in the Chesapeake Bay area, and several other seafood products also come under the auspices of the USPHS.

Processed Foods. There are four ways AMS inspectors ascertain the quality of processed fruits and vegetables:

1. The foods may be sent to an AMS laboratory for inspection. The results certify only the samples inspected, not the lot from which they came.

2. Random samples may be withdrawn from a warehouse. The entire lot may be certified on this basis.

3. If an inspector is in a processing plant at all times when foods are being processed, the inspection is called "continuous." All facets of the operation, including sanitation procedures, are inspected. If all standards are met, certificates of quality may be issued, or the federal shield that certifies the grade may be affixed. A facsimile of the shield appears as Exhibit 3-1.

4. If the federal inspector has several plants, the overall operations of which fall into his area of inspection, or if for some other reason he is only in the plant intermittently, the plant products may be certified by stamp only as to the grade (no certificate will be issued). Just because no certificate of grade accompanies a shipment does not mean that it has not been certified. A federal grade shield is adequate. If the buyer wishes the peace of mind associated with it, he may require his purveyors to provide both grade shield and certificate of inspection; he will, however, pay for what is almost a duplication of effort. In the case of meats, federal inspections, if required, must be continuous. Then the whole lot processed is, of course, certified.

There are three standards that are checked by the inspectors in verifying the grade of processed foods. They are quality, identity, and fill.

There are various objective and subjective tests for *standards of quality*, such as color, texture, tenderness, and freedom from defect. Generally a scale ranging from 1 to 100 is used, and a product must score 90 or above for an "A," 80-89 for a "B," 70-79 for a "C," and so on. The butter score is a familiar one: 92 is "AA"; 91 is "A." If minimum quality standards are not met, the product must be marked "below standard in quality," and a statement by the packer must accompany the notation, explaining why it is low. It should be noted that "below standard" does not mean "unwholesome," for, as A. A. Johnson argues, "the very presence of a food product for the marketplace indicates that the food is safe."

Broken fruit, skin blemishes, and other such natural phenomena, which would probably detract from use in an aspic salad, for instance, might be perfectly permissible used in diced form in a fruit glaze. This is another way of saying that one should "purchase for intended use." The buyer should look for such good buys, given a legitimate use for them.

Standards of identity distinguish a product. Certain regional or colloquial names have evolved until they are commonly accepted, both by the trade and by the patron. Because the public has a mental set as to what things go into such products as succotash, fruits-for-salad, fruit cocktail, and taco sauce, the AMS has set up specific standards as to what containers that display such names should contain. This country has done little in the area of reciprocal trade and identity-use agreements internationally, but the AMS has inadvertently provided some relief in this area. Products may not be called the name of another generic product, which meant that the Roquefort Cheese Association of France was able to take prominent restaurant owners from both New York City and San Francisco to federal court and win injunctions against the practice of using any other product and calling it "Roquefort cheese." They also collected damages. It is interesting that many restaurants of national repute suddenly either bought more genuine Roquefort cheese or changed their menus to read "blue cheese dressing" shortly after these decisions were handed down by the court. Similarly, the Coca-Cola Bottling Company successfully enjoined a major restaurant chain against using another cola product and calling it "Coke" or "Coca-Cola." If a person now goes to a restaurant featuring a cola product other than Coca-Cola, he will more than likely be told the brand name he will be getting. Operatives from both the Roquefort cheese and Coca-Cola companies are checking for further evidence of violation at all times.

Standards of identity must state exactly what a product is made of. If a product such as grape jelly contains simulated color, flavor, or other things, this must be spelled out with a descriptive adjective, such as "artificial," attached. If drained weight is a factor in identity, then it must appear in the identification of contents. The USDA sets standards of identity for meat, poultry, and egg products. The FDA does this for other foods.

If various *standards of fill* are not met, the product may be marketed, but only with the label "below standard in fill" and an accompanying explanation. Short or "slack" and deceptive filling is not tolerated. This does not mean, in the case of canned goods, that the product must be filled to the top. Normal "headspace" must be allowed for expansion of the product during thermalization.

Standards of identity and fill, unlike use of a federal grade, must be followed in every case where the product will move in interstate commerce. The possibility of criminal action and, upon conviction, the possible outcome of such litigation are usually strong enough incentives to prevent shoddy and illegal practices. A person so convicted may face fines, prison, or loss of his business; a corporation may be fined or put out of business and its officers imprisoned.

Other Regulatory Legislation

There are other laws that affect the buyer. The *Perishable Agricultural Commodities Act of 1930*, which licenses dealers and establishes fair trade practices governing both interstate and foreign commerce, is administered by the USDA. The *Tea Inspection Act* regulates importation of tea and establishes and administers, through the auspices of the FDA, the purity, quality, and fitness for human consumption of this commodity. There is a seven-member board of tea experts that meets yearly to establish the standards for the year, and the members are part of what is probably the world's smallest and most exclusive group of professionals. The *U.S. Warehouse Act* provides that agricultural and processed foods moving in interstate commerce must be certified for storage. AMS standards are followed for grading.

Good Manufacturing Practices (GMP's)

In 1970 the commission of the FDA introduced a set of regulations. The guidelines covered the maintenance of sanitary conditions for plants, grounds, equipment, utensils, facilities, controls and processes, and personnel obligations that, if they were abused, could lead to adulterated products. GMP's apply to specific processes for canning low-acid foods susceptible to botulism. There is one interesting development regarding the processing of low-acid foods. The GMP's were published in May 1973. By September 25, 1974, each worker having anything to do with packaging those foods had to attend an FDA school teaching the GMP specifications, whether he had a Ph.D or an eighth-grade education. Processes are also recommended for breading shrimp, smoking fish, bottling water, freezing foods, baking, and freezing fresh seafoods.

The Occupational Safety and Health Act of 1970

The purposes of the Occupational Safety and Health Act (OSHA) are stated as follows:

To assure safe and healthful working conditions for working men and women by authorizing enforcement of the standards developed under the act; by assisting and encouraging the states in their efforts to assure safe and healthful working conditions; by providing for research, information, education, and training in the field of occupational safety and health. . . .

All parties under the act have duties to perform. The employers have a general obligation to furnish each employee with a place of employment free from recognized hazards that might cause death or serious physical harm, as well as to adhere to specific standards set under the act.

The act is administered primarily through the Secretary of Labor. Power is vested, through him, in the OSHA review commission, which is a quasijudicial board made up of three members appointed by the President of the United States. Research and related functions are handled through the National Institute for Occupational Safety and Health (NIOSH), which is administered through the Department of Health, Education, and Welfare.

The Secretary of Labor promulgates and enforces job safety and health standards through inspections carried out by officials located in various regional offices of the federal government. The main consideration determining OSHA standards is the avoidance of hazards proven by research or experience to be harmful to personal safety and health. The objective has been to make general rules that might, at one time or another, apply to all employees. One example might be comprehensive fire protection standards, but other standards applicable to the food service industry are:

Aisles and passageways shall be kept clear and in good repair, with no obstruction across or in aisles that could create a hazard.

No employee shall be allowed to consume food or beverages in a toilet room nor in any area exposed to a toxic material.

All flour-handling equipment, each individual unit or the entire system collectively, shall be so constructed that all interior or exterior protruding corners are of a rounded nature.

Other standards of a more specific nature are: toxic materials or harmful physical agents may not "materially impair" health or functional capacity, even though the employee may be regularly exposed for his entire working life; descriptive labeling must be used to acquaint employees with packaged materials containing hazardous contents; suitable protective clothing is prescribed; warnings of potential hazards at places and intervals necessary for employee protection must be set up; types of medical examinations or other tests for employees exposed to health hazards must be performed as often as deemed necessary, and employees may request the results of such tests.

To register a complaint, any employee or a representative of an employee may submit a written and signed notice to the Department of Labor requesting an inspection where he believes that a violation of job safety or health standard exists. Inspectors may "enter without delay," at reasonable hours, any establishment to look for pertinent conditions or examine structures, machines, apparatus, devices, equipment, and materials, and they have the right to question any and all persons present. If a violation is found, the employer is issued a written citation describing the specific violation and setting a reasonable time to make necessary changes. Citations must be prominently posted near each place of violation. Notices, in lieu of citations, may be issued for *de minus* violations that have no direct or immediate relationship to safety or health. No citation may be issued when more than six months have elapsed since the violation occurred.

The act requires that employers keep and make available to the Department of Labor accurate records and periodic reports of work-related deaths, injuries, or illnesses. Injuries must be recorded if medical treatment is required, if there is a loss of consciousness, or if the injury restricts work or motion or necessitates transfer to another job. Exposure to potentially toxic materials or harmful physical agents also requires that records be kept. Imminent dangers may be restrained by U.S. District Court order, and employees who exercise their right to report suspected violations, imminent dangers, or other problems are protected.

Education and training programs for both employer and employee are authorized, and assistance provided through the Small Business Administration aids smaller firms in their efforts to comply with standards. There are other provisions covering advisory committees, review commissions, safeguards to protect businesses from divulgence of trade secrets discovered by OSHA inspectors, annual reports, and the setting up of an assistant secretaryship in the Department of Labor.

Grants are provided to encourage states to assume fullest responsibility for administering and enforcing their own OSHA laws, providing that the state laws are deemed equally as effective as those spelled out within the act and other constraints are met. Workmen's Compensation benefits under the Workmen's Compensation Act are not affected by OSHA. There is, however, a fifteen member National Commission on State Workmen's Compensation Laws to determine whether state laws provide an adequate, prompt, and equitable system of compensation for injury or death arising out of or in the course of employment.

GROUPS THAT AID IN REGULATION

Other federal agencies are concerned with the interstate and foreign commerce of foodstuffs. The Alcohol, Tobacco, and Firearms Division of the United States Treasury Department has jurisdiction over alcoholic beverages, and it uses many standards published by the AMS and the FDA in the conduct of its work. The IRS has other areas of general responsibility, either by law or through general regulatory power. If in doubt, it is wise to check.

The Bureau of Standards is concerned with control over weights and measures.

Exhibit 3-4. Recommended daily allowances as they would appear on the label of a food can (Courtesy: Del Monte Corporation, San Francisco, California)

It is looked to as the final authority by various state and local municipalities for guidance in "sealing" weights and measures, correct sizes, shapes, construction, and related matters.

The USPHS is not a policing agency with respect to foods; it does, however, aid other agencies in the enforcement of regulations regarding sanitation and food. The USPHS has many codes regulating the acceptability of meat, milk, shellfish, poultry, frozen desserts, and other items. They sponsor a public training program to enable those who handle foods to do so in a sanitary and safe manner. Individuals can attend school at the Sanitary Engineering Center in Cincinnati, or the USPHS will arrange field seminars.

The President of the United States has an Advisory Commission on Food and Fiber. This special group met at the request of President Lyndon Johnson in 1967, and the results of the meeting were published. Their report states that the nation is and must continue to be in the business of helping the "poverty class." To illustrate the scope of federal aid, in 1974 Arizona's help to the poor was approximately $150 million for an overall population of less than 2 million. In 1969, the USDA published its annual yearbook, which, for that year, was entitled *Food for Us All*. The theme was that we can produce the food needed for everyone, but there are other obligations as well. New regulations promulgated on May 15, 1973, went into effect in 1975. The main thrust was that we not only have an obligation to aid the "poverty class" monetarily, but we have a duty to help them understand the nutritive value of the food made available through the subsidies given. Specifically, the new regulations for package labeling (meaning cans and all other sealed containers) follow, as do present FDA regulations, the Recommended Daily Allowances (RDA) for nutrients. A can must be labeled with the ingredients by both avoirdupois measure and the percentage of the RDA each ingredient satisfies (see Exhibit 3-4).

The Food and Nutrition Board of the commission met in 1964 and established guides for investigating health hazards from microbiological contamination of food. They set down microbiological specifications (the maximum acceptable) and microbiological standards. Since that time the USPHS, the United States Quartermaster Corps, the FDA, and others have adopted similar measures that should substantially cut down on eruptions of food-borne illness and related problems.

There are other professional societies and trade associations that make recommendations and set standards for their own membership on the theory that lack of positive self-regulation will bring on public response and subsequent public regulation that may not be as efficacious as that instigated and administered internally. To mention just a few, these are the American Public Health Association, the International Association of Milk and Food Sanitation, the National Canners' Association, the American Meat Institute, and the American Dry Milk Institute.

DECISIONS AFFECTED BY FEDERAL AND STATE REGULATIONS

Because government regulations affect decisions made at every level of business, some of which are made every day, they are well worth contemplation by the food buyer in terms of:

Product
  Has it been altered?
  Is the design functional?
  Is the quality good?
  Is the labeling accurate?
Market
  Is there an exclusive dealership?
  Are there exclusive territorial distributorships?
  Are there tying agreements?
  Are there exclusive dealers' rights?
Promotion
  Is the advertising false or misleading?
  Is this bait advertising?
  How much should be allowed for promotion and promotional activities?
Price
  What should the price be?
  Is the price discriminatory?
  Is there a minimum price?
  Is a price increase warranted?
  Is the pricing structure deceptive?
Competition
  Should one think about expanding?
  How far should one go to maintain cooperative relations?
  What competitive practices can and should be used?

4 *The Purchasing Department in the Food Service Industry*

The food service industry is, to a great extent, a food manufacturing industry. There is, however, a continuing debate over whether food supplies should be purchased by a department that is separate from the manufacturing arm of the industry or by the food manufacturing department. It is taken for granted, in any other line of manufacturing, that a purchasing department is separate from the production department and that the function of the purchasing department is to obtain for the production department necessary supplies at the most economical prices. In the food service industry, however, it has been customary in many fields for the person in charge of food preparation also to be in charge of food purchasing. This has meant that chefs are actually chef-stewards; food production managers, food production manager-purchasing agents; dietary managers, dietary manager-purchasing agents.

ORGANIZATION IN THE FOOD SERVICE INDUSTRY

There is a basic plan that is generally followed in the food service industry, whether the facilities are institutional or commercial. It is patterned after the general plan used in most service industries and, to a great extent, manufacturing plants throughout the modern world.

Even though there is a commonly used general organizational plan in the food service industry, there are almost as many variations as there are types and sizes of operations within the industry. It is possible to overorganize smaller operations so that they become top-heavy with management personnel and lack operational personnel—a classic case of "too many chiefs and not enough Indians." On the other hand, a small operation, through skillful individual management, can grow. If, in such a case, the organizational scheme fails to keep pace with the growth of the operation, it can be undermanaged and overstaffed. Both situations can reduce profits and productivity. A balance between size of organization and size of operation is one of the measures of skillful management.

Size has little effect on the general plan of organization, even though some of the more highly structured of the responsibilities noted in larger operations are lost in

47

smaller food service establishments. The basic plan is summarized in Exhibit 4-1.

The general scheme of organization is that management is responsible for the overall operation, and there are four areas of operational activities under management: procuring of supplies, manufacturing or producing a product from the supplies obtained, selling the manufactured product, and policing the entire operation through a continuous review of the cost. How skillfully management operates the four different divisions and how expertly it coordinates the activities of the divisions are the keys to a successful venture, and a successful venture is one that produces the desired results within the budget allowed. One of the best illustrations of the division of operational responsibility can be found in a typical family-owned Chinese restaurant. In this instance, the father is generally the cook in charge of preparation; the mother is the bookkeeper and cashier; the daughter is in charge of dining room service; the son is bartender; Uncle Harry is in charge of purchasing, and everyone watches Uncle Harry.

THE PLACE OF THE FOOD PURCHASING DEPARTMENT

Institutions

The institutional field is by far the largest in the food service industry in the United States if amount of food and number of meals served are the measures used. Snack bars probably ring up more sales, but most of the food served in institutions does not involve cash sales. Hotels and restaurants, although they are important factors in the food service industry, are actually responsible for less than 10 percent of all meals eaten outside the home throughout the country.

One of the most important segments of the institutional field is the hospital. Exhibit 4-2 shows an organization chart for the dietary department of a medium- to large-size hospital. The organization breaks down into three of the four basic spheres of operation outlined earlier in this chapter. The fourth field of operation, sales, is not a factor in a hospital dietary department.

The dietary manager is not responsible for purchasing foods or other operational equipment, but he is responsible for food production and food service to the using outlets. The purchasing department is separate from and independent of the dietary manager, and the controller's department is also separate from and independent of both the purchasing and the dietary managers. The controller's department, in this particular case, is responsible for cost controls throughout the entire dietary department and is directly responsible for receiving and accounting for all incoming merchandise, for maintaining the general supply stockrooms, and for issuing merchandise to the using departments.

All three departments are under the control of a qualified department head who, in turn, reports to the hospital director for administration. It is the responsibility of the director to see that the three departments function efficiently and coordinate their activities to produce the lowest cost of operation compatible with the quality of service desired for the hospital.

A similar type of organization can be used for a college cafeteria, a large high school dining room, an industrial in-plant feeding operation, food service in a correctional institution, or food service in a retirement or nursing home.

Hotels

Over the last twenty-five years the size of the average hotel has varied. The facil-

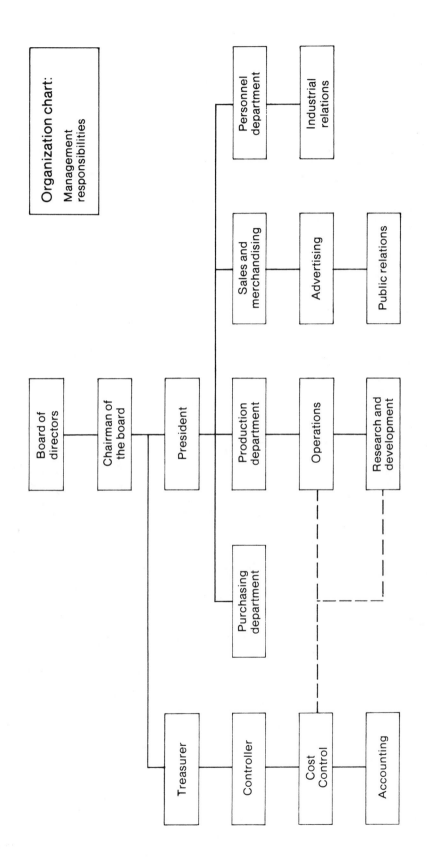

Exhibit 4-1. Chart showing management responsibilities in the general organization plan often used in the food service industry

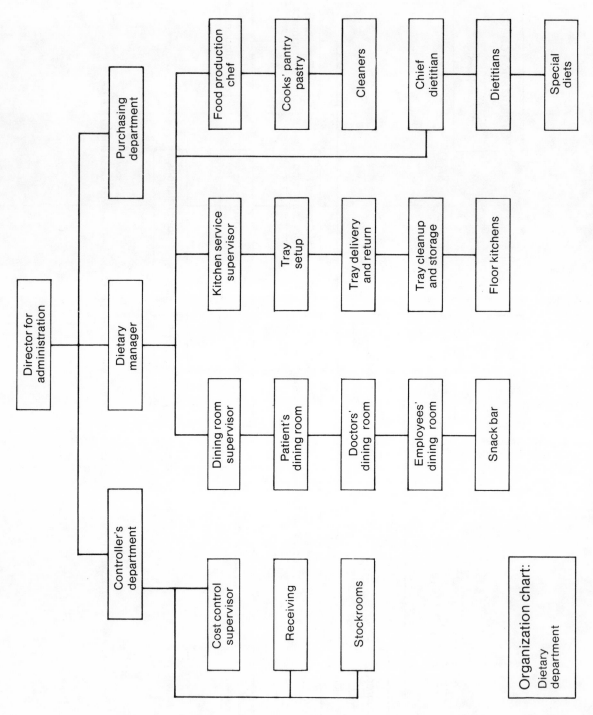

Exhibit 4-2. Chart showing an organization plan for the dietary department in a hospital

Organization chart:
Dietary department

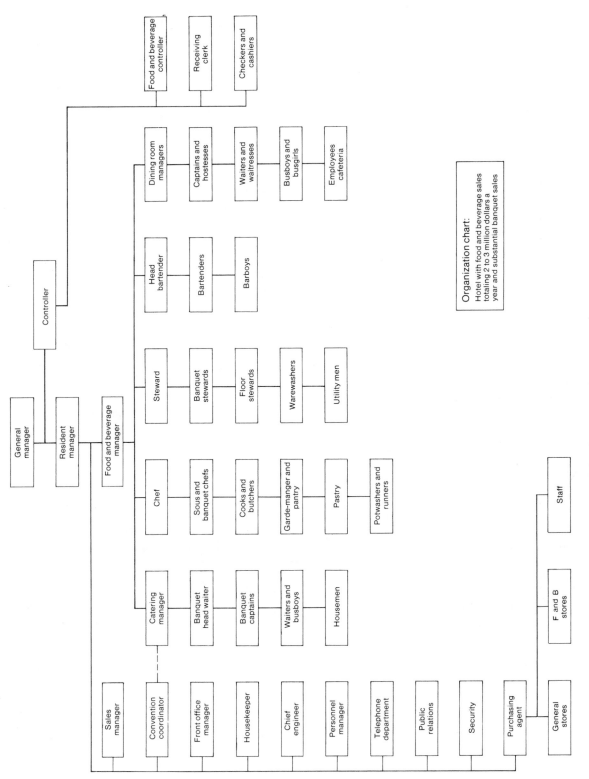

Exhibit 4-3. Chart showing an organization plan for a hotel

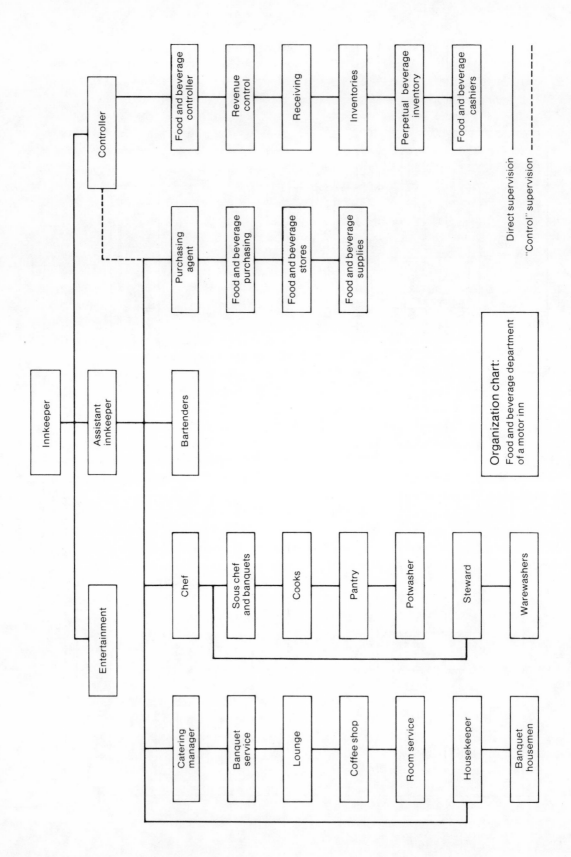

Organization chart:
Food and beverage department of a motor inn

Direct supervision ———
"Control" supervision - - - -

Exhibit 4-4. Chart showing an organization plan for the food and beverage department in a franchised motor inn

ity may be either very large or rather small, as exemplified by motor inns in suburban areas and along highways. A few years ago the typical metropolitan hotel had from 300 to 500 rooms, and, in a few instances, some chain hotels reached 700 to 800 rooms. Economy of operation then forced new metropolitan hotels to the point where any hotel with less than 1,000 rooms was considered economically unsound. There are instances where hotels of 2,000 or more rooms are able to operate at a profit largely because of revenues obtained from housing large conventions, with attendant food and beverage sales.

Experience has shown that a certain type of organization seems to produce the best results for a medium- to large-size hotel, and it is the one generally used, with some small variations to suit a specific property. Exhibit 4-3 shows how the organization is set up, how the various operating departments relate to each other, and how management communicates with each of the many departments.

The four general divisions of operations can be traced. The procurement department, the food production department, the sales department, and the controller's department are all set up as separate spheres of operation, and the heads report to the general manager of the hotel. The controller's department is in a position to exert cost controls throughout the entire operation and is directly responsible for receiving all supplies into the hotel, for the functioning of the food and beverage cost control office, and for all checkers and cashiers who handle funds throughout the entire house.

Motor Inns

Although there are many chain-operated motor inns in North America, most are privately owned or members of a franchised organization. The actual operation of even a franchised motor inn can be, and generally is, largely the responsibility of the owner. The franchisor prescribes certain standards that must be met, but, in actual practice, a franchised operation is seldom forced to surrender its franchise.

In spite of the relatively small size of a motor inn and its food and beverage department, the organizational patterns show only minor variations from those that form the basic pattern of the larger hotel. The form of organization for a food and beverage department in a group of better-organized and operated motor inns operating under a franchise is depicted in Exhibit 4-4. Again, the food and beverage department is set up in terms of four operational areas: procurement, preparation, sales, and control.

The purchasing department buys all of the food and beverage supplies, as well as the general operating supplies. The storage and issuing of food and beverage supplies is also the responsibility of purchasing in this instance. The preparation of food and beverages is under the direction of the chef and the head bartender. The sales department, which has responsibility for banquets and dining rooms, is under the direction of a catering manager. The independent control function is under the direction of a controller responsible for food and beverage control, revenue control, receiving, inventory, and the direction and control of persons handling money. Overall responsibility is the function of the general manager, who, in this particular case, is called an innkeeper. The resident manager is an assistant innkeeper.

This organization chart is satisfactory for a motor inn with 200 to 400 rooms. Even if there are only 100 rooms, with a proportionately smaller organization, it is possible to keep the four areas of operation separate. This is generally accomplished by having the innkeeper take over the responsibility for procurement; the chef, for production and storage: a dining hostess or dining room manager, for catering and bar service; a bookkeeper, for control. What better opportunity is there for controlling costs in a motor inn with 100 to 150 rooms than for the manager to buy food and beverage supplies?

Chains and Government Operations

Large chain operations, whether hotels, motor inns, or industrial food services, have clearly delineated areas of operation, operational controls, and operating guides so that there is no question about how the four basic spheres of operation are separated. Usually purchasing is a completely independent operation, and the purchasing office is located near the general market area. The purchasing department buys what is requested by the various operating units, and all supplies are clearly specified so that there are no questions concerning what is to be purchased. The control function in a large chain operation is much more important than it is in the individually operated hotel or institution. One possible criticism of the chain operation is that it may be overcontrolled because of the independent and detailed policing power wielded by the controller's department, and overcontrol tends to stifle individual initiative. The sales phase of the operation is clearly separate.

Governmental institutions and related agencies usually have a separate purchasing department that uses the bid contract and specification system of buying. Again, purchasing is under the scrutiny of a controller, an attorney general, a state auditor, or some other prescribed control department.

WHY A SEPARATE PURCHASING DEPARTMENT?

One decision facing many people in the food service industry today concerns whether or not to set up a separate food purchasing department. It is well to examine arguments for and against such a move before arriving at a conclusion.

Arguments against a Separate Department

One of the arguments most frequently used against setting up a separate purchasing department involves cost. Even though it is acknowledged that savings can be realized through the use of efficient purchasing methods, many people feel that the cost of setting up such a department outweighs the savings. Perhaps, where smaller food service operations are involved, this is a valid argument.

Opponents of a separate department claim that each department should do its own buying. Each department, it is felt, has a better concept of what is needed to produce a product of the quality and in the quantity needed. Since the technical information and the specifications required to produce a quality product are more familiar to those who work in the department, they should make the necessary purchases. It is also felt that the establishment of a separate purchasing department often creates an atmosphere of distrust and misunderstanding among workers.

Management, for its part, argues that, even if there were a separate purchasing department, the engineer, the food production manager, the kitchen manager, the chef, the head bartender, or the housekeeper would still have to make all of the decisions. Why, in that case, should they not do the buying and save the cost of a separate department? An attitude often expressed is: "Who cares if the buyer gets a little on the side—he can't get too much—he is happier and will do a better job if he is happy. Anyhow, he isn't being paid too much."

There are complaints that separate purchasing departments are not concerned about prompt delivery, which results in production delays. It also takes time to work out a detailed list of specifications for such a department. If a chef or a food production manager knows what is needed, it seems, again, a waste of time to draw up a set of specifications, to prepare a list of items for purchase, or to meet with the purchasing department to iron out difficulties.

Arguments for a Separate Department

There is another side to the argument. The purchasing of food supplies becomes more complicated all the time. Rapid changes are foreseen in the food industry, and it would seem that the purchasing of food will require a full-time, trained person to ensure an even flow of supplies and, of equal importance, to relay information concerning market conditions to management and the production department.

With today's lack of trained employees, a department head is hard pressed to keep his department working smoothly. If he must take time to do the purchasing, both the purchasing and the operation of the department can suffer unless the department head gains an assistant or two. When the chef or food production manager gets assistance to handle purchasing, other departments probably need such assistance, too. It is in this way that payroll costs soon mount.

As for management, a centralized pur-

chasing department is more responsive. It is much easier to communicate with one person than with several department heads, and a single purchasing department is more easily controlled and policed than several points of purchase. This makes the controller's and management's jobs easier and more effective.

A trained professional buyer can buy anything when supplied with specifications, when closely supervised by management, and when assisted by cooperating department heads. Such a buyer is interested in market research, price and supply forecasting, the obtaining and recording of price quotations, the monitoring of inventories, and the expediting of deliveries. It is through departmental purchasing committees that department heads can express their ideas, have a voice in setting up specifications, and select products for use by their department. To this extent, various department heads share in management decisions, using information furnished by the purchasing department as a result of market research and long-range forecasting.

Centralized purchasing has resulted in the development of innovative procedures, the securing of better prices and new and better products, and the maintaining of a steadier source of supply without interfering with legitimate direction by the heads of the using departments. It frees the person in charge of production to supervise the production process, to train employees involved in production, to balance food and payroll costs, and to budget and plan profit margins. Change has come slowly, and it will probably take many more years before the food service industry fully accepts the premise that purchasing should be separate from production, as it is in most other manufacturing and service industries.

Unless some new element enters the purchasing field of the food service industry, the trend is definitely toward separate purchasing departments. It is interesting that, even in smaller motels and motor inns around the country, the managers of the operation have taken over the food purchasing function, as well as purchasing for all other departments. This represents a variation of the idea of a separate purchasing department, even for small operations. It should also be recognized that there is a trend toward cooperative or group buying (see Chapter 6) that may render arguments for or against a separate purchasing department academic.

FUNCTIONS OF A FOOD PURCHASING DEPARTMENT

A food purchasing department not only buys necessary food supplies, but it also acts as an information center for a food operation. In the first instance, it is the task of the food purchasing department to obtain from the world food distribution system the food supplies, both as to quantity and quality, required by the operation, and to have the supplies delivered, when needed, at the best possible price. This is, of course, the function of any purchasing department, whether it is for the food industry, the steel industry, the airline industry, or the interplanetary space industry of the future. This function should be carried out in such a manner that the operation is able to make a profit, or, if profit is not a motive, to provide meals at the lowest possible cost for food supplies consumed.

In its capacity as an information center, a food purchasing department also serves as an exchange agency. The department, besides exchanging ownership and possession of goods, exchanges information in two ways. It sends back to the producers and growers information regarding customer preferences, reports on what is selling and what will sell. A purchasing department also passes back to the production department information concerning food supplies: quality to be expected, cost, adequacy of the supply, and any other information that might help the consumer or the management of an operation in making long-range plans.

The importance of the exchange function of a food purchasing department should not be overlooked. The information going back into the world food distribution system has an effect on the grower, the producer, the manufacturer, the advertiser, and the sales promotion agency. It influences government policy, union activities, and political platforms.

THE ROLE OF THE BUYER

There are six basic elements in the world food distribution system: the grower; the packer or manufacturer; the transporter; the wholesaler, broker, or commission man; the middleman, purveyor, or food supply house; and the buyer or consumer.

If one asks which is the most important and if one rules out politics, weather, wars, strikes, elections, revolutions, or other unexpected phenomena, the answer is, obviously, the buyer or consumer. That is the person who determines what is grown, what is packaged, and how it is manufactured, shipped, sold, and consumed. If it cannot be sold, it will not be grown, manufactured, or marketed. Actually, the buyer is many persons and elements. The buyer is the housewife, the corner druggist, the operator of a snack bar, the director of a hospital, the school dietitian, the buyer for a supermarket, the manager of a restaurant, the chef, the steward, and the owners of thousands of "mom and pop" food service facilities throughout the world.

These people are influential in the overall food distribution system. The bigger the job, the stronger the influence, and it must be used wisely. Influence should be used to benefit trade and not to gratify personal ego. There are always alarmists who point out the danger inherent in possessing too much power, but there has been little argument against having a separate purchasing department with a concentration of buying power that can be used for the benefit of both the company and the trade.

The purchasing department and the buyer have been viewed in relation to the overall organization that is to be found in the food service industry. Next, the buyer must be trained in terms of the purchasing department and the functioning of that department.

5 *The Food Buyer and His Job*

By now, it should be obvious that the person heading the purchasing department should not be just anyone available when the position is open if purchasing is to be done skillfully. The person, be it a woman or a man, must gain the cooperation of other department heads and be able to communicate with food service managers, dietary directors, chefs, catering managers, dietitians, medical personnel, professional agitators, political appointees, and people from every walk of life. He must be able to understand salesmen and learn from them without losing their respect. The person should be in good health, energetic, and free from personal habits that might interfere with performance. As for personality traits, he should be aggressive but not abrasive, honest but not scrupulous, confident but not conceited, innovative but not impractical, decisive but not inflexible. Since it is unlikely that anyone possess all these attributes, there must be compromise—another prime requisite for a good food buyer.

It was Mr. McCawber in *Oliver Twist* who said: "If you are right 51% of the time—happiness, but if you are wrong 51% of the time—misery." In order to select a food buyer, the person who is making the decision needs to know as much as possible about the food buyer's job. The objective of this chapter is to examine the job requirements, to consider the type of person needed to fill it, and to suggest ways to organize the job so that the position and the person will be as productive as possible. A wise decision does, indeed, make the difference between happiness and misery, or, more specifically in this instance, between profit and loss.

JOB DESCRIPTION

The first requirement for any job is a clear, detailed written statement of what the job entails and what is expected of the person filling it. Personnel people maintain that the main reason good executives fail on the job is because they do not understand what the boss expects. On the other hand, communications being what they are, it is always possible that the boss thinks the man on the job knows what the job is, whereas, in reality, it has never been spelled out. It is amazing how many executives or employees in such key positions as department heads find no job description available when they start in a new position and no one to accept the responsibility for preparing one. Many persons starting on a job that is not clearly outlined decide for themselves what to do and how to do it. If this does not please the boss, there are problems, and perhaps eventually there is a change in personnel.

A good job description not only helps the food buyer; it also helps clarify the responsibilities of those who work with him, and they are less likely to interfere with the purchasing function at the expense of their own jobs. The same job description enables a boss to rate the performance of the food buyer fairly and comprehensively, and it helps the food buyer evaluate his own performance. The role of the job description as a measure of proficiency is frequently overlooked.

A food scientist might describe a food buyer as "the link in the world food distribution system where the flow of goods moves from the supply chain to the production process and on to the end user." The food operator, on the other hand, would probably describe him as "the guy that gets what we want, when we want it, and at the best possible price." Both definitions are correct, but the second one leaves nothing to the imagination.

No one job description is perfect for all food buying jobs. It is doubtful that there are any two such jobs that are exactly alike anywhere in the world. Even though the basic requirements may be the same, each job has certain challenges that require a hand-tailored description.

The following job description, although it is designed for a food buyer in a hotel, could be modified for use in many large- or medium-sized food service organizations. The responsibilities would not change appreciably.

JOB DESCRIPTION
FOR
THE FOOD BUYER—
WITH STOREROOM
RESPONSIBILITY

I. Basic responsibility
   A. For purchasing, storage, and issuance of food (or other items designated by management)
   B. For security, cleanliness, and maintenance in all goods and beverage supply storage areas

II. Organizational relationships
   A. Reports to: General manager
   B. Supervises: Purchasing office staff
                   Supply storage personnel
   C. Functional relationships
      1. With food and beverage manager regarding department requirements
      2. With chef regarding food
      3. With receiving clerk regarding receiving of food, beverages, and other supplies and regarding training and policing in receiving
      4. With catering manager regarding group meals
      5. With dining room managers regarding their suggestions for food and beverage supplies
      6. With controller and food and beverage controller regarding cost controls
      7. With kitchen stewards regarding food and beverage supplies

8. With staff planner regarding scheduling

D. Lateral supervision
1. From general manager directly, or from resident manager or senior assistant manager in general manager's absence
2. From food and beverage manager and controller as their responsibilities relate to purchasing
3. From senior department heads, but only in terms of suggestions and requests for purchases

E. Authority
1. Under the supervision of the general manager makes decisions for the purchasing department in order to achieve an efficient overall operation
2. Has final approval of quality, price, quantity, and source of supply in keeping with house policy and purchase specifications

III. Functions and duties
A. Purchases food, beverages, and other supplies, either on own responsibility or after consultation with chef and other department heads
B. Visits
1. Markets to select and stamp meats for aging and to mark other products of specific nature and quality for delivery
2. Purveyors to inspect product quality and to keep up to date on available quality and seasonal products
C. Solicits and analyzes bids, places orders, and makes contracts with the approval of management

D. Selects purveyors on the basis of their ability to deliver specified quality merchandise at competitive prices, with the approval of management
E. Monitors receiving procedures and assists in training receiving personnel
F. Acts as chairman of testing committee and carries out a continuous program of product testing
G. Inspects supply storerooms for
1. Sanitation
2. Orderliness
3. Condition of stock
4. Rotation of supplies
5. Maintenance of parts
6. Security measures
H. Carries out internal accounting control procedures regarding purchasing, storing, and issuing of food and beverage supplies, in conjunction with food and beverage controller
I. Reviews and approves invoices as to prices paid, quantities ordered, and quality of merchandise received
J. Employs, instructs, and discharges purchasing office staff and supply storage personnel
K. Maintains reasonable, regular visiting hours for salespeople
L. Maintains a constant search for new and better supplies and for opportunities to economize
M. Maintains a good working relationship with other department heads and personnel throughout operations and solicits opinions and suggestions from others regarding operation of the purchasing department

IV. Requirements
   A. Personal
      1. Must have a cooperative attitude toward his job and other personnel
      2. Should have a "Let's try it and see" approach to problems
      3. Must have integrity and be completely honest
      4. Must possess a "curiosity factor" that pushes him to do things
      5. Must be an aggressive bargainer, but must not demand the impossible; an ability to recognize the "bottom price" is essential
      6. Must have the ability to resist flattery and avoid the "God Syndrome" (self-importance)
      7. Should be in good health with normal living habits
      8. Must inspire job loyalty in his associates and staff
      9. Must be able to do a good public relations job for his employer
   B. Experience and training
      1. Must read, write, and communicate well
      2. Should have at least two years in college or in a technical trade school
      3. Should have at least five years of experience in the back of the house, with at least one year of experience in food purchasing
      4. Must be thoroughly acquainted with food, beverages, supply products, specifications, and the market
      5. Should have some training in business law

FINDING A GOOD BUYER

A job can be set up with operating manuals, specification lists, checklists, internal controls, management supervision, and outside advisory services. But, if the food buyer is wrong for the job, whether the reason is personal, lack of experience, or poor technique, the job will not be as well done as it might have been.

The Search

A good buyer can frequently be promoted from within the organization, unless it is new. If an organization has been established for some time and there is no such person, management should realize that their policy regarding training needs revision. One of the marks of good management is to see that there is a backup person ready to step into all key department jobs throughout the entire operation. Department heads themselves, if they are really management minded, will have a trainee ready to take over in case of an emergency, ensuring continuity in policy in case of illness, retirement, or some other circumstance.

If it is necessary to seek a buyer from outside the organization, management should realize the importance of being patient and thorough in the search. The personnel department should not be expected to produce a suitable applicant in a few days or, in some cases, even a few weeks, and recommendations from purveyors should be ignored since such opinions might be biased. A hurried decision is costly if the wrong person is hired.

One of the easiest ways to get a good food buyer is to determine who is doing the best job for a successful food operation in the area. The offer of a higher salary or an increase in benefits might persuade that person to make a move. If he has been successful, however, a large part of that success is probably dependent upon cooperation from the boss and other department heads he is working with, and the person probably has a great sense of loyalty to his present employer. Sometimes a change in management creates a situation where an outstanding employee will entertain a bid from another company.

Another good place to look is among men working immediately under successful buyers. If such a person has been on the job for a while, he has usually been well trained and is probably looking for advancement. If advancement appears to be blocked in the present job, that person might entertain an outside offer.

There are many good executive search companies in the country that can be of considerable help in finding an applicant, but it is essential to establish the reputation of so-called "headhunters" before it is safe to use their services. Some of the sharp practices of these "talent scouts" are well known. Many of them are not above shuffling employees from one position to another just to collect the fee. Some send candidates for an interview without screening them or even calling former employers to learn the reason for termination or resignation.

Accounting firms and operational consultants to the food industry can generally be depended upon for an unbiased recommendation. They are also helpful in checking the background of an applicant.

As for salary, the food buyer should be paid enough to remove the temptation to steal. Perhaps the most common rationalization, if the buyer is underpaid, is that he "is making so much money for the company that he is entitled to part of it."

The Candidate

Personality Traits and Character. Such considerations as personality and character are probably as important as experience and formal training for the job when weighing a candidate for the position of food buyer. Anyone who is interested and has the basic qualifications can learn the trade, but personal attitudes and habits are not likely to change much. The many complications that confront a food buyer daily as he carries out his job require that he be flexible, easy to approach, and able to get along with people. Others' opinions, ideas, and wishes are not just important to the person who has them; they may even have merit. The good buyer listens and decides whether or how to use the "advice" that flows through his office daily.

Within the organization, management, even though unfamiliar with the finer points of food buying, is almost sure to become involved. The wise buyer encourages management to express wishes and opinions, for this puts him in a stronger position to get the job done without interference from other department heads.

Every food buyer also has to get along with chefs, whether they are men or women, young or old, trained in Europe or trained elsewhere. The pressures that chefs are subjected to can make them difficult to get along with at times. A buyer must make every effort to work with the chef on an amicable basis.

Finally, if the buyer does not have the cooperation of his fellow workers, they can ruin him by withholding necessary information and by constantly criticizing him behind his back. There are always people willing to listen to criticism, often those who are jealous of a job well done.

Conrad Hilton, who proved to be one of the world's leading hotel executives and who has demonstrated a keen ability to select excellent executives, addressed a graduation class at the Culinary Institute of America in New Haven, Connecticut. He indicated that the one thing he always looked for in a person was the curiosity factor: why a thing was being done the way it was, and how it could be done better. A good food buyer has to have an open mind about things and people. He has to be willing and able to listen objectively to salesmen and people in his own organization, and even to solicit suggestions. He has to be not only willing, but eager to try a new product, a change in procedure, or a change in a control if the new idea seems to offer opportunity for improvement.

And Abraham Lincoln's thought-provoking statement that "a stubborn man can stand adversity, but it takes a great man to stand success" certainly applies to the food buyer who is subject to all kinds of flattery from salesmen every day. It takes an objective viewpoint not to be affected by the feeling of importance attached to making decisions, as well as by the feeling of power that accompanies placing orders, often for large sums of money. The wise buyer sees himself as part of a team, working for the success of an operation of which he is a part.

Some people in the food buying business seem to think that a buyer's entire mission in life is to try to get a lower price. These people forget that there is a bottom price for everything. Anything below that price means that the seller cheapens something in order to protect his own business from failure. The food buyer should recognize that the honest purveyor is faced with problems related to delivery, financing, and labor relations. The purveyor is entitled to a fair profit, and the buyer who operates with this in mind will get better prices, service, and quality.

The good buyer should view his job as a game that must be played according to accepted rules—and won for the benefit of management. If management does not benefit, a new player will be introduced. The buyer must have self-control and be slow to anger. On many occasions he can be criticized, harassed by friends and friends of friends seeking favors, and, on occasion, his very reputation is at stake. Unless he can take such annoyances and pressures in stride, the job or even his health may suffer.

One way to maintain control in difficult situations is not to get so personally involved in a problem that one's judgment is affected. A good sense of humor is a real asset, for it can relieve a tense situation and permit a graceful retreat. This allows a buyer to strengthen his case and return at a later time to gain his point. Flexibility should be encouraged, but there are times when one must take a stand. It is a wise person who can distinguish between the principle that must be defended and the opinion or action that is open to discussion.

A food buyer cannot live with his job twenty-four hours a day, seven days a week, and expect to remain keen and alert, doing a sound, perceptive job. He must learn to close the office door and leave the pressures behind. Good management encourages department heads to enjoy their home life and participate in community affairs. Local politics should, however, be avoided since it can create additional pressures, which the food buyer does not need.

Finally, it must be acknowledged that the food buyer should be free of anything that might cause him to be subject to blackmail or any other pressure. Moderation, it seems, is the key.

Qualifications. Although the most important requirements for a professional food buyer are those reflected in personality and character, education and experience cannot be ignored. A top food buyer needs at least two years in college or in a technical trade school, plus at least five years of back-of-the-house experience and a minimum of one year as a buyer or as an assistant buyer in a large, first-class operation, whether it be institution, hotel, or restaurant.

Education. A few years ago almost everyone insisted that a college education was a prerequisite for success in modern society. Experience has shown that this is not necessarily so, and today the emphasis is on training appropriate to the individual's interests, desires, and capabilities. In terms of earnings, the graduate from a technical school can compete quite successfully with the graduate from a college in most fields of endeavor. Certainly there are professions such as medicine, law, theology, engineering, accounting, and teaching that require years of study and training, but, even then, education does not guarantee professional or personal success. It does, however, help a person to learn and enables him to organize his thoughts. It imparts a sense of accomplishment, instills confidence, and helps in developing the ability to live and work with others. It can also open doors for those seeking jobs.

Any person who has the drive to succeed in his chosen field will obtain the education he needs, wherever it is to be found and whether the source is formal or informal. For the food buyer, everyday experience is a continuous teacher.

Experience. Back-of-the-house experience covers all phases of the food operation: catering manager, restaurant manager, food and beverage controller, receiving clerk, storeroom manager, steward, food preparer, and even warewasher. Often, a young chef or sous chef eager to get into management will accept a food-

buying job as part of his training and development. Such a person usually is an excellent food buyer, but he is satisfied to stay with the job for only three to five years before seeking further advancement. He knows how the entire operation works, how one department relates to others, where to go for information, and, usually, whether the information is correct. He also "speaks the language." There is in such cases, much togetherness in a food operation, especially in the kitchen and preparation areas. A food buyer who knows the "lingo" has a much easier time than a person from the outside or from the front of the house.

A food buyer from the back of the house, who has a better understanding of quality and what is really needed, avoids such errors as buying the best canned tomatoes on the market for making tomato sauce or vegetable soup. Purveyors, cognizant of the buyer's experience, have more respect for his ability, admire his progress in the business, and are less apt to try to take advantage.

The good food buyer has to know all of the sources of supply in his own community. He should also know the supply situation in nearby communities. There are often "gentlemen's agreements" that the food buyer cannot cope with in a local community, and a nearby source of supply often proves useful. He also recognizes that transportation problems are greater than ever before, and fuel costs and ever-increasing traffic congestion threaten to increase such problems. Unions can also be an asset. If the buyer knows the rules and abides by them, he can persuade the union to do the same. Most locals will help if their problems and rights are recognized.

The buyer must have a thorough knowledge of current packaging, grading, sizes, and sectional and seasonal products, as well as considerable experience in making butcher and taste tests in order to set up purchase specifications. A fairly accurate knowledge of the relationship between food supplies as purchased and portions served, better known as portion cost factors, is also helpful.

Records are important, and some that the food buyer needs to keep in order to maintain an internal control system are purchase orders, receiving sheets, quotation sheets, invoices, requisitions, inventories, cost of money, and payments. Experience or training in the law governing contracts can also prove valuable.

An experienced food buyer knows, and a smart, inexperienced food buyer soon learns, that there is no point in trying to change the marketing system. By the time a buyer understands completely how the market works and knows how to make it work to his advantage, he qualifies as a professional food buyer.

FOOD BUYING AS A PROFESSION

A rapid turnover of people serving in the capacity of food buyer discourages competent people from entering the field. This is a costly problem for the food industry. If the food buyer has a reputation for honesty and is pleasant to work with, and if ownership or an immediate superior have not changed, why is this turnover so great? Often it is because the person in the job is not a professional food buyer; he is an order clerk.

An order clerk buys the merchandise needed and receives it in an orderly and routine manner. He gets the merchandise at a price that is not always the best, or the worst. He may or may not visit the market. He may or may not have regular hours for salesmen to visit, and he prob-

ably does not pay too much attention to salesmen. He may resist innovation. In short, he does a routine job of telephone buying.

The buyer who approaches his job professionally, whether he buys food or other supplies, is constantly on the alert to find a better way to do what he is doing. He constantly studies the market and reads newspapers, magazines, and other literature pertaining to products. He visits market sources on a regular basis, checks the quality and availability of products on the market, and anticipates market changes and trends. He is willing to learn and be educated by people in the market who, as a rule, know more about the products than he does. He exercises his curiosity factor by looking for new products, new ways to use products, and new purchasing techniques. This is what makes his work satisfying and challenging.

The Problem of Authority

One of the biggest sources of irritation for a professional food buyer is the lack of adequate decision-making authority. This complaint is heard from every department head in any type of business, and it is a common complaint, even of people in management. It is natural for everyone to seek greater authority because it makes the job easier to perform, and, in many instances, makes the job more secure.

Too much authority without checks and counterchecks is, however, dangerous. A food buyer who has been given complete authority for making all decisions can be a source of irritation to the people with whom he works. If disagreements arise over buying procedures, management must investigate the situation, find out what the problems are, and provide solutions. Neglect of such a situation can prove costly; it can even result in the manager's losing his job.

If, on the other hand, the food buyer's decisions are constantly criticized by the food service manager, the dietary director, the chef, the butcher, the pastry chef, the steward, the head storeroom man, and others, he may lose initiative and effectiveness in performing the job. Good job descriptions, which should be approved by management, spell out the responsibility and level of authority of all the various persons—food buyer, food service manager, chef, catering manager, food and beverage controller, and controller of the operation—involved in buying procedures. Such elucidation of authority is not only fair for the food buyer; it is also fair for the other people involved. They may try to contribute to the buying procedure with the best of intentions, but lack of knowledge, lack of time, or self-interest may mean that they actually hurt themselves, the food buyer, and the overall operation.

One of the best aids in avoiding problems in buying and in solving the problem of decision making is, again, the attention that management gives to the buying procedure. Management must be aware of what is going on all the time, even though it is not deeply involved in the day-to-day functioning of the purchasing department. Sometimes the food buyer must be supported even when he is wrong, but, if he is wrong too often, management must find either a new food buyer or some way to avoid mistakes in judgment.

The use of a committee, whatever name is given to it, working under the direction of management to establish purchasing specifications and to advise in areas of disagreement is probably one of the best ways to avoid misunderstandings among department heads and usurpation of authority by any one person. A continuous testing program keeps problems out in the open and encourages communications among all the people involved in the buying procedure.

The Need for Rigid Requirements

Time and again it has been proved that a professional approach to purchasing can easily save up to 10 percent of the total cost of purchases in a large food operation. Even if the operation is only large enough to use $500,000 worth of merchandise a year, this represents potential savings of $50,000. Food operations requiring food purchases of up to $4 million or $5 million a year are not uncommon. For an establishment to have become that large, the purchasing job being done is probably good, but a professional buyer, using modern techniques, may be able to effect savings amounting to hundreds of thousands of dollars per year. There is one recorded situation where a change in purchasing techniques meant a minimum saving of $200,000 per year in an operation that had the reputation for being one of the most proficient in the entire area. This was done by taking advantage of the large-quantity buying power of the operation after an expansion program increased volume about four times. Prior to the expansion, the volume of business was not large enough to permit quantity buying and deliveries.

When consulting firms are asked to find the probable causes of high food costs per dollar of sale or high cost per meal in an institution, they invariably look at the food buying situation for that is often the source of the problem. If high costs are the fault of the food buyer, it follows that the man is not suited to the job, perhaps because management did not take sufficient care in filling the position.

Keeping up with the Profession

Often, after several years of hard work, a food buyer may begin to feel complacent about his achievements. Such an attitude is fatal. A buyer should constantly make self-evaluations to be sure that he is doing everything possible to protect his job, to lay the groundwork for future promotion, and to increase his own sense of worth. The buyer and management should both realize that changes in markets, products, politics, strikes, trials, wars, and research make it impossible to get by on yesterday's knowledge. The buyer must keep up with the world and look forward to tomorrow.

The buyer should be permitted and encouraged to grow by attending conventions, seminars, and trade association meetings. He should read trade publications and daily newspapers for market information and for trade information, and, when possible, he should contribute articles to trade papers and participate in other trade association activities, as well as aid local community schools, night schools, and trade schools that are endeavoring to train youth. And, if management does not encourage the buyer to attend auxiliary training courses, the buyer should take the initiative in order to keep his "tools of the trade" in good working order.

Professional Honesty

Many of the pitfalls surrounding the food buyer are discussed in Chapter 11, but the subject of honesty in a food buyer can be settled very quickly and without much discussion. A *food buyer is honest, or he is not honest.* Books on purchasing that discuss this point at all frequently deviate from the commonly recognized concept of honesty. Some even go so far as to suggest that there are compromise positions providing certain conditions are met by both buyer and purveyor. Security services, on the other hand, stress that the first step down the path toward dishonesty is the first compromise with the basic concept, and every buyer caught up in some form of wrongdoing has stated that the first step was always that small compromise with honesty that he did not even recognize as being dishonest.

Several years ago, the food buyer retired from a large hotel chain famous for its accommodations and service, progressive innovations, profitability, and exemplary management. The farewell dinner was attended by six hundred persons, including every hotelman and purveyor who could obtain an invitation. The buyer had worked for the company for nearly forty years, having started in the storeroom of one of the first hotels built by the company in upstate New York. Over the years he had acquired a reputation for being one of the fairest, most honest, and most capable food buyers in New York City. The company had paid him well, he had invested wisely over the years, and his farewell gift of a generous number of shares of stock in the company ensured a comfortable retirement living. In this, he was almost unique. He was one of five food buyers in New York City at that time to achieve full retirement. His thoughts that night summarize the subject of honesty in buying.

"It's a great feeling," he said, "not to spend one moment worrying about what anyone thinks of you because of something you did the day before, about losing your job because someone finds out about some 'side money,' or about what your wife and kids and friends will think if you get caught."

He told of tragic situations where food

buyers had been unable to withstand pressure from purveyors, friends of purveyors in the organization, or friends of purveyors with potential business to offer, stressing the fact that accepting gratuities or favors could compromise a person's freedom of decision. In his opinion, a good reputation is the best asset that a person can have in the food buying business. Any compromise with honesty cannot be kept secret. One's reputation is public knowledge and, although a monetary value cannot be assigned to it, everyone is aware of it. The reward for the strictest standards of honesty, as he saw it, is the respect of people in the trade and in the profession and the pride and confidence that accompany a good reputation. During all the years that he was associated with buying, he never had to discuss salary with his boss, an indication that good employers apparently realize the importance of competence and honesty in the buying business.

He closed his remarks that night with the opinion that the most rewarding aspects of a foodbuyer's job are the many friends made on the job and the pleasant and often amusing memories of crises, challenges, successes, and failures over the years—all of which add up to a full and rewarding business life.

6 *The Mechanics of Buying Food*

There are prerequisites to the actual mechanics of food buying, and they concern management, the food buyer, and the organizations in which food buying procedures are performed. If a good job of food buying is to be done, as has already been pointed out, management must take an active part in the operation. Management's policies must be clear and concise if those policies are to be followed.

The food buyer should be set up as an independent buyer, reporting directly to the general manager or business manager of the operation. There should be a committee to work with the food buyer and the operating heads of the food department (this can be the same committee that is used for testing), and the controller's office should then have the independent control necessary to cover all phases of the food purchasing operation. These arrangements may be elaborate, involving several persons, or they may be simple. This depends on the size and scope of the operation. Once the system has been established, there are four basic considerations in the mechanics of food purchasing, and they are what, where, from whom, and how to buy.

WHAT AND HOW MUCH TO BUY

It is unfair to expect a food buyer to know exactly what is needed by operating departments and how much of it to buy. Even if he did know, it would be unwise to make this the responsibility of a single person, ignoring a production manager, the chef, a storeroom manager, and other operating department heads.

In setting up a new operation, the department manager or operator should meet with the purchasing agent, the production manager, the chef, the catering manager or equivalent person, and the storeroom manager in order to work out a commodity list for menus to be used in preparing food for the operation in question. After the list has been prepared, it is important that these same people agree on specifications covering the items listed. If there is a testing committee, any items requiring testing should be submitted to the committee before final approval of the specifications (see Chapter 7). After the list has been compiled and the specifications have been determined, it should be broken down further into staples and perishables.

The list of staples, which are normally considered grocery storeroom items, should be prepared for the storeroom manager's use with an indication of minimum and maximum supply for each item carried in the storeroom. Such a list is helpful in keeping inventory, in avoiding the problem of dead stock, and in preparing the storeroom manager's orders that go to the food buyer. The chef should have a copy to be sure that needed grocery items are in stock and available on short notice.

As for perishable items, there are two categories, fresh and frozen. Fresh perishables should be ordered as needed, based on specific intended use. Either they back up the daily menu, or they are for use at a function or a special event. Frozen items can be used to back up a par inventory stock.

In some operations the chef is expected to submit a daily list of all perishables that he wishes to have delivered for an immediate, specified use. If this proves too time consuming for the chef, the storeroom manager might be able to maintain the proper quantities of fresh fruits and vegetables by referring to banquet menus or a list of special requirements that can then be added to the average daily use of these items. The chef would then be responsible only for working up a list of requirements for meats, poultry, and fish. This list of requirements and the cost are key factors in determining the cost of food sold or the cost per meal served in the institutional field, and the chef is the person best qualified to prepare it.

The food and beverage controller can be very helpful in determining requirements for the amount of perishables needed to serve a given number of covers, that is, persons to be served. These amounts are generally figured in terms of pounds or units necessary to serve one hundred covers in dining rooms or for banquets. By making periodic tests, the food and beverage controller works with the food and beverage manager and the chef to estimate just how much of the many key items is needed to provide for the estimated number of covers required for the various food services, banquets, parties, or special diets.

The key to controlling food costs is to establish a relationship between pounds or units of food purchased to serve an accurately estimated number of persons on a day-to-day basis.

When purchasing frozen foods, some operators have found it helpful to set a minimum and maximum allowable stock on each frozen item to be carried. This aids in checking inventory turnover, helps in maintaining the level of usable stock, and eliminates the possibility of overlooking items because they do not appear on the required list in the chef's or catering manager's hands. In Chapter 9, on storeroom management, it is pointed out that a perpetual inventory on frozen storeroom items prevents costly losses.

WHERE TO BUY

Before a decision is made concerning where to buy, a market search should be made. Much depends on the country, or the part of the country, where the operation is located, what supplies are available, and the season of the year.

Location, which influences the quantities of food that must be purchased and stored, helps to determine mini-maxi limits. It also affects delivery schedules, and, since the cost of delivery is rising, limited delivery schedules worked out with suppliers could result in greater discounts, better quotations, or lower average unit delivery costs.

Other considerations are the amount of storage area available for the operation and whether or not there is a dependable source of energy for refrigeration and the maintenance of equipment or a reliable alternate source of power, such as a diesel generator or a standby steam-driven generator fired by coal or, in some parts of the world, by wood, for emergencies.

In deciding whether to buy locally, other questions arise. Are local suppliers large enough to carry adequate stocks? Are there enough local food purveyors to permit the buyer to get truly competitive prices? During particular times of the year, it should be recognized that the local farmers' market can be one of the best sources for certain perishables. Not only do you save money, but there is also an opportunity to improve relations with local people and to support the local economy. If an operation is close to a large metropolitan area, it should be recognized that large purveyors will make deliveries as far as a hundred miles from their base of operations, often delivering merchandise at considerably lower cost than if it is purchased locally.

Today, there is also the matter of contracts. Many large companies distribute nationally by working out satisfactory arrangements for the delivery of merchandise on a national or long-term basis.

FROM WHOM TO BUY

In Chapter 2 there was a general discussion of functions, including the supply function, of the market and of some of the functionaries who operate in it. It is important that the food buyer have a clear understanding of the respective functions of the suppliers with whom he does business.

In the case of meat, a *packer* may slaughter, clean, store, and sell. Today, some so-called packers buy animals from slaughterhouses (abattoirs) that specialize in killing and cleaning carcasses of meat animals. A *processor* generally turns raw food into finished products through canning, mixing, baking, or some other means. Sometimes packers process such items as hams, bacon, sausage, corned beef or tongues, and often, shortening and oil. Some large packers, for example, Swift, Armour, and Cudahy, do more processing and marketing than killing and breaking. Companies such as Iowa Beef Processors, Missouri Packing Company, Monfort, Oscar Mayer, Excel, Litvak, Spencer Packing, and a host of others engage in the killing, breaking, and marketing of boxed, ready-for-use meats and in sideline feedlot operations, bagging fertilizers for the garden and recycling food dropped in the feedlot in a pelletized form for cattle and pets. Chicken feathers have also proved to be an important commodity in the manufacturing of pet food.

A *breaker* is a company that specializes in buying carload lots of meat carcasses and "breaks" them into wholesale cuts that are then sold to meat supply houses, chain stores, grocery stores, and fabricators. The *fabricator*, who buys wholesale cuts of meat, makes them up on a custom order basis for wholesalers and processors or sells them directly to a user who pays his account on a weekly basis. (See Chapter 15 for a more detailed treatment.)

Dealers, purveyors, suppliers, and *wholesalers* perform similar services, and the titles are used interchangeably. They deal directly with the buyer, either by means of a house account (no salesman) or through a salesman. Most dealers specialize in a single item or a group of related items. In smaller communities, a supply house sometimes acts as a general supplier (a one-stop supply service).

Salesmen, the backbone of the food supply business, are probably the hardest working, least appreciated members of the marketing system. A commission house generally sells, on a commission basis, to purveyors or wholesalers who in turn sell to the food buyer. Most commission houses specialize in certain foods and seldom sell direct to a user, except for large accounts and food processors. *Commission men* generally buy or sell specialized items on a paper basis. They accept carload lots of lettuce, for example, from a cooperative in California and sell it, for a commission, in the best market while the goods are still en route. Sometimes a commission house speculates by buying a lot of merchandise and selling it at a profit or a loss.

A *broker* is a salesman who represents a manufacturer or a group of manufacturers by setting up a distribution point and selling, on a commission basis, to a regular food supply house. *Missionary salesmen* go out from headquarters to open up new accounts, to research and overcome resistance to a product, to introduce new products, or to start a new sales campaign, among other activities.

With all of these steps in the food supply line, it is a wonder that food does not cost more. Today, a quantity food buyer must investigate every legal and ethical way to "buypass" any step in the distribution chain. This is not easy because, even if a purveyor would benefit, he is not anxious to tamper with a "safe" situation.

Selecting Suppliers

The selection of suppliers is one of the most important decisions that management must make in setting up and oper-

ating any type of food operation, whether it be food processing, a hotel, a restaurant, a hospital or some other institution, or a catering service. Good management works with the food buyer and the testing committee before approving a list of purveyors. Management is stressed because the final decision as to who the supplier will be belongs to management alone.

The testing committee, which includes the production manager, the chef, the food and beverage manager, and other operating department heads, should also be concerned with which suppliers are chosen to furnish food to the operation. Through decisions as to what brand names or qualities are to be used in the operation, the committee influences selection, for its recommendations are reflected in the specifications. The wise food buyer is glad that he does not have the final say in selecting purveyors.

Before any selection is made, the reputations of the purveyors available in the area should be thoroughly investigated. One of the best ways to judge a purveyor is to find out who his customers are. If the operations he services have good reputations and competent management personnel, the chances are that the purveyor is reliable. A few telephone calls to other institutions or to hotel, restaurant, and food managers in the area, the local Better Business Bureau, the Chamber of Commerce, local trade associations, and local bankers often provide helpful information, and confidential reports can be obtained from companies that specialize in such activities. If the potential volume of business to be done is large, a complete, independent report on the reputation of the purveyor might be worthwhile.

Management can, in addition, visit the purveyor's premises with the food buyer, so that both can assess the size and the quality of the operation. By inspecting the quantities on hand and the quality of the merchandise, one can make a considered judgment as to whether a business association would be beneficial. The general manager can use his first visit to make clear to the purveyor that, if he is selected, his performance will be judged solely on the quality of merchandise delivered, the service rendered, and the prices quoted in competition with other dealers.

HOW TO BUY

Too many people buy food by sitting down with a list of needed items, phoning familiar dealers, placing an order, and asking the dealer to rush the order. There is little or no attempt to compare prices from different sources, but the buyer is secure in the knowledge that the dealers will give good service, that they will be nice to him around the holidays, and that the merchandise will be of good quality. As long as it gets the job done, everyone is satisfied, the operation shows a profit, and the manager goes along with it to keep peace, this type of buying continues. Of course, the fact that it costs anywhere from 10 to 20 percent more than it should is played down.

Other buyers meticulously call various purveyors and haggle over every price quotation before recording it on the daily market list. After several hours of telephoning, such a buyer goes over the quotation list and circles the prices he is willing to pay, thereby choosing his suppliers. The telephone is again used to place orders, and the supplies are delivered the next day. If this is the purchasing method, the receiving clerk or the food buyer should check deliveries as meticulously as prices were checked. This type of one-track buying also can cost a company money because no one system of buying suffices for all of the various kinds of merchandise used in a food service operation.

The professional food buyer uses different systems of buying, with different, detailed procedures, for different kinds of merchandise. A good buyer will also change his system from time to time to meet market conditions, to take advantage of dips in the market, and to flatten out purchase costs when uptrends are expected in the market. The good buyer also continues to add new purveyors to his list and drops those who are not interested enough in the account to perform satisfactorily. Even though all of the purveyors might be making an effort to keep the account, a good buyer gives some "vacations" to purveyors, but rotates the "vacations" so that no conscientious purveyor is eliminated from the list.

PURCHASING SYSTEMS

Systems most commonly used in the food industry today are:
1. farmers' market buying
2. supermarket buying
3. open market buying
4. fixed markup over daily trade quotation
5. buy and hold
6. average yearly (or shorter period) negotiated price
7. drop shipments from national purveyors
8. one-stop buying
9. cost-plus from best competitive dealers
10. formal written bid system
11. buying at auction
12. standing order system
13. acting as one's own distributor
14. cooperative or group buying.

The examination of each system that follows includes discussion of both its good and bad points. There are other systems and variations of systems that might be preferable to those listed, depending on circumstances. The personalities involved, the type of operation, distance from market sources, available transportation, the local and international political situation, availability of funds, and the season of the year—all influence the system used.

Farmers' Markets

These markets were the main source of supply for food in colonial days, and they continue to serve the food industry throughout the country. Although it is still called the farmers' market in some areas, it is perhaps better known now as the public market. Generally located near the wholesale market area, it can operate on a year-round basis, just on weekends in the off-season, or twenty-four hours a day at the height of the local harvest. In some areas fishermen supply local markets. In other areas the markets carry fresh eggs, dairy products, poultry, and smoked meats.

Although the institutional and hotel trade seldom patronizes a farmers' market, small-food operations, such as a motel, a restaurant, a nursing home, some schools, and small grocery stores, use the farmers' market as much as possible. The advantages are lower prices and fresher, often better-quality foods. Some restaurants make a point of promoting and serving local products (fresh Blue Lake green beans, Rockport melons, lima and butter beans, and actual vine-ripened tomatoes). The food buyer for Restaurant Associates, who operated outstanding restaurants in the central part of New York City, took full advantage of public markets located in Long Island and Jersey City. Even though the trip to the market took time, being able to get fresh seasonal fruits and vegetables was well worth the effort. To the vegetable enthusiast, nothing compares with fresh peas or fresh corn picked from the garden in the morning and served at dinner that same evening.

Recently, some farmers and cattle producers have opened a farmers' market-type of meat market in a cooperative effort to increase the farmers' and producers' portion of the dollar spent for food. By eliminating some of the middleman's profit and expense and certain transportation charges, the farmer-producer hopes to get the product to the consumer at lower cost to the consumer and greater profit to the farmer or producer. These markets are federally inspected, and they are rapidly increasing in number and scope. Any food operator in an area serviced by a cooperative should certainly investigate the possibility of using it as a steady source of supply.

Supermarkets

Many small food operators have used the local supermarket as a basic source of supply for years. The growing price pinch means that more small operators, and even some of the large ones, are taking a good hard look at the possibility of using supermarkets as a regular source of supply. The main advantage is that at least 90 percent of the food supplies needed by a small operator are under one roof and can be picked up daily in the exact amounts needed. This reduces the amount of money tied up in inventories, reduces dead stock to an absolute minimum, and, because such buying has almost built-in portion control, greatly reduces the problem of food cost. By merely adding up daily bills from the supermarket the operator can get an accurate food cost without worrying about cash flow or going into debt. Because bills are usually paid in cash, this is probably one of the best internal control systems for a small operator.

The question of quality may arise. Today, however, the demand for quality is such that the leading supermarket chains are carrying the finest meats, poultry, fruits and vegetables, canned goods, groceries, and frozen items available in the country at lower retail prices than small operators can often secure through regular wholesale channels because the supermarket chain has tremendous buying power.

There is a motel operator who has eighteen franchises from a leading company, and his system of food operation is based almost entirely on buying from the local supermarket. His food departments earn a profit, and his particular restaurants are so popular that, during certain slack seasons, the restaurant and bar carry the rooms department—an almost unheard-of situation in the motel business.

Open Market Buying

Open market buying, quotation buying, competitive market buying, or whatever the name, is the most popular means of buying food in the industry today. The system is basically one of ordering needed food supplies from a selected list of dealers based on either daily, weekly, or monthly price quotations. The quotations are based on a set of specifications in the hands of each dealer, and every day the buyer asks various dealers to quote a price for the quantities needed that particular day.

Even though the buyer may have been given a weekly list of prices on certain perishables, experience has shown that, because prices fluctuate on perishables, it is best to get a quotation for specific purchases. Because of the many grocery items involved, the average buyer does

use the dealer's monthly price submissions as the basis for deciding what to buy from each dealer. This system of buying simplifies controlling food costs as it permits the chef, the kitchen supervising dietitian, the food production manager, or the restaurant manager to decide daily what and how much of various food items should be purchased. The food buyer then makes the actual purchase.

Large institutions, food processors, and hotel and restaurant operations normally prepare a special purchase request listing items generally needed in their particular operation. This saves time in writing, serves as a reminder of items needed, and reduces mistakes to a minimum.

For smaller, perhaps average-sized food operations, probably the easiest and simplest way for the chef or those responsible for suggesting what to buy is to use a copy of the regular food requisition, listing the items and the amounts needed. The pantry, the butcher shop, and the pastry department could do the same, with the approval of the chef, and pass on requests to the food buyer. An example of such a form is shown in Exhibit 6-1. In larger, formalized operations, a form similar to a steward's daily market quotation list (see Exhibit 6-2) is used to indicate quantities required. The list is then passed on to the food buyer as a formal request for purchase. A previously prepared and duplicated list of grocery items can also be used by the storeroom attendant to indicate his requirements and can then be passed on to the purchasing department. In lieu of individual, formalized lists, standard forms are available from hotel stationery supply houses.

When the food buyer has received requests for purchase, he records them on a custom or a standard steward's daily market and quotation list (see Exhibit

Form 489	**FOOD REQUISITION**		S. L. 100 PADS 9/73

№   6253

Date _____

ARTICLE	QUAN.	PRICE	AMOUNT

_____
Department Head

_____

Exhibit 6-1. Form used to requisition food, items not listed

UNIFOOD CORPORATION   HOTEL   DATE

BEEF				PROVISIONS			
Rib CH 34-40, 10x9				Bacon, Canadian 5-8			
Rib CHOP 3x4 #107				Bacon, Sli. 18-20			
Rib CH RR 19-22 #109				Bacon, Sli. 20-24			
Strip CH 9" Bl				Sli. Dried Beef			
Strip CH #180				Bologna			
Tender, Long 8-9				Brisket, Corned 12-14			
Tender, Short 5½-6				Brisket, Fresh 12-14			
Tender, Peeled				Cooked Corned Beef			
Knuckleface, Tied				Frankfurts 8/1			
Top Rnd. CH Bnls 20/22				Frankfurts 10/1			
Bottom Rnd. Bnls 25/28				Frankfurts, Cktl.			
Round, S.S. CH				Ham B & R 10-12			
Chuck, Sq. Bnls. CH				Ham, RTE 12-14			
Top Sir. Butt CH 12/14				Ham, RTE 10-12			
Top Sir. Butt PR 12/14				Ham, "Cure 81"			
Hamburger Meat, Sher.				Ham, Danish Pear			
Patties, 4 oz.				Ham, Dom. Pear			
Patties, 5 oz.				Ham, Danish Pull.			
Patties, 8 oz.				Ham, Dom. Pullman			
Flank Steak 2-3				Ham, Prosciutto Bnls.			
Short Ribs, 10 oz.				Ham, Virginia			
Steer Livers 8-10				Ham, Fresh			
Sirloin Steaks				Knockwurst 7/1			
Sirloin Flanks				Liverwurst			
Tenderloin Steaks				Oxtails			
Rump Steaks 8 oz.				Pastrami			
Swiss Steaks 4 oz.				Pigs Knuckles			
Rib Cap Meat				Port Butts CT Bnls.			
Beef Bones				Pork Loins, Fresh			
				Pork Loins, Smkd.			
VEAL				Pork, Salt			
Veal Legs Sgl. 25/28				Pork Shoulders			
Veal Loins, Dbl.				Pork Tenders 3/4-1			
Veal Loins, Dbl. Bnls.				Salami, Genoa			
Veal Racks, Dbl.				Salami, Cooked			
Veal Shoulders				Sausage Link, 12 lb.			
Calves Liver 2-3				Sausage Link, Ckt.			
Sweetbreads				Sausage, Ital. Swt.			
Veal Cutlets, Leg				Sausage, Meat			
Cutlets, Breaded				Spareribs, 3 dn.			
Veal Tops				Sweetbreads			
				Tongue, Smkt. 4-5			
LAMB				Tripe, H.C.			
Lamb Legs, Sgl.							
Lamb Back, 16-18							
Lamb Rack, 6-8							
Lamb Loins							
Lamb Chucks (Fores)							
Lamb Chucks, Bnls.							
POULTRY				**POULTRY**			
Broilers, 2 1/4 lb.				Cornish Hens 14-16			
Broilers, 2 1/2 lb.				Breast Kiev 7 oz.			
Broilers 3 1/2 lb.				Breast Cor. Bleu, 7 oz.			
Roasters, 4 lb.				Duck Breast, 2 lb.			
Fowl, 6-6½ lb.				Chic Livers, lb.			
Ducks, 4-5				Chic Breast, 8 oz.			
Turkeys, 22-24				Chic Breast, 10 oz.			
Turkey Breast, 8-10				Chic Legs, 8 oz.			
Turkey Breast, 14 lb.				Giblets, lb.			
Turkey Breast, Cooked							

Exhibit 6-2. Form used to requisition food, items listed (Courtesy: Sheraton Corporation of America, Boston, Massachusetts)

FORM 1291   COPYRIGHT 1968

AMERICAN HOTEL REGISTER CO., 226 W. ONTARIO ST., CHICAGO, ILL. 60610

Inventory and Quotation L

ARTICLE	QTY ON HAND	QTY NEEDED	QUOTATIONS			ARTICLE	QTY ON HAND	QTY NEEDED	QUOTATIONS			ARTICLE	QTY ON HAND	QTY NEEDED	QUOTA
BEEF						**PORK (Cont.)**						**SHELL FISH**			
Brisket						Ham, Corned						Abalone			
Chipped Beef						Ham, Fresh						Clams			
Chuck						Ham, Polish									
Corned Beef						Ham, Smoked									
						Ham, Virginia						Crabs			
Fillets						Ham, Westphalia									
Foreshank															
Flank												Crawfish			
Ground Beef						Head Cheese						Lobster			
Kidney						Hock									
Liver						Lard									
Loin, Short						Loin						Mussels			
Ox Tails						Phila. Scrapple						Oysters			
Ribs						Pig's Feet									
Round						Pig's Head									
Rump						Pig's Knuckles						Scallops			
Shank												Shrimp			
Short Plate						Pig, Suckling									
Sirloin															
Smoked Beef						Salt Pork						Turtle			
Tongues						Sausage, Country									
Tongues, Smoked						Sausage, Frankfurter						**FISH**			
Tripe						Sausage, Meat						Bass, Black			
												Bass, Sea			
												Bass, Striped			
												Bloaters			
												Blowfish			
						Shoulder, Corned						Bluefish			
VEAL						Shoulder, Fresh						Bonito			
Brains												Carp			
Breast						Spare Ribs						Catfish			
Flank						Tenderloin						Cod			
Foreshank						Tongues									
Hindshank															
Kidney															
Leg												Eel			
Liver												Finnan Haddie			
Loin						**POULTRY**						Flounder			
Rib						Capons									
Shoulder						Chicken						Fluke			
Sweetbreads						Chicken, Roast						Frog's Legs			
						Chicken, Broiler						Haddock			
												Halibut			
						Cocks									
MUTTON						Duck						Herring			
Fore Quarters												Herring, Kippered			
Hind Saddle						Ducklings						Kingfish			
Kidney						Geese						Mackerel			
Leg						Gosling									
Rack						Guinea Hens									
Shoulder						Guinea Squab						Octopus			
						Pigeon						Perch			
						Squab						Pickerel			
						Turkey, Roasting						Pike			
						Turkey, Spring						Pompano			
LAMB												Red Snapper			
Breast												Salmon			

Exhibit 6-3. Inventory and quotation list for fresh and refrigerated items (Courtesy: American Hotel Register Company, Chicago, Illino

Fresh and Refrigerated Items

DATE _____

ARTICLE	QTY ON HAND	QTY NEEDED	QUOTATIONS			ARTICLE	QTY ON HAND	QTY NEEDED	QUOTATIONS			ARTICLE	QTY ON HAND	QTY NEEDED	QUOTATIONS		
VEGETABLES						VEGETABLES (Cont.)						CHEESE					
...okes						Tomatoes						American					
...gus												Bel Paese					
...gus Tips												Bleu					
...Green						Turnips, White						Brick					
...Lima						Turnips, Yellow						Brie					
...Wax						Watercress						Camembert					
												Cheddar					
...ops												Cheshire					
...li												Cottage					
...ls Sprouts												Cream					
...ge, Green																	
...ge, Red						FRUIT											
...s						Apples, Baking						Edam					
						Apples, Cooking						Feta					
...lower						Apples, Crab						Gouda					
						Apples, Table						Liderkranz					
...Knobs						Apricots						Longhorn					
...l						Avocados						Monterey Jack					
...ory						Bananas						Mozzarella					
...s						Blackberries						Muenster					
						Blueberries						Parmesan					
						Cantaloupe						Port du Salut					
...erries												Romano					
...ber						Cherries						Roquefort					
...lion												Swiss, Emmanthal					
...lant												Swiss, Gruyere					
...e						Chestnuts						Tilsit					
...ole						Coconuts											
...gon						Currants											
						Dates											
...adish						Figs											
						Gooseberries											
...bi						Grapes						DAIRY PRODUCTS					
												Butter, Cooking					
...s												Butter, Prints					
...ce												Butter, Sweet					
						Grapefruit											
												Buttermilk					
...am						Guava						Cream					
						Honeydew Melons						Half-and-Half					
...ooms						Huckleberries						Margarine					
						Kumquats											
						Lemons						Milk, homogenized					
...s						Limes						Milk, skim					
...muda						Mangos						Milk, 2%					
...l						Muskmelons						Milk, whole					
...llions						Nectarines											
...nish						Oranges						Sour Cream					
...te												Whipping Cream					
...low												Yogurt					
						Peaches											
...Plant												MISCELLANEOUS					
...ey																	
...ips						Pears											

6-3) in the quantities needed. Then he calls various dealers to get current quotations. Even though purveyors have a set of purchase specifications, it is good business for the food buyer to repeat basic specifications so that there is no cause for misunderstanding on the part of the purveyor.

After the market and quotation sheet is complete and the dealer is selected, orders are placed by telephone. Generally, the sheet is made out in duplicate. A copy is retained in the purchasing office, and the original is sent to the receiving department to verify delivery and from there to the chef or to the food and beverage manager for their information.

The system of buying is best on a year-round basis for the average food operation. It does, however, have certain shortcomings, and other forms of buying, properly pursued, may prove more beneficial.

One of the main objections to open market buying is that the buyer is limited to the stock available on the market. The purchase procedure, since it is completed in one day, does not give the buyer a chance to negotiate or take advantage of seasonal trends, and, unless the chef and others are familiar with the best buys in the market, they may request items out of season that are extremely expensive.

Another fault is that the system permits those purveyors being called regularly for price quotations to agree on prices. It is not unusual for a group of purveyors to take advantage of a buyer by getting together to apportion the business from a particular operation. They can then arrange bids or prices that enable them to divide the business at prices very advantageous to themselves.

A buyer may combat this practice by introducing new dealers from time to time. Visiting the market at least once a week enables him to examine what is available from other dealers and the prices for the current week, which leads to another shortcoming in this system of buying. Unless the food buyer has an assistant or a clerk to take care of all the paperwork, he may be too tied down to visit the market.

Fixed Markups

In the fixed-markup system, the buyer negotiates a fixed markup over current market price for items listed in daily market reports. Sometimes the price is tied to the market as reported in the daily newspaper, in the Urner Barry market report, *Producers Price-Current*, in one of the USDA bulletins, or in *Fresh Fruit and Vegetables Market News*, which is published in various metropolitan areas. This type of activity is pretty much restricted to butter, eggs, turkeys, turkey parts, broilers, ducks, poultry parts, and some game items.

Dealers willing to work on this basis normally do not become involved unless the volume of business is substantial. This system has worked well, especially for those who buy for large institutions or large food-processing companies. Buying in carload lots generally means a price from 1 cent to 3 cents a pound over the top spot market as reported in the market reporting service for turkeys, poultry, ducks, and poultry parts. Butter can generally be purchased from 5 cents to 7 cents a pound over the top side of the spot market, and fresh eggs will be priced from 4 cents to 8 cents over, depending on whether the eggs are Midwestern mixed or extra large double A Eastern whites. The markup for frozen eggs can be as low as 2 cents to 3 cents a pound over the top spot market.

Such arrangements are generally made for a period of three to six months, and, if both parties are satisfied, a renewal can easily be negotiated. Buyers who work out these arrangements are under pressure to divide this business up for one reason or another. A fair buyer will keep a record of the prices that he pays under this type of arrangement and give 80 percent to 85 percent of the business to the dealer with whom he has negotiated it, buying the other 15 percent on a daily quotation basis in order to determine whether he is making money by such an arrangement.

Where records have been kept, it has been found that the buyer can save from 3 percent to 5 percent over the year by negotiated markup over cost as against daily price quotation buying. Usually a purveyor in this line has to get from 15 percent to 25 percent markup over costs to run his business, and, of this amount, as much as a quarter or a third, or 5 percent to 8 percent, has to be set aside for promotion and selling costs. Most dealers would be willing to eliminate this selling cost if they could be assured of a sufficient volume of business from a negotiated markup over costs. The 5 percent to 8 percent is the food buyer's possible savings.

There is always the danger that such an arrangement will be exploited by a dishonest buyer or purveyor who cheats the boss through collusion on fixing the price. The simplicity of the system and the ease of checking the cost price and negotiated markup by any auditor seem, however, to discourage manipulation, and many of the best buyers do use this system to their advantage.

Exhibit 6-4 shows a sample of the *Producer's Price-Current* and a market report from a metropolitan daily newspaper. Most such market reports are put out by the Associated Press, and they are the same in all publications for each area throughout the country. It does not make much difference what source is used as a base, so long as it remains constant over the period of the arrangement.

Buy and Hold

A buyer who uses the buy-and-hold system must represent a large user, or there is no advantage. The system takes advantage of seasonal fluctuations in the market. At certain periods of the year, as at harvesttime, an excess of supply drives a price down so that a buyer with some money can make substantial savings by eliminating the middleman. The food buyer deals with the producer—frozen food manufacturer, canner, shrimp packer, production line meat fabricator, or large local purveyor—who has access to a lot of stock or has overbought and wants to reduce his inventory.

Usually the buyer has to pay cash for the amount of stock that he buys, and there are always problems involving storage, delivery, insurance, and losses through spoilage. In noninflationary times there is always the specter that the bottom will fall out of the market, leaving the buyer sitting there holding the bag.

Large chain operators, especially in certain fast food operations, take advantage of this type of buying. Buyers for large processors of convenience foods use it regularly. Even some large hotel and restaurant chains have found it worthwhile to follow the buy-and-hold method of food purchasing on occasion.

Some items that lend themselves to this type of buying are green headless shrimp or processed shrimp, lobster tails, any type of frozen fish, any cut of fabricated meat that can be used frozen, canned tomatoes and canned fruits, frozen fruits and vegetables (particularly peas, green beans, asparagus, and orange juice,

Producers' Price-Current

The Urner Barry Market

ESTABLISHED 1858 · MORE THAN A CENTURY OF MARKET REPORTING SERVICE

PUBLISHED DAILY EXCEPT SATURDAYS, SUNDAYS AND HOLIDAYS BY URNER BARRY PUBLICATIONS, INC.
34 EXCHANGE PLACE, JERSEY CITY, N. J. 07302 · N. J. PHONE 201 432 7777 · N. Y. PHONE 212 349 0240 · WIRE: JGC · TELETYPE: 710 730 5370

Second Class Postage Paid at Jersey City, N. J.

Copyright 1974 By Urner Barry Publications Inc

No. 103   THURSDAY, MAY 30, 1974

BUTTER
URNER BARRY QUOTATIONS

Based on extensive country-wide trade reports and other terminal market wholesale transactions.

TRUCKLOTS BULK (Deliv. East Spot Mkt.)

	SALT	SALES FROM WAREHOUSE	
		1 Pound Solids	1 Pound Quarters
62.00	93 Score (AA)	65.50-67.25	69.50-71.75
61.50	92 Score (A)	64.25-66.00	68.25-70.50
60.00	90 Score (B)	63.25-65.00	67.25-69.50

MIDWEST
LOADS & POOL LOADS DELIVERED

93 Score	92 Score	90 Score
59.75-60.00	59.25-59.50	57.25-57.50

IMPORTED
LOADS & POOL LOADS

Finest	1 st's	2nds

CHEESE
CHEDDARS - Whole Milk - lbs.

	Ex Sharp	Sharp	Medium	Mild
Blocks	$ .98-1.05	$ .92-1.02	$ .87-.90	$ .79-.83
Daisies			.88-.96	.86-.92
Splits	1.01-1.08	.95-1.05	.88-.94	.84-.87
Midgets	1.03-1.05	.97-1.07	.90-.96	.86-.92
Flats	1.00-1.06	.97-1.04		
5 lb. Loaf - Processed	.725-.840			
Known Brands	.725-.840	Muenster	.785-.860	
Other Brands	.745-.765			

OTHER VARIETIES

SWISS - Cuts
DOMESTIC

Grade A	$1.05-1.11
Grade B	1.01-1.08
Grade C	.95-1.03

IMPORTED —

Austria	1.03-1.09
Denmark	1.05-1.10
Finland	1.06-1.10
Switzerland	1.28-1.32
French	

FLUID MILK
TRUCKLOTS DELIVERED MET. NEW YORK
Bottling quality per 40 quart unit $

CONDENSED SKIM MILK
DELIVERED METROPOLITAN NEW YORK
Per lb. Solids (SNF) in tanklots $61.00-63.00

FLUID CREAM
CLASS II or MANUFACTURING
SPOT SALES DELIVERED MET. NEW YORK
Butterfat per lb in tanklots ¢.7800-.8175
Per 40 qt unit in tanklots $25.75-27.00

SPOT SALES DELIVERED PHILADELPHIA
Butterfat per lb in tanklots ¢7900-.8200
Per 40 qt unit in tanklots $26.05-27.05

SPOT SALES DELIVERED BOSTON
Butterfat per lb in tanklots ¢.7800-.8200
Per 40 qt unit in tanklots $25.75-27.05

BOSTON EQUIVALENT PRICE
May 19-25 .... $26.843

FLUID MILK & CREAM
Milk production trends upward and is at or near "peak" levels. This combined with poor bottling sales results in a very ample supply. Diversions to manufacture are heavy and these

Fats & Oils
MARGARINE
Less Carlots
Sales by First Receiver - Cents per lb.-

Vegetable Oil, 1 lb. Solids	37.00-38.00
Vegetable Oil, 1 lb. Quarters	38.00-39.00
Animal - Vegetable, 1 lb. Solids	32.00-33.00
1 lb. Quarters	33.00-34.00

Trucklots - Delivered East - Cents per lb -

Vegetable Oil, 1 lb. Solids	35.00-
Vegetable Oil, 1 lb. Quarters	36.00-

SOYBEAN OIL FUTURES
Chicago Board of Trade futures trading for previous day.

Deliv.	Open	High	Low	Close	Prev Close
July	27.20	28.05	27.20	28.05	27.10
Aug	26.10	26.85	26.10	26.85	25.90
Sept	25.15	25.88	25.15	25.88	24.90
Oct	24.15	24.80	24.10	24.80	23.80
Dec	22.90	23.60	22.90	23.60	22.65
Jan	22.15	22.75	22.15	22.65	22.00
Mar	21.95	22.40	21.90	22.35	21.70

WEDNESDAY, MAY 29, 1974
FRESH VEGETABLES
ARRIGULA
Local bchd 20-24s   2 50-3 00
Local lugs 20s   3 50-4 00
ARTICHOKES   5 00-7 00

Rubb-
Local W/bu cr   2 00-2 50
MUSHROOMS bkt-
Pa med-lg   2 50-3 00
Pa med-lg fair   2 00-2 25
Pa sm-med   2 00-2 25
Pa sm-med fair   -1 75

POULTRY S...
Carlot turkey market creased selling pressu and consumer sizes of to what improved for the but with available stock tone is highly unsettle is true on the consumer

Mid-sizes of toms are light offerings. Demand tious. Heavier weights hands.

Canner packs irregula selling pressure buildi Iced chickens full ste prices are asked for ne mand is sharply impro feature sales noted, port a firm undertone. Fowl and roasters is clearing the limited a

D.P.S.C. Purchases at C Turkeys Boneless Expor Domestic Cent. 63.83

NC greens
bu bake
NC bu bu
NC yellow
takot
NC yel bu
SC greens

Commodity Markets   July 10, 1975

THE WASHINGTON POST
Friday, July 11, 1975   D 11

Chicago Board of Trade
CHICAGO (AP) — Wheat, soybean and soybean oil futures soared to daily allowable limits on the Chicago Board of Trade Thursday, but fell back at the close under the liquidation.

Wheat and soybeans have advanced 20 cents a bushel around noon and oil was up 100 points, or 1 cent a pound. Corn was then just short of its 10 cent a bushel limit at about 8 cents higher while oats were up 5½ cents. Profit taking then took over and prices eased a little in the wheat, soybean and oil pits and closed mixed in corn and oats.

Some validity was given to reports that Russian agents were in the United States to buy grain. Senator Jackson of Washington said that this was so. Another report, unofficial, had Russians buying 200 million bushels of wheat and 80 million bushels of corn.

Trade was mixed in the major pits but sellers were very scarce throughout the day.

As the Russian buying gave prices a lift, the specter of a bearish government report dealing with small grain production, issued after the close, hung over the pits. Record production was expected in corn, wheat and soybeans but world needs for soybeans and products might not be met and trade bought these commodity futures.

Iced broilers closed steady to about ½ cent a pound higher after a lightly traded session. Domestic gold was about $1 to $1.50 lower.

At the close, wheat futures were 11½ to 17 cents a bushel higher, July 3.43½; soybeans were 8 to 14 higher, July 5.56; corn was 2 lower to ½ higher.

	Open	High	Low	Close	Prev Close
WHEAT (5,000 bu)					
Jul	3.35	3.52	3.32	3.43½	3.32
Sep	3.41	3.58½	3.39	3.51¼	3.38¼

Gold Trading
Here is the gold futures trading for Thursday, July 10, 1975:
Chicago Board of Trade
3 1-kilogram bars contracts

	Open	High	Low	Close	Prev Close
Jul	164.50	164.50	164.50	164.50	166.00
Aug	—	—	—	—	165.50
Sep	166.90	167.70	165.80	166.60	168.20
Nov	169.70	170.70	169.20	169.50	171.00
Jan	173.00	173.20	172.00	172.30	173.90
Mar	175.70	175.70	174.80	175.50	176.80
May	—	—	—	—	178.20 179.60
Jul	—	—	—	—	180.90 182.90

529 volume 3,435 contracts.

Chicago Mercantile Exchange
100-Troy ounce contracts

Sep	166.60	167.40	165.90	166.50	168.00
Dec	170.70	171.70	170.10	170.50	172.00
Mar	175.30	175.90	174.40	174.80	—
Jun	—	179.40	180.10	178.30	179.10 180.10
Sep	—	183.10	183.70b	182.70	182.70 184.00

Sales: Sep 1,565; Dec 345; March 52; June 36; Sep 3.

New York Commodity Exchange
100 troy ounce contracts

Jul	164.60	164.60	164.60	164.50s	166.00
Aug	165.90	165.90	164.60	165.30s	166.90
Oct	168.00	168.00	167.40	168.00s	169.50
Dec	171.10	171.30	170.10	170.70s	172.20
Feb	173.90				
.30	173.30	173.60s	175.00		
Apr	176.30	177.40	176.10	176.40s	177.80
Jun	179.30	179.30	179.30	179.20s	180.60
Aug	182.50	182.50	182.50	182.00s	183.40
Oct	184.20	184.20	184.20	184.80s	186.20

Sales: 2,323.
s-settling.

New York Mercantile Exchange
1 kilogram contracts

Jul	164.40	164.40	164.40	164.40	166.00
Aug	166.20	166.20	166.00	165.40s	166.60
Sep	167.60	167.60	166.20	166.20	168.00
Dec	171.00	171.00	171.00	171.00	172.20
Jan	173.60				

Mercantile Futures
CHICAGO (AP) — Futures trading on the Chicago Mercantile Exchange Thursday:

	Open	High	Low	Close	Prev Close
LIVE BEEF CATTLE (40,000 lbs)					
Aug	46.30	47.30	46.10	47.20	45.75
Oct	41.25	42.55	41.20	42.05	40.90
Dec	39.75	41.12	39.75	40.95	39.55
Feb	49.40	40.42	39.40	40.00	39.25
Apr	39.25	39.95b	39.20	39.60	38.95
Jun	39.40	40.50	39.35	40.50	39.40

Sales: Aug 5,260; Oct 3,072; Dec 1,407; Feb 1072; April 80; June 14.
Open interest: Aug 15,196; Oct 9,688; Dec 5,246; Feb 3,475; April 381; June 20.

FEEDER CATTLE (42,000 lbs)					
Aug	34.00	34.30	33.75	34.25	33.95
Sep	34.00	33.40	32.80	33.42	33.30
Oct	32.60	33.40	32.60	33.07	32.50
Nov	33.00	33.25b	32.60	33.20	32.50
Mar	—	—	—	—	33.40

Sales: Aug 20; Sep 14; Oct 157; Nov 44; March 0.
Open interest: Aug 211; Sep 141; Oct 1,299; Nov 277; March 0.

LIVE HOGS (30,000 lbs)					
Jul	55.80	56.80	55.50	56.80b	55.35
Aug	52.20	53.50	52.20	53.50b	51.95
Oct	46.90	47.82	46.60	47.65	46.30
Dec	46.70	47.65	46.45	47.65	46.20
Feb	45.35	46.62	45.35	46.62	45.10
Apr	42.30	43.25	42.30	43.25	42.25
Jun	43.00	43.80	42.70	43.60b	42.70
Jul	42.55	43.70b	42.55	43.70b	42.45

Sales: July 918; Aug 1,932; Oct 1,050; Dec 940; Feb 436; April 159; June 59; July 8.
Open interest: July 1,701; Aug 4,594; Oct 3,186; Dec 5,782; Feb 3,357; April 827; June 318; July 45.

SHELL EGGS (22,500 doz)					
Jul	—	—	43.60	43.60	
Aug	46.20	46.95	46.20	46.75	45.75
Sep	53.75	54.65	53.55	54.40	53.40
Oct	53.00	53.25	53.00	53.25	52.75
Nov	56.95	57.75b	56.30	57.50a	56.95

Government Securities
Treasury Bills

Due	Bid	Ask	Yld	Due	Bid	Ask	Yld
—1975—				11-13	6.26	6.08	6.29
7-17	6.06	5.28	5.35	11-18	6.24	6.10	6.30
7-24	5.96	5.36	5.34	11-20	6.27	6.11	6.34
7-29	5.96	5.30	5.38	11-28	6.26	6.14	6.35
8-7	5.97	5.35	5.44	12-4	6.30	6.14	6.39
8-14	5.87	5.45	5.55	12-11	6.20	6.16	6.35
8-21	5.90	5.54	5.65	12-16	6.30	6.16	6.34
8-26	5.93	5.63	5.75	12-26	6.30	6.16	6.34
9-4	5.95	5.73	5.86	—1976—			
9-11	5.94	5.78	5.88	1-2	6.41	6.27	6.56
9-18	5.95	5.75	5.89	1-8	6.38	6.22	6.50
9-23	5.92	5.70	5.84	1-13	6.43	6.27	6.60
9-25	5.96	5.80	5.95	1-31	6.49	6.31	6.62
10-2	6.05	5.89	6.05	2-4	6.49	6.31	6.62
10-9	6.16	5.96	6.13	3-4	6.51	6.33	6.67
10-16	6.15	5.96	6.17	4-6	6.57	6.37	6.75
10-21	6.17	6.01	6.20	5-4	6.57	6.37	6.75
10-23	6.21	5.95	6.24	6-1	6.51	6.33	6.69
10-30	6.21	6.05	6.25	6-29	6.51	6.45	6.89

Treasury Bonds and Notes
NEW YORK (AP)—Closing Over-the-Counter U.S. Treasury Bonds for Thursday.

Rate	Mat. date	Bid	Asked	Bid Chg	Yld
5⅞	Aug 1975 n	99.29	99.31	—.1	4.68
8¾	Sep 1975 n	100.12	100.16	—	5.86
8	Nov 1975 n	100.4	100.8	—	6.17
7	Dec 1975 n	100.6	100.10	—	6.29
5⅞	Feb 1976 n	99.13	99.17	+.1	6.70
6	Feb 1976 n	99.18	99.26	—.2	6.49
8	May 1976 n	100.25	100.29	+.1	6.48
5¾	May 1976 n	99.2	99.6	—	4.76
6½	May 1976 n	99.22	99.26	—	6.69

Exhibit 6-4. Examples of market reports (Courtesy: Urner Barry Publications, Inc., Jersey City, New Jersey; Associated Press, New York, New York)

and, for a certain type of chain operator, blueberries, cherries, apples, peaches, and other fruits for use in a pastry department).

A large buyer also keeps constant check on the future market and judges his buying to take advantage of long-term trends. If a drought is forecast, if a revolution in a coffee country seems imminent, if an unseasonal frost hits some area of the country, if it appears that a huge grain deal will be negotiated with a foreign country, then the large-quantity buyer steps in and protects himself for a reasonable period of time with a large buy-and-hold order.

Smaller buyers can take advantage of such a program by taking into consideration the two times of the year that meat prices are traditionally low and the two times of the year when meat prices are traditionally high. By buying, freezing, and holding certain items, it is possible for them to realize a considerable savings.

Beef prices, which are low about the middle of January, continue low through February. Then they start rising until after Easter and through May. They tend to stay high over the summer and start down again in the fall until, in November, they are generally at their lowest level. Right after Thanksgiving, however, the price of beef starts a rapid rise for the holidays and reaches a peak just before the Christmas-New Year season that holds until about the middle of January, when they again drop.

Most large chain hotel and restaurant operators lay in a supply of heavy beef items such as ribs, strips, filets, and top butts during the early part of November to avoid paying the premium price over the holidays. During the past few years, these savings have amounted to as much as 75 cents a pound, especially on strips and filets.

Negotiated Price

Buying at a negotiated price is more common where markets do not fluctuate widely. This system would be used oftener if purveyors were willing to gamble on the future. Buyers do occasionally work out a six-month's price on an item that they use in great quantity, and some purveyors are willing to risk a rise in price to obtain a large order.

An excellent, well-known restaurant in New York City that has been in the hands of one family for over six decades uses the average yearly price almost exclusively. The reputation of the owners secures the credit needed to make this type of buying profitable. Because needs are covered at a known fixed price for the year, except for some payroll costs, it is easy for management to set accurate selling prices and to keep fluctuation in menu prices at a minimum. This, in turn, reassures the customer. It also eliminates the need for daily quotations, checking prices, and worrying about ups and downs in supply. In fact, where ownership is able to help negotiate such prices, this type of buying can benefit the user.

Drop Shipments

Some large grocery houses and food processors, in order to secure a greater share of the market for their products, have devised a national marketing system. It can be helpful, from an economic standpoint, for the large-quantity food buyer.

National distributors tend to have knowledgeable salesmen. They know their business, they know their products, and their ethics are almost always above reproach. Such companies cannot afford any hanky-panky over the small markups that they receive, and they cannot be subject to the whims of an excitable food buyer or chef. They simply avoid these situations.

The salesmen work out delivery schedules with large-quantity buyers so that the maximum drop shipment can be made direct from a trailer truck. The price schedule is related to the size of the shipment: the larger the shipment, the better the price that the buyer gets. Shipments are programmed. Deliveries are made to certain areas on certain days of the week, and the record of the trucking concerns has been very good.

Savings can run, in some instances, as high as 10 to 15 percent against the average local purveyor's price, and, in some instances, the savings run as high as 25 percent. This type of buying lends itself to such items as canned tomatoes, canned fruits, cooking oil, salad oil, shortening for frying or pastry, mayonnaise, tomato juice, ketchup, olives, pickles—almost any type of item handled by a national grocery house. This system has not worked for meats, poultry, or other perishable items, or for commodities subject to wide price fluctuations.

One-Stop Buying

For years the idea of a one-stop buying and delivery service has intrigued both enterprising purveyors and forward-looking food buyers, especially in relation to large-institution and chain food operations. The idea made little progress until rising delivery costs made the concept more attractive in 1974.

The first company to offer this service in any depth was known as Foodco. The company started in New York about 1960, and it was made up of a number of purveyors who had been supplying hotels with meats, fish, produce, canned goods, groceries, butter, and eggs. They decided that a buyer would prefer to make one telephone call and purchase most of the items he needed. The overhead, delivery

costs, and selling and billing costs would be less than they were for several individual houses, and kickbacks could be eliminated. There would also be better control over quality. The savings realized could be passed on, at least in part, to the food buyer. Foodco launched the project with much enthusiasm and managed to stay in business for a number of years before the company had to be rescued by a large insurance company. The insurance company apparently found a way to make the system work profitably. One reason Foodco had difficulty was because the company refused to make or take payoffs.

There is always resistance to changing any system that is familiar and seems to work, and the established system tried to discredit the whole idea of one-stop buying. Local purveyors saw it as a threat to specialized businesses, and unions saw it as a threat to the job security of members. It was even rumored in New York City that, if Foodco succeeded, chefs in the city would ask for $10,000 more a year, and they would still lose money. Various chefs' organizations in the area strongly opposed this unfair allegation.

Top management in the institutional and hotel and restaurant fields was also reluctant to support the one-stop system. Although it seemed to be a good idea, there was fear of antagonizing the system that controlled all of food buying in the New York metropolitan area at that time. The institutional trade was, however, the first to venture into one-stop buying, and the idea is now winning acceptance in the hotel and restaurant trade. Mounting delivery charges may win further acceptance in the future.

It is a well-known "secret" that the average markup on meat, produce, fish, and almost any other commodity is from

15 percent to 25 percent over cost. Cost to the average purveyor means everything, including depreciation, business expense, and any personal living expenses that the Internal Revenue Service will allow. At first, the one-stop buying idea was to offer a service at a true 10 percent to 12 percent markup over cost before selling expense and delivery costs and, naturally, without any business promotion costs. At first, this markup was impossibly low because of high overhead in terms of salaries and high initial costs involved with warehousing, delivery, billing, and all of the unexpected routine work. These problems have been overcome, and the system has proved feasible. According to large food buyers, the one-stop system is actually saving 10 percent to 12 percent over the cost of using the individual purveyor system for food buying.

Cost-Plus

On first inspection, cost-plus buying appears to flaunt every rule laid down for buying procedures. In the hands of the right food buyer and when the volume of business is substantial, however, there is potential for significant savings. This system is used by large chain food operators and those in the institutional field. The chief difference between this system and one-stop buying is that the cost-plus plan can be worked out with the individual dealer who specializes in just one or two items such as beef, seafood, or frozen fruits and vegetables, fats, oil, dressings, and grocery items. Records of companies using the cost-plus system prove that they save, on a yearly basis, 10 percent to 12 percent on the purchase prices of commodities bought in this manner as against open market buying.

A buyer agrees with a purveyor to buy as much as 75 percent to 85 percent of the buyer's need for a particular classification of food from the dealer for a period of time based on a fixed markup over the dealer's cost. This might seem to be risky at first. Because the arrangement can be made for as little as thirty days or as much as six months, depending upon the situation, however, the whole arrangement can be open to bid among different dealers. An agreement can also be cancelled on short-term notice if something goes wrong. These arrangements are not new. Institutional food buying has been working for years on a negotiated markup over cost with food purveyors, but the same system has only recently been tried in the hotel and restaurant business.

Such a plan works only when the volume of business is large and deliveries are restricted, preferably to one location. If the arrangement involves meat, for example, the fewer items the buyer needs, the easier it is to control the procedure and the more accurate the costs.

The amount of markup over cost is not difficult to arrive at because this can be either the result of a bid or the result of negotiations. Purveyors normally operate on a 15 percent to 25 percent markup over their true cost, and, even for better customers with good credit and large orders, the markup over true cost is generally around 15 percent to 18 percent. When a customer has a poor credit rating, volume is small, or there are kickbacks, the markup can rise as high as 30 percent or more over cost.

Often a purveyor, when approached by a food buyer, will be skeptical of cost-plus purchasing, especially if he is one of the regular suppliers. The purveyor understands that such an arrangement cuts into the profit margin, but he must also realize that it is better to make a small markup doing a large volume of business than it is to lose the account. Most purveyors try to avoid the issue by saying that it is impossible to know costs closely enough to be able to work fairly with such an arrangement.

This is only a ploy. Every dealer who has been in business longer than a month knows exactly what his costs are. It is only a matter of laying it out on the table and arriving at a definition of cost with the buyer.

True cost generally works out to be the cost of material to the purveyor plus any costs of fabrication, change in packaging, or loss because of required trim, cooking, or shrinkage from aging. This is the true material cost to the purveyor, and it does not include any overhead, salesmen's salaries, delivery, cost of billing, promotion, taxes, or other nuisance charges, which are borne by the purveyor from his "markup over cost." If the purveyor receives 10 percent over cost, he stands to make about 5 percent profit before income taxes, which is better than average in the food business.

A workable markup over cost varies with the type of food being purchased. There are instances where meats, because of location, have to be purchased in the frozen state. In such instances markup over true cost from 8 percent to 10 percent can be obtained as against the normal markup of 15 percent to 20 percent on fresh, chilled meats. There are other instances where both the food buyer and the purveyor are satisfied with a markup of only 6 percent over cost in frozen fish, poultry, and ready-to-cook poultry items. Another arrangement of this type that has been used is based on a 10-cent-per-pound markup over cost on all items costing over $1.00 per pound and 5 cents per pound on any item merely transferred from the purveyor's source of supply to the food buyer

in its original box or shape. This arrangement has been successfully worked out with several meat dealers who receive 10 cents per pound over cost for fabricated and aged meats, and 5 cents per pound on items such as boxed bacon, hams, and packaged corned beef. In grocery houses a markup of 8 percent to 10 percent over cost seems to work.

The highly perishable nature of fresh produce makes it difficult for a purveyor to know true cost on any particular item. Also, the volume of business in produce is generally not so great that it is worth the time and effort required to work out a cost system.

Formal Written Bid

In the institutional field, in the food manufacturing and processing field, and especially in government procurement systems, the formal written bid is the key to practically all food buying. This system ensures a steady flow of merchandise at a nonfluctuating price, and it conforms with the requirements of most governmental agencies at both the national and local levels.

The formal bid system is easy to police, which goes far toward solving the problem of questionable ethics, and the possibility of misunderstandings as to quality, price, delivery, and packaging is practically eliminated. On the whole, this has proved to be an excellent system. There are, however, two basic problems. The system is rather cumbersome, and whatever purchasing is done has to be planned well in advance so that the buyer has a chance to get the bid forms out and the suppliers have a chance to line up stock and suggest a fair price. The bid system is fine for canned goods, frozen products, smoked meats, and other staple items. It is not practical for perishable items because market prices fluctuate from day to day.

This system, designed to ensure honesty in the purchasing system, does discourage petty manipulation, but it lends itself to larger manipulation, especially if the purchasing department and purchasing agent are open to political pressure. Because bids cannot be sent out to every dealer in the area who handles the type of merchandise required, there is generally a selected list of approved purveyors to whom requests for bids are sent. The names appearing on the list of approved dealers and who approves the dealers on the list are important decisions. It is not difficult to imagine what would happen to a large supplier if, during a drive for campaign funds, he did not make a substantial contribution to the potential winning candidate for a sensitive political office. All other dealers in the area expecting an opportunity to bid on supplies, since they are subject to the same pressure, would also contribute. Contributions are generally made to both party candidates and sometimes even to a third-party candidate who might possibly be elected to an office of power. Since this cost must be added to the cost of doing business, the bids are generally higher than they would be if political considerations were not a factor.

Sometimes formalized bids call for a supply of merchandise over a period of time at prices that fluctuate with the market. Without a provision allowing for flexibility, the prices submitted by all dealers must again be higher than they would be if the dealer could manipulate prices in accord with the market.

Most bids are, however, for a specific quantity of merchandise that the buyer withdraws and uses within a set period of time. A bid can be written so that the buyer pays for all at the time of purchase, or it can be paid for as it is withdrawn, with a suitable arrangement to cover the cost of storage and the cost of carrying the inventory in storage.

Many different forms are used in the written bidding system, but all of them are basically invitations to bid with the conditions of the bid clearly specified. Attached to the invitation is a listing of the merchandise needed, the quantities involved, and any conditions related to supply and fluctuations in the market. Any invitation to bid generally includes a copy of the purchase specifications set forth by the buyer so that there is no confusion over what is wanted by the buyer.

A typical request for bid appears in Exhibit 6-5. Generally, the bids are to be sent in by a specified date, and they are to be sealed. More often than not, the bids are reviewed by a committee rather than one person. In some cases the identity of the bidder is disguised so that the committee doing the reviewing and decision making cannot identify the successful bidder; thus, personalities have no effect on the decisions of the committee. After the identity of the successful bidder is revealed, a purchase order (see Exhibit 6-6) is issued to him. This is the formal closing of the deal and covers the various legal aspects involved. In this system withdrawal of stock, as needed, is authorized by the issue of a purchase order that refers to the accepted master bid.

This system is complete and effective, and it has the benefit of thoroughness, complete legality, and the almost total elimination of misunderstandings.

Auctions

Buying at auctions is another system that is now used by some large-quantity food buyers and could be used more widely if it were better understood.

FLORIDA INTERNATIONAL UNIVERSITY
TAMIAMI TRAIL
MIAMI, FLORIDA 33199
(305) 552-2161

Telephone Number:

STATE OF FLORIDA
INVITATION TO BID
Bidder Acknowledgment

Page 1 of _pages_	H. E. W. PROJECT NO. FLA.	STATE PROJECT NO.	FILE NO.	BID NO.

BIDS WILL BE OPENED

and may not be withdrawn within _____ days after such date and time.

All awards made as a result of this bid shall conform to applicable Florida Statutes.

BID TITLE

COMPANY NAME	REASON FOR NO BID

MAILING ADDRESS	PAYMENT TERMS	PROMISED DELIVERY DATE

CITY · STATE · ZIP	VENDOR NO.	AGENCY MAILING DATE:

AREA CODE	TELEPHONE NUMBER	CERTIFIED OR CASHIER'S CHECK IS ATTACHED, WHEN REQUIRED, IN THE AMOUNT OF: $ _____

I certify that this bid is made without prior understanding, agreement, or connection with any corporation, firm, or person submitting a bid for the same materials, supplies, or equipment, and is in all respects fair and without collusion or fraud. I agree to abide by all conditions of this bid and certify that I am authorized to sign this bid for the bidder.

AUTHORIZED SIGNATURE (MANUAL)

AUTHORIZED SIGNATURE (TYPED)   TITLE

GENERAL CONDITIONS

Bidder: To insure acceptance of the bid, follow these instructions.

SEALED BIDS: All bid sheets and this form must be executed and submitted in a sealed envelope. The face of the envelope shall contain, in addition to the above address, the date and time of the bid opening and the bid number. Bids not submitted on attached bid form may be rejected. All bids are subject to the conditions specified herein. Those which do not comply with these conditions are subject to rejection.

1. **EXECUTION OF BID:** Bid should contain a manual signature of an authorized representative in the space provided above. The company name and vendor number must also appear on each page of the bid as required. (If a vendor number has not been assigned to your company, contact this office immediately, in writing or at the telephone number shown above.)

2. **NO BID:** If not submitting a bid, respond by returning one copy of this form, marking it "NO BID", and explain the reason in the space provided above. Repeated failure to quote without sufficient justification shall be cause for removal of the supplier's name from the bid mailing list.
NOTE: To qualify as a respondent, bidder must submit a "NO BID", and it must be received no later than the stated bid opening date and hour.

3. **BID OPENING:** Shall be public, on the date and at the time specified on the bid form. It is the bidder's responsibility to assure that his bid is delivered at the proper time and place of the bid opening. Bids which for any reason are not so delivered, will not be considered. Offers by telegram or telephone are not acceptable.

4. **BID TABULATIONS:** Will not be furnished. Bid files may be examined during normal working hours.

5. **PRICES, TERMS and PAYMENT:** Firm prices shall be quoted; typed or printed in ink and include all packing, handling, shipping charges and delivery to the destination shown herein. Bidder is requested to offer cash discount for prompt invoice payment. Discount time will be computed from the date of satisfactory delivery at place of acceptance or from receipt of correct invoice at the office specified, whichever is later.

a) **TAXES:** The State of Florida does not pay Federal Excise and Sales taxes on direct purchases of tangible personal property. See exemption number on face of purchase order.
This exemption does not apply to purchases of tangible personal property made by contractors who use the tangible personal property in the performance of contracts for the improvement of state owned real property as defined in Chapter 192, F. S.

b) **MISTAKES:** Bidders are expected to examine the specifications, delivery schedule, bid prices, extensions and all instructions pertaining to supplies and services. Failure to do so will be at bidder's risk. In case of mistake in extension, the unit price will govern.

c) **DISCOUNTS:** Will be considered in determining the lowest net cost.

d) **CONDITION AND PACKAGING:** It is understood and agreed that any item offered or shipped as a result of this bid shall be new (current production model at the time of this bid). All containers shall be suitable for storage or shipment, and all prices shall include standard commercial packaging.

e) **SAFETY STANDARDS:** Unless otherwise stipulated in the bid, all manufactured items and fabricated assemblies shall comply with applicable requirements of Occupational Safety and Health Act and any standards thereunder.

f) **UNDERWRITERS' LABORATORIES:** Unless otherwise stipulated in the bid, all manufactured items and fabricated assemblies shall carry U.L. approval and reexamination listing where such has been established.

g) **PAYMENT:** Payment will be made by the buyer after the items awarded to a vendor have been received, inspected, and found to comply with award specifications, free of damage or defect and properly invoiced. All invoices shall bear the purchase order number.

4. **DELIVERY:** Unless actual date of delivery is specified (or if specified delivery cannot be met), show number of days required to make delivery after receipt of purchase order in space provided. Delivery time may become a basis for making an award (see Special Conditions). Delivery shall be within the normal working hours of the user, Monday through Friday.

7. **MANUFACTURERS' NAMES AND APPROVED EQUIVALENTS:** Any manufacturers' names, trade names, brand-model names, information and/or catalog numbers listed in a specification are for information, not to limit competition. The bidder may offer any brand for which he is an authorized repre-

Exhibit 6-5. Form used by all state agencies in Florida to request bids, with name of agency appearing in the top, left corner (Courtesy: Florida International University, Miami)

sentative, which meets or exceeds the specification for any item(s). If the bids are based on equivalent products, indicate on the bid form the manufacturer's name and number and indicate any deviation from the specifications. YOUR BID, LACKING ANY WRITTEN INDICATION OF INTENT TO QUOTE AN ALTERNATE BRAND, WILL BE RECEIVED AND CONSIDERED AS A QUOTATION IN COMPLETE COMPLIANCE WITH THE SPECIFICATIONS AS LISTED IN THE BID FORM.

8. **INFORMATION AND DESCRIPTIVE LITERATURE:** Bidders must furnish all information requested in the spaces provided on the bid form. Further, as may be specified elsewhere, each bidder must submit for bid evaluation cuts, sketches, and descriptive literature and technical specifications covering the products offered. Reference to literature submitted with a previous bid or on file with the buyer will not satisfy this provision.

9. **INTERPRETATIONS:** Any questions concerning conditions and specifications shall be directed to this office in writing no later than five (5) days prior to the bid opening. Inquiries must reference the date of bid opening and bid number.

10. **CONFLICT OF INTEREST:** The award hereunder is subject to Chapter 112, Florida Statutes. All bidders must disclose with their bid the name of any officer, director, or agent who is also an employee of the State of Florida, or any of its agencies. Further, all bidders must disclose the name of any State employee who owns, directly or indirectly, an interest of ten percent (10 percent) or more in the bidder's firm or any of its branches.

11. **AWARDS:** As the best interest of the State may require, the right is reserved to reject any and all bids and to waive any irregularity in bids received; to accept any item or group of items unless qualified by bidder.

12. **ADDITIONAL QUANTITIES:** For a period not exceeding ninety (90) days from the date of acceptance of this offer by the buyer, the right is reserved to acquire additional quantities up to but not exceeding the original bid quantity at the prices bid in this invitation. If additional quantities are not acceptable, the bid sheets must be noted "BID IS FOR SPECIFIED QUANTITY ONLY."

13. **SERVICE AND WARRANTY:** Unless otherwise specified, the bidder shall define any warranty, service and replacements that will be provided. Bidders must explain on an attached sheet to what extent warranty and service facilities are provided.

14. **SAMPLES:** Samples of items, when called for, must be furnished free of expense, and if not destroyed will, upon request, be returned at the bidder's expense. Request for return of samples shall be accompanied by instructions which include shipping authorization and name of carrier and must be received within ninety (90) days after bid opening date. If instructions are not received within this time, the commodities shall be disposed of by the State of Florida. Each individual sample must be labeled with bidder's name, manufacturer's brand name and number, State of Florida commodity number, bid number and item reference.

15. **NONCONFORMANCE TO CONTRACT CONDITIONS:** Items may be tested for compliance with specifications under the direction of the Florida Department of Agriculture and Consumer Services or by other appropriate testing Laboratories. The data derived from any tests for compliance with specifications are public records and open to examination thereto in accordance with Chapter 119, Florida Statutes, 1971. Items delivered not conforming to specifications may be rejected and returned at vendor's expense. These items and items not delivered as per delivery date in bid and/or purchase order may result in bidder being found in default in which event any and all reprocurement costs may be charged against the defaulted contractor. Any violation of these stipulations may also result in:

   a) Supplier's name being removed from the Division of Purchasing vendor mailing list.
   b) All State departments being advised not to do business with the supplier without written approved from the Division of Purchasing.

16. **INSPECTION, ACCEPTANCE AND TITLE:** Inspection and acceptance will be at destination unless otherwise provided. Title to or risk of loss or damage to all items shall be the responsibility of the successful bidder until acceptance by the buyer unless loss or damage results from negligence by the buyer.

17. **DISPUTES:** In case of any doubt or difference of opinion as to the items to be furnished hereunder, the decision of the buyer shall be final and binding on both parties. However, should an administrative hearing occur, the party requesting the hearing shall be held accountable for any and all costs relating thereto.

18. **GOVERNMENTAL RESTRICTIONS:** In the event any governmental restrictions may be imposed which would necessitate alteration of the material, quality, workmanship or performance of the items offered on this proposal prior to their delivery, it shall be the responsibility of the successful bidder to notify the buyer at once, indicating in his letter the specific regulation which required an alteration. The State reserves the right to accept any such alteration, including any price adjustments occasioned thereby, or to cancel the contract at no expense to the State.

19. **LEGAL REQUIREMENTS:** Federal, state, county, and local laws, ordinances, rules, and regulations that in any manner affect the items covered herein apply. Lack of knowledge by the bidder will in no way be a cause for relief from responsibility. Any corporation doing business with the State shall be on file with the Department of State in accordance with the provisions of Chapter 608, and/or Chapter 613, Florida Statutes as applicable; and all partnerships doing business with the State shall comply with the applicable provisions of Chapter 620, Florida Statutes.

20. **PATENTS AND ROYALTIES:** The bidder, without exception, shall indemnify and save harmless the State of Florida and its employees from liability of any nature or kind, including cost and expenses for or on account of any copyrighted, patented, or unpatented invention, process, or article manufactured or used in the performance of the contract, including its use by the State of Florida. If the bidder uses any design, device, or materials covered by letters, patent or copyright, it is mutually agreed and understood without exception that the bid prices shall include all royalties or cost arising from the use of such design, device, or materials in any way involved in the work.

21. **ADVERTISING:** In submitting a proposal, bidder agrees not to use the results therefrom as a part of any commercial advertising. Violation of this stipulation may be subject to action covered under Paragraph 15 of this document.

22. **ASSIGNMENT:** Any Purchase Order issued pursuant to this bid invitation and the monies which may become due hereunder are not assignable except with the prior written approval of the State.

23. **PUBLIC PRINTING (APPLIES ONLY TO PRINTING CONTRACTS(:** Florida Laws require that all printing of the State shall be done in the State. Bidder hereby certifies he will comply with Florida printing laws and all regulations applying thereto.

   a) **Bid Response:** Failure to respond to our invitation to Bid for three (3) consecutive bids will result in vendor's name being dropped from our classified bid list for the Florida Group Classification of Printing.
   b) **Manufactured in Florida:** In accordance with Class B Printing Laws and Regulations "All public printing required by any agency shall be manufactured in the State of Florida; provided, however, that in any case in which an agency shall make a determination that such printing cannot be manufactured by one of two or more competing qualified printing firms in the State of Florida, then the agency may purchase the item from the lowest responsible bidder regardless of his plant location. Indicate on Bid Sheet whether or not the printing included in your offer is to be manufactured in the State of Florida.
   c) **Contracts Sublet:** In accordance with Class B Printing Laws and Regulations "No contracts for printing shall be sublet through brokers, persons or firms not regularly engaged in the production of class printing called for by the agencies."
   d) **Disqualification of Bidder:** More than one bid from an individual, firm, partnership, corporation or association under the same or different names will not be considered. Reasonable grounds for believing that a bidder is involved in more than one proposal for the same work will be cause for rejection of all proposals in which such bidders are believed to be involved. Any or all proposals will be rejected if there is reason to believe that collusion exists between bidders. Proposals in which the prices obviously are unbalanced are subject to rejection.
   e) **Trade Customs:** Current trade customs of the printing industry are recognized unless excepted by Special Conditions or Specifications herein.
   f) **COMMUNICATIONS:** It is expected that all materials and proofs will be picked up and delivered by the printer or his representative, unless otherwise specified. Upon request, materials will be forwarded by registered mail.
   g) **Return of Materials:** All copy, photos, artwork, and other materials supplied by the purchaser must be handled carefully and returned in good condition upon completion of the job. Such return is a condition of the contract and payment will not be made until return is effected.
   h) **Quality-Performance Analysis:** The contractor on any purchase of printing in excess of $1000 shall complete and forward to the Division of Purchasing the analysis form that accompanied his purchase order together with an invoice copy.

24. **LIABILITY:** The supplier shall hold and save the State of Florida, its officers, agents, and employees harmless from liability of any kind in the performance of this contract.

NOTE ANY AND ALL SPECIAL CONDITIONS ATTACHED HERETO WHICH VARY FROM THESE GENERAL CONDITIONS SHALL HAVE PRECEDENCE.

FORM PUR. 2043 (Rev. 5/30/75)

This system is normally used in metropolitan areas where there are auctions of fruits, produce, and other food items.

Items that lend themselves to this type of purchasing are oranges, grapefruit, lemons, melons, grapes, potatoes, apples, peaches, pears, and almost any other produce item that can be purchased in quantity. Food manufacturers and processors of "ready" or convenience entrées use the auction system as their main source of supply.

A buyer for a food operation cannot, of course, simply walk into an auction house and bid because the bidding is only open to members of the auction who support the operation on an annual basis. The best way is to arrange with a member of the auction to act on the buyer's behalf for a commission fee. The auction member makes the purchase at the best price and sees that the merchandise is inspected before it leaves the auction floor and is transported to the buyer's premises for use.

The commissions are fixed either on a percentage basis or on a fixed amount for each unit (box, carton, case) purchased at auction. Depending on the arrangement made with the agent, the commission may run from as little as 10 cents a basket on mushrooms to 50 cents per box of oranges or apples. The commission covers the "racket" charges at the auction, which can total 10 cents to 15 cents a carton. These include the cost of transporting the merchandise from the auction floor to the auction dock, loading the merchandise from the auction dock onto the truck, delivery by truck to the user's dock, transport from the truck onto the user's dock, and, finally, transportation from the user's dock to the user's receiving point. There is no way to circumvent these transportation costs. The user pays them whether he buys from a purveyor or uses an agent at the auction.

This type of buying generally produces a net savings to the buyer almost equal to the commission per package paid to the auction member acting as agent. If the commission is 35 cents a package, which includes all transportation and side costs, the buyer can expect to make a net saving of an equal amount if he does not have to go through the regular wholesale distribution system.

Members of the regular wholesale market distribution system take a dim view of anyone using auction buying, and the pressure put on the buyer from all sources, including unions, can be strong. If auction buying is done, it is best to use one of the regular purveyors in the wholesale supply system to act as agent since practically all of the larger wholesalers in the area use the auction as their source of supply.

Standing Orders

This system is briefly discussed for the general edification of food buyers. It is used sometimes and, under certain circumstances, is the most practical way to handle some supply requirements. On the whole, however, the use of standing orders is dangerous and often proves costly, especially for hotels, restaurants, and smaller institutional users. Under such a system, a purveyor sends in a certain amount of merchandise every day or for a specific time, depending upon the volume of business being done by the user. It is, however, almost impossible to forecast volume of business accurately enough to use that as a basis for ordering any kind of food supply far in advance. As a result, stock builds up, and it is often wasted or pilfered because there is so much around. The employee feels justified because it would be "going in the garbage can anyway."

This is how coffee, bread and rolls, milk and cream, eggs, and even, on occasion, such things as watercress and mint are purchased. Certain seafood dealers on the East and West Coasts have worked out standing orders for their products for certain inland areas. With the advent of containerized air freight, this works out rather well if the food buyer is farsighted enough to make sure that the standing orders are short of what he really expects to sell.

In some of the smaller, more remote areas, certain suppliers load up a truck and make the rounds of their clients. They are permitted to replace merchandise used. The buyer is assured of his supply, and he does not have to keep inventory or place an order.

This system relies on the honesty of both the supplier and driver. Instead of replacing old stock, a driver can shuffle stock around and charge for stock not actually delivered. It is also possible for him to overstock. (See also "Agent Middlemen—Wholesalers" in Chapter 2.) This convenient but potentially costly system is seldom used by large food buyers or by companies with strong, well-operated internal control systems.

Acting as One's Own Distributor

Certain Federal Trade Commission regulations restrict suppliers, to some extent, in their negotiation for prices with large-quantity users as against buyers who do not have the purchasing power of the large buyer. The government seeks, of course, to prevent certain users from getting too much power, thereby affecting competition in the field. Most suppliers have learned to cope with this situation by publishing price schedules that depend on volume of business, the size of a drop shipment made at one point, and a distributor's price.

Some large buyers have found that they have the qualifications necessary to become a distributor, and they have taken advantage of a situation that is both legal and ethical. A distributor's price on a five-gallon can of salad oil is often as much as $1.00 to $1.50 less than the regular wholesale price. Savings can also range from 50 cents a gallon on salad dressing to as much as $1.00 a case on canned goods and some grocery items. When this system is applied to frozen fruits and vegetables, price savings can vary from 3 cents to 5 cents a pound on the most commonly used items, up to 25 cents and 30 cents a pound on such items as jumbo frozen asparagus.

This system of buying large quantities is being used more by large consumers, but it is not new. It has long been used in purchasing such supplies as china, glass, silver, linen, soap powders, and cleaning supplies.

Cooperative or Group Buying

The idea of cooperative buying is not new. Some years ago owners and managers of many types of food service operations planned cooperative buying centers. Except for certain charitable and denominational institutions where desire for savings overcame opposition, however, little progress was made.

There were three practical reasons why the concept did not gain wider acceptance. It seems, first of all, that the average buyer connected with the food industry is proud of his ability to negotiate and buy, and he is reluctant to surrender the prerogative. Unless management is firmly committed to take such a step, the idea is conveniently forgotten. Next, there is a realization that cooperative buying provides less opportunity for the questionable but lucrative practices discussed in Chapter 11. There would, of course, be opposition to any system that discouraged or eliminated such practices. Finally, it is well known that the federal government is suspicious of cooperative ventures, especially when they involve large food processors, restaurant chains, hotel and motor inn groups, and commercial franchise operations. These suspicions have been borne out in test cases before the courts, where it has been shown that cooperative buying efforts have often resulted in unfair practices that violate the antitrust laws. There is a failure, on the part of business, to recognize the need for self-restraint. Certainly the regulatory power of the government has deterred the commercial food industry from wholesale acceptance of cooperative buying.

In the institutional field, however, cooperative buying has worked well. It would be difficult to say just where it got started, but Catholic charitable organizations throughout the United States, Canada, and Mexico certainly played an active part in setting up and supporting cooperative buying offices. Most schools and institutions supported by city, state, and federal funds have used the cooperative approach, but independent institutions were somewhat slow in seeing the advantages. It was not until the inflationary spiral that began early in the 1960's that the idea of group buying became more widespread.

Hospital councils, such as the Chicago Hospital Council, formed in 1865, pioneered in the area of cooperative buying, and the trend will unquestionably continue, at least in the institutional field.

Summary

The systems of food buying outlined above cover current methods widely used to purchase food supplies, whether for the small "mom and pop" restaurant or the large food processing company with worldwide distribution. Variations of every system are in use, and, as was pointed out earlier, no one system can or should be utilized to the exclusion of all the other systems.

The good and bad points of each system, as they apply to an individual situation, must be weighed by management and the food buyer so that the operation gains maximum benefit.

VISITING THE MARKET

Regardless of the system used for buying food, a good buyer makes it his business to visit the market. He checks prices, the quality of perishables, and the availability of supply. It is also his opportunity to learn from dealers the expected long-term market trend as well as that for the immediate future. By knowing what is available in good supply on the market and what will be arriving in plentiful supply or "gathering short," the food buyer can relay this information to the chef or food service manager and to the food director so that menus can be planned to take advantage of market trends.

One of the things a good buyer should do on regular visits to the market is personally to select and stamp for delivery as many items as possible, especially heavy beef items such as ribs, strips, filets, rounds, legs of veal, lamb legs and racks, some fish items, and even cases of melons and hampers of vegetables that lend themselves to individual selection and stamping.

When one buys meat for aging, it is imperative that the buyer put his stamp on it before it goes into cryovac. When a buyer goes to the market, he can look for good buys, and he has first selection of quality. Today, with the rather wide latitude in grading beef, a buyer has an obligation to select and stamp his purchase of major meat items. There are five different yield grades and three different levels of U.S. Choice grade on the market. The best meat goes to the man in the market.

Sometimes there are three or four "marks" for honeydews or cantaloupes and eight or ten different labels for citrus fruits. The only way to know which is best is to go to the market and cut and taste.

Formerly a buyer would go to the market as early as 4:00 or 5:00 a.m. to get the pick of the market, but eventually everyone agreed to open the wholesale (suppliers) market at 6:00 a.m. Commission houses (those that sell to wholesalers) and auctions still keep early hours. In some areas these markets open the night before so that wholesalers can be stocked by 6:00 a.m. the next day.

Going to the market is not only worthwhile; it is fun! If a food buyer fails to see the advantage of frequent visits for his own edification, thereby sharpening the tools of his trade, it may be because of the burden of office work or a lack of initiative. Whatever the reason, such a buyer often does an inadequate job of buying. He also acquires the reputation of being a telephone order clerk, instead of a professional food buyer.

THE OFFICE

Management

The location of the food buyer's office is important. Unless it is a corporate buying office, with headquarters located in a remote city, the best location is on the premises of the operation involved. It should be adjacent to the storeroom and as near the receiving area as practical. If the buyer is responsible for the operation of food and beverage storerooms, his office should also allow him full view of the storerooms and access to them.

The office and furnishings have to be adequate and in keeping with the image that the operation is trying to project. The buyer who is expected to do a prestigious negotiating job for hundreds of thousands of dollars worth of merchandise should have a suitably attractive and comfortable office. Even if the buyer has only a few thousand dollars worth of merchandise to buy each week, he is at least entitled to privacy and some comfort.

The office should be divided into a reception area, where salesmen can wait in reasonable comfort, an area for assistant buyers if the operation is sufficiently large, and a private area where the buyer can carry on discussions with salesmen without being overheard. Recording equipment, if it is used to tape discussions related to contracts and quality as an aid to memory, should be in full view of everyone in the office, and the practice should be agreed to by both parties.

There should be a regular schedule of visiting hours for sales representatives. Usually one morning a week, from 8:00 until 12:00, is adequate for seeing salesmen, but, if the buyer has time, two mornings a week should be worked into the schedule. The best single morning seems to be Wednesday. If two mornings can be set aside, however, the best ones appear to be Tuesday and Thursday.

The food buyer intent on doing a good job also finds that it usually takes two visits to the market every week to keep abreast of market conditions. He can go either by himself or with a food production manager, a chef, the receiving clerk, or, on occasion, the general manager or the food and beverage manager.

The actual placing of telephone orders

and the routine solicitation of quotes should be delegated to a capable assistant. If the buyer himself has to spend much time making telephone calls, getting quotations, and placing orders, he does not have time to analyze the market, to explore ways of improving buying procedures, or to take advantage of market trends.

If a buying office is only large enough to support one buyer plus an assistant-secretary, as much detail as possible should be assigned to the secretary or, in some instances, to the head storeroom man. Using the head storeroom man to assist in purchasing procedures equips him to serve as a potential backup for the food buyer.

Records

Every transaction performed by a food buyer or his staff should be recorded in a systematic manner so that, at any time, any question regarding the conduct of the office can be answered in writing.

Requests for merchandise from the various departments should be signed by the proper department head and filed. Any quotation received from any dealer should be recorded on a properly authorized form or filed for ready reference. Every order placed should have a purchase order number or be duly recorded in an order book showing who was given the order, the item and the quantity ordered, and the price in reference to a specification. There should be a detailed description of any cost-plus contract or any arrangement made on a long-term basis showing competitive prices secured before signing a cost-plus contract or making a long-term purchase.

One weak point often found in a purchasing office is poor communications between that office and the receiving department. If the two offices are adjacent,

a copy of the quotation sheet used for determining orders can be given to the receiving clerk so that he can anticipate and check in the orders for the day. Many orders, such as those for bread and milk, are made by telephone. Others are based on long-term contracts. They are not shown on daily or weekly quotation sheets. In this case, the purchase book, which is filled out when the purchase is made, should be set up so that a copy can be taken from the book and sent to the receiving clerk's office.

Another weak point is the lack of a formalized method of recording grocery quotations. The good buyer will make sure that he has a properly organized quotation book to back up every purchase of groceries. It should show items, dealers, and current competitive prices in order that there can be no argument about what is proper and what is not. As much as 15 percent of the total dollar purchase can be in grocery items, and, with as many as four hundred or five hundred items in use, there must be a good, systematic way of recording quotations for easy reference. Otherwise, money may be lost to the operation because the buyer is unaware that the price quoted by one dealer is 25 cents or 30 cents a case less than that quoted by another dealer.

Procedures should be established so that each day the invoices from the receiving department, plus the original copy of the receiving sheet, come to the buyer's office for approval of price and quantity after the invoices are compared with the orders placed. After approval by the buyer, these records are then passed on to the accounting department.

The buyer should have at hand a complete list of discounts and credits; thus, he can make sure that any invoice showing regular prices bears a discount notation.

Then the accounting department will be sure to pick up the credit.

FINANCIAL ASPECTS OF PURCHASING

The Cost of Money

Every purveyor or salesman hopes to sell large orders of everything because it means more commissions and bigger profits. A food buyer who succumbs to this type of selling soon finds himself in trouble. Large quantities of dead stock in a storeroom or items that do not turn over in sixty to ninety days should cause concern.

Although there should be an immediate use for merchandise purchased, this does not mean that food must be bought on a hand-to-mouth or day-to-day basis. Delivery and the cost of handling bills often exceed the cost of having some money tied up for a reasonable period of time. Buying canned goods weekly on a rotating month's supply can save in terms of transportation costs and cost per unit. A wise buyer knows how to use his buying power. He saves money by buying large quantities of merchandise, but only when this is feasible.

Because of rising delivery costs, food buyers have found that weekly or semi-weekly deliveries of even such items as dairy products, meats, and produce are satisfactory as well as profitable. Money costs approximately 1 percent a month, and, if a food buyer can get a 10 percent discount by buying a six-month supply of a nonperishable item, he would not be doing his job if he did not make the purchase and realize the savings. A 4 percent net savings on a cost of 6 percent means a return on a cost of over 120 percent a year that can be realized if there is storage space and if the company can secure financing.

During an inflationary period, it is always good business to make sure that every possible way has been explored to get merchandise on hand, as long as it is nonperishable, to circumvent the inflationary trend. This has not been as much of a problem in the United States as it has been in other countries, where inflation is one of the biggest problems of the food buyer and management. In some areas inflation has made it expedient to buy an entire year's supply of canned goods and groceries and to make a year's commitment, if possible, on such items as liquors, soap powders, paper supplies, china, glass, silver, linen, and practically everything else a food operation requires.

Paying Bills

One of the best tools a food buyer has is his operation's good credit rating. It seems to be the nature of the food business that many operations are marginal. A poor credit rating means the buyer has to pay higher prices and will invariably get some lower-quality merchandise.

Most prices are quoted on a thirty-day credit basis with a ten-day grace period. This means a buyer can order for a period of one month or thirty days on credit, but he must have the bill paid by the end of the tenth of the following month. The dealer must get his bills out on the first or second of the month, and he can expect payment by the tenth or the eleventh of that month.

When a company is unable to pay bills on a thirty-day basis and goes to sixty or ninety days, purveyors either have to borrow money to pay their bills, or they have to assign the account to a factor who charges as much as 25 percent to 35 percent yearly. This cost must be borne by the buyer, for it is included in the price of the goods purchased. Paying food bills on time is vital, even though some other bills have to be postponed.

Some dealers, because of their financial setup, have to factor their bills every week, and, if a buyer is in a position to work with the dealer and pay on a weekly basis, the chances are he can get some substantial discounts, averaging anywhere from 2 percent to 5 percent, for weekly payment of bills. Every food buyer and management should look into this possibility if they are in a position to take advantage of such a situation.

WORKING WITH SALESMEN

Advice for Food Buyers

It does not take long for a good food buyer to learn that the salesmen or purveyors he contacts know much more about their own products than he will probably ever know. The average salesman or purveyor constantly works with the same few items, whereas the buyer works with hundreds. The buyer cannot hope to know as much about each product, and it would be foolish to try. The smart buyer quickly adopts a friendly attitude toward salesmen and purveyors so that he can use their knowledge to his own advantage.

This is not to advocate personal involvement of the buyer with salesmen or purveyors. A friendly business relationship, based on fairness and mutual cooperation, can exist without the buyer's showing the slightest favoritism, practicing any dishonesty, or earning any justifiable criticism. It is better to conduct business in a relaxed, friendly atmosphere than in a tense, highly competitive one.

Even though purveyors and salesmen are highly competitive, they will, when necessary, function as a group to deal with an unsatisfactory or unfair situation created by a food buyer or a group of

buyers. More than one buyer has been forced to leave a business because a group of purveyors joined forces against him and kept him from doing a satisfactory job. This situation occurs more often in smaller communities where the market is rather limited and the number of purveyors is small and becomes a close-knit group. It is wise, therefore, to stay on friendly business terms with purveyors.

Salesmen can, if they are so inclined, help the buyer, whether he is just starting on the job or has been doing it for a long time. The salesman not only educates the buyer in terms of his own products; he also keeps him abreast of the activity of competitors and up to date on market trends. A salesman can also use his influence to see that orders are given a bit of extra care. When a salesman is on good terms with the buyer, delivery service always seems to be a little better, and, if there is an emergency (and there always are in the food business), a salesman can have deliveries made on weekends, even if he has to make them himself.

The one time a food buyer inevitably needs a friend is during a strike. There is no friend like the salesman, who will, somehow or other, find a way to get deliveries to the buyer, often at considerable expense to himself. In strike situations the salesman may risk his own well-being to help a buyer who has treated him fairly.

A purveyor and his salesmen also spend money. Buyers for hospitals, other institutions, and charitable organizations that depend largely on financial contributions from the public must keep in mind that many purveyors have funds for such purposes, and they are more likely to make a liberal contribution if their representatives have been treated with consideration.

What, then, constitutes "fair," "proper,"

and "considerate" treatment? Salesmen are human beings, and they should be accorded respect and courtesy at all times. This means that they are entitled to present their product to the food buyer, and they should have his full attention. Lack of attention is not only unfair; it is rude.

The practice of having regular visiting hours for salesmen is also considerate, and a good buyer makes sure each salesman has approximately the same amount of time. There should be no obvious preferential treatment for any sales representative.

Salesmen should also, if possible, be provided with a suitable place to wait. In many operations the buyer's office is in the lower level of a building. It is not unusual for six or eight salesmen to be standing in a hot, dirty, ill-lighted hallway, waiting their turn to see the buyer. Perhaps nothing can be done about the location of the buyer's office, but the area in which the salesmen wait could be clean, freshly painted, bright, and well ventilated, with some seating provided.

Sometimes a salesman must prove himself to his boss. The best way to do this is to show the boss that he can call the buyer and make an appointment for himself and his boss. This happens only occasionally, but it means a great deal to the salesman if the buyer cooperates. The small favor is often repaid many times over by the salesman.

The wise buyer listens to rumors from salesmen and immediately puts them out of his mind. He never betrays the confidence of a salesman by divulging a price or telling a trade secret.

The buyer should immediately make clear that he is a one-price buyer, that he wishes to hear only the salesman's "lowball" price, and that there will be no opportunity to quote a second price if the first one is too high. The sale is made or lost on the first quote. The buyer who haggles over prices, going from one dealer to another in search of a lower price, can never be sure that he settled for the lowest one. Perhaps, because of lack of confidence on the part of the dealers, he was given too high a price in the beginning.

If any food buyer is to last in the business, he must avoid the reputation of being a chiseler. Certainly he must try to get the bottom price for the quantity and quality of merchandise needed, but he must also recognize when that point has been reached.

Salesmen and purveyors should not be imposed upon. It is important that a buyer never asked a personal favor that is not connected with business and that he keep emergency orders to a minimum.

The biggest concern of any salesman is to retain an account, even though the volume of business is small. He should be assured that the buyer will use his product as long as the salesman produces, that the account will not be lost through capriciousness on the part of the buyer or anyone else in the organization who might have an ulterior motive. With such assurance, the salesman will go out of his way to support the account.

Being a salesman is not easy. Selling is a tough job, both physically and emotionally. It is difficult to make a call, regardless of the weather or any other problem, only to be turned down by a buyer. Any doubts about the hardships of selling would be dispelled by Arthur Miller's *Death of a Salesman*. It takes an exceptional person to sell. It may even take more expertise than to buy. The buyer holds the power of decision, whereas the salesman has only his own personality, his products and his knowledge of them, and his ability to convince the buyer. However he does it, short of dishonesty, it is the salesman's job to get his product into use. It is unfortunate that many salesmen become overzealous in their attempt to succeed.

If a salesman tries to buy his way into an account by going behind the buyer's back, then the salesman has asked for rough treatment, and the buyer should dismiss him. A salesman who does not know his product and "trade puffs" should also be discouraged.

Advice for Salesmen

What, in the opinion of a food buyer, is the mark of a good salesman? What should the salesman do to make a sale?

The answer to the first question is that a good salesman comes to the buyer with a thorough knowledge of his product and what his product can do for the buyer. If a salesman calls on a buyer without even knowing whether the buyer can use the product, he is wasting his own and the buyer's time. A salesman should also try to determine whether a buyer is having a problem with some product or a line of products. If so, he may be able to offer a similar product. And, any salesman who tells a buyer that he should be using his products, rather than those of a competitor, implies that the buyer is not very smart if he is not using them—often the kiss of death for a salesman.

As to what motivates the purchasing of products, most buyers will say, first, that they need the product, and, second, that they have confidence in the salesman because of his knowledge of the product and what it can do. The best advice that can be given a salesman is to do his homework well. He should find out what the buyer needs and try to fill those needs. Price is usually not a consideration in placing first orders or in securing an account.

A fast-talking, fast-joking salesman

seldom wins the confidence of a good food buyer. If a salesman's feelings are easily hurt or if he is self-conscious for any reason, he has probably chosen the wrong occupation.

THE FOOD BUYER AND THE LAW

Under ordinary circumstances, the food buyer can carry on his activities for years and never require a legal settlement of a disagreement or a misunderstanding. As long as the buyer is dealing with local purveyors and deliveries are made in the dealer's trucks directly to the receiving department of the buyer's company within a day or two of when the order was placed, there is little risk of disagreement or need to resort to the law. Today, however, legal actions are becoming more common, and the professional food buyer should have a working knowledge of the law as it applies to his activities. Perhaps the most important thing for the buyer to know is when he needs help from a lawyer to avoid trouble and costly litigation.

The first line of defense for a food buyer is the purchase specifications worked out with the testing committee, approved by management, and distributed to all purveyors with whom he does business. These specifications protect both buyer and seller from misunderstandings about what is desired by the buyer.

There is more chance of trouble when merchandise has to travel a considerable distance by common carrier and in sufficient quantities that it requires the use of public storage. Another source of trouble is the contract covering an extended period of time. Perhaps by intent, but more often because the situation has changed, it becomes impossible to carry out the terms of the contract.

PURCHASE ORDER

BILL TO

S A M P L E

VENDOR

DO

NOT

USE

SHIP TO

Attention:

| PURCHASE ORDER NO. |
| REQUISITION NO. |
| PROJECT NO. |

THESE NUMBERS MUST BE SHOWN ON ALL PACKAGES, SHIPPING PAPERS, INVOICES, CORRESPONDENCE ETC.

PURCHASE ORDER DATE

All invoices must be submitted ATTENTION ACCOUNTS PAYABLE bill to above address in duplicate. Failure to comply may result in delay of payment.

Shipping & Handling Instructions

1. All orders must be acknowledged within 7 days of receipt of order.
2. All acknowledgements must state a shipping date, or the shipping date specified herein shall control.
3. Ship the least expensive method of parcel post, UPS, REA, Truck or Rail. Air freight may only be used if indicated in the ship via column.
4. You must use your name as the shipper on all orders.
5. Ship from the F.O.B. point indicated.
6. Ship transportation prepaid or collect as indicated in the 'ship via' column. If shipment is transportation prepaid, you must pay the carrier and you must bill us on your invoice. No other method is permitted.
7. All bills of lading, packing lists, pieces invoices and other documents must state our purchase order number.

These instructions must be followed. Any changes require our approval in writing.

SHIP DATE	REQ. AT SHIP TO	F.O.B.	CONTRACT #	SHIP VIA	TERMS

ITEM	QUANTITY	UNIT	CATALOG NO.	DESCRIPTION	UNIT COST	EXTENSION

TOTAL

SPECIAL INSTRUCTIONS

Authorized Signatures:

Hotel Controller   Hotel General Manager   Purchasing Agent

Date   Date   Date

PRINTED IN USA #573R

PURCHASING

Exhibit 6-6. Form used to order merchandise

Purchase Orders

If a purchase involves more than one delivery, the food buyer should make sure that a formal purchase order (see Exhibit 6-6) is issued to the purveyor. It should make clear the specifications of the product and all of the conditions involving payment. One of the most important parts of any written contract or purchase order is the method of payment. It should make clear who pays how much for what and when.

Not only should the purchase order spell out the specifications—price, manner of shipment, and quantities involved—and method of payment, but it should also clearly state who is responsible for insurance, timing of the delivery, follow-up, transportation schedules, claims, and so forth. A purchase order made out in this manner clearly defines when the title to the goods passes from the seller to the buyer, which is necessary information in every transaction of buying and selling. If there should be loss while the goods are being transported, it is necessary to know the legal owner of the merchandise at the time the loss occurred.

If the order, which is actually a sales contract, whether written or verbal, states that the merchandise is to be delivered to the buyer's place of business, there is no question as to who is responsible for any losses. If the seller fails to deliver on time, the buyer has at least a basis to claim damages, providing he actually suffered damages because the merchandise was not delivered as ordered and agreed upon.

If the merchandise was ordered FOB (free on board) from the city of the seller to a local carrier, it is the responsibility of the buyer, who actually took possession of the merchandise when it was delivered to the carrier, to file a claim with the carrier for adjustment or damages in case of loss.

Sometimes merchandise is purchased FAS (free alongside ship), which is basically the same as FOB except that, when the merchandise arrives at the port of destination, an additional carrier is involved. If the shipment is warehoused and later delivered from the warehouse to the ship, this involves a number of carriers and conditions. Because the title to such merchandise passes to the buyer when it is delivered alongside ship, it becomes the responsibility of the buyer to make sure that his shipment is insured, either by his own company or that of the various carriers involved. Losses from overseas shipments are notoriously high. It is largely because of these high losses that the idea of containerized shipments of all classes of food merchandise has won support, and the need to consolidate different classifications of food into a single shipment has encouraged the use of one-stop buying for overseas and off-mainland shipments.

A buyer can choose another procedure. He can purchase under a contract that has a CIF (cost, insurance, and freight) destination point stipulation. This means that the seller has to arrange for shipment of the merchandise and to pay the cost of transportation to the point of delivery, and any freight costs involved from the point of disembarkation. This plan is usually used to cover overseas shipment. All necessary papers are sent ahead to the buyer, and, when the merchandise arrives at the port, the buyer arranges for his own transportation and pickup at dockside. He is free of any charges and losses up to the time he actually takes physical possession of the merchandise.

Speculative Buying

When a buyer wants to procure a large quantity of a certain item, there can be cost savings if the merchandise is purchased at the source during the height of the harvest season, with storage in the buyer's city and deliveries spaced according to the buyer's needs.

The help of an experienced lawyer is necessary in preparing the contract for such a purchase. Provisions must be made for payment direct to the packer, generally in advance of any shipments from him. The specifications must be extremely clear as to amounts, prices, delivery schedules, and quality. Provisions concerning transportation must clearly state who is responsible for arranging the details as well as insurance and transportation costs. Details include where and how the merchandise is to be stored, who has title to the merchandise, and cost of storage (which can run as high as 2 cents to 3 cents a pound per month, plus 1 cent or 2 cents a pound for being placed in storage, plus an additional 1 cent or 2 cents a pound to get it out of storage). Finally, the terms concerning pickup and delivery to the buyer's operation have to be clearly set forth.

A prospective buyer should remember that some deterioration in the quality of merchandise is normal; it occurs between the time merchandise is packed and the time it is unpacked in the buyer's storeroom or kitchen. If the merchandise is not usable on delivery, the question of responsibility arises. When the litigation is over, it is usually determined that the buyer is responsible for the loss as it is almost impossible to determine when deterioration began in such items as shrimp, seafood, chickens, hams or bacon, canned goods, and frozen fruits and vegetables.

Contracts: The Promises Men Live by

A contract is a legally enforceable agreement between two or more persons involving mutual promises to do or not to do something. Whether it is implied or specific, it always involves an offer, consideration, and acceptance. Harry Sherman, a leading economist, in his book, *The Promises Men Live by*, remarks on the extraordinary number of times that people do things or fail to do things because they count on someone else to do something or not to do something. He also brings out the fact that many activities involve promises that are actually legal contracts, but they are never put in writing.

Just going into a restaurant and sitting down is an implied contract with the restaurant owner that you are there to buy food or beverages and to receive service and that you will pay for this service. When a person checks in to a hotel, there is an implied contract that he desires the services of the hotel and that he is in a position to pay for those services. He also implies that he will conduct himself in accord with the rules of the hotel and of the commonweal. Businessmen make contracts that are never recorded merely by meeting people on the street and discussing business deals with them, or they make telephone calls or write letters—all of which involve an implied contract.

Oral and Written Contracts. Remember that an oral contract, made in good faith, is legally binding and enforceable by law. Of course, neither all oral nor all written contracts are enforceable. Some, both oral and written, are illegal or against public policy or unenforceable because one of the parties is not competent to make a contract. If, for example, a seller is selling stolen merchandise, and the buyer, upon learning this, refuses to accept it or pay for it, the seller would then have no redress against the buyer. If a seller contracts to sell certain merchandise to a buyer and then fails to deliver because the producer failed to deliver to the seller, the buyer clearly cannot force the seller to produce the merchandise. The buyer does, however, have the right to sue the seller for damages as a result of nondelivery of the merchandise. The seller then has the option of trying to collect damages from the producer if the producer is in a position to pay damages or can even be located.

Expressed and Implied Contracts. Most contracts for the sale of merchandise are spelled out so that there is no question that they are expressed contracts. Even if a contract does not explicitly state everything regarding the merchandise, there is always an implied contract that the merchandise will be of the actual quality necessary to perform the intended function under ordinary circumstances.

The question of quality may arise because the person making the complaint has "exquisite" or "extraordinary" taste. The courts must then determine what the ordinary person would feel about the quality of the product. A food buyer should keep this in mind when he rejects a shipment because, in his opinion, the quality is not exactly right.

Other forms of contracts in which a food buyer might become involved are unilateral or bilateral contracts and voidable and unenforceable contracts. He might also be concerned with the legal capacity of parties (minors and incompetents) to make contracts, responsibility of partnerships, individuals, and legal corporations, assignment of contracts, inability to perform, rescinding of contracts, cancellation and surrender of contracts, substitution of new contracts, and breach of contract. If a food buyer is not careful, he might fall into these legal traps. When this does occur, he should seek professional help immediately.

The best protections a food buyer can have, again, are a good set of specifications, which are in the hands of the purveyors with whom he does business, and a written purchase order spelling out details of the transaction such as quality, price, length of contract, shipping instructions, and any other considerations that apply to the order.

7 *Specifications and Testing*

SPECIFICATIONS

One dictionary defines specifications as "a detailed list of requirements." According to the United States government, a specification is "a statement of particulars in specific terms." The author of a textbook explains that a specification is nothing more than a description of an item stated in such a way that a department's exact requirements can be understood by both buyer and seller, while another author sees a specification as a precise statement of what is required in a commodity in order to suit production needs. Yet another author suggests that specifications should be "written in such a way as to prevent inadvertent policy changes and to communicate accurately with purveyors." It has been further suggested that specifications should describe to purveyors exactly what is wanted, without exception. All of these definitions are correct, at least in part, and, taken together, they leave little room for misunderstanding. Specifications, in the fullest sense of the term, touch practically every phase of the food operation, regardless of type or size.

Specifications, or "specs," are a means of communication that travels all the way from the customer, to the waiter, into the kitchen, the storeroom, and the purchasing department, and on to the purveyor. They go far toward establishing both quality of food and type of operation. Specifications influence costs and profits, as well as the operation of the kitchen. Specifications help to control the movement of foods from the purchasing department through the checker; they aid the controller in the performance of his duties; they make it easier to requisition from the storeroom; and, above all, they answer purveyors' questions as to food buyers' requirements. There is another valuable, but often overlooked, benefit to be derived from clear specifications: they eliminate friction between the purchasing department and the using department because they reflect and set forth policies of management.

Basic Rules Governing Specifications

Specifications Must Be Used. The best specifications in the world mean absolutely nothing if they are not used. Since they belong to the operation, not to any one individual, no one should change specifications to suit a personal whim. Management should take an active part in preparing them and in "policing" to see that only those approved are used, if that should become necessary.

Specifications Are Management Policy. One outstanding hotel consulting firm, when asked to find out why an operation's food costs are high or why there is conflict among various department heads, invariably finds that there are no written specifications approved by management that represent management policy. Instead, the establishment is usually ordering a few items based on rather vague quality descriptions and weight ranges from a list prepared either by the purchasing agent, a receiving clerk, a chef, or, perhaps, a former chef.

Specifications Must Comply with Current Standards. A set of specifications should comply with standards already in use—set either by the federal government, by a state government, or by a marketing association. Today, it seems that every product has some sort of standard already written. To ask the food distribution system to change those standards not only does not work, but it costs money to try.

Specifications Must Be Based on Tests. Specifications should be the result of a carefully conceived and implemented plan of testing that involves the important decision makers in the food department. The formation of a testing committee and who should serve on such a committee are discussed later in this chapter. Some trade publications have published articles suggesting that specifications be prepared by a group of independent, disinterested persons without consulting either the chef or the purchasing agent of an operation.

Such a theory harks back to the days of "efficiency experts," who never worked in a food storeroom or kitchen and failed to recognize that good results depend on getting responsible people involved and interested in an operation.

One hotel company, when there was an important taste test involved, invited three or four guests to participate in the test. Some revealing and helpful observations that were not always in keeping with the general ideas of some of the production crew resulted. The broader the representation on a taste test panel, the more the test reveals.

Regular Test Panel Meetings Are Necessary. The testing panel should meet on a regular basis at a specified time under the direction and order of management, and certain testing procedures should be followed and observed at each meeting. It is also essential that at each meeting the program for the next meeting be outlined so that everyone who attends can come prepared to discuss the products involved.

Tests Must Be Accurate. One of the most important ground rules in making specifications based on tests is to have an understanding of the allocation of costs in make-or-buy decisions. It is unfortunate that this is often ignored. Time and again, testing groups indicate that there will be savings on butcher payroll costs if a pre-cut product is adopted when it is obvious, because there is often only one butcher on the payroll, that the purchase of some pre-cut meats would not save a cent on payroll costs.

Test groups that often spend hours deciding whether they should make a product or buy a product would also know, if they had read their union contract, that reduction in payroll costs was impossible; nor can the operation serve a product that was not made by the staff. This has affected bread making, roll purchasing, the filleting of fish, and even the use of oven-prepared ribs.

There is at least one instance where a management consultant went into a hotel operation, ordered the butcher shop to close, and directed that all meats formerly processed there were to be purchased in a portion-ready state. The confusion that resulted brought to light the following facts: the hotel was doing about $2.5 million worth of food business and was operating on a 40 percent gross food cost, which meant that they were purchasing about a million dollars worth of food a year, and, of that amount, about $300,000 worth of it was being processed in the butcher shop. It is a well-known fact that portion-controlled meats actually cost at least 15 percent more than "scratch meats" when trim, portion cutting, and packaging are considered and after the purveyor has added in the costs of butchering and the required personnel. The 15 percent of $300,000 represented additional costs of $45,000, or 1.8 percent of the gross sales of the department. Under normal circumstances, there would have been an increase of $45,000 in yearly costs. After three months of operation, however, food costs actually went up three full percentage points, which on a yearly basis, would have amounted to some $75,000. The actual cost of operating the butcher shop (the butcher, his helper, and benefits) had amounted to $18,000 a year. The hotel actually suffered a loss of some $57,000 by changing systems.

Not only did the hotel suffer a financial loss; its reputation for serving fine banquet food was also damaged when patrons realized that a poorer quality of meat was being served. The biggest loss in quality was in items that the butcher had been preparing: prime ribs of beef, steaks, top butts, and filets of beef. The butcher had also been fabricating stuffed breasts and legs of chickens, which were very popular and profitable, and he had been taking care of the dry aging of the ribs and steak meat. With the butcher shop closed, these functions became the responsibility of purveyors, who were not as concerned with quality. Loss of business at the hotel was actually a more serious problem than the increase in the cost of the food. Poor research had resulted in a very costly decision.

Specifications Must be Concise. Any list of specifications is likely to be lengthy. Those preparing such a list should cover essential information with a minimum amount of detailed description.

Purveyors Should Have a Copy of the Specifications. Purveyors should be given a complete set of specifications for any products the purchaser might buy, and they should be notified in writing that these specifications must be adhered to and that only the testing committee and management can change them.

Information Required in a List of Specifications

When setting up specifications, simpler items sometimes require a more detailed and lengthy description than more expensive and familiar items because of the nature of the item involved. Any specification should contain enough information so that there can be no misunderstanding, and it is better to have too much information rather than it is to have too little.

It is also better, in dealing with a certain classification of foods such as beef, to use terms commonly accepted in the trade. Whenever possible, the specifications should conform to those used by the government, the American Meat Institute, or some other group connected with the trade.

Certain information should be included in all specifications:

1. the common or usual trade name of the product;
2. the recognized federal, trade, or commonly accepted local grade;
3. the unit or container on which the price is quoted;
4. the name and size of the basic container;

Additional information often needed is:

5. the count and size of items or units in the container;
6. the weight ranges;
7. minimum or maximum trims;
8. the type of processing and packaging;
9. the degree of ripeness; and
10. additional information that would eliminate any possibility of misunderstanding.

The writer of specifications usually gets carried away when he reaches the last item and ends up with several pages describing a little-used one. When it is impossible to describe what an item is, the writer often has to resort to describing what the product is *not* in order to clarify his intent. A further explanation of these various factors should prove helpful.

Common or Trade Name. The common or trade name of an item is usually simple, but the name of some items, especially certain cuts of beef, differs in various parts of the country. A spec writer has to recognize this.

On the West Coast there is a long tenderloin known as a "Special K," whereas on the East Coast the nearest thing to a "Special K" tender is a Silverskin tender, which is referred to in the *Meat Buyer's Guide* as Specification #190 Full Tenderloin Special. A boneless top butt, western style, is different from a boneless top butt cut in the East. In fact, the value to the buyer of this item can vary from 10 to 14 percent, generally in favor of the western cut. A boneless square-cut hip is still common in the Midwest, whereas, on the East and West Coasts, the word "hip" is not commonly used in the trade. A lamb rack, hotel style, could well be a bracelet of lamb elsewhere, with consequent misunderstandings.

A Pullman ham is square; other canned hams are pear shaped. A corned brisket of beef means one thing in Boston and something else in New York and generally throughout the United States and Canada. Lemon sole is lemon sole in Boston, but it is Boston sole in New York City. Boston sole in Boston can be called yellowtail or dab.

One can get into a real argument trying to specify just what scrod is. Scrod is spelled s-c-r-o-d in Boston, but in Providence, Rhode Island, it is spelled s-c-h-r-o-d, and in New York City it is spelled both ways. If you order scrod in Boston, you can get baby cod, baby haddock, hake, cut-up cod, haddock, pollock, or Boston bluefish. In New England scrod sells well; elsewhere, it does not sell as well.

Another case in point is "striped bass." This excellent fish, which breeds in both fresh and salt water, is called rockfish from Baltimore to Charleston, South Carolina, but striped bass from Nova Scotia down through the Caribbean. In Puerto Rico, the rockfish is a large, warm-water fish that does not even resemble a bass.

Federal, Trade, or Commonly Recognized Local Grades. It has been accepted in the food service business that, if it can be eaten, the USDA has a grade for it. This is a fairly accurate statement, for U.S. grading standards are probably the best in the world, followed closely by those of Canada and Australia.

A more complete listing and discussion of federal, state, and local grading systems, packaging, distribution, and regulations pertaining to the marketing of food products, especially as the regulations apply throughout the United States, are available through the U.S. Department of Agriculture and trade groups. The enormity of the subject and its complicated nature can be partially appreciated when one considers some of the factors involved in grading:

Classification of Beef

Items covered by these specifications must be of the following (grades, types, weight ranges, and states of refrigeration, as specified).

Grade
(to be specified by purchaser)

U.S. Prime	U.S. Commercial
U.S. Choice	U.S. Utility
U.S. Good	U.S. Cutter
U.S. Standard	U.S. Canner

Division of Grade
(to be specified by purchaser)

The official U.S. standards are written in such a way that the purchaser may differentiate between the upper half or lower half of each grade. If this is not specified, the full range of the grade is considered acceptable.

Weight Range
(to be specified by purchaser)

This range can be based on dressed carcass weight or actual weight of the cuts in pounds (10-12 lbs., 20-24 lbs., etc.).

State of Refrigeration
(to be specified by purchaser)

A. Refrigerated   B. Chilled   C. Frozen

Yield Grade
Fat Limitations— Wholesale and Fabricated Cuts
(to be specified by purchaser)

For all wholesale and fabricated beef products, the purchaser must specify maximum average surface fat thickness limitations. For example:

Average thickness:

1 inch (1 1/4 inches maximum at any point except for seam fat)

3/4 inch (1 inch maximum at any point except for seam fat)

1/2 inch (3/4 inch maximum at any point except for seam fat)

Defatting must be done by smoothly removing the fat by following the contour of the underlying muscle surface.

Source of Product

Beef products described must come from sound, well-dressed, and quartered carcasses, or from sound, well-trimmed wholesale market cuts from carcasses. The beef must be prepared and handled in accord with good commercial practice and must meet the type, grade, style of cut, weight range, and state of refrigeration specified. Beef cuts that have been excessively trimmed to meet specified weights or that are substandard according to the specifications for any reason are excluded. The beef must be of good color for the grade and must be free of objectionable odors, blood clots, scores, mutilations (other than slight), discoloration, ragged edges, superficial appendages, blemishes, deterioration, damage, or mishandling. The beef also must be free from bruises and evidence of freezing or defrosting, and must be in excellent condition when delivered.

The Unit or Container on Which Price Is Quoted. This refers to whether the unit is a pound, liter, bushel, carton, box, crate, bunch, piece, case, barrel, hogshead, gallon, or any other unit in common use.

The Name and Size of the Basic Container. The size of the container could be a case holding 6 #10 cans, four single gallons, or 24 #2 cans, a 50-pound bag of carrots or cabbage, a 30-pound can of frozen apples, a 30-pound lug of tomatoes, a 28-pound hamper of string beans, or a 52-gallon barrel of vinegar.

Count or Size of Units in Container. The count or size of units in the container is usually essential. Some examples are: the 18- to-20-slice-pound of bacon; 23-size grapefruit; size 80-90 green olives; 5 x 6 packed tomatoes; jumbo asparagus; broccoli in 12- to 14-bunch crates; size 90 Idaho bakers; 45-size cantaloupes; 30 to 35 count for #10 canned Bartlett pears; 3-inch minimum yellow globe onions; 24 2-pound heads of iceberg lettuce; and 100-size Florida oranges.

Weight Ranges. This refers primarily to cuts of meat and sizes of poultry. Weight ranges are essential when specifying any cut of meat, especially oven-ready ribs of beef, steak-ready strips, broilers, turkeys, and fish. Portion-control meats and ready foods are all sold by weight and count, and this must be specified. Such a specification can also refer to the weight of the individual item, as in the case of melons, or the weights of bags, as in the case of carrots, cabbage, or beets, and minimum gross weights should be specified for cases of eggs, oranges, lemons, and other "open" containers. And, in order to check overrun, containers of ice cream are weighed.

Minimum or Maximum Trim. Practically every government or trade standard specifies trim. Those who draw up specifications should make sure that every detail of trim appears. The maximum length of trim, from the end of the eye of the meat on a strip loin is, for example, particularly

important because of the price of the item. The Yield Grade determining the allowable thickness of the fat covering on meats is also important. Altering the trim of beef is one way that some dealers take advantage of a food buyer. Just a quarter of an inch excess left on the end of the flank of a strip loin can mean as much as 15 cents a pound difference. Whole fish can come with heads, and broilers can come with necks and gizzards if removal is not specified. As for vegetables, the number of outer leaves left on a head of iceberg lettuce certainly affects the price, even though the minimum weight of the head and the number of heads that go into a carton of lettuce have been specified.

Processing. Usually the name of the item indicates whether it is fresh, frozen, dehydrated, canned, corned, or packed in a certain way. If this is not made plain in the specifications, an unscrupulous dealer can take full advantage. For example, a fresh fillet of red snapper can bring as much as $5.00 a pound in New York City, whereas a frozen one would sell for around $2.25. A careful dealer could thaw frozen fillet of red snapper, repack it nicely in shaved ice, claim that it was fresh, and deliver it, thereby making an additional profit.

About 90 percent of the bacon processed in the United States is from frozen pork bellies, which is a standard trade practice. It is not standard trade practice, however, to sell frozen pork products once they have been cured and processed, but it is a rare dealer who will not sell frozen sliced bacon as fresh processed if the specifications do not specifically prohibit it.

A common "market practice" is to thaw out frozen poultry, green shrimp, brook trout, scampi, pork loins, butter, lobster, crab meat, and salmon and sell these products as fresh. Specifications should make it clear that "fresh" means the time from harvest to buyer's loading dock.

Degree of Ripeness. Most dealers prefer to sell perishable fruits, melons, and produce such as tomatoes in the "hard ripe" stage. The dealer reduces his labor and passes his losses to his customer. Too often the "customer" then serves green tomatoes, peaches, melons, pears, and avocados to his guests who, if they knew, would prefer to patronize a restaurant where the specifications say "ready for use upon delivery."

Additional Information Required. Many subjects fall into this category, and often a minor detail such as specific gravity or drained weight can be critical. Many such factors result merely from personal preferences. If there are items on the market to satisfy these preferences, however, it is up to the testing group to determine whether a preference constitutes a requirement.

The amount of "Angus beef" that is sold every day in the United States is amazing. For some reason Angus beef is considered to be the best type, and everyone asks for it. Less than 15 percent of all beef slaughtered in the United States has Angus blood. As for purebred Angus cattle, so little of it is slaughtered that it is of no consequence. Many years ago it was found that crossbred beef was better for slaughter than purebred beef. Today, it is difficult to find a purebred animal in the large feedlots and pens of the Midwest. The better grades of cattle are made up of several different breeds, with each breed contributing something to the final product. Some of the more popular crosses are Angus-Hereford, Charolais-Angus, Brangus (Brahman-Angus), and Santa Gertrudis (Brahman-Shorthorn). As to which is the best-tasting beef, knowledge-

able cattlemen suggest that there be a Holstein bull in the more recent ancestry, for Holstein beef has a "beefier" taste than any other single breed of cattle, and Holstein calves constitute the best source of veal.

Nicholas is recognized as one of the best strains of turkeys, and crosses of White Rocks and Cornish are generally the standard for poultry. Leghorn chickens are regarded as being the best layers, but the poorest for the market.

The Big Boy tomato makes a wonderful field-grown tomato, but it does not ship or pack as well as a Rutgers or some of the new hybrids. Provider and Wade string beans freeze well, but the Tender Crop variety is a better one in the market. The best fresh sweet corn varieties (Butter and Sugar, Wonderful, or Golden Cross Bantam) are seldom considered for canning and freezing.

Even though some Eastern varieties of baking apples are lower in price than Western ones, the latter may be preferred. Public acceptance of better quality from certain growing areas in the country is reflected in the name of the product. California iceberg lettuce, Oregon delicious apples, Colorado-fed beef, Iowa-fed pork, Smithfield hams, New York greening apples, Boston lettuce, Florida grapefruit, California navel oranges, Idaho russet potatoes, New Brunswick cobbler, Louisiana strawberries, Vermont maple syrup, Michigan-pack tomatoes, Sacramento tomato juice, Maine chickens, Delmarva fowl, Vermont turkeys, Mexican white shrimp, and Hawaiian pineapple are just a few of the geographical areas preferred for quality.

A number of large companies have worked hard to establish their brand names as quality items, and some have succeeded. Many of the brand names that continue in use—Butterball, Chef's Pride, Primex, Frymax, Jewel, Star, Hostess, Cure 81, Brookfield, Orchid, Blue Goose, Plume de Veau, Birdseye, Snow Crop, Turlock, Heinz, L&P, A-1, Dickinson, Sara Lee, Sacramento, Idlewild Farm, and Ore-Ida, among others—have proved their worth.

Although it is not always possible to determine exactly how many pounds of a meat item like beef ribs are necessary to serve a hundred portions, guidelines related to such requirements assist the food buyer and help in cost control, and they may be included in the specifications. This is especially important for operations that have a large banquet business.

Other considerations can enter into the specifications. Should butter be sweetened or unsweetened, and how should it be packed (prints, boxes, chips)? Should jams and jellies be pure or imitation flavored? What is the specific gravity of tomato products? What is the percent of fat in ground meat and pork sausage products? What is the drained weight of fruits in fresh fruit sections? In what is the product packed (water, brine)? What is the syrup density (light, medium, heavy)? Is age (baby beef, yearling beef, young duckling, vine-ripened tomatoes) a factor? Is sex (steer, capon, hen) important? And, with the use of so many prepared and frozen items, complete specifications today might well include the temperature of the products upon delivery to the purchaser's dock or freezer.

Setting up a List of Specifications

Before a set of specifications can be drawn up, the buyer and any others involved must do considerable research if the job is to be done effectively. Some of the factors to be considered are discussed below.

Type of Operation. If the operation is a large industrial feeding service, there is no point in developing a set of specifications for prime ribs of beef, nor in specifying 18 percent butterfat ice cream when the selling price is to be 25 cents a portion. If the operation is a privately owned hospital with a variety of facilities and an employees' cafeteria serving one thousand people per day, the requirements will differ, of course, from those of a municipal hospital serving five hundred ward and semiprivate patients per day. Or, if the operation is a hotel or if it is going to be a hotel, then it is the type that sets the level of quality in the specification list. Is it a high-class resort, a high-class commercial hotel, a luxury hotel, a motor inn, or an economy motor inn?

A budget should be available for the use of the food buyer. It indicates the expected volume of business, the expected costs, and the expected ratio of profit to sales in a commercial enterprise.

The Organizational and Physical Setup of the Operation. A person preparing specifications needs to know the goals of the organization, and he must recognize the decision makers and whether the management of the operation is food oriented and will reinforce his decisions. He also needs to develop rapport with the food service manager, the chef, storeroom personnel, the food and beverage controller, and the accounting department. If a testing committee is involved, then the food buyer should also know that. The smart buyer will see that such a committee *is* built into the organization.

The physical setup of food facilities influences specifications. The amount of storage space, including dry storage for canned goods and groceries and freezer and refrigerator space, often determines what is to be purchased and the quantities. Today, some of the largest kitchens are set up without steam-jacketed kettles, potato peelers, a pastry shop, a butcher shop, or any refrigeration in the storeroom. If there is no butcher shop, it is not necessary to establish specifications based on primal cuts of meat and fish. If there is no pastry shop or bakeshop, then the demand for frozen fruits and canned goods and grocery items is less. If there are no stock kettles, either much time will be spent in making stock on top of a range or many canned soups and dehydrated soup bases will be used in preparing food.

Size and type of restaurant, size of banquet facilities in a hotel, and sizes of the various cafeterias and snack bars in any institution, as well as the dining room service facilities offered department heads, management, and subdepartment heads, influence the food buyer. In hospitals the ratio of patient to nonpatient service may be a factor.

Market Conditions. Distance to market sources and the commodities available in the market area are important. If a large hospital is located in rural Tennessee, the specifications list probably differs from that drawn up for a hospital located just outside Washington, D.C.

Delivery schedules and delivery facilities should also be scrutinized carefully. The energy problems facing the world now and probably for decades to come could require some adjustments in packaging and processing foods. It may even influence the variety of items available.

Another factor concerned with the market is the credit rating available to the food buyer. Larger purveyors with a wide range of products and delivery services sometimes have very strict credit rules. Unless payments can be made by the due date, the food buyer must look for an-

other group of dealers.

Menus. If exact menus are not available when specifications are formulated, the food buyer and those responsible should consult sample menus from similar types of operations. If sample menus are not available, a prototype or a series of menu outlines should be furnished by management for the use of the purchasing department.

Items Needed. If a new food buyer is updating and revising a set of specifications already in use, then it is a waste of time to create a new list of items. When one is setting up specifications for a new facility, he seldom finds a testing committee already in operation. It should be understood that any preliminary list is subject to approval and correction by a testing committee when one is formed. Perhaps the quickest and best way to formulate a list is for the food buyer to obtain lists of items available from various purveyors representing the different food delivery services in the area. After the buyer receives these lists, he should review them with the food service manager, the chef, and the steward or storeroom man and have all those affected indicate the items that are to be used in food preparation and service.

Testing Committee Should Be Activated. In a new operation, management should establish a testing committee prior to the opening of the facility, if that is possible. If it is not possible, management should designate the testing committee, determine how it is to function, and set a date for it to start operating. Such action sets the tone for the operation, and, later, when the committee starts to function, the groundwork will have been laid, and there will be less resistance to it.

"Borrowing" Specifications. Whenever a food buyer takes over an existing job, he is generally confronted with the preparation of a new set of purchase specifications. If another set is being used, it is usually out of date. Or perhaps the previous buyer took the specifications with him.

When the operation is part of a chain, the buyer need only update the company's basic specifications. In a new operation the food buyer or purchasing agent should design a good set of specifications for that particular facility, but often he simply does not have time to do so. Even if he did have time, the kitchen crew might be so busy trying to get the kitchen in operation that they would have no time to help with such specifications. Perhaps the most practical thing to do in such a situation is to determine who has the best operation in the area and ask to borrow its list. If this is not feasible, a dealer might have a set of specifications. It is important to pick the best competitor in the area since one of the probable reasons for his success is his list of specifications.

Preparing Individual Specifications. It is still best, of course, to prepare an individual set of specifications based on the requirements of a particular establishment. This might initially appear to be a formidable task because in the day-to-day operation of a food service establishment some four or five hundred items are generally used. Since most food items are already covered by standards set by individual companies, trade groups, or governmental agencies, however, only a few items must be tested to turn those standards into specifications for an establishment. Testing generally involves the selection of standards already established by the government or by trade practices.

There is help available for anyone charged with responsibility for assembling a set of specifications. The best and most complete source of information is government publications. Standards produced by the USDA cover nearly every item from fresh meats to canned goods and groceries currently available in the United States and often throughout the world (see Chapter 15 and Appendix I). Canada has had an excellent system of food grading since 1929, especially for meats, and that grading system has been expanded to cover all food items available (see Appendix III). The United States and Canada are not alone in devoting much time and effort to standards for food products. During the past few years Mexico, Venezuela, Brazil, Argentina, Australia, Singapore, Turkey, Egypt, West Germany, Italy, Spain, France, England, Denmark, and Sweden have also developed good standards. While these countries may have fewer food items available for sale, their standards of grading are adequate in relation to availability. Any buyer who purchases foods for export or who plans to fill a position in another country should become familiar with that country's grading standards.

Trade publications sponsored by such groups as the National Association of Meat Purveyors and publications of manufacturers such as Blue Goose, Inc., include specifications. Finally, commercial publishers have put out volumes that are helpful in drawing up specifications (see Chapter 15).

A PRACTICAL TESTING PROGRAM

The old army saying "Your way, the Army way, and the Right way" states the philosophy for the testing program discussed here.

Because any testing program is built around a testing committee, the first consideration is the purpose or mission of the program and the committee. Activities of the program and the committee cover most phases of the procuring, processing, preparing, and serving of food, but this wide range of activities can be reduced to three basic functions: to assist in setting up purchase specifications based on house requirements; to assist in making "buy-or-make decisions"; and to maintain a continuous testing program to monitor costs, quality, taste, and presentation of food used and served in the operation.

Composition of the Committee

The testing committee in a typical, large, commercial hotel will be used to demonstrate the organization and activities of such a committee. It can be easily adapted to practically any type of large food operation.

The top decision maker of any operation should be the executive chairman of the testing committee. This would mean the general manager of a hotel, restaurant, or motor inn, the director of a dietary department in a hospital, the general manager of an institutional food service, or any other person in a position to back up decisions of the food testing committee.

The regular chairman of the committee should be the food service manager of the hotel or his counterpart in other operations. In Holiday Inns, for example, the assistant innkeeper is often in charge of the food and beverage department. In some companies the resident manager is the active supervisor of the department, and in still others the executive-assistant manager for food and beverage operations is responsible.

The executive secretary of the committee (not the secretary who keeps the notes) does most of the research and work, and this position should be filled by the company's purchasing agent or food

buyer. The balance of the committee consists of persons from the various departments, for they are more likely to reflect the taste and wishes of the general public than a committee made up entirely of persons in the food production department.

Certainly the committee should include the production manager, the chef, the steward, the catering manager, a dining room manager, if available, the food and beverage controller, the receiving clerk, the head stockroom man, the housekeeper, the senior room clerk, the public relations manager, and, on a rotating basis, the sous chef, the bell captain, a room clerk, a cook, a pantry person, a butcher if one is used, and a guest of the hotel who volunteers to serve, if this can be arranged.

Basic Requirements of the Program

If a testing program, backed by a testing committee, is to prove effective and worth the time and expense involved, there are a few basic requirements or ground rules that should be observed throughout the program. The most important one, perhaps, is that the findings and decisions of the committee must be accepted by all committee members and by management. Management must then see that the decisions are enforced. Complete written minutes of all committee meetings should be kept and signed by management.

Testing should be done in a suitable environment. An adequate test kitchen is rarely available, and the tendency is to meet in a kitchen where it is convenient to cook or cut up some item. This is, of course, wrong. Participating members cannot help but be distracted; there are too many comments from persons who are not involved; and, because the facilities are uncomfortable, there is a tendency to rush decisions. An operation large enough to support such a program generally has at least one banquet kitchen that can be set up as a suitable test kitchen. An employees' cafeteria can often be used in the afternoon. And, when butcher tests are being made, the butcher shop is an ideal place for the committee to meet.

Many large food-processing corporations have complete test kitchens with both gas and electric ranges, fluorescent and incandescent lighting, and even provision for ultraviolet lights to disguise the appearance of food when making taste tests. Although such an elaborate testing environment may be necessary for large institutional food-processing companies, it is not necessary for the average hotel, hospital, or restaurant.

The committee should meet regularly, with provision for special meetings when a question arises that needs immediate action. If a department head who is a member of the committee is unavailable, there should be an alternate who can attend the meeting and has the power to vote.

Testing should be done on a blind basis and should be carried out in accord with specific procedures. There are three stages: the first should be restricted to selection of quality; the second, to price; the third, to identifying the product and supplier if necessary.

During the first stage when the quality or the appearance of a prepared dish is being considered, the committee should conduct the procedure in silence so that no one will influence another person's thinking. Unless strict silence is maintained, an aggressive person in a responsible position could influence the activities of the committee, thereby making the committee's activities useless and the specifications worthless. If an employee with special interests has a chance to offer a comment in a testing committee meeting, he is in a position to pursue questionable

activities. Nor should anyone know the cost of products being tested until after quality selection has been made. The price often reveals the source.

A committee should not limit itself to just one selection. There are often two or three products of equal quality or of a quality suitable for the needs of the operation. By providing the purchasing department with an alternative, the food buyer can "shop" within a quality and a price range. The voting of the committee should be a matter of record, and voting procedures should be set.

Other requirements should be kept in mind by the testing committee. Any samples should resemble each other as closely as possible (aging in beef, cut and trim on meats, size of boxes or cans, method of cooking). Samples should also be selected from regular stock, and no purveyor should be informed that a test is planned or be permitted to send in a special sample. If new products are to be tested, it is advisable for the food buyer either to buy samples from a retail outlet, obtain them from another hotel or operation, or go to the purveyor's place of business and pick samples at random.

Samples should be identified by code numbers or letters, and only the buyer and the committee chairman should be able to identify them. It is preferable for the buyer not to vote or express an opinion, and the chairman should not open the identification envelopes until at least a quality standard has been established. An important decision should never be based on a single test; a series of tests is needed to arrive at a fair decision.

"Make-or-Buy" Decisions

These decisions represent one of the most important responsibilities of the testing committee. Whether to make a food item or to buy it prepared and whether to buy primal cuts of meat and butcher them or to buy precuts may depend on a number of factors. The decision is occasionally determined by the physical setup of the kitchen and storage areas or by the type and nature of the food service. The decision may also depend on either economic or quality considerations, though one is frequently sacrificed for the other. The following questions must be asked in order for decisions to be made.

Will the Customer Buy It? If the quality of a prepared item is not up to the standards of the operation, then the answer is obvious. Often, however, there is so little difference between the item to be made and the item already made that the decision requires very objective thinking by committee members. If the vote of the committee results in a tie, management has to decide.

Will Labor Costs Really Be Reduced? One case where a wrong decision was based on faulty research has already been cited in this chapter. Many similar decisions have been made without full consideration of contributing circumstances.

Some time can be saved in buying a product that is already prepared, but it is not a saving unless it is reflected on the time card. If an employee cannot be eliminated, overtime cannot be reduced, or the saved time cannot be used to improve quality or relieve another department, thus resulting in improved sales and profits, there is no saving.

Sometimes a decision has to be made as to whether to open or close a butcher shop, a pastry shop, or a bakeshop. With delivery costs soaring, some operators have decided to reopen pastry shops and bakeshops and to expand their butcher shops. Within today's market, any full-menu operation in a hotel or restaurant making $2.5 million in gross business (or an institution doing an equal volume of business) can support a bakeshop as well as a pastry shop. One making $1.5 million in gross business should take a hard look at the possibility of opening or closing butcher and pastry shops. This seems to be the point at which a decision is required.

Institutional operations, which are often smaller and have limited menus, have generally found it impractical to operate their own butcher shops. They find that it is more to their advantage to purchase prefabricated, fresh meats.

Are Food Costs Really Being Controlled? There are many who claim it is easier to control food costs by using "prefab" meats and "prepared" foods. It goes without saying that this makes it easier to determine portion costs and to control portion sales—on paper. It must be recognized, however, that the use of such products also makes it easier to pilfer. Loss from pilferage can exceed the savings involved. According to some successful hotel operators, whenever controlled tests have been made during the past thirty years food costs have gone up from two to four points as a result of the introduction of prefab, preprepared, or preportioned foods.

Another consideration intrudes at this point. Most authorities on personnel and production standards claim that, as far as can be determined, one-half of the average employee's time on duty is nonproductive. Even if this claim is only half true, the possibilities for savings and increased production based on this nonproductive time might reduce the number of previously prepared items needed. The next question, then, is: "How good is the control system?" That is management's problem, not the testing committee's.

Is the Merchandising Plan Well Developed? There are instances where the

BUTCHER TEST CARD

Item_____ _____Grade_____Date_____

Pieces_____Weighing_____lbs._____oz.   Average weight_____

Total cost $_____at $_____per_____Supplier_____Hotel_____

Breakdown	No.	Weight		Ratio to total weight	Value per pound	Total value		Cost of each		Portion		Cost factor per	
		lb.	oz.					lb.	oz.	Size	Cost	Pound	Portion
Total													

Item   Portion size   Portion cost factor

COOKING LOSS

Cooked_____ Hours_____ Minutes at _____ Degrees

_____ Hours_____ Minutes at _____ Degrees

Breakdown	No.	Weight		Ratio to total weight	Value per pound	Total value		Cost of each		Portion		Cost factor per	
		lb.	oz.					lb.	oz.	Size	Cost	Pound	Portion
Original weight													
Trimmed weight													
Loss in trimming													
Cooked weight													
Loss in cooking													
Bones and trim													
Loss in slicing													
Salable meat													
Salable meat													
Remarks:													

Item   Portion size   Portion cost factor

Exhibit 7-1. Butcher test card: (*a*) Front, uncooked item; (*b*) Back, cooked item (Courtesy: Sheraton Corporation of America, Boston, Massachusetts)

TASTE TEST—SCORE SHEET

Product: _____   Date: _____

Item	First (5 points)	Second (3 points)	Third (2 points)	Fourth (1 point)	Remarks	Total points
A						
B						
C						
D						
E						
F						
G						
H						
I						
J						
K						
L						
M						
N						

Grading to be based on flavor, tenderness, color, shrinkage, aroma, juiciness, and general appearance.

Additional remarks: _____
_____

_____
Signature

Exhibit 7-2. Score sheet for taste test

FOOD PURCHASE AND RECEIVING SPECIFICATIONS

Company: _____

Date: _____

Item	Unit	Trade specs.	U.S. Grade	Detailed requirements	Weight or count	Required per 100 portions
BEEF						
Rib, roast ready	lb.	#109	Choice	Top half of grade, cryovac aged three weeks from date of kill, three-inch trim on loin end, four-inch trim on chuck end, no fat over one-inch	20-22 lbs.	150 lbs.
Rib-eye roll, boneless	lb.	#112	Choice	Top half of grade, three weeks aged, all outside fat removed except one grade stamp	10-12 lbs.	50 lbs.
Strip loin—boneless, short cut	lb.	#180	Choice	Top half of grade, cryovac aged three weeks from date of kill, three-inch trim at rib end, two-inch trim at butt end, no fat over one inch, average 1/2 inch	12-14 lbs.	100 lbs.
Strip loin—boneless, steak ready	lb.	#180 Modified	Choice	Same as #180 above except trim one inch from eye of meat	10-12 lbs.	85 lbs.
Top sirloin, butt, boneless	lb.	#184	Choice	Top half of grade, cryovac aged four weeks from date of kill, one inch maximum fat, cut western style	12-14 lbs.	75 lbs.
Full tenderloin, regular	lb.	#189	Steer	Fat not to exceed 3/4 inch at gland, tenderloin to be 1/4 naked, no scores over 1/2 inch, must be three inches minimum at center of cut	7-8 lbs.	50 lbs.
Short loin, regular	lb.	#173	Choice	Top third of grade, dry aged three weeks from date of kill, soft bone cut with no cartilage from hip, fat covering not to exceed one inch, flank not to be over six inches from eye of meat	36-38 lbs.	150 lbs.
Full tenderloin special (also known as silver skin)	lb.	#190	Steer	Same as #189 above except all fat removed leaving silver skin	5-6 lbs.	40 lbs.
Square-cut chuck boneless clod cut	lb.	#116	Choice	Lean, fat not to exceed one inch at any surface, fresh cut	58-65 lbs.	50 lbs.
Round-rump and shank off	lb.	#164	Prime	Must be aged three weeks minimum, fat not to exceed one inch at any surface, cut through round bone posterior to ball joint	60-75 lbs.	60 lbs.
Round inside—top round boneless	lb.	#168	Prime	Must be aged three weeks minimum, fat not to exceed one inch at any surface	22-25 lbs.	50 lbs.

Item	Unit	Spec	Grade	Specification	Size/Weight	Pack
Round bottom—gooseneck boneless	lb.	#170	Choice	Must be aged three weeks maximum, fat not to exceed one inch at any surface, top 1/2 of grade	25-30 lbs.	50 lbs.
Corned brisket—deckle off boneless	lb.	—	Choice	Lean-cured kosher-style brisket, to be trimmed to specification, cryovac packaged	12-14 lbs.	60 lbs.
Ground beef special	lb.	#137	—	25 percent trimmable fat, ground twice, final grind 1/2 to 3/16 inch holes in plate, no bull, stag, cow, or variety meats, no additives, fresh-ground on day of delivery	—	40 lbs.
POULTRY						
Chickens, broilers	lb.	Fresh	A	Eviscerated, no necks or giblets, White Cross preferred, ice packed	2, 2½, or 3 lbs.	50 birds
Chickens, roasting	lb.	Fresh	A	Eviscerated, no necks or giblets, White Cross preferred, ice packed	4, 4½, or 5 lbs.	100 lbs.
Fowl, stewing	lb.	Fresh	A	Eviscerated, White Rocks preferred, ice packed	5-6 lbs.	75 lbs.
Turkeys, toms, roasting	lb.	Fresh or frozen	A	Eviscerated, Beltsville or Wagon strain, northern-raised birds preferred, cryovac wrapped, box packed	22-24 lbs. 24-26 lbs.	75 lbs. 70 lbs.
Duckling	lb.	Frozen	A	Eviscerated, Peking strain, no necks or giblets, cryovac wrapped, box packed	4½-5 lbs.	50 birds
Turkeys, hens, roasting	lb.	Fresh or frozen	A	Same specs as turkeys, toms, roasting	10-12 lbs. 12-14 lbs.	75 lbs.
EGGS						
Boiling, white	Doz.	Extra large	AA	Clean, not oiled, white or cream-colored shells, 30 dozen, cardboard cases	54 lbs., gross 48 lbs., net	½ case
Cooking, white	Doz.	Large	A	Clean, not oiled, white shells only, cardboard cases, 30 dozen	52 lbs., gross 46 lbs., net	½ case
Bakers, mixed	Doz.	Large	A	Clean, mixed colors permitted, no cracks or checks, 30 dozen, wood or cardboard cases	52 lbs., gross 46 lbs., net	½ case

Exhibit 7-3. Table showing food purchasing and receiving specifications, by item

Item	Unit	Trade specs.	U.S. Grade	Detailed requirements	Weight or count	Required per 100 portions
FRESH VEGETABLES						
Asparagus—jumbo	Crate	Fancy	Fancy	Loose or bunch as specified, fresh, 90 percent all green stems, crisp, no spreading tips, 5/8 inch minimum diameter per spear	35 lbs., gross 30 lbs., net	2 crates
String beans	Hamper	Fancy	Fancy	Round, uniform size, clean, fresh, crisp, tender, dark green color, free of leaves and stems, length of beans four inches to six inches	35 lbs., gross 28 lbs., net	1 hamper
Onions, Spanish	Bag	#1	#1	Mature, firm, uniform shape and size, free from damage or decay, three inches minimum diameter	50 lbs., net	Cooking or slicing, 10 lbs.
Potatoes, baking	Box	Fancy	Fancy	Idaho Russets when available, Russet Burbanks and Norgold Russets acceptable, packed 70-80-90 as specified, uniform in size and shape, free of cuts, dirt, and decay	Box filled, count not to vary over 3 percent as ordered, minimum 55 inches gross	100 potatoes
Tomatoes, fresh	Lug	Fancy	#1	Firm ripe, good red color, uniform size, color, and condition, free of scab, nailhead, bruises, and rots, order by size 5 x 6, 6 x 6, or 6 x 7	33 lbs., gross 30 lbs., net	1 lug for salads
Lettuce, iceberg	Carton	Fancy	#1	California or Arizona lettuce preferred, heads to be fresh, firm, and green, free from decay, burn, mildew, dirt, and burst, wrapper leaves not to exceed eight, twenty-four heads per carton	43 lbs., gross 40 lbs., net	1 carton for salads
CANNED GOODS						
Green beans	Case	Fancy	A	Blue Lake variety preferred, cut or whole as ordered, whole beans No. 2 sieve	6 No. 10 per case or 24 No. 2½	4 No. 10 or 20 No. 2½
Carrots, whole	Case	Fancy	A	Specify 100 or 125 count or 200 or 250 count per No. 10 can, good color, no broken or blemished carrots, water and light sugar pack	6 No. 10 per case	4 No. 10
Tomatoes, cooking	Case	Extra-standard	B	Jersey, Michigan, or midwestern pack preferred, minimum drained weight per No. 10 can, 63.5-68 oz., tomatoes to be 70 percent whole	6 No. 10 per case	6 No. 10 or for cooking

Item	Unit	Grade	Grade	Description	Pack	Size
Tomato juice	Case	Fancy	A	Fancy California tomato juice preferred, Sacramento brand where available, red, heavy, sweet juice specified	12 No. 5 per case	10 No. 5
Green olives (queen)	Case	Fancy	A	Fancy Spanish queen olive desired (colossal—80/90 per kilo, 200/225 per gallon, jumbo—100/110 per kilo, 250/275 per gallon), minimum drained weight per gallon, 86 oz., packed stuffed, whole, or pitted as ordered	6 gallons per case	2 gallons 3 gallons
Peaches, yellow cling	Case	Choice	Choice	Specify halves, quarters, or sliced, packed in medium syrup, size 30 to 35 in No. 10 can, full pack with minimum of syrup	6 No. 10 per case	6 No. 10

Exhibit 7-3. *(continued)*

merchandising plan affects a food operation. Sometimes a pastry shop or a butcher shop operates far below capacity and at a loss because neither the menu nor the menu merchandising promotes the products of those departments. In properties doing a large banquet business, for example, it is often easier for the banquet manager to sell an "Ice Cream Bombe, Fantasia" than an "Angel Cake with Fresh Strawberries."

For years the Plaza Hotel in New York City featured a "Stuffed Breast of Capon à la Plaza" (made from a whole chicken) that cost the hotel just half the price of a prefab product, and they had the legs at no cost for other dishes. Employees often appreciate a freshly made chicken potpie instead of leftover roast, and potpie costs must less than pot roast.

Butcher Test Card

"Make-or-buy" decisions have to be based on recorded butcher and cooking loss tests, plus consideration of the labor and merchandising aspects. It is fortunate that the procedures and records used in making such tests are fairly well standardized and followed.

Large operators often have their own testing records, but all establishments need certain basic information. The sample shown in Exhibit 7-1 is a typical butcher and cooking loss test card. Providing the information on this card is the food and beverage controller's responsibility, but the testing committee should insist that the tests be made and the results recorded.

Score Sheets

Score sheets for taste tests (see Exhibit 7-2) should provide room for com-

ments that can be used by the scorer to support his vote. This forces the committee member to give full attention to the test so that he can support his opinion. Analysis of the comments is often revealing and more useful than the arithmetical score.

Some Facts Based on an Actual Testing Program

From an actual series of fifty tests on various food items, the following interesting facts and perhaps a valuable lesson were learned:

1. Only two times out of fifty was the highest-priced item judged to be of the best quality.
2. In eighteen times out of fifty the lowest-priced item in the test was judged to be of the best quality.
3. At no time was the lowest-priced item judged to be last in quality.
4. At no time was it impossible to accept as an alternate a nearly equal item, and thirty-five times out of fifty it was possible to accept a third alternate item as being of nearly equal quality.
5. At no time did any one product receive all first-place votes.
6. The average saving in purchase price between the product selected and the highest-priced item in each category was 28 percent.

Testing, it would appear, is worthwhile.

Sample Specifications

Excerpts from a set of specifications now in use in a large chain food operation are shown in Exhibit 7-3. Many of the points shown there have been discussed throughout this chapter.

8 *Receiving: A Hidden Hard Spot*

In the corporate vernacular, a hard spot is an opportunity for a profit that has been overlooked. This definition certainly justifies the title of this chapter.

It has long been recognized in the food business that the receiving clerk is often overworked, poorly trained, unappreciated, and underpaid. Often many millions of dollars worth of merchandise pass through the hands of a receiving clerk, whose job it is to see that it is accounted for and that it meets all specifications. That person is probably the sole judge of 90 percent of the merchandise delivered. In large operations purchasing several million dollars worth of food per year, the receiving of merchandise is often left to a storeroom clerk, a timekeeper, or a kitchen steward and sometimes to the food buyer. Under such circumstances, there is no way that a satisfactory receiving job can be done.

Even when a receiving department is properly set up under the control and supervision of the accounting department, the receiving department is often left to fend for itself. Too often the receiving clerk is given a few directions and then

practically forgotten by the controller, which means that he is often adopted by the food and beverage controller, the kitchen manager, the chef, the steward, or some other interested party.

In terms of the food purchasing function in the food business, it is said that a good food buyer constitutes the head, while a good set of specifications is the backbone. It should also be recognized that the receiving clerk serves as the arms and the legs and that he must be ambitious, honest, and alert. Because of this, it should also be recognized that the person should be well trained and well paid.

When a scandal related to purchasing erupts in some food department, it appears that the trouble generally starts in the receiving department. The findings of outside investigators generally show that, where there are problems involving the receiving function, receiving clerks are somewhat vague as to who their boss is and are poorly supervised; the receiving office is poorly located in relation to the storeroom and receiving dock; scales are inadequate; there are no written instructions as to how the department should be operated; accounting forms are inadequate; and there is no backing from management.

Merchandise enters the food operation through the receiving department so that is where short weights begin, poor quality is passed, double billing is made, prices are inflated, excessive trims and mislabeled merchandise are accepted, substitutes for size and quality are passed, spoiled merchandise is dumped, inflated orders are accepted, home deliveries start—any of which could encourage a series of nonviolent crimes. Investigations have shown that food costs can rise by as many as five or six points because of practices that start in a receiving department. That is where small things begin and grow to serious proportions.

A GOOD RECEIVING SYSTEM

Before any receiving system can be set up, management has to outline a plan that suits the operation involved. It should be patterned after a system that has proved satisfactory elsewhere in the food industry, and then it should be followed by all involved. Unless the plan is written out in sufficient detail to establish responsibility for each part and unless there is a time schedule for the completion of the plan, there is little chance for success. If management cannot handle such an assignment, outside professional assistance should be sought. The major concerns are:

1. proper organizational relationships among the receiving department, the accounting department, and operations;
2. adequate facilities and proper tools in a convenient location;
3. the need for a competent, trained receiving clerk adequately compensated; and

4. continuous checks by those within the house and outsiders on receiving.

The receiving of all food, beverages, and operating supplies is traditionally the responsibility of the accounting department under the controller. The receiving clerk should be a recognized member of the accounting department, directly responsible to the controller and assisted by the food and beverage manager. It is imperative that management support the independence of the receiving clerk's office. The prerogatives of the receiving clerk with relationship to the food buyer, the chef, the food and beverage manager, and other department heads should be clearly spelled out in the organization chart and in the operating manual covering the operation.

A receiving clerk cannot be any better than the controller to whom he reports. Many controllers are not particularly interested in the food business, and they do not take the time to give the proper backing and supervision to the receiving clerk. This minimizes the effectiveness of the receiving department. Some controllers arrive at their office around 9:00 a.m. or even 10:00 a.m., but they work later in the evening. By the time he arrives, three-fourths of the merchandise going through the receiving department is already checked in and is in the storeroom.

Facilities

Location. The receiving clerk's office and receiving area should be located as near as possible to the receiving dock and adjacent to the storeroom and the food and beverage control office. The receiving office should not be either in the storeroom or in the food control office; it should be located adjacent to them. The front of the receiving clerk's office should be glass in order that, as he works at his desk, he can see all of the activity at the entrance to the storeroom. And all of the merchandise coming in or leaving the property should pass his office. There should be enough space outside the office so that merchandise does not pile up, thereby making the receiving function a rush job.

Equipment. In larger operations the receiving clerk should be provided with adequate scales built into the floor. They facilitate loading and unloading. There should also be a small platform scale, perhaps table mounted, for weighing smaller items (see Exhibit 8-1).

For the average-sized operation there are varied sizes and types of scales designed to serve specific needs. These range from the plan "balance arm" platform model to the sophisticated automatic recording ones with ounce calibrations and fluid recording. Some scales can even be programmed into a central, in-house computer, complete with scanner, but such equipment would only be needed in a large warehouse operation.

The office and receiving area should be well lit and should meet the sanitary requirements of the Occupational Safety and Health Act (see Chapter 3), and both the office and its contents should be adequately secured.

The receiving office should be equipped with such other "tools of the trade" as rulers and other measuring devices; receiving sheets; receiving tickets and dispenser; credit memo forms; forms for goods received without invoice; an operation manual for the receiving department; a complete set of receiving specifications (duplicating the purchasing specifications); instant-reading thermometers; strap cutters, crate hammers, small crowbars, a cardboard box cutter, and a sharp knife or two for cutting merchandise for inspection; and adequate filing cabinets.

THE RECEIVING CLERK

What kind of person usually takes a position as a receiving clerk? A young, ambitious person might use the position to gain experience needed to take on a better job, or a semiretired or a handicapped person proud of being able to work can often perform the tasks. Then there are the "sharpies" looking for a place to "make a fast buck" and move on; the lazy incompetents who do only what they must to hold a job; and others who might or might not be capable of doing the job, depending upon the amount of training and supervision needed and provided.

The personnel department should take the initiative in locating and screening applicants for the position, checking qualifications and experience. Then the applicant should be approved by the controller, the personnel department, and the operation manager. If an applicant has had good experience and is unemployed for no clear reason, one should be wary. A good receiving clerk with a good record is seldom available through the open job market.

The best way to find a good candidate is often by promotion from within the present storeroom staff, the food and beverage control staff, the accounting office, or the steward's department. Sometimes a cook who has had institutional training is interested in obtaining managerial experience to further his career, and he is willing to start in the receiving department.

One successful chain food operator has a policy of paying key department heads 25 percent more than the normal rate. This includes the receiving clerk.

Exhibit 8-1. Examples of scales used in the receiving department (Courtesy: Hobart Food Equipment, Troy, Ohio)

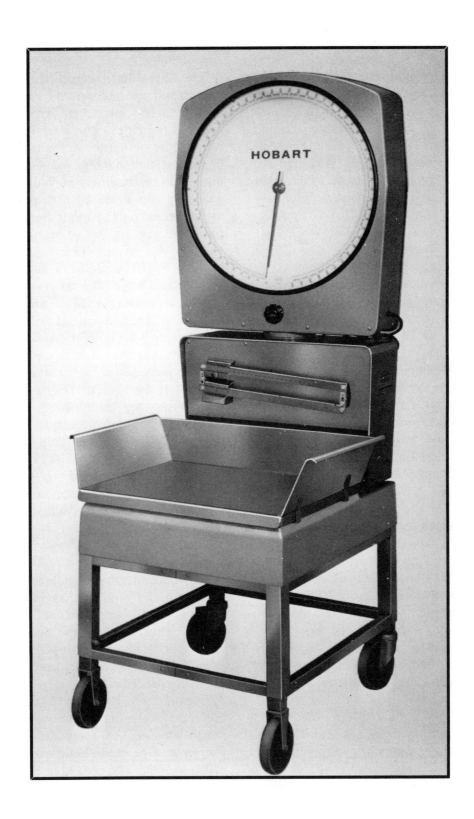

The policy has apparently paid off many times.

Even if a receiving clerk is experienced in food operations and has a good background in food receiving, management should provide for a continuous training program. Some large food operations have a program whereby certain positions are rotated on a periodic basis. This plan works quite well when there is adequate supervision.

Continuous Training

Once a receiving clerk has been given a set of purchase specifications that he can use for receiving, he should understand that these specifications cannot be changed by any one individual unless such a change has been passed by the purchasing committee and approved by management. Because he is involved with the food buyer, the food production manager, the chef, storeroom personnel, and the food and beverage controller, the receiving clerk might find that these people will contribute to his training and knowledge.

Because the quality of fresh foods varies so much from week to week, the food buyer should, on a regular basis, take the receiving clerk to the market to round out his training. It is a good idea to include the chef on occasion. Then food buyer, chef, and receiving clerk look at the same merchandise at the same time and agree on the quality that is acceptable. If the food buyer does not ask the receiving clerk to accompany him, the controller should suggest to the general manager that the food buyer do so. One very wise food buyer invites the receiving clerk to sit with him while he meets with salesmen. It is well known that salesmen are among the best trainers in the business, whether the training be good or bad.

THE RECEIVING OPERATION

The hours that the receiving operation is open and manned should be coordinated with delivery practices. In downtown areas of big cities, where traffic is heavy, it might be necessary to open the receiving department at 6:00 a.m., and all receiving, other than emergency deliveries, is generally completed by 3:00 p.m. In suburban areas, on the other hand, delivery trucks might not arrive until midmorning. There is no point in having the receiving dock open if no deliveries are expected.

The food buyer should cooperate with the receiving clerk and the various dealers to work out a schedule of deliveries that is satisfactory to both the dealer and the receiver. Because of high delivery costs and the prospect of higher ones, the food buyer may be able to realize substantial savings just by establishing economical delivery schedules with purveyors. The advisability of having deliveries every other day, twice a week, or weekly has already been reviewed in Chapter 6, along with possibilities for savings in the monthly purchasing of canned goods and other food supplies.

Saturday and Sunday deliveries should be made only if there is a real emergency. When there are many such emergencies, the controller and management should investigate. Either someone is not determining the needs of the operation in a systematic manner, or someone is intentionally bypassing normal purchasing and receiving procedures.

Even if there is a regular schedule for the receiving office to be open and for most deliveries to be made, some deliveries may be made before the receiving office is open. The receiving clerk should work out specific instructions for that person in the food department who will be signing for such deliveries and checking on the shipment. Someone in a position of responsibility should check periodically to determine how well this early morning or late evening receiving is being executed.

The set of purchasing specifications that also serves as receiving specifications should be posted behind glass so that every page can be seen by everyone involved, including deliverymen, the receiving clerk, or anyone working with the receiving clerk who performs the receiving functions. If the receiving clerk is referring to the specifications on a regular basis, truck drivers notice this and report the fact back to the dealers, which is exactly the intent of a good receiving department.

When there is a blind receiving system, deliverymen bring only a list of the items in the shipment. The receiving clerk must then count and weigh everything that comes in to complete the receiving sheet. The theory is that the invoice, with the dealer's weights and prices, is sent to the accounting department, where it is matched with the prices quoted to the food buyer and the receiving tickets. If everything matches, monthly statements can be paid after management approves them. Some receiving systems even include scales that stamp weights on delivery slips. Computerized scales and scanners are also being used in the receiving function. Blind receiving has not proved practical because it is difficult to match invoices with delivery slips, and extra staff is needed to compare the various records.

A receiving clerk should be in a position to accept or reject merchandise on the spot. If there are any weight shortages or there is a disagreement on count or specification, he should be able to adjust the delivery slip or invoice at once or reject questionable items. Most satisfactory receiving systems in use today require that the deliveryman bring an invoice with merchandise so that it can be checked for accuracy at the time of delivery. Any variations can be handled either with a credit memorandum or a statement of goods received without invoice.

FORMS IN USE

Receiving Sheets and Tickets

A properly organized receiving department for any type of operation, including a food service, should be charged with receiving all merchandise that enters the building. One point of entry makes it easier to check everything into the building, keep the proper control records, and see that all merchandise meets the specifications and matches the orders, that invoices are complete, and that pricing is accurate.

In some operations where highly technical merchandise is delivered, it is sometimes preferable to set up a food and beverage receiving point near the food and beverage storeroom and another receiving point near the engineering department, medical storeroom, or housekeeping department. Regardless of where the receiving point is located and what is received at any one point, there are certain basic requirements for good receiving that must be met to avoid possible losses. This chapter, which deals with the receiving of food and food supplies, also shows how the receiving of beverages fits.

Everything that passes through the receiving department in a day should be listed on a receiving sheet on which are recorded the activities of the department. These records can always be used as the basis for establishing accounting controls needed to safeguard a company's assets.

There does not appear to be a single form of receiving record that is really adequate for writing up food and beverage items and other food department supplies, such as soap powders, paper supplies, china, glass, silver, pots and pans, and some three hundred to four hundred other items used in the operation of the food department. The three forms in general use today have been utilized for some time, and they comprise the receiving clerk's daily report (Exhibit 8-2), which is used for all incoming food. Miscellaneous supplies can be written up either on the regular receiving sheet or on a receiving ticket, and a copy then attached to the delivery slip or invoice that accompanies the incoming merchandise.

A separate sheet is generally used for the receiving of alcoholic beverages because many states require certain information regarding the purchasing and receiving of them. It is best to record this information for the accounting department on what is commonly known as the beverage receiving clerk's daily report (Exhibit 8-3) at the point where the beverages enter the operation.

A receiving sheet (see Exhibit 8-4) should be written up in detail so that there is no question as to what came into the operation, what goods were received without invoice, what credits were taken for any merchandise that did not arrive according to the invoice, and what merchandise was taken out through the receiving department. Some receiving clerks merely write down the name of the dealer and the total of the bill on the receiving sheets "to save time" but, for all practical purposes, this type of entry is useless.

After the receiving sheet has been completed, showing dealers, items, quantities, prices, and extensions, the columns should be totaled and the sheets signed by the receiving clerk each day. The receiving sheet is normally prepared in duplicate. The original, with copies of all invoices, credit memorandums, and lists of goods received without invoice, is sent first to the food and beverage control office, then to the food buyer, the general manager, and on to the controller for payment. The copy is retained in the receiving department. In larger operations it has proved helpful to prepare it in triplicate, with one copy being forwarded to the general manager's office and on to the controller, the second being kept at the receiving point, and a third copy being used by the food and beverage controller.

Individual receiving tickets are useful when there are only a few large shipments of supplies, but the difficulty of handling the many separate pieces of paper that would be required for receiving food makes this system impractical.

Receiving Stamps

Each invoice attached to the original of the receiving sheet should be stamped with a receiving stamp that has space for the date, the initials of the persons approving price, quantity, quality, and extensions, the controller's initials, and the general manager's final approval for payment.

The receiving stamp should be set up to show the following:

Date _____
Received by _____
Weight and count OK _____
Prices OK _____
Quality OK _____
Food and beverage control OK_____
General manager OK_____

This may seem to be a lot of work, but if approvals are not obtained on a regular

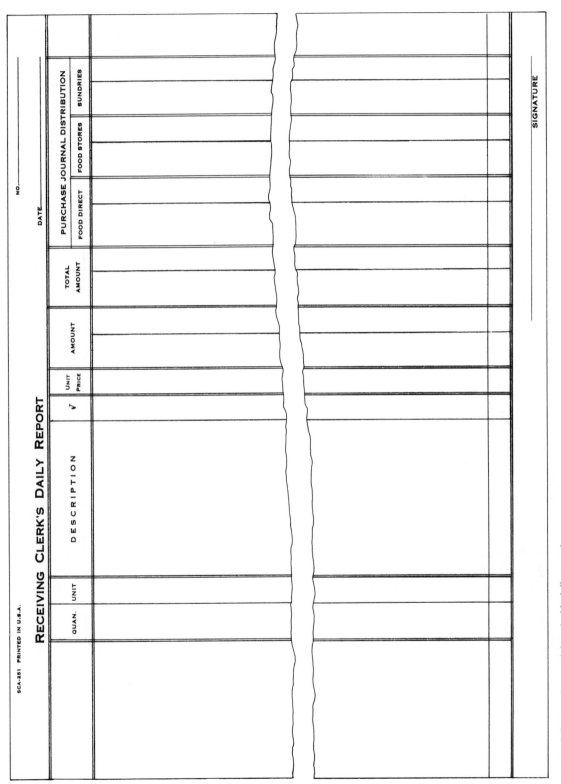

Exhibit 8-2. Form for receiving clerk's daily report

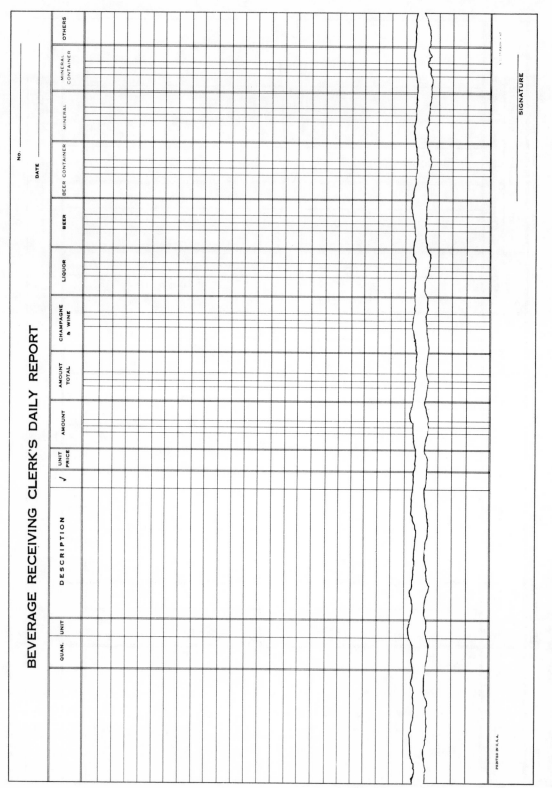

Exhibit 8-3. Form for beverage receiving clerk's daily report

RETURN TO
ACCOUNTING DEPT

RECEIVING RECORD

No. 55006   Date_____

Received from_____

Address_____

Order No._____ Complete Delivered to_____ Dept.
                    Partial

No.	DESCRIPTION	Via	Freight	Prepaid C.O.D.
			Parcel Post	
			Express	
			City	
		Charges	$	
		Total	$	
		Weight		

Receiving Clerk

Quantity	ARTICLES	Amount
	1	

Counted, inspected and received in stock _____19____

By_____Department Clerk

7/64E O-325451-T

Exhibit 8.4 Form for recording merchandise received

HOTEL_____

CITY_____ DATE_____

NOTICE OF ERROR CORRECTION

PURVEYOR_____

SHIPPER_____

GENTLEMEN:
CORRECTIONS HAVE BEEN MADE ON YOUR INVOICE AS SHOWN BELOW.

INVOICE NO._____ DATE_____

ITEM	REASON FOR CORRECTION	UNIT PRICE	YOUR BILLING	CORRECTED BILLING	DIF-FERENCE

KINDLY ADJUST YOUR RECORDS ACCORDINGLY.

HOTEL_____

BY_____

TITLE_____

TOTAL CORRECTIONS

TOTAL YOUR INVOICE

OUR CORRECTED TOTAL

SCA 315   PRINTED IN U.S.A.

Exhibit 8-5. Form used for correcting an invoice

daily basis, a control system eventually breaks down, with resulting operational losses.

It is important that the general manager of the operation get the receiving sheet and invoices every day so that he is aware of what is being purchased. A good general manager can spot irregularities, excess purchases, changes in cost prices that necessitate menu changes or changes in dealers, and many other variants from the norm.

Credit Memorandums

Most good receiving systems provide for the use of a credit memorandum (see Exhibit 8-5) when merchandise is returned, when credit is taken for a short weight or count, when a price is corrected, or when salvage, such as grease, bones, or egg cartons, is sold. Some receiving

clerks merely make a notation on the invoice, but this system breaks down when there is no invoice or the deliveryman does not turn in the corrected delivery slip.

The credit memorandum is generally prepared in duplicate, with the original going back to the purveyor via the deliveryman and the copy being sent on with the invoices to the controller after being noted on the receiving sheet.

Goods Received without Invoice

To avoid the complications and disagreements that arise when merchandise is received without an invoice, the receiving clerk should fill out a goods received without invoice (GRWI) form (see Exhibit 8-6). The form is generally made up in duplicate, with the original going to the accounting department after being

```
          SHERATON  CORPORATION  OF  AMERICA

              GOODS RECEIVED WITHOUT INVOICE
                                              N⁰

  RECEIVED FROM:_____

  _____        DATE_____

 QUANTITY |      ITEM      | UNIT PRICE | AMOUNT
          |                |            |
          |                |            |
          |                |            |
          |                |            |

                              Signature
 SCA-314                              Printed in U.S.A.
```

Exhibit 8-6. Form indicating goods received without an invoice (Courtesy: Sheraton Corporation of America, Boston, Massachusetts)

noted on the receiving sheet and the duplicate remaining with the receiving clerk.

When the invoice arrives, the accounting department, having been forewarned, sends the invoice to the receiving clerk, who attaches the duplicate GRWI to the invoice, writes the invoice up completely on the receiving sheet, and sends the invoice, plus the duplicate GRWI form, through the regular channels for payment.

FUNCTIONS OF THE DEPARTMENT

Weighing, Counting, and Measuring

These functions are the most important activities of the receiving department

and the main reason for having an independent department. The words seem simple, but this is where questionable practices carried on by smart dealers are begun and the worth of a good receiving clerk is demonstrated.

The following are good rules for any receiving clerk to follow:

1. Remove the paper or containers from turkeys, meats, and other wrapped items or take a standard allowance that is agreeable to the purveyors.

2. Never accept weights stamped on a box or container if it can be opened and weighed or counted.

3. Check the weights of such incoming merchandise as eggs, oranges, lemons,

lettuce, tomatoes, butter, and coffee against the weights that appear in the receiving specifications.

4. Weigh containers of frozen foods on a spot-check basis.

5. Count or weigh bags containing such items as carrots, beets, cabbage, potatoes, dry beans, rice, and flour to determine whether the weights match the invoices.

6. Check individual weights of melons to see if they meet the specifications.

7. Count baking potatoes, melons, tomatoes, grapefruit, lemons, oranges, apples, and any other items sold by size or count.

8. When weighing large quantities of like items such as hams, ribs, strips, top butts, and poultry, weigh the total gross and then spot-check individual items to see that weight ranges are according to specifications.

9. If using meat tags, average individual weights for the shipment to save time.

10. Keep a ruler tied to the scale for checking length and trim of meats so that when the receiving clerk finds excess trim and the dealer says that the meat stretched in handling, even though it has a bone in it, the company will know enough to get a new dealer.

11. Weigh sealed cases since a case can be opened and two or three bottles or cans removed without leaving a mark on the case, or the count could have been short when the case was originally closed.

Judging Quality

The judging of quality at the receiving point is the most difficult part of the receiving clerk's work. More disagreements arise over quality than any other single phase of the receiving procedure.

For many years, the kitchen manager, chef, or a food and beverage manager passed on the quality of merchandise. This prac-

tically eliminated any need for an independent receiving department. In an efficient department, however, a receiving clerk is trained by the food buyer, in cooperation with the chef, to reflect the opinion of the food buyer, the food and beverage manager, and the chef in judging quality. If there is a real question as to the quality of some product, the problem should be referred to the purchasing committee for final decision, subject to the general manager's approval. The smart receiving clerk calls for help when there is a doubt in his mind and it is this sharing of decision making with others that builds confidence in his decisions and avoids many problems.

A Few Points to Remember

Deliverymen have eyes and ears, and they report back to the dealer everything that the receiving clerk does. If the receiving clerk knows his business, properly weighs and counts the merchandise, observes the quality of the merchandise, and checks the bottom layers of packages containing such items as lettuce and tomatoes for quality, then dealers are not going to take many chances and try to pass short weights or poor-quality merchandise. If, on the other hand, the receiving clerk just waves the delivery in, as often happens, then the dealers know that the receiving is carelessly handled and can take advantage.

Deliverymen usually try to hurry the receiving clerk. Sometimes this is a deliberate attempt to confuse the receiving clerk so that he will overlook some short weights or other discrepancies. In other instances, it is simply because there is a parking problem or the deliveryman is faced with a heavy schedule. The receiving clerk occasionally must help the deliveryman by setting merchandise aside to be checked thoroughly later. This is risky, but, if necessary, it can be done, and purveyors will accept credits taken under such circumstances.

When first-of-the month deliveries are made for groceries and other items bought in large quantities, it is only fair for the food buyer to work out a delivery schedule with purveyors to avoid undue delays at the receiving dock. There is no reason why large deliveries must be made on the first of the month; they can be spaced out through the month by design.

Emergency delivery costs are high. The receiving clerk should advise the controller and management if the number of emergency deliveries exceeds one or two a day.

The strict maintenance and constant use of various accounting forms in the receiving department are what make the receiving process work. If corners are cut there, the effectiveness of the department will suffer.

The receiving clerk should be of such stature and the receiving system should be so efficient that the receiving clerk should feel free at all times to discuss anything questionable with the controller. He should also be in position to request to talk with both the general manager and the controller if the need arises.

CONTROLS IN THE SYSTEM

No system of any kind has ever been devised that has been able to eliminate completely the part played by human error. Someone has to police the receiving system, or the system, somewhere along the line, breaks down. Any receiving system, the manner in which the system functions, and the policing of the system are the unqualified responsibility of the accounting department and the controller.

The receiving clerk and the food and beverage controller are both part of the accounting department. In order to avoid the charge of collusion, however, the receiving clerk should not report directly to the food and beverage controller. The food and beverage controller should be in a position to observe the functioning of the receiving system. If the receiving clerk is not performing his job satisfactorily, the food and beverage controller should report his observations to the receiving clerk and the controller. In this manner, an independent person other than the controller, who might not have adequate time or perhaps training in receiving, is checking on the receiving clerk, thereby eliminating a possible weakness in the system.

By freeing the food and beverage controller of responsibility for receiving, that person is in a position to act as a controller. If he were responsible for the receiving clerk, he would be part of the operation and should not be performing a control function. Many controllers have, unfortunately, given this responsibility to the food and beverage controller with some rather disastrous results. Even though accounting department employees are supposed to be trustworthy and are thoroughly investigated, they are human. It is very easy for a receiving clerk and a food and beverage controller to join forces, to the detriment of the company.

In a well-managed and disciplined operation, the receiving department and the receiving clerk work under the scrutiny of a good food buyer. Any reputable chef also continuously checks on the receiving department to be sure that sloppy practices do not affect the cost or quality of food that he is to prepare, and a good controller manages to find time to spend a few minutes with the receiving clerk and at the receiving dock every normal working day. The dedicated, outstanding controller finds some time to be at the receiving dock at odd hours and on days not normally regarded as working days. It is unfortunate that many controllers are prone to work from 9:00 a.m. to 5:00 p.m., five days a week. Such a schedule does not allow much time for checking on the receiving department, and such people are not ideal controllers. They are more bookkeepers with the title of controller.

The director of food services in a hospital or an institution, a general manager of a hotel, a food and beverage director in a hotel, or a manager of a restaurant is always a busy person in any operation. He should, however, find time daily or at odd intervals to observe how the receiving department is operating.

According to a leading security service manager who specializes in this phase of the food industry, whenever a breakdown in the purchasing system occurs it generally starts with poor receiving practices. Perhaps there is an adequate system, but there is no one policing the system.

In large operations, regardless of whether they are hospitals, institutional food services, or hotels, it is always good to have outside auditors do spot checks of the receiving function from time to time on a nonregular schedule. Accounting companies that offer these services have qualified, trained personnel who in one day can measure the efficiency of a receiving department. This surprise check is a valuable, relatively inexpensive management tool. One of the best-organized and carefully hidden systems devised to steal from a large chain hotel company was uncovered when the president of the company engaged a spot-check service from an outside auditing firm to look at the receiving department, as he said later, "just for the hell of it."

Another part of a good receiving system is the use of a visitor's logbook at the receiving office. Good management encourages the controller, the chef, the food-purchasing agent, the head storeroom man, the food and beverage director, and even the catering manager to visit the receiving dock if for no other reason than to show the receiving clerk that he is being watched and that his work is appreciated. There should be a logbook in the receiving office, and the receiving clerk should insist that all visitors sign in, with the date and time of their visit. Management can then review the logbook from time to time. If the visits by responsible people are frequent, then the manager has just one more good management tool working for him.

In small operations, where buying, receiving, storing, and issuing are done by one employee and any independent checking is done by the controller and manager or perhaps even by the senior room clerk, the logbook system is even more essential.

THE ROLE OF GOVERNMENT

Some of the problems involved in food purchasing, transportation, and receiving are discussed in Chapter 11. Because of the existence of these problems and efforts to solve them, many institutions and large companies, especially companies operating outside the United States, turned to the government for help. In addition to establishing complete grade standards, the government has set up an acceptance service within the USDA concerned with meats and meat products. This service is designed to assure purchasers that available products comply with detailed specifications approved by the USDA. After bids have been submitted by purveyors and accepted by a buyer, a grader from the Department of Agriculture inspects the beef or any other meats or meat products to ascertain whether the products comply with the specifications. If they do comply, an inspector accepts them, and the federal grader certifies that they have been accepted. The containers are then marked and sealed so that the purchaser receiving the merchandise can be reasonably sure that the products being received are the products shipped and that the products comply with government standards.

The cost of this service is normally nominal. It generally averages less than two or three cents per pound depending on the size of the shipment, and this is generally offset by peace of mind where the exporting or shipping of large quantities of meat from one area to another is concerned.

In certain parts of the world, primarily the United States, Canada, and Europe, there are accredited and, in some cases, licensed accounting firms, consultants, and sanitarians who act as independent receiving agents or spot-receiving agents for companies that need this type of service. These people are generally highly trained, competent, and, on the whole, conscientious and honest. They help to maintain standards when they might not otherwise be maintained.

Why, one might ask, if there is a professional food buyer involved in the buying process, is it necessary to hire specialists to check on food buyers or other persons involved? The answer, which goes back to the weaknesses of "human nature," is the main concern of Chapter 11.

9 *The Storeroom: A Place to Make Money*

BASIC FUNCTIONS

Since there are many ways to save money in a good storeroom operation, it is fair to say that a storeroom is "a place to make money." Whether it is for food, beverages, or supplies, the storeroom operation has two basic functions of equal importance. They are supply and control.

Supply

This function, when it is efficiently handled, is the means of supplying an operation with what is needed, when it is needed, and in the amount needed. It resembles the purchasing phase of the operation, and the two activities are interrelated. A reserve stock of nonperishable goods kept in a storeroom helps maintain price levels by making it unnecessary for the food buyer to purchase under the pressure of need. If sufficient space is available for storage, a good buyer can always negotiate for better prices on large-quantity deliveries and avoid purchasing when a commodity is in short supply.

Delivery schedules were not a great problem in the past. There was no shortage of fuel to move trucks at low cost. That cost factor is becoming increasingly important. In the 1960's the average delivery to a food operation in a metropolitan area cost $5.00. By 1970 this had increased to $15.00 per delivery, and the current average cost per delivery is approximately $30.00 and headed toward $50.00. A well-run storeroom with sufficient space available can operate with weekly and monthly deliveries on many items, greatly reducing delivery charges.

Control

It is while performing this function that the amount of merchandise put into the production stream can be checked most easily by the food production manager, the chef, the food and beverage manager, or whoever is responsible for monitoring the cost of merchandise issued from the storeroom. It is unfortunate that many people in management have not mastered the art of controlling costs at the storeroom level. Too often employees are permitted to sign out merchandise and put it into production in quantities unrelated to the true needs of the operation. Storeroom controls and their use are discussed later in this chapter and again in Chapter 10.

THE STOREROOM OPERATION

As in all other operating departments, the general manager of any food operation or facility has the final responsibility for operating the storeroom. It is his responsibility to set up a proper organization or to see that one is set up, to see that written instructions cover all phases of storeroom operations, to see that the department manager is suitable, and to see that proper controls are provided and maintained and that proper inspections of the storage areas are made. If the general manager cannot do all of this personally, he should delegate the responsibility for working with the storeroom staff to other department heads.

If the food buyer or purchasing agent has an office in the storeroom or nearby, he is generally in charge of the storeroom, the wine cellar, and general food stores. If that person is not located nearby, it is best to appoint a storeroom manager who reports to the food and beverage manager or someone responsible for the overall operation of the food and beverage department. Pricing of requisitions can be the responsibility of the storeroom manager, but the controller should see that the pricing is accurate. Actual control should, however, be exercised through the food and beverage manager, who would then be responsible for setting up the proper systems of issuing, planning for the security of the storeroom, securing the keys, and seeing that properly authorized signatures appear on all issues from the storeroom. An ambitious controller occasionally takes over the operation of the storeroom, but this is poor policy for the controller is then responsible for both operation and control. Over an extended period of time this could lead to a conflict of interest. It is independent control that ensures

against losses.

The controller is responsible for setting up the control system over storeroom operations, for supervising the system, and for taking independent, month-end inventories. Taking these inventories is the sole responsibility of the controller's office unless the controller delegates it to the food and beverage controller in cooperation with the storeroom manager. Such an arrangement is satisfactory, providing the controller or another capable person from the accounting department is present and verifies the quantities of the month-end food and beverage inventories.

Personnel

Anyone who works in the storeroom should be thoroughly screened by the personnel department, investigated by a security service, and bonded against any form of thievery or shortages in the storeroom. Upgrading job titles for positions in the storeroom seems to have a beneficial effect on storeroom operations. One suggestion has been to call the head storeroom man a storeroom manager and the other people who work with him storeroom attendants or food supply clerks.

Schedules

Storeroom hours depend on a number of circumstances. Since the storeroom must be open to receive incoming merchandise, the location of the food operation in relation to the market influences when the storeroom opens in the morning. Normally, milk, bread, and some produce deliveries start arriving at about 6:00 a.m. Most storerooms, therefore, open at that hour six days a week since there are milk and bread deliveries on Saturday. If the food operation is some distance from the market area, deliveries do not arrive until 8:00 or 9:00 a.m. In that case, the storeroom can open as late as 8:00 a.m. Because deliveries are not usually made on Sunday, it should be possible to arrange for the kitchen to requisition supplies on Saturday for use on Sunday; then the storeroom can be closed.

Most food storerooms in large operations remain open from 6:00 a.m. to 8:00 or 9:00 p.m., requiring two shifts. When storerooms are open so long each day and so many days of the week, it is usually for the purpose of servicing departments that are continually running out of supplies—a bad habit that should not be encouraged. Careful planning on the part of kitchen and storeroom management to schedule issues to the various kitchen departments can usually eliminate the need for such long hours of operation, in which case the following schedule might prove more effective:

> Monday through Saturday: 6:00 a.m. to 2:00 p.m., closed 2:00 p.m. to 4:00 p.m., reopened 4:00 p.m. to 7:00 p.m.
> Sundays and holidays: 6:00 a.m. to 2:00 p.m., closed the rest of the day.

The two-hour break in the afternoon should be used for cleanup and arranging and taking inventory of the stock as a basis for the next day's ordering.

Well-managed kitchens and storerooms have an ordering schedule that requires each kitchen department to submit a daily requisition. If the requisitions are submitted to the chef in the afternoon, he can review them, make necessary changes, and approve them. In late afternoon the storeroom personnel fill all of the various orders and place them on a truck or trucks for delivery or pickup the first thing in the morning. Not only does this increase the

degree of control over the issue of merchandise, but it also reduces the food supplies in the kitchen at night, when losses are more likely to occur.

Equipment

Shelving. The equipment needed to operate a good-sized storeroom is rather simple and inexpensive after refrigeration is installed in the necessary areas (see Exhibit 9-1). Perhaps the most immediate need is adequate shelving (see Exhibit 9-2).

The shelves should be 18 inches to 20 inches deep, and there should be 16 inches to 18 inches between them. The bottom shelf should be at least 6 inches off the floor to permit air circulation and cleaning. The top shelf should not be more than 6½ feet from the floor for ease in loading and unloading.

All shelving must meet local sanitary codes where the operation is located and the sanitary codes set by the Occupational Safety and Health Act (see Chapter 3). Some shelving should be of the modular type for easy arrangement or rearrangement. The best shelving is made of stainless steel, but, because it is extremely expensive, manufacturers have produced shelving made of alternative materials for the refrigerated area and for other storeroom areas.

For refrigerated areas, vinyl-coated, louvered shelving is acceptable, as is the old standby, galvanized, slotted metal shelving. The use of perforated or slotted shelving in the refrigerated area has the advantage of allowing better air circulation than solid shelving. Some manufacturers have introduced "embossed" shelves with raised ridges that allow air to circulate around the pans without any foreign materials dropping into the food below (which is why most sanitary codes require

① METRO SOLID SUPER "ERECTA" SHELVING
② METRO WIRE "ERECTA" SHELVING

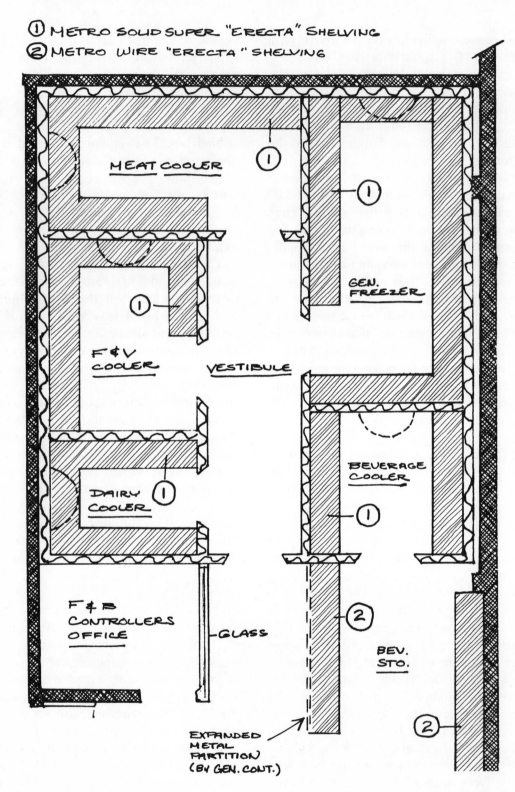

Exhibit 9-1. Sketched layout for refrigerated storage area (Courtesy: Sheraton Equipment Company, Boston, Massachusetts)

Exhibit 9-2. Various types of shelving for storage (Courtesy: Southern Equipment Corporation, St. Louis, Missouri; Metropolitan Wire Goods Corporation, Wilkes-Barre, Pennsylvania)

Exhibit 9-2. *(continued)*

that any food be covered during storage in the refrigerator).

A very good shelving for the dry storage area, whether it be food, liquor, or other supplies, is made of chrome-plated wire. It is available under a variety of trade names. This shelving is strong, light-weight, and can be put up and taken down easily. It is, however, unsatisfactory for refrigerating and freezing areas because it tends to rust under damp conditions. Some operators have turned to solid painted metal shelving for dry storage areas, but it requires painting about every three years to control rust on worn sur-faces. In areas where sanitary codes permit, for supplies other than food, wooden shelving is satisfactory, provided it is tight, well painted, and free from breaks where vermin can hide.

Solid metal or wooden shelving is good for storing liquor, but vinyl-coated, lou-vered, or flat shelving is best for storing refrigerated wines. There is also a vinyl-coated, honeycomb shelving for storing refrigerated wines in a horizontal posi-tion to keep the corks moist.

Kitchen architects or kitchen equip-ment contractors often fill the storeroom with too much shelving. Not only does this cost more than it should, but it interferes with storeroom operations. It is advisable, in fact, not to equip over 50 percent of the area with shelving. Some merchandise can be stored in cases, with only the top case being open. This reduces labor costs and facilitates taking inventory. It also contributes in a small way to better secur-ity.

Pallets or Dunnage Racks. Nothing should be stored directly on the floor of either the storeroom or the refrigerated areas. It is usually a sanitary code viola-tion to do so. Pallets or dunnage racks (Exhibit 9-3) of lightweight materials can

be used to keep stored items off the floor. Wooden skids are also satisfactory and relatively inexpensive.

Trucks. If the storeroom is large enough, an electric motorized truck can be used to move skids and dunnage racks, or a motorized forklift truck with a small turning radius is ideal. (See Exhibit 9-4.) A few metal hand trucks should also be available for moving storeroom stock, as should two- or three-deck trucks for use by purveyors, even though most delivery-men have their own small hand trucks.

One type of truck, often overlooked or forgotten entirely in setting up a storeroom area, is the small two-deck delivery truck (Exhibit 9-5) used by a storeroom man to deliver merchandise to the kitchen or used by the runner from the kitchen in picking up his stock. In hotel operations room service tables are generally pressed into service, but they are fragile and expensive. The price for not having proper storeroom delivery trucks is high.

Scales. Even though the receiving area is equipped with large floor-type scales (see Exhibit 8-1), the storeroom should be equipped with a floor scale capable of weighing up to approximately two hundred pounds. It does not necessarily have to be embedded in the floor. In addition, the storeroom should have a table-model scale that can be used for checking smaller weights and weighing small quantities of bulk merchandise that is to be rebagged and issued to the kitchen. This type of scale is also important in operations that utilize the central ingredient room con-cept where no one has access to the store-room except those who weigh out all ingredients for recipes—a system that is gaining acceptance in large hospitals today.

Other Equipment. The storeroom man-ager should be provided with a suitable

Exhibit 9-3. Pallets or dunnage racks used to keep stored items off the floor (Courtesy: Eastern Steel Rack Corporation, Boston, Massachusetts)

Exhibit 9-4. Motorized vehicles for storeroom work (Courtesy: Clark Equipment Company, Battle Creek, Michigan)

Exhibit 9-5. Three-deck hand truck for storeroom deliveries (Courtesy: Southern Equipment Corporation, St. Louis, Missouri)

desk, a chair, a file case, and a small cabinet where he can lock up small, valuable merchandise that might otherwise be lost. There should be a work table with a stainless steel top where merchandise can be examined and where large, bulky packages can be broken down into smaller portions for use in the kitchen.

Storeroom personnel should be issued uniforms to improve the appearance of the area, to provide better sanitation, and to upgrade the job. Freezer coats are necessary for individuals working in the freezer area.

FOOD STORAGE AREAS

Basic Requirements

The average storeroom operation falls into the same category as the receiving operation. It is there, it is busy, and a lot of valuable merchandise is received, stored, and issued from there, but no one seems to know or to care much about what goes on there unless things go very wrong. When that happens, however, there are reverberations.

Often food storage areas are inadequately planned when the initial layout is made, and they are invariably the first places to suffer when funds are allocated. if the usual pattern is followed, the storage area is usurped for engineering needs, for housekeeping supplies, and for paper and cleaning supplies, leaving about half the space that is needed for food and liquor. Sometimes the various storage areas for the food department are far apart, even on different floors. Under such circumstances, it is little wonder that there is less control over the merchandise. Those responsible for setting up a storeroom and planning storeroom areas should give consideration to location and size.

Location. The storeroom should be between the kitchen and the receiving area. Because of building layouts, however, this is often difficult to achieve. If the kitchen or kitchens are located on different floors, it is preferable to have the storeroom next to the receiving area to facilitate delivery of supplies to the storeroom after the shipment has been checked through the receiving area. Once the merchandise is in the house, various departments may pick up their supplies from the storeroom as needed.

In the past, storerooms have usually been located in the first or second basement of a building but new building codes are forcing architects to relocate storerooms on street and upper-floor levels so that there is light and ventilation. Backed-up sewer lines have caused problems, especially in areas where there is danger of flood, another reason why storage areas should be located on upper floors.

Size. There is a direct relationship between size of storeroom area required and type of operation, between size of operation and proximity to supply sources. An operation in a large school, which uses mainly convenience foods, requires larger freezer and canned goods storage areas

than a full-service restaurant or hotel using large quantities of fresh meats, poultry, and produce. A resort hotel in the Caribbean requires about twice the usual amount of space for canned and frozen items, and the storage area needed for fresh produce and dairy products is determined in accordance with local laws.

In the initial planning stage, the planner must make an educated guess as to what the requirements will be many years in the future. Once the walls are finished, there is little chance that the storage area will ever be made larger, though it can easily be made smaller.

Space Requirements. Every kitchen architect has a schedule showing space allocations for storage that he uses in kitchen planning, and the standards are changed to fit the needs of the operation being planned. How skillfully these adaptations are made depends largely upon the ability of management and the kitchen architect to determine the future needs of the operation.

Whether the requirements are based on cubic feet per hundred covers served per day, the dollar volume of business, or the size of the kitchen area and, thereby, the dining area, the final decisions are always tied to the volume of business expected and the distance to and adequacy of the market to be used.

One system commonly used by kitchen layout men to determine the amount of storage and refrigerated space required for a proposed hotel or motel operation is an average percentage allotment of the total space to be provided for the entire operation. The total space includes dining area, banquet service, bar (if a part of the setup), and back of the house. Some adjustments have to be made for a bar, cocktail lounge, and banquet service in a hotel serving liquor that are unneces-

Facility	Number of seats		Square feet per seat		Square feet in area
Coffee shop	125	x	12	=	1,500
Dining room	150	x	20	=	3,000
Subtotal					4,500
Employees' cafeteria	60	x	15	=	900
Bar and lounge	125	x	20	=	2,500
Ballroom	600	x	12	=	7,200
Private dining rooms	200	x	15	=	3,000
Subtotal					13,600
Divided by a use factor of 6 (rounded)					2,300
Total determining area (4,500 + 2,300)					6,800
Multiplied by allocation for back of the house (2) to get total basis for storage area					13,600
Multiplied by 10 percent to determine size of storage area					1,360

Exhibit 9-6. Working out the formula for space requirements in a food service facility

Area	Allocation (percent)		Storage area (square feet)		Allocation (square feet)
Dry storage (including liquors and mineral waters)	50	x	1,360	=	680
Freezer	15	x	1,360	=	204
Meat refrigeration	10	x	1,360	=	136
Fruits and vegetables	8	x	1,360	=	109
Dairy	5	x	1,360	=	68
Liquor refrigeration	5	x	1,360	=	68
Vestibule outside refrigerated area	7	x	1,360	=	95
TOTAL	100				1,360

Exhibit 9-7. Allocation of storage area in a food service facility

sary in a large commercial or institutional food service. Because any plan is affected by location, distance from market, type of business, personnel involved, and other factors, professional help is needed in designing and planning any food operation.

To illustrate this system of space allocation, assume the following circumstances:

125-seat coffee shop
150-seat dining room
60-seat employees' cafeteria
125-seat bar and lounge
600-seat ballroom
200-seat accommodations in private dining rooms
kitchen, with pastry shop
storerooms, no butcher shop

A rule of thumb is that storage area should constitute 10 to 12 percent of the square foot area of the entire facility. Because of the limited food service in the bar and lounge and some function areas, a lower percentage of storage and refrigerated area is needed there. For determining the correct amount of space, the following formula is useful:

Total dining area plus ⅙ of bar and function room area multiplied by 2 (to allow for back of house) and the result multiplied by 10 percent. (See Exhibit 9-6.)

The space thus determined is the total space required for storage, including dry, refrigerated, and freezer. Space is further allocated (see Exhibit 9-7) as:

	Percent
Dry storage (including liquors and mineral waters)	50
Freezer	15
Meat refrigeration	10
Fruits and vegetables	8
Dairy	5
Liquor refrigeration	5
Vestibule outside refrigerated area	7
TOTAL	100

This somewhat detailed treatment of the storage areas has been included to emphasize the many facets that must be considered in designing those areas. The ability and the judgment of architect and management are as clearly reflected in well-planned storage areas as they are throughout the rest of the establishment. No one method or formula covers all of the many types of food service operations found throughout the world. Ultimately space requirements should be based on the type of food service, purchasing and inventory policies, the menu, the availability of production and service personnel, and the location of the establishment and the effectiveness of distribution systems.

Temperature Ranges

The following is a list of temperature ranges for various storage areas normally provided in temperate zones:

Storage areas	Temperature Range Fahrenheit	Celsius
Nonrefrigerated		
Dry grocery storage	50°-70°	10°-22°
Liquor storage, whiskeys	50°-70°	10°-22°
Wine storage, red	50°-70°	10°-22°
Wine storage, white	50°-70°	10°-22°
Beer storage	50°-70°	10°-22°
Mineral waters	50°-70°	10°-22°
Refrigerated		
Vestibule	50°-60°	10°-15°
Meats	30°-35°	0°-2°
Poultry	30°-35°	0°-2°
Fish and seafood	30°-35°	0°-2°
Smoked meats	30°-35°	0°-2°
Dairy products	30°-35°	0°-2°
Butter and eggs	30°-35°	0°-2°
Fresh fruits and vegetables	36°-40°	2°-4°
Delicatessen	36°-40°	2°-4°
Wine storage, white	40°-45°	3°-5°
Beer and mineral waters	40°-45°	3°-5°
Freezer storage	0°-(-)10°	(-)18°-(-)24°

Where dry storeroom temperatures exceed 70°F., it is necessary to air-condition the storeroom to prevent excessive losses from spoilage of wines, beers, and canned goods. Cereal grains and flour should be stored where the temperature can be kept below 65°F. to prevent growth of weevils.

Storage Times

The length of time for safe storage of frozen foods depends on the storage temperature and how well it is maintained, the nature of the items stored, and the manner in which the items are packaged. Fluctuating temperatures reduce the life expectancy of frozen foods, and small packages are more susceptible to freezer burn and dehydration than larger, well-packaged items. Some foods such as pork, especially hams and bacon, do not freeze well because of the soft content.

Once a frozen packaged item has been thawed, it should not be refrozen unless necessary because there is deterioration in quality. Any refrozen item, even though packaged, should not be kept over thirty days. The following storage time limits, although they are not maximum, are considered safe.

Frozen item	Safe storage time limits*
Raw beef, lamb, veal	Up to 1 year
Cooked beef, lamb, veal	Up to 3 months
Pork, fresh	Up to 6 months
Pork, cooked, smoked	Up to 1 month
Sausages, smoked	Up to 1 month
Raw poultry, fish	Up to 6 months
Cooked poultry, fish	Up to 3 months
Chopped meats, any	Up to 3 months
Fruits and vegetables	Up to 1 year
Cooked fruits and vegetables	Up to 3 months
Ice cream	Up to 6 weeks
Frozen entrées	Up to 3 months
Sandwiches	Up to 2 weeks

*0°-(-)10°F. or (-)18°-(-)24°C.

Refrigerated item	Safe storage time limits
Meats, fish, poultry	
Beef, aging (cryovac)	1 month
Beef, other	10 days
Lamb	1 week
Veal	1 week
Pork	5 days
Poultry	3 days
Smoked meats	10 days
Fish and seafood	3 days
Dairy products	
Butter	10 days
Eggs	5 days
Milk and cream	3 days
Smoked meats	10 days
Cheese, hard	30 days
Cheese, soft	10 days
Cheese, cottage	3 days
Fruits	
Apples, oranges, grapefruit, lemons, limes	1 month
Pears, peaches, apricots, pineapples, grapes, plums, cherries, nectarines	2 weeks
Grapefruit, oranges, pineapple, and mixed fruit sections in gallons	1 week

Berries	
Strawberries, raspberries, blackberries	48 hours
Blueberries	72 hours
Cranberries	1 month
Melons, ripe	
Cantaloupes, Crenshaw, Spanish, Persian, honeydew, Rockport, muskmelon	1 week
Watermelon	2 weeks
Avocado, papaya	1 week
Vegetables	
Onions (dry storage)	3 months
Peas, stringbeans, peppers, lima beans, broccoli, cauliflower, eggplant, asparagus, sprouts, summer squash, cucumbers, radishes, parsley, cress	10 days
Spinach, chard	72 hours
Corn	48 hours
Beets, carrots	1 month
Lettuce, escarole, romaine, endive, chicory, celery	10 days
Tomatoes, ripe	1 week
Mushrooms	3 days
Peeled potatoes	3 days

Vestibule storage	
Bananas	72 hours
Sweet potatoes	10 days
Potatoes, sack	1 month
Mayonnaise	2 months
Salad dressings	2 months
Oils and shortening	3 months
Dry beans, rice, cereal, grains	2 months

Canned goods and groceries

Most items can be kept six months but not over a year. Canned fish and seafood, canned meats, stews, and hash should not be kept longer than three months.

Storage Areas

The following paragraphs discuss specialized storage areas and how they are used.

Dry Storage Area. This general area should be separated further into storage of dry foods, liquor, mineral water, cleaning supplies, and, in some instances, operating equipment such as pots and pans, china, glass, silver and paper supplies, and cooperage supplies. Sometimes accounting supplies are kept in a locked area in the food storeroom, to which only the controller has the key.

It is unfortunate that the food storeroom often becomes a catchall for old accounting records, old menu stock, broken equipment, and other junk when no one has authorized proper disposal of such items. Management could well authorize the head storekeeper to sell as salvage or throw out anything not belonging in the area that has been there for 120 days.

Refrigerated Area. Such an area is generally divided to accommodate fresh meats and poultry, fresh fruits and vegetables, and dairy products. In larger storage facilities the refrigerated area is sometimes separated further, allotting areas to smoked meats, delicatessen items, and a fish box.

Freezer Area. This was formerly a small box at the back of the meat area, but, with the increased use of frozen merchandise, a separate freezer for storing meats, fruits, vegetables, and other convenience foods is needed. A well-designed freezer area has one section for meats and poultry, another for fruits, vegetables, and seafood, and a third for frozen convenience foods of various types.

Vestibule. In any well-planned food storeroom all of the refrigeration and freezer areas open into a vestibule that in turn opens into the storeroom proper. This vestibule helps to reduce loss of refrigerated air and to maintain steady refrigerator temperatures and reduces the amount of outside air entering the freezer and refrigeration areas. It can also be used for the storage of such items as bananas, lemons, sweet potatoes, avocados, grapefruit, oranges, potatoes, onions, and other items not normally refrigerated.

Exhibit 9-1 shows an actual layout of the refrigerated area of a storeroom. In this particular layout, management placed the food and beverage controller's office in the food and beverage storeroom as a means of strengthening internal control. The purchasing office and the receiving office were located at the receiving dock three floors below, along with the storeroom and the production kitchen. The storeroom attendant had a work table, a scale, a desk, and a file for his records and packaging activities.

Commissary Area. In larger, newer storeroom setups, provision has been made for a small butcher shop and a salad and vegetable preparation area so that the storeroom acts as a commissary for the preparation and distribution of these items to the using kitchens throughout the operation. There are fewer distractions in the storeroom, and the output per man per hour increases so much that there is no question of the value of this arrangement.

One very large hotel, which does over $5 million worth of business per year, found it possible to reduce its butcher shop crew from six men to two when the butcher shop was moved to the storeroom area.

Another large hotel, which takes in $8 million in annual food revenue, found that one butcher working eight hours a day was able to do all the butchering for the hotel. This particular hotel fabricated its own beef strips, top butts, filets, and chucks, ground its own hamburger, cut all of its lamb chops and ham steaks, made all of its veal cutlets, prepared all of its pork roasts, cut all of its calves liver, cut all of its fish for fillets, and in some cases, even bought its own fish dressed and finished its own portion cutting.

In larger institutions it has been standard practice for many years to have a single vegetable and salad preparation area, sometimes in the storeroom and sometimes in an isolated place in the kitchen, but use of the storeroom has only recently been adopted widely by hotels. Today, as a matter of fact, hotels doing as much as $6 million to $8 million worth of food business a year are preparing all bulk salads needed for the operation, including cole slaw, potato salad, vegetable salads, fruit salads, and greens, as well as cleaning and cutting all of the fresh vegetables needed for the operation.

Ingredient Rooms. Where it is possible to use standard recipes and sales forecasts, ingredients in the exact amount required by any one department for an entire day's production can be set out in the storeroom and issued as needed. Large institutions and food processors have for some time been rearranging their storerooms to allow for ingredient rooms. This trend, more prevalent in hospital and nursing home kitchens, now is gaining acceptance in large hotels. Not only is it an effective cost control measure, but it also helps in maintaining higher standards of quality.

Such a system has become feasible through the use of minicomputers, which makes ingredient and recipe control practical. The University of Massachusetts has been a leader in the development of this system.

Reserved Kitchen Storage Areas. It costs money to keep the main storeroom open, and it also costs money to have kitchen runners going to the storeroom to pick up a can of this and a box of that and a small bag of something else that another department has overlooked. Many large food operations have arranged to have a small, locked reserve storage area in each department where a par stock is maintained for daily use, and the keys are held by the head of the kitchen department.

Such a reserve area eliminates costly trips to the storeroom.

Garbage and Trash Areas. Until a few years ago, the storage of garbage and trash and its disposal was one of the most unsanitary and least satisfactory phases of any food operation. Modern storage and disposal methods have greatly improved sanitary standards in the back areas of food operations.

In cities where sewage systems will permit, garbage is now ground by a very powerful garbage grinder and flushed down the drain. Only heavy bones are held out to be disposed of by other methods. Where the sewage system does not allow this, the old problem of collecting the garbage and transporting it to a refrigerated area or a dumpster container located at the back door still exists. Most city codes do, however, require that all garbage cans have liners and that the liner be closed and tied when the can is full. In this manner, fewer flies and vermin are attracted.

It is doubtful that many cities in the United States and Canada lack a trash removal system based on a portable compactor parked at the rear entrance of the operation. This system has even spread to the individual home and the apartment complex, and it is standard procedure for larger food operations.

Sanitary Requirements

Sanitary considerations are normally part of the responsibility of the architect and the kitchen contractor. All existing sanitary codes should be followed in laying out, designing, and constructing the storage and refrigerated areas. Details overlooked could result in problems for the operator after the establishment opens.

Floor and wall surfaces in storage and refrigerated areas should be constructed so that they are resistant to heavy trucks, easy to keep clean, and grease- and moistureproof. The best material for floors appears to be red quarry tile properly installed. In extremely wet areas Carborundum quarry tile is best suited to the purpose. There are substitutes, including poured mastic floors and treated cement floors, but they have not proved to be as satisfactory.

The best wall surface is glazed tile, but it is expensive. A special bonded cement or a glazed building block that can be easily cleaned is more often used in modern construction projects. Regardless of the wall surface used, it is best to have bumper guards to protect the walls; in time low and high trucks break through a building block wall or a metal surface refrigerator.

Local building codes normally specify the height of the ceiling—generally a minimum of eight feet from floor to ceiling. If the cost of airconditioning the storage area is not allowed for in the budget, then there must be adequate forced-air ventilation. There must also be adequate lighting. Again, local building codes guide the architect in planning these details.

Operators should check the plans for the storeroom and refrigerated areas to make sure that there is drainage to facilitate cleaning refrigerators and scrubbing storeroom floors and walls.

Security and Control Measures

Securing against Entry. A well-planned food and beverage storeroom has one entrance through which everything enters and leaves. When the storeroom is locked, the key, which ought to be kept on a large ring, should be left at the front office in a large, sealed envelope, and there should be a record showing the name of the person who delivered it and the name of the person who received it.

The morning storeroom attendant should sign his name to the record when he receives the key, and, if the seal on the envelope has been broken, he should note that fact in the record. The controller should ascertain why it was necessary to use the key during the previous evening. Certainly emergencies do occur at night that require opening the storeroom. That is why the key is kept in the front office, under seal.

Another key to the storeroom should be kept in the vault in a sealed envelope and should be issued to the controller, the general manager, or the night manager, depending on the policy of management, but this should also be recorded and the general manager of the operation notified in writing.

The storeroom should be divided into three areas, each separately locked if possible. If the liquor storeroom is within the food storeroom area, then it is absolutely necessary that there be a separate key, with one man responsible for both the key and the liquor stock. When that man leaves, he should also lock the area, put the key in a sealed envelope, and leave it at the front office where it should be handled in the same way as the main storeroom keys. A liquor storeroom, whether it is inside the food storeroom or separate, should be as secure as a bank.

It is wise to have another small locked area in the dry storeroom to accommodate small valuable grocery items such as anchovy filets, boneless and skinless sardines, truffles, small jars of cocktail olives, smoked oysters, individual jars of jam for room service, and, in some parts of the country, certain bottled condiments.

A small locked area in one of the refrigerators is also advisable with the key in possession of the storeroom manager.

Items most likely to be stolen, such as caviar, pâté de foie gras, small packages of smoked meats, and costly spices can be stored there. The keys to both small areas should be in the possession of the storeroom manager.

In large operations there should be a recording time lock on the door to the storeroom, and the tape from the time lock should go to the controller each day for review. Time locks can be useful. For example, a large New York hotel inexplicably lost about $1,500 a month from the storeroom. Everyone was blaming the figures except the control department. As a last resort, they installed a time lock on the storeroom door, and it was found, as a result, that the morning storeroom attendant was opening the storeroom forty-five minutes before the scheduled time. When questioned, he explained that he needed the extra time to prepare the storeroom for morning deliveries. The controller decided to give the morning storeroom man an afternoon shift so that he would not have to get up so early in the morning. The first day he was to work on the new schedule the storeroom attendand did not report for work, and it was subsequently learned that he had left the country. The storeroom shortages stopped immediately. Investigation revealed that the attendant had been removing valuable merchandise and concealing it around the hotel for friends to pick up during the day. For this "service" he received about half of the retail value of the merchandise.

The main entrance to the storeroom can be a Dutch door, with the lower half being closed at all times. All except storeroom personnel and deliverymen, who should be observed when they are in the storeroom, can be excluded. Large issues on trucks can be delivered outside the

door, and small issues can be handed over the shelf on it. The watchman's key punch station for the area should be near the entrance, and, if there is liquor stored in the food storeroom, the watchman should punch in hourly at this point.

If possible, there should be no electrical panels and water control valves in the food storage area, and, if there are any ventilating shafts passing through the storeroom, they should be secured against entry into the storeroom. Any head space above drop ceilings should be thoroughly secured.

Perpetual Inventory Checks. The food and beverage manager should keep perpetual inventories on other "sensitive" items in the food storeroom such as bacon, tuna fish, anchovies, butter, expensive condiments, and cut meats and a complete perpetual inventory on all alcoholic beverages. Physical inventory checks on food stocks should be varied from month to month so that no one except the food and beverage controller knows what items are being spot-checked. A typical perpetual inventory card is shown in Exhibit 9-8.

Freezer stock should be controlled by a permanent perpetual inventory, including dating, to facilitate prompt use. Otherwise, freezer stock is an unknown quantity as it is difficult to get an actual count. Storeroom attendants are reluctant to spend much time in the freezer, even when provided with proper clothing. Security people should be instructed to check the freezer storage area occasionally since it is an out-of-the-way place for concealing merchandise stolen elsewhere.

Requisitions. The primary rule governing the control of all storeroom stock is that everything that goes into the store-

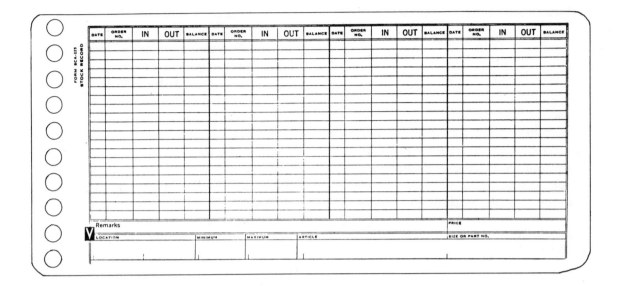

Exhibit 9-8. Perpetual inventory stock record

room be entered on a receiving sheet and everything that goes out leave upon receipt of a signed requisition. The simplest basic control is the monthly storeroom difference, which is determined by adding total storeroom purchases during the month to the opening storeroom inventory and subtracting merchandise issued from the storeroom for the month. The resultant theoretical inventory stock is then compared with the actual closing inventory.

If the difference between the theoretical inventory and the actual inventory is more than half of a percent of the closing inventory value, the food and beverage controller and the controller of the operation should investigate why this difference is greater than the minimum allowed.

A storeroom shortage can be the result of many different things that occur in the daily operation of the storeroom, or it can be the result of spontaneous or organized thievery. Some shortages occur because storeroom personnel are lax in getting a requisition for every item, be-

cause a requisition is unclear as to the size of the container, because there are inaccuracies in the number of cans or items issued, because items issued by weight may be carelessly weighed or repackaged or requisitions may be mispriced. Occasionally the merchandise was never placed in the storeroom, and that fact was not noted for one reason or another.

Every requisition (see Exhibit 9-9) should bear the signature of a person designated by management as having the authority to sign it. A sample list of qualified signers, such as the one that appears below, with copies of the signatures, should be posted at the storeroom entrance behind sealed glass so that storeroom personnel can compare signatures on requisitions with the approved originals. Nothing should be issued without an approved signature, and the person signing the requisition should draw a line from the last item listed on a requisition to his signature so that no one can add items to the approved requisition.

Office of the General Manager

Date _____

To all department heads:

The following named department heads are authorized to sign requisitions for food supplies from the storeroom. Storeroom personnel will not issue any stock unless one of the following signatures is on the requisition.

_____
John C. Smith—Food and Beverage Manager

_____
Anthony B. Brown—Chef

_____
Porter F. O'Brien—Sous Chef

_____
Gene A. Stryker—Night Chef

_____
Herman G. Shultz—Relief Chef

_____
Bertha A. Cotten—Pantry Supervisor

_____
Michael Lyzinski—Steward

_____
General Manager

Storeroom personnel should initial requisitions when they fill them. At the end of the day all requisitions should be totaled, clipped together with an adding machine tape, and sent to the food and beverage control office.

Most instructions on food and beverage controls say that requisition numbers should be closely regulated. The controller's department should account for all requisitions every day. This works well for liquor requisitions, but, under normal circumstances, accounting for all food requisition numbers is too costly. It is better to have a series of requisition books, in which each department is represented by its own distinct color, and to keep a continuous record from month to month. The food and beverage controller can run a series of spot checks on one color per week. In this way, adequate control is exercised over the numbers with a minimum of effort and expense.

Every piece of merchandise in the storeroom should bear a price on the package or on a meat tag (which is only needed in a large operation) attached to the merchandise. This enables storeroom personnel to price the requisition as the merchandise is issued, thereby providing more accurate daily food costs and eliminating storeroom differences at the end of the month. A broad, felt-tip pen is best for this purpose, although some storerooms use what are called supermarket pricing stamps. The two hours that the storeroom is closed in the afternoon is the best time to bring the pricing up to date, and slow evening periods can also be used to fill requisitions and price merchandise.

The month-end inventory can be priced according to the price of the merchandise that was received last. This saves averaging prices from different lots. From month to month, the total difference proves negligible.

Chapter 12 outlines new, computerized methods of storeroom control. New systems are being rapidly installed in the larger institutional and commercial food operations.

Rotation of Stock. Good storeroom management and operation insists on a true rotation of stock to avoid loss from

Form 489

FOOD REQUISITION

S. I. 100 PADS 7-75

№ 6254

Date _____

	ARTICLE	QUAN.	PRICE		AMOUNT	

_____   _____
Department Head

Exhibit 9-9. Typical storeroom requisition form

spoilage, shrinking, and deterioration of quality. This is especially important for perishable foods and even more vital for such short-lived commodities as calves liver, melons, tomatoes, fresh strawberries, raspberries, and blueberries, fish and seafood, milk, butter, cream, certain cheese items, and certain delicatessen items. A good storeroom manager, working with the chef and the food buyer, requests that these highly perishable items be purchased almost on a daily basis to avoid large losses.

During the past few years there have been a number of changes in storeroom operations because of changes in the packaging of food supplies. Many perishable items that originally came in large, bulk containers had to be sorted as soon as they were checked into the storeroom, with bruised and injured merchandise going directly to the kitchen for immediate use. Merchandise in good condition was generally repackaged in smaller units and held for issue when needed. Today practically everything is packaged in containers ready for storage. These containers protect the merchandise against damage and can be used for issuing merchandise to the using departments. This virtually eliminates "cooperage" accounts and many losses from inaccurate weighing and spoilage.

Since most merchandise now comes in containers that are more practical in size and shape, the amount of shelving, both in storerooms and in refrigerators, can be reduced to about half of that formerly needed. The merchandise in containers can be stacked on skids or pallets, and either the full container can be issued or the amount requisitioned can be removed from the top container. This method not only saves work; it also expedites daily taking of inventory to determine supplies needed and aids in taking the month-end inventory.

Good storeroom management also requires that all containers be stamped with the date or coded by color, with one color being reserved for each day of the week.

The date stamp is better for long-term storage, but color codes on perishable items have worked quite well, especially when storeroom personnel are unable to read or write.

Packaging can, however, be carried to extremes. It is costly, and many dry bulk items such as rice, beans, sugar, or specialty flours can be bought at a lower cost per pound in large units. The large containers can then be broken down into small packages, labeled, date stamped, and issued in smaller quantities in the storeroom. A net saving of as much as 30 percent is possible by repackaging bulk dry merchandise in the storeroom.

Even though items such as melons, tomatoes, apples, and other fruits are purchased "ready for use," it is always necessary, before issue, for storeroom personnel to unpack the containers, sort or trim the merchandise, or allow it to ripen, as required. This requires some shelving and tables for handling the merchandise. Some operations even have ultraviolet lamps with an off-and-on electrical control to ripen melons and certain fruits and berries.

Each storeroom shelf and storage area should be labeled with the name of the item to be stored and maximum and minimum stock levels. The minimum stock level is the point where storeroom personnel should request purchases to raise stock to the maximum level. Nothing ordered should be on hand more than ninety days except with the approval of management. At times when shortages are imminent and inflationary prices are expected, purchases of stock that exceed the ninety-day use period are desirable, almost necessary.

One category that always seems to be in excess supply is spices. Sometimes supplies of such things as mace, bay leaf, tarragon, and oregano adequate for three to four years of use are found. For some unknown reason there is sure to be too much poultry seasoning in almost every storeroom.

There are always those special items that some chef or banquet manager simply "has to have." As soon as a large quantity is on hand, however, the whole project is forgotten, and, unless the dead stock is recorded on a monthly basis and forced into the kitchen for use, it is eventually thrown out.

Inventory Taking. Month-end inventory taking can be an ordeal. Often it is so rushed that the results are inaccurate and unreliable. Frequently the work is assigned to someone who is poorly trained or uninterested, and errors result. Manipulating the figures to make them look accurate may well be the next step, and, as soon as this situation exists, someone is sure to see the possibilities in a systematic removal of stock.

The final responsibility for the taking of the month-end inventory lies with the controller and the accounting department. The controller, with the help of the head storeroom attendant and the food and beverage controller, must ensure a true and accurate accounting of all merchandise in the storeroom.

It is generally sufficient for the head storeroom attendant or storeroom manager working with the food and beverage controller to take the food and beverage inventory. From time to time, however, an independent representative from the accounting department should be present, and several times during the year the controller himself should participate in the taking of inventories.

The storeroom should be shut down during the taking of inventories, and it is helpful to have the storeroom crew count the merchandise and leave a ticket on each that shows the amount of merchandise on each stack of supplies. The inventory should be taken in a permanently bound inventory book with the items listed in the book in the order that the stock is arranged in the storeroom to facilitate a speedy and accurate count. The figures should be listed in the inventory book with a pen, and, once an entry is made, any change should be initialed by both the head storeroom attendant and the food and beverage controller.

Even though freezer stock should have a perpetual inventory, it is advisable to spot-check actual stock against the perpetual inventory on about a quarter of the items in the freezer. A different list of items should be spot-checked each month.

The liquor inventory, also perpetual, must be checked, item for item, against the actual inventory. This can be done at a later time by the food and beverage controller, who then determines overages or shortages by item.

One word of caution: the food and beverage inventory book should always be in the possession of the food and beverage controller. Once the book is priced, extended, and totaled, it should be kept under lock and key in the accounting office. Some large storeroom differences have been concealed by changing the storeroom inventory count when the book was available either in the storeroom or in the food and beverage control office. In one instance, the book was altered by a member of the accounting department who happened to have a taste for fine brandy.

Inspections. An inspection checklist should be prepared for management by the food and beverage manager in cooperation with the controller and the chief engineer. It should cover all require-ments of the Occupational Safety and Health Act (see Chapter 3) and of local building codes. In addition to sanitary requirements in the storeroom operation, the checklist should cover all phases of the operation, including controls, hours of service, security measures, and any other pertinent information.

A copy of the major provisions of the local sanitary codes should be posted in the storeroom as a constant reminder to the staff. A regular cleaning schedule and a daily schedule of cleaning responsi-bilities should also be posted so that the storeroom would be ready for inspection by anyone at any time (see Exhibit 10-7).

A good general manager of a hotel or large food operation will find time in his busy schedule to inspect the storeroom weekly. This does not have to be a formal matter; simply walking through the area helps to keep an operation alert.

Most food operations are required to conduct a formal monthly inspection and file a written report in the manager's office. The best inspections are often made by a team composed of two or three other department heads and the store-room manager. Their checklist can be filed and used by outside inspectors.

Another practice has worked well for some large facilities. The general manager invites the local or state health inspector to visit the premises to help train the self-inspection team so that an effective month-

ly inspection can be made. This gives the health inspectors confidence in the at-titude of management, and, if problems arise later, the operation is able to request the help of the health inspector who participated in the training process.

Other large operators have hired outside sanitation consultants on a regular basis to make a complete and thorough sanitary inspection of the premises and provide a written report with recommendations on compliance with local, state, and national health codes. Not only do these consultants help keep the premises in good shape; they can also help if there are any problems. The fact that management is interested enough to secure outside help often discourages lawsuits and keeps legal judgments at a low level.

In addition to regularly scheduled storeroom and sanitary inspections, there should be an understanding that certain department heads are expected to visit the storeroom, look over the operations, and offer any helpful comments or sugges-tions that they might have. These surprise inspections can be made by the food and beverage manager, the kitchen manager, the food buyer, the chef, the controller, the head bartender, the catering man-ager, or anyone else designated by the general manager of the operation.

Any reports from such inspections should be made to the general manager of the operation, as well as to the store-room staff.

10 *Controls and Checklists*

In Chapter 4 it was pointed out that practically all food service industries are divided into four main areas: procurement, manufacturing, sales and service, and controls. This chapter is concerned primarily with the control function and how it relates to the professional food buyer.

If a controller is, indeed, "responsible for the control and the security of all of the assets of the company," his authority is broad. He must be involved in the daily activities of all the departments in any food service operation. In addition, he is responsible for the accounting office and all members of the accounting staff.

The control department keeps a set of books and accounts as prescribed by law and recommended by the trade industry. It collects all income, accounts for bank deposits, pays all bills, and keeps payroll records. The controller is responsible for establishing an internal control system and seeing that it works, auditing all incoming bills for accuracy, seeing that all payments are properly approved by management before payments are made, issuing daily operational reports, making

special analyses for management, issuing regular monthly reports and annual tax reports, exerting necessary payroll controls, and assisting management in dealing with the unions. As if these duties were not sufficient, the controller is expected to act as an operations analyst and to advise management on decisions affecting the success or failure of the business. The controller or his department basically observes, records, and reports every transaction of the entire operation. From these reports the controller is most competent to act as confidential adviser to management on financial matters.

This chapter is by no means an attempt to outline the operation of a control department. Instead, it represents an attempt to make the professional food buyer aware of how the controller and that department function in relation to his own job. The chapter also deals with the internal control system of a food service operation and how it operates on a day-to-day basis in departments that are under the direction of the food buyer and points out why some of the steps in the internal control system are necessary.

INTERNAL CONTROL

The first control function related to food buying is the request from the various departments to the food buyer stating items and quantities needed. Then there are forms for recording price quotations, requests for bids, and purchase orders. There are additional forms for receiving incoming merchandise, including receiving sheets, receiving tickets, credit memorandums, and forms used for merchandise received without invoice. The checking of incoming bills, the checking of merchandise against specification sheets, the control of the requisitions for the issue of merchandise, the keeping of necessary perpetual inventories and month-end inventories, as well as the proper pricing or requisitions and inventories, the issuing of dead stock reports, the issuing of storeroom reports on overages and shortages, and the securing of the storeroom are further control measures. Even after merchandise is issued to the production department from the storeroom, the controller sees that it is prepared according to the standards of the testing committee and that necessary production records are maintained. The controller's function continues until food is served to the guest and the bill is paid. The sections that follow represent an attempt to relate control functions to purchasing functions.

Specifications

Even though the controller is not responsible for preparing specifications, he should recommend to management that such a list be prepared and used by the purchasing and receiving departments. The food and beverage controller, who does help the food buyer prepare purchase specifications, is under the direct supervision of the controller. The controller also checks to see that the testing committee meets regularly and does the job expected of it. Information is relayed to the controller through the food and beverage controller.

The receiving clerk, who is also under the direct supervision of the controller, should have a copy of the specifications and be trained in its use. The controller is responsible for seeing that the specifications are used by receiving personnel. If specifications are not being adhered to, the receiving clerk should report this to the controller, who then takes the matter up with the food buyer, and, if necessary, with management.

Price Quotations

In Chapter 6 it was pointed out that the wise food buyer made sure that he could support every price that he paid with a written record of competitive or negotiated competitive quotations. The controller reviews the records of the buyer to be sure that the required records are kept and, if necessary, reports lack of proper records to management. The controller sees that necessary purchase orders are issued and that orderly numerical files are kept on purchase orders and contracts. He also makes certain that the receiving department gets necessary information on incoming merchandise from the buyer in order to compare a shipment with an order showing item, amount, and price.

Receiving Sheets

Internal control systems in the food service industry generally require the use of receiving sheets or tickets that give in detail the name of the purveyor and a listing of merchandise by item, quantity, price, and extensions. This information is supported by invoices properly stamped with a receiving stamp and approved by the respective department as to price, quality, and amounts received.

A good internal control system also assures that the receiving department uses credit memorandums and records goods received without invoice.

Storeroom Controls

The value of storeroom stocks for a food service operation can range from a few hundred dollars to several hundred thousand dollars and include stocks of food, beverages, and operating supplies such as china, glassware, silverware, linen, utensils, and paper and cleaning supplies. Practically all items carried in the food service operation's storeroom have a re-sale value, and, unless there is close security, there can be substantial losses from pilferage. A complete and detailed internal control system is designed to keep storeroom shortages to a minimum.

The system begins with the receiving sheet where all items that come into the operation are recorded as to quantity and price. Effective storeroom operation dictates that, as soon as merchandise is in the storeroom, it be date stamped or marked and priced at cost so that requisitions can be priced properly by the storeroom staff as issues are made.

The next step is concerned with a properly made out and signed requisition bearing the signature of a department head authorized to make withdrawals from the storeroom. Nothing should be issued without such a requisition.

Then there is a record of the minimum and maximum amounts of stock to be carried in the storeroom. This mini-maxi stock list is used as a basis for reordering as well as for keeping the stock value within the storeroom budget. The food and beverage controller, if there is one, the bookkeeper, or someone else from the controller's office should maintain a perpetual inventory on certain storeroom items such as liquor, freezer contents, and china, glassware, and silverware.

At the end of each month, a complete storeroom inventory of food and beverages must be taken by the controller's office. (This duty can be delegated to the food and beverage control office.) The month-end inventory is used for determining accurate costs for the month, and, in addition, it is the basis for preparing an overage and shortage report on items kept on perpetual inventory (see Exhibit 10-1).

Inventories on china, glassware, silverware, and linen are generally taken on a quarterly basis, and any necessary adjustments of the month-to-month cost of such items are made at that time.

The controller's department sees that production inventories are taken throughout the various departments of the operation. Most of these inventories are taken by the department head, assisted, on a spot-check basis, by someone from the controller's office. The taking of a production inventory can be a very sensitive matter as there is always some question about what is of value once it is in production. Vagueness of terms used in production inventories sometimes conceals high costs or pilferage.

There must be a storeroom reconciliation, made by the controller's department, on both food and beverages that lists storeroom adjustments (sales made from the storeroom at cost, food spoilage, transfers at cost to other departments, employees' meals, public relations, and gratis foods). Any difference between the calculated month-end inventory and the actual month-end inventory has to be reconciled.

Another step in the internal control system is the dead stock report. It should be made out on a monthly basis for man-

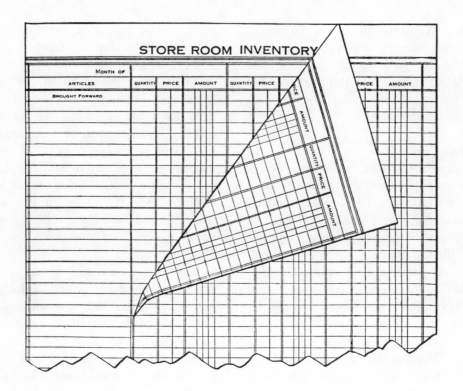

Exhibit 10-1. Pages from typical storeroom inventory books

agement's and the operating department's information. The dead stock report lists items that have been on hand in the storeroom for ninety days or more that, for one reason or another, are not being used in production. Management may be able to "sell" the production department on the use of dead stock items on a regular basis, but often this stock has to be forced into the production line to ensure use before spoilage. Some operators sell these items at cost or below cost to the staff, creating a further problem for the controller's department.

One of the more important facets of the internal control system in the storeroom is the logbook, kept where storeroom keys are turned in every night for security reasons. This logbook records the signatures of anyone who withdraws the keys, and the controller's office must investigate any withdrawal of the storeroom keys except to open the storeroom in the morning.

In large food service operations, management often authorizes the controller's department to bring in outside consultants for surprise inventories and for surprise receiving checks. Consulting firms doing this type of work are not necessarily the same ones that do year-end audits for the operation. Receiving checks must be done by people trained in purchase specifications, and some accounting firms do not even offer this service.

Other Activities Related to the Control System

Internal control in a food service operation also includes production controls in the kitchen or manufacturing plant, portion counts, recipe and portion-size control, daily food costs either in relation to sales or, in the institutional field, cost per meal served, and the estab-

lishment of a potential beverage cost. This information is expressed either as percentages or in cost per meal served. Maintaining food and beverage control and production work sheets (and reports issued thereon), checking and cashiering of all cash revenue and control of checks, taking register readings, reconciling cash and charges, and accounting for all funds also require internal control.

Controls in the Small Operation

The cost of an elaborate control system is unwarranted in a small operation. Management, generally the owner, can use visual control in place of a more detailed plan. Actually, an alert owner, with the help of family members or a partner, can exert a tight system just by staying constantly alert. If the operation is large enough to afford a fulltime bookkeeper, that person can take care of some controls such as control of cash, checking of invoices, and taking of inventories.

In a medium-sized operation that is large enough to warrant a small controller's department, a fairly complete internal control system can be maintained by the controller through the spot-check method. If the controller's department varies the spot checks, the element of surprise can be almost as effective as an actual continuous control system.

A Word of Warning

The most elaborate internal control system possible means absolutely nothing unless it is correctly and fully used, with the controller ensuring such use. Management must also take a very active part in policing the internal control system. One reason many food operations are in trouble today is that management was lulled into a false sense of security by a control system that has been allowed to deteriorate.

Another reason could be that the controller or someone in the controller's office or department is dishonest, and the question, then, is: Who is watching the controller? In addition to the management of the operation, outside auditors and consultants should come in occasionally on a spot-check basis to make sure that nothing is going wrong with the controller or the controller's department. The failure to have outside checkers has resulted in heavy losses and business failures. Operators have learned the value of outside spot checks on a reasonable cost basis.

The Controller's Role in Inspection Teams

Some parts of a food service operation do not require that the controller or a representative from the controller's department be on the self-inspection team, but any part of the operation involving the food buyer should have the controller or a representative of that department as a member of any inspection team.

Any checklist concerned with the activities of the purchasing department should give attention to purchase requests by the various using departments, price quotations, butcher and cooking tests, specifications, receiving practices, requisitions for merchandise, pricing, and inventories. These are all part of the internal control system, and the controller is basically responsible for the manner in which that system is carried out.

CHECKLISTS

In a seminar on food and beverage purchasing during a summer school session at Cornell University, a well-known and highly regarded food buyer for a large industrial feeding operation was discussing the value and use of checklists. He attached great importance to their use, stressing that they help to make a person's job easier as well as more efficient. At one point the speaker stated that the use of checklists could save one's life. In the face of a rather skeptical reaction from his audience, the speaker went on to tell how the use of a checklist had done that. During World War II he was a passenger in a single-engine aircraft when the plane became lost in a heavy overcast so charged with electricity that neither radio nor direction finder could be used. As the pilot circled, in the hope that weather conditions would change and permit radio contact, the single engine quit. Pilot and passenger prepared to parachute from the plane, but not before the pilot, who had been trained in the use of an emergency checklist, proceeded to follow it. Within a few seconds the engine caught again, and twenty minutes later the pilot made radio contact and landed safely at an airport only two hundred miles from the intended destination. It was later discovered that the gas in the main tank had been exhausted, even though the gas gauge showed an ample supply. One of the procedures to be followed on the emergency checklist was to throw the emergency pump onto the reserve gas tank.

A food buyer may not owe his life to a checklist, but it is well known that one's best efforts are devoted to those phases of a job that are checked by others. A good checklist, properly used by both the departments and management, proves to be a helpful guide to both the operator and management.

One problem can arise in the use of checklists. If the person using the checklist considers himself to be perfect, he can cause difficulties for the operator. It

Date: _____ Institution: _____

FOOD AND BEVERAGE PURCHASING CHECKLIST

Satis-factory	Unsatis-factory	N/A	Item description	Comments
			What specifications were used for purchasing?	
			Do all vendors have copies of the specifications for items they handle?	
			Are competitive bids being received from a minimum of two vendors on all items purchased competitively?	
			Are price quotations recorded on a market quotation list?	
			Are these lists kept on file for a period of one year?	
			Are the quantities to be purchased determined by forecasts?	
			Does the chef approve the quantities to be purchased before orders are placed?	
			Is a grocery price book maintained showing competitive prices?	
			Is the grocery price book up to date?	
			Is there a file supporting the decision to purchase certain products from single purveyors?	
			Are orders for fresh fish phoned to the vendor's office no later than 11:00 a.m. for delivery the next day?	
			Are orders for meats, provisions, poultry, fresh fruits and vegetables, frozen foods, and dairy items phoned to the vendor's office no later than 1:00 p.m. for the next day's delivery?	
			Are orders for canned goods and dry stores on a twice a month schedule?	
			Are orders for canned goods and dry stores phoned to the vendor's office at least forty-eight hours before desired delivery date?	
			Does the institution provide the vendor with a weekly forecast of requirements for ribs, strips, and top sirloin butts every Monday?	
			Are requirements given one week in advance for ribs and two weeks in advance for strips and top butts to allow the proper aging?	
			Are requirements for melons given to the vendor one week in advance to allow dealers time to purchase, select, and ripen melons?	
			Has the vendor furnished the institution with an approved vendor list?	
			Is there any deviation from this list?	
			Which major food items are not bought through the vendor? _____ _____ _____	
			Are certain perishable items that are used in small quantities bought by the pound or at retail instead of by the case lot?	
			Is no more than a three-month supply of spices bought to assure freshness and eliminate waste?	

Exhibit 10-2. Checklist for purchasing food and beverages (Courtesy: Sheraton Corporation of America, Boston, Massachusetts)

Date: _____ Institution: _____

FOOD AND BEVERAGE PURCHASING CHECKLIST

Satis-factory	Unsatis-factory	N/A	Item description	Comments

			How many days has the oldest supply of the following items been in the storeroom?
			
			Strawberries —————— Lemons ——————
			Chicken —————— Tomatoes ——————
			Oranges —————— Eggs ——————
			Grapes—————— Grapefruit ——————
			Butter—————— Romaine ——————
			Avocados—————— Coffee ——————
			
			Does the food purchaser verify invoices for agreement of amounts, prices, and items with orders placed?
			
			Has the quantity purchasing program to gain price advantage been implemented?
			
			Are the following items being purchased in accordance with Mr. Jones's memorandum of August 1973?
			
			     Texas brown shrimp, 21-15 count?
			     Sliced bacon, 21-14 count?
			     Breakfast sausages, 14-16 size?
			     Grade "A," large eggs?
			     Vitality frozen orange juice?
			     Instant hot cereal?
			     Maple syrup, 15% blend?
			
			Are beverage purchase orders approved by the general manager before being placed?
			
			Are quantities ordered determined by par stock and banquet orders?
			
			Are all private and exclusive label beverages being purchased?	

Exhibit 10-2 *(continued)*

Date: _____ Institution: _____

FOOD RECEIVING INSPECTION CHECKLIST

Satis-factory	Unsatis-factory	N/A	Item description	Comments
			Is the receiving clerk responsible to the controller?	
			Is there a list of the items to be received showing vendor, items, quantities, and prices?	
			Are all items received (including those without invoices) written on the receiving sheet showing item, quantity, price, and total?	
			Are returns written on the receiving sheet?	
			List three items returned during the past week.	
			a)_____	
			b)_____	
			c)_____	
			What were the percentages of returns to total food purchases for the past two months?_____ % _____%	
			Are receiving sheets completed and added up daily?	
			Who prepares the receiving sheet?	
			Name: _____ Title: _____	
			Are food receiving specifications posted in the receiving areas?	
			Are they readable from the scale?	
			Are the persons receiving food items familiar with the receiving specifications?	
			Does the general manager or food and beverage manager check the food receiving weekly?	
			Are the scales checked periodically by an inspector? Date: _____	
			Is a ruler attached to the receiving scale to measure the trim of the meat?	
			Is there an adequate scale for weighing merchandise received?	
			Are all items weighed in total and individual weights checked?	
			Are all meats, poultry, and fish items stripped of their wrappings before being weighed?	
			Are fruits and other items bought by size and count spot-checked to make sure that the size of the fruit is according to USDA grading marked on the box?	
			When receiving fruits, is the net weight as well as the count checked?	
			Are melons and pineapples taken out of their containers and checked for decay and ripeness?	
			Are unripened melons returned?	

Exhibit 10-3. Checklist for inspecting food and beverages received (Courtesy: Sheraton Corporation of America, Boston, Massachusetts)

Date: _____ Institution: _____

FOOD RECEIVING INSPECTION CHECKLIST

Satis-factory	Unsatis-factory	N/A	Item description	Comments
			Are berries checked as to net weight per pint?	
			Are cartons of oranges, grapefruit, and lemons turned over to see that the quality is consistent throughout?	
			When receiving lettuce, is at least one head of lettuce cut to check quality and see that it is free from decay?	
			Are fresh beans taken out of their containers and the net content weighed?	
			Are all perishable items date stamped?	
			Is ice cream weighed to check the overrun?	
			Is butterfat content checked on milk, cream, butter, and ice cream? Date of last check:_____	
			Are butter and coffee spot-checked for weight?	
			Are eggs weighed?	
			What merchandise was received before the food receiver came on duty?	
			Dealer Item Quantity Price Total _____ _____ _____ _____ _____	
			What merchandise was received after the food receiver usually goes off duty?	
			Dealer Item Quantity Price Total _____ _____ _____ _____ _____	
			Were the early morning and late afternoon deliveries emergency orders?	
			Is a "goods received without invoice" prepared when merchandise is received without invoice?	
			Is there a "notice of error and correction" prepared when merchandise is returned or an invoice is corrected?	
			Does the receiving clerk stamp and sign invoices?	
			Is incoming beverage merchandise checked against the purchase order?	
			Are cases of liquor weighed on a spot-check basis to find missing or broken bottles?	

Exhibit 10-3 *(continued)*

Date: _____ Institution: _____

FOOD AND BEVERAGE STORAGE AND ISSUING CHECKLIST

Satis-factory	Unsatis-factory	N/A	Item description	Comments
			Are designated opening and closing hours of the food and liquor storeroom maintained?	
			Is there a logbook maintained at the front desk recording the "in and out" of storeroom keys during the time the storeroom is closed?	
			Are all containers priced to facilitate inventory taking and costing of requisitions?	
			Are inventory items rotated, i.e., issued on a "first-in, first-out" basis?	
			Are sugar, spices, nuts, etc., prepackaged and priced in the quantities usually requisitioned?	
			Are items on shelves placed in order according to the inventory books?	
			Do the food and beverage storerooms operate out of single opened containers as far as possible?	
			Is a written requisition signed by an authorized person required for all items?	
			Is there a list of authorized signatures posted in the food store-room?	
			Are requisitions signed by the person issuing the merchandise?	
			Are food requisitions priced by the storeroom clerk on a daily basis?	
			Are the keys to the liquor storeroom under the control of one person?	
			Is there an emergency key to the liquor storeroom in a sealed envelope at the front desk, and is it controlled by a signed in and out log?	
			Is the beverage perpetual inventory handled by a person other than the one who has the liquor storeroom keys?	
			Are bar requisitions handled as outlined in the food and beverage control manual?	
			a) Are the requisitions made out and signed by the bartender, are original and duplicate copies of the order sent to the wineroom, and is the third copy retained at the bar?	
			b) After filling the order, are the original and duplicate copies of the requisition signed by the wineroom storekeeper?	
			c) Does the bar boy sign the original and duplicate of the requisition before delivering the order?	
			d) Does the original requisition accompany the order to the bar and is the duplicate kept in the beverage storeroom?	
			e) Is the original rechecked and signed by the bartender on duty?	

Exhibit 10-4. Checklist for issuing food and beverages stored (Courtesy: Sheraton Corporation of America, Boston, Massachusetts)

Date: _____ Institution: _____

FOOD AND BEVERAGE STORAGE AND ISSUING CHECKLIST

Satis-factory	Unsatis-factory	N/A	Item description	Comments
			f) Is the signed original requisition forwarded to the food and beverage control office in a sealed envelope?	
			Is there a separate banquet bar used for the return and reissue of banquet stock to the regular bars?	
			Is there any open beverage stock in the wineroom?	
			Have storeroom operating hours been reduced to a minimum?	
			Are food, liquor, and general storeroom functions combined?	
			Has such a combination been examined for practicality?	

Exhibit 10-4 *(continued)*

Date: _____ Institution: _____

FOOD AND BEVERAGE SECURITY CHECKLIST

Satis-factory	Unsatis-factory	N/A	Item description	Comments
			Is there only one set of keys to the storeroom in circulation?	
			Does the morning storeroom man take the storeroom keys home with him so that he will have them to open next morning?	
			Are the storeroom keys kept locked at the front desk when the storeroom is closed?	
			Are the storeroom keys kept in an unlocked drawer of the assistant manager's desk in the lobby?	
			Is there only one set of keys to the kitchen spaces in circulation?	
			Do the kitchen keys hang on a nail in the main kitchen all day and night till closing?	
			Are the kitchen keys kept locked at the front desk when the kitchen is closed?	
			Does the breakfast cook have a personal set of kitchen keys for speedy opening in the morning?	
			Is a logbook kept at the front desk to record the signing in and signing out of keys?	
			Are two signatures required for each entry: the person signing the keys in or out and the desk clerk?	
			Has anyone checked the entries in the front office key logbook during the past month?	
			When the storeroom must be opened after hours in an emergency situation, does the assistant manager accompany the person requesting merchandise to the storeroom?	
			Is a busboy or food runner sent alone to the kitchen for emergency withdrawals of food after the storeroom is closed?	
			Are designated opening and closing hours of the food storeroom maintained?	
			Do salesmen inventory the food purchases and tell the purchaser the institution's requirements?	
			Is a written requisition signed by an authorized person required for all items?	
			Does the storeroom man add forgotten items to food requisitions which are phoned in by a cook?	
			Is there a list of authorized signatures in the food storeroom?	
			Are food requisitions complete as to date, department, item, quantity, and size?	
			Are requisitions signed by the persons issuing the merchandise?	
			Is one responsible person entrusted with signing out kitchen keys?	

Exhibit 10-5. Checklist for securing food and beverages stored (Courtesy: Sheraton Corporation of America, Boston, Massachusetts)

Date: _____ Institution: _____

FOOD AND BEVERAGE SECURITY CHECKLIST

Satis-factory	Unsatis-factory	N/A	Item description	Comments
			Is a responsible person assigned the responsibility of locking all kitchen spaces at closing?	
			Are kitchen refrigerators left unlocked overnight?	
			Is there an established routine for putting all production food in locked areas overnight?	
			Are more employees' meals eaten in the main kitchen than the employees' cafeteria?	
			Are employees required to enter and leave through an employee entrance?	
			Are all bundles inspected before being taken from the premises?	
			Is there an organized method of salvaging usable butter, cream, and relishes from banquets?	
			Are restaurant and room service condiments stored in locked areas during hours when there is no service?	
			Are usable items salvaged from room service and restaurants during and at the close of operations?	

Exhibit 10-5 *(continued)*

Date: _____ Institution: _____

FOOD AND BEVERAGE COST CONTROL SYSTEM CHECKLIST

Satis- factory	Unsatis- factory	N/A	Item description	Comments

			Manager's spot checks
			
			Is the food and beverage control in this institution being carried out according to standard food and beverage control standards of the institution?
			
			Do the general manager, food and beverage manager, chef, and banquet manager receive a daily flash food cost report?
			
			Do the general manager, food and beverage manager, and controller receive a monthly summary of beverage sales, potentials, and costs (bar potential report)?
			
			Is a monthly report of overages and shortages from the beverage perpetual inventory sent to the general manager and controller?
			
			Are the monthly food and beverage inventories taken by the food and beverage cost controller and a representative designated by the controller?
			
			Are menu prices adjusted on a quarterly basis to reflect fluctuating costs?
			
			Is there a complete list of portion sizes posted at all points of service in the kitchen?
			
			Are weekly cover forecasts prepared and distributed to the concerned department heads on a regular weekly basis?
			
			Does the general manager receive the previous day's food and beverage invoices after they are properly approved by the purchasing agent, receiving clerk, and food and beverage controller?
			
			Is the general manager getting current banquet information regarding: a) Food and beverage costs
			                 b) Guarantees
			                 c) Special prices
			
			Is there a regularly scheduled weekly meeting of the general manager and food and beverage controller to review current food and beverage costs and trends?
			
			Is there a weekly food and beverage meeting that the general manager attends?
			
			Food and beverage cost control procedures
			
			What standard system of food and beverage control is in use?
			
			   For large operation _____
			   For small operation _____
			   One-sheet control _____
			
			Is the appropriate food and beverage control manual available to all concerned?
			
			Is the manual understood by the persons responsible for controls?	

Exhibit 10-6. Checklist used in establishing cost controls for food and beverages (Courtesy: Sheraton Corporation of America, Boston, Massachusetts)

Date: _____ Institution: _____

FOOD AND BEVERAGE COST CONTROL SYSTEM CHECKLIST

Satis-factory	Unsatis-factory	N/A	Item description	Comments
			Does the food and beverage cost controller report to the general manager?	
			Is the food and beverage cost controller responsible to the controller for carrying out accounting control procedures as prescribed in policy and procedures?	
			Are invoices written up completely on the receiving sheets showing the date, purveyor, item, quantity, price, and total?	
			Are receiving sheets completed and totaled daily?	
			Is the minimum practical number of items on direct charge?	
			Are the receiving sheets verified by the food and beverage controller before being sent to the auditing office?	
			Are controller's food and beverage purchase figures balanced monthly with the total purchases shown on the receiving sheets?	
			Are requisitions required for all food items issued from the storeroom?	
			Are meats issued by requisitions?	
			Are food requisitions complete as to date, department, item, quantity, size, and authorized signature?	
			Are requisitions signed by the person issuing the merchandise?	
			Are food requisitions priced by the storeroom clerk on a daily basis?	
			Is the standard (three copies) bar requisition used as prescribed in the food and beverage control manual?	
			Is the banquet beverage requisition in use?	
			Are monthly food and beverage inventories taken by the food and beverage cost controller and a representative of the controller?	
			Are the monthly food and beverage inventories recorded in pen in bound books which are secured in the auditing office when not in use?	
			Are all corrections of changes in the inventory books initialed by a representative of the controller?	
			Is the food production inventory taken according to policy and procedure?	
			Is the beverage perpetual inventory kept by the food and beverage cost controller?	
			Is a monthly beverage report of overages and shortages from the perpetual inventory prepared by the food and beverage cost controller and sent to the controller and general manager?	
			Do the general manager, food and beverage manager, banquet manager, and chef receive a daily flash food cost report?	

Exhibit 10-6 *(continued)*

Date: _____ Institution: _____

FOOD AND BEVERAGE COST CONTROL SYSTEM CHECKLIST

Satis-factory	Unsatis-factory	N/A	Item description	Comments
			Is the monthly summary of beverage sales, potentials, and costs prepared by the food and beverage cost controller and sent to the food and beverage office and to the general manager and controller?	
			Are the food and beverage reconciliations prepared by the food and beverage cost controller and sent to the food and beverage department and to the general manager and controller?	
			Is the monthly report of private label usage prepared by the food and beverage cost controller and sent to the food and beverage department and to the general manager and controller?	
			Are employees' meals accounted for and costed as explained in the policies and procedures?	
			Food and beverage cost control procedures—operations	
			Is there a file of competitive menus in the food and beverage control office?	
			Is there a regular monthly program of butcher tests and recipe costing?	
			Is there a list of portion sizes for all restaurant and banquet menu items?	
			Is a portion control maintained for steaks and other high-cost items?	
			Are menu prices adjusted on a quarterly basis to reflect fluctuations in purchase prices?	
			Are food covers forecast monthly by outlet and by meal period?	
			Are food covers forecast weekly by outlet and meal period?	
			Does the food and beverage controller furnish food costs by outlet as his contribution to the preparation of the quarterly profit and loss by outlet?	
			Are marked menus furnished to the chef of the institution on a continuing daily basis?	
			Are marked menus used in planning food production?	
			Is the chef's daily order and production record for the butcher shop used?	
			Is the chef's daily order and production record for the pastry shop used?	
			Is the nonproductive items control in effect?	
			Is the alcohol content of liquor spot-checked on a monthly basis with a hydrometer?	
			Are banquets costed daily?	

Exhibit 10-6 *(continued)*

Date: _____ Institution: _____

FOOD AND BEVERAGE COST CONTROL SYSTEM CHECKLIST

Satis-factory	Unsatis-factory	N/A	Item description	Comments
			Are banquet checks compared with production records and the number charged verified for accuracy?	
			Internal accounting control	
			Are restaurant and bar checks signed for by waiters, waitresses, and captains when issued to them?	
			Are amounts posted by a cash register on bar checks by the bartender after each round of drinks is prepared and served to bar customers, and are the checks placed face down on the bar in front of the customers?	
			Are properly posted bar checks presented after each round of drinks to table guests by the waitress (waiter) by placing the check face down on the table after the service of drinks?	
			Are bar checks rung back through the cash register when checks are paid?	
			Are used bar checks put in a locked box?	
			Is there a daily missing check report prepared by the auditing office?	
			Are cash registers locked and readings taken only by representatives of the auditing office?	
			Is a cash register used in the coffee shop?	
			Control procedures—purchasing	
			Are revised purchase specifications used for purchasing?	
			Do all vendors have copies of specifications used for the items they handle?	
			Are competitive bids being received from a minimum of two vendors on all items purchased competitively?	
			Are these quotations recorded on a market quotation list?	
			Does the chef approve the quantities to be purchased before orders are placed?	
			Is a grocery price book maintained showing competitive prices?	
			Is the grocery price book up to date?	
			Is there a file supporting the decision to purchase certain products from single purveyors?	
			Does the purchasing agent verify invoices for agreement of amounts, prices, and items with orders placed?	
			Is the beverage purchase order approved by the general manager before being placed?	

Exhibit 10-6 *(continued)*

Date: _____ Institution: _____

FOOD AND BEVERAGE COST CONTROL SYSTEM CHECKLIST

Satis-factory	Unsatis-factory	N/A	Item description	Comments
			Are butterfat and bacteria tests taken on milk, cream, and ice cream on a quarterly basis?	
			Control procedures—receiving	
			Is the receiving clerk responsible to the controller?	
			Are receiving procedures being carried out as directed by the controller?	
			Are receiving specifications posted?	
			Has the receiving clerk been instructed in the use of the specifications?	
			Does the receiving clerk receive a list from the purchasing agent of items, amounts, and prices of orders placed to compare with the invoices for merchandise received?	
			Is there an adequate scale for weighing merchandise received?	
			Is the scale checked periodically by an inspector and a verifying seal attached to the scale?	
			Is a ruler attached to the receiving scale to measure the trim of meat?	
			What standard food and beverage receiving sheets are used?	
			Is the food receiving sheet filled out showing dealer, item, quantity, price, and extensions and totaled daily?	
			Is a "goods received without invoice" prepared when merchandise is received without invoice?	
			Are items received without an accompanying invoice recorded on the receiving sheet?	
			Is there a "notice of error and correction" prepared when merchandise is returned or an invoice is corrected?	
			Are corrections and returns noted on the receiving sheet?	
			Does the receiving clerk stamp and sign invoices?	
			Are all cartons and containers date stamped when received?	
			Are weights of certain items, e.g., eggs, written on the carton along with the date received?	
			Is incoming beverage merchandise checked against the purchase order?	
			Are cases of liquor weighed on a spot-check basis to find missing or broken bottles?	
			Are receiving procedures checked by the food and beverage controller?	

Exhibit 10-6 *(continued)*

Date: _____ Institution: _____

FOOD AND BEVERAGE COST CONTROL SYSTEM CHECKLIST

Satis-factory	Unsatis-factory	N/A	Item description	Comments
			Control procedures—storing and issuing	
			Are designated opening and closing hours of the food and liquor storerooms maintained?	
			Is there a logbook maintained at the front desk recording the "in and out" of storeroom keys during the time the storeroom is closed?	
			Are all containers priced to facilitate inventory taking and costing of requisitions?	
			Are inventory items rotated, i.e., issued on a "first-in, first-out" basis?	
			Are sugar, spices, nuts, etc., prepackaged and priced in the quantities usually requisitioned?	
			Are items on shelves placed in order according to the inventory book?	
			Do the food and beverage storerooms operate out of single opened containers as far as possible?	
			Is a written requisition signed by an authorized person required for all items?	
			Is there a list of authorized signatures posted in the food store-room?	
			Are requisitions signed by the person issuing the merchandise?	
			Are food requisitions priced by the storeroom clerk on a daily basis?	
			Are the keys to the liquor storeroom under the control of one person?	
			Is there an emergency key to the liquor storeroom in a sealed envelope at the front desk and is it controlled by a signed in and out log?	
			Is the beverage perpetual inventory handled by a person other than the one who has the liquor storeroom keys?	
			Are bar requisitions handled as outlined in the food and beverage control manual?	
			a) Are the requisitions made out and signed by the bartender original and duplicate copies of the order sent to the wine-room, and is the third copy retained at the bar?	
			b) After filling the order, are the original and duplicate copies of the requisition signed by the wineroom storekeeper?	
			c) Does the bar boy sign the original and duplicate of the requisition before delivering the order?	
			d) Does the original requisition accompany the order to the bar and is the duplicate kept in the beverage storeroom?	

Exhibit 10-6 *(continued)*

Date: _____ Institution: _____

FOOD AND BEVERAGE COST CONTROL SYSTEM CHECKLIST

Satis-factory	Unsatis-factory	N/A	Item description	Comments
			e) Is the original rechecked and signed by the bartender on duty? f) Is the signed original requisition forwarded to the food and beverage control office in a sealed envelope? Is there a separate banquet bar used for the return and reissue of banquet stock to the regular bars? Is there any open beverage stock in the wineroom?	

Exhibit 10-6 *(continued)*

would be better not to have a checklist than to use it in this manner.

The best system for the preparation and use of a checklist is for the department head, with the help of his staff, to compile one for the department and submit it to management. Once the checklist has been approved, department head and staff should be willing to use it because they designed it.

It is best to have teams from within the department make inspections, rather than a single individual. A team made up of one or two representatives from the operating department plus representatives from other departments helps to lessen the demoralizing effect. The self-inspection teams should fill out the checklist and review it with the department head before filing it in the department. Management can, on occasion, refer to this checklist when comparing its own inspection report with those of the self-inspection teams.

Sample Checklists

Food service personnel may be charged with preparing an operational checklist or lists covering a food and beverage purchasing operation. Exhibits 10-2 through 10-7 are examples of checklists now being used. These checklists, as they are set up, actually constitute a brief, condensed operating manual based on all the proven and successful methods of operation for a typical food service facility. If any food service operator could answer affirmatively all the items on these checklists covering purchasing, control, and sanitation, he would have an almost perfect operation, at least in terms of the areas checked.

The checklists for the food and beverage cost control system start with a list of "manager's spot checks," followed by a rather comprehensive list of questions that a manager should insist be answered in the affirmative so that he can be assured that back-of-the-house operations, especially the purchasing, receiving, storing, and issuing functions, are under control and that the food buyer is carrying out his responsibilities.

Sanitation requirements outlined in the Occupational Safety and Health Act (see Chapter 3) will probably become more

SURVEY REPORT
FOOD SERVICE ESTABLISHMENTS

CITY, COUNTY OR DISTRICT	NAME OF ESTABLISHMENT	ADDRESS	OWNER OR OPERATOR

REFERENCE GUIDE: 8G, 7F, 7E, 7C, 7D, 6B1-3

SECTION B. FOOD
1. FOOD SUPPLIES

Column headers: Specify: Bakery products / Poultry and poultry products / Meat and meat products / Frozen desserts / Shellfish / Milk and milk products / REFERENCE GUIDE / Demerit Points

Item		Reference Guide	Demerit Points
1	Approved source		6
2	Wholesome - not adulterated		6
3	Not misbranded		2
4	Original container; properly identified		2
5	Approved dispenser		
6	Fluid milk and fluid milk products pasteurized	6B2	6
7	Low-acid and non-acid foods commercially canned	8H1	6

2. FOOD PROTECTION

Column headers: Preparation / Storage / Display / Service / Transportation / Reference Guide / Demerit Points

Item		Reference Guide	Demerit Points
8	Protected from contamination	8A1	4
9	Adequate facilities for maintaining food at hot or cold temperatures	8A2	2
10	Suitable thermometers properly located	8A2	2
11	Perishable food at proper temperature	8B1	2
12	Potentially hazardous food at 45° F. or below, or 140° F. or above as required	8B2,3	6
13	Frozen food kept frozen; properly thawed	9B5	2
14	Handling of food minimized by use of suitable utensils	9C1	4
15	Hollandaise sauce of fresh ingredients; discarded after three hours	9B4	6
16	Food cooked to proper temperature	9C3-6	6
17	Fruits and vegetables washed throroughly	9C2	2
18	Containers of food stored off floor on clean surfaces	10D1,2	2
19	No wet storage of packaged food	10D3	2
20	Display cases, counter protector devices or cabinets of approved type	10E1	2
21	Frozen dessert dippers properly stored	11E3	2
22	Sugar in closed dispensers or individual packages	11E4	2
23	Unwrapped and potentially hazardous food not re-served	11E5	4
24	Poisonous and toxic materials properly identified, colored, stored and used; poisonous polishes not present	11G 1-7	6
25	Bactericides, cleaning and other compounds properly stored and non-toxic in use dilutions	12G4	

SECTION C. PERSONNEL
1. HEALTH AND DISEASE CONTROL

| 26 | Persons with boils, infected wounds, respiratory infections or other communicable disease properly restricted | 12B | 6 |
| 27 | Known or suspected communicable disease cases reported to health authority | 12B | 6 |

2. CLEANLINESS

28	Hands washed and clean	12C1-3	6
29	Clean outer garments; proper hair restraints used	13D1,2	2
30	Good hygienic practices	13E	4

3364 1-66

REFERENCE GUIDE: 13A2, 13A2, 13A2, 13A3, 13A3, 13A1, 3, 14A, 4, 5, 9-11, 14A6-8

SECTION D. FOOD EQUIPMENT AND UTENSILS
1. SANITARY DESIGNS CONSTRUCTION AND INSTALLATION OF EQIUPMENT AND UTENSILS

Column headers: Good repair, no cracks / No chips, pits or open seams / Cleanable, smooth / Approved material / No corrosion / Proper construction / Accessible for cleaning and inspection / REFERENCE GUIDE / Demerit Points

Item		Reference Guide	Demerit Points
31	Food-contact surfaces of equipment		2
32	Utensils		2
33	Non-food-contact surfaces of equipment		2
34	Single-service articles of non-toxic materials	15A12	2
35	Equipment properly installed	15B1-3	2
36	Existing equipment capable of being cleaned, non-toxic, properly installed, and in good repair	16C	2

2. CLEANLINESS OF EQUIPMENT AND UTENSILS

37	Tableware clean to sight and touch	16D1	
38	Kitchenware and food-contact surfaces of equipment clean to sight and touch	16D2	4
39	Grills and similar cooking devices cleaned daily	16D2	
40	Non-food-contact surfaces of equipment kept clean	16D3	2
41	Detergents and abrasives rinsed off food-contact surfaces	16D4	2
42	Clean wiping cloths used; use properly restricted	16D5	2
43	Utensils and equipment pre-flushed, scraped or soaked	17F1	
44	Tableware sanitized	16E1	
45	Kitchenware and food-contact surfaces of equipment used for potentially hazardous food sanitized	16E2	4
46	Facilities for washing and sanitizing equipment and utensils approved, adequate, properly constructed, maintained and operated	17-19 F	4
47	Wash and sanitizing water clean	17F3	
48	Wash water at proper temperature	17F3	2
49	Dish tables and drain boards provided, properly located and constructed	18F7	2
50	Adequate and suitable detergents used	17F2	2
51	Approved thermometers provided and used	18F6	
52	Suitable dish baskets provided	18F5	
53	Proper gauge cocks provided	18F10B	
54	Cleaned and cleaned and sanitized utensils and equipment properly stored and handled; utensils air-dried	19G1,2	2
55	Suitable facilities and areas provided for storing utensils and equipment	20G2	2
56	Single-service articles properly stored, dispensed and handled	20H1,2	2
57	Single-service articles used only once	20H3	
58	Single-service articles used when approved washing and sanitizing facilities are not provided	20H4	6

SECTION E. SANITARY FACILITIES AND CONTROLS
1. WATER SUPPLY

59	From approved source; adequate; safe quality	20A1	6
60	Hot and cold running water provided	20A2	4
61	Transported water handled, stored; dispensed in a sanitary manner	21B1,2	6
62	Ice from approved source; made from potable water	21C1	6
63	Ice machines and facilities properly located, installed and maintained	21C1	2
64	Ice and ice handling utensils properly handled and stored; block ice rinsed	21C2	2
65	Ice-contact surfaces approved; proper material and construction	21C4	

Exhibit 10-7. Example of a report on food service sanitation (Courtesy: American Mutual Insurance Company, Wakefield, Massachusetts)

PAGE 2

Item	2. SEWAGE DISPOSAL	REFER. GUIDE	Demerit Points
66	Into public sewer, or approved private facilities	21A1	6
	3. PLUMBING		
67	Properly sized, installed and maintained	22A1	2
68	Non-potable water piping identified	22A2	1
69	No cross connections	22A1-3	6
70	No back siphonage possible	22A3	
71	Equipment properly drained	22B1-3	2
	4. TOILET FACILITIES		
72	Adequate, conveniently located, and accessible; properly designed and installed	23A 1-3	6
73	Toilet rooms completely enclosed, and equipped with self-closing, tight-fitting doors; doors kept closed	23A3	2
74	Toilet rooms, fixtures and vestibules kept clean, in good repair, and free from odors	23B1	2
75	Toilet tissue and proper waste receptacles provided; waste receptacles emptied as necessary	23B2	2
	5. HAND-WASHING FACILITIES		
76	Lavatories provided, adequate, properly located and installed	23A1-3	6
77	Provided with hot and cold or tempered running water through proper fixtures	24A4	4
78	Suitable hand cleanser and sanitary towels or approved hand-drying devices provided	24B1	2
79	Waste receptacles provided for disposable towels	24B1	2
80	Lavatory facilities clean and in good repair	24B2	2
	6. GARBAGE AND RUBBISH DISPOSAL		
81	Stored in approved containers; adequate in number	24A1,4	2
82	Containers cleaned when empty; brushes provided	24A3	2
83	When not in continuous use, covered with tight fitting lids, or in protective storage inaccessible to vermin	24A2	2
84	Storage areas adequate; clean; no nuisances; proper facilities provided	25B1-3	2
85	Disposed of in an approved manner, at an approved frequency	25D1	2
86	Garbage rooms or enclosures properly constructed; outside storage at proper height above ground or on concrete slab	25B4	2
87	Food waste grinders and incinerators properly installed, constructed and operated; incinerators areas clean	25C,D2	2
	7. VERMIN CONTROL		
88	Presence of rodents, flies, roaches and vermin minimized	26A1,2	4
89	Outer openings protected against flying insects as required; rodent-proofed	26B1-3,C	2
90	Harborage and feeding of vermin prevented	26A2	2

Item	SECTION F. OTHER FACILITIES 1. FLOORS, WALLS AND CEILINGS	REFER. GUIDE	Demerit Points
91	Floors kept clean; no sawdust used	26A1	2
92	Floors easily cleanable construction, in good repair, smooth, non-absorbent; carpeting in good repair	26A2,4	1
93	Floor graded and floor drains, as required	27A3	2
94	Exterior walking and driving surfaces clean; drained	27A5	2
95	Exterior walking and driving surfaces properly surfaced	27A5	1
96	Mats and duck boards cleanable, removable and clean	27A6	2
97	Floors and wall junctures properly constructed	27A7	2
98	Walls, ceilings and attached equipment clean	27B1	2
99	Walls and ceilings properly constructed and in good repair; coverings properly attached	27B3-5	1
100	Walls of light color; washable to level of splash	27B2	2
	2. LIGHTING		
101	20 foot-candles of light on working surfaces	28A1	
102	10 foot-candles of light on food equipment, utensil-washing, hand-washing areas and toilet rooms	28A1	2
103	5 foot-candles of light 30" from floor in all other areas	28A1	
104	Artificial light sources as required	28A1	2
	3. VENTILATION		
105	Rooms reasonably free from steam, condensation, smoke, etc.	28A1	2
106	Rooms and equipment vented to outside as required	28A2	2
107	Hoods properly designed; filters removable	28A3	2
108	Intake air ducts properly designed and maintained	28A4	1
109	Systems comply with fire prevention requirements; no nuisance created	28A5	2
	4. DRESSING ROOMS AND LOCKERS		
110	Dressing rooms or areas as required; properly located	29A1	1
111	Adequate lockers or other suitable facilities	29A2	1
112	Dressing rooms, areas and lockers kept clean	29A3	2
	5. HOUSEKEEPING		
113	Establishment and property clean, and free of litter	29A1	2
114	No operations in living or sleeping quarters	29A2	2
115	Floors and walls cleaned after closing or between meals by dustless methods	29B1	2
116	Laundered clothes and napkins stored in clean place	29C1	2
117	Soiled linen and clothing stored in proper containers	29C2	1
118	No live birds or animals other than guide dogs	30D1	2

REMARKS —

Note: This checklist indicates what areas are examined in a sanitation survey of food service establishments. The American Mutual Insurance Companies' engineering department has prepared a manual (**Food Service Sanitation: Valuable Information for Persons Concerned with the Food Service Industry**) that accompanies the checklist, and the numbers that appear as "Reference Guides" refer to page number and section where related information appears in the manual (e.g., 6B 1-3 refers to page 6, section B, subsections 1-3 on "Milk and Milk Products"):

1. All milk and milk products, including fluid milk, other fluid dairy products and manufactured milk products, shall meet the standards of quality established for such products by applicable State and local laws and regulations.

2. Only pasteurized fluid milk and fluid-milk products shall be used or served. Dry milk and milk products may be reconstituted in the establishment if used for cooking purposes only.

3. All milk and fluid-milk products for drinking purposes shall be purchased and served in the original individual container in which they were packaged at the milk plant, or shall be served from an approved bulk milk dispenser: **Provided,** That cream, whipped cream or half and half, which is to be consumed on the premises, may be served from the original container of not more than one-half gallon capacity or from a dispenser approved by the health authority for such service, and for mixed drinks requiring less than one-half pint of milk, milk may be poured from one-quart or one-half gallon containers packaged at a milk plant.

Exhibit 10-7 *(continued)*

rather than less strict. The wise food operator will insist that his establishment be clean and sanitary at all times, and the best way to ensure this is to have a regular sanitation inspection, using an inspection checklist that covers all angles of the sanitation problem.

The food service operator not only needs a good reference manual on food service sanitation; he should also provide one for his staff, to serve as a guide for their daily activities and also as a guide for inspection. Such a manual has been prepared as an aid to the food service industry by the American Mutual Insurance Company's engineering department. The food service sanitation checklist (Exhibit 10-7), which is part of this publication, has been adopted by over forty states as a uniform and acceptable sanitation guide. It has also been accepted by the federal government and is used in many government-operated food services.

11 *Common Market Practices: Ethical Considerations*

This controversial subject is treated superficially, or it is not discussed at all, in many texts on purchasing. Perhaps in some businesses loss from "nonviolent crime" is of little concern. In the food business, however, losses from carelessness, indifference, bad habits, poor market practices, and deliberate thievery can determine whether a business continues to operate. Often the amount of money involved reflects the greater share of the profit. Knowing how to reduce losses to a minimum and keep them under control is an important responsibility of management today, especially in the food business. Many thoughts on this subject have appeared in books and articles concerned with the great white-collar rip-off; the security service business has mushroomed; sophisticated machines, cameras, and surveillance equipment are used; business psychologists attempt to provide "moral stabilization"; millions of dollars have been spent on seminars. Still, the "old payola" goes on.

Call it what you will: graft, payoff, payola, point system, cooperation, grease, nonviolent crime, rip-off, *comme-ca*, 2 percenters, 5 percenters, on the take, in the business, one of the boys, handouts, pig, easy mark, side money, black hat, or white hat. Whatever the name, it comes out of the boss's pocket, and he passes it along to the customer.

After reading this chapter, one might feel that all dealers are dishonest, that every executive and employee spends his working hours devising systems to "take" the boss, and that every customer is a potential thief. That is not the intent. Large losses do, indeed, occur as a result of dishonesty and carelessness in the food business, but, on the whole, that business differs little from any other "buy and sell" business. There are, however, far more "loopholes and opportunities" than would be present in most other businesses.

The real purpose of this chapter is to make management and employees alike aware of how large such losses can be, why they occur, and some methods of control. With awareness comes the potential for preserving not only one's job, but, on occasion, entire businesses.

THE HIGH COST OF DISHONESTY

No one really knows exactly how much the white-collar rip-off costs the customer and business today. There have, however, been some indepth studies of this problem, and figures based on these studies, said to be conservative, are staggering.

Nonviolent crimes cost the American businessman and customer approximately $40 billion a year. Such crimes include employee theft, shoplifting, kickbacks, "promotional expense," and common practices that constitute cheating wherever they occur in the entire market system. This total is four times greater than all of the armed robberies, break-ins, muggings, purse snatching, and pocket picking combined. It would give every child in the United States, under eighteen, a four-year college education, complete with books, tuition, room and board, travel, and a hundred dollars each month for spending money.

No business is immune from this problem. A number of examples can be found that relate to one type of insurance or another. It has been reported that 90 percent of the body shops in the United States cooperate with their customers to steal from automobile insurance companies. This may cost every person who has automobile insurance as much as twenty dollars per year, and the total mounts to approximately $1.5 billion a year. Losses from arson, largely covered by insurance, may reach between $4 billion and $5 billion a year. In only about half of the instances, however, is arson proved and the culprit punished. Of the approximately 75 million shoplifting violations committed per year, which total about $2 billion in value, many go unprosecuted. And, the advent of federally subsidized health benefits for older people has opened up one of the most lucrative sources of nonviolent crime the country has ever known, but doctors and lawyers who abuse such programs are seldom barred from practice when the abuses are discovered by a government investigator or some other security agent. There are indications that the legal and medical professions plan to initiate their own controls rather than submit to outside pressure.

Similar abuses, whether the business involved is television, the theater, trucking, or food, are not difficult to find. About 18,000 businesses go broke each year from a combination of employee and management thievery. About a quarter of the instances involve some facet of the food industry, whether it is a restaurant, a hotel, or some other enterprise. This helps to explain why four out of five restaurants fail in the first five years of operation. The situation in the hotel and motel business is even more discouraging. Approximately 8 cents out of every dollar spent for products delivered to a hotel or restaurant go to pay for some form of theft. Currently, hotel, motel, and restaurant facilities purchase about $1.25 billion worth of food and food supplies a year, and this figure does not include the amount spent in hospitals, correctional institutions, or the snack business. Allowing 8 cents on every dollar spent in the hotel and restaurant business results in a loss of $98 million a year owing to nonviolent thefts. That is about 15 percent of the total net operating profit reported by the hotel and motel industry during 1975. If the institutional food business and the snack business were to be included, the loss could easily come to $150 million or $200 million a year.

Such losses cannot continue for any long period of time, or almost every business in the country would go bankrupt.

Awareness of the problem throughout the manufacturing and service industries of the United States has led to steps to control it, which have also proved expensive. In 1972 those businesses spent some $5 billion to combat the problem. This amount increased to $15 billion by 1975, and it is anticipated that it will continue to increase by a billion dollars per year until the country is spending somewhere between $25 billion and $30 billion a year on security measures. There are no figures as to the proportion spent by the food service and lodging industries, but it has to be assumed that expenditures must at least relate to their proportion of sales.

The security business has enjoyed a greater rate of growth in recent years than any other business. Technological advances include use of the computer to allow exchange of information among agencies, use of lie detecting equipment, and use of television cameras for surveillance. Candidates for employment are screened, and their records with previous employers are checked before they are hired. Innumerable shopping services have been started. Trade associations have initiated programs to help members combat the problem. Federal and local laws have been passed making bribery a felony, and undercover agents are used to detect problems.

Certain purveyor groups have set up codes of ethics, but no way has yet been discovered to make such codes effective.

WHO STEALS?

Even the most cynical person must find it difficult to accept the fact that seven out of ten employees steal or have stolen from their own company, starting at the highest levels of management and reaching down to the lowest-ranking employee.

Many guests or customers of a food operation also steal if they have an opportunity. There are innumerable records of bills not paid, bad checks passed, signatures forged, and stolen credit cards used. It has also been estimated that one customer in every fifty has managed to get away with free drinks, an extra course or two with dinner, towels, silverware, napkins, blankets, light bulbs, bathroom fixtures, wall decorations, statues, radios, and any other item that can be removed without a hand truck. Even security personnel, hired to protect property, are not above practicing a little dishonesty on their own. The percentage of people caught stealing in the security business is somewhat lower than the general average, but there is also an effort to conceal such figures.

No one really looks like a criminal. Nor is stealing limited to any age group, sex, color, creed, educational level, or social status in a community or an organization. Some managers say that it is best to trust no one until a person has proved worthy of trust. Others profess to trust everyone until they can prove that a person no longer deserves to be trusted. Perhaps the best preventive measure is to remove temptation wherever it exists and to set up the kind of control within an organization that will, at reasonable cost, make it difficult to steal at any level in the organization. Many employees have defended their actions by claiming that the boss made it too easy and that the temptation was too great to resist. Unions have supported this defense, and many cases have been decided by the courts in favor of the defendant on the basis of lax management and lack of control.

WHY DO PEOPLE STEAL?

During a recent symposium on the problem of stealing in banks, one of the heads of a large, successful New York bank was asked this same question. His reply, though it was no answer, was simple and direct: he said that he did not know. He went on to say that he knew the reasons people gave for stealing, but he doubted if they were the real ones. In his opinion, if a man had the urge to steal, sooner or later he would do so, and he would be caught. If, on the other hand, a man were basically honest, he would not steal under any circumstances.

Modern research has opened this theory to question. If honesty or dishonesty had been left to chance in the makeup of human nature, then 50 percent of people would steal and 50 percent would not. Statistics have shown, however, that about seven out of ten employees are stealing or have stolen from the boss. Security officials have produced a varied list of reasons why people steal and reasons that they give for stealing. The most important of the reasons given are reviewed briefly below.

Mountain climbers, when asked why they risk climbing a mountain, have long responded, "Because it's there." An astronaut, when asked why he wanted to walk on the moon, said, "Because it's there." This reasoning seems to prevail in the food business, as well as in nearly every other enterprise. A cashier, when asked why she systematically took ten dollars out of the till every night for a short period before she was caught, replied, "Because it was there." When psychologists researched this answer in the context of stealing, they found that some people simply cannot resist temptation, as others cannot resist challenges.

Often employees begin stealing from the boss by "borrowing" a wrench, a dollar, a few bricks and pieces of lumber from the storage area, or a bottle of whiskey for a party. They originally intended to return the item, but somehow they never got around to it. If borrowing stopped at this point, there would be fewer people jailed, less money stolen, and fewer businesses bankrupted. Sometimes it does not, however, and employees who have been caught have said that the first dime was the hardest to steal. After that, it became easier.

Real or imagined resentment toward management or the company is another reason employees often give for stealing. Some feel that the company is not concerned about their welfare, that they are not being paid a fair wage, that the boss is stealing, or that the boss does not deserve their respect for some other reason. If unfair practices are tolerated at higher levels, this toleration will be used as justification for questionable activities at other levels.

Then there is a desire to belong that starts early in life, a desire that society reinforces by stressing group participation, beginning at the kindergarten level. As children grow older, they often get into trouble because of the need to be "one of the gang." Even if the student manages to avoid trouble before he enters the business world, he is still conditioned to the need for belonging and being accepted. Sometimes this need makes him vulnerable to temptation or pressure from those working with him.

The most frequent reason employees used to give for stealing was that they had a need for money. Fringe programs—unemployment benefits, group insurance, medical benefits, extended time payments, and more lenient terms for obtaining loans—are now available to fill some legitimate needs, but many employees still feel a real or an imagined need, and this leads them to steal.

There are other needs. People are driven to prove, either to themselves or to friends, how smart or how brave they are. They convince themselves that nothing can happen to them because they are such important personages. Closely allied with this need is the effort to impress others with new clothes, an extravagant life-style, expensive entertainment, or a winter vacation. People get trapped into living beyond their means, as do those who support a girlfriend or a wife with expensive tastes, those who attempt to supply their children with all of the "advantages", those who must pay off large debts, or those who have costly habits. When they see an opportunity to obtain the money that they need, they cannot resist temptation.

Other people cannot, for some inexplicable reason, resist the desire to get something for nothing. Stealing becomes almost a game with them. They may start in a small way, they get hooked, and eventually they are caught.

When the economy suffers reverses or business is in decline and unemployment levels are high, many people are tempted to steal in order to gain security. Benefits available to the unemployed and to senior citizens have helped to reduce instances of stealing for these reasons, but it is still one of the most important motives.

Then there are the stories, reported daily in the press, of people who do foolish things and even risk their lives in a search for excitement. Some people steal because it gives them the same sort of thrill.

Finally, there is the "Robin Hood" type of person who steals from the boss to help those who are less fortunate.

While a concern for one's fellowman is commendable, it must be recognized that such reasoning is often motivated by a need for the approval of one's associates, rather than their welfare.

QUESTIONABLE PRACTICES IN THE FOOD MARKET

Some practices in this market are questionable, and others are patently dishonest. In dealing with questionable practices, the food buyer should heed the ancient warning: *Caveat emptor* (Let the buyer beware). Some practices have been used by dealers, their salesmen, and their deliverymen for so long that they have become standard operating procedure (SOP), in U.S. Army terms, and dealers have developed arguments to support their position. They insist that they must cut a few corners to offset shortcuts on the part of others in a competitive pricing situation. Many dealers claim that they do not like to do business in this way, but they feel that, if they do not, they must quote higher prices and risk losing business. It is recognized that a dealer needs just "one large, careless account to pay the rent"; additional business is profit.

These arguments lose credence if it is realized that many dealers do stay in business and meet competition without taking all of the shortcuts available to them. Some of the shortcuts or profit builders most commonly used today are listed below, but the buyer should be aware that new ones may show up at any time.

Upgrading Quality

Upgrading quality is not only the most commonly used shortcut, but it is the hardest to prove. The dealer can always argue that, in his opinion, the quality grade was correct but that he replaced the products with a better grade. This practice is most common in the produce business and the portion-cut meat business. It seems, however, that each category of foods is vulnerable to some form of upgrading.

Produce. Because produce has the shortest storage life, it is not unusual to get spoiled commodities along with the good if one is not careful, even though the quotation was based on the assumption that everything would be good upon delivery. The "sharp" dealer attempts to pawn off one- or two-day-old merchandise to the unsuspecting customer at top prices, whereas dependable dealers sell it for exactly what it is to certain types of operations that can use lower-quality produce.

Ice Cream and Sherbet. A little extra profit can be made by the dealer who delivers ice cream with a lower butterfat content than was specified and billed. True fruit-flavored water ices and sherbets are more costly to manufacture than artificially flavored products, and the sharp dealer takes advantage by substituting artificial flavorings for true fruit ones.

Not long ago ice cream was usually made with a minimum of 10 percent butterfat and at least 40 percent milk solids, not to exceed a 100 percent overrun. In spite of the law, some dealers knowingly reduce standards for extra profit. Ice milk, which can contain as little as 2 percent butterfat, is sometimes substituted for ice cream. The best protection against substitution in the product category is to have an outside testing laboratory take a sample of the ice cream and sherbet being used and compare the product with the specifications every two months.

Milk and Cream. As with ice cream, a questionable practice is to deliver milk with a lower butterfat content than that specified by the buyer and often lower

than that required by law. It is easy to substitute half and half for coffee cream, even though the container is labeled light cream. Light cream can be substituted for medium cream. A little stabilizer added to medium cream makes it whip fairly well and brings the whipping cream price. These practices are illegal, but some dealers are willing to take the risk. Another big problem concerned with the delivery of milk and cream is bacteria count. In spite of all the sanitary steps taken, this grows from day to day. A customer careless enough to accept a high bacteria count in milk and cream can be a blessing to a dealer when products have a bacteria count that is too high to pass inspection. Although dairy companies claim that it does not pay to make substitutions because they cost more than they are worth, substitutions have been made in the past, and they are still being made. Again, the best protection against such practices is to have the outside laboratory that checks the butterfat content of ice cream and sherbet do the same for milk and cream and, at the same time, determine the bacteria count. This protects both the food buyer and customers.

Butter and Eggs. As far as butter is concerned, it is simple to substitute a lower score for the higher one quoted and billed. Most quotations are based on 92-score butter, but no one ever seems to mention 90-score or 91-score butter. In some cases butter scored at 92 has been shown to be "fit for human consumption" and nothing more. When butter was being stored by the U.S. government in the Kansas salt caves, it was a common practice to substitute frozen storage butter for fresh sweet cream butter, and the fifteen ounce "pound" of butter is still quite in vogue. Butter in patties deteriorates rapidly, and another favorite practice is to deliver "old" butter as patties.

Upgrading eggs is another favorite way of getting a little extra profit from unsuspecting customers. The "sharp" dealer substitutes large eggs for extra-large ones, and does a one-size substitution on down the scale. He also substitutes Grade A eggs for double A, and makes a similar one-grade substitution on through the grades. Nor is it much of a problem to substitute ungraded farm eggs for graded ones. Buying ungraded eggs for cooking may be allowable during the fall and winter if the food buyer can locate a dependable dealer who knows how to handle his product, but it should be avoided in the summer because of heat. Some dealers also risk handling uncandled eggs.

Another practice, which has diminished but still goes on, is the substitution of brown eggs for white in all parts of the country except Boston, where the brown egg is considered to be more desirable from the customer's viewpoint. In Boston, white eggs are substituted for brown eggs when possible.

Federally inspected and graded eggs are supposed to be delivered to the buyer in carefully and clearly marked cartons. This is a great protection. Occasionally, however, federally inspected eggs are repacked before delivery, and the cartons contain only Grade B and Grade C eggs in a sealed carton marked U.S. Grade A.

In the egg business a process known as oiling helps to maintain freshness in eggs, especially when they are to be transported long distances. A dealer should not, however, substitute an oiled egg that may be a cold storage one if the specification calls for a fresh, nonoiled egg.

One dealer, after he sold his business, admitted that he had never delivered a Grade A egg to some of the biggest and best accounts in New York City and that every pound of butter that had been delivered was storage butter. In some cases he had to cut off the mold before he reprocessed and repackaged the butter. By following these practices, he was able to pay as high as 8 percent of sales to the management, food buyers, and chefs in the various operations as payoffs. In one instance, he admitted that he paid a chef $20,000 a year over a period of five years and that he increased the payoff to $25,000 a year as a "cost-of-living increase."

Poultry. Another questionable practice of the "sharp" dealer is to "slack out" frozen poultry, repack it in ice, and sell it as being fresh. This can be done with turkeys, ducks, guinea fowl, and Cornish, as well as poultry. Some dealers do not even bother to "slack out" the product; they just repack it in ice and send it along to the careless buyer. If the ice is included in the weight, that brings another bit of extra profit. It is around holidays, when there is a great demand for fresh-killed poultry, that the "sharp" dealer really makes a profit.

Unless the person receiving poultry is well trained, it is rather difficult to distinguish a Grade B broiler from a Grade A one, especially when it is packed in ice. Although it is legal to sell ungraded poultry, reputable dealers should deliver graded products if a good buyer insists that the standard be met.

Fish and Seafood. Because of the highly perishable nature of fish and seafood and because there are many similar varieties, getting what one pays for is somewhat problematical. A clear understanding between the food buyer and the dealer, a good set of specifications, and a well-trained receiving clerk are the best guarantee of a good buy in the fish and seafood business. The two most common practices are the substitution of frozen for fresh fish and the substitution of similar, cheaper varieties for better-eating, more expensive ones.

The practice of "slacking out" frozen fish, repacking it in ice, and selling it as fresh can easily be spotted in whole fish because of the sunken appearance of the eyes and the grayness of the gills if the head is left on. If the head is off, the buyer should, without question, refuse delivery. It is somewhat more difficult to tell fresh fillets from previously frozen ones, especially after they have been treated with a salt water bath. A good receiving clerk can, with a little practice, tell, from the feel of the fillet, whether it has been frozen or not.

The substitution of frozen green shrimp for fresh green shrimp is rather common in cities like New York, Boston, and Philadelphia, where there is a heavy demand for fresh shrimp. Some dealers have an elaborate system for thawing out frozen shrimp. They tumble them in a large wooden wash wheel while running seawater over them, bag them in net bags, repack them in ice, and deliver them as fresh shrimp. If this is done only for the benefit of the dealer, it is certainly questionable. Because of the substantial profit involved, such a substitution may well indicate a substantial payoff to someone in the customer's organization.

Other common upgrading practices involve substitution of varieties: brown and pink Gulf shrimp for Mexican whites, smaller-size shrimp for larger ones by re-marking boxes, Caribbean and African lobster tails for Australian, grouper for red snapper, mango snapper for red snapper or grouper. Gulf and Pacific snapper for Florida red snapper, haddock for cod and vice versa, pollock for haddock and cod, cusk for haddock or cod, flounder and fluke for gray and lemon sole, fluke for eastern sole, gray sole for lemon sole, lox for smoked salmon, and salmon from the Pacific Northwest, Canada, and Alaska for so-called Atlantic salmon.

Another favorite substitution is to cut up sea scallops and sell them as bay scallops or Long Island scallops. Alaskan scallops have recently been introduced; they are cut up and sold as sea scallops.

Regular back fin crab meat can easily be repacked in a can with a jumbo crab meat identification and delivered for a little extra profit. Special crab meat can also be repacked and delivered as lump crab meat by some dealers, and, for a while, pasteurized crab meat was being substituted for fresh back fin lump crab meat.

Coffee. Coffee companies frequently complain that they lose money with the sale of every pound of coffee, but, if a coffee company fails, the owner must be either a poor businessman or a poor salesman. Blending coffee is a highly specialized business. Large national distribution companies will not compromise their blends. Their coffees are blended according to certain basic standards and tastes, and there is no deviation. Because it is almost impossible for the user to know what he is getting, however, the "sharp" blender can take advantage of the situation. Less scrupulous companies submit coffees for testing that contain a high ratio of Colombian and some very aromatic African coffees. If they get the business, they gradually reduce the ratio of Colombian coffee in the blend until the dealer profits. It is not difficult to decrease the dealer's cost by as much as 20 cents a pound without making a change in taste and aroma too noticeable.

Other dealers have found it easy to hold out an ounce of coffee from each bag. It is advisable for receiving clerks to weigh coffee frequently. Another "sharp" practice is for dealers to tell prospective users that fourteen ounces of their brand makes better coffee than a pound of a standard brand. The price of one of the smaller bags is, of course, the same as a full pound.

In order to save on the cost of delivery, some companies provide a user with a special packaged coffee that is meant to last for three to four weeks. It usually does not last as long as the dealer claims, but he saves much money in delivery costs.

If the code of the coffee roasting dates is changed, a user will be unaware of receiving stale coffee. This enables an unscrupulous dealer to pick up coffee from one account and redeliver it as fresh coffee to another account.

Some large national dealers pick up old coffee from their bigger accounts and re-sell it to institutions such as prisons and low-priced catering services at a considerably lower price. No one saw anything wrong with this practice until some dealers offered this coffee as a bargain to their better accounts. After it was discovered, the practice did not last long, but it did cause a lot of confusion in the coffee business.

Meats. Many publications, some of which are mentioned in Chapter 15, are devoted to quality in meats and how to recognize it. This is expecially true for beef. Defining quality or guaranteeing quality is, however, almost impossible. Generally a definition ends by saying what quality is not, rather than what it is.

Some factors involved in determining quality in beef are breeding and blood lines in the animal, age, type of food, whether the animal is range or grass fed or a finished steer. If it is a finished steer, the length of time the steer was fed grain or grass and even the type of grain are important, as are the area where the animal was raised, care in slaughtering, transporting, fabricating, and aging, and the amount of fat covering the meat.

Some beef items have three distinct qualities within one grade. For example, choice grade may be top, average, or low within the grade. In addition, there are five fat coverings that affect the quality and price of beef.

Following are some of the factors that allow unscrupulous meat dealers to bene-fit. It seems, in the first place, that the new ink used in grading stamps disappears in a short time, leaving only a faint tint of color on the fat. An attractive piece of choice meat can be sold as prime if a customer accepts it. As for the three levels of quality in the choice grade, it is a rare dealer who will volunteer to ship any customer all of his top choice, even though the customer is paying for it. Substituting a packer grade for a U.S. Choice quality grade is not unusual, even though packers' grades do not necessarily mean anything when it comes to quality. It is also a matter of record that "fed cows" have been substituted for steers, and such substitutions often go undetected.

As for pork, the meat from grain-fed animals tastes and eats better than meat from animals fed refuse, but it is difficult to detect the latter without special training. Veal is, again, difficult to cope with, especially when fabricated cuts or pre-portioned convenience items are involved.

The possibility of upgrading in prefab portion-controlled meats is as common as it is in the case of produce. The easiest way for a dealer to upgrade quality is during the cutting. It is not difficult to use

U.S. Top Choice strips and cut "prime" sirloin steaks and to use U.S. Good strips and cut "choice" sirloin steaks. Some well-fed cows produce a strip that looks good. If the meat has been aged long enough and treated, the steaks are quite tender and might pass as choice steer steaks. The substitution of cut filet steaks from cows and "cheaters" for steer filets is so common that no one pays much attention unless he is truly a professional buyer.

To take another example, a specification for prefab veal cutlets can read "cutlets to be fabricated from U.S. Choice veal and cut from the rib, loin, rump, or hind leg of the veal." It is a rare dealer, who, when cutting up veal for cutlets, does not include every muscle that can be cleared of connective tissue, even up into the shoulder, foreshank, and neck. Fabricators even shred the meat, layer it with a gelantinous substance, and then force the shreds together to resemble a veal cutlet. Most dealers do not try to sell these as true cutlets, but, unless the buyer is alert, he will get them. Few dealers would cut up a U.S. Choice or Prime veal for cutlets. Most prefab cutlets come from good, utility, and, of course, "bobbed" (unborn) veal.

Other upgrading practices found in the portion-control business are the substitution of New Zealand lamb for American lamb, Australian beef for cube steaks, and for boned, rolled, and tied roasts. "Ungraded steers" are often used in cutting small luncheon steaks and other bargain steaks featured in low-priced steak houses.

Upgrading in portion-cut meats is the biggest drawback to buying these products. If an operation decides to use portion meats, then it is doubly important for the buyer to find the dealer with the best reputation in the area. Even then it re-quires the concerted efforts of both the buyer and the receiving clerk to be sure the operation gets what it pays for.

Some meat products freeze quite well, and practically every meat dealer hedges during certain periods of the year when prices are low by buying large quantities of meat and putting them aside in a freezer to sell later. There is certainly nothing wrong with this practice; many good food buyers do the same thing to protect against periods of low supply over the year. If the food buyer has not made such arrangements, however, he should not be sent frozen meats when he has ordered fresh, especially pork products, veal, and some cuts of lamb that do not freeze well.

The biggest "joke" in the meat business involves the hamburger or ground meat product. Some reliable dealers have built a reputation and a profitable business by scrupulously blending the beef in ground meats and maintaining strict standards for fat content. There is a difference of opinion as to the best formula, but it is hard to beat ground beef made from two-thirds fresh choice lean chuck and one-third choice top round. Another excellent product is two-thirds ground lean choice steer chuck and one-third boned cow rounds. The amount of fat that goes into hamburger can vary from 10 percent to 40 percent, but a fat content of somewhere between 20 percent and 25 percent produces a juicy product that does not dry out on a hot grill.

Some questionable meat products are often used in ground beef. All dealers know that frozen Australian and South American beef liver, Australian fores and South American chucks, and boned American cow and bull necks, flanks, and brisket meat are used. Although lungs, brains, and kidneys are not supposed to be used, they are often included, and, if all else fails, there is that latest profit-improving product known as soybean meal. There is, of course, a legitimate place for meat additives, but the buyer should specify when these are suitable. A purveyor should not add meat extenders without the buyer's knowledge.

Short Weights and Counts

Directly behind the upgrading of quality comes another frequent abuse: short weights and counts. Many dealers make no attempt to weigh the contents of boxes of poultry, meats, and other packed items; they merely take the weight shown on the box and put it on the invoice sent along to the consumer. If someone cheats them, they get their money back by charging the customer. It behooves a good receiving clerk, therefore, to open boxes and weigh and count the contents. This should be one of the easiest practices to detect, but it is amazing to watch seemingly well-trained receiving clerks merely wave deliverymen past the scale and into a refrigerator without bothering to weigh anything or count the number of cases being delivered.

Sometimes receiving clerks fail to weigh or count shipments because their scales are inadequate. It is easy for dealers to take advantage of short weights and measures in such instances. Fourteen-ounce and fifteen-ounce "pounds" of butter and coffee have already been discussed. Now that margarine is so expensive, it is necessary to add that to the list of items to be checked.

Many produce items have standard weights and measures accepted in the trade: hampers of string beans, lugs of tomatoes, cases of oranges, lemons, grapefruit, lettuce, escarole, and various greens, containers of ice cream and sherbet. Most apples, avocados, pears, and baking potatoes not only have the count on the box, but there is a standard weight that goes with the count. Again, the receiving clerk should make sure that containers are weighed, both gross and net, and he should keep a complete list of gross weights to facilitate checking.

Receiving clerks usually note any credit due (for short weight, back orders, or some other reason) on the invoice that accompanies the delivery. A similar note is made on the copy that goes back to the dealer. The dealer may try to ignore the note on the delivery slip, and, if the operation pays the invoice without deducting the credit, then the dealer will continue to ignore it. The best way to combat this practice is for the receiving clerk to make out a separate credit memorandum each time one is needed. The controller's department can then check the file of credit memorandum each time one is needed. The controller's department can then check the file of credit memorandums against the monthly statement from each dealer.

Invoices can show weights that include ice or wrappings in the weight of the products. In a sizable shipment of beef such extras can amount to from twenty to twenty-five pounds at a cost of up to $2.00 per pound. When the buyer takes the dealer to task for this, the dealer may say, "Well, that's the way I bought them, and that's the way I sell them." If that is his attitude, it is best to look for another dealer.

Excessive Trim

Trim applies to meats. Excessive trim can mean excess fat covering, length of fat trim, or even the method of breaking the carcass down into wholesale cuts of meat. Unless specifications are clear and the receiving clerk is diligent, a dealer can pick up 10 percent additional profit on the excess fat left on prime ribs, strips, filets, lamb racks, top butts, rounds, and pork loins. The buyer may be unaware of his loss if the violation is not flagrant enough to be clearly visible at a glance.

Length of trim on the flank end of strips, ribs, and cut steaks can mean as much as 50 cents a pound over a quoted price if it is excessive. As little as one-quarter of an inch of excess trim on strips and ribs can mean as much as 15 cents a pound, and a half-inch in excess trim on a sirloin strip can mean 25 cents a pound over the quoted price.

The method of cutting meat also plays an important part in the cost relationship between trim and price. Chicago-cut rounds are entirely different from New York-cut rounds, and a regular trimmed long filet in New York contains as much as one pound more than a regular trimmed filet in Chicago or Boston. On the other hand, a Boston strip is cut on the bias whereas, throughout the rest of the country, it is square cut on the soft bone, which is more economical.

A favorite market practice has long been to cut strips, shell strips, and short loins from the diamond bone instead of the soft bone, the latter being the proper method. The dealer gets the steak price, instead of the sirloin butt price, for this extra inch of excess trim—a difference of as much as 15 cents a pound.

Some breakers, probably at the request of a dealer, leave two ribs on the strip and then cut one rib higher into the chuck in order to have the prescribed seven ribs on a prime rib roast, a practice often carried over into veal and hotel lamb racks. The number of nine-rib lamb racks on the market today is amazing. Again, a half-inch excess on the length of the rib of the lamb rack costs 15 cents to 20 cents a pound more. The "sharp" dealer is quick

to send the kidneys along in a loin of lamb, even though the price quoted was on kidney-out loins. It is the responsibility of the receiving clerk to check for these violations.

Other Practices

Price Changing. Unless the receiving clerk and the buyer are alert, a dealer can quote one price and then send the invoice through at another price. One should suspect the dealer who never seems to be able to get out a complete invoice with a delivery, but merely sends along a delivery slip showing pounds or count without the price.

Brand and Label Substitution. Substituting brands of bacon, sausage, canned goods, oils, salad dressings, frozen goods, melons, oranges, grapefruit, lettuce, or any other item is a favorite way for the dealer to get a price advantage. If questioned, he probably will claim that it was a mistake, that he thought the brand delivered was better than the one ordered, or that he was just trying to do the customer a favor.

Substituting labels on canned goods is illegal, but it is still done by some dealers. Some get so bold that they do not even bother to remove the original label. They place their own on top of the original and hope that no one will notice.

Packaging and Processing. Every packer or purveyor repacks merchandise with the best side forward or the best products on top; it is up to the buyer and the receiving clerk to look beneath the first layer. Some dealers have been known to glue packages shut and to twist wires especially tight to discourage receiving clerks from opening packages to inspect merchandise.

The amount of liquid in a gallon of fruit sections can be varied by the dealer. The receiving clerk also has to be alert to see that he does not get hot-packed fruit sections after paying for cold-packed fruit sections, which are preferred.

Upgrading Sizes. This practice is quite easy, especially where lemons, oranges, limes, grapefruit, and melons are involved. One simply removes the top of a 23-size grapefruit carton and puts it on a 27-size grapefruit box. The dealer must then remember to take out four grapefruit and shake up the box. Receiving clerks should, from time to time, spot-check the gross weight of the cartons and open some to count the fruit.

Substituting 10-size Cranshaw or honeydew melons for 8's and 8's for 6's or 5's is almost standard operating procedure. A good packer can make a 36-size crate of cantaloupes look full by using 45's.

DISHONEST PRACTICES IN THE FOOD MARKET

Whenever a questionable practice continues for any length of time, it is likely that at least one person in an organization is working with a purveyor or purveyors in some sort of dishonest scheme. Sometimes it takes two, often three, people in an organization to arrange a payoff scheme. Invariably someone is caught, but seldom is he prosecuted. It is usually the boss who both pays and loses.

Purveyors

Purveyors in the food industry are either scrupulously honest, inherently dishonest (known as "whores" in the trade), or simply do what is expected of them in order to make a sale. They are not likely to be naive. If they have lasted through their training period, they know all the rules. Many have forgotten more about chicanery than the most experienced food buyer may ever know, and, by the time

any dealer is big enough to amount to anything in the trade, he has already decided whether he is going to be honest or dishonest or whether he will "play both sides of the street." It is unfortunate that so many dealers fall into the third category.

Most dealers conduct themselves and their business in such a manner that they are favored by food buyers and companies that insist on strict honesty. There are enough honest dealers to give an honest food buyer competitive prices.

Most large food manufacturers, packers, and food distributors do business in an honest and straightforward manner. Such companies as Swift, Armour, Standard Brands, General Foods, Campbell, Heinz, Kellogg, Morton, and many others are so strict and have trained their sales representatives so thoroughly that they avoid doing business with a food buyer who mentions "contributing" to his favorite charity.

Then there are always the few dealers that, for one reason or another, simply do not know how to or will not do business in an honest manner even when offered the opportunity to do so. These companies are generally high-pressure organizations with overenthusiastic salesmen. Because the business was built on this type of policy, there is little reason to change at the risk of losing clients.

A few years ago the Supreme Court rendered a decision in favor of a defendant accused of illegal and unethical practices and income tax evasion by the Internal Revenue Service. The accused dealer had been withholding 10 percent of his gross business for "business promotion purposes." When questioned about the practice and the amount, the dealer said that, in order to compete, he had to pay that amount to those who were in a position to influence purchasing. He also claimed that the practice was so generally accepted that it was a legitimate business expense. The Supreme Court decision in favor of the accused dealer has not, however, worked out quite as expected. By identifying itself, the company was immediately labeled for just what it was. No self-respecting food buyer would have his name associated with that company, and many large companies have refused to do business with it.

Though it is likely that most dealers would prefer to do business in a straightforward and honest manner, they are in the business to make a profit. If they have to make some sort of arrangement with the food buyer, the owner, or someone else in order to make a sale, most will do so. There does, however, seem to be an unwritten but almost universal law among this group of dealers that, if the dealer gives his word to an owner or a food buyer that he will conduct his business in an honest manner, he either keeps his word or drops the account.

Food Buyers

There are only two categories of food buyers: honest and dishonest. This is discussed in greater detail in Chapter 5.

The Bait

After a dealer has made an effort to become a regular supplier and has not succeeded, the next step is usually to suggest how the dealer can be of service to the buyer: use of a credit card, tickets to an annual dinner or to sports events, rigged card games, a friendly foursome for golf, a boat maintained for weekend use, dinner and nightclub entertainment, or membership in an exclusive social club with perhaps a few dollars thrown in. If the relationship with the buyer progresses, there is always the trip to Florida when the weather is especially bad in the North, then the Caribbean trip, and eventually a trip to Europe with all expenses paid. For the interested golfer, the purveyor picks up initiation fees, club dues, and often a large share of the cost of enjoying the game.

Some dealers take the direct approach. They find out exactly how much the purchasing agent wants, and the bidding generally begins at around 2 percent of the gross business from the dealer. The amount can increase to 5 percent, and, in some cases, it goes even higher. Some dealers have admitted paying 8 percent and, in one particular case, the amount was 28 percent across the board.

Stories about the three-room suites maintained by some companies are also true. If a buyer has unusual sex habits, he is vulnerable when dealing with a purveyor who lacks a precise definition of honesty.

Sometimes a buyer is approached by an "attractive sales representative," but the smart buyer sees through this quickly if the sales representative is better looking than knowledgeable.

If the aggressive dealer still does not succeed in getting on the approved purveyor list, other methods can be tried. The food buyer's boss may be approached with the promise of business brought to the hotel through the dealer's connections with a real or mythical organization. This is very persuasive if the food buyer works under a food and beverage manager or catering manager who is struggling to keep sales up, and it is one reason why it is dangerous to put the buyer under the direct responsibility of anyone except the general manager of the hotel. If the dealer is able to pick up club dues for the general manager or to compromise management in some other way, then the food buyer either compromises his principles or resigns.

In smaller operations a purveyor often arranges a business loan for an owner who might be having temporary financial problems. Naturally, the owner pays back part of the loan by giving business to the purveyor, thus, the purveyor makes an extra profit beyond his contribution.

Often, especially in hotels with a sizable convention and banquet business, there are sales representatives who feel that they are underpaid. They can usually be persuaded to put pressure on the food buyer at least to give a purveyor the chance to bid or quote, starting with a small order to see how the purveyor works out.

Few companies admit that they indulge in such practices. They claim that a salesman works on his own. If he chooses to spend commissions and expense money on such things, that is his business. It does not necessarily represent the policy of the company.

Finally, there are dealers who are not above writing an anonymous letter to a food buyer's boss accusing the buyer of dishonesty or incompetence. The letter further indicates that the organization could get better prices if it used another set of dealers. The name of the dealer who wrote the letter is always included in the list of the better dealers.

The government rightfully takes a dim view of trade associations, chambers of commerce, and other professional membership groups using their influence to exclude noncontributors from doing business with their members, but it is

tried. Some triple damage awards have slowed down this practice.

Payoffs

It has been said that payoffs in the food business go all the way from peanuts to penthouses. It is, however, difficult to prove anything, and, as long as bonding companies and kind-hearted bosses fail to prosecute, there will be more fiction than fact concerning payoffs. Only cases that have stood up under investigation can be termed fact, some of which are mentioned below.

One of the most highly publicized cases involved the food service director in a New York City hospital. He took $45,000 over a period of three years, or at least that is the amount he admitted having taken when he was caught. The hospital chose not to prosecute him after he made restitution in the amount of $5,000.

Then there was the hotel steward whose salary was $198.67 a week. The summer before he was caught he went on a four-week trip to Europe, taking his family and his Oldsmobile 98 sedan. A catering manager, who was not very smart, drove a Lincoln Continental to work each morning—on a salary of $250.00 a week!

The receiving clerk and purchasing agent in a large metropolitan hotel worked together. At the end of a year the hotel had been overcharged some $38,000 for certain food supplies—their shared payoff from a single dealer. The two were not prosecuted; they were allowed to resign.

The chef for a large hotel in a metropolitan area, whose specialty was "French" loins, took his usual summer vacation in Europe. When he heard that the Internal Revenue Service was investigating his income tax returns, he found it prudent to remain there. It seems that "French" loins always cost 10 cents to 15 cents a pound more than ordinary strip loins, and the only difference that anyone could determine was that the "French" loins were cut into the hip through the diamond bone instead of the soft bone, which raised the price another 15 cents to 20 cents a pound. The overcharge cost the hotel about $20,000 a year for four years.

One hotel steward retired to devote his time to a real estate business and the operation of two large parking garages, which he happened to own. The fact that he was only forty-two years old and had been working for only ten years contributed to his success story. Another steward retired when the large metropolitan hotel in which he was working was sold. He has not worked since and is said to have been living on his investments for about twenty years.

One hotel with problems found that its chef was able to retire in five years. As there were questions about some of the purchasing practices, the hotel brought in an "honest" chef, who retired in four years. Neither chef, although living comfortably, has found it necessary to work since. It was at this hotel that the butter and egg dealer complained that he was forced to pay 8 percent of the gross business done with the hotel directly to the chef. The catering manager, who was able to put together a $500,000 portfolio in eight years, has among his specialties a certain ice cream bombe purchased from a certain company at one dollar higher than a similar bombe purchased from anyone else.

The fruit section business is apparently quite profitable. One purveyor was able to give a $20,000-a-year commission to the buyer in a large hotel who decided that his fruit was better than fruit bearing the same label and coming from the same company in Florida as that handled by other dealers in the city.

A clerk, who had worked at the receiving dock in a large hotel for many years finally died. There was some question as to who was to get the 25 cents that he had been collecting over the years for every package of goods received into the hotel. Of course he had been forced to share the estimated $25,000 to $35,000 a year with certain other people.

In contrast, a receiving clerk in another hotel was offered $200 a month because he favored a certain company's merchandise. Being an honest person, he reported this to the management. It was arranged that he accept the money for two months while a close watch was kept. The company immediately started to send short weights and merchandise of questionable quality. When asked to explain, the purveyor claimed that this was the way his company was forced to do business, it was the way it did business, and it would not change its way of doing business even for a hotel that was willing to conduct business in an honest manner. When the purveyor was told that the hotel would no longer do business with him, he said that his many friends in the organization would not allow that to happen, and the purveyor was right.

There is no question about the authenticity of the story concerning the purchasing agent for a leading airline who required a down payment of $50,000 from any liquor purveyor who wished to do business with that airline, or the story concerning the $10,000 worth of blue-chip stocks delivered to another food buyer by "mistake." The company that sent the stock was surprised when it was returned by registered mail, return receipt requested. At least there was no attempt to raise the ante.

One of the nicest thirty-two-foot cabin cruisers on the Ohio River belonged to the purchasing agent for a company that owned some restaurants and a couple of hotels. A fire destroyed the boat shortly after the purchasing agent found it advisable to resign from his job.

Newspapers have reported instances where executives have formed an outside supply company to sell merchandise to their own company at prices profitable to themselves. Two executives in competing hotel companies formed an outside one-stop buying service that sold to their own companies at 15 percent to 20 percent higher prices than competitive purveyors offering the same supplies. This arrangement was broken up, but the offenders were not prosecuted.

Not long ago the management teams in two large metropolitan hotels were dismissed because of improper purchasing practices. Those affected included the general manager, the purchasing agent, the chef-steward, the chief engineer, and the controller.

These cases have been mentioned to show that questionable or dishonest practices are widespread, that practically every phase of a food operation is affected, and that the amounts involved are substantial. Such practices are almost sure to be discovered, especially if more than two persons are involved.

PROTECTION AGAINST DISHONESTY

Whether top management feels that it has a problem or not, it is folly not to have a security program in operation. Professional security men agree on certain basic requirements for a good program, and the requirements are, surprisingly, relatively simple.

1. *Management must set an example.* Norman Jaspen, head of what is probably one of the best security organizations in the country, states emphatically that the biggest single contribution to employee dishonesty is dishonesty on the part of management. The best way to encourage honesty throughout an organization is to remove any aura of dishonesty from the ranks of management.

If those who enjoy executive privileges are dishonest or behave in an avaricious or undignified manner, employees use this to justify their own similar actions.

2. *Management should let everyone know that honesty is the only policy.* If management has its own house in order, then the next step is to let everyone know, and to keep on letting them know, that there is no room for any kind of skimming process. Instant dismissal should result if such practices are discovered, even if only small amounts are involved, and any major form of dishonesty should, without exception, be prosecuted to the fullest degree.

3. *Management should be vigilant.* Management should be neither paranoid nor complacent. There is a lesson to be learned from the saying "Only thee and me are honest, and, at times, I doubt thee." Management has learned, often the hard way, that no one is immune from being approached, and the record shows that seven out of ten listened to the siren's call. Ernest Henderson, who with Robert Moore built the Sheraton chain of hotels, talked one night to a group of executives, as part of a monthly dinner, about an unpleasant situation that had been uncovered in the company. The speaker shared responsibility with other executives who had been at fault, or at least

lax, in their supervision. In his opinion, the most effective deterrent to employee dishonesty is a good employer who commands the respect and loyalty of his workers. The employer should establish and maintain the kind of atmosphere in which dishonesty is impractical and unacceptable. He, along with all management and supervisory personnel, must set and follow the highest standards of business morality and efficiency. The company should maintain job discipline and morale while using all security measures needed and making certain that all employees know that such measures are in effect. Adequate benefits, good working conditions, and equal opportunity for advancement must be provided. If, under these circumstances, an executive or employee succumbs to temptation, he should be prosecuted, not as an act of vengeance but more in keeping with a sense of justice and obligation to those who remain honest.

4. *Management should maintain good employee relations.* This important responsibility has often been shifted to unions, trade associations, government regulators, or poorly trained personnel managers because it requires constant attention. Maintaining good employee relations has become one of the top jobs of management, for wages and benefits are not the only concerns. Other matters—employee meals and dining rooms, employee locker rooms and toilet facilities (as well as their care and maintenance), group participation in sports and other activities, and Christmas parties, children's parties, and similar social functions—are also of prime importance.

5. *Management should be available to employees.* Management that isolates itself from department heads, especially those in sensitive positions, is asking for

trouble. In one case, management waited three years to sit down with the vice-president in charge of all food and beverage purchases for the company, amounting to some $20 million a year, to discuss company policy. Management here was either trusting, disinterested, or naive. The door cannot be open at all times to all department heads or employees, but it is possible to talk to people on the job or to insist that department heads do this so that employees have a chance to express themselves regarding management policy and other matters.

6. *Management should seek the support of unions.* Occasionally a union will support a dishonest employee, but this support usually comes only when poor management has contributed toward the employee's dishonesty. When the facts indicate a case of dishonesty, it is a rare union that does not support dismissal and prosecution. Progressive management groups have found that they can often get their message about honesty across to employees faster and more effectively by enlisting union help.

7. *Management should make the final decision regarding dealers.* One of the biggest mistakes management can make is to leave to someone else the final decision as to what dealers should put on the accounts payable list. Management should visit its purveyors, get to know them, and make clear to them that they do business with the operation because it is a management decision and not the decision of anyone else in the organization.

8. *All department heads should be thoroughly investigated.* Rarely does a prospective department head lack an available record of his background. An employer can check on his past employment, his credit rating, his bank account, his hobbies, and how he lives. His drink-

ing habits, his religion (if any), his marital relations, and his family life are also often known. If management prefers, there are public firms that specialize in character reference investigations.

9. *Department heads should be paid well enough to enable them to resist temptation.* Paying over-scale or above-custom wages does not assure honesty, but a well-paid, happy, and satisfied employee is less likely to make deals or accept bribes. This certainly applies to the buyer, the receiving clerk, and the production manager or chef in any operation.

10. *Specifications should be clear and complete.* They should be based on tests and approved by a testing committee, with final approval from management. Any purveyor doing business with the operation should be furnished with a set of specifications and should be notified in writing that they cannot be changed except by top management.

11. *There should be a good operations manual and checklist.* The purpose of such a manual and checklist is obvious, but it should be recognized that both tools are a waste of time if they are not used and supported by management.

12. *There should be regular inspections.* This is where the operations manual and a security checklist are needed. Self-inspection is helpful, but group inspection or inspection by another department head is more effective.

13. *The internal control system should be adequate and effective.* If the internal control system is inadequate, it is wise to hire the best accounting firm that specializes in control and have that firm set up a complete system, install it, and operate it until it runs smoothly. The best available controller should be hired, and he should report to top management. Any internal control system should include food and beverage control, and a food and beverage controller should be part of the controller's department. The receiving clerk should also be part of the controller's department, and he should be independent of the food buyer, the food service director, the production manager, the chef, the catering manager, the food and beverage manager, and everyone else in the operation except the controller and top management.

14. *An outside inspection service should be used.* Periodic use of an outside inspection service is well worth the expense. All management personnel and employees and the union representative should be aware that such services are being used.

15. *Offenders should be prosecuted.* One of the most disturbing things about the whole matter of dishonesty is that so few persons are caught, and, even those who are caught are often permitted to resign. They are seldom prosecuted. There is, however, a growing realization that efforts made to punish offenders, even if such efforts are time-consuming and expensive, serve as a means of discouraging further crime.

12 *The Face of Things to Come*

When the first exploration of the moon was in its final planning stage, one of the planners, an electronics expert, stated that, whatever other results there might be, the world would never be the same again. The vast number of improvements in electronic equipment required to put a man on the moon would affect the life of every man. Certainly nothing since the development of the alphabet and the adoption of the Arabic system of numerals has affected business more than the computer. Hardly a single aspect of modern civilization remains untouched. It can be argued that the effects have not always been good and the cost to many businesses has been extremely high, but the overall effect has proved beneficial.

This chapter does not represent an attempt to describe how a computer works, how it is programmed, how it runs, or how it is maintained. The attempt is, rather, to show how the computer can be used in the food service industry and how it can help the professional food buyer in his job.

A COMPUTER-CONTROLLED SYSTEM

Today, a complete food and beverage cost control system is available to any company with a large food service operation. In addition to stockroom control reports, a complete system shows food costs broken down according to the various kitchens, menu sales analysis, portion costs, and a daily food cost report showing income from all sources, actual daily food cost, and potential daily food cost based on actual sales. This is in addition to a daily report on bar operations that shows income from all bar sales by outlet, the actual cost of beverages by outlet, and the potential cost of each outlet. Through proper programming, the computer can record sales as they leave the kitchen, account for all cash and charges from customers, set up the city ledger for local charge accounts, print and send out monthly statements based on the city ledger, transfer charges in a hotel dining room to the guest's account in the front office, and, at the end of the month, prepare a complete operating statement and make out the balance sheet based on operating statements and all asset and liability accounts.

When the computer is free, it can be used to make out payrolls, issue payroll checks, keep any necessary guest histories, and prepare budgets based on information fed into it. It can also provide statistics on how many paper napkins were used per hundred patients served, how many teaspoons were stolen by guests, how many towels disappeared when guests checked out of a hotel, or how many pounds of detergent were used to wash dishes for a thousand prison inmates. A computer can supply almost endless amounts of information on a wide variety of problems that concern those who operate food services.

It is obvious that the computer has made a tremendous contribution to the food service industry and to the professional food buyer. There are, however, drawbacks to a computerized system, the most important being cost. The computer, plus input station wiring, can amount to several hundred thousand dollars. Then there is the matter of programming and operation, which requires that trained people be located and hired. The period required to install the system and to train employees is long. Management must also be trained to use the information to advantage since the average manager has been operating without most of the information available to him through a computerized system.

Obsolescence is another consideration. As far as computers are concerned, they are probably to the stage of the biplane as compared with the jumbo jet. The cost of obsolescence is a tremendous factor in determining whether a company should adopt computerized controls.

A related problem is the possibility of breakdown. Even though computerized equipment is being improved daily, breakdowns can be disastrous in a fast-moving food service industry. Any operation doing business with the public should have a manual system available for use when the computer system breaks down. This factor is especially important in large hotels when literally hundreds of people are checking in and out and thousands of transactions are going on throughout the house at any one moment. In one hotel a completely automated computer control and accounting system had to be abandoned because there were too many breakdowns. The confusion and customer complaints that resulted were unacceptable.

On the positive side, a completely automated control system can be depended on to work many times faster than accountants and controllers, to work inexhaustibly, to work irregular hours without complaint, to be completely accurate, to write legibly, to be honest, to be inexpensive when weighed against the amount of work done, and not to talk back.

The present state of the technology tends to indicate that there never will be a foolproof electronic system. To compensate, in the case of the moon flights, scientists developed backup systems. When the first-line system breaks down, reserve equipment takes over, thereby guaranteeing the integrity of the overall system with no interruption of service. Any redundancy capability built into a system obviously costs more. It is necessary to weigh possible "down time" using a single set of input-work-output mechanisms against the increased costs and relevant cost benefits of back-up equipment.

Computers, however they are constructed, are not as expensive as they were at one time, but it is becoming increasingly apparent that, apart from the questionable prestige accruing from ownership, most companies do not need to own the entire system. This realization stems from the fact that all computerized activity is not performed at the same rate of speed.

Inner data massaging, that is, mathematical computation, can be performed many times faster than either input or output. To use an analogy, if the system were compared to a short-order restaurant, a digital computer system works much like a restaurant that seats a thousand people and has one slow waitress and five hundred journeyman short-order cooks, with one slow cashier recording sales at the end of the food delivery sequence. The cooks could not work at the peak of their efficiency because they would have little or nothing to do. To translate this analogy into a generally known system, one can look at computerized airline reservations.

The American Airlines SABER system was the first and still is the classic reservation system that has been copied and refined by all airlines since it was first set up in the early 1960's. It is actually a perpetual inventory system scrupulously maintained by two computers, one having redundancy capability, set up in Westchester County, New York. Hundreds of terminals (input-output stations) are located all over the country. When a person goes to an airport or calls for a reservation, the clerk types into an input machine, asking the computer if there is a space on that flight. The computer searches its "inventory sheet" and flashes back the answer at the speed of light, and it appears before the clerk on a cathode-ray tube that looks like a television screen. The reservation having been made, the computer then removes one seat from inventory and records any other information that is pertinent, such as the request for a vegetarian meal for the person booking the flight. This all seems to be happening instantaneously, and unquestionably *is* fast. In terms of the computer's capabilities, however, it resembles the five hundred bored cooks.

There is a master computer that revolves continuously, checking all input terminals. When a request is typed into the machine, the request is accepted in order. Where actual mathematical computations are performed, even though the machine is seldom without anything to do for relatively long periods of time, it actually is pausing often. How can this be? It seems that, although the person operating the terminal may be typing at a speed of sixty words per minute, the computations are made in nanoseconds (a billionth of a second), which means that a bit of information, say, a five-letter word, may be processed in 1/2 of a nanosecond, or two billionths of a second. It is no wonder that the master control can search several hundred terminals, take care of all requests, and still have periods of inactivity.

And the SABER system is a relatively unsophisticated one today. The fact that a computer can potentially do much more work than it is generally called upon to do is what makes it possible to use one without buying it. By going on line with someone else's computer, it means that the computer is busy when it might otherwise be "bored." All that is needed to make use of a cooperative system is an input-output interface device, plus some leased telephone line (using a low level of activity on the line that is not audible). Costs are thereby greatly reduced. Once the system is set up, a thousand-bed hospital can go on line at night, and, in less than five minutes, completely update its food inventory at a cost that makes a perpetual inventory of all food feasible for the first time in history. This off-hour service has been possible for years; the main reason why more food service facilities have not utilized it is probably because of institutional inertia and conservatism rather than because of price, capability, or availability of on-line, leased computer time.

THE COMPUTER AND FOOD PURCHASING

Use in the Purchasing Department

The computer can give management and the food buyer complete control over every transaction involved in purchasing, receiving, storing, issuing, and preparation. In addition, it can do the necessary record keeping required in selling food to the customer, serving meals to patients, or selling processed foods to the buyer. On the basis of menus, house counts, and volume of business, a computer can project the probable number of portions of each item on the menu to be served and suggest the quantities needed to take care of the indicated business.

The computer, when properly programmed, can go even further. It can make out daily requisitions for supplies from the storeroom and purchase requisitions to keep storeroom stock at normal levels. It is now also possible for the computer automatically to place orders with approved dealers who submitted the best price for the items and quantities needed. A computer can alert management when prices paid are not the best ones quoted by approved dealers, and it can let both management and the food buyer know when quantities purchased exceed prescribed limits for storeroom stock. The computer can also issue a dead stock report every month showing merchandise that has not moved in thirty days, sixty days, or ninety days, or any other time set by management.

Besides overages and shortages, the computer can supply the food buyer with additional helpful analyses. It can tell him exactly how many units of any item were purchased from any one dealer and whether every purchase was made at the best-quoted price. It can tell the buyer and management how much of any one item was used during the month and what should have been used according to actual sales during the month. This potential cost report is based on standard portion sizes and recipes as well as on menu sales. As a final step, the computer can check incoming monthly statements against receiving records and invoices, complete the accounts payable for the month, and issue checks in payment for all purchases.

The computer can also indicate how many man-hours of labor were actually used to produce food in the kitchen and can compare the actual hours used with the number of hours that should have been used according to standard accepted work practices. This information is helpful when deciding upon the feasibility of buying previously prepared foods or foods to be prepared in the kitchen.

One might think that computers could mean the elimination of purchasing agents throughout industry. This is, however, unlikely to happen. The element of reasoning required in the event of market changes and the necessary time lapse before information can be stored in the computer demonstrate the need for an intelligent mind to control the computer.

Use in the Receiving Department

Once an order is placed, the computer

can furnish the receiving department with copies so that the department can be prepared for incoming merchandise. At the same time the computer can indicate any item ordered that does not conform to accepted purchase specifications.

When the merchandise arrives and is checked in at the receiving point, the computer, properly activated, can write out receiving sheets and receiving records in completed form, total the receiving sheets, and deduct proper credits for returns and merchandise received without invoice. This makes further checking of receipts by the receiving clerk unnecessary.

A simple example will show what happens when just one transaction is entered into the computer for processing. Assume that one case of six #10 cans of Sexton canned tomatoes, purchased from Jones and Company Grocers in the amount of $8.47, have just come into the receiving department.

The first step would be to punch the preceding information, coded in a prearranged manner, into the computer terminal. This single entry activates the following:

1. The purchase is registered in the purchase journal.
2. The purchase is recorded as emanating from a particular vendor, Jones and Company.
3. An entry is made in an accounts payable ledger.
4. The inventory of Sexton cooking tomatoes is increased by one case or six cans.
5. The area or storeroom where the inventory is being stored and from which the issue will be made is indicated.
6. The extension on the invoice is checked.
7. The perpetual inventory of total tomatoes is updated.
8. The original invoice number on which the case of tomatoes appeared is recorded.
9. The purchase passes through the entire accounting cycle to provide a final summation of the transaction, including payment of the statement and the issuing of a check for payment.

All of this is completed in a split second, illustrating the speed at which computers work. To have performed the same tasks manually could have required as much as four hours.

Use in the Storeroom

Once merchandise passes through the receiving office and, properly coded, enters the storeroom, the computer can tell management, at any time, exactly how much of every item should be in the storeroom. A series of spot inventories can be fed into the machine to obtain an immediate report on any storeroom differences.

The computer can record any issues from the storeroom at the proper price, control all requisition numbers, indicate the department for which the items were intended, show who took what items, and check signatures on requisitions for authenticity by using an electronic scanner. Some hospitals use the computer to determine how much of each food to issue from the storeroom through the use of standard recipe cards and volume forecasts.

OTHER THINGS TO COME

Looking into the future is always fascinating, even though the forecast is based on past experience or on history.

Perhaps one of the reasons we are unable to glimpse the future is that we might not like what we see, but projections based on what is happening today are attempted here. These projections are, however, limited to areas that affect the professional food buyer and his job.

The Universal Product Code (UPC).

History. A linear bar code system is not really new. It was used both by the railroads in the control of freight cars for several years prior to 1973, and by steel mills for manufacturing control and warehousing.

In the 1930's, when the National Live Stock and Meat Board was putting together the forerunner of the *Meat Buyer's Guide*, a group of retail trade executives created a committee to consider whether or not a universal product code symbol would benefit the entire food industry. Though there were several false starts, just before World War II the committee made specific recommendations concerning such a code. For example, a numbering system was recommended to the grocery and food-packing industry as a necessary first step in automation and control of food supplies in the retail trade. The system was based on a ten-digit, all-numeric code, which should be a standard machine-readable symbol or manifestation if it were to be adopted.

With the advent of war, the whole idea was set aside, to be picked up after the war when the *Meat Buyer's Guide* was published. Little progress was made, however, until a practical computerized system and an electronic scanner were available. The IBM card index system, even though it had been available for years, was slow, cumbersome, and expensive to install and operate, and the early scanners available were entirely impractical and unsatis-

factory. Then came the space program and the rapid development of electronic equipment, including the minicomputer and the optical scanner. The UPC was resurrected, and in April 1973 a linear bar code was selected as the standard symbol for the food industry. By 1973 practically all large manufacturers in the country were utilizing this type of code to control merchandise because it eliminated the need to activate a computer terminal in the storeroom.

The System. The UPC system may look complicated and mysterious, but, when broken down into its component parts, it becomes quite simple and logical. A typical symbol appears in Exhibit 12-1, with identification of the areas of the symbol.

In the ten-digit UPC number, the first five numbers identify the manufacturer. The second five numbers identify the item. The bar code symbol, which is only machine readable, represents the number series. Normally the code symbol is approximately 1½ inches square, but current equipment will take codes up to double that size and handle codes as small as an inch square.

The bar code, as translated by the computer will print out the price of the item, package size, and any other information pertinent to the product that has been fed into the computer. The computer can then print out a completed food requisition or a sales receipt, and, at the same time, adjust inventory records and issue a list of items that need to be restocked. All computer action is triggered by the use of a scanner, whether the merchandise is passed over the scanner or the scanner is a portable pencil- or gun-type that can be carried around by the storeroom staff.

The UPC system was originally designed for supermarket and manufactur-

This is a Typical Universal Product Code Symbol

Number System Character ——— 0

Check Digit

May or may not be printed on the symbol

41174 00100

Manufacturer Number | Item Identification Number

Assigned by Distribution Codes, Inc. | Numbers 00000 to 99999 assigned to Products at discretion of manufacturer or supplier.

Typical Layout of Corrugated Shipping Carton

REGULAR PACK

FLAKES		ƎMIꓤᑫ	
		12345-67890	
12345-67890	12345-67890	12345-67890	12345-67890
PRIME FLAKES	**PRIME FLAKES**	**PRIME FLAKES**	**PRIME FLAKES**
24-12 OUNCE	24-12 OUNCE	24-12 OUNCE	24-12 OUNCE
SƎꓘA⅃Ⅎ		**PRIME** 12345-67890	

Portion of Invoice Using UPC Numbers

	FREIGHT PREPAID—SELLER'S EXPENSE	
	SHIPPING POINT CHICAGO	**SHIPPED VIA** ZIPPO TRUCKING
UPC CASE CODE	**DESCRIPTION, PACK, SIZE**	
12345	MANUFACTURER ID FOR FOLLOWING ITEMS	
49102	PRIME FLAKES - 24 12 OZ.	
49101	PRIME FLAKES - 12 24 OZ.	
35207	FLASH CHIPS - 12 6 OZ.	
54321	MANUFACTURER ID FOR FOLLOWING ITEMS	
35266	FLASH CHIPS - 24 12 OZ. DEAL 5¢ OFF	
12601	BRIGHT DONUT MIX - 12 6 OZ.	

Exhibit 12-1. Typical Universal Product Code symbol (*a*), as used on a corrugated shipping carton (*b*), and on an invoice (*c*) (Courtesy: *Institutions Magazine,* Terre Haute, Indiana)

ing control use, but there is a food service version used in many large operations that maintains complete, item-by-item control over all storeroom stocks, accepts returned merchandise, verifies receipts and issues checks, posts accurate credits from any refunds, and prints all of this information for use by management.

Benefits to the industry include maintenance of accurate inventory records, an indication of stock shortages, better communications in terms of specifications (see Chapter 7), information on product movement, aid in portion costing, assistance in making nutritional analyses, and better control of vending machines.

Prior to adoption of the standards contained in the *Meat Buyer's Guide*, the specifications on a strip loin might cover half a page and contain up to thirty variations, any of which might be subject to misunderstanding. With the advent of the *Meat Buyer's Guide*, the food buyer could specify exactly what he wanted by quoting the number (such as a 180 strip), thus reducing the specification to one line. The same idea is contained in the UPC. If the code number calls for a 1.06 specific gravity tomato puree, that is what the product should be, and there should be no question in anyone's mind about the details. When one realizes that a dealer may have as many as twenty-five different packs for olives and that a convenience food supplier may have as many as two thousand convenience food entrees that vary in size, packaging, and quality, it can readily be seen how the UPC system can aid in the food-buying process.

Where the UPC system has been adopted on coded items, order processing has been accelerated, time and manpower costs have been reduced, and records and payments are more accurate. Food cost control is greater. Delivery performance has improved, with fewer misunderstandings between buyer and supplier as to quality, price, and pack of merchandise.

Use. At first, the UPC was intended to expedite the handling of groceries in supermarkets, but it soon became apparent that it could be used to control the movement of merchandise from warehouses and to automate the handling of storeroom stocks.

Invoices printed out by computer as merchandise passes electronic scanners make it possible for invoices to accompany delivery. This means that receiving is simpler and more accurate. Incoming merchandise again passes a scanner that activates the terminal and puts necessary information into the computer. No longer must people in storerooms punch prices and issue information into the computer. And, to issue merchandise from the storeroom, it is only necessary for the merchandise to pass the scanner, which again activates the computer to perform storeroom control activities. At the end of the month, when an actual inventory is taken and fed back into the computer, the computer prepares a storeroom difference report that shows exactly what merchandise is missing from the storeroom according to the computer's records.

Nor is it necessary to have the staff do a physical count of the inventory; they merely pass a portable scanner over the inventory stock. The scanner automatically takes the inventory and feeds the results back into the computer. This system is as yet rather sophisticated and costly for use in the average food service operation, but it is already being employed in many large institutional storerooms and by many meat-processing packers. It can be used on any produce where a surface measuring one and a half inches to three inches in size can be provided. It is coming to be a way of life in wholesale grocery houses, liquor warehouses, and general supply warehouses. The code now appears on boxed, smoked, and fresh meats, almost all frozen products available for use in the food service industry, and some perishable products such as boxes of apples, lettuce, oranges, grapefruit, and similar items. Even though the UPC code is not yet functioning throughout the food service industry, it is likely that there will eventually be a direct application of the system in common use. There seems to be little question that most large food service operations, including hotels, restaurants, and institutional food services will soon be using the UPC system to control the entire purchasing function of the operation.

Electronic Stock Control Registers

The National Cash Register Company, IBM, and at least eight other companies are already producing an electronic stock control register, and they are being used in some of the largest retail establishments, such as Montgomery Ward, Sears Roebuck, Macy's, and Marshall Field's. The register is tied in with a centralized computer that provides a complete record of all inventories. Though this would be ideal for use in the food service industry, the cost is too great for general acceptance at this time.

The National Cash Register Company and others, such as Sweda, IBM, and Bunker Ramo, have developed small electronic registers that can be placed in the storeroom and used to "ring in" all merchandise that goes into the storeroom and "ring out" all merchandise requisitioned. The equipment gives complete stock control by item, compares actual against mini and maxi stock levels, and

produces a daily cost of issues, plus a number of other information guides, as programmed.

This equipment, which is actually a minicomputer, is simple and lacks ultrasophisticated controls. It can be put into service for approximately $5,000, an acceptable price range for medium- to large-sized food service storerooms. Practically all operations in the food service industry except the very small ones will probably soon be using such equipment for the control of storerooms and purchasing, and the system will also be utilized for beverage supplies and such miscellaneous items as paper, linen, silver, glassware, and cleaning supplies.

The food service industry may be forced to carry larger inventories to allow for less frequent deliveries and to protect against shortages brought about by economic as well as political forces. As has already been mentioned in Chapter 2, this situation, which will encourage one-stop buying, will also increase the need for more accurate records and greater inventory control.

The World Supply of Food

World Power. Because of the demand for food throughout the world (see Chapter 14), the United States and Canada are in a position to influence world policy. Whether or not they seek a dominant role, the ability to produce food in great quantities means that such a role is theirs, and it will grow stronger.

Changing Standards. Stabilizing the economies of emerging nations will increase the demand for food around the world. This could influence present standards. For example, standards governing the percentage of additives followed in food might be altered if research on additives can establish whether or not they harm the world's food supply.

There will almost certainly be some further lowering of the grading standards on meats that rely on grain for finishing, such as beef and pork. There are too many hungry people in the world to waste grain fattening hogs and cattle for no better reason than to ensure a better-tasting steak for the few people able to afford it.

The Changing Market

Streamlining the System. Marketing costs will probably continue to increase. There will be a concerted effort by government as well as the consumer to reduce that part of the dollar going to the middleman rather than to the farmer, the producer, or the consumer. Food buyers will attempt to bypass the wholesaler by buying directly from the breaker or even from the packer or producer if the buyer has the necessary purchasing power. Growers, packers, breakers, and fabricators have already begun a joint effort to market their merchandise or product directly to the buying public or the food service industry. These cooperatives are causing great concern among wholesalers. The fact that many large food service operators have already gone directly to the source of supply is evidenced by the rapid growth of companies in the cattle feeding, packing, distribution, and supermarket businesses. Monfort, Iowa Beef Packers, Missouri Packers, American Packers, and Central Packing are just a few of the names to be reckoned with in this line of marketing.

Use of Precut Meats. There has been a virtual elimination of butcher shops in the food service industry, and there is no reason to expect a reversal of the trend. The sale of wholesale cuts to the food service industry is, therefore, likely to become a thing of the past.

The Disappearance of Vegetables. Another trend that will unquestionably continue is the disappearance of vegetables from the average institutional and hotel and restaurant menu. Menus in hospitals are following this trend since patients do not eat vegetables served to them, primarily because they are not in the habit of eating them. Patrons of food service establishments seem to prefer salads to the poorly cooked, warmed-over vegetables normally found even in the best restaurants. Vegetables often appear simply as a garnish for the entrée. This trend might be reversed if cooking methods were improved.

Food Service for the Future

Convenience Foods. The use of convenience foods in the food service industry (see Chapter 13) will continue to grow until it comprises a preponderance of foods used in the industry. Resistance to preprepared entrées is apt to diminish as the quality improves and consumers become more familiar with them. There will, however, continue to be people who, because they enjoy fine dining and can afford to pay for it, will insist upon good white-tablecloth restaurants, with the foods prepared on the premises. Truth-in-menu laws may be needed to protect the public.

Fast Food Service Establishments. In this category are snack bars, drive-in restaurants, and roadside diners, and there is every indication that they will continue to increase. Certainly such establishments produce foods that maintain life at a lower cost than can be done in a general service restaurant. This is what some people prefer and all that some people can afford.

Specialty Restaurants. These may well be an outgrowth of the fast food service establishments discussed above. The specialty may be steak, seafood, or so-called organic foods, or it may be based on something else besides food. Older companies, like Marriott, are turning toward specialty-theme restaurants. They are training or retraining employees and remodeling older facilities, based on a single theme.

Single-Service Supplies. Along with the growth of the snack bar business, there has been almost a revolution in single-service, disposable supplies. With the tremendous increase in the price of silver, china, glassware, and the cost of labor for warewashing, plus the money tied up in the inventories of such items, it is little wonder that the fast food industry has turned to disposable materials. The variety now being offered in size, shape, quality, price, and purpose of paper goods and plastics far exceeds that available in china, glass, and silver. There is little doubt that single-service supplies will be used almost exclusively in the institutional field and in fast-food service. It may even dominate in white-tablecloth establishments. Familiarity is likely to lessen resistance to use of single-service supplies. Earlier resistance from conservationists to disposable supplies has diminished since most paper supplies of this nature come from managed forest farms. Undergrowth must be cut, and it was formerly wasted. Now it is turned into the raw pulpwood that is used to manufacture single-service paper supplies.

Plastics have also made great strides forward, but scarcity and the high cost of petroleum have slowed development. Stainless steel has already largely replaced plated flatware and holloware. Now plastics are being used in place of stainless flatware. It appears that this trend will continue.

The Outlook for Food Service Employees

It appears that there will be continuous improvement in the monetary position of employees, with increased wages and benefits, at least for those who have jobs. It is possible that labor will eventually price itself out of the market, as some people have predicted, but this does not appear to be happening.

One thing, however, that is happening in the food service and other industries is that the knowledge and expertise of employees are being increasingly recognized and utilized at the policy-making level. The average employee knows more about his job than management, and, with the proper motivation, he can help management plan more effectively. It seems that employees who have helped to plan their own work often do a better job at less cost than those who have had no opportunity to make a contribution at the planning stage.

Improved management skills, respect for the role of labor, and a desire to increase profits will mean increased use of the employee for planning and self-inspection. This, in turn, will contribute to upward mobility and increased job skills within the organization. Management has finally learned the value of self-motivation.

It seems fair to conclude that there will continue to be changes in the food service industry. And it appears that such changes will occur with ever-increasing frequency.

13 *Convenience Foods: An Alternative*

DEFINITION

Convenience foods, depending upon the definition of the term, have been available for many years. Through much of that time, perhaps even now, they have prompted controversy within the industry, and there is as yet no firm consensus as to their acceptability in use. There is not even a universally accepted, exact definition of the term "convenience food." However, for the purpose of this discussion, the following definition is offered: *a convenience food item is one in which all or part of the labor otherwise necessary for preparation is "built into" the product prior to purchase.* If this definition is accepted, a convenience food item is one that requires *less* on-site labor to preprepare, prepare, or otherwise make ready for service than would a nonconvenience counterpart.

This definition excludes some natural food items—shell eggs, nuts, fresh berries, apples—since no alternate, nonconvenience forms are available. It is interesting to note that even natural food items can be purchased in convenience form.

For example, peanuts can be purchased with or without shells; fresh apples can be purchased in skinned and sliced form. The number of foods used in the exact form in which they are grown, in most operations, is small relative to other items purchased, and so, in reality, this particular controversy is not significant. What is significant is that, when a food purchaser has a choice between a food item that requires less on-site labor for its preparation or service than another market type of the same food item, he is purchasing a convenience food product when he selects the former.

According to Bruno Maizel, there are three major types of convenience foods:

Minimally processed—food items that have some processing labor built in but that require additional on-site labor. They are generally designed to eliminate some semiskilled labor. Examples: peeled, whole potatoes; shredded, cleaned cabbage; various vegetable salad ingredients.

Partially processed—food items processed more extensively where profitable use is often related to such nonlabor factors as waste, by-products of processing, personnel scheduling. Examples: preportioned meats; breaded fish products.

Completely processed—the undisputed "convenience" foods that require little, if any, further preparation after purchase. Examples: salad dressings; frozen, fresh-baked pies.

Minimally processed items can often be evaluated according to standards used to evaluate fresh products. Partially processed items should be evaluated relative to their suitability for the operation. There are, however, different criteria for completely processed products, and they are examined later in this chapter.

Many terms are used when referring to convenience foods, including fast foods, efficiency foods, ready-to-serve foods, ready service foods, frozen foods, prepared foods. Some of these terms are inaccurate when applied to the broader concept of convenience foods. For instance, not all convenience foods are frozen. Nor are all convenience foods ready to serve since some preparation may be necessary prior to service. It is this inability to arrive at an accepted definition which, in part, contributes to the continuing controversy over convenience foods.

For example, a purchaser may well encounter complaints about the poor quality of a preprepared, frozen beef stew because the establishment lacks the equipment to reheat it satisfactorily. If so, he should be aware of other market forms or intermediate types of products. In the case of a beef stew, there are canned products available, or it might be better to purchase intermediate components such as precut beef cubes, a prepared base for the gravy, canned vegetables, dehydrated chopped onion pieces and to incorporate these items into the beef stew recipe. The point is that there are many options, and, if any one or a com-

bination of these products proves acceptable, the purchaser may well be less resistant to the general idea of using convenience foods. A negative bias toward one form (frozen) might be offset by the availability and suitability of other types of nonfrozen, convenience food products.

Perhaps it would be more helpful to consider convenience foods in terms of a raw-to-ready scale devised by B. Smith. The concept is based on the amount of on-site labor required before a food item is ready to serve. The linear (straight-line) scale or continuum begins with 1 and ends with 10, as shown below:

Raw   *Ready*

1   2   3   4   5   6   7   8   9   10

The higher on the scale a food item appears, the less on-site labor is required to prepare it for service. Conversely, an item that is placed at or close to the beginning of the scale requires more on-site labor before it can be served. Judgments as to where specific items appear on a raw-to-ready scale are frequently arbitrary. Exhibit 13-1 gives examples placed on points 1, 5, and 10 of the scale. The exhibit serves to indicate that there is a broad spectrum of convenience products available for purchase and that there are alternative forms of many individual items.

Even this simple scale is not correct in all instances. For example, some operations (such as some institutional feeding programs) may grow their own beef animals and fruit and vegetable products for on-site processing or harvesting. In this instance primal meat cuts and fresh fruits and vegetables would appear higher on the scale than they are placed in Exhibit 13-1 since no on-site labor is required for the growing and butchering of beef or the planting and harvesting of fruits and vegetables.

Raw		Ready
1	5	10

Primal meat cuts
Flour, shortening,
  yeast, etc., used in
  preparation of bread
  and roll items
Fresh fruits and
  vegetables to be used
  in salads
Oils, seasonings,
  etc., to be used in
  house salad dressings
Fresh whole (round)
  fish to be butchered
  on-site
	Preportioned, uncooked,
	  ground meat patties
	Frozen bread dough and
	  related products
	Canned tomato and other
	  sauces used as a base
	  for on-site preparation
	  of house sauces
	"Instant" rice, macaroni,
	  and similar products
	Gravy bases and similar
	  products that are
	  built up to yield
	  finished gravy and
	  sauce products
		Baked pies, cookies,
		  and other desserts
		Baked, sliced bread
		Canned, ready-to-serve
		  pie fillings and
		  puddings
		Sweet rolls and
		  doughnuts
		Ice cream and
		  prepared toppings
		Bottled salad
		  dressings
		Milk and similar
		  products

Exhibit 13-1. The location of sample food items on a raw-to-ready scale

Many food items commonly considered convenience foods lie somewhere between point 5 (perhaps the point at which a food item that is somewhat complicated to prepare is made considerably less difficult to prepare) and point 10 (ready to serve). For example, canned and frozen vegetables, as well as other items, must generally be opened or unpackaged, placed into a pan or vessel for heating, and portioned prior to serving, and the vessel must also be washed. Preparing these items for service is somewhat more complicated or at least more time consuming than it is for items close to or at point 10 on the scale.

Perhaps, with some exceptions in individual operations, items at point 10, which represents the epitome of convenience, are perishable in nature and tend to be purchased for immediate use rather than for inventory or storage purposes. Other items—fresh fruits, nuts, and other natural foods—might also be placed at point 10 on the scale, but even they require some preparation (washing, shelling, sorting) before service. They have been excluded from the raw-to-ready scale in order to satisfy the definition of convenience foods that does not consider items for which no alternative market forms are generally available.

When individual food items are considered higher on the raw-to-ready scale, this indicates that less on-site labor is necessary. For example, one might choose to purchase primal meat cuts that require in-house processing or bulk ground beef or portioned meat patties or even precooked, portioned meat patties. Each choice affects the amount of on-site labor required.

Where on the continuum a food product falls must be determined for each food service operation, and the purchaser must have a clear understanding of the operation's exact needs. For example, frozen baked pies, which require thawing and, perhaps, warming, cannot be purchased if the operation needs a product that is at or at least very close to point 10 on the scale. In that case, fresh pies that require no warming before service might be purchased since they will require less equipment and labor time to make them ready for service (although the need to cut and dish each piece of pie and, perhaps, to wash the serving dish and utensils must be considered).

The raw-to-ready scale has been used by James Keiser and Elmer Kallio to illustrate the extent to which an *entire* food service operation makes use of convenience foods. For example, at the low point (1) of the scale no (or very few) convenience foods are used; at the high point (10) of the scale an operation makes maximum use of all convenience food items available. Operations at the lower end of the scale generally require more skilled personnel, more specialized equipment, and more production time. Operations at the higher end of the scale generally require less-skilled employees, different kinds of equipment, and less production time. Many "gourmet," full-service restaurants probably rank low on such a scale, while a simple, fast food operation probably ranks high. An "average" operation, depending upon the number of convenience food items utilized, probably ranks close to the middle (from point 4 to point 6) on the raw-to-ready scale.

TRENDS IN THE USE OF CONVENIENCE FOODS

Most observers agree that there is a recognizable trend indicating an often dramatic increase in the number of convenience foods being utilized. Marvin Thorner reported in the *Cornell Hotel and Restaurant Administration Quarterly* that, by the late 1960's, more than half of all food establishments in the United States were using convenience food products. If this is true, then it would appear that now, almost ten years later, most operations use at least some types of convenience foods. It can also be noted that the use of convenience foods does not require a total commitment. Few operations make either complete or no use of convenience foods; most make individual decisions about specific food items based on their own unique needs.

The adoption of convenience foods is spurred by advantages that are perceived in their use, a topic discussed later in this chapter. The present rate of use reflects a long history that began when earliest man first started eating and then preparing natural foods. Methods of processing and preserving foods gained sophistication over the years. The modern age of convenience foods began in the 1920's. While fruits and vegetables were frozen with limited success, frozen orange juice concentrates gained acceptance during the 1940's, and frozen french fries and complete meals ("TV dinners") gained popularity in the 1950's and into the 1960's. It was the later developments that demonstrated the immense possibilities for using convenience foods in commercial and institutional establishments.

Today there are more than 2,500 nationally distributed convenience food items available according to M. Finn (1975). This list, of course, continues to grow, and the food purchaser must stay abreast of the wide variety of items available in every conceivable category and within every reasonable price range.

Thorner has divided the seemingly endless number of convenience food items into product categories and provided examples of items within each category. A sample of foods within each category follows.

Appetizers, snacks, and hors d'oeuvres: juices, fruit cocktail, patés, egg rolls, stuffed cabbage, cheese puffs.

Soups: chowders, bisques, purées, minestrone, vegetable, chicken, cream of potato, green pea with ham, wonton.

Entrées: seafood, beef, poultry products, lamb, pork, pasta, casseroles, meat pies.

Specialty entrées: nationality foods such as beef Stroganoff, ravioli, cacciatore, lasagna, tortillas, tamales, chow mein, chicken Kiev, chicken Polynesian, sauerbraten, beef Burgundy.

Vegetables: potato dishes, onions, rice

dishes, spinach soufflé, varieties of vegetables.

Salads: fish, meat, tossed, fruit.

Bread and rolls: French toast, muffins, breads, rolls.

Desserts: puddings, fritters, cakes, pies.

Nonalcoholic beverages: iced tea (dispenser), soft drinks and juices (postmix dispensers), coffee (freeze-dried).

This list can only suggest the wide variety of convenience food items currently available.

One aspect of food service operations has always separated that industry from other businesses. The manufacture and sale of food service products have been confined to one site while most other businesses manufacture their product in one location and sell it in another (for example, clothing may be made by a garment manufacturer on the East Coast or the West Coast or even in another country and sold elsewhere). As the use of convenience foods becomes more widespread, the food service industry will also find itself purchasing food items made elsewhere. This permits the food service establishment to concentrate on serving and selling, rather than on manufacturing, food products.

FACTORS AFFECTING "MAKE OR BUY" DECISIONS

There are two types of make or buy decisions. If a food service system is to make total use of convenience foods, this affects the design of a new facility or leads to the remodeling of an existing one. On the other hand, convenience foods can be adopted on an item-by-item basis. There are some elements common to both approaches.

Price and Quality

Value is, according to Lendal Kotschevar and others, a function of price and quality. Value analysis suggests that value increases as price, relative to quality, decreases; value decreases as price, relative to quality, increases. These two factors—quality and price—are of the utmost importance in make or buy decisions. Quality in this sense is a subjective judgment by the food service manager as to how well the taste, appearance, consistency, or other aspects of a product meets the standards set for that product by the operation (the standard may be how well the operation itself can prepare the item).

Quality also reflects the food service manager's perception of the extent to which the customer will accept a product. If quality is not judged acceptable, a product *will not* be purchased regardless of price. If quality is acceptable, the product *may* be purchased if the price can be justified, or the product *will* be purchased if it cannot be prepared on-site. Quality and price cannot be separated when the decision to purchase convenience foods is made.

The price-quality difference between convenience foods and items prepared on-site was the basis for considerable early debate. There were allegations (perhaps accurate in many instances) of poor quality at a high price when convenience foods were being considered. Lack of precedent, defense of the status quo, fear for job or professional status, lack of proper equipment and other factors also affected the make or buy decision during the 1960's and early 1970's. A number of these same factors may remain important considerations today.

It is unfortunate that many food service operators do not make a careful, objective analysis of either quality or price when considering whether to make or buy. It is true that such an analysis can be complicated and time consuming. And, especially in large operations, this may constitute a further justification for establishing a separate purchasing department wherein a purchasing specialist might conduct a thorough analysis important in making the wisest decision. It is also true that, even in small operations, some objective study is critical to the decision-making process.

Quality analysis can require the use of taste panels. Specifications that suit the operation must be developed. Eligible suppliers must be selected. Proper receiving, storing, and issuing practices must be followed. The best preparation and service techniques must be determined. These responsibilities are of equal importance whether the food purchased is in convenience or more traditional form.

Price analysis, presuming equal quality, constitutes an attempt to identify and assess all costs relating to the use of on-site, prepared items and to compare that cost to the cost of using convenience food items. (This topic is discussed in a later section of this chapter.)

In addition to the obvious factors of price and quality, there are other factors involved in the make or buy decision. Each food service operation, being unique, will have specific concerns integral to its operation. Management experience is probably the best key to understanding these unique features, and the relationship between management and the purchasing department, if they are not the same, is an important one.

Acceptability

Some restaurant operators fear (and their fears are sometimes borne out) that customers will disapprove when they discover that entrees and other menu items were prepared off the premises. This disapproval stems, in part, from attitudes developed in the early days of convenience foods when quality was often low or inconsistent. There is also anxiety on the part of many operators that customers will discover that convenience foods are being used.

Actually a dichotomy appears to exist. What is widely acceptable in fast food or low-check average family, table service operations is frowned upon by customers in higher-check average gourmet table service restaurants. Operators must know their market and understand when convenience foods will be judged acceptable. Food service personnel are not generally anxious to educate their customers as to the quality available in convenience products. They must, therefore, utilize such products when it is assumed that they will be acceptable to the customer.

This problem is aggravated by requirements of the Federal Trade Commission and state and local governmental agencies relating to advertising. The spirit and intent of these regulations are that the customer should know exactly what he is buying so that he can make an informed choice between alternatives. Closely aligned to this need is recent legislation in some areas of the country where there is concern for "truth in menus." If a menu indicates that toasted cheese sandwiches, for example, are available, then processed cheese food products cannot be used; nor can ice cream be ice milk. These are just two of many possible examples. Some areas have even considered legislation requiring that menus indicate where items offered for sale have been prepared. This need to inform the public is another important consideration when one is deciding whether to make a food item or buy a convenience food alternate.

Other Considerations

Certainly the above concerns are common in any establishment. Other considerations peculiar to each establishment include: equipment, the number and availability of qualified personnel, time available for preparation, size and type of available packaging of convenience food products, consistent availability and quality of product, versatility in use, and the reputation of the supplier. The following questions should be asked by those who purchase food in order that they might be more discerning in their selection of convenience products:

Is specialized equipment needed to prepare or serve on-site, or must equipment be purchased?

If equipment is to be purchased, is there space for it?

Is skilled labor available for on-site preparation?

Is food service management aware of all operational changes required if convenience food items are to be incorporated into the menu?

Which type of packaging is best suited to the needs of the establishment? (For example, beef stew can be purchased in a "boil-in-the-bag" form. It can be canned or frozen in containers that vary in size.)

Is a food item easy to serve?

Do changes in preparation or service (such as batch cooking or cooking to order) create problems in inadequately designed production-serving areas?

Are the food items, in amounts needed by the operation, consistently available?

Is the product consistent in quality, or does quality vary in each shipment?

Are the suppliers who handle the product reputable?

Can the product be varied, given available personnel skills, to make it distinctive from the same product used by a competitor?

All factors involved in the make or buy decision are important. The task is difficult when menu items are considered separately. The task is monumental when decisions involve the initial design and construction of an establishment that is or is not to be "total convenience."

ADVANTAGES AND DISADVANTAGES IN USING CONVENIENCE FOODS

The trend toward increased use of convenience foods within the food service industry must be an indication that food service operators are finding convenience foods more acceptable, but a complete discussion of this topic is difficult because food service operations vary. No listing of advantages or disadvantages can apply to all operations. In addition, there have been continuous improvements in product, distribution, and processing procedures that serve to reduce perceived disadvantages. The following represents an attempt, in spite of the difficulty, to list some possible advantages and disadvantages. Many of these have been enumerated by Thorner.

Advantages

It is appropriate to begin with the advantages that might accrue to management from the use of convenience foods. For one thing, more attention can be devoted to the merchandising and serving of menu items rather than to preparation of the products. Also, equipment malfunction and supply problems are less likely to occur or, if they do occur, they are often easier to resolve.

In terms of purchasing, the computation

of food costs and the keeping of records are simpler since there is not the same need for high levels of raw material purchase, alertness in receiving, extensive inventory and complicated preparation. Reliable suppliers—often fewer are needed—and manufacturers' representatives may assist with problems stemming from the initiation or daily operation of a convenience product or system. Purchasing can be done in quantities and assortments that meet the needs of an operation, and packaging requests can be meshed into the general operation. Waste as a result of shrinkage, spoilage, pilferage, careless handling, or theft can be more carefully controlled. And, if nutritional information is needed, it is available on the label.

Less production space is needed when an efficient work system design is incorporated into the facility. This is especially true for a new facility that is planned around the use of convenience foods. Production needs during the peaks and valleys of meal service can be scheduled more accurately, and menus can be varied without a corresponding increase in planning and production effort. The ability to prepare food in batches can reduce or eliminate overproduction, and there is more control over portion sizes.

The time lag between production and service of a food item also decreases, and this improves the quality of the item being served. Proper processing, distribution, storage, and reconstitution of a convenience food item may be less detrimental than on-site preparation followed by hours of holding at a high temperature level. The quality of a convenience product is more likely to remain consistent from day to day and from cook to cook, and some larger operations can develop their own standards of quality for convenience products.

Production personnel need not have high skill levels (purchased by management at a high wage or salary level) if convenience products are used and the gross number of labor hours needed for production decreases. Working conditions on-site improve, with fewer odors, lower humidity, and cooler temperatures emanating from production equipment.

The food service operator is always concerned about sanitation in food production and service. The number of sanitation and cleaning tasks in the care of facilities and of large and small equipment is reduced. With the production process (or much of it) eliminated, there could be less danger of food-borne illness. Food service personnel must still be concerned about and follow all proper food-handling procedures when convenience foods are used, but there is some assurance that convenience food products entering the facility will be wholesome and not contaminated. It has been pointed out by Karla Longree that, with proper handling and care of precooked, frozen food items, the quality component involving high sanitation levels can be met.

Disadvantages

Careful analysis and adequate planning are critical before introducing a convenience food item. This takes time, and frequently the assistance available to management is limited. Certainly the purchase of new equipment or the remodeling of facilities may require increased capital. That equipment is often complicated and requires highly skilled personnel to repair malfunctioning units, and, even then, the machinery often does not work smoothly at first. For these and other reasons implementation of a new convenience food item or system does not always produce an immediate increase in business or profits. One additional threat is strikes by employees of manufacturers and shippers. Obviously the convenience system cannot be as closely controlled as is possible within a single establishment.

There are also some disadvantages in the purchasing area. There is no effective standardization of product quality or size and type of packaging between products offered by competing manufacturers. Comparing the merits of, for example, a beef stew or a poultry casserole item being offered by two different manufacturers is difficult. The availability of so many convenience items can also be confusing and result in inadequate or incorrect merchandising and sales programs. Certainly there is reliance on specific manufacturers and suppliers for quality, and consistent, reliable product distribution may be limited in some instances to metropolitan areas. As a general rule, the overstocking of convenience foods because of "special buys" is not economically justifiable.

Disadvantages in the production area relate, first, to customer dissatisfaction. Quality must be maintained or the reputation of the establishment suffers. Improper handling or processing of a convenience product, on or off the premises, can affect quality, and instructions accompanying a product may be inadequate or not carefully followed. Although the people preparing the product may not need to be as highly skilled, they must be creative in their approach so that the convenience product becomes more acceptable to the customer.

Convenience systems, are often implemented with improperly or inadequately trained management, production, and serving personnel. This situation is not improved when employees see convenience foods as a threat to job security, as limit-ing creative ability, or as "cheating" the customer. In order to reassure them, union contracts or other personnel agreements may prohibit the termination of employees or any reduction in employee hours worked because of the increased use of convenience foods. Such documents may be specifically worded to prohibit the closing of any preparation department or prohibit the use of any convenience foods unless the facility operates as a "totally convenience" operation.

IMPLICATIONS OF THE USE OF CONVENIENCE FOODS

Careful analysis of all factors involved in the potential use of convenience foods is important as make or buy purchasing decisions are made. Many of these factors, as well as possible advantages and disadvantages to the use of convenience foods have been noted, but there are several additional matters that should be considered if convenience programs are to be implemented in existing food operations.

Employee training in the proper procedures for handling convenience items is critical to the success of any implementation program, and training should begin with a defense and justification of operational changes in order to counter any existing prejudice against their use. Apprehension about job security must also be relieved. Training must be thoroughly planned and involve everyone from top management through storeroom personnel. It might be wise to experiment with different handling techniques before procedures are standardized. As was noted earlier, some existing equipment may need to be replaced by items specifically designed for heating and reconstituting convenience foods. It is often tempting to try to make do with available equipment, but it should be recognized that this could compromise the quality of the finished product. Existing operational procedures may need to be changed as convenience foods are used. These changes affect far more than work flow and employee scheduling in the production area. Purchasing systems, receiving methods, storage facilities and practices, record-keeping, and other activities are affected, and change in these areas must also be accommodated. It must by now be obvious that there is a great need for commitment to convenience foods as expressed by an allocation of sufficient time and monies to the implementation or conversion task.

One additional point to be considered is the time saved by using convenience foods. Exhibit 13-2 indicates the general impact on prime costs (food and direct labor) of traditional and convenience food systems. The exhibit suggests that, if convenience foods are used, a food service operator can generally expect a higher food cost than if nonconvenience food items are prepared on-site. This seems reasonable since processing and other costs incurred by the manufacturer are passed on to the buyer. These charges are not usually present when raw products are purchased.

On the other hand, the food service operator can generally expect lower labor costs when convenience foods are used than when nonconvenience food items are utilized. This also appears logical since at least some processing was done prior to purchase and does not need to be repeated on-site. It is this labor cost reduction that, in many instances, encourages the purchaser to choose the convenience product.

Even a cursory review of Exhibit 13-2 should suggest that any analysis of prime costs must be carefully undertaken in order to determine whether total prime costs (food and labor) are higher or lower when a convenience alternate (either an item or an entire system) is proposed. This discussion of prime cost analysis presumes equal quality in the convenience and nonconvenience food item being considered. This discussion likewise excludes the very necessary analysis of financial and other factors unrelated to prime cost discussed earlier in this chapter.

But, in the opinion of Michael Coffman, many food service operators in different establishments find themselves comparing food, labor, and other expenditures without considering operational differences that contribute to variable costs. Thus, to find that a neighboring establishment is working on a higher or lower food cost percentage is not usable information in itself. There may be easily explainable reasons for differences. Certainly an establishment utilizing convenience foods can expect to operate on a higher food cost percentage than one making less use of convenience foods. One must then look further, determining costs for other categories in order to assess the true fiscal status of an operation. For example, the operation with a higher food cost percentage may well have a much lower labor cost percentage than the neighboring establishments, which has the net effect of lowering the total prime cost.

"Paper" savings in labor costs when convenience foods are used are meaningless unless the actual number of dollars spent for labor decreases. If the amount spent for labor does not decrease and if food costs increase, the food service operation will find itself in an unsatisfactory financial position. The question then becomes: What do we do with the labor hours saved through the use of convenience foods? (This same question applies when labor-saving equipment is being con-

Cost category	When convenience foods are used	When convenience foods are not used
Food cost Labor cost	Will be higher Will be lower	Will be lower Will be higher

Exhibit 13-2. Fiscal implications of convenience foods use on prime costs

sidered for purchase.) Ideally, hours can be reduced through employee attrition, but, if this is not feasible, then other alternatives must be carefully reviewed and decisions made prior to the implementation of a convenience foods program.

Potential problems in employee scheduling must also be considered and resolved during the make or buy decision-making process. For example, if a convenience food item is used on some days but not on others, can employee schedules reflect this vacillation in need for man-hours? Perhaps cleaning, training, or other activities can be scheduled for days when it is necessary to utilize man-hours saved. There are other ways to redirect and reschedule employee hours in order to accommodate the changes that come as a result of using convenience foods, but these must be planned for by management if available labor is to be used most efficiently.

The implications that the use of convenience foods have for the entire fiscal and operational structure of the food service operation are great. Time must, therefore, be spent in planning, employee training, supervision, and operational monitoring if there is to be a successful transition to the use of convenience foods.

COST ANALYSIS IN A MAKE OR BUY DECISION

Assuming that the quality of food items prepared on-site and those purchased in convenience form is equal or at least ac- ceptable, cost differences must be considered. The typical food service operator probably does not have the time, the ability, or access to complicated measuring equipment required to conduct sophisticated tests of time, energy, and other factors to be considered when the usefulness of convenience products is analyzed. It is possible, however, to conduct a reasonable study and analysis of major cost differences between alternate purchase forms of menu items. It is also possible to consider, even if only subjectively, many other factors before substituting a convenience food item for one prepared on-site. The following examples show how this analysis can be done.

Example 1

A small restaurant prepares 12 pecan pies daily. It has sufficient equipment (ovens and mixer) to produce the pies since the equipment needed is multipurpose and is used for many other production tasks. The assistant cook who prepares this item is scheduled to retire, and the decision has already been made to purchase several other bakeshop items needed. It is necessary to decide whether to continue on-site preparation of the pies. What are the prime cost implications of preparing and buying pecan pies (assuming that an item of equivalent quality is available)?

First, calculate the standard food cost from the standardized recipe that is (or at least should be) used in preparing the pecan pies. Labor time can be determined from personal observation, interviews with production personnel, time-motion study, or, perhaps, a combination of these procedures. The results of such an analysis appear in Exhibit 13-3.

The time necessary to portion slices, plate, perhaps heat, serve, wash plates, or other activity is the same regardless of whether the pie is purchased or prepared on-site. There are other costs that have not been considered. Utility charges apply for on-site preparation, and the cost of disposing of pie tins must be considered for the prepared product. The large cost differential, however, indicates that there may be an economic advantage to the continued on-site production of the pecan pies. Other noneconomic factors to consider in this make or buy decision were examined earlier in this chapter.

Example 2

The same food service operator was informed by a friend at a restaurant convention that money could be saved by purchasing a canned spaghetti sauce and modifying it on-site with additional spices and seasonings. Since there always seemed to be production bottlenecks on days when spaghetti sauce was being prepared, the alternative certainly seemed worth considering. The analysis that appears in Exhibit 13-4 would be appropriate in this instance.

The cleaning time for the work area and the equipment for either alternative would be similar. Utility costs may be higher for the on-site item since the range oven or steam kettle will be used for a longer period of time. Time for preparing spaghetti and portioning costs would be the same. Since the cost of the convenience item is less and the quality is acceptable and since use would, with operational changes, help to eliminate production bottlenecks, it might be wise, after evaluating all other factors,

to buy the convenience item. However, unless scheduling results in an actual reduction in employee time spent in production, these are "paper" savings, as noted earlier, which do not, in themselves, reduce labor cost. In this case, the expense involved in utilizing the convenience item may be acceptable even without a subsequent reduction in employee time because of the elimination of the bottleneck in work procedures.

THE SUPPLIER'S PERSPECTIVE

The advantages and disadvantages of using convenience foods have thus far been seen from the viewpoint of the food purchaser. The suppliers who sell the products also have interesting viewpoints. Suppliers who offer full-line service (different market forms of many different products) have noted a trend toward significant increases in convenience food sales. Growth rates of 300 percent or more in convenience food sales within a period of several years are not uncommon. Many suppliers suggest that more convenience products are used in institutional food service operations than in their commercial counterparts.

Suppliers often hear the following four reasons why an operator decides to adopt a convenience item:

1. Convenience foods are frequently used as the basis for preparing meals for employees of the food service operation.
2. Convenience foods are more consistent in quality than the corresponding product prepared on-site.
3. There is less waste than with on-site preparation.
4. Convenience foods can be used to reduce labor costs.

The primary disadvantage of conve-

Cost	Make pie		Buy pie	
	Time (minutes)	Money (dollars)	Time (minutes)	Money (dollars)
Standard food cost		2.11		2.95
Production				
Prepare dough	15			
Roll out 12 shells	11			
Prepare filling	8			
Portion pies	4			
In/out oven	2			
Check-in process	1			
Clean equipment, work station	5			
Wash pie pans	4			
Total	50			
Labor (per pie)*		0.23		0.00
TOTAL (per pie)		2.34		2.95

*The bakery employee is paid $2.90 per hour, plus an additional 10 percent fringe benefit ($2.90 + $0.29 = $3.19). Thus, the labor cost for preparing 12 pies is 50/60 × $3.19 = approximately $2.66. For one pie, then, the cost is $2.66 ÷ 12 = $0.23.

Exhibit 13-3. Example of a cost analysis to determine whether to make or buy twelve pecan pies

nience foods, from the viewpoint of the supplier, is that many food purchasers complain about quality. During the early years of fast growth, many convenience foods were of inferior quality. As these items entered the marketplace, food purchasers experimented, found the products inferior, and returned to the use of nonconvenience foods. Attitudes formed then still remain with purchasers today, even though there have been many improvements. Larger, nationally known, reputable companies that started slowly in terms of convenience foods now, in many instances, dominate the field. Products produced by these companies are of higher quality, and, as use increases, suppliers believe that there will be fewer complaints.

Cost	Make sauce		Buy sauce	
	Time (minutes)	Money (dollars)	Time (minutes)	Money (dollars)
Standard food cost (36 cups or approximately 3 #10 cans)		$ 9.85		$11.15
Additional seasonings		0.00		0.29
Estimated total		$ 9.85		$11.44
Production				
Clean, weigh, chop, saute vegetables)	40			
Add canned tomato sauce, other ingredients, stir, season to taste	15			
Measure or weigh and add seasonings, stir			10	
Total	55		10	
Labor*		2.78		.51
TOTAL		$12.63		$11.95

*The assistant cook is paid $2.75 per hour with an additional 10 percent in fringe benefits ($2.75 + $0.28 = $3.03). Thus, with on-site preparation labor, the cost is 55/60 x $3.03 = approximately $2.78. Labor for the convenience food product raises the cost 10/60 × $3.03 = $0.51. The preparation labor when the convenience food item is used is, then, $0.51.

Exhibit 13-4. Example of a cost analysis to determine whether to make spaghetti sauce or to buy and modify a prepared product

Although suppliers readily agree that the quality of the convenience product has not always been satisfactory, they also point out that longtime users of convenience products are generally pleased, with few subsequent problems reported to the supplier. This suggests that there is frequently an awkward period between the time a convenience food is tried for the first time and the time it is accepted for use. Such periods are trying for both the operator and the supplier. Suppliers share the feeling that growth in the use of convenience foods will continue, primarily because product quality will improve through advances in technology. As for handling convenience products, suppliers find it easier. Perishability and sanitation concerns are lessened, and shelf life is increased. Most suppliers work hard to overcome the suspicions of food purchasers and encourage the use of high-quality convenience products.

THE BUYER'S PERSPECTIVE

The Product

Considering convenience foods from the perspective of the food purchaser has prompted most of the comments in this chapter so far. The purchaser must recognize that acceptability varies according to the type of operation. Also, because quality levels may be different, the purchaser must make comparisons and choose reliable suppliers if he is to obtain a high-quality product that can overcome any subsequent customer resistance. Even if there is little chance or desire to convert an entire operation to the use of a convenience system, it is possible to defend the purchase and use of many individual convenience items in terms of consistent quality, lower labor costs, lower capital costs, and ease of operation.

Equipment

One benefit that comes from the use of convenience foods is that such products require less equipment for reheating or reconstituting than would be required for more traditional processing. This seems logical since some (or all) of the food preparation task is performed off-site, but it is also true that convenience foods often require more specialized equipment for highest quality presentation of the item to the customer. Many properties must, however, use older, more traditional equipment to prepare convenience foods, at least until the use of these items increases enough to justify purchase of new equipment.

There are three major concerns when purchasing specialized equipment:

1. Some equipment may need to be purchased (if not already available) as a convenience foods program is implemented.
2. Equipment models constantly change or improve. Newer items have many options or features not available on older models.
3. The wide variety of equipment available makes selection difficult.

The criteria used to select equipment used in the processing of convenience foods does not differ greatly from criteria used in the purchase of most other food service equipment. These criteria have been identified by Kotschevar and Margaret Terrell as:

Need (Will the addition of an equipment item help to improve the quality, increase the quantity, or reduce time for or cost of the operation being performed?)

Cost (Can the equipment be cost justified not only in terms of initial purchase expense, but also in terms of subsequent installation, repair and maintenance, operating, and other charges?)

Performance (Does the equipment perform adequately, from the purchaser's perspective, the job it is supposed to do?)

Satisfaction of need (Does the equipment have the proper capacity and operational ability to fill present and future needs?)

Safety and sanitation (Is the equipment safe to use and easy to clean? Does it have the approval of recognized agencies such as Underwriter's Laboratories [electrical] and the National Sanitation Foundation [cleanliness]?)

Appearance and design (Does the equipment fit into the operation, and does its design provide for simple operation, maximum space utilization, and other needs?)

General utility value (Are mobility, size, quietness of operation, or some other factor matters of concern?)

With these criteria in mind, one can consider equipment items as they relate to convenience foods systems.

Refrigeration. Preparation facilities planned years ago generally provide for considerably more refrigerated storage (32° to 40°F.) than for frozen (−10° to 0°F.) storage. With the dramatic increase in the use of convenience foods (especially frozen food items) this relationship has changed. Newly designed operations frequently contain more frozen than refrigerated storage space. Walk-in refrigerated and frozen units have proved more useful for bulk or central storage. Upright, under the counter, reach-in, and pass- or roll-through units can often be justified in work and serving centers in terms of increased employee productivity and efficiency.

Several types of "thawing" units are also available for fast, sanitary thawing of frozen foods. These units are designed for automatic thawing of frozen foods and subsequent holding at a proper, preset temperature. There are units that can also be programmed to cook, bake, or otherwise heat for service the items being held. It is known that proper storage and thawing of frozen foods are important to protect the quality of the frozen product. Odd tastes, poor texture, shrinkage, discoloration, and spoilage can frequently be traced to improper storage and thawing. It is important to follow closely instructions provided by the supplier for the storage and processing of convenience items, and this might require specialized storage, heating, or serving equipment.

Heating. Many convenience items must also be heated prior to service. Often traditional bake or roast deck ovens, rotary ovens, or range ovens already on the premises must be used as convenience food programs are being implemented. It should be recognized, however, that several new and improved types of equipment are available:

Convection ovens. These units utilize one or more fans inside the oven cavity to circulate heated air through the oven chamber. It is the convection current created that gives rise to the name. This oven enables the operator to prepare items at a lower temperature and in a shorter period of time than is possible with a conventional oven. These features, along with compact size, enable more efficient utilization of space. (A stacked convection oven [two units] can hold approximately twenty-two 18" x 26" pans of hamburger patties, cookies, or some other item, using less floor space than a single-tier conventional oven holding just two such pans would require.) Convection ovens lend themselves to fast reheating of rather large quantities of convenience food products, and the sale of these ovens is increasing. In fact, traditional ovens are not being placed in many facilities being constructed or re-modeled today.

Microwave ovens. These ovens make use of short radio waves (hence, the name microwave) produced by magnetron tube(s) in the oven unit. Molecules in foods placed in the oven absorb this energy, and it is the friction generated by the fast-moving molecules within the food that produces heat. The molecular movement occurs deep within the food item at the same time that the surface is being heated. This greatly shortens the required cooking time. These ovens can heat on an order-by-order basis or in somewhat greater bulk items for subsequent service. The advantages have been listed by Julie Wilkinson as:

1. ability to heat small amounts of food quickly,
2. capacity to complement existing equipment,
3. fast thawing of frozen items,
4. fast cooking, and
5. reduction in labor costs because there is less food handling.

There are disadvantages to the use of micro-wave units. For example, bulk preparation of large amounts of food is not generally possible; some items, such as breaded products, do not lend themselves to micro-wave cookery; position, size, shape, con-sistency of thaw, and weight of items to be cooked must be considered to ensure con-sistent quality in the product being cooked (heated); browning is impossible without a special attachment.

The advantages, however, frequently outweigh the disadvantages. It has been estimated by Thorner that, by the end of the 1970's, 80 percent of all food service operations will be making some use of microwave heating units. With personnel trained to utilize equipment correctly, entire systems can eventually be designed around microwave ovens. With the in-creased use of convenience foods, it seems

likely that there will be a corresponding increase in the use of microwave ovens for the heating of those foods.

Infrared (quartz) ovens. These ovens were originally designed to reconstitute bulk-pack frozen foods, but they are also used to heat, roast, and brown. They are much faster than convection ovens, but do not heat as quickly as microwave ones. They have the advantages of both types since they brown and can satisfy quantity needs. A quartz plate at the top of the oven diffuses infrared rays around the ambient area. This provides uniform heat transfer. The ovens are useful for broiling and are particularly good for finishing dishes that may have been heated in a microwave oven and are then browned and crisped in the quartz oven (in much the same fashion as occurred with the more traditional "sal-amander" or back-shelf broiler units). This piece of equipment comes close to being perfect for cooking to order in a large-volume operation.

Re-Con ovens. These ovens can be used to reconstitute frozen, prepared entrees, or they can be used as high-speed, conven-tional ovens that, because of the tempera-ture range, can broil or roast as needed. Because of their flexibility and because they are offered in various sizes (from a small unit that produces forty portions to one that can yield six hundred breasts of chicken at one time), this piece of equipment has been well received and is gaining wide use by institutions, airlines, catering opera-tions, and hotels and restaurants.

Steam equipment. Self-contained steam equipment units are in frequent use today since efficient, centrally located sources of live, clean steam are not always avail-able. Self-contained units are usually cleaner, less expensive to operate, energy saving, and faster than direct hookup counterparts. Local ordinances may re-quire that a licensed engineer be on the premises whenever high-pressure steamers are used, but these ordinances can usually be bypassed if self-contained units are employed.

High steam pressure means more efficient and faster cooking, with less nutrient loss. Several different types of steam cooking equipment are available that make it possible to do both basic cooking and reheating of convenience foods. There are stationary or tilting models that range in size from several quarts to many gallons. Traditional compartment steamers are of a low-pressure type (approximately five pounds of pressure per square inch). They range in size from one to four compartments (each of which can be separately controlled and will hold several steam table pans) and can be used for the heating of canned and frozen vegetables and many other convenience items. A faster-operating model (called a high-pressure steamer since it operates at approximately fifteen pounds of pressure per square inch) is also available. It is frequently smaller than low-pressure units and cooks much faster, thereby lending itself to small batch or "to order" cooking requirements. Small counter top units, which generate steam in a spray and can be used for single-order purposes, are also available. These units can frequently be moved between work stations and are utilized in many fast food operations for such purposes as melting cheese on hamburgers and warming buns. A recent innovation in terms of steam heating equipment is the convection steamer, which circulates steam around food products placed within the cooking compartment. It does not operate under pressure, and it is useful for cooking and heating many types of convenience food products.

Specialty Equipment. There are many specialty equipment items available for use in the processing of convenience foods. Examples include: spaghetti-handling equipment that cooks, washes, stores, and reheats spaghetti products; water-heating units developed to heat "boil in the pouch" items; hot dog and hamburger cookers; "computerized" deep fryers that automatically adjust to quantities and types of food items being fried (some have automatic lowering and lifting devices for fryer baskets).

Other Items. Depending upon the market form and the amount of preparation built into the convenience foods being purchased, many items of traditional equipment (steam kettles, tilting fry pans and grills, ovens) can and are used in the on-site processing of convenience food items. As volume of production-service increases, there are equipment items (even if of a single-purpose, specialty nature) available for use in the more efficient processing of convenience products.

THE FUTURE OF CONVENIENCE FOODS

After many years, during which the use of convenience foods by the food service industry has increased, there is still some debate about the worth of convenience items. This makes it even more difficult to look into the future and make predictions about the use of convenience foods. We do know that the American public is spending more money and eating more meals away from home. It has been estimated that, by the 1980's, 40 percent or more of all meals consumed by Americans will be eaten outside the home.

We also know that there is, and probably will continue to be, a proliferation in fast food, family-style, table service restaurants. That is the area where company-owned and franchised operations are most active. Since it is these types of operations that make the fullest use of convenience foods, and since, in terms of numbers of meals and dollars of sales, these operations are growing, this indicates a continued, even dramatic, increase in the use of convenience items.

Other operations (fast food hamburger, chicken, and similar counter-service types) are designed around the complete, or almost complete, use of convenience foods. This type of operation, which enables owners to invest less capital in equipment and space and to make use of unskilled workers, is actually growing quickly *because of* the availability and utilization of convenience foods.

The future may also see still greater variety in the types of convenience foods available. The most striking increase in variety may be seen in the area of more elaborate cuisine items. High-quality items such as beef Wellington, elegant canapes, and beef Stroganoff are already available. There will be more such items as procedures used in the processing of simple items are adapted to the more difficult ones.

The quality of convenience foods will improve still further in the future. New methods of reheating (probably accompanied by still newer equipment or, at least, further modifications in existing equipment) or for other processing tasks on-site will also be developed.

Some observers envision (perhaps still very far off in the future) credit cards being used to activate a keyboard from which one selects a complete meal, reserves a table, and is billed. Two or three employees (really technicians) would be needed to operate a computerized kitchen that automatically prepares food items for service. After dinner the table is automatically cleaned, sanitized, and reset.

Other observers, probably thinking of the more immediate future, do not see "kitchenless" facilities. They see food service operations in which facilities are modified, using new and different types of equipment, and management tasks are redesigned to allow for new methods of purchasing, receiving, storing, issuing, and, obviously, production-service.

Perhaps kitchens will be viewed as "assembly points," rather than the more traditional "processing units," again with the result that management emphasis can be placed on merchandising, selling, and service, rather than, as at present, needing to be split between these same duties and actual production.

The restaurateur who operated a facility twenty years ago but who has not been in a commercial kitchen since would probably be amazed at the equipment now being used and the many alternate market forms of food items available for purchase. It appears that the restaurateur of today who "leaves the scene" for twenty years would, should he return about the year 2000, be equally amazed. It is likely that there will still be gourmet, high-check, average operations still preparing a large percentage of their food items on-site. There will not, however, be the growth in this segment of the food service industry to compare with that in fast food, lower-check, average properties making maximum (perhaps, in the near future, even total) use of convenience foods. This being the case, then, the percentage of food service dollars used to purchase convenience foods will increase dramatically, to the end that the vast majority of all dollars spent will be used to purchase convenience items. Convenience foods, then, it would appear, will be important in the future of the food service industry.

14 *The World's Food Supply: Today and Tomorrow*

The oil shortage shocked most middle-aged, middle-class Americans, but the total effect was probably somewhat less than it might have been because they were faced, at the same time, with other failures in their hitherto secure world. No longer were such sayings as "sound as the dollar" or discussions of "our great wheat surpluses" and "our world leadership in electronic technology" relevant.

As critical as the oil shortage was and potentially still is today, especially when it is properly linked with potential profit margins in the food service and lodging industry, that shortage seems to be more one of defining terms. The world has apparently fallen into a kind of marketing myopia wherein shortages of energy are confused with shortages of oil that were largely brought about when oil-producing nations first collectively joined forces in a successful bid for recognition as a world power through the world market. Taking into consideration all available options (including, by definition, all the sources under the sun), there are viable alternatives with which to solve energy needs. In the areas of food and the real existent and potential world shortages of it, however,

there is no comparably wide set of options. It is true that the same sun that is the ultimate source of all known energy can also potentially provide the energy for an almost unlimited increase in the world's food supply, but the other main components required for the growing of food—land and sea in which to grow it—are limited.

Mrak (1975) argues that there is a real link between the basic use of energy and the production of food energy:

> It may seem far removed from food production but the future of energy production in the United States does have a spin-off effect on food production. The great concern about nuclear plants—whether or not we will have them—off-shore oil, the use of coal for the production of electrical energy, strip mining, and so on, do have constraining reverberations clear down to the farm. These may not be direct constraints, but they certainly are indirect constraints.

If the thesis that we have possible answers to our basic needs holds true, then we do not have to worry much about the linkages between basic energy needs and food energy needs; the former will satisfy the needs of the latter by providing the energy needed to produce fertilizers and to plant, irrigate, cultivate, harvest, transport, process, prepare, and market food. It seems that it is the limitation of space—our main delimiting resource—to which attention should first be directed. When the task of allocating and husbanding this resource in the interests of assuring an adequate and continuing supply of food and energy is accomplished, the needs of the world will be met.

A limited discussion of the world's food supply is appropriate in any book concerned with food. It should interest the professional food purchaser because, according to the latest statistics, about 37 cents out of every food dollar in the United States is spent away from home, and this figure is estimated to be 50 cents by 1980. If these figures are accurate, the food service facilities of the United States have and will continue to have a tremendous influence on nutritional adequacy of American diets. It makes everyone who is in any way connected with the food service and lodging industry a "nutritionist" of sorts, with or without benefit of nutritional education and training. A second reason to be concerned about the world's potential food supply comes from the related fact that increasing numbers of people have all or most of their food intake mandated (those in educational facilities, industrial food programs, residences for the elderly, child care centers, among many others). Such a situation is largely due to social legislation. Those involved literally will become what they are as a direct result of the combination of available food supplies selected and prepared for them. As Leverton (1968) contends: "Food becomes you."

THE REASONS FOR FOOD SHORTAGES

First of all, shortages can be attributed to "shrinkage of land." In this section attention is devoted to the land situation in the United States. Remarks regarding the food resources of other countries mainly appear in the sections concerned with the future. In the forty-eight contiguous United States there are about 1.9 billion square miles of land and roughly 30.1 million square miles of water. These are fixed quantities, but the population is not fixed. When the pilgrims landed, the Indians had about 2,500 acres per person, but today we have, at best, only about 11 acres per person.

There are other reasons for this per capita decline besides the obvious fact that there are more people than there were in the seventeenth century. Urbanization, road building, and changes in eating habits (more real income shifts purchases from grains as the main source of energy toward meats, which take, on the average, seven to ten pounds of cereal to equal one pound of meat) are among them.

Storage is another reason for shortages. It is claimed that many people starve, not because of the lack of adequate levels of food, as because of the lack of adequate storage methods for foods that are potentially available. The United States has, for instance, shipped many tons of cereals and flour to other countries, but perhaps as little as half of it reaches the ultimate consumer. Much is lost through pilfering and political corruption and through damage from insects, rodents, rain, and mold. When the chairman of the Rockefeller Commission was on a tour of Latin America, the President of Nicaragua indicated the great need for information on how to store rice. Apparently their rice production had increased, but storage losses (insects, rodents, and mold) were so great that the increase was meaningless.

Distribution systems (or the lack of them) also affect shortages of food. The starvation rate in many emerging nations can, at least to some extent, be attributed to the failure to distribute available food properly rather than to food shortages as such. Official corruption, bureaucratic incompetence, hoarding, and black markets are often found in such situations.

There has already been an allusion to the part energy plays in present food shortages. Energy inputs vary from crop to crop, but it is fair to say that, the more mechanized a country becomes, the more energy supplied by manual labor is replaced by energy supplied by fuel. Energy shortages must surely, then, increase the cost of producing food, thereby perhaps cutting the supply. It must be remembered, however, that the original thesis is that energy needs can be met with changes in priorities.

One factor that contributes to optimum utilization of land for food production is the availability of adequate amounts of fertilizer. World production of fertilizers grew as much as 90 percent in some of the developing nations during the last decade, but total production still lags behind the need.

Environmental constraints are another influence. During the early 1970's the timber harvest in the West was hampered by laws requiring that environmental impact statements be presented and approved before any cutting could be done. This process has slowed the production of lumber and other wood products, and it has also raised prices in the construction industry. Both results tend to depress the supply of related products. Other kinds of governmental constraints have also had the same effect. The day may not be far off when the farmer may be required to do an environmental impact study before he can change from the production of corn to the production of tomatoes. The rationale might be that tomatoes encourage the development of fruit flies that, in turn,

could invade homes in the surrounding areas. This line of thought, although it does not explain what has caused shortages in the past, is a logical extension of the kind of constraints that have influenced the availability of goods. In this category we might also list the Food and Drug Administration's monitoring of pesticides and strains of faster-growing plants and the impact of the Occupational Health and Safety Act of 1970, which stipulates that the safety of the farm worker must be the responsibility of the farmer himself. Regulatory provisions have, indeed, been made to protect the health and welfare of mankind. At the same time it must be recognized that such constraints place an additional burden on the productive potential of limited land and sea resources.

The economics of agriculture and the financing of farm products have also served to limit production and thereby contribute to shortages. The end result of all the factors mentioned has been to raise the price of each calorie of food energy delivered both here and abroad. Balance of trade deficits during the last decade have served to deflate the value of currency to the point where imports of products needed to accelerate food production have become prohibitive in price. All developed nations have felt this price squeeze, while the emerging nations seeking loans and other methods of financing in their search for more modern production methods find it even harder to borrow money. Several South American countries, for instance, are in the beef production business, but are short on per capita consumption of protein. They are unhappy that the United States does not import more of their beef so that they can acquire the money needed to add to their overall purchasing power. Although the United States may not be importing much beef currently, it does, on the other hand, import almost all of the world's production of canned tuna, usually from countries that could use the tuna, but feel that they need the money more.

Weather has also been a consideration. Experts might say that the weather that we have experienced during the last few years is, on balance, no better or worse than it has ever been. Whatever the facts may be, the combination of longer winters, floods, and off-season rains in the major food-producing regions of the United States and Canada have greatly restricted food production.

Food habits and cultures have played a part. Eating habits change as more money becomes available in the food budget. Generally, the higher up the scale one goes in the food chain, the more inefficient is the food energy source. Then there is the matter of culture. Valid cases can be cited where potentially satisfying and nutritious foods have been rejected because of ethnic, religious, or other taboos. One case seems to make the point clearly. A fairly new variety of corn, known as "opaque," has not been received well in one area of South America where the consumption of protein is low. The new variety was introduced because it was relatively high in protein and because it was about the lowest-priced source of protein that genetic research had identified as compatible with the soil and other growing conditions in the area. The fact that it does not make up into a tortilla that tastes as good as less nutritious corn is the reason for its lack of acceptance.

Water, or lack of it, is a critical factor. About 320 billion gallons are used in the United States each day, approximately 35 percent of it for irrigation. Projected needs are for twice that amount well before the year 2000, and yet water tables in several areas of the country already are receding. At present, less than 4 percent of the total world rainfall is diverted for irrigation. The remaining water is limited by geographical distribution of river systems, and it can be made available only through vast engineering projects. Even if a fiscal commitment were made toward that end, any decisions would still require a full study of the environmental impact. Modern technological advances, great though they have been, are still far from taming the rampaging waters of the Missouri-Mississippi River Valley. And, at the same time, vast sums of money are being spent by conservation groups in efforts to stop flood-control projects in these and other areas. Then there is the pollution problem. Much available water is still being contaminated by industrial and other man-related wastes, as well as by pesticides used to increase food production.

One final area, the use or misuse of grazing lands, seems worth mentioning if for no other reason but to illustrate available options. Efforts now being made to control the wild animal population may have to be directed toward protecting those animals that can be used to supplement man's food supply or more carefully guarding domestic animals that now constitute man's food supply.

This is, admittedly, a simplistic view of the reasons for present food shortages. It should at least establish the fact, however, that there are shortages. Though this is a relatively new concern in the United States, it has been an ever-present specter in other areas of the world. Now it is important to consider the future.

THE IMMEDIATE FUTURE

The world population is increasing by about 219,000 persons each day. While the rate of increase in developed countries is down, that of developing countries averages about 2.5 percent—a record rate that seems, however, to be on a slight decline. Population growth continues, however, for a considerable time even after fertility has fallen to a level that would, in the long run, just assure population replacement, and a rapid decline in death rates has further accelerated the population rise in many parts of the world. If the more developed areas maintain fertility at or below replacement level and developing countries attain that level by the end of the century, the total population of the world might level off in seventy years at about 8 billion, more than 80 percent of it in presently developing countries.

Members of the world community must face one of two possibilities. Eventual attainment of an average rate of increase is inevitable. What is uncertain is the size of the total population when growth does cease and how the balance will be maintained: a high birthrate and with an average duration of life of less than thirty years, or a low birthrate with an average duration of life of seventy years or more. This is admittedly left-handed Malthusian theory, but the facts, as presented by such bodies as the World Health Organization (WHO), the Food and Agriculture Organization (FAO), the United Nations Children's Fund (UNICEF), the Protein Advisory Group, and the World Bank, all seem to come to the same fundamental conclusions.

In a few of the developing nations, often where there has been government support of family planning, there has been a decline in fertility. People's expectations had to undergo drastic change before such programs were accepted. Where the life expectancy of children is short, families tend to be larger. This reflects either a need or a desire to perpetuate society. Until people are convinced that large families are neither necessary nor to be desired, it is unlikely that the problems inherent in overpopulation will be resolved.

Any predictions concerning food supplies in the future must be tentative. Certainly the pattern established in 1972, of intermittent shortages of at least some foods for the next few seasons, has been set. Although the harvest of fish from the seas has been increased at a rate nearly twice that of world population growth in the last few decades, this has increased total protein intake from fish to only 6 percent, and there is danger of overfishing the oceans. The world fish harvest, which reached a peak of 70 million metric tons in 1970, has declined in three successive years for which accurate records have been available since 1970. Many marine biologists feel that the global catch of table-grade fish may have reached or even surpassed maximum sustainable limits. There is as yet no firm basis for these statements. Nor is it known how much pollution and other factors will affect the oceans and inland seas or how much can be done to change present conditions. Whether or not these assumptions prove accurate, the food buyer of the immediate future will not have the wide selection that has been available in the past few decades. Planning ahead will also be limited because fluctuation in supply leads to fluctuation in price. This example will certainly affect contract buying, as it did in the summer of 1973 when price controls were imposed upon foods. These were intended to keep the general rise in prices to an average of about 3 to 4 percent during the fall, winter, and spring of 1973-74. Many major contract food firms were able to renegotiate bids with at least the larger institutions around the nation, based on the projected rise. As fall and winter passed and the price constraints moved from phase to phase, prices soared. By spring, prices were about 8 to

12 percent above what they had been in the summer of 1973, and food service corporations ended the year with a huge loss. This has made them all wary of settling on a contracted price for a whole year, and the yearly increases that are negotiated are high enough to avoid the risk of disaster. The result of such situations, which can be directly attributed to food shortages, has been higher prices and lower consumer acceptance. The food service industry has suffered, and it appears that similar situations will continue to arise in the immediate future.

LONG-TERM PERSPECTIVE

Leaders in the areas of food and nutrition research and in other disciplines that have a stake in shaping the quality and quantity of the world's food supply in the future seem to point out three main areas of need. They are: to increase food production in the poorest, least developed countries, to devise a better system of world food security, and to improve the nutrition of the poorest and most vulnerable people in the world.

The crux of the food problem is that limited resources are unevenly distributed among burgeoning populations in a world divided by jealously guarded rights and boundaries. The problem is seen to have not only nutritional and agricultural significance; there are also demographic, financial, economic, social, psychological, and political ramifications. Only through collective planning and sharing of food and other resources and through the balancing of population and resources does definite progress appear likely.

The World Food Conference

On the basis of the assumptions and assessments outlined above, a World Food Conference was held in Rome, November 5-16, 1974. This conference brought together the 130-member governments of the United Nations, about 100 nongovernmental entities, and approximately 1,200 members of the press. A "Universal Declaration on the Eradication of Hunger" was produced. It states: "Every man, woman, and child has the inalienable right to be free from hunger and malnutrition in order to develop fully and maintain their physical and mental faculties."

The conference passed a number of resolutions. Taken as a whole, the resolutions, if followed by those bodies of the world community to which they were directed, probably comprise the best pattern for continued and lasting improvement in the world food picture. Several that dealt directly or indirectly with the subject at hand are outlined below:

Resolution 1, "Objectives and Strategies of Food Production," called on developing countries to plan and promote changes in rural socioeconomic structures in order to facilitate increases in food production. Developing countries and various international bodies were asked to assist in these goals.

Resolution 2, "Priorities for Agricultural and Rural Development," called for agrarian reforms and improvements to generate employment and integrated development. Such reforms included education, status of women, land tenure, and credit.

Resolution 3, "Fertilizers," called for immediate financial and material assistance to the thirty-two poorest and most seriously affected countries in order to improve the efficiency of existing fertilizer plants, to construct new plants in developing countries, and to establish storage and distributive facilities. The existing International Fertilizer Supply Scheme of the Food and Agricultural Organization (FAO) of the

United Nations was called upon to carry out this work, in addition to analyzing long-term supply and demand. All governments were urged to promote efficient use of fertilizers of all types and to reduce uses for noncritical purposes.

Resolution 4, "Food and Agricultural Research and Extension and Training," used "extension" in the sense of the extension services established in the United States under the Morrill Land Grant Act. The resolution called for programs to utilize more effectively all resources, especially water, soil, and plant and animal genetic materials. It also called for a substantial enlargement of the International Agricultural Research Consultative Group to include remote sensing and to obtain and use funds from national and international sources to further agricultural research, extension, and training in developing countries.

Resolution 5, "Policies and Programs to Improve Nutrition," had at its heart the goal of reducing world hunger and malnutrition, although these themes run throughout all conference documents. It recommended that each government formulate integrated food and nutrition plans and policies based on careful assessments of need. All United Nations agencies, including FAO, WHO, the World Bank, UNICEF, and the Protein Advisory Group were called on to propose, by mid-1975, a project to assist governments in developing food and nutritional plans for each member nation. This resolution seemed to be at the heart of possibilities for progress, as it suggested ways to ameliorate all of the complex, interlocking problems spelled out briefly herein. The resolution asked, specifically, that governments use national, binational, and international facilities to initiate and strengthen nutrition programs. They were to provide nutritional educa-

tion, strengthen health and family services, improve water supplies and environmental conditions, treat malnutrition, encourage breast feeding, improve the status of women, establish special feeding programs (especially for children and for pregnant and lactating women), maximize local food production, decrease nutrient deficiencies by fortification of staple foods, modernize food legislation, support the Codex Alimentarius Commission, encourage applied nutrition research, and cooperate with all nutrition-related activities. WHO was asked to undertake a global program to reduce the deficiencies of the fat-soluble Vitamins A and D, iodine, iron, folate, riboflavin, and thiamine. FAO was requested to inventory noncereal vegetable resources and to study the possibilities of increasing the production of those foods, as well as distribution and consumption. A joint FAO-WHO food contamination-monitoring program was recommended. The resolution also proposed an international nutrition surveillance system to monitor food and nutritional conditions, as well as an internationally coordinated nutritional research program.

Resolution 6, "World Soil Charter and Land Capability Assessment," recommended conservation and protective measures. It specifically asked FAO to establish a World Soil Charter to assure rational use of the world's limited land resources. All relevant United Nations organizations were invited to cooperate in assessing land resources that might be used to produce food.

Resolution 7, "Scientific Water Management: Irrigation, Drainage, and Flood Control," urged the World Meteorological Organization, FAO, and other groups to assess climate, water, irrigation potential, hydropower potential, energy requirements, and other facets of the subject.

Some of the problem areas that these bodies were asked to consider were brackish water and areas affected by water logging, salinity, and alkalinity. They were asked to identify and exploit ground water resources (flood control measures, drainage systems, and irrigation) and to develop better technology and delivery systems in all these areas.

Resolution 8, "Food and Women," urged that governments involve women in the decision making for food production and nutrition policies and that they promote equal rights and adequate access to medical and social services.

Resolution 9, "Achievement of a Desirable Balance between Population and Food Supply," called for support from governments and people everywhere to support "rational policies." The conference did not *directly* address itself to areas of population control, believing that it was beyond its direct field of inquiry. It did, however, make a strong plea for such measures.

Resolution 10, "Pesticides," spelled out the lack of these priority farm inputs as being the cause of enormous food losses. The resolution also listed recommendations aimed at reducing uses of pesticides for "noncritical" purposes and suggested research in the areas of soil fertilizers and plant growth.

Resolution 12, "Seed Industry Development," called for development of high-yield, disease-resistant varieties of food plants. It also asked for policy and legislation in the areas of production, processing, quality control, distribution, and education.

Resolution 13, "International Fund for Agricultural Development," called for an investment of $5 billion per year to aid developing countries. By terms of the resolution, this fund could only be estab-

lished after the Secretary-General of the United Nations determined that adequate funding would be provided on a continuing basis. Whether or not the fund were established, the conference proposed that a consultative group on food production and investment be charged with increasing, coordinating, and improving financial and technical assistance, bilateral and multilateral, to agricultural production in developing countries.

Resolution 14, "Reduction of Military Expenditures for Increasing Food Production," recommended that governments implement United Nations resolutions pertaining to the reduction of military expenditures and allocate more money both to finance food production in developing countries and to establish reserves for emergencies. As can be imagined, there was wide diversity of support among member nations.

Resolution 17, "International Undertaking on World Food Security," endorsed the objectives, policies, and guidelines of this body, which affirmed the common responsibility of the international community to provide food security. It saw a world network of national grain reserves coordinated through international consultations and exchanges of information. Needy countries were to be assisted in building up and maintaining stocks. The basis of the system was a global information and early warning system on food and agriculture, and the resolution calls for all governments to furnish information on crop forecasts, production, stocks on hand, and trading intentions.

Resolution 18, "An Improved Policy for Food Aid," called for a mutual annual goal of 10 million tons of grains, beginning in 1975, in addition to other foods. The World Food Program (WFP) was to be used as a channeling agency, and it was further asked to provide as many outright grants as possible. The resolution further recommended that gifts of cash, grain stocks, or both be earmarked for emergency use by the WFP in accord with guidelines that would supply food to the neediest and the most vulnerable as quickly as possible.

Resolution 19, "International Trade and Adjustment," called for all countries to expand and liberalize trade, especially to benefit developing nations. The United Nations Conference on Trade and Development was urged to make international commodity arrangements that would improve access to markets of developed countries by those now being developed.

Resolutions not summarized here were of a specific nature and not germane to this discussion, or they are no longer of interest because they have been superseded. Remarks made by Howard Cottam (1975) at the fifty-eighth Annual Meeting of the American Dietetics Association concern the conference:

Obstacles to Nutritional Adequacy

At the 57th Annual Meeting of the American Dietetic Association, I affirmed that "to strive toward an adequate diet for everyone everywhere seems to be a reasonable objective." My on-the-spot view of the World Food Conference did not change my viewpoint. But it dampened my hopes. The global political will to abolish hunger quickly was not evident.

Neither strong nor weak, rich nor poor, large nor small countries are willing adequately to relinquish enough sovereignty to permit a *bona fide* global food policy. Each understandably insists on sovereign control of its resources, its boundaries, its political-economic system, and its cultural practices, including population control. Each spends disproportionately on armaments while urging others to relax defense.

Developing countries demand recompense for prior colonial exploitation and a new economic order, yet sovereign rights are jealously guarded. Socialist countries attribute world hunger and the poverty which underlies it to decadent social systems. Yet the largest socialist states adamantly refuse to share basic information on food stocks to permit orderly global food security planning. Market-economy states depend on supply-demand forces with minimum regulation; they emphasize efficiency more than social goals.

Food-exporting countries, while willing to share food, insist that others share costs, especially because they pay dearly for petroleum and other "scarce" commodities. Oil-rich countries want to catch up on development and attain permanent security as their exhaustible oil reserves dwindle. They are unaccustomed to the role of donor.

The poorest countries, "most seriously affected" (M.S.A.) by scarcities, seem to realize that only they themselves can ultimately solve their food, population, and development problems. But, desperately, they need and seek help.

Without an agreed world food policy which supersedes parochial sovereignty, the interdependence which characterized the World Food Conference will remain more fancy than fact. Universally adequate nutrition may not be achievable in our lifetime.

The United States and World Food

Beyond the obvious areas of providing as much food as possible for others under the guidelines of the World Food Conference, the United States has the potential for a particularly vast input into the future of food in the world in the area of improved efficiency of agricultural production systems. Although the methods used in the past to implement advances in these areas are open to serious question, a rational rapprochement seems likely. Among future unique inputs into solving the food and nutritional problems of mankind will probably be research into areas concerned with promoting the genetic improvement of food crops and lessening the genetic vulnerability of crops and livestock. This includes the maintenance of genetic pools and genetic stocks. There will probably also be intensified research on nonleguminous nitrogen fixation, including the possible introduction of the enzyme nitrogenase in the interest of finding new avenues toward sufficient levels of protein adequacy in the world. Other areas where additional research is likely are: crop and livestock diseases, biological and chemical means of pest control, studies of climatic variations as they may affect food production, agricultural practices that would conserve and make optimal use of energy resources and natural resources, agriculture in cleared tropic forests, and improved methods of harvesting, transporting, storing, processing, and marketing.

The United States has no monopoly on attempts to carry out these plans, but it does have a stake in these areas because of past performance. If the efforts are to succeed, however, the entire developed world, through communications technology, research capacity, trained and public service-oriented experts, and financial resources, must expand its collaboration with the developing world.

The outlook for meeting overall food needs for the next few years appears manageable, provided there are no serious production setbacks in the principal food-producing regions. The outlook for subsequent decades is alarming unless real progress can be made in resolving the problems of overconsumption and undersupply.

The Responsibility of the Purchasing Agent

The majority of important decisions in a capitalistic economy are based primarily upon the premise that a business enterprise must be in a positive position to compete successfully in the money market for operating capital. Most modern textbooks still point out the continuing need for this type of competition as the only realistic approach to business health and viability, but there is a note of restraint that is based upon responsibility to the environment.

No longer can forests be indiscriminately raped of virgin fruits, with no thought of the long-term consequences, and the major lumber firms are the first to admit it, to do something about it, and to pass the resultant costs on to the buying public.

The restaurateur whose place of business was bypassed in the great freeway-building boom of the late 1950's and 1960's was probably one of the first in the hospitality business to question traditional premises regarding the allocation of basic resources. There should be no dichotomy between the capitalistic system and newer ideas (to the business community) of conservation and optimum utilization of resources. Indeed, if a buyer has one main thrust toward alleviating world hunger and guarding against malnutrition, it is in areas where the best buyers have traditionally excelled: setting specifications for specific uses, searching the market, ordering maximally, receiving intelligently, storing properly, and issuing in necessary and sufficient amounts the food entrusted to his care and stewardship. If those receiving foods from the United States had the expertise and facilities of the best food buyers at their disposal, the percentage of food sent and eventually issued to users might well approach 100 percent, rather than the 50 percent often reported as the norm.

Buyers must, further, be willing to support management and the concerted efforts of the entire industry in an active search for viable alternatives in the race between food and famine. This may mean developing new sets of specifications for presently unused forms of plant and animal life to be purchased and utilized in food service facilities. Certainly the buyer must be willing and ready to accept the responsibility of leadership in promoting the use of more forms of protein than are now customary in the United States and

Canada. The transition is already being made easier by a growing population of aware young people who are beginning to make their wants and needs felt in the business community. Menus for any food facility in high schools or colleges reflect, both in variety and in percentage of total consumption, the acceptance of vegetarian dishes and unusual foods.

These are not stumbling blocks in the pathway of the future food buyer. The fast-paced and far-reaching implications of the world food situation should present stimulating new challenges.

15 *Food as Commodities: Sources of Information*

The quality of a food-purchasing system reflects a lot, including the efficiency of the receiving room, the effectiveness of the managerial structure, and the care with which specifications are developed and used. Ultimately, however, the reputation of the professional food buyer is no better than the quality of the food purchased. And, when purchasing quality products, there is no substitute for knowledge. A knowledgeable buyer who knows the standards for a given food product can distinguish between substandard, average, and outstanding products and can construct a set of meaningful specifications for an item needed. On-the-job experience under informed, trained supervision can, of course, be an immensely valuable way to gain the knowledge needed. There is, however, another way to learn—often far less costly than the school of mistakes. The alternative method involves the use of the many sources of information available to the food buyer. This information can enhance the capabilities of the relatively new food buyer and can sharpen those of the experienced buyer.

A recent publication, Raymond Pedderson's *Specs: The Comprehensive Food Service Purchasing and Specification Manual* (1977) is a most complete guide to drawing up a list of specifications, and, therefore, the prospective food buyer should be aware of the availability of this extensive work. There is detailed information on topics covered more succinctly in this volume: purchasing policies, meat, poultry, eggs, dairy products, fish, convenience foods, produce, groceries, quality control and regulation, and storage and handling.

The conscientious buyer's need to educate himself never ends. This chapter serves only as an introductory guide to the mountain of material available to the food buyer.* The aim is to provide a beginning point in the search for accurate information on buying foods.

GENERAL SOURCES

Information on food bombards us. Billboards, television and radio commercials, and advertisements in the printed media constantly stress food products. The daily newspaper supplies recipes, information

---

*For assistance in locating materials, see this chapter and the Selected Bibliography (pages 333-349). Additional information is available through libraries.

on new food products, and the availability of such items as fruits, vegetables, and beverages through articles by food editors, through advertisements, and through market information. Newspapers can, particularly on a daily basis, do much to educate and aid the buyer, but they are bulky and only a small part of any particular edition contains information important to a food buyer. It is also often difficult to find earlier articles if they are needed for reference at a later time. The quality of the information also varies according to the reliability and expertise of the person who wrote it. Probably market reports (see Exhibit 6-4) constitute the most dependable source of information, and they should be read daily by the professional food buyer.

Popular magazines also publish articles that have potential value for the food buyer. Although periodicals like *Good Housekeeping, Better Homes and Gardens,* and *Consumer Reports* are obviously aimed at the individual consumer, they may contain articles that would interest any buyer, large or small, responsible for the selection of quality foods and food products. *Consumer Reports* has, over the years, analyzed in detail not only food products but the newer forms in which foods are processed. For example, an article entitled "Food Dating: Now You See It, Now You Don't," *Consumer Reports* (June 1972) discusses the need for and the usefulness of open dating on perishable food and provides a glossary for the various dating methods currently in use (for example, pack date, shelf life, pull date, freshness date, expiration date, and shelf-display date). Articles in popular magazines such as these are more readily accessible than most newspaper articles because the *Reader's Guide to Periodical Literature* (available in most public libraries) indexes

widely read magazines. By consulting this index a buyer can quickly learn what has recently appeared in this type of periodical on a particular subject. Another bibliographic source that is helpful is "A Bibliography: Hotel and Restaurant Administration and Related Subjects," published annually in the August issue of the *Cornell Hotel and Restaurant Administration Quarterly*. This outstanding listing of publications, alone, justifies an annual subscription to the periodical.

Perhaps the next most common sources of information are federal and state governmental agencies. The United States Department of Agriculture (USDA), which is the most prolific of these agencies, publishes or otherwise makes available a vast quantity of information literally on everything from soup to nuts. It is the USDA that finally fixes the standards that determine, for example, whether a beef carcass will be graded choice or prime. The USDA publishes both the specific standards that apply to each commodity from almonds to watermelons and general information about grading and food quality. Three examples of these general information pamphlets from the USDA are: (1) *How to Use USDA Grades in Buying Food* (1977), a concise guide to the various grades for dairy products, poultry, eggs, fruits, vegetables, eggs, beef, lamb, and veal; (2) *Your Money's Worth in Foods* (1977), by Betty Peterkin and Cynthia Cromwell, a booklet aimed at the family consumer but one containing charts useful in comparing costs of similar foods; and (3) *Food Purchasing Guide for Group Feeding* (1965), by Betty Peterkin and Beatrice Evans, a pamphlet mainly of charts useful in estimating quantities of food needed in group feedings for a wide range of products. These and other USDA publications are commonly available from the Superintendent of Documents in Washington, D.C., from a Government Printing Office (GPO) bookstore (only found in larger cities), or from the issuing agency.

The National Marine Fisheries Service (in the Department of Commerce) is the federal counterpart to the USDA for seafood. While much less active than the USDA in publication, it nevertheless can occasionally aid the buyer of freshwater and ocean fish, mollusks, and crustaceans. The *Monthly Catalog of U.S. Government Publications* indexes the publications put out by the agencies. Many of the publications are also available at the larger public, college, and university libraries that serve as depositories for government documents. The complete set of federal regulations as they relate to the food industry (see Chapter 3) may be found in the most recent edition of the *Code of Federal Regulations*, particularly in Titles 7, 9, 21, and 50. These are the regulations of the USDA, the Food and Drug Administration (FDA), and the National Marine Fisheries Service.

The USDA is also responsible for compiling a marvelously thorough annotated bibliography on the subjects of food service and nutrition. This bibliography, the *Food and Nutrition Information and Educational Materials Center Catalog* and the supplements to it, all from the Food and Nutrition Information and Educational Materials Center (FNIC), list and describe relevant publications from public and private, governmental and trade sources that FNIC or the National Agricultural Library has collected. Its materials include books, journal articles, pamphlets, government documents, special reports, proceedings, and bibliographies. FNIC also maintains a collection of films, filmstrips, slides, charts, audiotapes, and video cassettes. The nonprint media are available only to groups as specified in the *Catalog*. Besides

being thorough, the *Catalog* and its supplements are easy to use because there is an extensive subject index in each volume. A cumulative subject, author, and title index that appeared in 1975 provides references for all accessions by the center from April 1971 through February 1975. Additional supplements have been issued twice a year since 1975. The *Catalog* and supplements are available upon request from FNIC.

Although specifically designed to disseminate information on school food service training and nutrition education, the FNIC's services are available to other members of the food service industry. Circulating books are loaned for a period of one month. In addition, in lieu of loan of the journals themselves, FNIC will photocopy up to six journal articles at one time for one person. Journals and some other materials at FNIC are not loaned. Requests for information or materials should be addressed to the Food and Nutrition Information and Educational Materials Center, National Agricultural Library, Room 304, Beltsville, MD 20705.

State agencies issue valuable publications that define various state standards for such products as ice cream, ice milk, and sherbets. While it is impossible to list the names and addresses of all the various agencies within all fifty states, the state departments of agriculture, the agriculture extension services, and the state agricultural colleges within a given state are often excellent places to begin the search for information on how to evaluate and buy a food item. These institutions may also be able to provide names and addresses for relevant out-of-state agencies and institutions.

In addition to government publications, private industry, with its various promotional, educational, and public relations outlets, frequently prints relevant pamphlets, booklets, and leaflets. Some of these publications are purely promotional and do not deserve a food buyer's attention since they are designed more to stimulate the salivary glands than the brain cells. Others, however, provide by far the best information on a given product. The variety of organizations that industry has created is enormous. They range from the California Avocado Advisory Board to the Idaho Bean Commission to the United Fresh Fruit and Vegetable Association. These associations, while scarcely impartial, nevertheless supply valuable, precise information about their products and the marketing of them.

There are also specialized journals that are directed at a highly specialized food buyer. Again the great number of publications makes a complete listing impossible, but the types of journals that fit in this category are illustrated by several randomly chosen titles: *Quick Frozen Foods, Purchasing, Modern Packaging, Vending Times, Cooking for Profit, Hospitality, Baker's Digest,* and the *Cornell Hotel and Restaurant Administration Quarterly.* Each of these publications is related to a specific industry and is likely to deal with technical aspects of particular, narrow problems. While the articles in these journals are unlikely to appeal to all buyers, one with a particular focus may be valuable to a buyer with specific needs relating, for example, to buying frozen foods for a large grocery chain. In short, let the buyer be aware that potential sources of information lurk under every book and magazine cover.

The buyer should be aware that current prices on many foods and food products are listed in the Urner Barry (4340 Redwood Highway, Suite 237, San Rafael, CA 94903; or P.O. Box 389, Toms River,

NJ 08753) publication *Producer's Price-Current* (see Chapter 6, Exhibit 6-4). Another of its publications that is useful for most buyers is the *Restaurant Buyers Guide,* a weekly (with East and West Coast editions) that includes current prices for shell eggs; butter; margarine; selected cheeses; mayonnaise; oils; various cuts of beef, lamb, pork, and veal; turkeys; fresh fryers; roasters; and selected fresh fruits, vegetables, and seafood. The semiweekly *Seafood Price-Current* provides a more detailed price list for fresh, frozen, and smoked fish and fresh and frozen shellfish.

There are two other categories of reference works that occasionally help the new buyer or the buyer who must begin purchasing foods with which he has had no previous acquaintance. These two categories are, first, multivolume encyclopedias, such as the *Encyclopaedia Britannica*; and, second, cookbooks of all kinds. If a buyer's employer, for example, decided to expand his beverage list to include gourmet coffees, the buyer unfamiliar with coffees other than those vacuum packed by large corporations could benefit from an encyclopedia article on coffee and a glance through the beverage section of a cookbook like *Joy of Cooking*. While that would scarcely provide the buyer with everything he or she needed to know, it might well supply enough information to get started. Because an encyclopedia article also usually contains a brief bibliography, just the book or article needed to inform the buyer fully about a particular item might be listed.

General sources of information are quite useful to the buyer, but expert buyers will inevitably assemble their own libraries based on specific foods to be bought or particular situations in which they find themselves. In this chapter the discussion is organized around the foods available for purchase: meats; poultry and eggs; dairy products and dairy substitutes; fish and shellfish; grains, cereal products, nuts, and spices; fats and oils; fresh fruits and vegetables; processed fruits and vegetables; convenience foods; and beverages.

MEATS

Meat is one of the most important food groups for anyone buying food in the United States. A high proportion of the food budget is channeled into the purchase of meat. Despite the large quantities of meat served, however, the average consumer still has only a vague idea of what the various names and cuts signify, and, for a long time, the lack of standardized names for the various cuts fostered this confusion. Fortunately, several excellent publications are now available to educate the buyer and to eliminate much of the guesswork from meat purchasing. One such basic publication is *Lessons on Meat* (4th ed., 1976) from the National Live Stock and Meat Board. It offers fundamental information and illustrations for meat identification and meat buying and includes charts for identifying beef, veal, port, and lamb cuts. It also includes a section on "Meat in Other Forms" (for example, sausage products) and a brief discussion of variety meats such as heart, tongue, and liver. Additional aid in evaluating meat is available in the *Meat Evaluation Handbook* (1976) from the National Live Stock and Meat Board. This beautifully illustrated guide to evaluating meat according to quality, yield (cutability), and maturity also includes suggestions for judging carcasses and wholesale cuts for beef, pork, and lamb, including hams and veal. A third publication, the *Meat Buyer's Guide to Standardized Meat Cuts* from the National Association of Meat Purveyors

(NAMP), gives specifications and illustrates in color standard meat cuts as defined by the USDA's Institutional Meat Purchase Specifications (IMPS) for beef, lamb, veal, and pork. The standardization of cuts is particularly valuable for institutional buyers because it offers greater assurance that the cuts purchased are uniform. Thus, after specifying grade, yield, weight range, state of refrigeration, and fat limitations, the buyer may order a particular cut number (for example, #123, for short ribs, trimmed) at a specified width. Each such cut ordered should then closely approximate the specifications for that cut number. NAMP also offers the *Meat Buyer's Guide to Portion Control Meat Cuts*, a valuable addition to a meat purchaser's library. Portioned meats that are pretrimmed and sized allow precise cost control. They are available in a wide range of cuts. One national meat firm advertised that it was currently marketing more than thirty portioned cuts for beef alone.

The USDA operates a voluntary acceptance service based on IMPS for fresh beef, lamb and mutton, fresh veal and calf, fresh pork, cured pork, cured beef, edible by-products, sausage products, and portion-cut meat products. A basic description of this service, which can be particularly valuable for contract purchasers, is available in the USDA pamphlet entitled *USDA's Acceptance Service for Meat and Meat Products* (1970).

Grades for various meats are further explained in publications prepared by the USDA itself: *USDA Yield Grades for Beef* (revised ed.; 1974); *USDA Yield Grades for Lamb* (1970); *USDA Grades for Pork Carcasses* (1970); *USDA Grades for Slaughter Swine and Feeder Pigs* (1970); and *Meat and Poultry: Standards for You*. The quality and yield standards for beef are detailed in the latest edition of the

Official United States Standards for Grades of Carcass Beef, which is updated as the standards are amended. Similar publications are available for other products.

The National Live Stock and Meat Board has also published a pamphlet that briefly presents the revisions in beef grading that went into effect in February 1976. This pamphlet, *Beef Grading: What It Is; How It's Changed* (1976), also explains the difference between grading for quality and grading for yield.

In addition, the USDA in its "Home and Garden Bulletins" has published several pamphlets in which meat purchasing figures prominently. Among these are *How to Buy Beef Roasts* (1968), *How to Buy Beef Steaks* (1976), *How to Buy Lamb* (1971, by Sandra Brookover), and *How to Buy Meat for Your Freezer* (1976). All of these are aimed at the individual consumer, but they provide accurate, concise information supplemented with illustrations and charts that are equally beneficial to the professional buyer. *How to Buy Meat for Your Freezer* is especially valuable, even if freezing is not contemplated, since it discusses buying beef, lamb, and pork and includes charts picturing the cuts available from each. It also examines the alternatives of buying by the whole carcass, by the side, by the quarter, by the wholesale cut, or by the retail cut. Furthermore, it provides a guide to calculating and comparing the actual cost of usable beef bought in carcass form with that of beef bought in retail cuts. Finally, the yield grades for beef are explained in terms of the minimum and maximum percentage yields theoretically available in retail form from a carcass. Yield Grade 1, for example, means that the carcass will yield at least 79.8 percent in retail cuts, while Yield Grade 5 will yield 65.9 percent or less. The publications of the USDA are fre-

quently available *in single copies*, without charge, from the Office of Communication, U.S. Department of Agriculture, Washington, D.C. 20250.

The professional buyer's choice between purchasing beef by the carcass, side, quarter, wholesale cut, or portion-control cut from a meat purveyor or by the retail cut from a local supermarket may not be as obvious as it appears, especially for the comparatively small-scale buyer. A comparative study of costs conducted by Consumers Union (the organization that publishes *Consumer Reports*) revealed that bulk buying of meat (at least on a small scale) was rarely cheaper than buying at the supermarket after allowance was made for waste in bulk purchases. Research carried out by Consumers Union, moreover, casts some doubt on the reliability of the USDA quality and yield grades. Its investigations and those of researchers at Texas A&M question whether taste and tenderness in beef correlate with USDA quality grades. The study by Consumers Union showed little correlation between designated yield grade and actual yield. One Yield Grade 4 side of beef even had much less waste than most Yield Grade 2 sides checked in the tests. A Yield Grade 2 side or carcass should provide between 75.2 and 79.7 percent yield; yet the *most* any USDA Yield Grade 2 side provided in this study was 70 percent. Several Yield Grade 2 sides showed yields of only 60 percent, which, according to USDA standards, would place it well down in the Yield Grade 5 range. The results of that study, which also indicated that there are, indeed, dishonest meat dealers, are published in "Buying Beef: Bulk Buying vs. the Supermarket," and "Buying Beef: What a Good Label Can Tell You," *Consumer Reports* (September 1974).

An earlier Consumers Union study ("A

Close Look at Hamburger," *Consumer Reports* [August 1971]) also warned of the need to be wary in purchasing ground beef both because of putrefaction in some samples purchased and because of the unpredictable percentage of fat in packages labeled ground beef, ground chuck, ground round, and ground sirloin. Obviously the buyer is well advised to choose his source for meat supplies with great care and to review the products received continually.

Two other articles published in 1970 (and therefore slightly dated) deserve to be mentioned. J. J. Wanderstock's "Meat Purchasing," *Cornell Hotel and Restaurant Administration Quarterly* (November 1970) concisely and cogently discusses meat purchasing for a restaurant. He makes helpful suggestions for developing purchase requirements; discusses meat inspection on the federal, state, and local level; gives a brief history of the U.S. government grading system for beef up to 1970; explains what packer grades are and how they differ from federal grades; describes the USDA meat acceptance program, the aging or ripening of meat, and the receiving and storing of meat. He also provides an outline of what should be included in beef specifications. The second article, Louis Szathmary's "Beef—Some Answers," also in the *Cornell Hotel and Restaurant Administration Quarterly* (November 1970), is a practical guide to buying, storing, and using steaks. It discusses sirloin steaks, tenderloin steaks, chateaubriand, filet mignon, tournedos, chuck steaks, and others. Both articles stress that, unless a food service operation can utilize all parts of a carcass, there is no reason to buy carcass meats in view of high labor costs and a shortage of trained butchers. Szathmary, a restaurateur, strongly defends buying portion-controlled steaks.

There are two other publications of particular value in buying pork. One, the USDA's *Pork in Family Meals: A Guide for Family Meals* (1975), provides an excellent summary of the basics for buying and storing pork and pork products. It includes a pictorial guide for identifying pork cuts, both fresh and cured; a brief discussion of the inspection and grading system for pork; and a description of common sausages and variety meats available from pork. The second publication on pork, an outstanding article, is Robert E. Rust's "How to Buy Pork," *Cornell Hotel and Restaurant Administration Quarterly* (August 1973). It is concerned precisely with the needs of the quantity food buyer. Rust emphasizes that pork is not graded beyond the carcass and that USDA grades are of little value to the user. In giving advice on selecting pork, he suggests that with modern pork production methods, heavier cuts are not necessarily from older animals and that heavier pork loins (14 to 17 lbs.) and hams (14 to 18 lbs.), for example, are likely to have less waste than their lighter counterparts with no sacrifice in quality. He also notes that the best quality indicators in pork are a slight amount of marbling and a grey-pink color. Moreover, he lists some specialty cuts of pork that are especially appropriate for quantity food service operations. Both of these publications offer good advice on storage requirements for pork and a word on pork as a safe food (*Trichinella spiralis*, a microscopic parasite found in pork, is easily killed by the low temperature of 140°F.).

Other publications that a buyer may find useful, especially in buying variety meats and processed meats are: the USDA's *Beef and Veal in Family Meals: A Guide for Consumers* (1975) and *Lamb in Family Meals: A Guide for Consumers* (1974); "Canned Hams," *Consumer Reports* (October 1970); "Frankfurters," *Con-*

sumer Reports (February 1972); "How Good Is the Bologna in That Sandwich," *Consumer Reports* (March 1976); and Albert Levie's *The Meat Handbook* (3d ed., 1970).

Finally, useful both in understanding definitions and in constructing specifications for meat and poultry items is John C. de Holl's *Encyclopedia of Labeling Meat and Poultry Products* (3d ed., 1976). De Holl uses standards of the federal government in deciphering labels for these products and in identifying hundreds of terms. For instance, chili is described as a product that, to be labeled chili, must contain a minimum of 40 percent meat, with head meat, cheek meat, and heart meat composing no more than 25 percent of the meat component. The implications of knowing the exact, official definitions for various products when constructing purchasing specifications is obvious.

One study of the use of soy proteins as a beef substitute or extender may be found in Linda M. Nielson and Agnes Frances Carlin's article, "Frozen, Precooked Beef and Beef-Soy Loaves," *Journal of the American Dietetic Association* (July 1974).

POULTRY AND EGGS

Poultry is considerably less complicated to purchase than meat since variation among chicken breasts, for example, is much less than among various beefsteaks. There are, nevertheless certain things a buyer should be acquainted with before beginning to purchase poultry. The buyer should certainly be aware of the distinctions between frying and stewing chickens, between young Tom turkeys and yearling turkeys, and between a roaster duckling and a mature duck. Two aids in learning these distinctions as well as distinguishing between U.S.

Grade A and U.S. Grade B birds are the USDA's *How to Buy Poultry* (1968) and *Poultry in Family Meals: A Guide for Consumers* (1974). The latter also describes the many forms in which poultry products are marketed—chilled or frozen, stuffed or unstuffed, canned or precooked, boneless roasts and rolls, and whole birds or poultry parts. All poultry sold in the United States is inspected for wholesomeness either by the federal government or by an equivalent state system.

The National Turkey Federation has published a promotional booklet, *The Turkey Handbook* (undated), which gives a full listing of the many forms in which turkey is now available, including whole, steaks, cutlets, preportioned, as parts, as roasts, and in pastrami, salami, bologna, and franks. It also includes a price per serving calculator based on cost per pound and portion size. "Turkey off the Assembly Line," *Consumer Reports* (November 1973), also discusses processed turkey products and gives a brand-name ranking for whole turkeys, turkey breasts, and turkey roasts. Because there is constant change in the way turkey is processed, these rankings are probably outdated. Other sections of the article remain valuable, however, in alerting the buyer to possible pitfalls when purchasing poultry. Processing can, for example, make a considerable difference in the quality and price per edible pound of the end product. These differences include the amount of water absorbed or injected into the bird during processing, the amount of sodium per serving, and the addition of sugar to the bird (these last two would be of special importance when buying food for a hospital). The *Consumer Reports* article also warns of the need for vigilance on the part of the buyer as to the labeling and grading of poultry products. The USDA grading system takes no account of flavor, tenderness, or juiciness since USDA inspectors determine grade mainly by appearance. If a bird fails to conform to USDA standards for Grade A, moreover, the processor may simply omit any grade labeling at all. Consumers Union concluded that USDA grade labeling bore little relationship to the taste and tenderness of the turkey products examined in its study. The buyer again must be warned to monitor the poultry he is receiving continually, to conduct taste tests as regularly as possible, and to read all labels carefully. Reading the label can reveal, for instance, that Swift & Co.'s Butterball turkeys contain no butter whatsoever.

For information on buying eggs in quantity, an inexpensive publication of the Cooperative Extension Service, University of Massachusetts (available from the Hotel, Restaurant, and Travel Administration, Flint Laboratory, University of Massachusetts, Amherst, MA 01003), is probably the best place to begin. This pamphlet, *Purchasing Eggs for Food Service Establishments* (1968), by Robert M. Grover and Charles E. Eshbach, discusses the parts of an egg; the quality, grades, and sizes for shell eggs; egg prices; specifications for buying eggs; and egg storage and use. In addition to this concise presentation of vital information on purchasing shell eggs, the brochure also provides a brief outline of essentials on egg products and their availability, sanitation, packaging, and care.

The USDA has also published pamphlets that describe and depict important qualitative distinctions in eggs. Among these publications are *Shell Egg Grading and Inspection of Egg Products* (1964), *Egg Grading Manual* (1977), *Know the Eggs You Buy* (1967), and *How to Buy Eggs* (1975). The first two of these four give precise definitions of U.S. standards for shell, air cell, white, and yolk — the parts of an egg. They also discuss differences between consumer grades, wholesale grades, procurement grades, and export grades. Finally, they explain the federal-state grading program and labels. The last two publications give the basic information about three egg grades (Grade AA or Fresh Fancy, Grade A, and Grade B) and about six sizes (ranging from Jumbo eggs, which have a minimum weight per dozen of 30 ounces, to Peewee eggs, with a minimum weight of 15 ounces per dozen). USDA publications strongly emphasize watching for the USDA grade shield as a guide to quality. One rigorous investigation of egg grading ("Do Eggs Make the Grade," *Consumer Reports* [February 1976]), however, revealed weaknesses in both state and federal egg-grading systems. One-fourth of all eggs tested in New York state, for example, failed to meet that state's standards for Grade A eggs, the quality grade under which the eggs were sold. Of the eggs purchased in California (and sold as meeting California standards for Grade AA), 15 percent failed even to meet the standards for federal Grade A. In fact, only 9 percent of the California Grade AA egg cartons bought at the retail level contained a dozen eggs conforming to federal Grade AA standards. It must be noted at the same time, however, that there was no similar discrepancy in the stated weight and size standards of the eggs examined in the same study.

Federal standards, which apply to eggs that are moved in interstate commerce, are quite demanding as written. In practice, however, the USDA shield may prove to be no more reliable than state standards. Grading, it would appear, serves as an indication of quality in whole, fresh eggs, but this is only one consideration.

Freshness when delivered and used and

constant refrigeration during grading, after packing, and in transit and storage are equally important in keeping a Grade AA egg at that quality level. Hence, careful selection of a purveyor, close observation of the handling of eggs, and specifications requiring a packing date for all eggs delivered also help to maintain quality. If large quantities of eggs are to be used for baking, it is also wise to consider and experiment with lower-grade eggs and egg products since they are less expensive.

Eggs are available in forms other than fresh, whole eggs. The American Egg Board has published an informative pamphlet on alternative forms for egg products. This publication, *A Scientist Speaks about Egg Products* (1974), is especially useful in acquainting the professional food buyer with the various forms in which eggs may be purchased (such as dehydrated or frozen whole egg solids, yolk solids, and white solids). It also discusses storage conditions and the properties of fresh eggs affected and unaffected by processing.

Because of medical concern with the effect of eggs on human health (the question remains controversial), egg substitutes came on the market in the 1970's. For a discussion of one of these substitutes and its qualities compared to eggs, see "Egg Beaters: Do They Beat Real Eggs?" *Consumer Reports* (March 1974).

For Canadian food buyers, an excellent summary of basic information on egg purchasing is available: H. L. Orr, and D. A. Fletcher, *Eggs and Egg Products: Production, Identification, Retention of Quality*, Publication 1498 (Ottawa: Canada Department of Agriculture, 1973). This booklet is available from the Information Division, Canada Department of Agriculture, Ottawa K1A 0C7. A similarly informative—but unfortunately outdated—Canadian publication on poultry is Earle S. Snyder, and Henry L. Orr, *Poultry Meat: Process-*

ing, Quality Factors, Yields, Publication 9 (Toronto: Ontario Department of Agriculture, [1964?]).

DAIRY PRODUCTS AND DAIRY SUBSTITUTES

Milk and milk products are, like eggs, among the foods with the widest and most varied uses and forms. Milk itself can be whole, low in fat content, nonfat, concentrated, sweetened condensed, dried, flavored, or filled. Fresh cream may be sold as half-and-half, coffee cream, light cream, or whipping cream. In addition, milk or cream can be transformed into yogurt, buttermilk, acidophilus milk, butter, sour cream, cheese, ice cream, ice milk or sherbet—to mention only some of the possibilities. A food buyer for many large and small institutions will encounter most, if not all, of these dairy products and needs to know of the alternatives available and what distinguishes one from another. Fortunately, introductory guides to these products are readily available.

A good introductory guide is the University of Massachusetts's Food Management Leaflet 15, entitled *Purchasing Dairy Products for Food Service Establishments* (undated), by Frank E. Potter. It is available at small cost from the Hotel, Restaurant, and Travel Administration, Flint Laboratory, University of Massachusetts, Amherst, MA 01003. This leaflet discusses the purchase of the entire range of dairy products, offering clear, helpful advice on both general and specific buying problems. Fluid milk beverages, packaging, bid purchasing of milk, coffee cream, whipping cream, cottage cheese, butter, cheese, nonfat dry milk, dry whole milk, ice cream, ice milk, sherbets and water ices, and soft serve or ice cream mix are all judiciously analyzed.

The USDA publishes two pamphlets

that give basic federal definitions for the most common dairy products. These are: *How to Buy Dairy Products* (1974) and *Milk in Family Meals: A Guide for Consumers* (1974). The National Dairy Council has a leaflet, *Milk* (1975), providing similar information but also mentioning specialty milks such as multivitamin, multimineral, certified, and low sodium. The standard procedures for judging and grading milk and all other common dairy products, including butter, cheese, ice cream, fermented milk, cream, concentrated milk, and dry milk are treated in depth in John A. Nelson and G. Malcolm Trout, *Judging Dairy Products* (4th ed.; 1964). "Instant Nonfat Dry Milk," *Consumer Reports* (January 1977), gives a quality ranking for nineteen brands of nonfat dry milk based on flavor, aroma, color, texture, and ability to be easily reconstituted.

The most complex facet of buying dairy products comes in purchasing cheese. When confined to only the products most frequently consumed in the United States, cheese buying offers little challenge, but interest in more complex and distinctive cheeses has been growing. The number of cheese stores and delicatessen sections of supermarkets featuring gourmet cheeses is increasing. Considering the hundreds of cheeses that are made and marketed around the world, cheese can become a complicated subject, indeed. Cheeses may be classified in countless ways—as unripened or ripened; as soft, semisoft, hard, or very hard; and as blue, spiced, or processed. Several publications offer introductions to the world of cheeses. The National Dairy Council's publication, *Cheese* (1975) is a compact chart of thirty-four cheeses with their place of origin, texture, color, shape, flavor, ripening period, and uses all displayed. It also provides helpful information on storage of cheese and lists which cheeses can be

successfully frozen. Two similar brochures from the USDA are: *How to Buy Cheese* and *Cheese in Family Meals: A Guide for Consumers*. The first of these gives a brief description of the cheese-ripening classifications, followed by a chart listing twenty-eight varieties of natural cheese along with their place of origin, ripening times, flavor, texture, color, and uses. It also, albeit too briefly, describes pasteurized process cheese, pasteurized process cheese food, and pasteurized process cheese spread. The most important distinction between these various products is in the butterfat content. Thus, while an American cheddar cheese must have a minimum of 31 percent butterfat and a maximum of 39 percent moisture, a process cheese spread may have as little as 20 percent butterfat and as much as 60 percent water. For a fuller discussion of the distinctions between cheddar cheese, process cheese, cheese food, cheese spread, process imitation cheese spread, and process cheese product, see "Milk: In Cheese, It's Disappearing," *Consumer Reports* (January 1974), and Pamela J. Nystrom, *et al.*, "Cheese Products: Protein, Moisture, Fat and Acceptance," *Journal of the American Dietetic Association* (July 1974). The latter of these two is useful in showing appropriate uses for such cheese products as cheese spread.

For the buyer who needs more detailed information about cheeses, there are several options. One of these is Peter Quimme's *The Signet Book of Cheese* (1976), an inexpensive paperback that is an excellent guide to some of the best American and imported cheeses. It includes informative chapters on buying and storing cheeses, a glossary of terms, and an extensive dictionary of cheeses. In this dictionary over two hundred cheeses are either listed briefly or described in depth. The fuller descriptions contain buying hints and information on taste, aroma, texture, length of usable life, and interior and exterior appearance. The USDA also has a detailed description of individual cheeses entitled *Cheese Varieties and Descriptions* (1974; slightly revised version of a 1953 ed.). Being concerned with the exact methods of manufacture of the various cheeses more than their taste, aroma, or appearance when in optimum condition, this book is more useful to the turophile (cheese lover) than the professional food buyer. The USDA has indicated, however, that it will be reissued with major revisions at a future date.

W. S. Arbuckle's *Ice Cream* (1972) and Philip G. Keeney's *Commercial Ice Cream and Other Frozen Desserts* (n.d.) provide more information on ice cream, ice milk, sherbet, and mellorines (frozen vegetable fat desserts) than the average buyer is likely to need. Both give standard definitions for the various products. Keeney's publication is less expensive and shorter in length, but it does provide the essential information on ingredients and identifies which ingredients make for a quality product. Less technical and briefer, but nevertheless of high quality, is the article "Ice Cream," *Consumer Reports* (August 1972), which, in concise fashion, analyzes the modern manufacture of ice cream, ice milk, and mellorines, the question of bacteriological impurity in ice cream, the fat content (one indicator of quality) of the various categories of frozen dairy desserts, the distinctions between such labels as "vanilla ice cream," "vanilla-flavored ice cream," and "artificially flavored ice cream." It suggests qualities to look for in evaluating any ice cream, such as weight per unit, color, texture, taste, and melting characteristics. It also explains the meaning and significance of "overrun" (the amount of air incorporated into ice cream, thereby increasing the volume).

The brand ratings included are outdated.

Two frequent nondairy product substitutes deserve to be mentioned. These are nondairy creamers in liquid and powder form and margarine. Nondairy coffee creamers have won a substantial share of the market away from dairy products because of shelf life and economic and dietary considerations. Perhaps the single best analysis of these products to date is "Coffee 'Creamers,'" *Consumer Reports* (March 1975). If coffee creamers come in two forms, margarine comes in at least five (regular, soft, whipped, diet-imitation, and liquid), and those five forms of margarine together outsell butter in the United States at a rate of more than two to one. The components, flavor, purity, spreadability, frying characteristics, and percentage of polyunsaturated fats are all discussed in "Choosing a Margarine for Taste and Health," *Consumer Reports* (January 1975).

In terms of drafting institutional specifications for dairy products, the standards set forth by the United States Department of Agriculture and the United States Department of Health, Education, and Welfare (HEW) provide guidance. The following USDA publications provide examples of those standards as published: *The Grade A Pasteurized Milk Ordinance* (1973), *Standards for Frozen Desserts* (1968), and *Standards for Butter* (1960). HEW publishes *Standards of Identity for Dairy Products* (various dates).

FISH AND SHELLFISH

Americans in the 1970s eat far more meat and poultry than fish. In fact, annual per capita consumption for beef and poultry was 116 pounds and 52 pounds, respectively, in 1973, compared to only 12 pounds for seafood. Nevertheless, this country since colonial days has had a large fishing industry as well. Fish and shellfish, however, are now available more conveniently, in many more forms, and in many more geographic areas than was possible prior to the development of modern processing, refrigeration, and transportation systems. The buyer is no longer limited to purchasing the fish or shellfish available in his particular state or region. Without giving a thought to the technological structure required, a restaurateur today may feature on his menu lobster tails from South Africa, shrimp from the Gulf of Mexico, Middle Atlantic sea scallops, salmon from the Pacific Coast, and rainbow trout from hatcheries west of the Rocky Mountains. For the seafood lover, this wide choice poses no problems. For the professional food buyer, on the other hand, this horn of plenty filled with fresh, frozen, dried, and canned fish and shellfish brings added responsibilities and the need for considerable knowledge.

As might be expected, there is no single source to which the buyer can turn for a quick lesson on buying all of the products contained in the waters of the world. There are several government pamphlets and circulars available from the National Marine Fisheries Service (NMFS) in the National Oceanic and Atmospheric Administration (NOAA), an agency of the U.S. Department of Commerce (USDC). While these publications will hardly satisfy the needs of a buyer deeply concerned with purchasing seafood, they will at least help. Two readily available NMFS booklets aimed at the consumer are *Let's Cook Fish! A Complete Guide to Fish Cookery* (1976) and *How to Eye and Buy Seafood* (1976). The first of these, as is obvious from the title, is primarily concerned with the various methods of cooking fish. It does, nevertheless, describe the forms in which fresh and frozen fish are marketed (for example, whole, dressed, fillets, steaks, chunks, raw breaded fish portions, fried fish portions and fish sticks) and the characteristics these various forms exhibit when in optimum condition. Whole or dressed fresh fish should have firm flesh; shiny skin; bright, clear eyes; red gills that are free of slime; and a fresh, mild odor. Frozen fish should be frozen solid, free of discoloration on the edges, and wrapped in moisture and vaporproof material. Fresh fillets and steaks should have a fresh-cut appearance with no traces of discoloration or dehydration. *Let's Cook Fish*! also briefly discusses canned tuna and canned salmon. It notes that canned tuna is sold either as "white meat" tuna or as "light meat" tuna. Only one tuna species, albacore, may be marketed as "white meat." The other species (mainly yellowfin, bluefin, and skipjack) are all labeled as light meat. Tuna is sold in solid, chunk, flaked, and grated forms, and it may be packed in olive oil (rare), any other vegetable oil (the kind is rarely revealed on labels), or water. The salmon canned on the Pacific coast are of five distinct species, each of different value. In descending order of price (and degree of redness and oil content), they are: red or sockeye salmon, chinook or king salmon; coho or silver salmon; pink or humpback salmon; and chum or keta salmon.

How to Eye and Buy Seafood is even more valuable to the buyer, because, in addition to including much of the information published in *Let's Cook Fish*, it adds excellent basic information for buying shellfish. It divides shellfish into its two classifications—crustaceans and mollusks—and discusses the common varieties of each in some detail. (The most abundant crustaceans are shrimp, lobster, and crabs. The most abundant mollusks are sea scallops, clams, and oysters). It also gives some hints on storing and cooking these seafoods.

Although unavailable from the Superintendent of Documents, the NMFS has other publications useful to the buyer. These publications (discussed below) are currently available directly from the National Marine Fisheries Service, National Oceanic and Atmospheric Administration, U.S. Department of Commerce, Washington, D.C. 20235. Because fishery products, unlike meat and poultry, are not subject to any mandatory inspection to ensure that they are wholesome and of acceptable quality, NMFS in recent years has been striving to increase the amount of fishery products passed through its voluntary inspection program. All food products, including fish, that move in interstate commerce must meet Food and Drug Administration regulations. This prohibits the addition of poisonous substances, the production, packing, or handling of food under unsanitary conditions, and the shipment of foods that are filthy, putrid, or decomposed.

The NMFS inspection program can also be a valuable aid in buying wholesome and (where rigorous grade standards have been established) high-quality fishery products. Federal inspectors check fishery products for quality, quantity, condition, and packaging. Two major types of inspection—continuous inspection and lot inspection—are available. Products processed under the continuous inspection program may bear USDC inspection marks and, if grade standards exist, a grade designation such as U.S. Grade A or U.S. Grade B. Under a lot inspection program, a government inspector examines products from a representative number of samples to determine grade, quality, and condition; condition only; or compliance with other factors requested by the applicant. At present this voluntary inspection program covers about 40 percent of the fishery products processed in the United States.

To aid the buyer in understanding the types of voluntary inspection it offers and the grading system it uses, the NMFS has published several brief descriptive leaflets: (1) *Federal Inspection Marks for Fishery Products* (Food Fish Facts No. 50); (2) *U.S. Grade Standards for Fishery Products* (Food Fish Facts No. 51); (3) *Fish Portions and Fish Sticks* (Food Fish Facts No. 53); (4) *Breaded Shrimp* (Food Fish Facts No. 54); (5) *Protection through Inspection* (1974); and (6) "NMFS's New Inspection Services" (mimeographed). In addition, NMFS has available a reprinted article from *NOAA* (January 1975), the quarterly magazine of the National Oceanic and Atmospheric Administration, entitled "Helping the Housewife Choose," by Gerald D. Hill, Jr. It describes how the inspection system works within a fishery processing plant. Moreover, it must be noted that the NMFS through its National Consumer Educational Services Office (100 East Ohio Street, Room 526, Chicago, IL 60611) has in recent years developed and published more than fifty descriptive leaflets in its "Food Fish Facts" series. These leaflets together constitute one of the best descriptive sources on individual species, their habitat, and their culinary uses. Each leaflet dealing with a specific food fish carries an illustration of that particular item. The items described in separate leaflets include: red snapper, rainbow trout, haddock, Dungeness crab, North Pacific halibut, oysters, Pacific salmon, shrimp, channel catfish, Maine sardines, smelt, flounder, ocean perch, blue crab, American shad, surf clam, gray sole, scallops, king crab, American pollock, rockfish, whiting, sablefish, tuna, swordfish, black or striped mullet, Atlantic cod, Atlantic mackerel, menhaden, Spanish mackerel, striped bass, weakfish, scup or porgy, lake trout, snow crab, Pacific sea herring, pompano, yellow perch, lingcod, Pacific cod, squid, Atlantic croaker, geoduck clam, Jonah crab, ocean quahog clam, sunray venus clam, and red crab.

Two other NMFS sources can assist the buyer. "Institutional Purchasing Specification for the purchase of Fresh, Frozen, and Canned Fishery Products" (mimeographed, 1976; by Jack B. Dougherty) is a circular providing a set of institutional specifications in sample form for the procurement under a bid system of fishery products. It can easily be adapted to suit individual needs and is potentially of great value to anyone constructing or revising specifications. In addition, in its introduction to the specifications, it lists the categories of fishery products that carry the USDC inspection marks and those for which grade standards and federal specifications exist. A second noteworthy publication is the *Approved List, Sanitarily Inspected Fish Establishments* (semi-annual). This document lists all fishery processing plants that have voluntarily subscribed to the USDC inspection program, have met its standards of sanitation, and have demonstrated the ability to produce safe, wholesome fishery products. The document lists by category (1) those plants that have been approved for sanitation, and (2) those that have been approved for sanitation and that produce fishery products that have been inspected and bear the official USDC inspection or grade marks. The establishments that produce specific inspected fishery products are also listed. Thus, the buyer interested in purchasing precooked batter-dipped fish portions can quickly learn which approved firms process this product, under what brand name, and in what general package sizes.

The Texas Parks and Wildlife Department has also published a book (*Seafood Retailing*, by Samuel M. Gillespie and William B. Schwartz) that is especially helpful to the fish retailer but that includes one chapter on buying and caring for fish and shellfish that is extremely valuable to any seafood buyer. This chapter contains a solid guide to recognizing quality and quality defects both for fresh and frozen fish and shellfish, as well as an outstanding section on the care of fresh and frozen seafood. It also includes a glossary of popular fish and shellfish items and a brief discussion of the NMFS inspection program.

The National Fisheries Institute also offers a free publication entitled *Fish Nets Profit*! It is primarily designed to encourage restaurateurs to offer fish and seafood on their menus. However, it also has an informative guide to more than forty species of white-fleshed ocean fish and other popular species and shellfish. It gives a listing of the various names in common use for a single species, tells where each is caught, and describes the forms in which each is marketed.

Other sources that essentially repeat information found in *Seafood Retailing* and the NMFS publications include: "Fish and Seafood Basics," *Better Homes and Gardens* (April 1977); *Good Housekeeping* (July 1975); and "Buying Guide to Lesser-known Fish Varieties," *Good Housekeeping* (October 1973). This last article discusses less expensive fish varieties that can be used as substitutes for flounder (turbot) and haddock (pollock) or as tasty, inexpensive alternatives (whiting, mackerel, and ocean perch).

Consumers Union in recent years has twice studied frozen shrimp, once as breaded shrimp and once as unbreaded shrimp in their various market forms. Both of these articles point out the enormous importance of immediate and constant refrigeration for all harvested seafood and of the grave effect any delays in freezing or any fluctuations in freezer temperatures have on shrimp. These articles are: "Frozen Breaded Shrimp," *Consumer Reports* (January 1972), and "Frozen Shrimp," *Consumer Reports* (March 1974). Consumers Union has also analyzed and ranked canned tuna and canned sardines by brand. See "Canned Tuna," *Consumer Reports* (November 1974), and "Canned Sardines," *Consumer Reports* (February 1976).

GRAINS AND CEREAL PRODUCTS

Although Americans are renowned as meat eaters, any balanced diet also includes products from such cereals as wheat, rice, and corn. Although corn and rice are common staples in the United States, wheat is the most commonly used cereal because it is the basic ingredient in most bakery products. Wheat is not the single uniform grain many people assume it to be. There are, for example, fourteen species of wheat with either seven, fourteen, or twenty-one chromosomes. Three of these fourteen species (common, club, and durum), however, account for 90 percent of the world's wheat production. The flours made from these different species—and the products, in turn, made from these flours—reflect the characteristics of each specie. Thus, hard red spring wheat and durum wheat do not produce flour appropriate for delicate cakes and pastries. And soft red winter wheat produces a flour poorly suited to French bread. Fortunately, the full story of wheat, wheat flours, and wheat products is available at modest price from the Wheat Flour Institute. Although the institute's beautifully illustrated publication, *From*

Wheat to Flour (revised ed.; 1976), contains some information unneeded by the buyer, it provides a wealth of information on the kinds of flour and wheat products available to the buyer. It clearly explains the factors that affect the handling and baking characteristics of the various flours. It mentions the U.S. standards of identity for wheat and related products. And it discusses, in favorable terms, the effects of bleaching and enriching on flour, bread, self-rising products, and pasta.

Because of increased concern with nutrition, the number of breads made from whole wheat or whole grain flours has increased dramatically in recent years. Many bakers have developed special "natural food" breads that seek to profit from this trend. Is there sufficient substance to the claims to warrant a professional buyer's serious attention? One study that forcefully shows a need for caution in accepting advertising claims of nutritional superiority for this or that product is: "Bread: You Can't Judge a Loaf by Its Color," *Consumer Reports* (May 1976). This investigation might surprise uncritical proponents of whole grain breads.

Consumers Union has also tested various breakfast cereals for nutrition—not taste. See "Which Cereals Are Most Nutritious," *Consumer Reports* (February 1975). Again, the results do not follow the advertising claims.

For buying and storing rice, the Rice Council of America has one especially informative booklet entitled *Rice in Foodservice* (no date). It supplies the basic information on the types of rice available (for example, regular milled white rice, brown rice, parboiled rice, and precooked rice) and their respective characteristics. A less thorough introduction to rice may be found in Steve Weiss's

"Rice: Going with the Grain for Profit," *Institutions/Volume Feeding Management* (November 1, 1975).

NUTS

The most frequently used nuts are thoroughly covered in Jasper Guy Woodroof's *Tree Nuts: Production, Processing and Products* (2 vols.; 1967). Almonds, Brazil nuts, cashew nuts, chestnuts, filberts, macadamia nuts, pecans, and English and black walnuts all receive attention. There is discussion of the use of nuts in restaurants as well as of their culture, harvesting, storage, and processing. For a far briefer, but competent discussion of nuts and peanuts, see the USDA's *Nuts in Family Meals: A Guide for Consumers* (1971). For a complete analysis of peanuts (which are not really nuts, but a relative of the pea), see Jasper Guy Woodroof's *Peanuts: Production, Processing, Products* (1973). For a somewhat dated brand ranking of peanut butter on the basis of flavor, aroma, texture, and appearance, see "Peanut Butter," *Consumer Reports* (May 1972).

SEASONINGS

Long before Marco Polo reported seeing ginger growing in China and cinnamon in Ceylon, spices and herbs had been flavoring the cuisines of the world. Their use in American cooking has increased substantially in recent decades, and spices that are previously unknown to all but professional chef are now widely available. The broad term "spices" actually includes several categories. Spices, more narrowly defined, are parts of perennial plants such as dried seeds, buds, flavor parts, or the bark or roots of plants. Herbs are the leafy parts of annual and perennial shrubs. Aromatic seeds are the seeds of lacy annual plants such as anise, caraway, and fennel. Seasonings are blends of spices, herbs, aromatic seeds. Finally there are what are called the vegetable spices: garlic, onion, paprika, chili peppers, horseradish, mushrooms, and others. Spices are sold in whole or ground forms. Strength of flavor and aroma, quality of flavor and aroma, and proper color are primary buying considerations. The shelf life of spices varies with the spice itself, the form in which it is purchased, and the conditions under which it is stored. Spices keep for a longer period if they are stored in cool, dry places and in airtight containers. Under favorable conditions, according to a leaflet, *Seasoning with Spices and Herbs* (1972), from the USDA's Consumer and Food Economics Institute (Hyattsville, MD 20782), spices keep maximum aroma and flavor up to six months. Whole spices, however, retain their flavor almost indefinitely. Herbs are most sensitive to flavor loss. In general, spices should be purchased in quantities that can be utilized fairly quickly. Among the best guides to the spices themselves is *Spice Islands Guide to Your Spice Shelf* (1975), which is available from Specialty Brands Inc. (850 Montgomery St., San Francisco, CA 94133). It provides guidance on buying only for a few of the fifty-one spices it discusses. Still, it is quite valuable in acquainting a buyer with the various forms in which spices are sold and in alerting the spice buyer to certain facts about spices. Curry powder, for example, is a blend of many spices, not one single spice. Thus, curry powders will vary greatly from blend to blend. Because the Spice Islands product line does not include such vegetable spices as horseradish and mushrooms, no information is provided on these spices. Other sources of information on spices are: Craig Claiborne (ed.), *The New York Times Cook Book* (1961); Frederic Rosengarten, Jr., *The Book of Spices* (abridged ed.; 1973); Steve Weiss, "A Dash of Spice . . .," *Institutions/Volume Feeding Management* (December 1, 1975); and Tom Stobart, *The International Wine and Food Society's Guide to Herbs, Spices, and Flavourings* (1973).

FATS AND OILS

Fats and oils are vital components of every quantity food operation, and, therefore, items most buyers will have to purchase. Both fats and oils are composed mainly of triglycerides, but fats, at room temperature, are solid, while oils are liquid. Scientists, who group both fats and oils under the term "fats," divide fats into visible and invisible edible fats. Invisible fats are those found in such foods as eggs, meat, poultry, fish, dairy products (excluding butter), and fruits and vegetables. Visible fats such as lard, shortening, butter, margarine, and cooking and salad oils, which constitute about 40 percent of the fat consumption in the American diet, are the ones with which this section is concerned. Butter and margarine are discussed in the section on dairy products.

Again, no single source exists that can answer the food buyer's questions on edible fats and oils. Several publications combined, however, will provide the buyer with a solid background from which to proceed. *Food Fats and Oils* (4th ed.; 1974), by the Institute of Shortening and Edible Oils, is the most technical of the recommended publications. Although somewhat difficult for persons without a background in chemistry and

although aimed more at the nutritionist than the food buyer, it nevertheless provides much essential information for understanding the primary differences between various fats and oils. It fully defines such terms as "hydrogenation," "bleaching," and "saturation," as well as the properties of treated fats. Moreover, it describes several of the products (for example, salad and cooking oils, shortenings, mayonnaise, and salad dressing) prepared from fats and oils, giving information on the fats from which these products are usually derived.

For information specifically on cooking fats, two publications are especially valuable. These are: Peter Rainsford, Paul Beals, and James C. White, "A Comparative Study of Six Commercial Fats," *Cornell Hotel and Restaurant Administration Quarterly* (August 1976); and "Cooking Oils and Fats," *Consumer Reports* (September 1973). The first of these articles studied fats used for *pan frying* and grill work, taking into consideration packaging and ease of handling that package, appearance, odor, absorption of fat by food, sticking of food, splattering, taste, smoke point, free fatty acid content (which can cause "off" flavors or odors in fats or foods cooking in them, at times even exceeding the human toxicity level) and color changes when heated. Although the study does not give brand names for the fats and oils checked, it does reach conclusions on what characteristics the ideal product should have. These characteristics can undoubtedly be helpful to the buyer. The Consumers Union study also investigated cooking oils and fats, but its main concern was to evaluate and rank by brand thirty-six fats and oils for *deep-fat frying*. It concluded that the most important indicator of a fat's quality for deep-fat frying was its smoke point. The higher the smoke point, in this case, the better, for the smoke point goes down with continued use of the frying medium. A fat or oil with a high initial smoke point (for example, 500°F. or above) is apt to have a longer usable life than one with a lower smoke point. "Cooking Oils and Fats" also includes some comments about fats and oils that may be helpful in evaluating them for use in vinegar-and-oil salad dressings or in pastry. In general, Consumers Union notes that the better a fat or oil is for deep-fat frying, the less suited it is for use as a shortening in baking. Thus, a good shortening would be one with a *low* smoke point. It should also be noted that for pan frying and grill work, smoke point is of less consequence than in deep-fat frying.

Consumers Union has also analyzed two other items with high vegetable oil contents—mayonnaise and salad dressing. Mayonnaise must contain 65 percent vegetable oil to meet federal standards, while salad dressings (not to be confused with such dressings as "thousand island" or "French" dressings) must contain a minimum of 30 percent vegetable oil. For the results of this study, see "Mayonnaise (and Things That Look like It)," *Consumer Reports* (March 1977).

FRESH FRUITS AND VEGETABLES

In purchasing fresh fruits and vegetables the American buyer confronts a variety and supply that is the envy of most of the world. There is also an abundance of excellent publications. The USDA provides two high-quality, if brief, publications specifically aimed at the purchaser of fresh fruits and vegetables. They are: *How to Buy Fresh Fruits* (1967) and *How to Buy Fresh Vegetables* (1967). Following some general buying hints, these two pamphlets provide specific suggestions for buying more than forty common fruits and vegetables. With each product listed is a statement noting both when each is available and which characteristics indicate superior and inferior quality.

If the USDA has produced competent buying guides to fresh fruits and vegetables, private groups associated with these commodities have published outstanding sources of information. William C. Moyer's *The Buying Guide for Fresh Fruits, Vegetables, Herbs, and Nuts* (6th ed.; 1976), published by Blue Goose, Inc., is an outstanding book on the subject. A thorough discussion of fruits and vegetables is accompanied by helpful color photographs—an attractive publication at reasonable cost. Not far behind in terms of the quality of their information are two publications from the National Restaurant Association. These booklets are both written by R. A. Seelig and Marshall Neale—from the United Fresh Fruit and Vegetable Association—and bear the titles *Buying, Handling, and Using Fresh Fruits* (no date) and *Buying, Handling, and Using Fresh Vegetables* (no date). These together describe more than 60 items available for restaurant use. They give information about the sources of supply, monthly availability, uses, grades, varieties, storage requirements, and other buying considerations. The authors stress that buyers should have specifications detailing grade quality, variety, size, price, brand, and growing area. They also indicate that a full set of U.S. Grade standards for fresh fruits and vegetables can be obtained free by writing the Fresh Products Standardization Section, Agricultural Marketing Service,

United State Department of Agriculture, Washington, DC 20250.

In addition, there is a thorough treatment in the *Packer's Produce Availability and Merchandising Guide* (Kansas City, Mo.: Vance Publishing Corp., 1976), and a national weekly newspaper put out for the fruit and vegetable industry (*The Packer*) and published by the same company.

Two sources of current information on supplies of individual fruits and vegetables are available: The USDA publishes both the *Weekly Summary of Shipments-Unloads* and an annual *Fresh Fruit and Vegetable Unloads for 41 Cities*. The second source is the United Fresh Fruit and Vegetable Association's *Monthly Supply Letter*, which covers the average monthly availability of fresh fruits and vegetables.

Other publications of potential value to the buyer of fresh fruits and vegetables include the USDA's *How to Buy Potatoes* (1972), by Lawrence E. Ide; Sunkist Growers' *Sunkist Fresh Citrus Buying Guide* (1975), a guide to fresh oranges, lemons, grapefruit, tangerines, and limes from California and Arizona only; *Florida Citrus for Healthy Profits* (1975), a reprinted advertisement available from the State of Florida's Department of Citrus.

Finally, there is a popular, inexpensive, and interesting guide to more than 120 fruits and vegetables in Joe Carcione and Bob Lucas' *The Greengrocer: The Consumer's Guide to Fruits and Vegetables* (1972). It also tells when the produce is most plentiful and provides guidelines for detecting imperfect merchandise.

PROCESSED FRUITS AND VEGETABLES

Many fruits and vegetables have a limited, seasonal availability in their fresh, unprocessed forms. Thanks to the development of canning, freezing, and dehydration methods, however, fruits and vegetables are readily obtainable all year long, but the techniques for buying fresh apricots, for example, cannot be applied, obviously, to buying canned or dried apricots. Certain information can help to minimize the differences between processed produce and fresh produce. Basic buying and storage information may be found in two publications from the USDA: *How to Buy Canned and Frozen Fruits* (1971) and *How to Buy Canned and Frozen Vegetables* (1975). In addition to discussing more than forty individual fruit and vegetable products, these two pamphlets describe U.S. grade standards and their meaning. These grade standards for fruits and vegetables are used more at the processing and wholesaling level than at the retail level and thus are infrequently found on the package label itself. *How to Buy Canned and Frozen Vegetables* also contains a guide to industry terminology for various can sizes (a 46 oz. can, for instance, is called a No. 3 Special) and a description of styles in which various items are available. Two other USDA publications give additional information on storage requirements for fruits and vegetables in their various forms. These are: *Fruits in Family Meals: A Guide for Consumers* (1975), and *Vegetables in Family Meals: A Guide for Consumers* (1975).

A good introduction to the buying of canned fruits and vegetables is *Purchasing Canned Fruits and Vegetables for Food Service Establishments* (1966), by Robert F. Lukowski, which is an inexpensive publication of the Cooperative Extension Service, University of Massachusetts. It gives the basic information on grades, can sizes, label requirements, and standards of identity, as well as helpful advice on taste testing and institutional purchase specifications. It is available from the Hotel, Restaurant, and Travel Administration, Flint Laboratory, University of Massachusetts, Amherst, MA 01003.

In addition to these general sources for buying processed fruits and vegetables, numerous other publications deal with individual items. One such work is the USDA pamphlet *How to Buy Dry Beans, Peas, and Lentils* (1970), products that nutritionally are among the world's best food bargains. Dried beans also illustrate the thorns with which the USDA grading system can afflict the buyer. As Consumers Union pointed out in its article, "In Praise of Dried Beans," *Consumer Reports* (July 1975), not only is the USDA grading system for beans optional and thus too infrequently used, but the nomenclature employed to grade dried beans in their various forms is ridiculously and needlessly confusing. For most beans, including kidney beans, U.S. No. 1 is the top grade. For navy (pea) beans, however, U.S. No. 1 indicates third quality, following U.S. Choice Handpicked and U.S. Prime Handpicked—where choice and prime indicate the reverse of what they mean in terms of beef. Moreover, for lima beans yet another system is added. U.S. No. 1 is second to U.S. Extra No. 1. Only the wary buyer will emerge unscathed from this obstacle course.

Two other articles dealing with a single item are "Instant Potatoes," *Consumer Reports* (July 1971), and "Frozen French Fries," *Consumer Reports* (October 1971). The first of these, though it is now dated, rates various brands of instant mashed, au gratin, scalloped, and hash brown potatoes. It is particularly helpful in comparing costs with homemade potato dishes and in warning of the danger of getting old products well past their prime.

Two pamphlets of use in buying raisins are: The USDA's *Marketing California Raisins* (1975), by Joseph C. Perrin and Richard P. Van Diest; and the California Raisin Advisory Board publication, *A Raisin Is a Dried Grape* (no date), which mainly portrays raisin production and marketing. The first of these is perhaps the more helpful to the buyer.

For an analysis and comparison of orange juice in its various forms—as well as a glossary of the types of oranges and their seasonal availability—see "Orange Juice: Frozen, Canned, Bottled, Cartoned, and Fresh," *Consumer Reports* (August 1976).

For a similar comparative analysis of fresh, frozen, and canned green beans, see "Green Beans," *Consumer Reports* (July 1977).

CONVENIENCE FOODS

Chapter 13 of this volume presents the basic information about convenience foods, their advantages and disadvantages, and selected equipment needed to reconstitute them. Consequently, this discussion of sources lists only materials complementing that basic information. Two longer studies of convenience foods are Marvin E. Thorner, *Convenience and Fast Food Handbook* (1974). Thorner is especially thorough in discussing convenience equipment and its effect on foods. A booklet is also available from the Economic Research Service of the USDA that is directed principally at the processor of convenience foods but that is quite helpful in surveying the introduction, use, and discontinuance of convenience foods. This booklet is entitled *Convenience Foods for the Hotel, Restaurant, and Institutional Market: The Processor's View* (1976), by Harold R. Linstrom and N. Seigle.

Because the variety of convenience foods is so great, it is impossible for an individual buyer to be aware of all of them. Several sources aid the buyer in surveying the scope of convenience products available for use in the quantity food operation. Marvin E. Thorner's article, "Convenience Foods," *Cornell Hotel and Restaurant Administration Quarterly* (May 1975) contains a detailed list of categories of convenience foods available as appetizers, soups, entrées, specialty entrées, vegetables, salads, breads, desserts, and nonalcoholic beverages. *Institutions/ Volume Feeding Management* assists the purchaser of convenience foods in two ways. First, it contains a large number of advertisements from convenience foods manufacturers. These ads help keep the buyer abreast of the new products available for purchase. Moreover, each issue of this magazine contains an "Information Retrieval Card" correlated with the advertisements in that issue. Thus, finding an item that might be useful for his operation, a buyer may easily request additional information through this service. Second, *Institutions/Volume Feeding Management* in 1975 published three articles listing by manufacturer both frozen and nonfrozen convenience foods. These articles, "Your Guide to Frozen Convenience Foods," (February 1, 1975, and April 15, 1975), and "Your Guide to Non-Frozen Convenience Foods," (August 15, 1975), range from frozen convenience entrées, appetizers, and pastries to canned, freeze-dried, and dehydrated items. Obviously many new convenience foods have appeared since 1975, but these guides still present a compact summary and guide to many of the products available.

For further insights into the problems and rewards of using frozen convenience entrées in institutions (especially hospital and university food services), both in terms of quality and cost, see Clinton L. Rappole, "Institutional Use of Frozen Entrées," *Cornell Hotel and Restaurant Administration Quarterly* (May 1973).

BEVERAGES

Like most other commodities the food buyer purchases, beverages, upon closer examination, are more complex than an initial glance would suggest. Some buyers may only need to buy one kind of coffee, one kind of tea bags, regular milk, a cola product, and a cocoa beverage. For these buyers, beverages pose few problems. Buyers for other operations, such as tablecloth restaurants, however, face far greater demands on their purchasing skills. They may have to decide which of several coffee blends to buy, which teas to feature, and—most complex of all—which wines would be most compatible with the menu of the establishment.

For a general survey of nonalcoholic beverages, the buyer may turn to Marvin E. Thorner and Ronald J. Herzberg's *Food Beverage Service Handbook* (1970). It includes chapters on coffee (and its brewing), soft drinks, dairy beverages, juices, tea, and cocoa beverages. It will not, however, answer as many questions about the actual purchase of beverages as it will about their preparation and handling. For the detailed information needed to purchase such things as coffee and tea intelligently, the buyer must turn to more specific publications.

As with cheeses, more and more Americans are taking an interest in specialty coffees and teas. This increase in public interest and sophistication has been matched by a commensurate increase in the number of books analyzing coffees and teas. One excellent, inexpensive volume that discusses both coffee and tea is Peter Quimme's *The Signet Book of Coffee and*

Tea (1976). For coffee it provides a thorough description of the two main types of coffee beans, the growing regions and their respective reputations as coffee-growing areas, and roasting and brewing methods. It discusses how to buy and store coffee and some of the pitfalls that await the unwary. In addition, the section on tea describes the types of teas available, the grading system used for tea, and the proper way to buy tea. This book also includes a valuable glossary of terms for both tea and coffee. Two alternative, but more expensive sources for information on coffee are John Svicarovich, Stephen Winter, and Jeff Ferguson, *The Coffee Book: A Connoisseur's Guide to Gourmet Coffee* (1976); and Kenneth Davids, *Coffee: A Guide to Buying, Brewing, and Enjoying* (1976). For tea, an excellent, brief summary of basics every buyer needs to know is included in "Tea," *Consumer Reports* (September 1977). The article defines the three broad types of tea (green, black, and oolong), the various grades of tea (both by quality and size), and several generic varieties (for example, American black, English breakfast, Earl Grey's, Lapsang Souchong, Russian, Darjeeling, and Irish breakfast). In addition, it describes what qualities constitute a good tea according to the tasters' standards and gives a brand ranking of twenty teas—nineteen of these in tea bags. The Tea Council of the USA also offers a free leaflet on tea varieties and grades entitled *Two Leaves and a Bud: The Story of Tea* (undated). One rather dated ranking of instant coffees is "Instant Coffees," *Consumer Reports* (January 1971).

For a comparative ranking of several cocoa beverages, see "Chocolate Drink Mixes," *Consumer Reports* (September 1976).

"Orange Drink Mixes," *Consumer Reports* (February 1977), gives a similar comparison for several imitation orange juice products such as "Tang" and "Awake."

The beverage that is undoubtedly the most varied in the world and potentially the most complex is wine. Buyers for large wine stores practically spend their lives learning about the constantly changing qualities and nuances of wines. Fortunately, one need not be a French or California vintner to find one's way through the grapes. Two inexpensive paperbacks provide a general introduction to wines of the world and of the United States. Alexis Bespaloff's *The Signet Book of Wine: A Complete Introduction* (1971) provides a quite readable introduction to the wines of the world. It is especially strong in discussing the wines of France and Germany, but it has sections on Italy, Spain, Portugal, and other European wine-producing countries. American wines receive rather little attention, in part because the United States (ranked sixth in world wine production) produces only about 3 percent of the world's wine. The wines of the two main wine-producing countries of South America, Chile and Argentina, also are mentioned. Sparkling wines, brandies, and such fortified wines as sherry, port, and vermouth also receive brief discussion. Peter Quimme's *The Signet Book of American Wine*, as is obvious from the title, has a much narrower focus, but it, like other food books by the same author, is well organized, clearly written, and informative. Especially helpful are the sections describing the principal grape varieties grown in the United States and the wines they produce, the meaning of American wine labels, the proper handling and storing of wines, and the wineries and wines of the United States. In the guide to wineries and wines California receives three-fourths of the attention, while New York and other wine-producing areas receive attention approximately proportionate to their current production. One inexpensive alternative to Bespaloff's book is *The Vintage Wine Book* (1975), by William S. Leedom. More detailed and generally more expensive books on wine are available in such profusion that they cannot even be listed. Information on wines from particular countries is sometimes available from ambassadorial, consular, or commercial offices of the various wine-producing countries. For example, the Italian Trade Commission (One World Trade Center, Suite 2057, New York, NY 10048) has several excellent free publications on Italian wines, including the *Italian Wine Guide* (1976); *Denominazione* (2d ed.; 1977), a description in English of the Italian quality control system and its use on labels; and a *Vintage Guide to Fine Italian Wines* (1977), by Pier Garoglio. These, it must be remembered, are intended to be promotional in nature.

In addition, there are now several rather costly wine newsletters, such as *Robert Finigan's Private Guide to Wines* (100 Bush St., San Francisco, CA 94104), that help identify wines of note. Magazines like *Vintage Magazine* and *Wine World* also can provide some guidance, although they aim primarily at the wine connoisseur.

Paul Beals' article, "Distilled Spirits and the Beverage Operator," *Cornell Hotel and Restaurant Administration Quarterly* (November 1976), which is part of a forthcoming book on beverage management, presents an excellent introduction to distilled alcoholic beverages and their purchase. It discusses the basic processes used in the production of distilled spirits and how these processes affect the beverage. It also describes the federal definitions for straight Bourbon whiskey and the distinctions between it and such appelations as Tennessee whiskey, bottled-in-bond whiskey, blended whiskey, Canadian whiskey, Scotch whiskey, and Irish whiskey. The author also includes basic information on gin, vodka, rum, brandy, cognac, tequila, and cordials. Other noteworthy sources on alcoholic beverages include *The Consumers Union Report on Wines and Spirits* (1972); Alex Lichine, *New Encyclopedia of Wines and Spirits* (1974); and (Harold J.) *Grossman's Guide to Wines, Spirits, and Beers* (6th Rev.; 1977). Grossman's *Guide* is considered by many to be the authoritative guide in this area.

One recent volume devoted solely to beers is Michael A. Weiner's *The Taster's Guide to Beer: Brews and Breweries of the World* (1977). While the strong opinions expressed on the beers are apparently those of the author alone and thus intensely personal, it nevertheless provides an in-depth survey of the world's beers.

Appendix I Guides to Purchasing Food

Table 1. Portion and Yield Factors for Meats, Poultry, Fish, and Shellfish

Wholesale Cut	IMPS Code Number	Entrée	Yield Factor (percent)	Portion Factors		
				Size and State	Cost	Average Number of Servings
MEATS						
Beef						
Rib, primal (regular, 34 to 38 lb.)	103	Roast ribs of beef	26	15 oz., cooked	3.60	10
				11 oz., cooked	2.64	14
				9-½ oz., cooked	2.23	16
				8-½ oz., cooked	2.04	18
Oven ready (20 to 22 lb.)	109		44	15 oz., cooked	2.10	10
				11 oz., cooked	1.49	14
				9-½ oz., cooked	1.32	16
				8-½ oz., cooked	1.17	18
Top round (roast ready), 19 to 23 lb.)	168	Pot roast	55	8 oz., cooked	.91	23
				6 oz., cooked	.68	30
		Round steak	65	10 oz., raw	.96	21
				8 oz., raw	.77	27
		Roast round	57	8 oz., cooked	.88	23
				6 oz., cooked	.66	31
				4 oz., cooked	.44	47
Bottom round (25 to 28 lb.)	170	Pot roast	55	8 oz., cooked	.91	28
				6 oz., cooked	.68	37
		Hamburger	90	8 oz., raw	.55	47
				6 oz., raw	.42	63
				5 oz., raw	.35	76
Strip loin (bone in, 10-inch trim, 18 to 20 lb.)	175	Sirloin steak (2-inch tail, 1/8-inch fat)	50	16 oz., raw	2.00	10
				14 oz., raw	1.75	12
				12 oz., raw	1.50	14
				10 oz., raw	1.25	16
				8 oz., raw	1.00	20
Strip loin (boneless, 12 to 14 lb.)	180	Sirloin steak (2-inch tail, 1/8-inch fat)	70	16 oz., raw	1.42	10
				14 oz., raw	1.24	12
				12 oz., raw	1.06	14
				10 oz., raw	.89	16
				8 oz., raw	.71	20
Top sirloin butt (boneless, 12 to 14 lb.)	184	Top butt steak	62	10 oz., raw	1.01	12
				8 oz., raw	.81	16
				6 oz., raw	1.01	20
		Roast top sirloin	75	8 oz., cooked	.67	20
				6 oz., cooked	.50	26
				4 oz., cooked	.34	38

277

Table 1 *(continued)*

Wholesale Cut	IMPS Code Number	Entrée	Yield Factor (percent)	Portion Factors		
				Size and State	Cost	Average Number of Servings
Tenderloin (full, 7 to 9 lb.)	189	Tenderloin steak	50	10 oz., raw	1.25	5 to 7
(short, 5 to 6 lb.)	192			8 oz., raw	1.00	7 to 9
				6 oz., raw	.75	9 to 12
		Roast tenderloin	40	8 oz., cooked	1.25	5 to 7
				6 oz., cooked	.94	7 to 9
				4 oz., cooked	.63	11 to 14
Corned brisket (kosher style, 12 to 14 lb.)	120	Corned beef	45	8 oz., cooked	1.11	10 to 12
				6 oz., cooked	.83	14 to 16
				4 oz., cooked	.56	21 to 25
Fresh brisket	120	Same as corned brisket				
Chuck (square cut, boneless, 62 to 72 lb.)	116	Pot roast	66	8 oz., cooked	.76	82 to 95
				6 oz., cooked	.57	109 to 126
				4 oz., cooked	.38	163 to 190
		Stew meat or hamburger	90	8 oz., raw	.56	111 to 129
				6 oz., raw	.42	148 to 172
				4 oz., raw	.28	220 to 380
Veal						
Veal leg (single, 25 to 28 lb.)	334	Roast leg	40	8 oz., cooked	1.25	20 to 22
				6 oz., cooked	.94	26 to 28
				4 oz., cooked	.63	40 to 42
		Veal cutlets	47	8 oz., raw	1.06	23 to 26
				6 oz., raw	.80	31 to 35
				4 oz., raw	.64	47 to 52
		Veal stew	68	12 oz., raw	1.10	22 to 25
				10 oz., raw	.92	27 to 30
Veal rack (double, trimmed, 10 to 12 lb.)	306	Veal chops	60	10 oz., raw	1.08	9 to 11
				8 oz., raw	.86	12 to 14
		Roast loin	38	8 oz., cooked	1.32	7-½ to 9
				6 oz., cooked	.99	10 to 12
				4 oz., cooked	.66	15 to 18
Veal chuck (square cut, 8 to 12 lb.)	309	Veal stew	68	12 oz., raw	1.10	7 to 10
				10 oz., raw	.92	8 to 13
				8 oz., raw	.74	10 to 16
		Roast shoulder	40	6 oz., cooked	.94	10 to 12
				4 oz., cooked	.63	14 to 16
Calves liver (3 to 5 lb.)	Fresh	Calves liver	85	6 oz., raw	.44	4 to 6
				4 oz., raw	.30	6 to 10
Sweetbreads (12 to 16 oz. a pair)	Frozen	Sweetbreads	50	6 oz., raw	1.00	1
				6 oz., raw	.75	1
Veal kidneys (4 to 5 oz. each)	Fresh	Veal kidneys	40	8 oz., raw	1.25	4 per serving
				6 oz., raw	.94	3 per serving
Lamb						
Lamb chuck (15 to 17 lb.)	206	Lamb stew	55	12 oz., raw	1.37	11 to 13
				10 oz., raw	1.14	13 to 15
				8 oz., raw	.91	16 to 18
Lamb rack (6 to 8 lb.)	204	Lamb chops	50	8 oz., raw	2.00	6 to 8
				6 oz., raw	.87	8 to 10
				4 oz., raw	.50	12 to 16
		Roast rack	45	8 oz., cooked	1.11	5 to 7
				6 oz., cooked	.83	7 to 9
				4 oz., cooked	.56	10 to 14
Lamb leg (16 to 18 lb.)	233	Roast leg	44	8 oz., cooked	1.14	14 to 16
				6 oz., cooked	.85	18 to 21
				4 oz., cooked	.57	28 to 31
Pork						
Ham (fresh, 12 to 14 lb.)	401	Baked ham	55	8 oz., cooked	.91	14
				6 oz., cooked	.68	19
		Ham steak	80	10 oz., raw	.78	16
				8 oz., raw	.62	21
Ham (pullman, 7 to 9 lb.)	Trade	Ham, ready to eat	85	8 oz., raw	.59	12 to 15
				6 oz., raw	.44	16 to 20
Prosciutto (bone in, 12 to 14 lb.)	Trade	Hors d'oeuvres	50	4 oz., raw	.50	24 to 28
				2 oz., raw	.25	48 to 56

Table 1 *(continued)*

Wholesale Cut	IMPS Code Number	Entrée	Yield Factor (percent)	Portion Factors		
				Size and State	Cost	Average Number of Servings
Shoulder (4 to 8 lb.)	404	Roast shoulder	40	8 oz., cooked	1.25	3 to 6
				6 oz., cooked	.94	4 to 8
				4 oz., cooked	.63	6 to 12
Pork loin (10 to 12 lb.)	411	Pork chops	82	8 oz., raw	.61	16 to 19
				6 oz., raw	.46	22 to 26
		Roast loin	50	8 oz., cooked	1.00	10 to 12
				6 oz., cooked	.75	13 to 16
				4 oz., cooked	.50	20 to 24
POULTRY						
Roasting chicken (3 to 4-½ lb.)	N.A.	Roast chicken	30	4 oz., cooked	.83	3 to 5
				3 oz., cooked	.75	4 to 7
				2-½ oz., cooked	.53	5 to 8
		Breast of chicken	—	11 oz., raw	1.43	—
				10 oz., raw	1.30	—
				9 oz., raw	1.17	—
		Chicken leg	—	11 oz., raw	.73	—
				10 oz., raw	.66	—
				9 oz., raw	.59	—
Fowl (5-½ to 6-½ lb.)	N.A.	Chicken pot pie	25	4 oz., cooked	1.00	5 to 6
				3 oz., cooked	.90	7 to 8
Turkey (22 to 26 lb.)	N.A.	Roast turkey or turkey salad	23	6 oz., cooked	1.63	13 to 16
				4 oz., cooked	1.08	20 to 24
				3 oz., cooked	.98	26 to 32
Duckling (4-½ to 5 lb.)	N.A.	Roast duckling	—	½ per serving	2.38	2
Broiling chicken	N.A.	Broiled or fried chicken	—	1 per serving	—	—
FISH						
Bass, sea (whole, 1 to 1-¼ lb.)	N.A.	Sea bass, fillet	48	8 oz., raw	1.04	1
				6 oz., raw	.78	1-½
Bass, striped (whole, 8 to 12 lb.)	N.A.	Striped bass, fillet	40	8 oz., raw	1.25	6 to 9
				6 oz., raw	.94	8 to 12
Bluefish (whole, 3 to 8 lb.)	N.A.	Bluefish, fillet	40	8 oz., raw	1.25	2-½ to 6
				6 oz., raw	.94	3 to 8-½
Codfish (whole, 5 to 8 lb.)	N.A.	Codfish, fillet	40	8 oz., raw	1.25	4-½ to 6
				6 oz., raw	.94	6 to 8-½
Flounder (whole, ¾ to 2 lb.)	N.A.	Flounder, fillet	33	8 oz., raw	1.52	½ to 1
				6 oz., raw	1.14	½ to 1-½
Haddock (whole, 3 to 8 lb.)	N.A.	Haddock, fillet	36	8 oz., raw	1.39	2 to 5-½
				6 oz., raw	1.04	3 to 7-½
Halibut (whole, 10 to 12 lb.)	N.A.	Halibut, fillet	55	8 oz., raw	.91	11 to 13
				6 oz., raw	.68	15 to 17
		Halibut, steak	81	8 oz., raw	.91	16 to 19
				6 oz., raw	.68	21 to 25
Mackerel (whole, 1 to 2 lb.)	N.A.	Mackerel, fillet	50	8 oz., raw	1.00	1 to 2
				6 oz., raw	.75	1 to 2-½
Pompano (whole, 1 to 1-¼ lb.)	N.A.	Pompano	40	8 oz., raw	1.25	1
				6 oz., raw	.94	1-¼
Red snapper (whole, 8 to 12 lb.)	N.A.	Red snapper, fillet	40	8 oz., raw	1.25	6 to 9
				6 oz., raw	.94	8 to 12
Salmon (head off, 8 to 12 lb.)	N.A.	Salmon, fillet	65	8 oz., raw	.77	10 to 15
				6 oz., raw	.58	14 to 20
		Salmon, steak	85	8 oz., raw	.59	13 to 20
				6 oz., raw	.44	18 to 27
Scrod (whole, 5 to 7 lb.)	N.A.	Scrod, fillet	40	8 oz., raw	1.25	4-½ to 5
				6 oz., raw	.94	6 to 6-½
Shad (fillet, ½ to 1 lb.)	N.A.	Shad, fillet	100	8 oz., raw	.50	1 to 2
				6 oz., raw	.37	1 to 2-½
Shad, roe (pair, 6 to 14 oz.)	N.A.	Shad roe	100	8 oz., raw	.50	1 to 1-½
				6 oz., raw	.37	1 to 2
Sole, English (whole, 1 to 2 lb.)	N.A.	Dover sole	100	1-½ lb., raw	1.50	1
				1 lb., raw	1.00	1
Swordfish (center cut)	N.A.	Swordfish, steak	90	8 oz., raw	.55	—
				6 oz., raw	.42	—
Whitefish (whole, 2 to 3 lb.)	N.A.	Whitefish, fillet	50	8 oz., raw	1.00	2 to 3
				6 oz., raw	.75	2½ to 4

Table 1 *(continued)*

Wholesale Cut	IMPS Code Number	Entrée	Yield Factor (percent)	Portion Factors		
				Size and State	Cost	Average Number of Servings
SHELLFISH						
Clams, cherrystone (320 to 360 per bu.)	N.A.	Clams, fresh	95	6 per serving	.019	50 to 55
Clams, little neck (600 to 700 per bu.)	N.A.	Little neck clams	95	12 per serving	.019	48 to 55
				6 per serving	.009	95 to 110
Crab meat (1 lb. tin)	N.A.	Cocktail or entrée	95	5 oz.	.33	3
				3 oz.	.24	5
Crab meat (frozen)	N.A.	Cocktail or entrée	95	6 oz.	.39	2-½
				4 oz.	.26	4
Live lobster	N.A.	Whole lobster	100	2 lb., raw	2.00	—
				1-½ lb., raw	1.50	—
				1-¼ lb., raw	1.25	—
		Lobster cocktail or lobster meat	20	6 oz., cooked	1.87	—
				4 oz., cooked	1.25	—
				2 oz., cooked	.63	—
Lobster meat (fresh)	N.A.	Lobster cocktail or lobster meat	95	6 oz., cooked	.39	2-½
				4 oz., cooked	.26	4
				2 oz., cooked	.13	8
Lobster meat (frozen, 14 oz. can)	N.A.	Lobster meat	80	6 oz.	.47	2
				4 oz.	.31	3
Oysters, Chatham	N.A.	Oysters in half shell	95	12 per serving	.52	15 to 20
				6 per serving	.26	30 to 40
Scallops, Long Island (480 to 640 per gal.)	N.A.	Cape Cod scallops	100	24 per serving	.04	20 to 26
				18 per serving	.03	26 to 35
Scallops, sea (8 lb. per gal.)	N.A.	Sea scallops	95	6 oz., raw	.05	20
				5 oz., raw	.04	24
Shrimp (headless, frozen, 16 to 20 lb.)	N.A.	Shrimp cocktail or entrée	—	10 per serving	.55	1-½ to 2
				7 per serving	.39	2 to 3
				5 per serving	.27	3 to 4

Note: N.A. indicates not applicable. Lines indicate that there is too much variation to be specific.

Table 2. Amounts of Foods for 50 Servings

Food and Purchase Unit	Amount per Unit	Approximate Serving Size	Servings per Pound (AP)	Amount to Buy for 50 Servings	Comments
MEATS					
Beef					
Rib roast, rolled, boned, 7-rib	12 to 15 lbs.	2-½ to 3 oz. cooked (3-½ to 4-½ inch slice)	2-½ to 3	17 to 20 lbs.	May use sirloin butt, boned
Rib roast, standing, 7-rib	16 to 25 lbs.	3 to 3-½ oz. cooked	2 to 2-½	20 to 25 lbs.	
		4 to 5 oz. cooked	1-⅓ to 1-⅔	27 to 36 lbs.	
Chuck pot roast, bone-in, top	9 to 12 lbs.	3 to 3-½ oz. cooked	2 to 2-½	20 to 25 lbs.	
Chuck pot roast, bone-in, crossarm	6 to 9 lbs.	3 to 3-½ oz. cooked	2 to 2-½	20 to 25 lbs.	Top chuck is more tender
Round steak		4 to 4-½ oz. clear meat, uncooked	2-½ to 3	17 to 20 lbs.	Bottom round requires longer cooking than top round
Stew, chuck and plate, clear meat		5 oz. stew	3 to 5	10 to 17 lbs.	Yield per lb. of raw meat depends on amount of vegetables added to stew
Lamb					
Leg roast	6 to 8 lbs.	2-½ to 3 oz. cooked (3-½ to 4-½ inch slice)	1-½ to 2-½	20 to 35 lbs.	Great variation is due to difficulty in carving
Shoulder roast, boneless	4 to 6 lbs.	2-½ to 3 oz. cooked (3-½ to 4-½ inch slice)	2-½ to 3	15 to 20 lbs.	
Stew, shoulder and brisket, clear meat		5 oz. stew	2-½ to 3	17 to 20 lbs.	Yield per lb. of raw meat depends on amount of vegetables added to stew
Pork					
Loin roast, trimmed	10 to 12 lbs.	2-½ to 3 oz. cooked (3-½ to 4-½ inch slice)	2 to 2-½	20 to 25 lbs.	
Ham					
Fresh, bone-in	12 to 15 lbs.	3 to 3-½ oz. cooked	2 to 2-½	20 to 25 lbs.	
Smoked, tenderized, bone-in	12 to 15 lbs.	3 to 3-½ oz. cooked	2-½ to 3	17 to 20 lbs.	Smoked shoulder may be substituted for ground or cubed ham in recipes
Canned, boneless, ready-to-eat	2 to 9 lbs.	3 oz. cooked	4 to 5	10 to 12 lbs.	
Veal					
Leg roast	15 to 20 lbs.	3 to 3-½ oz. cooked	1-½ to 2-½	20 to 35 lbs.	Great variation is due to difficulty in carving
Shoulder roast, boneless	8 to 14 lbs.	3 to 3-½ oz. cooked	2-½ to 3	17 to 20 lbs.	
Cutlet		4 to 5 oz. uncooked	3 to 4	12 to 17 lbs.	May use frozen cutlets
Ground Meat					
Patties	1 lb. raw meat measures 2 C. packed	4 to 5 oz. uncooked (1 or 2 patties)	2-½ to 3	17 to 20 lbs.	May use one kind of meat only or combinations, such as 10 lbs. beef and 5 lbs. veal or pork, or 10 lbs. fresh pork and 5 lbs. smoked ham

Table 2 *(continued)*

Food and Purchase Unit	Amount per Unit	Approximate Serving Size	Servings per Pound (AP)	Amount to Buy for 50 Servings	Comments
Loaf or extended patties	1 lb. raw meat measures 2 C. packed	4 to 4-½ oz. cooked	3-½ to 4	12 to 15 lbs.	May use one kind of meat or a combination
Bacon					
Sliced	30 to 36 medium or 15 to 20 wide strips per lb.	3 strips	10 to 12	5 to 6 lbs.	1 lb. cooked and diced measures 1-½ C.
		2 strips	7 to 10	5 to 7 lbs.	
Canadian, sliced	12 to 16 slices per lb.	2 or 3 slices	5 to 8	7 to 10 lbs.	
Liver		4 oz. cooked	3 to 4	13 to 17 lbs.	
Sausage					
Links	8 to 9 large per lb.	3 links	3	17 to 20 lbs.	Yield varies with proportion of fat that fries out in cooking
Cakes		6 to 8 oz. raw (2 cakes)	2 to 2-½	20 to 25 lbs.	
Wieners	8 to 10 per lb.	2 wieners	4 to 5	10 to 11-½ lbs.	
POULTRY					
Chicken					
Fryers, dressed	2-½ to 3-½ lbs.	¼ fryer		35 to 40 lbs.	Dressed means bled and with feathers removed
Fryers, eviscerated	1-¾ to 2-½ lbs.	¼ fryer		25 to 30 lbs.	Eviscerated means ready to cook
Fowl					
For fricassee, dressed	3-½ to 6 lbs.	4 to 6 oz. bone-in	1 to 1-½	35 to 50 lbs.	
For fricassee, eviscerated	2-½ to 4-½ lbs.	4 to 6 oz. bone-in	1-¼ to 2	25 to 35 lbs.	
For dishes containing cut-up cooked meat, dressed		1 to 2 oz. clear meat	2-½ to 3	17 to 20 lbs.	4 lbs. raw yield about 1 lb. cooked boned meat
For dishes containing cut-up cooked meat, eviscerated		1 to 2 oz. clear meat	3 to 4	13 to 17 lbs.	3 lbs. raw yield about 1 lb. cooked boned meat
Turkey					
Young tom, dressed	12 to 23 lbs.	2 to 2-½ oz. clear meat	1 to 1-½	35 to 50 lbs.	1 lb. raw yields 4 to 5 oz. sliced clear meat or 5 to 6 oz. cooked boned meat
Young tom, eviscerated	10 to 18 lbs.	2 to 2-½ oz. clear meat	1-½ to 2	25 to 35 lbs.	Yields of all turkeys depend on type and size of bird: broad-breast and larger birds yield more than standard type and smaller birds
Old tom, dressed	20 to 30 lbs.	2 to 2-½ oz. clear meat	1 to 1-½	35 to 50 lbs.	
Old tom, eviscerated	16 to 25 lbs.	2 to 2-½ oz. clear meat	1-½ to 2	25 to 35 lbs.	

Table 2 *(continued)*

Food and Purchase Unit	Amount per Unit	Approximate Serving Size	Servings per Pound (AP)	Amount to Buy for 50 Servings	Comments
FISH					
Fresh or Frozen Fillets		4 to 5 oz.	3 to 4.	14 to 17 lbs.	
Oysters					
For frying	24 to 40 large per qt.	4 to 6 oysters		7 to 8 qts.	
For scalloping	60 to 100 small per qt.			4 to 5 qts.	
For stew	60 to 100 small per qt.	4 to 6 oysters		3 qts.	
VEGETABLES					
Asparagus, by lb. or in bunches	2 to 2-½ lbs. per bunch; 32 to 40 stalks per bunch	3 oz. or 4 to 5 stalks	3 to 4	12 to 16 lbs.	Yield may be increased if tough part of stalk is peeled
Beans, green or wax, by lb.	1 lb. measures 1 qt. whole or 3 C. cut up	2-½ to 3 oz. or ½ C.	4 to 5	10 to 12 lbs.	
Beets by lb.	4 medium per lb. (1-½ to 2 C. cooked and diced)	2-½ to 3 oz. or ½ C.	4 to 4-½	12 to 14 lbs.	
by bunch	4 to 6 medium per bunch	2-½ to 3 oz. or ½ C.	4 to 4-½	12 to 14 lbs.	
Broccoli, by lb. or in bunches	1-½ to 2-½ lbs. per bunch	2-½ to 3 oz.	2-½ to 3	17 to 20 lbs.	Yield may be increased if tough part of stalk is peeled
Brussels sprouts, by qt. berry basket	1 to 1-¼ lbs. per basket	2-½ to 3 oz.	4 to 6	10 baskets or 12 lbs.	
Cabbage, by lb. Raw	4 to 6 C. shredded per lb.	1 to 2 oz.	8	8 to 10 lbs.	
Cooked	2 qts. raw shredded per lb.	2-½ to 3 oz. or ½ C.	4	12 to 15 lbs.	
Carrots, by lb. Cooked	6 medium per lb.	2-½ to 3 oz. or ½ C.	3 to 4	14 to 16 lbs.	1 lb. raw yields 2 C. cooked and diced; after cooking, 3-¼ C. diced weigh 1 lb.
Raw		strips, 2 to 3 inches long		2 to 2-½ lbs.	3-½ C. diced raw weigh 1 lb.
Cauliflower, by head, trimmed	1 to 3 lbs. per head	3 oz. or ½ C	2	28 to 32 lbs.	A 3-lb. head yields 3 qts. raw flowerets
Celery, pascal, by bunch Cooked	1 medium bunch weighs 2 lbs.	2-½ to 3 oz. or ½ C.	3 to 4	7 to 10 bunches	1 medium bunch yields 1-½ qts. raw diced
Raw	1 medium bunch weighs 2 lbs.		8 to 10	3 to 4 bunches	1 qt. raw diced weighs 1 lb.
Cucumbers, single	1 cucumber weighs 10 to 14 oz.	5 to 7 slices (¼C.)		8 to 9 cucumbers	1 medium yields 1-¾ to 2 C. of peeled slices

Table 2 (continued)

Food and Purchase Unit	Amount per Unit	Approximate Serving Size	Servings per Pound (AP)	Amount to Buy for 50 Servings	Comments
Eggplant, single or by dozen	1 small eggplant weighs 1 lb.	2-½ oz. (1-½ slices)	4	10 to 12	A 1-lb. eggplant yields 8 to 9 slices
Lettuce, by head	1 medium head weighs 1-½ to 2-½ lbs. before trimming	⅙ to ⅛ head		4 to 5 heads for garnish; 6 to 8 heads for salad	10 to 12 salad leaves per head; 1 head untrimmed yields 1-½ to 2 qts. shredded;. 2 qts. shredded weigh 1 lb.
Mushrooms, by lb. or basket	1 basket weighs 3 lbs.				1 lb. raw sliced tops and stems measures 7 C.; 2-½ C. sautéed weigh 1 lb.
Onions, by lb.	4 to 6 medium per lb.	3 to 3-½ oz. or ½ C.	3 to 4	14 to 16 lbs.	1 lb. yields 2-½ to 3 C. chopped; 1 C. chopped weighs 5 oz.; 1 C. sliced weighs 4 oz.
Parsley, by bunch	1 bunch weighs 1 oz.				1 medium bunch yields ¼ C. finely chopped; 1 C. chopped weighs 3 oz.
Parsnips, by lb.	3 to 4 medium per lb.	2-½ to 3 oz.	3 to 4	15 lbs.	
Peppers, single or by lb.	5 to 7 per lb.				1 lb. yields 2 C. finely diced; 1 C. chopped weighs 5 oz.
Potatoes, sweet, by lb.	3 medium per lb.	3-½ to 4 oz.	2-½ to 3	17 to 20 lbs.	
Potatoes, white by lb.	3 medium per lb.	4 to 4-½ oz. or ½ C. mashed or creamed	2 to 3	15 to 20 lbs.	1 lb. yields 2-¼ C. diced
by bushel	1 bu. weighs 60 lbs.	4 to 4-½ oz. or ½ C.	2 to 3		
by bag	1 bag weighs 50 lbs.	4 to 4-½ oz. or ½ C.	2 to 3		
Rutabagas, by lb.	1 to 2 per lb.	3 to 3-½ oz. or ½ C.	2 to 2-½	20 to 25 lbs.	1 lb. yields 1-½ C. mashed or 2-½ C. diced
Spinach, by bag or bushel	10 or 20 oz. per bag	3 to 3-½ oz. or ½ C.	2-½ to 3	17 to 20 lbs. home-grown or 12 to 15 10-oz. bags cleaned	A 10 oz. bag yields 2 qts. raw, coarsely chopped for salad
Squash Summer, by lb.		2-½ to 3 oz. or ½ C.	3 to 4	13 to 16 lbs.	
Winter, by lb.		3 oz. or ½ C. mashed	2	25 to 30 lbs.	
Tomatoes, by lb., 8 lb. basket, or 10-lb. carton	3 to 4 medium per lb.	3 slices raw	5 (sliced)	10 lbs. for slicing	1 lb. yields 2 C. diced or cut in wedges
Turnips, white, by lb.		3 oz. or ½ C.	3 to 4	15 to 20 lbs.	

FRUITS

Food and Purchase Unit	Amount per Unit	Approximate Serving Size	Servings per Pound (AP)	Amount to Buy for 50 Servings	Comments
Apples by lb.	2 to 3 medium per lb.	½ C. sauce		15 to 20 lbs. for sauce or pie	1 lb. before peeling yields 3 C. diced or sliced; 4-½ to 5 C. pared, diced, or sliced weigh 1 lb.
by pk.	1 pk. weighs 12 lbs.	½ C. sauce		15 to 20 lbs.	1 pk. (12 lbs.) makes 4 to 5 pies, 4 to 5 qts. of sauce, 7 to 8 qts. of raw cubes

Table 2 *(continued)*

Food and Purchase Unit	Amount per Unit	Approximate Serving Size	Servings per Pound (AP)	Amount to Buy for 50 Servings	Comments
Apples (continued) by bu.	1 bu. weighs 48 lbs.	½ C. sauce		15 to 20 lbs.	
by box	1 box contains 80 to 100 large or 113 to 138 medium	½ C. sauce		15 to 20 lbs.	
Bananas, by lb. or dozen	3 to 4 medium per lb.	1 small	3 to 4	15 lbs.	1 lb. yields 2 to 2-½ C. sliced thin or 1-¼ C. mashed; for 1 C. sliced or diced, use 1-⅓ medium; for 1 C. mashed, use 2-¼ medium
Cranberries, by lb.	1 lb. measures 1 to 1-¼ qts.	¼ C. sauce	12 to 14 for sauce	4 lbs. for sauce	1 lb. makes 3 to 3-½ C. sauce or 2-¾ C. jelly
Grapefruit, by dozen, box, or half-box	54 to 70 medium per box; 80 to 126 small per box				1 medium-small yields 10 to 12 sections or 1-¾ C. broken sections
Lemons, by dozen, box, or half-box	210 to 250 large per box; 300 to 360 medium per box; 392 to 432 small per box			25 to 30 lemons (1-¼ qts. juice) for 50 glasses of lemon-ade	1 medium yields ¼ C. juice and 1 t. grated rind; 4 to 5 medium yield 1 C. juice
Oranges, by dozen, box, or half-box	80 to 126 large per box; 150 to 200 medium per box; 216 to 288 small per box	½ C. sections		40 to 50 oranges	Use medium oranges for table and salad; 1 medium yields 12 sections and ½ to ⅔ C. diced
Peaches by lb.	3 to 5 per lb.	3 oz. or ½ C.	4	10 to 12 lbs. for slicing	1 lb. yields 2 C. peeled and diced
by pk.	1 pk. weighs 12-½ lbs.	3 oz. or ½ C.	4		
by ½ bu.	½ bu. weighs 25 lbs.	3 oz. or ½ C.	4		
Pineapple, single	1 medium weighs 2 lbs.	½ C. cubed		5 medium	1 medium yields 3 to 3-½ C. peeled and cubed
Rhubarb, fresh, by lb.		½ C. sauce	5	10 lbs.	10 lbs. yield 6 qts. sauce
Strawberries, by qt.	1 qt. yields 3 C. hulled	½ C.		10 to 13 qts.	1 qt. yields 4 to 5 servings of fruit
	1 qt. yields 1 pt. hulled and crushed	⅓ C. for shortcake		8 to 10 qts.	1 qt. yields 6 servings of sauce for shortcake

STAPLES

Food and Purchase Unit	Amount per Unit	Approximate Serving Size	Servings per Pound (AP)	Amount to Buy for 50 Servings	Comments
Cocoa	1 lb. measures 4 C.; 1 C. weighs 4 oz.			2 C. (½ lb.) for 50 C. beverage (2-½ gals.)	
Rice	1 lb. raw measures 2-⅛ C.	1 no. 16 or no. 12 scoop	15 to 20	2-½ to 3 lbs.	1 lb. cooked measures 1-¾ qts.
Sugar Cubes	50 to 60 large or 100 to 120 small cubes per lb.	1 large or 2 small	50 to 60	¾ to 1 lb.	
Granulated	1 lb. measures 2-⅛ C.; 1 C. weighs 7 oz.	1-½ t. to sweeten coffee	50 to 60	¾ to 1 lb.	

Table 2 *(continued)*

Food and Purchase Unit	Amount per Unit	Approximate Serving Size	Servings per Pound (AP)	Amount to Buy for 50 Servings	Comments
Bread, by loaf					
White and whole wheat	1-lb. loaf yields 18 slices	1-½ slices to accompany meal	12	4 loaves	
	2-lb. club loaf yields 24 slices	1-½ slices	8	3 loaves	
	2-lb. Pullman (sandwich) loaf yields 36 slices	1-½ slices	12	2 loaves	
Rye	1-lb. loaf yields 17 slices	1-½ slices	11	4-½ loaves	
	2-lb. short loaf yields 29 slices	1-½ slices	10	5 loaves	
	2-lb. long loaf yields 36 slices	1-½ slices	12	2 loaves	
Butter	1 lb. measures 2 C.; 1 oz. measures 2 T.		48 to 60	1 to 1-½ lbs.	Available in wholesale units cut into 48 to 90 pieces per lb.; 60 count gives average size cut
Cheese					
Brick	1 brick weighs 5 lbs.	1-oz. thin slices for sand-wiches	16	3-¼ lbs. for sandwiches	
		4/5-oz. cubes for pie	20	2-½ lbs. for pie	
Cottage	1 lb. measures 2C.	no. 10 scoop (approximately ½ C.)	8 to 9	6 lbs.	1 lb. yields 12 to 13 of the no. 16 scoops and 25 of the no. 30 scoops
Coffee					
Ground	1 lb. drip grind measures 5 C.			1 lb.	Makes 50 C. when added to 2-½ gals. of water
Instant				2-½ C.	Add to 2-½ gals. of water
Cream					
Heavy (40 percent) to whip		1 rounded T.		1 pt. (yields 1 qt. whipped)	Doubles its volume in whipping
Light (20 percent) or top milk for coffee	1 qt. yields 64 T.	1-½ T.		1-¼ qts.	
Fruit or vegetable juice	1 46-oz. can measures approximately 1-½ qts.	4-oz. glass or ½ C.		4-⅓ 46-oz. cans (6-½ qts.)	
	1 no. 10 can measures 13 C. or 3-¼ qts.	4-oz. glass or ½ C.		2 no. 10 cans (6-½ qts.)	
Fruits, dried					
Prunes	1 lb. contains 40 to 50 medium	4 to 5 for stewed fruit		5 to 6 lbs.	
Honey	1 lb. measures 1-⅓ C.	2 T.		5 lbs.	
Ice cream					
Brick	1-qt. brick cuts 6 to 8 slices	1 slice		7 to 9 bricks	Available in slices individually wrapped
Bulk, by gals.		no. 10 scoop		2 gals.	1 gal. yields 25 to 30 servings
Lemonade		8-oz. glass (¾ C.)		2-½ gals. (25 to 30 lemons for 1-¼ qts. of juice)	
Peanut butter	1 lb. measures 1-¾ C.			4 lbs. for sand-wiches	
Potato chips	1 lb. measures 5 qts.	¾ to 1 oz.		2 lbs.	

Table 2 (continued)

Food and Purchase Unit	Amount per Unit	Approximate Serving Size	Servings per Pound (AP)	Amount to Buy for 50 Servings	Comments
Salad dressings Mayonnaise, by qt.		1 T. for salad		1 to 1-½ qts. for mixed salads; 3 to 4 C. for garnish	
French				¾ to 1 qt.	
Sandwiches Bread	2 lb. (14-in.) loaf cut 30 to 35 medium or 35 to 40 very thin slices	2 slices	7 to 8 medium; 9 to 10 very thin	3 loaves	
Butter, by lb.		spread on 1 slice		¾ lb.	
		spread on 2 slices		1-½ lbs.	
Fillings		2 T. or no. 30 scoop		1-¾ to 2 qts.	
		3 T. or no. 24 scoop		2-½ to 3 qts.	
Tea, iced	1 lb. measures 6 C.			3 oz.	Makes 50 glasses when added to 2-½ gals. water and chipped ice
Vegetables, dried Beans, navy	1 lb. measures 2-½ C.			5 to 6 lbs.	

Source: Marion Wood Crosby and Katharine W. Harris, *Purchasing Food for 50 Servings*, rev. ed., Cornell Extension Bulletin no. 803 (Ithaca: New York State College of Home Economics, 1963). Reprinted by permission.

Table 3. Summary of Federal Standards for Grading Meats, Poultry, Fish and Shellfish, Eggs, Dairy Products, Fruits, and Vegetables

MEATS

Beef

USDA grade	Steers and heifers	Cows	Bullock (young bull under 18 months of age)	Bull or stag (old bulls graded only for yield)
Prime	X	—	X	—
Choice	X	X	X	X
Good	X	X	X	X
Standard	X	X	X	—
Commercial	X	X	—	X
Utility	X	X	X	X
Cutter	X	X	—	X
Canner	X	X	—	X

	Quality grades				
Grading considerations:	Prime	Choice	Good	Standard	Commercial
Conformation					
Length of legs (short to long)	1	2	3	4	5
Width of hips and back (broad to narrow)	1	2	3	4	5
Body width to length (high to low)	1	2	3	4	5
Plump rounded body (blocky to lean)	1	2	3	4	5
Filled in cavities (fully to partially)	1	2	3	4	5
Fat covering (adequate to globy)	1	2	3	4	5
Quality factors					
Texture of meat	Very smooth	Fairly smooth	Slightly smooth	Slightly ropey	Ropey
Firmness of flesh	Very firm	Quite firm	Firm	Slightly firm	Soft
Marbling and fat	Abundant	Medium abundant	Moderate	Slight	Traces
Color of flesh	Bright cherry red	Medium cherry red	Red	Bluish red	Dark bluish red
Age (condition of bone, 1-½ to 3 years)	1	2	3	4	5
Buttons (feather bones)	Large, soft decreasing to hard, small.				

Yield (ratio of usable meat to total carcas weight)

	Yield grades				
	Most usable				Least usable
Quality grades	1	2	3	4	5
Prime	—	X	X	X	X
Choice	X	X	X	X	—
Good	X	X	X	—	—
Utility	X	X	—	—	—
Cull	X	X	—	—	—

Veal

USDA grade	Calf	Veal (under 3 months of age)
Prime	X	X
Choice	X	X
Good	X	X
Standard	X	X
Utility	X	X
Cull	X	X

No yield grades for veal.

Table 3 (continued)

Lamb

USDA grade	Lamb (under 1 year old)	Yearling 1 to 1-¼ year old)	Mutton (over 1-¼ year old)
Prime	X	X	—
Choice	X	X	X
Good	X	X	X
Utility	X	X	X
Cull	X	X	X

	Yield grades				
	Most usable				Least usable
Quality grade	1	2	3	4	5
Prime	—	X	X	X	X
Choice	—	X	X	X	X
Good	X	X	X	X	X
Utility	X	X	X	X	X

Pork

USDA grade	Barrow	Gilt	Stag	Boar
Fresh				
No. 1	X	X	—	—
No. 2	X	X	X	X
No. 3	X	X	X	X
No. 4	X	X	X	X
Utility	X	X	X	X
Smoked (hams, bacon, picnics, loins, Canadian-type bacon)				
No. 1	N.A.	N.A.	N.A.	N.A.
No. 2	N.A.	N.A.	N.A.	N.A.

No yield grades for pork.

POULTRY
(includes chickens, turkeys, ducks, geese, guinea fowl, and squab pigeons)

USDA grades for ready to cook carcasses	USDA grades for wholesale market
A	Extra
B	Standard
C	Trade

Grading considerations:
  Physical condition (edible)
  Properly cleaned (inside and out)
  Fleshing (full)
  Conformation (no abnormalities)
  Fat (well covered)
  Pinfeathers (free)
  No defects (broken bones, skin tears, freezer burns)

FISH AND SHELLFISH

USDA grades for fresh fish
  A
  B
  Substandard (SS)

Standards for classification as to:

Source (all fish and shellfish marketed in the United States must come from waters approved by the U.S. Health Department)
  Salt water
  Fresh water
  Fresh and salt water
  Cultivated or farm fish

Condition
  Fresh
  Frozen
  Canned
  Dried
  Processed

Table 3 *(continued)*

Market form (fresh fish)
  Whole or round (as caught)
  Drawn (eviscerated and scaled)
  Dressed (eviscerated, head, tail, fins off)
  Steaks (cross sections of dressed fish)
  Fillets (flesh cut lengthwise off back bone)
  Chunks (pieces of drawn or dressed fish)
  Sticks (fillets cut into pieces)

EGGS

USDA grades for fresh shell eggs

  AA (fresh, fancy)
  A
  B (all eggs below this grade are sold to processors)

Fresh shell eggs

Size	Weight	
	Minimum net weight per dozen (ounces)	Gross weight per case (including 4-pound allowance for carton) (pound)
Jumbo	30	60
Extra large	27	54
Large	24	49
Medium	21	43
Small	18	38
Peewee	15	28

Classification of eggs:
  Fresh shell (under 29 days old)
  Storage shell (over 29 days old)
  Processed storage (shell oiled before storage)
  Frozen—mixed whole
       —whites only
       —yolks, plain
       —yolks, sugar added (9:1)
  Dried—freeze-dried
      —dehydrated

DAIRY PRODUCTS

Butter
USDA grades

  AA
  A
  C
  Cooking (CC)

Classification of butter:
  Sweet cream (made only from sweet cream)
  Sweet (contains no salt, but can be made from sour cream)
  Creamery (factory made from milk and cream from many sources)
  Salted (contains salt, also called lightly salted butter)
  Farm (generally made on a farm and often unpasteurized)
  Sour cream (made from naturally soured cream)

Milk (all milk products must conform to state and federal standards for pasteurization, addition of vitamins, and coliform and bacteria counts)
Classification of milk:
  Fresh, whole (contains a minimum of 3-¼ percent milk fat and 8-¼ percent nonfat milk solids)
  Homogenized
  Pasteurized
  Nonfat
  Buttermilk
  Acidophilus
  Dried
  Cream
    Light (contains 16 to 18 percent milk fat)
    Table (contains 20 to 30 percent milk fat)
    Whipping—light contains 30 to 34 percent milk fat
          —heavy contains 34 to 40 percent milk fat
    Half and half (mixture of milk and light cream, about 10 percent milk fat)

Table 3 *(continued)*

Ice Cream and Frozen Desserts

	Product				
Government standards	Vanilla ice cream	Flavored ice cream	Ice milk	Sherbet	Ices
Minimum percent milk fat	10	8	2	1	0
Minimum percent milk solids	20	16	11	2	0
Minimum weight per gallon (in pounds)	4.5	4.5	4.5	6	6
Percentage of overrun	80 to 100	80 to 100	80 to 100	35 to 40	25 to 30

FRUITS

Fresh	USDA grades at the wholesale level
Apples	Extra Fancy, Fancy, No. 1, No. 1 Cookers, No. 1 Early, Utility
Apricots	No. 1, No. 2
Avocados, Florida	No. 1, Combination
Cantaloupes	No. 1, Commercial
Cherries, sweet	No. 1, Commercial
Cranberries	Grade A (Consumer grade)
Dewberries and blackberries	No. 1, No. 2
Grapes, American bunch	
Grapes, European, sawdust pack	Fancy, Extra No. 1, No. 1
Grapes, table	Fancy No. 1
Grapefruit (California and Arizona)	Fancy No. 1, No. 2, Combination, No. 3
Grapefruit (Florida)	Fancy, No. 1, No. 1 Bright, No. 1 Golden, No. 1 Bronze, No. 1 Russet, No. 2, No. 2 Bright, No. 2 Russet, No. 3
Grapefruit (Texas)	Fancy, No. 1, No. 1 Bright, No. 1 Bronze, Combination No. 2, No. 2 Russet, No. 3
Honeydew and honeyball melon	No. 1, Commercial, No. 2
Lemons	No. 1, Combination, No. 2
Limes (Persian), Tahiti	No. 1, Combination, No. 2
Nectarines	Fancy, Extra No. 1, No. 1, No. 2
Oranges (California and Arizona)	Fancy, No. 1, Combination, No. 2
Oranges and tangelos (Florida)	Fancy, No. 1 Bright, No. 1, No. 1 Golden, No. 1 Bronze, No. 1 Russet, No. 2 Bright, No. 2, No. 2 Russet, No. 5
Oranges (Texas)	Fancy, No. 1, No. 1 Bright, No. 1 Bronze, Combination No. 2, No. 2 Russet, No. 3
Peaches	No. 1, No. 2
Pears, summer and fall	No. 1, Combination, No. 2
Pears, winter	Extra No. 1, No. 1, Combination, No. 2
Pineapples	Fancy, No. 1, No. 2
Plums and prunes	Fancy, No. 1, Combination, No. 2
Rhubarb	No. 1, No. 2
Strawberries and raspberries	No. 1, No. 2
Tangerines	Fancy, No. 1, No. 1 Bronze, No. 1 Russet, No. 2, No. 2 Russet, No. 3
Watermelon	No. 1, Commercial, No. 2

Processed	USDA grades	Trade grades
Canned and frozen	A or Fancy	
	B or Choice	
	C or Standard	
	Below U.S. Standard (water packed)	
Dried	A or Fancy	Good
	B or Choice	Reasonably good
	C or Standard	Fairly good

Table 3 *(continued)*

VEGETABLES	
Fresh	USDA grades at the wholesale level
Artichokes, globe	No. 1, No. 2
Asparagus	No. 1, No. 2 (Washington No. 1, Washington No. 2 are more used in the markets)
Beans, lima	No. 1, Combination No. 2
Beans, snap	Fancy, No. 1, Combination, No. 2
Beets	No. 1, No. 2
Beet greens	No. 1
Broccoli, Italian sprouting	Fancy, No. 1, No. 2
Brussels sprouts	No. 1, No. 2
Cabbage	No. 1, Commercial
Carrots, bunched	No. 1, Commercial
Carrots, topped	Extra No. 1, No. 1, No. 2
Carrots, short-trimmed tops	No. 1, Commercial
Cauliflower	No. 1
Celery	Extra No. 1, No. 1, No. 2
Collard or broccoli greens	No. 1
Corn, green	Fancy, No. 1, No. 2
Cucumbers	No. 1, No. 1 large, No. 2
Cucumbers, greenhouse	Fancy, No. 1, No. 2
Dandelion greens	No. 1
Eggplant	Fancy, No. 1, No. 2
Endive, escarole, chicory	No. 1
Garlic	No. 1
Kale	No. 1, Commercial
Lettuce	No. 1, No. 2
Lettuce, greenhouse leaf	Fancy, No. 1
Mushrooms	No. 1
Mustard greens and Turnip greens	No. 1
Okra	No. 1
Onions, Bermuda, Granex	No. 1, No. 2, Commercial
Onions, Creole	No. 1, No. 2, Combination
Onions, northern grown	No. 1, No. 1 Boilers, No. 1 Picklers, Commercial No. 2
Onions, green	No. 1, No. 2
Parsley	No. 1
Parsnips	No. 1, No. 2
Peas, fresh	Fancy, No. 1
Peppers, sweet	No. 1, No. 2
Potatoes	Fancy, Extra No. 1, No. 1, No. 2, Commercial
Potatoes sweet	Extra No. 1, No. 1, Commercial, No. 2
Radishes	No. 1, Commercial
Romaine	No. 1
Rutabagas or turnips	No. 1, No. 2
Shallots, bunched	No. 1, No. 2
Spinach, fresh	Extra No. 1, No. 1, Commercial
Squash, fall and winter type	No. 1, No. 2
Squash, summer	No. 1, No. 2
Tomatoes, fresh	No. 1, Combination, No. 2
Tomatoes, greenhouse	Fancy, No. 1, No. 2

Processed	USDA grades	Trade grades
Canned and frozen	A or Fancy	
	B or Extra Standard	
	C or Standard	
	Below U.S. Standard (water packed)	
Dried	A or Fancy	Good
	B or Choice	Reasonably good
	C or Standard	Fairly good

Table 4. Approximate Quantities Required for Some Common Fruits and Vegetables

Item	Shipping Container	Approximate Net Weight in Pounds, as Purchased per Container	Miscellaneous Shipping or Portioning Data	Portion Size as Served	Portions per Pound as Purchased	Approximate Amount to Purchase as Purchased for 100 Portions
FRUITS						
Apples, whole	Western box, 113's	44		1 each	2.3	44 lbs. (1 box)
Apples, baked	Western box, 88's	44		1 each	1.8	55 lbs. (1-¼ box)
Apples, for pies	Bu. basket	48	20 pies per bu.; 2-½ lbs. used per 9-in. pie	1 pie slice[a]	2.5	40 lbs.
Apples, rings	Western box, 113's	44	5 rings per apple	2 rings	6.7	15 lbs. (⅓ box)
Apple salad, Waldorf	Western box, 113's	44	15 slices per apple	½ C. diced	4.5	22 lbs. (½ box)
Apple slices, small	Western box, 113's	44	16 to 20 qts. per bu.	3 slices	14.0	7-½ lbs. (20 apples)
Applesauce	Bu. basket	48	8 to 12 per lb.	½ C.	2.8	36 lbs. (¾ bu.)
Apricots, whole	Till, 60's	5	100 apricots per lug	2 each	5.0	20 lbs. (4 till)
Apricots, whole	Los Angeles lug	20		2 each	2.5	40 lbs. (2 lugs)
Avocados, half	Flat, 18's	13		half	2.0	52 lbs. (4 flats)
Avocados, sliced	Flat, 24's	13	30 slices per avocado used in grapefruit salad	4 slices	25.0	4 lbs. (8 avocados)
Bananas, whole	Box	40	3 per lb.	1 each	3.0	33 lbs. (.8 box)
Bananas, sliced	Box	40	2 to 2-½ C. per lb. or 30 slices per banana	½ C.	4.0	25 lbs.
Blackberries	Crate, 24 qts.	30	(use 1 qt. per pie for pies)	½ C. with cream	6.0	17 lbs. (13 boxes)
Blueberries, for pies	Crate, 12 qts.	8	¾ qt. per 9-in. pie	1 pie slice[a]	7.0	15 lbs. (24 pts.)
Blueberries, pudding	Crate, 24 qts.	30		½ C.	12.1	8-¼ lbs. (6-½ qts.)
Cherries, sweet, whole	Lug	15		12 cherries	5.0	20 lbs. (1-⅓ lug)
Cherries, sour, pie	Bushel	54	1-¼ qt. per 9-in. pie	1 pie slice[a]	3.3	33 lbs. (⅔ bu.)
Cranberries, sauce	Box	25	Cooked sauce	¼ C.	3.5	7-½ lbs.
Cranberries, sauce	Box	25	Chopped raw	½ C.	6.0	17 lbs.
Figs	Flat, 48's	6		3 medium figs	2.8	36 lbs. (6 boxes)
Grapes, Concord, whole	Basket	6		¼ lb.	4.0	25 lbs. (4 baskets)
Grapes, European, whole	Box	28	70 grapes per lb.	½ C.	3.6	28 lbs. (1 box)
Grapefruit	⅘ bu. carton, 32's	40	12 sections per grapefruit	Half	0.8	125 lbs. (3-⅛ boxes)
Grapefruit, sections	⅘ bu. carton, 32's	40	6-½ qts. juice per carton	6 sections (salad)	0.8	125 lbs. (3-⅛ boxes)
Grapefruit, juice	⅘ bu. carton, 40's	40	For lemonade: 1 pt. juice per dozen; 8 qts. per carton	4 oz.	1.3	80 lbs. (2 boxes)
Lemons, juice	⅘ bu. carton, 85's	38		2 oz. juice	3.6	28 lbs. (12 doz.)
Lemons, slices	⅘ bu. carton, 85's	38	8 slices per lemon	1 slice	40.0	2-¼ lbs. (1 doz.)
Lemons, wedges	⅘ bu. carton, 85's	38	6 wedges per lemon	1 wedge	25.0	3-½ lbs. (1-½ doz.)
Limes, juice	Dozen		For limeade	1-¾ oz. (1 lime)		9 doz.
Limes, wedges	Dozen		4 to 5 wedges per lime	1 wedge		2 doz.
Melons						
Cantaloupe[b]	Crate, 45's	70 to 80		half	.8 to 1.0	90 lbs. (1.2 crates)
Cantaloupe, rings	Crate, 45's	70 to 80	8 rings per melon, each ring used to hold chopped fruit for salad	1 ring	4.0	22 lbs. (13 melons)
Cantaloupe, balls	Crate, 45's	70 to 80	30 balls per melon; used for melon ball cup	9 balls	1.8	51 lbs. (30 melons)

Table 4 (continued)

Item	Shipping Container	Approximate Net Weight in Pounds, as Purchased per Container	Miscellaneous Shipping or Portioning Data	Portion Size as Served	Portions per Pound as Purchased	Approximate Amount to Purchase for 100 Portions
Cantaloupe, diced	Crate, 45's	70 to 80	10 oz. meat per melon	3 oz.	1.8	51 lbs. (30 melons)
Casaba, wedge[c]	Crate, 8's	50		1/8 melon	1.3	82 lbs. (13 melons)
Watermelon, slice	Individual melon	35		1 lb.	1.0	100 lbs. (3 melons)
Nectarines, whole	Lug, 120's	20		2 whole	2.4	34 lbs. (1-2/3 lug)
Oranges, whole	Carton, 88's	38		1 whole	2.3	43 lbs. (8-1/3 doz.)
Oranges, juice	Carton, 88's	45	10-1/2 qts. per carton	4 oz.	2.2	55 lbs. (1-1/4 cartons)
Oranges, slice	Carton, 88's	45	6 slices per orange for salad	3 slices	4.0	26 lbs. (50 oranges)
Oranges, sections	Carton, 88's	38	9 sections per orange	6 sections	w	28 lbs. (5-1/2 doz.)
Peaches, sliced	Lug	20	4 per lb.; 6 C. sliced per lb.; 8-1/2 qts. sliced per lug	1/2 C.	3.6	60 lbs. (3 lugs)
Peaches, pie	Basket, 20's	5 to 6	3 pies per basket; 2 C. per pie	1 slice pie[a]	1.7	30 lbs. (5 to 6 baskets or 2/3 bu.)
Peaches, pudding	Bushel	45		1/2 C.	3.4	18 lbs.
Pears, whole	Box, 120's	40	3 per lb.	1 whole	5.5	34 lbs.
Pears, diced	Bushel	48		1/2 C.	3.0	32 lbs. (3/4 bu.)
Persimmons, whole	Flat, 28's	14	(6 sections can be obtained per persimmon)	1 each halved	3.0	50 lbs. (8-1/3 doz.)
Pineapple, diced	Crate, 24's	70	20 oz. diced per pineapple	1/2 C.	2.0	60 lbs. (20 pineapples)
Pineapple, sliced	Crate, 24's	70	10 round slices per pineapple	1 slice	1.7	30 lbs. (10 pineapples)
Plums, whole	Basket, 5 x 5	5	18 to 24 medium per basket	3 medium	3.3	22-1/2 lbs. (4-1/2 baskets)
Plums, pie	Basket, 4 x 5	5	2-1/2 to 3 9-in. pies per basket	1 pie slice[a]	4.4	30 lbs. (6 baskets)
Raspberries	Crate, 24 pts.	18		3 oz. (2/3 C.)	3.3	16 lbs. (20 pts.)
Raspberries, pie	Crate, 16 qts.	20	3/4 qt. per pie	1 pie slice[a]	6.3	17 lbs. (13 qts.)
Raspberries, cobbler	Crate, 16 qts.	20		1/2 C.	6.0	10 lbs. (8 qts.)
Rhubarb, hothouse	Flat	5	Used for sauce	1/2 C.	10.0	20 lbs.
Rhubarb, pie	Crate	40	3 C. rhubarb sliced per pie	1 pie slice[a]	4.0	15 lbs.
Strawberries	Crate, 24 qts.	30	6 servings to qt.	2/3 C.	6.6	20 lbs. (17 qts.)
Strawberries, pie	Crate, 24 qts.	30	1 qt. per pie	1 slice pie[a]	5.0	20 lbs. (17 qts.)
Strawberries, sauce	Crate, 24 pts.	18		1/4 C.	5.0	10 lbs. (13 pts.)
Tangerines	Crate, 125's	40		1 tangerine	10.0	35 lbs.
Tangerines, sections	Crate, 125's	40	10 sections per tangerine; used for salad	5 sections	3.0	16 lbs. (4-1/4 doz.)

VEGETABLES

Item	Shipping Container	Approximate Net Weight in Pounds, as Purchased per Container	Miscellaneous Shipping or Portioning Data	Portion Size as Served	Portions per Pound as Purchased	Approximate Amount to Purchase for 100 Portions
Artichoke, globe	Artichoke box, 72's	40		1 each	1.8	56 lbs. (8-1/3 doz.)
Asparagus	Crate	29	1 bunch is 2-1/2 lbs. and contains 24 stalks	3 oz. (3-4 stalks)	2.6	38 lbs.
Beans, lima, Fordhook	Bu. basket	30	Yields 8 qts. shelled	3 oz. (1/2 C.)	2.1	48 lbs.
Beans, lima, baby	Bu. basket	28	Yields 8 qts. shelled	3 oz. (1/2 C.)	2.2	45 lbs.
Beans, lima, fava	Bu. basket	28	Yields 8 qts. shelled	3 oz. (1/2 C.)	2.1	48 lbs.
Beans, lima, shelled	Basket	1/4		3 oz. (1/2 C.)	5.3	19 lbs.
Beans, snap	Bu. basket	30		3 oz. (1/2 C.)	4.5	22 lbs.

Item	Market unit	Count	Description	Serving	Per unit	Weight
Beets, with tops	Crate, 36 bunches	45		3 oz. (½ C.)	2.1	46 lbs.
Beets, topped	Bu. basket	52		3 oz. (½ C.)	4.0	25 lbs.
Beet greens	Bu. basket	18		3 oz. (½ C.)	2.3	43 lbs.
Broccoli	Crate, 18 bunches	63	1 bunch is 2 to 2-½ lbs.	3 oz. (½ C.)	2.9	35 lbs.
Brussels sprouts	Drum	27		3 oz. (½ C.)	4.1	24 lbs.
Cabbage, shredded	Bag	50	Cooked 1 lb. shredded cabbage yields 2-½ C.	3 oz. (½ C.)	4.0	25 lbs.
Cabbage, shredded	Bu. basket	40	Raw 1 lb. shredded cabbage equals 3-½ C.	½ C. slaw	6.5	15 lbs.
Cabbage, Chinese	Bu. basket	40	Diced raw	2-½ oz. (½ C.)	4.0	25 lbs.
Carrots, with tops	Crate, 36's (bunches)	45		3 oz. (½ C.)	2.8	35 lbs.
Carrots, with tops	Crate, 36 bunches	45	Strips raw	2 oz. (4 strips)	4.3	23 lbs.
Carrots, topped	Bag	50		3 oz. (½ C.)	3.9	26 lbs.
Carrots, topped	Bag	50	Strips raw	2 oz. (4 strips)	5.8	17 lbs.
Cauliflower	Crate, 12's	24		3 oz. (½ C.)	2.0	50 lbs.
Chard	Bu. basket	18		3 oz. (½ C.)	3.7	27 lbs.
Celery	Crate, 30's	30		3 oz. (½ C.)	3.7	27 lbs.
Celery	Crate, 30s	30	Stalk pieces raw (small)	2 oz. (2 stalks)	6.0	17 lbs.
Cucumbers, pared	Bu. basket	45	75 cucumbers; 1 9-in. cucumber yields 25 to 30 slices	2-½ oz. (5 slices)	5.8	18 lbs.
Cucumbers, unpared	Bu. basket	45		2-½ oz. (5 slices)	7.6	13 lbs.
Endive, Belgium, chopped	Basket	5	15 to 25 heads	2 oz. (½ or ⅓ head)	7.1	14 lbs.
Collards	Bu. basket	20	12 bunches	3 oz. (½ C.)	4.3	23 lbs.
Corn on the cob	Wirebound crate	40	5 doz. ears each ear approximately 10 to 12 oz. as purchased	7 oz. (1 ear)	1.7	60-75 lbs. (8-⅓ doz.)
Corn, kernels from cob	Wirebound crate	40		3 oz. (½ C.)	1.5	66 lbs.
Eggplant	Bu. basket	40	24 to 30 eggplant; eggplant pared and steamed	3 oz. (½ C.)	4.0	25 lbs.
Eggplant, sliced	Bu. basket	40	Unpared, batter-fried	3-½ oz. (1 slice)	4.3	23 lbs.
Escarole, diced, raw	Bu. basket	25	2 doz. heads	2 oz.	5.8	17 lbs.
Chicory, curly leaf	Bu. basket	22	2 doz. heads	2 oz.	6.0	17 lbs.
Kale	Bu. basket	19	3 to 5 per lb.	3 oz. (½ C.)	3.7	27 lbs.
Kohlrabi	Bu. basket	22	18 bunches, 3 to 5 per bunch	3 oz. (½ C.)	2.9	35 lbs.
Leeks	Bu. basket	18		3 oz. (½ C.)	2.2	45 lbs.
Lettuce, iceberg	Carton, 24's	25	Chopped raw	2 oz. (½ C.)	5.9	17 lbs.
Lettuce, iceberg	Carton, 24's	25	Underliners for salad; 12 per head average		11.1	9 lbs.
Lettuce, leaf	Bu. basket	18	Raw	2 oz.	5.3	19 lbs.
Lettuce, Boston or Bibb	Bu. basket	24	Raw	2 oz.	5.1	20 lbs.
Mushrooms, chopped	Carton	1		1 oz. (2 T.)	11.1	9 lbs.
Mustard greens	Bu. basket	18		3 oz. (½ C.)	3.1	32 lbs.
Okra	Bu. hamper	38	Diced and cooked	3 oz. (½ C.)	5.1	20 lbs.
Onions, dry	Sack	50		3 oz. (½ C.)	4.0	25 lbs.
Onions, dry	Sack	50	French-fried	2-½ oz.	5.0	20 lbs.
Onions, dry	Sack	50	Raw diced or sliced	2 oz.	7.1	14 lbs.
Onions, green	California ⅔ crate		8 doz. bunches to the crate	1-½ oz. (2 onions)	3.9	25 lbs.
Parsnips	Bu. basket	45		3 oz. (½ C.)	4.2	24 lbs.
Peas, green	Bu. basket	28	8 qts. shelled	3 oz. (½ C.)	1.9	53 lbs.

Table 4 *(continued)*

Item	Shipping Container	Approximate Net Weight in Pounds, as Purchased per Container	Miscellaneous Shipping or Portioning Data	Portion Size as Served	Portions per Pound as Purchased	Approximate Amount to Purchase as Purchased for 100 Portions
Peppers, green	Sturdee crate, 1-¼ bu.	30	Chopped raw	1 oz.	13.1	8 lbs.
Peppers, green	Sturdee crate, 1-¼ bu.	30	Halves steamed	2 halves	4.0	25 lbs.
Potatoes, Irish	Sack	100	Whole, pared	1 (5 oz.)	2.6	39 lbs.
Potatoes, Irish	Sack	100	Baked	1 (7 oz.)	2.1	47 lbs.
Potatoes, Irish	Sack	100	Hash brown	4 oz.	2.3	44 lbs.
Potatoes, Irish	Sack	100	Mashed	4 oz.	3.3	30 lbs.
Potatoes, Irish	Sack	100	Raw-fried	4 oz.	1.7	59 lbs.
Potatoes, Irish	Sack	100	French-fried	3 oz.	2.7	37 lbs.
Potatoes, sweet	Bushel	50	140 potatoes; mashed	4 oz.	3.3	30 lbs.
Potatoes, sweet	Bushel	50	Candied	4 oz.	3.4	30 lbs.
Potatoes, sweet	Bushel	50	Baked	6 oz.	2.7	36 lbs.
Pumpkin	Bushel	40		3 oz. (½ C.)	3.4	30 lbs.
Radishes	Dozen bunches	10	Raw	1 oz.	10.0	10 lbs.
Rutabagas	Bushel	45		3 oz. (½ C.)	3.8	27 lbs.
Spinach	Bushel	18		3 oz. (½ C.)	3.2	31 lbs.
Spinach, trimmed and washed	Bushel	18		3 oz. (½ C.)	4.0	25 lbs.
Squash, summer	Bushel	40		3 oz. (½ C.)	4.2	24 lbs.
Squash, acorn	Bushel	50	50 squash	1 half	2.0	50 lbs.
Squash, Boston marrow	Pound		Mashed	3 oz. (½ C.)	4.1	24 lbs.
Squash, Boston marrow	Pound		Baked	4 oz.	2.9	35 lbs.
Squash, butternut	Pound		Mashed	3 oz. (½ C.)	2.4	41 lbs.
Squash, butternut	Pound		Baked	4 oz.	1.7	59 lbs.
Squash, Hubbard	Pound		Mashed	3 oz. (½ C.)	3.1	33 lbs.
Squash, Hubbard	Pound		Baked	4 oz.	2.2	46 lbs.
Tomatoes, unpeeled	Lug, 5 x 5	30	75 tomatoes; raw	3 oz.	4.9	20 lbs.
Tomatoes, peeled	Lug, 5 x 5	30	Raw	3 oz.	4.7	21 lbs.
Turnips, topped	Bushel	50		3 oz. (½ C.)	4.0	25 lbs.
Turnips, with tops	Crate, 18's	36		3 oz. (½ C.)	3.3	31 lbs.
Watercress	Basket, 14 bunches		Raw	2 oz.	5.9	17 lbs.

Note: All vegetables cooked unless otherwise noted.
[a] Each pie cut 6.
[b] Yield on honeyball melons is same as for cantaloupes if 45 per crate.
[c] Yield on honeydew and Persian melons is same as for casabas if 8 per crate.
Source: U.S. Department of Agriculture.

Table 5. Egg Equivalency Table

Fresh or frozen:
1 whole egg. . . . . = 3 T.
8 whole eggs. . . . . = 1½ C.

Fresh or frozen:
16 egg whites. . . . . = 1 pt.
24 egg yolks. . . . . = 1 pt.

Dried whole egg powder:
   Sifted. . . . . ½ oz. or 2½ T.
+ Water. . . . . 2½ T.
= Number of eggs. 1

Dried whole egg powder:
   Sifted. . . . . 4 oz. or 1⅓ C.
+ Water. . . . . 1⅓ C.
= Number of eggs. 8

Dried whole egg powder:
   Sifted. . . . . 6 oz. or 1 pt.
+ Water. . . . . 1 pt.
= Number of eggs. 12

Dried whole egg powder:
   Sifted. . . . . 12 oz. or 1 qt.
+ Water. . . . . 1 qt.
= Number of eggs. 24

Source: Recipes and Menus for All Seasons (Chicago: John Sexton and Co., n.d.). Reprinted by permission.

Table 6. Milk Conversion Table

Nonfat dry milk	13 oz.
+ Water	7¾ pts.
= Liquid skim milk	1 gal.

Nonfat dry milk solids	1½ oz.
+ Water	14½ oz.
= Liquid skim milk	1 lb.

Nonfat dry milk	3¼ oz.
Butter	1⅔ oz.
+ Water	1 qt.
= Whole milk	1 qt.

Dry whole milk	1 lb.
+ Water	7¼ pts.
= Liquid whole milk	1 gal.

Dry whole milk	2 oz.
+ Water	14 oz.
= Liquid whole milk	1 lb.

Dry whole milk	4½ oz.
Sugar	6½ oz.
+ Water	5 oz.
= Sweetened condensed whole milk	1 lb.

Nonfat dry milk solids	4 oz.
Sugar	7 oz.
+ Water	5 oz.
= Sweetened condensed skim milk	1 lb.

Source: Recipes and Menus for All Seasons (Chicago: John Sexton and Co., n.d.). Reprinted by permission.

Table 7. Dipper Equivalency Measures

Dipper Size	Equivalent
No. 8	½ C. or 8 T.
No. 10	⅖ C. or 6 T.
No. 12	⅓ C. or 5⅔ T.
No. 16	¼ C. or 4 T.
No. 20	⅕ C. or 3⅓ T.
No. 24	⅙ C. or 2⅔ T.
No. 30	⅛ C. or 2 T.

Source: Recipes and Menus for All Seasons (Chicago: John Sexton and Co., n.d.). Reprinted by permission.

Table 8. Common Container Sizes

Industry Term	Approximate Amount Contained			Principal Content	Approximate Number of Servings
	Net Weight	Fluid Measure	Cups		
8 oz.	8 oz.		1	Fruits, vegetables, specialties[a] for small families	2
Picnic	10-½ to 12 oz.		1-¼	Mainly condensed soups. Some fruits, vegetables, meat, fish, specialties[a]	2 to 3
12 oz. (vacuum)	12 oz.		1-½	Principally for vacuum-pack corn	3 to 4
No. 300	14 to 16 oz. (14 oz. to 1 lb.)		1-¾	Pork and beans, baked beans, meat products, cranberry sauce, blueberries, specialties[a]	3 to 4
No. 303	16 to 17 oz. (1 lb. to lb. 1 oz.)		2	Principal size for fruits and vegetables. Some meat products, ready-to-serve soups, specialties[a]	4
No. 2	20 oz. (1 lb. 4 oz.)	18 fl. oz. (1 pt. 2 fl. oz.)	2-½	Juices,[b] ready-to-serve soups, some specialties, pineapple, apple slices. No longer in popular use for most fruits and vegetables	5
No. 2-½	27 to 29 oz. (1 lb. 11 oz. to 1 lb. 13 oz.)		3-½	Fruits, some vegetables (pumpkin, sauerkraut, spinach and other greens, tomatoes)	5 to 7
No. 3	33 oz. (2 lbs. 1 oz.)		4	Some juices	
No. 3 cylinder or 46 fl. oz.	51 oz. (3 lbs. 3 oz.)	46 fl. oz. (1 qt. 14 fl. oz.)	5-¾	Fruit and vegetable juices,[b] pork and beans. Institutional size for condensed soups, some vegetables	10 to 12
No. 5	56 oz. (3 lbs. 8 oz.)		7		
No. 10	6-½ lbs. to 7 lbs. 5 oz.		12 to 13	Institutional size for fruits, vegetables, and some other foods	25

Notes: Strained and homogenized foods for infants, and chopped junior foods, come in small jars and cans suitable for the smaller servings used. The weight is given on the label. Meats, poultry, and fish and seafood are almost entirely advertised and sold under weight terminology. The labels of cans or jars of identical size may show a net weight for one product that differs slightly from the net weight on the label of another product, due to the difference in the density of the food. An example would be pork and beans (1 lb.), blueberries (14 oz.), in the same size can.

[a] A specialty is usually a food combination such as macaroni, spaghetti, Spanish-style rice, Mexican-type foods, Chinese foods, tomato aspic, etc.

[b] Juices are now being packed in a number of can sizes.

Sources: National Canners Association; *Recipes and Menus for All Seasons* (Chicago: John Sexton and Co., n.d.).

Table 9. Food Servings per Container

Commodity	Approximate Content of Container			Approximate Size of Each Serving
	Net Weight or Volume	Cups or Pieces	Number of Servings	
FRUITS				
Apples, apple sauce, berries, cherries, grapes, grape fruit and orange sections, fruit cocktail, fruits for salad, sliced peaches, pears, pineapple (chunks, crushed, tidbits)	8-½ to 8-¾ oz.	1 C.	2	½ C.
	16 to 17 oz.	1-¾ to 2 C.	3 to 4	½ C.
	1 lb. 4 oz.	2-¼ to 2-½ C.	5	½ C.
	1 lb. 13 oz.	3-¼ to 3-½ C.	5 to 7	½ C.
	6 lbs. 2 oz. to 6 lbs. 12 oz.	12 to 13 C.	25	½ C.
Apricots (whole, medium size)	16 to 17 oz.	8 to 14 pcs.	3 to 4	2 to 3 pcs.
	1 lb. 13 oz.	15 to 18 pcs.	5 to 7	2 to 3 pcs.
	6 lbs. 10 oz.	50 to 60 pcs.	25	2 to 3 pcs.
Apricots (halves, medium size)	8-¾ oz.	6 to 12 pcs.	2	3 to 5 pcs.
	16 to 17 oz.	12 to 20 pcs.	3 to 4	3 to 5 pcs.
	1 lb. 13 oz.	26 to 35 pcs.	5 to 7	3 to 5 pcs.
	6 lbs. 10 oz.	95 to 130 pcs.	25	3 to 5 pcs.
Peaches (halves), pears (halves)	16 to 17 oz.	6 to 10	3 to 4	2 medium pcs.
	1 lb. 13 oz.	7 to 12	5 to 7	1 large pc.
	6 lbs. 10 oz.	45 to 65	25	2 medium pcs.
Pineapple (slices)	9 oz.	4 pcs.	2	2 pcs.
	1 lb. 4 oz.	10 pcs.	5	2 pcs.
	1 lb. 14 oz.	8 pcs.	8	1 large pc.
	6 lbs. 12 oz.	28 to 50 pcs.	25	1 large or 2 small pcs.
Plums, prunes (whole)	8-¾ oz.	7 to 9 pcs.	2	2 to 3 pcs.
	16 to 17 oz.	10 to 14 pcs.	3 to 4	2 to 3 pcs.
	1 lb. 14 oz.	12 to 20 pcs.	5 to 7	2 to 3 pcs.
	6 lbs. 10 oz.	40 to 60 pcs.	25	2 to 3 pcs.
Figs (whole)	8 to 9 oz.	6 to 12 pcs.	2	3 to 4 pcs.
	16 to 17 oz.	12 to 20 pcs.	3 to 4	3 to 4 pcs.
	1 lb. 14 oz.	18 to 24 pcs.	5 to 7	3 to 4 pcs.
	7 lbs.	70 to 90 pcs.	25	3 to 4 pcs.
Cranberry sauce	6 to 8 oz.	¾ to 1 C.	4	¼ C.
	1 lb.	2 C.	8	¼ C.
	7 lbs. 5 oz.	12 to 13 C.	50	¼ C.
Olives, ripe (whole)	4-½ oz.	—	—	3 pcs.
	9 oz.	—	—	3 pcs.
	1 lb. 2 oz.	—	—	3 pcs.
	4 lbs. 2 oz.	—	—	3 pcs.

VEGETABLES

Food	Net weight	Approximate measure	Servings	Size of serving
Asparagus cuts, beans (green and wax, kidney, lima), beets, carrots, corn, hominy, okra, onions, peas, peas and carrots, black-eyed peas, pumpkin, sauerkraut, spinach and other greens, squash, succotash, sweet potatoes,ᵃ tomatoes, mixed vegetables, potatoes (white, cut, sliced)	8 to 8-½ oz.	1 C.	2	½ C.
	12 oz.	1-½ to 1-¾ C.	3 to 4	½ C.
	16 to 17 oz.	2 C.	3 to 4	½ C.
	1 lb. 4 oz.	2-¼ to 2-½ C.	5	½ C.
	1 lb. 13 oz.	3-¼ to 3-½ C.	5 to 7	½ C.
	6 lbs. 2 oz. to 6 lbs. 12 oz.	12 to 13 C.	25	½ C.
Asparagus (spears, medium size)	10½ oz.	9 to 12 pcs.	2	4 to 6 pcs.
	14-½ to 16 oz.	16 to 28 pcs.	3	4 to 6 pcs.
	1 lb. 3 oz.	20 to 38 pcs.	5	4 to 6 pcs.
	4 lbs. 4 oz.	115 to 145 pcs.	25	4 to 6 pcs.
Potatoes (white, peeled, whole, small)	16 to 17 oz.	8 to 12 pcs.	3 to 4	2 to 3 pcs.
	6 lbs. 6 oz.	55 to 65 pcs.	25	2 to 3 pcs.
Beans (baked, with pork, in sauce)	8-¾ oz.	1 C.	1 to 2	½ to ¾ C.
	1 lb.	1-¾ C.	3 to 4	½ to ¾ C.
	1 lb. 10 oz.	3 C.	4 to 6	½ to ¾ C.
	6 lbs. 14 oz.	12 to 13 C.	16 to 25	½ to ¾ C.
Mushroomsᵇ	2 oz.	⅓ C.	1	⅓ C.
	4 oz.	⅔ C.	2	⅓ C.
	8 oz.	1-½ C.	4	⅓ C.
	4 lbs. 4 oz.	12 to 13 C.	36	⅓ C.
Pimientos, peppers (red, sweet)	2 oz.	¼ C.	—	—
	4 oz.	½ C.	—	—
	7 oz.	1 C.	—	—
	6 lbs. 13 oz.	12 to 13 C.	—	—

JUICES

Food	Net weight	Approximate measure	Servings	Size of serving
Apple, cherry, cranberry, grape, grapefruit, grapefruit-orange, loganberry, nectars, orange, pineapple, prune, tangerine, carrot, sauerkraut, tomato, vegetable, vegetable cocktail	6 to 8 oz.	¾ to 1 C.	1 to 2	4 to 6 oz.
	12 fl. oz.	1-½ C.	3 / 2	4 oz. / 6 oz.
	1 pt.	2 C.	4 / 3	4 oz. / 6 oz.
	1 pt. 2 fl. oz.	2-¼ to 2-½ C.	5 / 3	4 oz. / 6 oz.
	1 pt. 7 fl. oz.	3 C.	6 / 4	4 oz. / 6 oz.
	1 qt.	4 C.	8 / 5	4 oz. / 6 oz.
	1 qt. 14 fl. oz.	5-¾ C.	12 / 8	4 oz. / 6 oz.
	3 qts.	12 C.	24 / 16	4 oz. / 6 oz.
Lemon, lime	5-½ to 6 oz.	¾ C.	—	—

Table 9 *(continued)*

Commodity	Approximate Content of Container: Net Weight or Volume	Cups or Pieces	Number of Servings	Approximate Size of Each Serving
	SOUPS			
Condensed	10-½ to 12 oz.	1-¼ C. (2-½ C. prepared)	3	¾ C.
	3 lbs. 2 oz.	5-¾ C. (11-½ C. prepared)	12 to 16	¾ C.
Ready-to-serve	8 fl. oz. individual	1 C.	1	1 C.
	12 fl. oz.	1-½ C.	2	¾ C.
	15 fl. oz.	2 C.	3	¾ C.
	1 pt. 5 fl. oz. to 1 pt. 9 fl. oz.	2-½ to 3 C.	4	¾ C.
	3 qts.	12 C.	20	¾ C.
	MEATS AND POULTRY			
Chili con carne, chili con carne with beans	15 to 16 oz.	2 C.	3 to 4	½ to ⅔ C.
	1-½ lb.	3 C.	4 to 5	½ to ⅔ C.
	6 lb. 12 oz.	12 to 13 C.	18 to 24	½ to ⅔ C.
Corned beef	12 oz.	—	4	3 oz.
	6 lbs.	—	30	3 oz.
Corned beef hash	8 oz.	1 C.	1 to 2	½ to ⅔ C.
	1 lb.	2 C.	3 to 4	½ to ⅔ C.
	1-½ lb.	3 C.	5 to 6	½ to ⅔ C.
	5 lbs. 8 oz. to 5 lbs. 14 oz.	12 to 13 C.	18 to 24	½ to ⅔ C.
Deviled ham	2-¼ to 3 oz.	⅓ C.	3 to 4	1-½ T.
	4-½ oz.	½ C.	5 to 6	1-½ T.
Deviled meat, potted meat, meat spreads	2 to 3-¼ oz.	⅓ C.	3 to 4	1-½ T.
	5-½ oz.	¾ C.	8	1-½ T.
Luncheon meat	12 oz.	—	4	2 slices (3-½ in. x 1-¾ in. x ⅜ in.)
	6 lbs.	—	32	
Tongue (beef, lamb, pork)	6 oz.	—	2	3 oz.
	12 oz.	—	4	3 oz.
	1 to 2 lbs.	—	5 to 10	3 oz.
Hams (whole, small)	1-½ to 4 lbs.	—	3 to 4 (per pound)	2 slices (4 in. x 3 in. x ⅛ in.)
(whole, medium)	6 to 8 lbs.	—		
(whole, large)	9 to 14 lbs.	—		
Poultry, boned (chicken, turkey)	5 to 6 oz.	—	2	3 oz.
	12 oz.	—	4	3 oz.
	1 lb. 14 oz.	—	10	3 oz.
	2 lb. 3 oz.	—	12	3 oz.

Food	Net weight	Measure per container	Servings	Size of serving
Sausages (pork links), frankfurters	8 oz.	11 to 12 pcs.	3 to 4	3 pcs.
Stew (beef, lamb)	12 oz.	8 to 9 pcs.	4	2 pcs.
	1 lb.	2 C.	2	¾ C.
	1 lb, 4 oz.	2-½ C.	3	¾ C.
	1-½ lb.	3 C.	4	¾ C.
Vienna sausage	4 oz.	8 to 10 pcs.	2	4 to 5 pcs.
	9 oz.	16 to 20 pcs.	2	4 to 5 pcs.

FISH AND SEAFOOD

Food	Net weight	Measure per container	Servings	Size of serving
Clams	7-½ oz.	1 C.	2	½ C.
Crab meat	5-½ to 7-½ oz.	¾ to 1 C.	2 to 3	⅓ to ½ C.
Mackerel	1 lb.	2 C.	4	½ C.
Oysters	8 oz.	1 C.	2	½ C.
Salmon	7-¾ oz.	1 C.	2	½ C.
	1 lb.	2 C.	4	½ C.
Sardines	3-½ to 4 oz.	6 to 10 pcs.	1-½	5 to 7 pcs.
Sardines, pilchards	15 oz.	6 to 7 pcs.	4	1-½ C.
Shrimp[b] (medium)	4-½ to 6-½ oz.	25 to 35 pcs.	3 to 4	10 to 12 pcs.
(jumbo)				6 to 8 pcs.
Tuna in oil	6 to 7 oz.	1 C.	2	½ C.
	13 oz.	1-¾ C.	4	½ C.

INFANT FOODS

Food	Net weight	Measure per container	Servings	Size of serving
Vegetables and fruits (infant: strained, homogenized; junior: chopped)	4-¾ oz.	½ C.	—	—
	6-½ oz.	¾ C.	—	—
	8 oz.[a]	⅞ C.	—	—
Meats (infant: strained; junior: chopped)	3-½ oz.	7 T.	—	—
Soups (infant; junior)	4-¾ oz.	½ C.	—	—
	8 oz.	⅞ C.	—	—

Note: The net weight of various foods in the same size can or glass jar will vary with the density of the food. For the most part only minimum weights are shown in the table. Cups or pieces and servings in the table have been given in approximates, and sizes of servings are given in rounded numbers in order to furnish a practical guide.
aSweet potatoes also come in 1 lb. 2 oz. to 1 lb. 7 oz. cans.
bDeclared as drained weight. The number of olives per container varies as to size of the olives.
Source: National Canners Association. Reprinted by permission.

Table 10. Substituting One Can Size for Another

Quantity	Approximate Equivalent of One No. 10 Can— Type	Weight
7	No. 303 or No. 1 tall	1 lb.
5	No. 2	1 lb. 4 oz.
4	No. 2-½	1 lb. 13 oz.
2	No. 3 cylindrical	46 to 50 oz.

Source: American Canners Association; *Recipes and Menus for All Seasons* (Chicago: John Sexton and Co., n.d.).

Table 11. Guide to Cost per Serving for Canned Foods

Cost per 6 Cans	Cost per Can	Cost per Serving, According to Number of Servings per Can									
		5	10	15	20	25	30	35	40	45	50
2.00	.33	.066	.033	.022	.017	.013	.011	.009	.008	.007	.007
2.25	.38	.076	.038	.025	.019	.015	.013	.011	.010	.008	.008
2.50	.42	.084	.042	.028	.021	.017	.014	.012	.011	.009	.008
2.75	.46	.092	.046	.030	.023	.018	.015	.013	.012	.010	.009
3.00	.50	.100	.050	.033	.025	.020	.017	.014	.013	.011	.010
3.25	.54	.108	.054	.036	.027	.022	.018	.015	.014	.012	.011
3.50	.58	.116	.058	.039	.029	.023	.019	.017	.015	.013	.012
3.75	.63	.126	.063	.042	.032	.025	.021	.018	.016	.014	.013
4.00	.67	.134	.067	.045	.034	.027	.022	.019	.017	.015	.013
4.25	.71	.142	.071	.047	.035	.028	.024	.020	.018	.016	.014
4.50	.75	.150	.075	.050	.038	.030	.025	.021	.019	.017	.015
4.75	.79	.158	.079	.053	.040	.032	.026	.023	.020	.018	.016
5.00	.83	.166	.083	.055	.042	.033	.028	.024	.021	.018	.017
5.25	.88	.176	.088	.059	.044	.035	.029	.025	.022	.020	.018
5.50	.92	.184	.092	.061	.046	.037	.031	.026	.023	.020	.018
5.75	.96	.192	.096	.064	.048	.038	.032	.027	.024	.021	.019
6.00	1.00	.200	.100	.067	.050	.040	.033	.029	.025	.022	.020
6.25	1.04	.208	.104	.069	.052	.042	.035	.030	.026	.023	.021
6.50	1.08	.216	.108	.072	.054	.043	.036	.031	.027	.024	.022
6.75	1.13	.226	.113	.075	.057	.045	.038	.032	.028	.025	.023
7.00	1.17	.234	.117	.078	.059	.047	.039	.033	.029	.026	.023
7.25	1.21	.242	.121	.080	.061	.048	.040	.035	.030	.027	.024
7.50	1.25	.250	.125	.083	.063	.050	.042	.036	.031	.028	.025
7.75	1.29	.258	.129	.086	.065	.052	.043	.037	.032	.029	.026
8.00	1.33	.266	.133	.089	.066	.053	.044	.038	.033	.029	.027
8.25	1.37	.274	.137	.091	.068	.055	.046	.039	.034	.030	.027
8.50	1.41	.282	.141	.094	.070	.056	.047	.040	.035	.031	.028
8.75	1.45	.290	.145	.097	.072	.058	.048	.041	.036	.032	.029
9.00	1.50	.300	.150	.100	.075	.060	.050	.043	.037	.033	.030
9.25	1.54	.308	.154	.103	.077	.062	.051	.044	.038	.034	.031
9.50	1.58	.316	.158	.106	.079	.063	.053	.045	.039	.035	.032
9.75	1.62	.324	.162	.108	.081	.065	.054	.046	.040	.036	.032
10.00	1.66	.332	.166	.111	.083	.066	.055	.047	.041	.037	.033
10.25	1.70	.340	.170	.113	.085	.068	.057	.049	.042	.038	.034
10.50	1.75	.350	.175	.117	.087	.070	.058	.050	.044	.039	.035
10.75	1.79	.358	.179	.119	.089	.072	.060	.051	.045	.040	.036

Table 11 *(continued)*

Cost per 6 Cans	Cost per Can	Cost per Serving, According to Number of Servings per Can									
		5	10	15	20	25	30	35	40	45	50
11.00	1.83	.367	.183	.122	.091	.073	.061	.052	.046	.041	.037
11.25	1.87	.374	.187	.124	.093	.075	.062	.053	.047	.041	.037
11.50	1.91	.382	.191	.127	.095	.076	.064	.054	.048	.042	.038
11.75	1.95	.390	.195	.130	.097	.078	.065	.056	.049	.043	.039
12.00	2.00	.400	.200	.133	.100	.080	.067	.057	.050	.044	.040
12.25	2.04	.408	.204	.136	.102	.081	.068	.058	.051	.045	.040
12.50	2.08	.416	.208	.138	.104	.082	.069	.059	.052	.046	.041
12.75	2.12	.424	.212	.141	.106	.084	.070	.060	.053	.047	.042
13.00	2.16	.432	.216	.144	.108	.086	.072	.061	.054	.048	.043
13.25	2.20	.440	.220	.146	.110	.088	.074	.062	.056	.048	.044
13.50	2.25	.450	.225	.150	.112	.090	.075	.064	.056	.050	.045
13.75	2.29	.458	.229	.152	.114	.091	.076	.065	.057	.050	.045
14.00	2.33	.466	.233	.155	.116	.093	.077	.066	.058	.051	.046
14.25	2.37	.474	.237	.158	.118	.094	.079	.067	.059	.052	.047
14.50	2.41	.482	.241	.160	.120	.096	.080	.068	.060	.053	.048
14.75	2.45	.490	.245	.163	.122	.098	.081	.070	.061	.054	.049
15.00	2.50	.500	.250	.166	.125	.100	.083	.071	.062	.055	.050
15.25	2.54	.508	.254	.169	.127	.101	.084	.072	.063	.056	.050
15.50	2.58	.516	.258	.172	.129	.103	.086	.073	.064	.057	.051
15.75	2.62	.524	.262	.174	.131	.104	.087	.074	.065	.058	.052
16.00	2.66	.532	.266	.177	.133	.106	.088	.076	.066	.059	.053
16.25	2.70	.540	.270	.180	.135	.108	.090	.077	.067	.060	.054
16.50	2.75	.550	.275	.183	.137	.110	.091	.078	.068	.061	.055
16.75	2.79	.558	.279	.186	.139	.111	.093	.079	.069	.062	.055
17.00	2.83	.566	.283	.188	.141	.113	.094	.080	.070	.062	.056
17.25	2.87	.574	.287	.191	.143	.114	.095	.082	.071	.063	.057
17.50	2.91	.582	.291	.194	.145	.116	.097	.083	.072	.064	.058
17.75	2.95	.590	.295	.196	.147	.118	.098	.084	.073	.065	.059
18.00	3.00	.600	.300	.200	.150	.120	.100	.085	.075	.066	.060
18.25	3.04	.608	.304	.202	.152	.121	.101	.086	.076	.067	.060
18.50	3.08	.616	.308	.205	.154	.123	.102	.088	.077	.068	.061
18.75	3.12	.624	.312	.208	.156	.124	.104	.089	.078	.069	.062
19.00	3.16	.632	.316	.210	.158	.126	.105	.090	.079	.070	.063
19.25	3.20	.640	.320	.213	.160	.128	.106	.091	.080	.071	.064
19.50	3.25	.650	.325	.216	.162	.130	.108	.092	.081	.072	.065
19.75	3.29	.658	.329	.219	.164	.131	.109	.094	.082	.073	.065
20.00	3.33	.666	.333	.222	.166	.133	.111	.095	.083	.074	.066

Source: Recipes and Menus for All Seasons (Chicago: John Sexton and Co., n.d.). Reprinted by permission.

Table 12. Food Serving Chart

CANNED VEGETABLES

Cans per Case and Container Size	Food	Style	Type	Approximate Net Weight	Range in Contents per Container	Suggested Portion per Serving	Approximate Portions per Container	Approximate Drained Weight	Miscellaneous Information
6/5 squat	Asparagus	Colossal all-green spears	California	4 lbs. 1 oz.	50 to 60	2 spears	25 to 30	2 lbs. 14 ozs.	
6/5 squat	Asparagus	Mammoth large all-green spears	California	4 lbs. 1 oz.	85 to 95	3 to 4 spears	21 to 34	2 lbs. 14 ozs.	
6/5 squat	Asparagus	Blended mammoth large all-green spears	California	4 lbs. 1 oz.	80 to 85	3 to 4 spears	20 to 26	2 lbs. 8 ozs.	About 25 percent tips
6/10	Asparagus	Cut, all-green	Michigan	6 lbs. 5 ozs.	300 to 375	½ C.	24	3 lbs. 15 ozs.	
6/5 squat	Asparagus	Colossal whole green-tipped and white	California	4 lbs. 1 oz.	50 to 60	3 to 4 spears	12 to 15	2 lbs. 10 ozs.	
6/5 squat	Asparagus	Mammoth whole green-tipped and white	California	4 lbs. 1 oz.	60 to 70	4 to 5 spears	12 to 14	2 lbs. 14 ozs.	
6/10	Beans, green	Tiny whole	Northwest Blue Lake	6 lbs. 5 ozs.		½ C.	29	3 lbs. 13 ozs.	No. 1 sieve
6/10	Beans, green	Small whole	Northwest Blue Lake	6 lbs. 5 ozs.		½ C.	30	3 lbs. 13 ozs.	No. 2 sieve
6/10	Beans, green	Salad whole	Northwest Blue Lake	6 lbs. 5 ozs.	420	12 to 14 pieces	30 to 35	3 lbs. 13 ozs.	No. 3 sieve
6/5 squat	Beans, green	Whole vertical pack	Northwest Blue Lake	4 lbs.	200	10 to 12 pieces	18 to 20	2 lbs. 8 ozs.	No. 4 sieve
6/10	Beans, green	French-style	Northwest Blue Lake	6 lbs. 5 ozs.		½ C.	30	3 lbs. 13 ozs.	
6/10	Beans, green	Cut	Northwest Blue Lake	6 lbs. 5 ozs.		½ C.	26	3 lbs. 15 ozs.	1½-inch cuts. No. 3 sieve
6/10	Beans, green	Cut	Northwest Blue Lake	6 lbs. 5 ozs.		½ C.	26	3 lbs. 15 ozs.	No. 4 sieve
6/10	Beans, kidney	Dark red		6 lbs. 12 ozs.		½ C.	24	4 lbs. 12 ozs.	
6/10	Beans, lima	Garden run Fordhook	Eastern Fordhook	6 lbs. 9 ozs.		½ C.	24	4 lbs. 8 ozs.	Fresh
6/10	Beans, lima	Small green	Eastern Henderson Bush	6 lbs. 9 ozs.		½ C.	24	4 lbs. 8 ozs.	Fresh
6/10	Beans, lima	Medium green	Eastern Henderson Bush	6 lbs. 9 ozs.		½ C.	24	4 lbs. 8 ozs.	Fresh
6/10	Beans, oven-baked		New England	6 lbs. 14 ozs.		½ C.	25	6 lbs. 14 ozs.	New England pack with salt pork
6/10	Beans, red		Idaho Red	6 lbs. 12 ozs.		½ C.	24	5 lbs. 2 ozs.	No. 3 sieve
6/10	Beans, wax	Cut	King Horn Variety	6 lbs. 5 ozs.		½ C.	24	5 lbs. 15 ozs.	
6/10	Beets	Cubed	Eastern Detroit Red	6 lbs. 8 ozs.	400 to 450	½ C., 15 cubes	26 to 30	4 lbs. 7 ozs.	¾-inch cubes
6/10	Beets	Diced	Eastern Detroit Red	6 lbs. 8 ozs.		½ C.	27	4 lbs. 7 ozs.	
6/10	Beets	Julienne	Eastern Detroit Red	6 lbs. 8 ozs.		½ C.	30	4 lbs. 8 ozs.	
6/10	Beets	Sliced	Northwest Detroit Red	6 lbs. 8 ozs.	200 to 250	½ C., 10 slices	20 to 25	4 lbs. 8 ozs.	
6/10	Beets	Whole	Oregon Detroit Red	6 lbs. 8 ozs.	Over 250	6 to 8 pieces	30 to 40	4 lbs. 5 ozs.	
6/10	Beets, rosebud		New York	6 lbs. 8 ozs.			30	5 lbs.	
6/10	Cabbage, red	Sweet-sour		6 lbs. 9 ozs.		½ C.	28	4 lbs. 8 ozs.	
6/10	Carrots	Diced	Northwest Chantenay	6 lbs. 9 ozs.		½ C.	29	4 lbs. 8 ozs.	
6/10	Carrots	Julienne	Northwest Chantenay	6 lbs. 9 ozs.	86	½ C.	28	4 lbs. 8 ozs.	
6/10	Carrots	Quartered	Northwest Chantenay	6 lbs. 9 ozs.		3 pieces		4 lbs. 8 ozs.	
6/10	Carrots	Small sliced	Northwest Chantenay	6 lbs. 9 ozs.	325 to 375	6 to 8 slices	43 to 54	4 lbs. 3 ozs.	
6/10	Carrots	Tiny whole	Northwest Chantenay	6 lbs. 9 ozs.	Over 200	6 to 8 pieces	30 to 35	4 lbs. 6 ozs.	1½ inch diameter
6/10	Carrots	Small whole	Northwest Chantenay	6 lbs. 9 ozs.	Over 100	6 to 8 pieces	24 to 30	4 lbs. 6 ozs.	
6/10	Celery	Cut	California	6 lbs. 2 oz.		½ C.	23	4 lbs. 2 ozs.	Packed in brine
6/10	Corn, cream-style	Little kernel Country Gentleman	Midwest White	6 lbs. 10 ozs.		½ C.	25	6 lbs. 10 ozs.	
6/10	Corn, cream-style	Golden sweet	Midwest	6 lbs. 10 ozs.		½ C.	25	6 lbs. 10 ozs.	
6/10	Corn, whole grain	Golden sweet	Midwest	6 lbs. 9 ozs.		½ C.	26	4 lbs. 1 oz.	
6/10	Hominy	Golden	Southern	6 lbs. 9 ozs.		½ C.	22	4 lbs. 12 ozs.	
6/10	Kale	Chopped	Wisconsin	6 lbs. 8 ozs.		½ C.	23	3 lbs. 12 ozs.	
6/10	Mixed vegetables			6 lbs. 8 ozs.		½ C.	25	4 lbs. 1 oz.	Carrots, potatoes, celery, green beans, peas, corn, lima beans
6/10	Mustard greens	Chopped	Southern	6 lbs. 2 ozs.		½ C.	20	3 lbs. 12 ozs.	
6/10	Okra	Cut	Southern	6 lbs. 3 ozs.		½ C.	25	4 lbs. 1 oz.	
6/10	Onions	Tiny whole	Eastern	6 lbs. 5 ozs.	Over 200	10 pieces	20	4 lbs.	
6/10	Onions	Small whole	Eastern	6 lbs. 5 ozs.	Over 100	5 pieces	20	4 lbs.	
6/10	Peas, early June	Extra sifted	Wisconsin Alaska	6 lbs. 9 ozs.		½ C.	24		No. 2 sieve
6/10	Peas, early June	Sifted	Wisconsin Alaska	6 lbs. 9 ozs.		½ C.	24		No. 3 sieve

Table 12 *(continued)*

Cans per Case and Container Size	Food	Style	Type	Approximate Net Weight	Range in Contents per Container	Suggested Portion per Serving	Approximate Portions per Container	Approximate Drained Weight	Miscellaneous Information
			CANNED VEGETABLES *(continued)*						
6/10	Peas, alsweet	Sifted	Wisconsin Alsweet	6 lbs. 9 ozs.		½ C.	24		No. 3 sieve
6/10	Peas, telephone	Sweet	Wisconsin Sweet	6 lbs. 9 ozs.		½ C.	25		No. 5 sieve
6/10	Potatoes, white	Tiny whole	Midwest	6 lbs. 6 ozs.	Over 150	6 pieces	25	4 lbs. 6 ozs.	
6/10	Potatoes, white	Small whole	Midwest	6 lbs. 6 ozs.	Over 100	4 pieces	25	4 lbs. 6 ozs.	
12/3 cyl.	Potatoes, sweet	Small whole	Louisiana yams	3 lbs. 3 ozs.	20 to 25	2	10 to 12	2 lbs. 3 ozs.	In heavy syrup
6/10	Sauerkraut		Midwest	6 lbs. 3 ozs.		½ C.	37	5 lbs.	
6/10	Spinach	Leaf	California	6 lbs. 2 ozs.		½ C.	18	3 lbs. 12 ozs.	
6/10	Spinach	Sliced	California	6 lbs. 2 ozs.		½ C.	15	3 lbs. 12 ozs.	
6/10	Tomatoes	Italian-style	California	6 lbs. 6 ozs.	28	1 whole	28	4 lbs. 4 ozs.	Trace of calcium chloride added
6/10	Tomatoes	Whole	Midwest	6 lbs. 6 ozs.	20	1 whole	20	4 lbs. 8 ozs.	Trace of calcium chloride added
6/10	Tomato paste	Sweet	California blended, round and plum tomatoes	6 lbs. 15 ozs.			12 cups	6 lbs. 15 ozs.	30 percent solids
6/10	Tomato puree	Extra heavy	California	6 lbs. 9 ozs.			12 cups	6 lbs. 9 ozs.	1.07 specific gravity
6/10	Tomato puree	Superb	California	6 lbs. 9 ozs.			12 cups	6 lbs. 9 ozs.	1.06 specific gravity
6/10	Turnip greens	Chopped	Southern	6 lbs. 2 ozs.		½ C.	20	3 lbs. 12 ozs.	
			DEHYDRATED VEGETABLES						
6/1¾ #	Onions, white	Slices		1 lb. 12 ozs.					Yields 2½ gallons when reconstituted
6/10	Potatoes	Flakes		1 lb. 12 ozs.		½ C.	90		
6/10	Potatoes	Instant	Powdered	6 lbs.		½ C.	112		
			CANNED FRUITS						
6/10	Apple sauce		New York State	6 lbs. 12 ozs.		½ C.	26	6 lbs. 12 ozs.	Heavy coarse finish
6/10	Apricots	Unpeeled halves	Blenheim	6 lbs. 14 ozs.	75 to 85	3 halves	25 to 28	4 lbs. 2 ozs.	In syrup
6/10	Apricots	Whole peeled	Blenheim	6 lbs. 14 ozs.	40 to 50	2 pieces	20 to 25	4 lbs. 4 ozs.	In syrup
6/10	Apricots	Sliced, peeled	Blenheim	6 lbs. 14 ozs.		⅓ to ½ C.	20 to 25	4 lbs. 2 ozs.	In syrup
6/10	Boysenberries		California Genuine Variety	6 lbs. 12 ozs.		12 berries	26	3 lbs. 7 ozs.	In syrup
6/10	Cherries, bing	Unpitted	Pacific Northwest	6 lbs. 12 ozs.	220	11 cherries	20	4 lbs. 5 ozs.	In syrup
6/10	Cherries, bing	Pitted	Pacific Northwest	6 lbs. 14 ozs.	300 to 350	11 cherries	27 to 32	4 lbs. 2 ozs.	In syrup
6/10	Cherries, red	Pitted	Michigan Montmorency	6 lbs. 14 ozs.		½ C.	23	4 lbs. 12 ozs.	In syrup
6/10	Cherries, Royal Ann	Light sweet unpitted	Pacific Coast	6 lbs. 12 ozs.	250 to 300	11 cherries	23 to 27	4 lbs. 2 ozs.	In syrup
6/10	Cranberry sauce	Home-style	Cape Cod or Wisconsin	7 lbs.		¼ C.	50		2 ozs. or No. 48 souffle
6/10	Cranberry sauce	Strained	Cape Cod or Wisconsin	7 lbs.		¼ C.	50		2 ozs. or No. 48 souffle
6/10	Figs	Whole	California Kadota	7 lbs.	70 to 90	3 pieces	23 to 30	4 lbs. 4 ozs.	Slice of orange added in syrup
6/10	Fruit cocktail		California Fancy	6 lbs. 14 ozs.		⅓ C.	27	4 lbs. 8 ozs.	In syrup
6/10	Fruit for salad		California Fancy	6 lbs. 14 ozs.		½ C.	20	4 lbs. 6 ozs.	Peach slices, pear slices, grapes, apricot halves, pineapple tidbits, maraschino cherries in syrup
12/3 cyl.	Grapefruit	Segments	Florida	3 lbs. 2 ozs.	50 to 60	4 segments	12 to 15	2 lbs. 1 oz.	In syrup
12/3 cyl.	Grapefuit and orange	Segments	Florida	3 lbs. 2 ozs.	65 to 75	5 segments	13 to 15	2 lbs.	In syrup
6/10	Grapes	Seedless	California Thompson	6 lbs. 14 ozs.		½ C.	22	4 lbs. 3 ozs.	In syrup
12/3 cyl.	Orange	Segments	Florida Valencia	3 lbs. 2 ozs.	65 to 75	6 segments	11 to 13	2 lbs. 1 oz.	In orange juice syrup
6/10	Orange, mandarin	Segments	Japanese	6 lbs. 6 oz .	425 to 450	½ C.	20	4 lbs. 3 oz.	In syrup
6/10	Peaches, ambrosia	Halves	Ambrosia yellow cling California	6 lbs. 14 ozs.	25 to 30	1 half	25 to 30	4 lbs. 10 ozs.	In syrup
6/10	Peaches, ambrosia	Sliced	Ambrosia yellow cling California	6 lbs. 12 ozs.		6 slices	16	4 lbs. 10 ozs.	In syrup
6/10	Peaches, yellow cling	Diced	Midsummer yellow cling California	6 lbs. 12 ozs.		½ C.	21	4 lbs. 5 ozs.	In syrup

6/10	Peaches, yellow cling	Halves	Midsummer yellow cling California	6 lbs. 14 ozs.	30 to 35	1 half	30 to 35	4 lbs. 2 ozs.	In syrup
6/10	Peaches, yellow free	Halves	Yellow free Elberta California	6 lbs. 14 ozs.	25 to 30	1 half	25 to 30		In syrup
6/10	Peaches, yellow free	Sliced	Yellow free Elberta California	6 lbs. 14 ozs.	150	6 slices	25		In syrup
6/10	Pears, Bartlett	Halves, peeled	Pacific Northwest Bartlett	6 lbs. 10 ozs.	30 to 35	1 half	30 to 35	4 lbs. 2 ozs.	In syrup
6/10	Pears, Bartlett	Halves, peeled	Pacific Northwest Bartlett	6 lbs. 10 ozs.	35 to 40	1 half	35 to 40	4 lbs. 3 ozs.	In syrup
6/10	Pears, Bartlett	Halves, unpeeled	Pacific Northwest Bartlett	6 lbs. 10 ozs.	25 to 35	1 half	25 to 35	3 lbs. 10 ozs.	In syrup
6/10	Pe. .s, Bartlett	Diced	Pacific Coast Bartlett	6 lbs. 10 ozs.		½ C.	21	4 lbs. 9 ozs.	In syrup
6/10	Pears, Kieffer	Halves	Michigan Kieffer	6 lbs. 10 ozs.	40 to 50	2 halves	20 to 25	3 lbs. 15 ozs.	In syrup
6/10	Pineapple	Crushed	Hawaiian Cayenne	6 lbs. 12 ozs.		½ C.	20	5 lbs. 5 ozs.	In syrup
6/10	Pineapple	Crushed	Hawaiian Cayenne	6 lbs. 11 ozs.		½ C.	18	4 lbs. 10 ozs.	In juice
6/10	Pineapple	Dessert cut	Hawaiian Cayenne	6 lbs. 12 ozs.	250 to 300	8 pieces	31 to 37	4 lbs. 5 ozs.	In syrup
6/10	Pineapple	Sliced	Hawaiian Cayenne	6 lbs. 13 ozs.	52	1 slice	52	4 lbs. 8 ozs.	In syrup
6/10	Pineapple	Sliced	Hawaiian Cayenne	6 lbs. 13 ozs.	66	1 slice	66	4 lbs. 3 ozs.	In syrup
6/10	Pineapple	Tidbits	Hawaiian Cayenne	6 lbs. 12 ozs.	850 to 900	½ C.	23	4 lbs. 12 ozs.	In syrup
6/10	Plums, Green Gage	Whole unpeeled	California	6 lbs. 14 ozs.	27 to 35	2 pieces	13 to 17	3 lbs. 12 ozs.	In syrup
6/10	Plums, Green Gage	Whole peeled	California	6 lbs. 14 ozs.	27 to 35	2 pieces	13 to 17	3 lbs. 12 ozs.	In syrup
6/10	Plums, prune	Whole unpeeled	Northwest Italian	6 lbs. 14 ozs.	60 to 70	3 pieces	20 to 23	4 lbs.	In syrup
6/10	Prunes	Prepared	Santa Clara	6 lbs. 14 ozs.	150 to 160	5 pieces	30 to 32	4 lbs. 7 ozs.	40 to 50 cut out prunes per pound
6/10	Prunes	Ready-to-serve	San Jose	7 lbs.	110 to 115	4 to 5 pieces	30 to 35	5 lbs. 2 ozs.	Water and sugar added
6/10	Rhubarb		Michigan	6 lbs. 9 ozs.		½ C.	18	4 lbs. 1 oz.	U.S. certified food coloring added in syrup

VACUUM-PACKED SHELLED NUTS

6/3#	Almonds	Sliced	Blanched	3 lbs.	3 qts.				
12/1#	Almonds	Slivered	Blanched	1 lb.	1 qt.				
6/4#	Nut topping			4 lbs.	4 qts.				Peanuts, cashews, almonds, pecans
6/3#	Pecans	Halves		3 lbs.	3 qts.				
6/3#	Pecans	Pieces		3 lbs.	3 qts.				
6/2¾#	Walnuts	Halves and pieces	Light California	2 lbs. 12 ozs.	2¾ qts.				
12/1#	Walnuts	Halves and pieces	Light California	1 lb.	1 qt.				
12/1#	Walnuts, black	Kernels	Eastern	1 lb.	1 qt.				

DRIED FRUITS

6/2#	Apple	Pie slices	Low moisture fruit	2 lbs.	1½ gal.		5—9-in. Pies		Used 1 quart for each pie
6/2½#	Apple	Sauce nuggets	Low moisture fruit	2 lbs. 8 ozs.	3¼ gals.	½ C.	104		
30# Carton	Apricots	Dried	Blenheim	30 lbs.	2550	6 to 7 pieces	364 to 425		
6/10	Apricots	Slices	Low moisture fruit	3 lbs. 8 ozs.	2¼ gals.	½ C.	72		
30# Carton	Figs	Dried	Calimyrna jumbo	30 lbs.	702	3 pieces	234		
5# Bag	Figs	Dried	Calimyrna jumbo	5 lbs.	117	3 pieces	39		
6/10	Fruit cocktail mix		Low moisture fruit	2 lbs. 12 ozs.	2¼ gals.	½ C.	72		Maraschino cherries, apricots, peaches, apples, grapes
30# Carton	Fruit	Dried	Mixed	30 lbs.	690 prunes 432 apricots 114 peaches 84 pears	5 pieces	264		Blenheim apricots, Lake County pears, Muir peaches, Santa Clara prunes
30# Carton	Peaches	Dried	Muir	30 lbs.	1134	3 pieces	378		
30# Carton	Prunes	Dried	Santa Clara	30 lbs.	540 to 720	2 pieces	270 to 360		Size 18/24
5# Can	Prunes	Dried	Santa Clara	5 lbs.	90 to 120	2 pieces	45 to 60		Size 18/24
30# Carton	Prunes	Dried	Santa Clara	30 lbs.	600 to 900	3 pieces	200 to 300		Size 20/30
5# Can	Prunes	Dried	Santa Clara	5 lbs.	100 to 150	3 pieces	33 to 50		Size 20/30
30# Carton	Prunes	Dried	Santa Clara	30 lbs.	900 to 1200	4 pieces	225 to 300		Size 30/40
5# Can	Prunes	Dried	Santa Clara	5 lbs.	150 to 200	4 pieces	37 to 50		Size 30/40
30# Carton	Prunes	Dried	Santa Clara	30 lbs.	1200 to 1500	5 pieces	240 to 300		Size 40/50
5# Can	Prunes	Dried	Santa Clara	5 lbs.	200 to 250	5 pieces	40 to 50		Size 40/50

Table 12 (continued)

Cans per Case and Container Size	Food	Style	Type	Approximate Net Weight	Range in Contents per Container	Suggested Portion per Serving	Approximate Portions per Container	Approximate Drained Weight	Miscellaneous Information
PREPARED PIE FILLINGS									
6/10	Apples		Greenings	7 lbs. 4 ozs.			3—9-in. Pies		Apple slices, sugar, lemon juice and water. Used 1 quart for each pie.
6/10	Blueberry		Maine	7 lbs. 4 ozs.			3—9-in. Pies		Contains blueberries, sugar, lemon juice, starch, salt and water. Used 1 quart for each pie.
6/10	Cherry		Michigan	7 lbs. 8 ozs.			3—9-in. Pies		Contains cherries, cornstarch, sugar, lemon juice, food coloring and water. Used 1 quart for each pie.
6/10	Lemon			7 lbs. 14 ozs.			3—9-in. Pies		Sugar, corn syrup, eggs, cereal, lemon juice, stabilizers, vegetable shortening, salt, fruit acid, lemon flavoring. Used 1 quart for each pie.
6/10	Peaches	Sliced	Yellow cling	7 lbs. 4 ozs.			3—9-in. Pies		Freestone peaches, sugar, starch, lemon juice and water. Used 1 quart for each pie.
PIE FILLINGS									
6/10	Apples	Sliced	York Imperial	6 lbs. 12 ozs.			16⅓ C.	6 lbs. 12 ozs.	No syrup
6/10	Apricots	Unpeeled halves	Blenheim, Royal or Tilton	6 lbs. 10 ozs.			11¼ C.	6 lbs. 10 ozs.	Preheated solid pack pie apricots, no syrup
6/10	Blackberries		Washington State Evergreen	6 lbs. 7 ozs.			12⅔ C.	4 lbs. 15 ozs.	Packed in water
6/10	Black raspberries		Michigan	6 lbs. 6 oz.			8 C.	3 lbs. 3 ozs.	Packed in water
6/10	Blueberries		Maine or Canada	6 lbs. 6 ozs.			9¼ C.	3 lbs. 12 ozs.	Packed in water
6/10	Boysenberries		Genuine Variety California or Oregon	6 lbs. 7 ozs.			6¾ C.	3 lbs. 6 ozs.	Packed in water
6/10	Cherries, red sour	Pitted	Michigan or Wisconsin Montmorency	6 lbs. 7 ozs.			11¼ C.	4 lbs. 7 ozs.	Packed in water
6/10	Gooseberries		Northwest or Michigan	6 lbs. 5 ozs.			11½ C.	3 lbs. 13 ozs.	Packed in water
6/10	Mincemeat		Olde English	7 lbs. 12 ozs.			13½ C.	7 lbs. 12 ozs.	Contains raisins, evaporated apples, sugar, boiled cider, candied fruits, beef suet, cider vinegar, spices
6/10	Peaches, yellow cling	Halves or slices	Midsummer or Phillips yellow cling California	6 lbs. 8 ozs.			14 C.	6 lbs. 3 ozs.	Preheated solid pack pie peaches, no syrup
6/10	Pumpkin		California	6 lbs. 10 ozs.			14 C.	6 lbs. 10 ozs.	Dry pack
SPICED FRUITS									
6/10	Apples, spiced	Rings	Jonathan	6 lbs. 10 ozs.	70 to 80	1 ring	70 to 80	3 lbs. 13 ozs.	Colored, unpeeled, cored in heavy syrup
6/10	Apricots, spiced	Whole peeled	California Blenheim	6 lbs. 14 ozs.	35 to 40	1	35 to 40	4 lbs. 4 ozs.	Pit loosened in extra heavy syrup
6/10	Cantaloupe, preserved	Cubed		8 lbs.	214	2	107	5 lbs. 11 ozs.	In heavy syrup
6/10	Crab Apples, spiced	Whole	Michigan Hyslop	6 lbs. 10 ozs.	50 to 60	1	50 to 60	4 lbs. 1 oz.	Colored red, cored in heavy syrup
12/5	Honeydew melon, preserved	Cubed		8 lbs.	226	2	113	5 lbs. 8 ozs.	In heavy syrup
6/10	Kumquats, preserved	Whole	Florida	3 lbs. 8 ozs.	70 to 75		70 to 75	2 lbs. 8 ozs.	In syrup
6/10	Peaches, yellow cling, spiced	Whole	California	6 lbs. 14 ozs.	25 to 30	1	25 to 30	4 lbs. 10 ozs.	Pit loosened in extra heavy syrup
6/10	Pears, Bartlett cinnamon-flavored	Halves	California	6 lbs. 12 ozs.	25 to 30	1	25 to 30	3 lbs. 10 ozs.	Colored red in extra heavy syrup

(Table continued from preceding page)

Pack	Commodity	Style	Variety	Net weight / contents	Approx. count per container	Size of serving	Approx. servings per container	Drained weight	Remarks
6/10	Pears, Bartlett peppermint-flavored	Halves	California	6 lbs. 12 ozs.	25 to 30	1	25 to 30	3 lbs. 10 ozs.	Colored green in extra heavy syrup
6/10	Pears, Kieffer, spiced	Whole	Michigan	6 lbs. 10 ozs.	40 to 50	1	40 to 50	3 lbs. 15 ozs.	Colored red in extra heavy syrup
6/10	Pears, Seckel, spiced	Whole	New York Seckel	6 lbs. 12 ozs.	70 to 80	1	70 to 80	4 lbs. 9 ozs.	In extra heavy syrup
6/5	Prunes, spiced	Whole	D'Agen	3 lbs. 4 ozs.	62	1	62	2 lbs. 10 ozs.	Sometimes available in No. 10 cans
6/10	Watermelon, preserved	Cubed		8 lbs.	194	2	97	5 lbs. 9 ozs.	

FRUIT JUICES, NECTARS, AND BEVERAGE BASES

Pack	Commodity	Style	Variety	Net contents	Size of serving	Approx. servings per container	Remarks
4/1 gal.	Apple	Cider	Unsweetened	1 gal.	4 oz.	32	
12/46 oz.	Apple	Juice		46 oz.	4 oz.	11½	Sugar added
12/46 oz.	Cherry	Juice	Red	46 oz.	4 oz.	11½	Sugar added
4/1 gal.	Cranberry	Juice	Cocktail	1 gal.	4 oz.	32	Sugar added
12/46 oz.	Grape	Juice	Concord	46 oz.	4 oz.	11½	Unsweetened
12/46 oz.	Grape	Juice	Concord	46 oz.	4 oz.	11½	Unsweetened
12/46 oz.	Grapefruit	Juice	Texas or Florida	46 oz.	4 oz.	11½	Unsweetened
12/46 oz.	Orange	Juice	Florida Valencia	46 oz.	4 oz.	11½	Unsweetened
12/46 oz.	Orange and grapefruit	Juice	Florida	46 oz.	4 oz.	11½	Sugar added
12/46 oz.	Pineapple	Juice	Hawaiian	46 oz.	4 oz.	11½	Unsweetened
12/46 oz.	Prune	Juice		46 oz.	4 oz.	11½	Unsweetened juice of dried prunes
12/46 oz.	Tangarine	Juice	Florida	46 oz.	4 oz.	11½	Sugar added
6/10	Tomato	Juice	Eastern or California	3 qts.	4 oz.	24	
12/46 oz.	Vegetable	Juice	Eastern or California	46 oz.	4 oz.	11½	
12/46 oz.	Apricot	Nectar	Eastern	46 oz.	4 oz.	11½	Sweetened
12/46 oz.	Boysenberry	Nectar	California	46 oz.	4 oz.	11½	Sugar added
12/46 oz.	Loganberry	Nectar	Northwest	46 oz.	4 oz.	11½	Sweetened
12/46 oz.	Peach	Nectar	California Elberta	46 oz.	4 oz.	11½	Sugar added
12/1 qt.	Pear	Nectar	Oahu		8 oz.	27	Sugar added
4/1 gal.	Punch	Beverage base	Oahu	8 oz.	8 oz.	96	Pineapple juice, orange juice, apricot nectar, loganberry nectar
12/1 qt.	Syrup	Beverage base	Concord Grape	8 oz.	8 oz.	28¼	Pineapple juice, orange juice, apricot nectar, loganberry nectar
12/1 qt.	Syrup	Beverage base	Lemonade	8 oz.	8 oz.	24	Sugar, water, corn syrup, concentrated lemon juice, lemon oil, ascorbic acid, certified artificial color, and 1/10 of 1 percent benzoate of soda
12/1 qt.	Syrup	Beverage base	Refresh-O-Orange Press	8 oz.	8 oz.	30	

PICKLES

Pack	Commodity	Style	Variety	Net contents	Approx. count per container	Size of serving	Approx. servings per container	Remarks
6/10	Pickles	Sweet, circles	Kurley Kut (serrated)	3 qts.	360 to 400	3	120 to 133	1½-inch diameter
6/10	Pickles	Sweet	Miniature	3 qts.	425	2 to 3	130	About 1½-inch length
6/10	Pickles	Sweet	Tiny	3 qts.	230 to 240	2	125	About 1¾-inch length
6/10	Pickles	Sweet	Midget	3 qts.	160 to 165	2	80	About 2-inch length
6/10	Pickles	Sweet, chips	20th-Century cross cuts	3 qts.	461	3 to 4	150	Small-type pickle, 1¾-inch diameter
6/10	Pickles	Sweet	Quartered stix	3 qts.	170 to 180	2	75 to 80	
6/10	Pickles	Sweet	Tidbits	8 lbs.	315 to 320	1 oz.	88	Watermelon, cantaloupe, Burr gherkin halves, pickle rings, tiny sweet gherkins, diced red peppers
6/10	Pickles	Sweet	Mixed	3 qts.	357	1 oz.	70	70 percent cut mixed pickles, 20 percent cauliflower, 10 percent onions
6/10	Cucumber	Sweet, circles	Cross cut	3 qts.	225 to 235	2 to 3	110 to 120	
6/10	Pickles	Sweet	Whole No. 60	3 qts.	115 to 120	1 to 2	58 to 112	About 3-inch length
6/10	Pickles	Sweet, whole	Small No. 36	3 qts.	55 to 60	1	55 to 60	Fresh cucumber pickles
6/10	Pickles	Home-style	Circles	3 qts.	390	4	95 to 98	bread-and-butter style

Table 12 (*continued*)

PICKLES (*continued*)

Cans per Case and Container Size	Food	Style	Type	Approximate Net Weight	Range in Contents per Container	Suggested Portion per Serving	Approximate Portions per Container	Approximate Drained Weight	Miscellaneous Information
6/10	Pickles	Home-style	Quartered, stix	3 qts.	140 to 150	2	70 to 75		Bred-and-butter style
6/10	Pickles	Dill, sweet	Circles, cross cuts	3 qts.	280 to 300	2 to 3	140 to 150		
6/10	Pickles	Dill, genuine	Circles	3 qts.	225 to 235	2	110 to 115		
6/10	Pickles	Dill, genuine	Whole. No. 18	3 qts.	32 to 35	⅔	75 to 80		About 3½-inch length
6/10	Pickles	Dill, genuine	Whole. No. 12	3 qts.	20 to 24	¼	80 to 90		About 4-inch length
6/10	Pickles	Dill, genuine	Whole. No. 18. garlic-flavored	3 qts.	30 to 35	¼	80 to 90		About 3½-inch length

OLIVES

Cans per Case and Container Size	Food	Style	Type	Approximate Net Weight	Range in Contents per Container	Suggested Portion per Serving	Approximate Portions per Container	Approximate Drained Weight	Miscellaneous Information
4/1 gal.	Olives	Colossal	Queen, plain	5 lbs. 8 ozs.	180 to 190	1	180 to 190		Imported Spain. Size: 60-60
4/1 gal.	Olives	Jumbo	Queen, plain	5 lbs. 12 ozs.	200	1	200		Size: 70-80
4/1 gal.	Olives	Mammoth	Queen, plain	5 lbs. 14 ozs.	220	1	220		Imported Spain. Size: 80-100
4/1 gal.	Olives	Giant	Queen, plain	5 lbs. 12 ozs.	250	1	250		Size: 90-110
4/1 gal.	Olives	Large	Queen, plain	5 lbs. 4 ozs.	280	1 to 2	140 to 280		Imported Spain. Size: 100-110
4/1 gal.	Olives	Medium	Queen, plain	5 lbs.	330	2 to 3	110 to 165		Size: 130-150
4/1 gal.	Olives	Fancy, pitted	Queen, plain	5 lbs. 12 ozs.	260	1	260		Size: 90-100
4/1 gal.	Olives	Colossal	Queen, stuffed	5 lbs. 14 ozs.	200	1	200		Imported Spain stuffed with bright red Spanish pimiento. Size: 70-80
4/1 gal.	Olives	Jumbo	Queen, stuffed	6 lbs.	225	1	225		Size: 80-90
4/1 gal.	Olives	Mammoth	Queen, stuffed	5 lbs. 12 ozs.	250	1	250		Imported Spain stuffed with bright red pimiento. Size: 90-100
4/1 gal.	Olives	Large	Queen, stuffed	5 lbs. 12 ozs.	300	1 to 2	150 to 200		Imported Spain stuffed with bright red pimiento. Size: 100-130
4/1 gal.	Olives	Medium	Queen, stuffed	5 lbs. 4 ozs.	330	2 to 3	110 to 165		Size: 130-150
4/1 gal.	Olives	Medium	Manzanilla, stuffed	5 lbs. 12 ozs.	700	3 to 4	175 to 233		Size: 240-260
4/1 gal.	Olives	Small	Manzanilla, stuffed	5 lbs. 2 ozs.	800 to 822	4 to 5	160 to 200		Imported Spain. Size: 300-320
6/10	Olives	Super colossal	Ripe	4 lbs.	128	1	128		Sevilliano variety
6/10	Olives	Colossal	Ripe	4 lbs.	152	1	152		
6/10	Olives	Large	Ripe	4 lbs.	404	1 to 2	202 to 404		Mission variety
6/10	Olives	Medium	Ripe	4 lbs. 2 ozs.	460	2 to 3	153 to 230		
6/10	Olives	Medium	Ripe, pitted	3 lbs. 4 ozs.	480	1 to 2	240 to 480		
24/5½ oz.	Olives	Medium	Ripe, pitted	5½ oz.	50 to 52	1 to 2	26 to 52		

JAMS[a]

Cans per Case and Container Size	Food	Style	Type	Approximate Net Weight	Range in Contents per Container	Suggested Portion per Serving	Approximate Portions per Container	Approximate Drained Weight	Miscellaneous Information
6/10	Apple	Butter		7 lbs. 8 ozs.		No. 45 souffle 1 oz.	120		Made from evaporated apples
6/4¾#	Cherry	Jam	Red chopped	4 lbs. 12 ozs.		No. 45 souffle 1 oz.	76		
6/4¾#	Grape	Jam	Seedless	4 lbs. 12 ozs.		No. 45 souffle 1 oz.	76		
6/4¾#	Damson plum	Jam	Seedless	4 lbs. 12 ozs.		No. 45 souffle 1 oz.	76		
6/4¾#	Plum	Jam	Santa Rosa	4 lbs. 12 ozs.		No. 45 souffle 1 oz.	76		

JELLIES[b]

Size	Variety	Type	Weight	Description	Container	No.	Notes
6/4½#	Apple	Jelly	4 lbs. 8 ozs.		No. 45 souffle / 1 oz.	72	
6/10	Apple	Jelly	8 lbs.		No. 45 souffle / 1 oz.	128	
6/4½#	Apple	Jelly	4 lbs. 8 ozs.	Crab	No. 45 souffle / 1 oz.	72	Translucent
6/4½#	Black raspberry	Jelly	4 lbs. 8 ozs.		No. 45 souffle / 1 oz.	72	
6/4½#	Cherry	Jelly	4 lbs. 8 ozs.	Red	No. 45 souffle / 1 oz.	72	
6/4½#	Currant	Jelly	4 lbs. 8 ozs.	Red	No. 45 souffle / 1 oz.	72	
6/4½#	Elderberry	Jelly	4 lbs. 8 ozs.	Wild	No. 45 souffle / 1 oz.	72	
6/4½#	Grape	Jelly	4 lbs. 8 ozs.	Concord	No. 45 souffle / 1 oz.	72	Apple base
6/10	Grape	Jelly	8 lbs.		No. 45 souffle / 1 oz.	128	
6/4½#	Mint	Jelly	4 lbs. 8 ozs.		No. 45 souffle / 1 oz.	72	
6/4½#	Plum	Jelly	4 lbs. 8 ozs.	Winey	No. 45 souffle / 1 oz.	72	
6/4½#	Quince	Jelly	4 lbs. 8 ozs.		No. 45 souffle / 1 oz.	72	
6/4½#	Strawberry	Jelly	4 lbs. 8 ozs.		No. 45 souffle / 1 oz.	72	
6/10	Strawberry-cherry	Jelly	8 lbs.		No. 45 souffle / 1 oz.	128	

PRESERVES[a]

Size	Variety	Type	Weight	Description	Container	No.	Notes
6/4¾#	Orange	Marmalade	4 lbs. 12 ozs.	Sweet	No. 45 souffle / 1 oz.	76	Sugar, orange peel, orange juice, pectin, and citric acid
6/4¾#	Apricot	Preserves	4 lbs. 12 ozs.		No. 45 souffle / 1 oz.	76	
6/4¾#	Blackberry	Preserves	4 lbs. 12 ozs.		No. 45 souffle / 1 oz.	76	
6/4¾#	Cherry	Preserves	4 lbs. 12 ozs.	Black pitted	No. 45 souffle / 1 oz.	76	
6/4¾#	Cherry	Preserves	4 lbs. 12 ozs.	Red whole	No. 45 souffle / 1 oz.	76	
6/4¾#	Grape	Preserves	4 lbs. 12 ozs.	Concord pitted	No. 45 souffle / 1 oz.	76	
6/4¾#	Elberta peach	Preserves	4 lbs. 12 ozs.	Rocky Mountain	No. 45 souffle / 1 oz.	76	
6/4¾#	Peach	Preserves	4 lbs. 12 ozs.	Rio Osa	No. 45 souffle / 1 oz.	76	
6/10	Peach	Preserves	8 lbs. 4 ozs.	Elberta	No. 45 souffle / 1 oz.	132	
6/4¾#	Pineapple	Preserves	4 lbs. 12 ozs.		No. 45 souffle / 1 oz.	76	
6/4¾#	Pine apricot	Preserves	4 lbs. 12 ozs.		No. 45 souffle / 1 oz.	76	
6/4¾#	Plum	Preserves	4 lbs. 12 ozs.	Oregon pitted	No. 45 souffle / 1 oz.	76	
6/10	Plum	Preserves	8 lbs. 4 ozs.	Oregon pitted	No. 45 souffle / 1 oz.	132	
6/4¾#	Raspberry	Preserves	4 lbs. 12 ozs.	Black seedless	No. 45 souffle / 1 oz.	76	

Table 12 *(continued)*

Cans per Case and Container Size	Food	Style	Type	Approximate Net Weight	Range in Contents per Container	Suggested Portion per Serving	Approximate Portions per Container	Approximate Drained Weight	Miscellaneous Information
				PRESERVES *(continued)*					
6/4¾ #	Raspberry	Preserves	Red	4 lbs. 12 ozs.		No. 45 souffle 1 oz.	76		
6/4¾ #	Strawberry	Preserves		4 lbs. 12 ozs.		No. 45 souffle 1 oz.	76		
6/10	Strawberry	Preserves		8 lbs. 4 ozs.		No. 45 souffle 1 oz.	132		
				DESSERT POWDER BASES					
6/10	Dessert powder	Gelatin		5 lbs. 4 ozs.		4 oz.	128		Flavors: apple, wild cherry, citrus, grape, lemon, lime, melba, orange, black raspberry, red raspberry, strawberry. Dissolved in 3½ gals. of water
12/2½	Dessert powder	Gelatin		1 lb. 8 ozs.		4 oz.	32		Flavors: apple, wild cherry, citrus, grape, lemon, lime, melba, orange, black raspberry, red raspberry, strawberry. Dissolved in 1 gal. of water
6/10	Dessert powder			5 lbs.		4 oz.	70—½ C.		Flavors: butterscotch, chocolate, coconut, vanilla. Makes 6—9 in. pies. Used 2 gals. of water
6/10	Dessert powder		Lemon	5 lbs. 8 ozs.		4 oz.	70—½ C.		Makes 6—9 in. pies. Used 2 gals. of water
12/2½	Dessert powder			1 lb. 6 ozs.		4 oz.	20—½ C.		Flavors: butterscotch, chocolate, coconut, vanilla. Makes 2—9 in. pies Used 2¼ qts. of water
12/2½	Dessert powder		Lemon	1 lb. 8 ozs.		4 oz.	20—½ C.		Makes 2—9 in. pies. Used 2¼ qts. of water
12/2½	Dessert powder	Blancmange	Mix 'n serve	1 lb. 4 ozs.		4 oz.	30—½ C.		Flavors: chocolate, coconut. Used 2½ qts. of water
12/2½	Dessert powder	Blancmange	Mix 'n serve	1 lb. 8 ozs.		4 oz.	30—½ C.		Flavors: butterscotch, vanilla. Used 3 qts. of water
				SEAFOODS					
24/303	Clams	No. 1 Little Neck	Whole	1 lb. 4 ozs.	16 Whole 1¾ Cups			8 oz.	Liquor—1⅓ C.
24/2	Clams	No. 2 Little Neck	Whole	1 lb. 4 ozs.	66 Whole 1 Cup			10 oz.	Liquor— ½C.
12/5 Tall	Clams		Chopped or minced	3 lbs. 3 ozs.	4 Cups			1 lb. 7 ozs.	Liquor—3½ C.
24/1	Crab meat	King	Imported Japan	13 oz.	B & F—3⅓Cups C—2¾ Cups	2 oz. 4 oz.	6½ 3¼	10 oz.	Liquor—⅓ C.
12/2½	Fish flakes	Pollack		2 lbs.	5¾ Cups				Liquor—1¼ C.
24/1	Lobster		Imported Canada	10 oz.	B & F—2⅓Cups C—2¼ Cups	2 oz. 4 oz.	5 2½		Liquor—½ C.
48/1	Salmon	Sockeye	Fancy Red Alaska	1 lb.	B & F—2¼ Cups C—2 Cups	2 oz. (⅓—½ C.) 4 oz. (⅔—¾ C.)	5 2½		Liquor—⅓C. Color—deep red. Small firm flakes

12/4#	Salmon	Sockeye	Fancy Red Alaska	4 lbs.	B & F— ¼ Cups C—8½ Cups	2 oz. (⅓—½ C.)	21		Liquor—⅓ C. Color—deep red
						4 oz. (⅔—¾ C.)	12		
48/1	Salmon	Cohoe	Fancy	1 lb.	B & F—2¼ Cups C—2 Cups	2 oz. (⅓—½ C.)	5		Large flake. Color—pale pink
						4 oz. (⅔—¾ C.)	2½		
12/4#	Salmon	Cohoe	Fancy	4 lbs.	B & F—9⅓ Cups C—8¾ Cups	2 oz. (⅓—½ C.)	21		Large flake. Color—pale pink
						4 oz. (⅔—¾ C)	12		
48/Tall	Salmon	Pink	Choice	1 lb.	B & F—2¼ Cups C—2 Cups	2 oz. (⅓—½ C.)	5		
						4 oz. (⅔—¾ C.)	2½		
12/4#	Salmon	Pink	Choice	4 lbs.	B & F—9 Cups C—8⅓ Cups	2 oz. (⅓—½ C.)	21		
						4 oz. (⅔—¾ C.)	12		
48/1#	Salmon	Chum	Packers	1 lb.	B & F—2¼ Cups C—2 Cups	2 oz. (⅓—½ C.)	5		
						4 oz. (⅔—¾ C.)	2½		
12/4#	Salmon	Chum	Packers	4 lbs.	B & F—9 Cups C—8⅓ Cups	2 oz. (⅓—½ C.)	21		
						4 oz. (⅔—¾ C.)	12		
24/5 oz.	Shrimp	Jumbo	Cleaned	5 oz.	15 to 17	4 to 5	3 to 4		
24/13¼ oz.	Shrimp	Jumbo	Cleaned		42 to 48	4 to 5	8 to 10		
6/10 squat	Tuna	White meat	Domestic	66½ oz.	B & F-13¾ Cups C—11 Cups	2 oz—½ C. 4 oz.—1 C.	27 13½		In cottonseed oil
12/10 squat	Tuna	White meat	Japanese	66½ oz.	B & F-14¼ Cups C—12 Cups	2 oz.—½ C. 4 oz.—1 C.	27 13½		Solid-pack in brine
6/10 squat	Tuna	Light meat	Japanese	66½ oz.	B & F—14 Cups C—11 Cups	2 oz.—½ C. 4 oz.—1 C.	27 13		In brine

CONVENIENCE FOODS

6/10	Beans with frankfurters	In tomato sauce		6 lbs. 14 ozs.		6 oz.—¾ C.	18+		Navy beans, pork, beef, sugar, tomato paste, onions and seasonings
6/10	Beans in tomato sauce	Meatless		6 lbs. 14 ozs.		8 oz.—1 C.	12		Pea beans, tomato paste, salt, brown sugar, vinegar, spices
6/10	Beans in tomato sauce	With pork		6 lbs. 14 ozs.		8 oz.—1 C.	12		
6/10	Beans	Lima	Sea Breeze	6 lbs. 12 ozs.		3½ oz.—½ C.	23	4 lbs. 7 ozs.	Large soaked lima beans with salt added
6/5	Beef with gravy			3 lbs. 3 ozs.		6 oz.	7		Four 2-in. cubes beef per serving
6/5	Beef with barbecue sauce	Chopped		3 lbs. 4 ozs.		4 oz.—½ C.	12		½ C. equals No. 16 scoop. Suggest serving on a bun
6/5	Beef chop suey			3 lbs. 2 ozs.		6 oz.—¾ C.	7		Celery, bean sprouts, beef broth, beef onions, water chestnuts, bamboo shoots, mushrooms
6/5	Beef hash			3 lbs. 3 ozs.		6 oz.—1 C.	7		Beef, potatoes, onions. Baked 3-in. squares
6/10	Beef hash	Corned		6 lbs. 12 ozs.		6 oz.—1 C.	16		Beef, potatoes. Baked 3-in. squares
6/5	Beef hash	Corned		3 lbs. 3 ozs.		6 oz.—1 C.	7+		Beef, potatoes. Baked 3-in. squares

Table 12 (continued)

Cans per Case and Container Size	Food	Style	Type	Approximate Net Weight	Range in Contents per Container	Suggested Portion per Serving	Approximate Portions per Container	Approximate Drained Weight	Miscellaneous Information
			CONVENIENCE FOODS (continued)						
6/5	Beef stew			3 lbs. 3 ozs.		8 oz.—1 C.	6		Beef, potatoes, carrots, celery, onions, peas
6/5	Chicken a la king			3 lbs. 2 ozs.		6 oz.—¾ C.	7+		Chicken, peppers, mushrooms
6/5	Chicken chop suey			3 lbs. 2 ozs.		6 oz.—¾ C.	7+		Celery, bean sprouts, chicken, onions, water chestnuts, bamboo shoots, mushrooms
6/5	Chicken fricassee			3 lbs. 2 ozs.		6 oz.—¾ C.	8		Chicken in chicken gravy
6/10	Chili beans	In hot chili gravy	Meatless	6 lbs. 14 ozs.		8 oz.—1 C.	12		Beef, beans, spices, tomato puree, onion powder, garlic powder. Dilute with 3 to 4 C. water as desired
6/10	Chili con carne	With beans	Home-style	6 lbs. 12 ozs.		8 oz.—1 C.	16		Beef, beans, spices, tomato puree, onion powder, garlic powder. Dilute with 1½ C. water as desired
6/5	Chili con carne	With beans	Home-style	3 lbs. 2 ozs.		8 oz.—1 C.	7		Beef, tomato puree, spices, onion powder, garlic powder. Dilute with 1 pt. water as desired
6/10	Chili con carne	Without beans		6 lbs. 10 ozs.		8 oz.—1 C.	14		Chili con carne with beans and macaroni (beef, tomatoes, beans, macaroni, potato starch, sugar, spices and seasonings)
12/5	Chili mac			3 lbs. 3 ozs.		6 oz.—¾ C.	8+		
12/5	Potato salad	German	Old-fashioned	3 lbs. 2 ozs.		4 oz.—½ C.	11		Sliced potatoes, bacon, onions, vinegar, parsley flakes, seasoning
6/5	Pork in barbecue sauce	Chopped		3 lbs. 4 ozs.		4 oz.—½ C.	12		½ C. equals No. 16 scoop. Suggest serving on a bun
6/5	Rice	Spanish	Meatless	3 lbs. 2 ozs.		6 oz.—¾ C.	8		Rice, onions, pepper, tomato paste, sugar, salt, spices
12/5	Spaghetti in tomato sauce		Meatless	3 lbs. 2 ozs.		8 oz.—1 C.	6		Spaghetti, tomato paste, onions, sugar, vinegar, spices
6/10	Spaghetti sauce	Meatless		6 lbs. 10 ozs.		4 oz.—½ C.	26		Water, tomato paste, onions, malt vinegar, bread crumbs, sugar, olive oil, hydrolized vegetable proteins, salt, dehydrated mushrooms, spices, flavorings, worcestershire sauce, beet powder, algin derivatives, garlic, monosodium glutamate
6/5	Vegetarian chop suey			3 lbs. 2 ozs.		6 oz.—¾ C.	7+		Celery, bean sprouts, water chestnuts, onions, mushrooms, bamboo shoots
			CONDENSED SOUPS[C]						
6/10	Chicken	Broth		3 qts.		8 oz.—1 C.	24+		Chicken broth, hydrolized wheat protein, chicken fat, and fresh vegetable flavoring
12/5	Chicken	Broth		3 lbs. 2 ozs.		8 oz.—1 C.	12+		
12/5	Beef	Bouillon		3 lbs. 2 ozs.		8 oz.—1 C.	12		Beef stock, parsnips, carrots, beef extract, onions, and seasonings
12/5	Tomato	Bouillon		3 lbs. 2 ozs.		8 oz.—1 C.	12+		Tomato juice, sugar, salt, beef extract, vegetable oil, onion powder, and spices

							Ingredients
12/5	Chicken	Chowder		3 lbs. 2 ozs.	8 oz.—1 C.	12	Chicken broth, potatoes, carrots, chicken, celery, cornstarch, onions, peas, corn, tomatoes, red peppers, and seasonings
12/5	Clam	Chowder	Manhattan	3 lbs. 2 ozs.	8 oz.—1 C.	12	Potatoes, clams, carrots, clam juice, tomato paste, red peppers, onions, celery, parsley flakes, and seasonings
12/5	Clam	Chowder	New England	3 lbs. 2 ozs.	8 oz.—1 C.	12	Clams, potatoes, onions, and seasonings
12/5		Chowder	Red snapper	3 lbs. 2 ozs.	8 oz.—1 C.	12	Potatoes, red snappers, tomatoes, carrots, onions, clam juice, corn, celery, red peppers, rice
12/5	Asparagus	Soup	Cream of	3 lbs. 2 ozs.	8 oz.—1 C.	12	Asparagus, milk, salt, sugar, onions, butter
12/5	Bean	Soup	Navy	3 lbs. 2 ozs.	8 oz.—1 C.	12	Navy beans, tomatoes, smoked jowl bacon, carrots, onions, and seasonings
12/5	Beef	Soup		3 lbs. 2 ozs.	8 oz.—1 C.	12	Beef, carrots, potatoes, barley, tomatoes
12/5	Beef	Soup	Noodle	3 lbs. 2 ozs.	8 oz.—1 C.	12	Beef stock, beef, egg noodles, carrots, onions, celery, beef extract, and seasonings
12/5	Celery	Soup	Cream of	3 lbs. 2 ozs.	8 oz.—1 C.	12	Celery, milk, onions, carrots, and seasonings
12/5	Chicken	Soup	Cream of	3 lbs. 2 ozs.	8 oz.—1 C.	12	Chicken broth, chicken, carrots, cream, milk, celery, onions, and seasonings
12/5	Chicken	Soup	Gumbo	3 lbs. 2 ozs.	8 oz.—1 C.	12	Chicken broth, okra, tomatoes, rice, chicken, celery, tomato paste, green peppers, onions, seasonings
12/5	Chicken	Soup	Noodle	3 lbs. 2 ozs.	8 oz.—1 C.	12+	Chicken broth, egg noodles, chicken, celery, onions, and seasonings
12/5	Chicken	Soup	Rice	3 lbs. 2 ozs.	8 oz.—1 C.	12+	Chicken broth, chicken, rice, celery, onions, and seasonings
12/5	Mushroom	Soup	Cream of	3 lbs. 2 ozs.	8 oz.—1 C.	12	Mushrooms, milk, onions, and seasonings
12/5	Pea	Soup	Green	3 lbs. 2 ozs.	8 oz.—1 C.	13	Split peas, smoked pork, carrots, onions, and seasonings
12/5	Pepper pot	Soup		3 lbs. 2 ozs.	8 oz.—1 C.	12	Beef stock, beef tripe, potatoes, carrots, red peppers, macaroni, onions, tomato paste, beef fat, parsley flakes, and seasonings
6/10	Tomato	Soup		6 lbs. 9 ozs.	8 oz.—1 C.	28	Fresh ripe tomatoes, sugar, wheat flour, onions, cracker flour, vegetable oil, flavoring
12/5	Tomato	Soup		3 lbs. 2 ozs.	8 oz.—1 C.	12	Fresh ripe tomatoes, sugar, wheat flour, onions, cracker flour, vegetable oil, flavoring
6/10	Vegetable	Soup	With beef broth	6 lbs. 9 ozs.	8 oz.—1 C.	26+	Beef stock, tomatoes, potatoes, carrots, peas, sweet potatoes, okra, corn, cabbage, onions, celery, green beans, lima beans, macaroni, pea beans, peppers, barley, and seasonings
12/5	Vegetable	Soup	With beef broth	3 lbs. 2 ozs.	8 oz.—1 C.	12	Beef stock, carrots, potatoes, peas, tomato paste, corn, green beans, lima beans, onions, celery, barley, pea beans, macaroni, okra, red peppers, beef extract, and seasonings

Table 12 *(continued)*

318   **APPENDIX I**

Cans per Case and Container Size	Food	Style	Type	Approximate Net Weight	Range in Contents per Container	Suggested Portion per Serving	Approximate Portions per Container	Approximate Drained Weight	Miscellaneous Information
				CONDENSED SOUPS *(continued)*					
12/5	Vegetable	Soup	Beef	3 lbs. 2 ozs.		8 oz.—1 C.	12+		Beef broth, carrots, tomato paste, potatoes, beef, peas, celery, lima beans, corn, onions, and seasonings
6/10	Vegetable	Soup	Vegetarian	6 lbs. 9 ozs.		8 oz.—1 C.	26		Carrots, potatoes, peas, tomato paste, green beans, corn, cabbage, celery, lima beans, macaroni, okra, onions, red peppers, leeks, and seasonings
12/5	Vegetable	Soup	Vegetarian	3 lbs. 2 ozs.		8 oz.—1 C.	12+		Carrots, potatoes, peas, tomato paste, green beans, corn, cabbage, celery, lima beans, macaroni, okra, onions, red peppers, leeks, and seasonings
				READY-TO-SERVE SOUPS					
12/5	Scotch	Broth		3 lbs. 2 ozs.		8 oz.—1 C.	6+		Mutton broth, barley, mutton, carrots, turnips, and seasonings. A thick soup
12/5	Corn	Chowder		3 lbs. 2 ozs.		8 oz.—1 C.	6+		Cream-style corn, corn, potatoes, celery, pork fat, milk, onions, red peppers, and seasonings
12/5	Jellied	Consomme		3 lbs. 2 ozs.		5⅓ oz.—⅔ C.	9+		Tomato juice, gelatin, hydrolized vegetable protein, sugar, beef extract, onion juice, salt, MSG, and flavoring
12/5	Madrilene	Consomme		3 lbs. 2 ozs.		5⅓ oz.—⅔ C.	9+		Tomato juice, lemon juice, vegetable juices, beef extract, and seasonings
12/5	Minestrone	Soup		3 lbs. 2 ozs.		8 oz.—1 C.	6+		Potatoes, tomatoes, onions, cabbage, carrots, celery, green peas, green beans, dried garbanzo beans, dried lima beans, macaroni, tomato paste, split green peas, red kidney beans, navy beans, pork fat, spinach, and seasonings
12/5	Onion	Soup	French-style	3 lbs. 2 ozs.		8 oz.—1 C.	6+		Beef stock, onions, beef extract, hydrolized vegetable protein, butter, tomato paste, and flavoring
12/5	Vichyssoise	Soup		3 lbs. 2 ozs.		8 oz.—1 C.	8+		Potatoes, milk, onions, leeks, and seasonings. Add 2 ozs. of cream to each serving to give 8-oz. portion

[a] Prepared from Grade A fresh frozen fruit and pure cane sugar. Cooked in small batches to retain natural flavor and high color.
[b] Prepared from Grade A frozen juices, all single strength. Cooked in small batches to retain natural flavor and high color.
[c] Dilute with one can of water.

Source: Recipes and Menus for All Seasons (Chicago: John Sexton and Co., n.d.). Reprinted by permission.

Appendix II   Calcumetric: Anglo-Metric Converter

1. Temperature

Fahrenheit (F.)		Centigrade (C.)
212°	=	100°
32°	=	0°
0°	=	17.8°

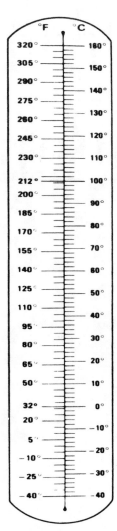

2. Length

inch/millimeter-centimeter

(in.)   (mm.)   (cm.)

1 in. = 25.4 mm. or 2.54 cm.

1 mm. = .03937 in.

1 cm. = .3937 in.

yard-foot/meter

(yd.) (ft.)   (m.)

1 yd. = .914 m.

1 m. = 1.093 yd.

1 ft. = .3048 m.

1 m. = 3.2808 ft.

mile/kilometer

(mi.)   (km.)

1 mi. = 1.609 km.

1 km. = .6214 mi.

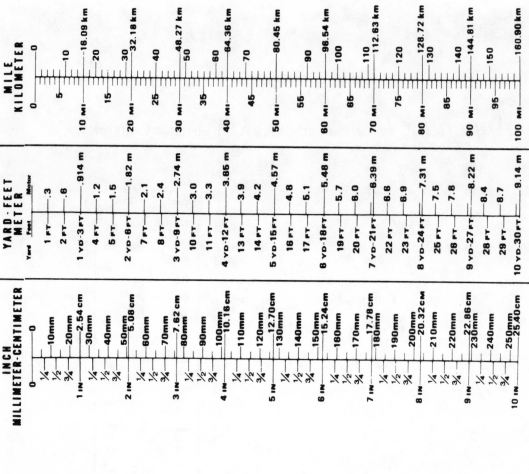

3. Area

square foot-square inch/square centimeter

(sq. ft.)   (sq. in.)   (sq. cm.)
1 sq. ft. = 144 sq. in. = 929.03 sq. cm.
1 sq. in. = 6.4516 sq. cm.
1 sq. cm. = .155 sq. in.

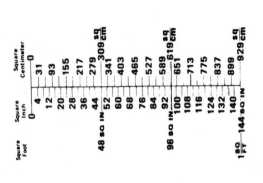

square yard-square foot/square meter

(sq. yd.)   (sq. ft.)   (sq. m.)
1 sq. yd. = 9 sq. ft. = .82 sq. m.
1 sq. ft. = .092 sq. m.
1 sq. m. = 10.8 sq. ft.

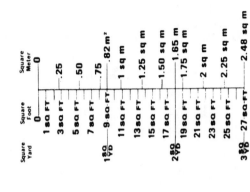

4. Capacity

Unit	UNITED STATES				METRIC		
	fluid ounce (fl. oz.)	liquid pint (liq. pt.)	liquid quart (liq. qt.)	cubic inch (c.i.)	cubic centimeter (c.c.)	deciliter (dl.)	liter (l.)
1 fl. oz.	1	.0625	.03125	1.8047	29.574	.2957	.0296
1 liq. pt.	16	1	.5	28.875	473.18	4.7316	.4732
1 liq. qt.	32	2	1	57.75	946.35	9.4633	.9463
1 c.i.	.5541	.03463	.01732	1	16.387	.1639	.0164
1 c.c. / 1 milliliter (ml.)	.0338	.00211	.00106	.06102	1	.01	.001
1 dl.	3.3815	.2113	.1057	6.1025	100	1	.1
1 l.	33.815	2.1134	1.0567	61.025	1,000	10	1

Note: The figures above have been rounded where full extension was impossible.

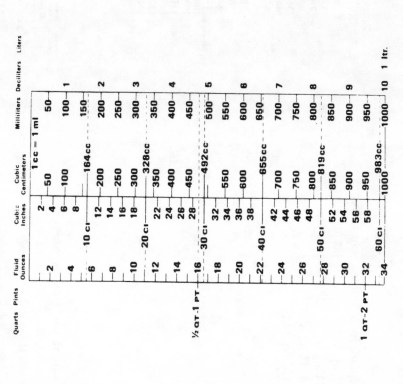

SHORT TON / METRIC TON

Short ton	Metric ton
0	0
¼, ½, ¾	.2, .4, .6, .8, .9 m ton
1 TON	1 m ton
¼, ½, ¾	1.2, 1.4, 1.6, 1.8 m ton
2 TON	2 m ton
¼, ½, ¾	2.2, 2.4, 2.6, 2.7 m ton
3 TON	2.8, 3 m ton
¼, ½, ¾	3.2, 3.4, 3.6 m ton
4 TON	3.8, 4 m ton
¼, ½, ¾	4.2, 4.5 m ton
5 TON	4.6, 4.8, 5 m ton
¼, ½, ¾	5.2, 5.4 m ton
6 TON	5.6, 5.8, 6 m ton
¼, ½, ¾	6.2, 6.3 m ton
7 TON	6.4, 6.6, 6.8, 7 m ton
¼, ½, ¾	7.2 m ton
8 TON	7.4, 7.6, 7.8, 8 m ton
¼, ½, ¾	8.1 m ton
9 TON	8.2, 8.4, 8.6, 8.8
¼, ½, ¾	9 m ton
10 TON	

POUND / KILOGRAM

Pound	Kilogram
0	0
¼, ½, ¾	.1, .2, .3, .4, .45 k
1 LB	.5, .6, .7, .8, .9 k
¼, ½, ¾	1 k
2 LB	1.1, 1.2, 1.3, 1.35 k
¼, ½, ¾	1.4, 1.5, 1.6, 1.7
3 LB	1.8 k
¼, ½, ¾	1.9, 2 k
4 LB	2.1, 2.2, 2.25 k
¼, ½, ¾	2.3, 2.4, 2.5, 2.6
5 LB	2.7 k
¼, ½, ¾	2.8, 2.9, 3 kg
6 LB	3.1, 3.15 k
¼, ½, ¾	3.2, 3.3, 3.4, 3.5
7 LB	3.6 k
¼, ½, ¾	3.7, 3.8, 3.9, 4 k
8 LB	4.05 k
¼, ½, ¾	4.1, 4.2, 4.3, 4.4
9 LB	4.5 k
¼, ½, ¾	
10 LB	

OUNCE / GRAM

Ounce	Gram
0	0
¼, ½, ¾	10, 20, 28 g
1 OZ	30, 40, 50, 57 g
¼, ½, ¾	60, 70, 80, 85 g
2 OZ	90, 100, 110, 113 g
¼, ½, ¾	120, 130, 142 g
3 OZ	150, 160, 170 g
¼, ½, ¾	180, 190, 198 g
4 OZ	200, 210, 220, 227 g
¼, ½, ¾	240, 250, 255 g
5 OZ	260, 270, 283 g
6 OZ	
7 OZ	
8 OZ	
9 OZ	
10 OZ	

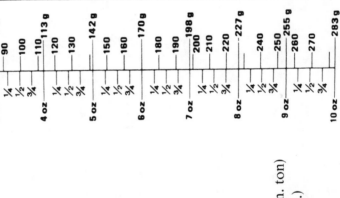

5. Weight

ounce/gram
(oz.)   (g.)
1 oz. = 28 g.
1 g. = .035 oz.

pound/kilogram
(lb.)   (kg.)
1 lb. = .45 kg.
1 kg. = 2.2 lb.

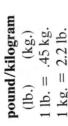

short ton (ton)/**metric ton** (m. ton)
(2,000 lb.)   (2,200 lb.)
1 ton = .907 m. ton
1 m. ton = 1.102 ton

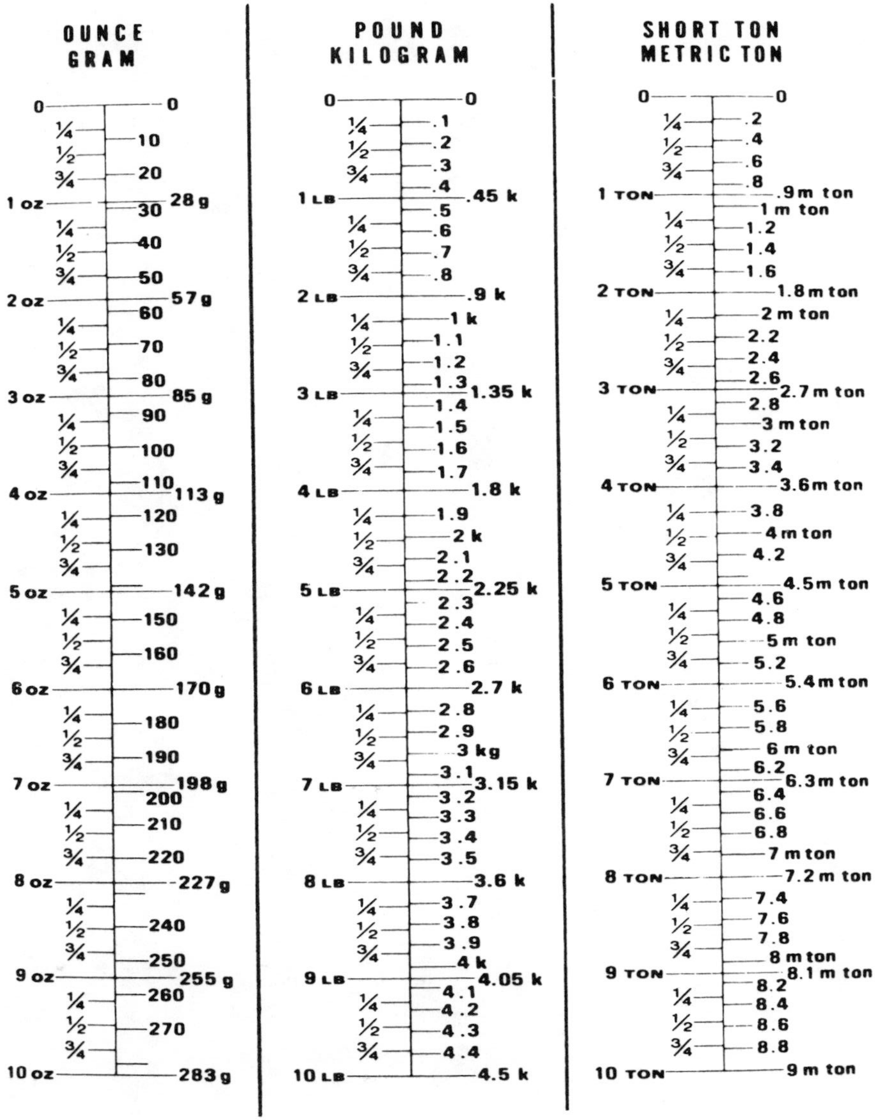

Appendix III   Canadian Food-Grading System

Food grading started in Canada shortly after the turn of the century when grades for apples, previously established only for export, were made applicable on the home market. Today we have grades for butter, cheddar cheese, instant skim milk powder, eggs, fresh and processed fruits and vegetables, honey, maple syrup, meat, and poultry.

Foods are graded according to national and provincial standards established by legislation. The Canada Department of Agriculture works in close cooperation with industry in developing the national standards. The word "Canada" in the grade name on the package or product means that the food is graded and packed in Canada in accordance with federal standards. The word "Canada" may not be used in a grade name on imported foods sold in their original containers, or on products not subject to federal grading regulations.

Before beef can be graded it must pass health inspection. Health-inspected meat and poultry products from plants registered with the Department's Health of Animals Branch are marked with the round Canada Approved or Canada inspection legend, which means the foods are wholesome but does not indicate that they are graded.

Federal grade standards apply to food exports, to imported foods of a kind produced in Canada, and to foods shipped from one province to another. Canada Department of Agriculture inspectors are responsible for enforcing federal grade standards.

The grading of foods produced and sold within a province is a provincial responsibility. However, where grade standards have been established under provincial authority, Canada Department of Agriculture inspectors collaborate with the provinces in enforcing provincial regulations.

Dairy Products

Creamery print butter and all packaged instant skim milk powder are graded and marked accordingly on the wrapper. Though grading of cheese for retail trade is not compulsory, most bulk cheddar cheese is graded, and sometimes it is sold by grade in consumer packages. All commercial packages of butter, cheddar cheese, and skim milk powder intended for interprovincial or export trade are sampled for composition and graded.

Grades

Canada Second Grade, Canada Third Grade, and Below Canada Third Grade butter and cheddar cheese are not usually available in retail stores.

Basis for Grades. Grades depend on the following:

Grading and Inspection. Federal dairy inspectors grade butter, cheddar cheese, and skim milk powder. The grade of creamery print butter may be declared by the manufacturer, but inspectors check the butter in creameries, warehouses, and retail outlets for accuracy of grading, composition, and weight. They also check the composition of cheddar cheese, process cheese, imported specialty cheeses, ice cream, and instant skim milk powder at wholesale and retail levels, and issue inspection certificates covering shipments of graded dairy products for interprovincial and export trade.

Most provinces have adopted legislation that is concurrent with federal grading regulations, but federal inspectors assign grades to the various products. Provincial dairy inspectors supervise the grading of raw milk and cream for use in manufactured products. Provincial legislation sets standards for pasteurization of fluid milk and cream and controls sanitation of these products.

Eggs

Eggs in the shell are sold by grade in all provinces. Grade marks must be shown on cartons and bulk displays in retail stores. All shell eggs that are imported, exported, or shipped from one province to another must be graded.

Grades

Canada Grade C and Canada Grade Cracks are not usually available in retail stores.

Basis for Grades. Eggs are graded on:
—weight
—cleanliness, soundness, and shape of shell
—shape and relative position of yolk within the egg, as viewed during candling
—size of air cell, an indicator of freshness
—presence of abnormalities, such as meat and blood spots

Grading and Inspection. A producer may grade his own eggs or have them graded at an egg-grading station registered with the Canada Department of Agriculture. Registered egg-grading stations must meet certain operating and sanitation requirements. Federal agricultural inspectors spot-check both producer premises and egg-grading stations to ensure that accurate grading is being done under sanitary conditions.

Federal agricultural inspectors check quality of eggs periodically at wholesale distributors, retail stores, restaurants, hospitals, other institutions, and military camps.

All provinces have regulations based on the federal grade standards for shell eggs. Federal agricultural inspectors are responsible for enforcing provincial legislation.

Fresh Fruits and Vegetables

Most Canadian fruits and vegetables grown in large quantities are sold by grade. Not all provinces require grading of the same fruits and vegetables, though all have regulations covering some. Provincial grades are similar to the federal grades outlined below, which are compulsory for interprovincial and export trade.

Grades

Apples

Apples must have a minimum diameter of 2¼ inches to meet federal standards. However, in certain years a 2-inch minimum is permitted for red and red-striped varieties of Canada Extra Fancy and Canada Fancy grades with 20 percent more color than normal color standards. Some provinces permit the sale of apples of some varieties in the size range of 2 to 2¼ inches provided they have Extra Fancy color.

Potatoes

Sizes for potatoes are as follows:

Canada No. 1	2¼ to 3½ inches in diameter for round varieties
	2 to 3½ inches in diameter for long varieties
Canada No. 1— Large	3 to 4½ inches in diameter
Canada No. 1— Small	1½ to 2¼ inches in diameter
Canada No. 1— New Potatoes	Before September 16 each year, new potatoes with a minimum diameter of 1-7/8 inches (both round and long varieties) may be graded Canada No. 1
Canada No. 2	1¾ to 4½ inches in diameter, with at least 75 percent of the lot having a diameter of 2 inches or larger

Basis for Grades. Fresh fruits and vegetables are graded on:
—uniformity of size and shape
—minimum and maximum diameter
—minimum length
—color
—maturity
—freedom from disease, injury, and other defects and damage
—cleanliness
—packaging

Grading and Inspection. Producers or packers grade their own fruits and vegetables. All products bearing federal grade names must meet grade and label specifications and must be in standard packages. All produce in bulk displays must meet grade specifications if a grade is declared. Bulk displays of apples must also indicate the variety when the grade is marked.

Federal fruit and vegetable inspectors check grades of fruits and vegetables at packing and shipping points and inspect and certify shipments for export. Grades are also checked by federal retail inspectors in food stores.

Ontario and Quebec have their own inspectors who collaborate with federal inspectors in checking grades of produce grown and sold in the province as well as that coming into the province. In the other provinces, where no provincial inspectors are appointed, federal inspectors check the grades of fruits and vegetables.

Processed Fruits and Vegetables

Most processed fruits and vegetables are sold by grade in Canada. About 95 percent of the production in every province is from plants registered for federal inspection and grading. Only federally registered plants may ship their products from one province to another or for export outside of Canada.

Nonregistered plants are not permitted to use a Canada grade name on their products. Sale of such products must be confined to the province in which they were produced.

Imported fruit and vegetable products for which grades are established must carry a grade mark, and they must meet the federal grade standard set out in the regulations for those products. Imported fruit and vegetable products cannot have Canada as part of their grade name when sold in original containers.

Grades

If a product fails to meet the lowest prescribed grade for it, yet is sound, wholesome, and fit to eat, it must be marked "Sub Standard." Products so labeled are not usually found in stores.

Basis for Grades. Processed fruits and vegetables are graded on:
—flavor and aroma
—color
—tenderness and maturity
—uniformity of size and shape
—consistency
—appearance of liquid media
—freedom from defects and foreign matter

Grading and Inspection. Processors grade their own products. Federal fruit and vegetable inspectors check the accuracy of their grading before labeling and shipping, and again in wholesale warehouses. Certificates of grade are issued on request. Grades are also checked by retail inspectors in food stores in cities across Canada.

In Quebec and the Maritimes, provincial inspectors see that provincial regulations are carried out in any processing plants not registered in those provinces for federal inspection and grading service.

Honey

Honey produced for sale in Alberta, British Columbia, Manitoba, Ontario, and Saskatchewan must be graded and classified as to color, except when sold directly to consumers at an apiary. All honey for export, and extracted honey in consumer containers of 8 pounds or less for interprovincial trade, must be graded and color-classified.

Grades and Color Classes. Color of honey does not affect grade, but is an indication of flavor; usually, the darker the honey, the stronger the flavor.

Grades: Canada No. 1, Canada No. 2, Canada No. 3

Color classes: White, Golden Amber, and Dark

Canada No. 2 and Canada No. 3 are not usually available in retail stores.

Honey that is wholesome but fails to meet Canada No. 3 requirements is marked "Sub Standard."

Basis for Grades. Honey is graded on:
—flavor
—freedom from foreign material
—keeping quality

Grading and Inspection. Honey is graded and color-classified by the packer.

Federal fruit and vegetable inspectors

check grades and color classifications claimed at retail, wholesale, and manufacturing levels and certify honey shipments for export trade. Federal retail inspectors also check honey in food stores in most large Canadian cities.

Canada Department of Agriculture inspectors are responsible for checking grades and color classifications of honey produced and sold within Alberta, British Columbia, Manitoba, and Saskatchewan. In Ontario, federal and provincial inspectors share this responsibility.

Maple Syrup

Maple syrup must be graded if it is to be sold in Quebec, but in other provinces grading is at the option of the packer. Grading is not compulsory for interprovincial or export trade. However, federal grades have been established, and products bearing a grade mark must meet the requirements laid down for composition and labeling.

Artificial maple products must bear the manufacturer's name and address, a list of ingredients, and the words "artificially maple flavored."

Grades. Canada Fancy, Canada Light, Canada Medium, and Canada Dark.

Quebec has an additional grade, Amber C, between Canada Medium and Canada Dark.

Basis for Grades. Maple syrup is graded on:
  — color
  — flavor
  — freedom from fermentation
  — percentage of solids

Grading and Inspection. Packers grade their own maple syrup except for that sold to companies or cooperatives in the Province of Quebec, which must be graded by provincial inspectors.

Federal fruit and vegetable inspectors check grades when declared, inspect for purity and proper labeling of maple syrup and artificially maple-flavored table syrups, and check composition of maple products at all levels of trade. On authority of the Quebec Department of Agriculture, they also assist provincial inspectors in checking grades and administering composition standards in Quebec.

Meat

Health Inspection. Health inspection by a federal meat inspector is necessary before meat can be moved in interprovincial or international trade. Inspection of meat bought or sold within the province in which it is slaughtered is the responsibility of the province.

Any meat plant in Canada that applies and meets the requirements may receive inspection service provided by the Meat Inspection Division of the Health of Animals Branch, Canada Department of Agriculture. In inspected plants, federal veterinarians examine meat animals before and after slaughter to ensure that all diseased or otherwise unwholesome meat is condemned as unfit for human consumption. Approved meat and meat products are stamped, tagged, or labeled with the official inspection legend—a round stamp bearing a crown in the center and, around the crown, the words "Canada Approved" or "Canada," plus the registered number of the plant. This stamp does not indicate quality or grade, but means that the food is fit for human consumption.

Some small plants not registered for federal inspection operate under provincial health inspection regulations, and in some areas medical health officers inspect meat at local or municipal levels. However, only meat inspected by federal inspectors in registered plants is stamped with the official inspection legend.

Grading. Animals slaughtered in packing plants under Meat Inspection Division, Health of Animals Branch, or provincial inspection are graded by inspectors of the Canada Department of Agriculture, Livestock Division. Beef, veal, and lamb carcasses are graded for producer payment and consumer information, but hog carcasses are graded only for producer payment.

Depending on provincial or municipal legislation, some cattle, hogs, and lambs are slaughtered in plants that do not meet the federal Health of Animals Branch requirements for inspection service. A small portion of these plants are approved for grading of hogs and lambs to provide the basis of payment to producers.

Grading is voluntary except in provinces that have passed grading legislation. British Columbia and Ontario have beef-grading regulations similar to federal regulations, and Alberta, Saskatchewan, Manitoba, and Ontario have branding regulations. In Saskatchewan, all lamb carcasses sold in Regina, Moose Jaw, Saskatoon, and Prince Albert must be grade-stamped under provincial legislation. Grading of carcasses produced and sold within each of these provinces is done by Canada Department of Agriculture officers.

Beef is usually sold by grade, and in some areas consumers may buy graded lamb and veal. Pork is not sold by grade in retail stores. A carcass of beef, when grade-stamped once on each major primal cut, must then be ribbon-branded with a continuous ribbonlike mark in a color indicating grade. The ribbon brand is applied in such a way that it appears on each primal and most retail cuts.

There are nine quality grades for beef and five for veal and lamb.

The main lamb grades available in retail stores are: Canada Choice, Canada Good, Canada Commercial, and Canada Utility.

Beef. All youthful carcasses are cut between the eleventh and twelfth ribs to expose the Longissimus dorsi muscle and permit the grader to make quality assessments and measure the fat *at a precise point* on the "rib eye." There are four fat levels in grades Canada A and Canada B.

Canada A—From youthful animals. The lean is firm, fine grained, and of a bright red color, and has at least slight marbling. The fat covers most of the exterior surface and is white to reddish amber in color.

As an example, a 550-pound carcass having all the quality factors for Canada A, and 0.5 inches fat at the "eye" between the eleventh and twelfth ribs would be graded and stamped Canada A2.

Canada B—From youthful animals. The lean is moderately firm with color ranging from bright red to medium dark. The texture of the flesh may be somewhat coarse and the exterior fat may range from white to pale yellow. Marbling is not necessary. Fat levels for Canada B grade are similar to those for Canada A, except that minimum fat for level 1 is reduced by 1/10 inch that is, .10 instead of .20, .20 instead of .30.

Canada C, Class 1—From youthful to intermediate age animals, including young cows and heifers of intermediate age, as well as youthful steers and heifers below 300 pounds carcass weight and those having below the minimum fat for Canada A or B. The lean can range in color from bright red to medium dark; the fat, from white to pale yellow.

Canada C, Class 2— Age same as Class

1. May be deficient in muscle development. The lean can range in color from bright red to dark; the fat, from white to lemon yellow. The texture of the flesh may be coarse.

Canada D—From mature cows and steers. Classes 1 to 4 are divided according to muscle development and quality, with Canada D4 having the lowest proportion of lean meat to bone. Canada D4 also includes excessively fat carcasses that would otherwise qualify for Canada C.

Canada E—Does not appear in retail stores. This grade is used mainly for manufacturing meat products.

Poultry

Grading of dressed and eviscerated poultry is compulsory for wholesale trade and sale in retail stores in most major cities. The grade mark is prominently indicated on a metal breast tag on fresh poultry or printed on the bag for frozen poultry. All eviscerated poultry that is imported, exported, or shipped between provinces must be graded and health inspected. All imported dressed and eviscerated poultry must meet equivalent Canadian grade standards.

Health Inspection. Health inspection is the responsibility of federal veterinarians stationed in eviscerating plants approved and registered by the Health of Animals Branch, Canada Department of Agriculture. Poultry found wholesome in plants operating under federal government inspection has the Canada Approved or Canada inspection legend on the tag, bag, or insert.

Grades

Canada Grade Special, Canada Grade C, and Canada Grade D are not usually available in retail stores.

Basis for Grades. Poultry is graded on:
—conformation, meaning presence of deformities that affect appearance or normal distribution of flesh, for example, a crooked keel bone
—flesh, meaning distribution and amount on the carcass
—fat covering, meaning distribution and amounts in specific areas
—dressing, meaning presence of defects such as discoloration, tears, pinfeathers, bruises, or other blemishes.

Grading and Inspection. Poultry may be processed and graded by producers registered to handle only their own products or at registered commercial poultry processing plants. Both types of registered premises must comply with strict operating and sanitation requirements. Federal agricultural inspectors check frequently to ensure that accurate grading is being done under strict sanitary conditions.

Periodic inspections of grade quality are made by federal agricultural inspectors at wholesale distributors, holding freezers, retail stores, restaurants, hospitals, other institutions, and military camps.

All provinces except Ontario have legislation that complements the federal regulations for grading and inspection of poultry. Federal agricultural inspectors are responsible for enforcing provincial legislation.

Selected Bibliography

Efforts to compile the information in this volume were greatly aided by the cooperation of many organizations designed to aid people working with foods and in food operations. Many have already been mentioned, but a list of those especially likely to have information helpful to the buyer, along with their addresses, follows.

American Egg Board
205 Touhy Avenue
Park Ridge, IL 60068

California Raisin Advisory Board
P.O. Box 5335
Fresno, CA 93755

College of Agriculture Extension Service
Pennsylvania State University
University Park, PA 16801

Educational Department
Blue Goose, Inc.
P.O. Box 46
Fullerton, CA 92632

Florida Citrus Commission
Florida Department of Citrus
P.O. Box 148
Lakeland, FL 33802

Food and Nutrition Information and
    Educational Materials Center
National Agricultural Library, Room 304
Beltsville, MD 20705

Food and Wines from France, Inc.
Information and Promotion Center
1350 Avenue of the Americas
New York, NY 10019

Hotel, Restaurant, and Travel
    Administration
Flint Laboratory
University of Massachusetts
Amherst, MA 01003

Information Division
Canada Department of Agriculture
Ottawa K1A 0C7

Institute of Shortening and Edible Oils, Inc.
1750 New York Avenue, N.W.
Washington, DC 20006

Italian Trade Commission
One World Trade Center
Suite 2057
New York, NY 10048

National Association of Meat Purveyors
252 West Ina Road
Tucson, AZ 85704

National Consumer Educational Services
    Office
National Marine Fisheries Service
U.S. Department of Commerce
100 East Ohio Street
Room 526
Chicago, IL 60611

National Dairy Council
6300 North River Road
Rosemont, IL 60018

National Fisheries Institute
111 East Wacker Drive
Chicago, IL 60601

National Live Stock and Meat Board
444 North Michigan Avenue
Chicago, IL 60611

National Marine Fisheries Service
National Oceanic and Atmospheric
  Administration
U.S. Department of Commerce
Washington, DC 20235

National Marketing Services Office
National Marine Fisheries Service
100 East Ohio Street
Chicago, IL 60611

National Restaurant Association
One IBM Plaza
Suite 2600
Chicago, IL 60611

National Turkey Federation
Reston International Center
11800 Sunrise Valley Drive
Reston, VA 22091

Office of Communications
U.S. Department of Agriculture
Washington, D.C. 20250

Rice Council
P.O. Box 22802
Houston, TX 77027

Sunkist Growers, Inc.
14130 Riverside Drive
Sherman Oaks, CA 91423

Superintendent of Documents
U.S. Government Printing Office
Washington, DC 20402

Tea Council of the USA, Inc.
230 Park Avenue
New York, NY 10017

Texas Parks and Wildlife Department
4200 Smith School Road
Austin, TX 78744

United Fresh Fruit and Vegetable
  Association
1019 Nineteenth Street, N.W.
Washington, DC 20036

Wheat Flour Institute
1776 F Street, N.W.
Washington, DC 20006

A great many other firms and associations connected with the food industry have been helpful and courteous in responding to our requests for information and assistance. Among these, a special note of appreciation must go to the American Mushroom Institute, the American Spice Trade Association, the Cling Peach Advisory Board, Coldwater Seafood Corporation, the Dried Fruit Association of California, the Idaho Bean Commission, the International Apple Institute, the Louisiana Sweet Potato Commission, the National Canners Association, the National Coffee Association of the USA, the National Soybean Crop Improvement Council, the New Bedford Seafood Co-operative, the Olive Administrative Committee, the Pacific Coast Canned Pear Service, the Roquefort Cheese Association, S & W Fine Foods, Inc., Thomas Lipton, Inc., the Tri-Valley Growers, and the U.S. Trout Farmers Association. This by no means exhausts the names of the organizations that made an effort to help. There are hundreds of private and public organizations to assist the buyer, and libraries and librarians are helpful in locating them. The names and addresses of many trade associations and publishers can be found in: (1) the latest edition of the *Encyclopedia of Associa-*

tions (Detroit: Gale Research Co.); and (2) the annual bibliography in the August issues of the *Cornell Hotel and Restaurant Administration Quarterly*, which contains a section entitled "Addresses of Organizations and Publishers."

As for published sources, it is hoped that the following listing will also prove helpful. Once again, it is by no means exhaustive. The listing is divided into government publications and other publications.

U.S. GOVERNMENT PUBLICATIONS

Department of Agriculture

Beef and Veal in Family Meals: A Guide for Consumers. Revised ed. Home and Garden Bulletin No. 118. Washington, D.C., 1975.

Cheese in Family Meals: A Guide for Consumers. Revised ed. Home and Garden Bulletin No. 112. Washington, D.C., 1976.

Cheese Varieties and Descriptions. Agriculture Handbook No. 54. Washington, D.C., 1974.

Convenience Foods for the Hotel, Restaurant and Institutional Market: The Processor's View. Agriculture Economic Report No. 344. Washington, D.C., 1976.

Egg Grading Manual. Agriculture Handbook No. 75. Washington, D.C., 1977.

Eggs in Family Meals: A Guide for Consumers. Revised ed. Home and Garden Bulletin No. 103. Washington, D.C., 1974.

Federal and State Standards for Composition of Milk Products (and Certain Non-Milkfat Products), as of January 1, 1974. Compiled and edited by Roland S. Golden. Revised ed. Agriculture Handbook No. 51. Washington, D.C., 1974.

Food and Nutrition Information and Educational Materials Center Catalog. National Agricultural Library. Food and Nutrition Information and Educational Materials Center. Washington, D.C., 1974-77. Catalog and Supplements 1-5.

Food Purchasing Guide for Group Feeding. Prepared by Betty Peterkin and Beatrice Evans. Agriculture Handbook No. 284. Washington, D.C., 1965.

Fruits in Family Meals: A Guide for Consumers. Revised ed. Home and Garden Bulletin No. 125. Washington, D.C., 1975.

Grade Names Used in U.S. Standards for Farm Products. Revised ed. Agriculture Handbook No. 157. Washington, D.C., 1965.

How to Buy Beef Roasts. Home and Garden Bulletin No. 146. Washington, D.C., 1968.

How to Buy Beef Steaks. Revised ed. Home and Garden Bulletin No. 145. Washington, D.C., 1976.

How to Buy Canned and Frozen Fruits. Home and Garden Bulletin No. 191. Washington, D.C., 1971.

How to Buy Canned and Frozen Vegetables. Revised ed. Home and Garden Bulletin No. 167. Washington, D.C., 1975.

How to Buy Cheese. By F. E. Fenton. Home and Garden Bulletin No. 193. Washington, D.C., 1971.

How to Buy Dairy Products. Revised ed. Home and Garden Bulletin No. 201. Washington, D.C., 1974.

How to Buy Dry Beans, Peas, and Lentils. Home and Garden Bulletin No. 177. Washington, D.C., 1970.

How to Buy Eggs. Revised ed. Home and

Garden Bulletin No. 144. Washington, D.C., 1975.

How to Buy Fresh Fruits. Home and Garden Bulletin No. 141. Washington, D.C., 1967.

How to Buy Fresh Vegetables. Home and Garden Bulletin No. 143. Washington, D.C., 1967; reprinted 1976.

How to Buy Lamb. By Sandra Brookover. Home and Garden Bulletin No. 195. Washington, D.C., 1971.

How to Buy Meat for Your Freezer. Home and Garden Bulletin No. 166. Washington, D.C., 1976.

How to Buy Potatoes. By Lawrence E. Ide. Home and Garden Bulletin No. 198. Washington, D.C., 1972.

How to Buy Poultry. Home and Garden Bulletin No. 157. Washington, D.C., 1968.

How to Use USDA Grades in Buying Food. Revised ed. Home and Garden Bulletin No. 196. Washington, D.C., 1977.

Institutional Meat Purchase Specifications for Sausage Products Approved by USDA. Agricultural Marketing Service, Livestock Division. Washington, D.C., 1976.

Know the Eggs You Buy. Consumer and Marketing Service. Washington, D.C., 1967.

Lamb in Family Meals: A Guide for Consumers. Home and Garden Bulletin No. 124. Washington, D.C., 1974.

Marketing California Raisins. By Joseph C. Perrin and Richard P. Van Diest. Marketing Bulletin No. 58 [Washington, D.C.?], 1975.

Meat and Poultry: Labelled for You. Home and Garden Bulletin No. 172. Washington, D.C., 1969.

Meat and Poultry: Standards for You. Home and Garden Bulletin No. 171. Washington, D.C., 1973.

Meat and Poultry Inspection Program. Animal and Plant Health Inspection Service. Washington, D.C., 1974.

Milk in Family Meals: A Guide for Consumers. Home and Garden Bulletin No. 127. Washington, D.C., 1974.

Nutritive Value of Foods. Revised ed. Agriculture Handbook No. 8. Washington, D.C., 1963.

Nuts in Family Meals: A Guide for Consumers. Revised ed. Home and Garden Bulletin No. 176. Washington, D.C., 1971.

Official United States Standards for Grades of Carcass Beef. Agriculture Marketing Service. Washington, D.C., [1975?].

Pork in Family Meals: A Guide for Consumers. Home and Garden Bulletin No. 160. Washington, D.C., 1975.

Poultry in Family Meals: A Guide for Consumers. Revised ed. Home and Garden Bulletin No. 110. Washington, D.C., 1974.

Regulations Governing the Grading and Inspection of Poultry and Edible Products Thereof and United States Classes, Standards, and Grades with Respect Thereof. Washington, D.C., 1971.

Regulations Governing the Grading of Shell Eggs and United States Standards, Grades, and Weight Classes for Shell Eggs [effective July 1, 1974]. Poultry Division. Washington, D.C., 1974.

Regulations Governing the Inspection of Eggs and Egg Products. Washington, D.C., 1972.

Seasoning with Spices and Herbs. Agricultural Research Service, Consumer and Food Economics Institute. Hyattsville, Md., 1972.

Shell Egg Grading and Inspection of Egg Products. Poultry Division, Agricultural Marketing Service. Washington, D.C., 1964.

Tips on Selecting Fruits and Vegetables. Marketing Bulletin No. 13. Washington,

D.C., 1967.

USDA's Acceptance Service for Meat and Meat Products. Marketing Bulletin No. 47. Washington, D.C., 1970.

USDA's Acceptance Service for Poultry and Eggs. Marketing Bulletin No. 46. Washington, D.C., 1971.

USDA Grade Names for Food and Farm Products. Agriculture Handbook No. 157. Washington, D.C., 1967.

USDA Grades for Pork Carcasses. Marketing Bulletin No. 49. Washington, D.C., 1970.

USDA Grades for Slaughter Swine and Feeder Pigs. Marketing Bulletin No. 51. Washington, D.C., 1970.

USDA Standards for Food and Farm Products. Revised ed. Agriculture Handbook No. 341. Washington, D.C., 1976.

USDA Yield Grades for Beef. Revised ed. Marketing Bulletin No. 45. Washington, D.C., 1974.

USDA Yield Grades for Lamb. Marketing Bulletin No. 52. Washington, D.C., 1970.

Vegetables in Family Meals: A Guide for Consumers. Revised ed. Home and Garden Bulletin No. 105. Washington, D.C., 1975.

Your Money's Worth in Foods. By Betty Peterkin and Cynthia Cromwell. Revised ed. Home and Garden Bulletin No. 183. Washington, D.C., 1977.

Department of Commerce. National Marine Fisheries Service.

Food Fish Facts Nos. 1-56, 62. Developed at the National Consumer Educational Services Office, National Marine Fisheries Service. [Chicago?], undated.

How to Eye and Buy Seafood. Washington, D.C., 1976. "Institutional Purchasing Specification for the Purchasing of Fresh, Frozen, and Canned Fishery Products." By Jack B. Dougherty. [Washington, D.C.?], undated.

Let's Cook Fish! A Complete Guide to Fish Cookery. Fishery Market Development Series No. 8. Washington, D.C., 1976.

Protection through Inspection. Washington, D.C., 1974.

Department of Health, Education, and Welfare.

An Experimental Guide for Personnel Training Requirements of Technicians in Future Food Irradiation Technology Industries: Final Report. By Philip G. Stiles. Washington, D.C. Project No. OEG-1-8-08A007-0034-058.

Food Service Manual. Public Health Service. Washington, D.C., undated.

Department of the Interior. Fish and Wildlife Service.

Fishery Product Inspection. Bureau of Commercial Fisheries. Washington, D.C., 1965.

Guide to Buying Fresh and Frozen Fish and Shellfish. Revised ed. Bureau of Commercial Fisheries. Washington, D.C., 1965.

How to Cook Salmon. By Kathryn L. Osterhaug and Rose G. Kerr. Test Kitchen Publication No. 4. Washington, D.C., 1951.

How to Cook Scallops. By Dorothy Keller, and others. Test Kitchen Bulletin No. 13. Washington, D.C., 1964.

How to Cook Tuna. By Kathryn L. Osterhaug, and others. Test Kitchen Publications No. 12. Washington, D.C., 1964.

OTHER PUBLICATIONS*

Alberts, Robert C. *The Good Provider: H. J. Heinz and His 57 Varieties.* Boston:

---

*References in text are keyed to last name of author and date of publication.

Houghton Mifflin Co., 1973.

Aldrich, Daniel. "Feeding a Hungry World." Paper presented at the Food Symposium, California State University, Chico, April 1975.

Amendola, Joseph. *The Baker's Manual*. 3d rev. ed. Rochelle Park, N.J.: Hayden Book Co., Inc., 1972.

American Can Co. *Purchase and Use of Canned Foods: A Guide for Institutional Buyers and Meal Planners*. New York: American Can Co., undated.

American Dry Milk Institute. *Nonfat Dry Milk in Quantity Food Preparation for Groups of 25 or Less*. Handbooks No. 705-706. Chicago: American Dry Milk Institute, Inc., 1963.

American Egg Board. *A Scientist Speaks about Egg Products*. Park Ridge, Ill.: American Egg Board, 1974.

American Hospital Association. *Food Service Manual for Health Care Institutions*. Chicago: American Hospital Association, 1966.

————. *Manual of Specifications for Canned Fruit and Vegetables*. Chicago: American Hospital Association, reprinted 1961.

American Meat Institute. *Mushrooms: The Versatile Vegetable*. Kennet Square, Pa.: American Mushroom Institute, 1964.

Arbuckle, W. S. *Ice Cream*. Westport, Conn.: Avi Publishing Co., Inc., 1972.

Armbruster, Gertrude, and others. *Game Care and Preparation in the Field and Home*. Rev. ed. Ithaca, N.Y.: Cornell University Press, 1964.

Armour and Co. *Convenience Concept for Food Service Systems*. Chicago: Armour Food Service Systems, 1972.

Artichoke Advisory Board. *All about Artichokes*. Santa Cruz, Calif.: California Artichoke Advisory Board, undated.

Axler, Bruce H. *Buying and Using Convenience Foods*. Indianapolis, Ind.: ITT Educational Publishing, 1974.

Ayers, J. C., and others (eds.). *The Safety of Foods*. Westport, Conn.: Avi Publishing Co., 1968.

Baker, H. A. (ed.). *Canned Food Reference Manual*. New York: American Can Co., 1939.

Balls, A. K. "Enzyme Action in Food Products at Low Temperatures," *Ice and Cold Storage*, 41 (1938), 143.

Bardach, John E., and others. *Aquaculture: The Farming and Husbandry of Freshwater and Marine Organisms*. New York: Wiley-Interscience, 1972.

"A Basic Guide to Buying Fish," *Good Housekeeping*, 161 (October 1965), 169.

Beals, Paul. "Distilled Spirits and the Beverage Operator," *Cornell Hotel and Restaurant Administration Quarterly*, 17 (November 1976), 76-85.

Beard, James. *Beard on Bread*. New York: Alfred A. Knopf, 1973.

————. *James Beard's Fish Cookery*. New York: Warner Books, 1954.

Beau, Francis N. *Quantity Food Purchasing Guide*. Rev. ed. Boston: Cahners Books International, 1974.

Benson, Norman G. (ed.). *A Century of Fisheries in North America*. Washington, D.C.: American Fisheries Society, 1970.

Berne, Eric. *Games People Play*. New York: Grove Press, 1964.

Bespaloff, Alexis. *The Signet Book of Wine: A Complete Introduction*. New York: New American Library, 1971.

"Best Buys in Fish and Seafood," *Good Housekeeping*, 181 (July 1975), 127-28.

Binstead, Raymond, James D. Devey, and John C. Dalin. *Pickle and Sauce Making*. 2d ed. London: Food Trade Press, Ltd., 1972.

Blair, Eulalia C. *Fish and Seafood Dishes for Foodservice Menu Planning*. Boston: Cahners Books International, 1975.

Blaxter, K. L. "Efficiency of Feed Conversion by Different Classes of Livestock in Relation to Production," *Proceedings* (Federation of American Societies for Experimental Biology and Medicine), 20 (No. 1, 1961).

Bloch, Jacques W. "What Makes a Successful Food Buyer?" *Hospitals: JAHA*, 40 (July 1966).

Bramah, Edward. *Tea and Coffee*. London: Hutchinson, 1972.

"Bread: You Can't Judge a Loaf by Its Color," *Consumer Reports*, 41 (May 1976), 256-60.

Brodner, Joseph, and others. *Profitable Food and Beverage Operation*. Rev. ed. New York: Ahrens Publishing Co., Inc., 1962.

Broten, Paul R. "Progress in 'Ready Foods,'" *Cornell Hotel and Restaurant Administration Quarterly*, 15 (May 1974), 37-40.

Brown, Bob. *The Complete Book of Cheese*. New York: Gramercy Publishing Co., 1955.

Bull, Sleeter. *Meat for the Table*. New York: McGraw-Hill Book Co., 1951.

Burger, Marie. *Cost Finder for Institutional Use*. Lakeland, Fla.: Florida Citrus Commission, 1956.

Burns, Marjorie, and others. *Fish and Shellfish: Selection, Care, and Use*. Ithaca, N.Y.: Cornell University Press. 1962.

"Buying Beef: Bulk Buying vs. the Supermarket," *Consumer Reports*, 39 (September 1974), 659-63.

"Buying Beef: What a Good Label Can Tell You," *Consumer Reports*, 39 (September 1974), 664-65.

"Buying Guide to Lesser-Known Fish Varieties," *Good Housekeeping*, 177 (October 1973), 190-91.

California Avocado Advisory Board. *All about the California Avocado*. Newport Beach, Calif.: California Avocado Advisory Board, 1974.

———. *Avocado Adventure*. Costa Mesa, Calif. California Avocado Advisory Board, 1967.

California Raisin Advisory Board. *A Raisin Is a Dried Grape*. Fresno, Calif.: California Raisin Advisory Board, undated.

"Canned and Dry-Mix Soups: Tomato, Chicken Noodle, Vegetable Beef, and Bean," *Consumer Reports*, 36 (September 1971), 536-40.

"Canned Hams," *Consumer Reports*, 35 (October 1970), 581-85.

"Canned Sardines," *Consumer Reports*, 41 (February 1976), 71-75.

"Canned Tuna," *Consumer Reports*, 39 (November 1974), 816-19.

Carcione, Joe, and Bob Lucas. *The Greengrocer: The Consumer's Guide to Fruits and Vegetables*. New York: Pyramid Books, 1972.

"Care and Use Tips for Frying Fats," *Cooking for Profit*, 41 (September 1972), 42+.

Carpenter, Ross (ed.). *Make or Buy*. Boston: Cahners Books, for *Institutions/Volume Feeding Management*, 1970.

"Chili: Canned vs. Homemade," *Consumer Reports*, 39 (October 1974), 716-20.

"Chocolate Drink Mixes," *Consumer Reports*, 41 (September 1976), 499-503.

Chocolate Information Council. *Consumer's Guide to Cocoa and Chocolate*. New York: Chocolate Information Council, undated.

Chocolate Manufacturers Association. *The Story of Chocolate*. Washington, D.C.: Chocolate Manufacturers Association, 1960.

"Choosing a Margarine for Taste and Health," *Consumer Reports*, 40 (January 1975), 42-47.

Claiborne, Craig (ed.). *The New York Times Cook Book*. New York: Harper and Row, 1961.

———, and others. *Classic French Cooking*. New York: Time-Life Books, 1970.

Clawson, Augusta H. *Equipment Maintenance Manual*. New York: Ahrens Publishing Co., 1951.

"A Close Look at Hamburger," *Consumer Reports*, 36 (August 1971), 478-83.

Coffee Brewing Center. *Facts about Coffee*. New York: Coffee Brewing Center, undated.

"Coffee 'Creamers,'" *Consumer Reports*, 40 (March 1975), 196-98.

Committee for Fisheries. *Market for Frozen Fish in O.E.C.D. Countries*. Paris: O.E.C.D. Publications, 1969.

The Consumers Union Report on Wines and Spirits. Mount Vernon, N.Y.: Consumers Union, 1972.

Cook, L. Russell. *Chocolate Production and Use*. Rev. ed. New York: Books for Industry, Inc., 1972.

"Cooking Oils and Fats," *Consumer Reports*, 38 (September 1973), 553-57.

Cottam, Howard R. "The World Food Conference," *Journal of the American Dietetic Association*, 66 (April 1975).

Crosby, Marion W., and Katharine W. Harris. *Purchasing Food for 50 Servings*. Rev. ed. Cornell Extension Bulletin No. 803. Ithaca, N.Y.: Cornell University Press, 1963.

Dahnke, Mary. *The Cheese Book*. New York: A. A. Wyn, Inc., 1950.

Davids, Kenneth. *Coffee: A Guide to Buying, Brewing, and Enjoying*. San Francisco: 101 Productions, 1976.

Davis, J. G. *Basic Technology. Volume I: Cheese*. New York: American Elsevier, 1965.

Dedrick, B. W. *Practical Milling*. Chicago: National Miller, 1924.

de Holl, John C. *Encyclopedia of Labeling Meat and Poultry Products*. 3d ed. St. Louis: Meat Plant Magazine, 1976.

Desrosier, Norman W. *The Technology of Food Preservation*. Westport, Conn.: Avi Publishing Co., 1972.

"Do Eggs Make the Grade?" *Consumer Reports*, 41 (February 1976), 71-75.

Dried Fruit Association of California. *The Story of California Dried Fruit and Tree Nuts*. Santa Clara, Calif.: DFA of California, undated.

Duns (Dun and Bradstreet Publications Corporation), June 1967.

Dukas, Peter. How to Plan and Operate a Restaurant. 2d rev. ed. Rochelle Park, N.J.: Hayden Book Co., Inc., 1973.

Economics Laboratory. *Food Equipment Sanitation Cleaning Procedures, Institutional Division*. New York: Economics Laboratory, Inc., 1965.

———. *Food Service Operators Sanitation Checklist*. New York: Economics Laboratory, Inc., 1965.

Edwards, Corwin, and others (eds.). *Public Policy toward Competition*. New York: National Conference Board, Inc., 1962.

"Egg Beaters: Do They Beat Real Eggs?" *Consumer Reports*, 39 (March 1974), 192-93.

Ell Vee Dee, Inc. *All about Scallops . . . and How to Cook Them*. New Bedford, Mass.: Ell Vee Dee, Inc., undated.

Escoffier, August. *The Escoffier Cookbook*. 25th rev. ed. New York: Crown Publishing Co., 1964.

Eshbach, Charles E. *Food Service Management*. 2d ed. Boston: Cahners Books International, Inc., 1976.

———. and Albert L. Wrisley. *Purchasing Food for Food Service Establishments*. Food Management Leaflet 10. Amherst: Cooperative Extension, College of Agriculture, University of Massachusetts, 1965.

Fay, Clifford T., Jr., and others. *Managerial*

Accounting for the Hospitality Service Industries. Dubuque, Iowa: Wm. C. Brown Co., 1971.

Fearn, David A. *Food and Beverage Management*. London: Butterworth, 1973.

Ferrando, R. "The Aura of the Future?" *FAO Nutrition Newsletter*, 12 (July-December 1974).

Finn, M. "Has the All-Convenience-Food Restaurant Come of Age?" *Hospitality—Food and Lodging* (April 1975).

"Fish and Seafood Basics," *Better Homes and Gardens*, 55 (April 1977), 142.

Florida Department of Citrus. *Florida Citrus for Healthy Profits*. n.p.: State of Florida, Department of Citrus, 1975.

Flower, Barbara, and Elisabeth Rosenbaum. *The Roman Cookery Book*. London: George Harrup and Co., Ltd., 1958.

"Food Dating: Now You See It, Now You Don't," *Consumer Reports*, 37 (June 1972), 391-94.

Food Grading in Canada. Revised ed. Publication No. 1283. [Ottawa]: Canada Department of Agriculture, 1973.

"Frankfurters," *Consumer Reports*, 37 (February 1972), 73-79.

Freudenberger, C. Dean. "Crises and Deeds: Responding to the Global Problem of Hunger and Famine." Paper presented to the Food Symposium. California State University, Chico, April 1975.

Frooman, A. A. *Five Steps to Effective Institutional Food Buying*. Chicago: Institutions Publications, Inc., 1953.

"Frozen Breaded Shrimp," *Consumer Reports*, 37 (January 1972), 27-32.

"Frozen French Fries," *Consumer Reports*, 36 (October 1971), 632-34.

"Frozen Shrimp," *Consumer Reports*, 39 (March 1974), 259-64.

Gardner, Jerry G. *Contract Foodservice/Vending*. Boston: Cahners Books, 1973.

Geer, Thomas. *An Oligopoly: The World Coffee Economy and Stabilization Schemes*. New York: Dunellen Publishing Co., Inc., 1971.

Gelatin Manufacturers Institute of America. *Standard Methods for the Sampling and Testing of Gelatins*. New York: Gelatin Manufacturers Institute of America, undated.

Gilbert, Phileas. "Vatel," in *Larousse Gastronomique*, ed. Prosper Montagne. New York: Crown Publishers, Inc., 1961.

Gillespie, Samuel M., and William B. Schwartz. *Seafood Retailing*. 2d ed. Austin: Texas Parks and Wildlife Department, 1977.

Grampp, William D., and Emanuel T. Weiler. *Economic Policy*. Homewood, Ill.: Richard D. Irwin, Inc., 1956.

"Green Beans," *Consumer Reports*, 42 (July 1977), 392-95.

Griswold, Ruth M. *The Experimental Study of Foods*. Boston: Houghton Mifflin Co., 1962.

Grossman, Harold J. *Grossman's Guide to Wines, Spirits, and Beers*. 6th ed. Rev. by Harriet Lembeck. New York: Charles Scribner's Sons, 1977.

Grover, Robert M., and Charles E. Eshbach. *Purchasing Eggs for Food Service Establishments*. Food Management Leaflet 17. Amherst: Cooperative Extension, College of Agriculture, University of Massachusetts, 1968.

Guide to Food Grades. Publication No. 1500. Ottawa: Canada Department of Agriculture, 1972.

"A Guide to the Dairy Counter," *Consumer Reports*, 39 (January 1974), 74-75.

Hannum, Horst, and Robert S. Blumberg. *Brandies and Liqueurs*. Garden City, N.Y.: Doubleday and Co., 1976.

Hansen, R. Gaurth. "Calories with Nutrients: Prescription for Progress." Paper presented to the Food Symposium,

California State University, Chico, April 1975.

Hayes, Kirby M., and others. *Frozen Foods in Food Service Establishments*. Food Management Leaflet 2. Amherst: Cooperative Extension, College of Agriculture, University of Massachusetts, 1970.

Hazlitt, W. Carew. *Old Cookery Books and Ancient Cuisine*. London: Elliot Stock, 1886 (reprinted by Gale Research Corp., Detroit, Mich., in 1968).

Heid, J. L., and Maynard A. Joslyn. *Food Processing Operations, Their Management, Machines, Material, and Methods*. 2 vols. Westport, Conn.: Avi Publishing Co., Inc., 1963.

Heilbroner, Robert L. *The Worldly Philosophers*. New York: Simon and Schuster, 1953.

Hilton, Conrad N. *Be My Guest*. Englewood Cliffs, N.J.: Prentice-Hall, Inc., 1957.

Horwath, Ernest B., and others. *Hotel Accounting*. Rev. ed. New York: Ronald Press, 1970.

"How Good Is the Bologna in That Sandwich," *Consumer Reports*, 41 (March 1976), 126-29.

"How Nutritious Are Fast-Food Meals?" *Consumer Reports*, 40 (May 1975), 278-81.

Huet, Marcel. *Textbook of Fish Culture: Breeding and Cultivation of Fish*. London: Fishing News (Books), Ltd., 1971.

"Ice Cream," *Consumer Reports*, 37 (August 1972), 495-502.

Idyll, C. P. *The Sea against Hunger: Harvesting the Oceans to Feed a Hungry World*. New York: Thomas Y. Crowell Co., 1970.

"In Praise of Dried Beans," *Consumer Reports*, 40 (July 1975), 426-27.

"Instant Coffees," *Consumer Reports*, 36 (January 1971), 32-35.

"Instant Nonfat Dry Milk," *Consumer Reports*, 42 (January 1977), 19-21.

"Instant Potatoes," *Consumer Reports*, 36 (July 1971), 435-37.

Institute of Shortening and Edible Oils, Inc. *Food Fats and Oils*. 4th ed. Washington, D.C.: Institute of Shortening and Edible Oils, Inc., 1974.

Jacobs, H. E. *Six Thousand Years of Bread*. Garden City, N.Y.: Doubleday, Doran, and Co., Inc., 1954.

Jennings, William H. "Confucius 'Analects Book XIII,'" in *Oriental Literature*, Volume 4. New York: Colonial Press, 1899.

Johndrew, O. F., Jr., and R. C. Baker. *Producing High Quality Eggs on the Farm*. Ithaca, N.Y.: Cornell University Press, 1965.

Johnson, A. A. (ed.). *Buy for Health: Meat, Fish, Poultry, Eggs, Dry Beans and Peas, Peanut Butter*. Ithaca, N.Y.: Cornell University Press, undated.

Johnson, Hugh. *The World Atlas of Wine*. Fireside ed. New York: Simon and Schuster, 1971.

Johnson, Ogden C. "The Food and Drug Administration and Labeling," *Journal of the American Dietetic Association*, 64 (May 1974), 471-75.

Judd, Robert W. (ed.). *Soybean Farming*. Revised ed. Urbana, Ill.: National Soybean Crop Improvement Council, 1966.

Kahrl, William L. *Advanced Modern Food and Beverage Service*. Englewood Cliffs, N.J.: Prentice-Hall, Inc., 1977, esp. p. 222.

———. *Foodservice Productivity and Profit Ideabook*. Boston: Cahners Books, 1975.

Kazarian, Edward A. *Work Analysis and Design for Hotels, Restaurants, and Institutions*. Westport, Conn.: Avi Publishing Co., Inc., 1974.

Keeney, Philip G. *Commercial Ice Cream and Other Frozen Desserts*. University

Park, Pa.: College of Agriculture, Pennsylvania State University, undated.

Keiser, James, and Elmer Kallio. *Controlling and Analyzing Costs in Food Service Operations.* New York: John Wiley and Sons, Inc., 1974, esp. pp. 108-109.

Keister, Douglas C. *Food and Beverage Control.* Englewood Cliffs, N.J.: Prentice-Hall, Inc., 1977.

———, and Ralph D. Wilson (eds.). *Selected Readings for an Introduction to Hotel and Restaurant Management.* Berkeley, Calif.: McCutchan Publishing Corp., 1971.

Kenison, Jean M. *Sexton Appetizers for Everyone.* Chicago: John F. Sexton and Co., undated.

Kent-Jones, D. W., and A. J. Amos. *Modern Cereal Chemistry.* 6th ed. London: Food Trade Review, 1967.

Klippenstein, Ruth N. *The Versatile Egg.* Ithaca, N.Y.: Cornell University Press, 1965.

Koo, Ted S. Y. *Studies of Alaska Red Salmon.* Seattle: University of Washington Press, 1962.

Korzybski, Alfred. *Science and Sanity: An Introduction to Non-Aristotelian Systems and General Semantics.* 4th ed. Lakeville, Conn.: Institute of General Semantics, 1958.

Kosikowski, Frank V. *Cheese and Fermented Milk Foods.* 2d ed. Westport, Conn.: Avi Publishing Co., 1977.

Kotler, Philip. *Marketing Management: Analysis, Planning and Control.* Englewood Cliffs, N.J.: Prentice-Hall, Inc., 1967.

Kotschevar, Lendal H. *Frozen Gold.* Chicago, Ill.: Frozen Potato Products Institute, undated.

———. *Management by Menu.* Chicago, Ill.: National Institute for the Foodservice Industry, 1975, esp. pp. 307-308.

———. *Quantity Food Purchasing.* 2d ed. New York: John Wiley and Sons, Inc., 1976, esp. pp. 3-4.

———, and Margaret E. Terrell. *Food Service Planning: Layout and Equipment.* 2d ed. New York: John Wiley and Son, Inc., 1977.

Kraft-Phenix Cheese Corp. *Romance of Cheese.* Chicago: Kraft-Phenix Cheese Corp., 1939.

Kreck, Lothar A. *Menus: Analysis and Planning.* Boston: Cahners Books, 1975.

Krueckeberg, Harry F. "Ten Steps to Effective Purchasing of Food and Supplies," *Cooking for Profit,* 44 (November 1975), 18-21+.

Larkin, Peter A., and others. *The Fisheries of North America.* Washington, D.C.: North American Fisheries Council, 1965.

Lawrie, R. A. (ed.). *Proteins as Human Food.* Westport, Conn.: Avi Publishing Co., 1970.

Leedom, William S. *The Vintage Wine Book.* Rev. ed. New York: Random House, 1975.

Leverton, Ruth M. *Food Becomes You.* 3d ed. Ames Iowa State University Press, 1965.

Levie, Albert. *The Meat Handbook.* 3d ed. Westport, Conn.: Avi Publishing Co., 1970.

Levitt, Theodore. "Marketing Myopia," *Harvard Business Review,* 38 (July-August 1960).

Lichine, Alex. *New Encyclopedia of Wines and Spirits.* New York: Alfred A. Knopf, 1974.

Lipton, Thomas J., Inc. *The World of Tea.* Englewood Cliffs, N.J.: Thomas J. Lipton, Inc., undated.

Longree, Karla (ed.). *Quantity Food Sanitation.* 2d ed. New York: Wiley-Interscience, 1972.

Louisiana Yam Commission. *The Yam.*

Opelousas: Louisiana Yam Commission, undated.

Ludvigson, Verna. *An Exciting New World of Microwave Cooking*. Minneapolis: Pillsbury Publications for Litton Microwave Cooking Center, undated.

Lukowski, Robert F., and others. *Receiving Practices in Food Service Establishments*. Food Management Program Leaflet 3. Amherst: Cooperative Extension, College of Agriculture, University of Massachusetts, 1965.

————, and others. *Using Storage in Food Service Establishments*. Food Management Program Leaflet 4. Amherst: Cooperative Extension, College of Agriculture, University of Massachusetts, 1966.

————. *Purchasing Canned Fruits and Vegetables for Food Service Establishments*. Food Management Program Leaflet 14. Amherst: Cooperative Extension, College of Agriculture, University of Massachusetts, 1966.

McCoy, John H. *Livestock and Meat Marketing*. Westport, Conn.: Avi Publishing Co., 1972.

MacKenzie, Donald S. *Prepared Meat Product Manufacturing*. Rev. ed. Ann Arbor, Mich.: Edwards Brothers, Inc., 1966.

Mackinney, Gordon, and Angela Little. *Color of Foods*. Westport, Conn.: Avi Publishing Co., 1962.

McLaughlin, Daniel J., Jr., and Charles A. Mallowe (eds.). *Food Marketing and Distribution*. New York: Chain Store Publishing Company, 1971.

McWilliams, Williard F., and Thomas T. Stout. *Economics of the Livestock-Meat Industry*. New York: Macmillan Co., 1964.

Magoon, Charles E. *Supply Guide: Average Monthly Availability of Fresh Fruits and Vegetables*. 9th rev. ed. Washington,

D.C.: United Fresh Fruit and Vegetable Association, 1975.

Maizel, Bruno. *Food and Beverage Purchasing*. New York: ITT Educational Services, Inc., 1971, esp. pp. 181-85.

Markel, Michael F. "The Food Scientist and the Law," *Food Technology* (March 1974).

Marquis, Vivienne, and Patricia Haskell. *The Cheese Book*. New York: Simon and Schuster, 1965.

Matz, S. A. (ed.). *Bakery Technology and Engineering*. Westport, Conn.: Avi Publishing Co., 1960.

————. *Cookie and Cracker Technology*. Westport, Conn.: Avi Publishing Co., 1968.

"Mayonnaise (and Things That Look like It)," *Consumer Reports*, 42 (March 1977), 148-51.

Mead, Margaret. "The Changing Significance of Food," *American Scientist*, 58 (1970), 176.

Merory, Joseph. *Food Flavorings, Composition, Manufacture and Use*. 2d ed. Westport, Conn.: Avi Publishing Co., 1968.

"Milk: In Cheese, It's Disappearing," *Consumer Reports*, 39 (January 1974), 74-75.

Milne, P. H. *Fish and Shellfish Farming in Coastal Waters*. London: Whitefriars Press, Ltd., 1972.

Milner, Max (ed.). *Protein-Enriched Cereal Foods for World Needs*. St. Paul: American Association of Cereal Chemists, Inc., 1969.

Minifie, Bernard W. *Chocolate, Cocoa, and Confectionary: Science and Technology*. Westport, Conn.: Avi Publishing Co., 1970.

Morgan, William J., Jr. *Supervision and Management of Quantity Food Preparation*. Berkeley, Calif.: McCutchan Publishing Corp., 1974, esp. p. 13.

Moyer, William C. *The Buying Guide for

Fresh Fruits, Vegetables, Herbs, and Nuts. 6th ed. Fullerton, Calif.: Blue Goose, Inc., 1976.

Mrak, Emil. "National and International Constraints to Increased Food Production." Paper presented at the Food Symposium, California State University, Chico, April 1975.

National Association of Meat Purveyors. *Meat Buyer's Guide to Portion Control Meat Cuts.* Tucson, Ariz.: NAMP, 1967.

_____. *Meat Buyer's Guide to Standardized Meat Cuts.* Tucson, Ariz.: NAMP, 1961.

National Canners Association. *Facts on Canned Foods.* Washington, D.C.: National Canners Association, 1966.

_____. *It's on the Label.* Washington, D.C.: National Canners Association, 1971.

National Fisheries Institute. *Fish Nets Profit!* Chicago: National Fisheries Institute, undated.

National Dairy Council. *Cheese.* Chicago: National Dairy Council, 1975.

_____. *Milk.* Chicago: National Dairy Council, 1975.

National Live Stock and Meat Board. *Beef Grading: What It Is; How It's Changed.* Chicago: National Live Stock and Meat Board, 1976.

_____. *Facts about Beef.* Chicago: National Live Stock and Meat Board, undated.

_____. *It's Beef for Food-Time USA.* Chicago: National Live Stock and Meat Board, undated.

_____. *Lessons on Meat.* 4th ed. Chicago: National Live Stock and Meat Board, 1976.

_____. *Meat Evaluation Handbook.* Chicago: National Live Stock and Meat Board, 1976.

_____. *Meat Manual: Identification, Buying, Cooking.* 5th ed. Chicago: National Live Stock and Meat Board, 1952.

National Restaurant Association and American Spice Trade Association. *A Guide to Spices.* 2d rev. ed. Technical Bulletin 190. Chicago: National Restaurant Association, undated.

National Turkey Federation. *Turkey: A Dish a Day.* Mt. Morris, Ill.: National Turkey Federation, undated.

_____. *The Turkey Handbook.* Reston, Va.: National Turkey Federation, undated.

Nelson, John A., and G. Malcolm Trout. *Judging Dairy Products.* 4th ed. Westport, Conn.: Avi Publishing Co., 1964.

Nestlé Co., Inc. *The History of Chocolate and Cocoa.* White Plains, N.Y.: The Nestlé Co., Inc., undated.

Nielsen, Linda M., and Agnes Frances Carlin. "Frozen, Precooked Beef and Beef-Soy Loaves," *Journal of the American Dietetic Association,* 65 (July 1974), 35-40.

Nystrom, Pamela J., and others. "Cheese Products: Protein, Moisture, Fat, and Acceptance," *Journal of the American Dietetic Association,* 65 (July 1974), 40-42.

Oliver, Raymond. *Gastronomy of France.* Cleveland, Ohio: World Publishing Co., 1967.

"Orange Juice: Frozen, Canned, Bottled, Cartoned, and Fresh," *Consumer Reports,* 41 (August 1976), 435-42.

"Orange Drink Mixes," *Consumer Reports,* 42 (February 1977), 68-70.

Orr, H. L., and D. A. Fletcher. *Eggs and Egg Products: Production, Identification, Retention of Quality.* Publication 1498. Ottawa: Canada Department of Agriculture, 1973.

Packer's Availability and Merchandising Guide. Kansas City: Vance Publishing Corporation, 1976.

Padberg, Daniel L. "Food Distribution Research Approaches for the 1970's," in *Food Marketing and Distribution*. Ed. Daniel J. McLaughlin and Charles McLaughlin. New York: Chain Store Books, 1971.

Page, Edward B., and P. W. Kingsford. *The Master Chefs*. London: Edward Arnold, Ltd., and Sons, 1971.

Paul, Pauline C., and Helen H. Palmer (eds.). *Food Theory and Applications*. New York: John Wiley and Sons, Inc., 1972.

Paul, the Apostle. "The Second Epistle of Paul the Apostle to Timothy," in *The Golden Book Edition of the Holy Bible*. Chicago: Consolidated Book Publishers, 1901.

"Peanut Butter," *Consumer Reports*, 37 (May 1972), 286-89.

Pedderson, Raymond B., *Specs: The Comprehensive Food Service Purchasing and Specification Manual*, ed. Jule Wilson (Boston: Cahners Books, 1977).

Pellegrini, Angelo M., and others. Chapter in *American Cooking: The Melting Pot*. Ed. James P. Shenton and others. New York: Time-Life Books, 1971.

Potter, Frank E. *Purchasing Dairy Products for Food Service Establishments*. Food Management Program Leaflet 15. Amherst: Cooperative Extension, College of Agriculture, University of Massachusetts, undated.

Price, L. E. "The Convenience Food Experience at Luther College," in *Selected Readings for an Introduction to Hotel and Restaurant Management*. Ed. Douglas C. Keister and Ralph D. Wilson. Berkeley, Calif.: McCutchan Publishing Corp., 1971, pp. 151-57.

Pyke, Magnus. *Catering Science and Technology*. London: John Murray Publishers, Ltd., 1974.

Quimme, Peter. *The Signet Book of American Wine*. New York: New American Library, 1975.

_____. *The Signet Book of Cheese*. New York: New American Library, 1976.

_____. *The Signet Book of Coffee and Tea*. New York: New American Library, 1976.

Rainsford, Peter, Paul Beals, and James C. White. "A Comparative Study of Six Commercial Fats," *Cornell Hotel and Restaurant Administration Quarterly*, 17 (August 1976), 18-21+.

Ramey, Berne. *Pocket Dictionary of Wines*. Skokie, Ill.: Wineco Publishing Co., 1970.

Rappole, Clinton L. "Institutional Use of Frozen Entrées," *Cornell Hotel and Restaurant Administration Quarterly*, 14 (May 1973), 72-88+.

Rausch, Alma G., and others (eds.). *The Guide to Convenience Foods*. Chicago: Patterson Publishing Co., Inc., 1968.

Reitz, Carl A. *A Guide to the Selection, Combinations, and Cooking of Foods*. Volume 1: *Selection and Combinations of Foods*. Westport, Conn.: Avi Publishing Co., Inc., 1961.

_____, and Jeremiah J. Wanderstock. *A Guide to the Selection, Combination, and Cooking of Foods*. Volume 2: *Formulation and Cooking of Foods*. Westport, Conn.: Avi Publishing Co., Inc., 1965.

Rice Council of America. *Facts about American Rice*. Revised ed. Houston, Tex.: Rice Council of America, 1968.

_____. *Rice in Foodservice*. Houston, Tex.: Rice Council of America, undated.

Rogers, John L. *A "Course" in Canning*. 4th ed. London: Food Trade Press, Ltd., 1966.

_____. *Production of Pre-Cooked Frozen Foods for Mass Catering*. London: Food Trade Press, 1969.

Rosengarten, Frederic, Jr. *The Book of Spices*. Abridged ed. New York: Pyramid Books, 1973.

Rykoff, S. E., and Co. *Complete Food Service Dictionary*. Los Angeles: S. E. Rykoff and Co., undated.

Sacharow, Stanley, and Roger C. Griffin, Jr. *Food Packaging*. Westport, Conn.: Avi Publishing Co., Inc., 1970.

Samuelson, Paul A. *Economics: An Introductory Analysis*. 3d ed. New York: McGraw-Hill Book Co., Inc., 1955.

Schultz, H. W. (ed.). *Food Enzymes*. Westport, Conn.: Avi Publishing Co., Inc., 1960.

Seelig, R. A., and Marshall Neale. *Buying, Handling, and Using Fresh Fruits*. Chicago: National Restaurant Association, undated.

_____. *Buying, Handling, and Using Fresh Vegetables*. Chicago: National Restaurant Association, undated.

_____. *Conserving Nutrients in Handling, Storing and Preparing Fresh Fruits and Vegetables*. Washington, D.C.: United Fresh Fruit and Vegetable Association, undated.

_____. *How the Fresh Fruit and Vegetable Marketing System Contributes to Optimum Nutrition*. Washington, D.C.: United Fresh Fruit and Vegetable Association, undated.

Sexton, John, and Co. *Recipes and Menus for All Seasons*. Chicago: J. Sexton and Co., undated.

Shalleck, Jamie. *Tea*. New York: Viking Press, 1972.

Shulman, David. "Motels," in *Selected Readings for an Introduction to Hotel and Restaurant Management*. Ed. Douglas C. Keister and Ralph D. Wilson. Berkeley, Calif. McCutchan Publishing Corp., 1971.

Sivetz, Michael, and H. Elliott Foote. *Coffee Processing Technology*. Volume 1: *Fruit, Green Roast, and Soluble Coffee*. Westport, Conn.: Avi Publishing Co., Inc., 1963.

_____. *Coffee: Origin and Use*. Corvallis, Ore.: Coffee Publications, 1974.

Slanetz, L. W., and others. *Microbiological Quality of Foods*. Proceedings of a Conference Held at Franconia, N.H., August 27-29, 1962. New York: Academic Press, 1963.

Smith, B. "A New Language for Today's System Implementation," *Food Service Magazine*, 33 (Nos. 6, 8, 1971).

Smith, Laura L., and Lewis J. Minor. *Food Service Science*. Westport, Conn.: Avi Publishing Co., Inc., 1968.

Smith, Ora. *Potatoes: Production, Storing, Processing*. Westport, Conn.: Avi Publishing Co., Inc., 1968.

Snyder, Earle S., and Henry L. Orr. *Poultry Meat: Processing, Quality Factors, Yields*. Toronto: Ontario Department of Agriculture, [1964?].

Snygg, Donald, and Arthur W. Combs. *Individual Behavior: A New Frame of Reference for Psychology*. Rev. ed. New York: Harper and Row, 1959.

Solomon, K. and N. Katz. *Profitable Restaurant Management*. Englewood Cliffs, N.J.: Prentice-Hall, Inc., 1974, esp. p. 203.

Southwestern Grocery Co. *Purchase Guide*. Tucson, Ariz.: Southwestern Grocery Co., undated.

Specialty Brands, Inc. *Spice Islands Guide to Your Spice Shelf*. New York: Dell Publishing Co., 1975.

Splaver, Bernard R. *Successful Catering*. Boston: Cahners Books, 1975.

Stare, Frederick, and Margaret McWilliams. *Living Nutrition*. New York: John Wiley and Sons, Inc., 1973.

Stein, Bob. *Marketing in Action for Hotels-Motels-Restaurants*. New York: Ahrens Publishing Co., Inc., 1971.

Stobart, Tom. *The International Wine and Food Society's Guide to Herbs, Spices, and Flavourings*. New York: McGraw-

Hill, 1973.

Stokeley-Van Camp, Inc. *Institutional Frozen Foods Quantity Recipes and Reference Manual*. Oakland, Calif.: Stokely-Van-Camp, Inc., undated.

Stokes, John W. *How to Manage a Restaurant or Institutional Food Service*. Dubuque, Iowa: Wm. C. Brown Co., 1967.

Storck, John, and Walter D. Teague. *Flour for Man's Bread*. Minneapolis: University of Minnesota Press, 1928.

Sultan, W. J. *Practical Baking*. Westport, Conn.: Avi Publishing Co., Inc., 1965.

Sunkist Growers, Inc. *Sunkist Grower's "Sunkist/Fish N'Seafood."* Los Angeles: Institutional Division, Sunkist Growers, Inc., undated.

———. *Fresh Citrus Quantity Service Handbook*. Los Angeles: Institutional Division, Sunkist Growers, Inc., undated.

———. *Sunkist Fresh Citrus Buying Guide*. Sherman Oaks, Calif.: Sunkist Growers, Inc., 1975.

Svicarovich, John, Stephen Winter, and Jeff Ferguson. *The Coffee Book: A Connoisseur's Guide to Gourmet Coffee*. Englewood Cliffs, N.J.: Prentice-Hall, Inc., 1976.

Swift and Co. *Cuts of Meat: How You Can Identify Them*. Agriculture Research Bulletin No. 7. Chicago: Swift and Co., undated.

Szarthmary, Louis. "Beef—Some Answers," *Cornell Hotel and Restaurant Administration Quarterly*, 11 (November 1970), 49-59.

"Tea," *Consumer Reports*, 43 (September 1977), 502-504.

Tea Council of the USA, Inc. *Two Leaves and a Bud: The Story of Tea*. New York: Tea Council of the USA, Inc., undated.

Tellus, Barbara. *Let's Cook for a Crowd with Fresh Fruits and Melons*. Los Angeles: Western Growers Association, undated.

Terrell, Margaret E. *Professional Food Preparation*. New York: John Wiley and Sons, Inc., 1971.

Thorner, Marvin E., and Ronald J. Herzberg. *Food Beverage Service Handbook*. Westport, Conn.: Avi Publishing Co., Inc., 1970.

———. *Convenience and Fast Food Handbook*. Westport, Conn.: Avi Publishing Co., 1973, esp. pp. 122, 270-71.

———. "Convenience Foods," *Cornell Hotel and Restaurant Administration Quarterly*, 16 (May 1975), 59-63+.

Topel, David G. (ed.). *The Pork Industry: Problems and Progress*. Ames: Iowa State University Press, 1968.

Tressler, Donald K., and M. A. Joslyn. *Fruit and Vegetable Juice Processing Technology*. Westport, Conn.: Avi Publishing Co., Inc., 1961.

———, and others. *The Freezing Preservation of Foods*, Volumes 1-4. 4th ed. Westport, Conn.: Avi Publishing Co., Inc., 1968.

"Turkey off the Assembly Line," *Consumer Reports*, 38 (November 1973), 664-70.

Ukers, William Harrison. *All about Coffee*. 2d ed. Detroit: Gale Research, 1976.

United Fruit Co. *Answers to Questions Frequently Asked about Bananas*. New York: United Fruit Co., 1958.

U.S. Trout Farmers Association. *A Handbook of Handling/Cooking/Serving U.S. Mountain Trout*. N.p.: U.S. Trout Farmers Association (P.O. Box 171, Lake Ozark, MO 65049), n.d.

United States Brewers Association. *A Guide to Game Cookery*. New York: U.S. Brewers Association, undated.

Van Zante, Helen J. *The Microwave Oven*. Boston: Houghton-Mifflin Co., 1973.

Vilella, Joseph A. *The Hospitality Industry —The World of Food Service*. 2d ed. New York: McGraw-Hill, 1975.

Wanderstock, J. J. "Meat Purchasing,"

Cornell Hotel and Restaurant Administration Quarterly, 11 (November 1970), 60-64.

Ward, Barbara. *Spaceship Earth*. New York: Columbia University Press, 1966.

Warren, Jean, and Alice Briant. *Meal Management with a Freezer*. Cornell Extension Bulletin No. 1025. Ithaca: Cooperative Extension Service, New York State College, 1961.

Weiner, Michael A. *The Taster's Guide to Beer: Brews and Breweries of the World*. New York: Collier Books, 1977.

Weiser, Harley H. *Practical Food Microbiology*. Westport, Conn.: Avi Publishing Co., Inc., 1962.

Weiss, Steve. "A Dash of Spice . . .," *Institutions/Volume Feeding Management*, 77 (December 1, 1975), 42-43.

———. "Rice: Going with the Grain for Profit," *Institutions/Volume Feeding Management*, 77 (November 1, 1975), 43-44.

Wellman, Frederick L. *Coffee Botany, Cultivation and Utilization*. New York: Interscience Publishers, Inc., 1961.

Wenzel, George L. *How to Control Costs*. Austin, Texas: privately printed by George L. Wenzel, Sr. (403 Riley Road), 1971.

West, Bessie Brooks, and others. *Food Service in Institutions*. 5th ed. New York: John Wiley and Sons, Inc., 1977.

Wheat Flour Institute. *From Wheat to Flour: The Story of Man in a Grain of Wheat*. Washington, D.C.: Wheat Flour Institute, 1976.

"Which Cereals Are Most Nutritious?" *Consumer Reports*, 40 (February 1975), 76-82.

Wilkinson, Jule. *The Complete Book of Cooking Equipment*. Rev. ed. Boston: Cahners Books, 1975, esp. p. 72.

Winter, A. R., and P. Clements. "Cooked Edible Meat in Ready-to-Cook Poultry,"

Journal of the American Dietetic Association, 33 (1957).

Witt, P. R., Jr. *The Chemistry and Technology of Cereals as Food and Feed*. Westport, Conn.: Avi Publishing Co., Inc., 1970.

Witzky, Herbert K. *Practical Hotel-Motel Cost Reduction Handbook*. New York: Ahrens Publishing Co., Inc., 1970.

Woodroof, Jasper Guy. *Peanuts: Production, Processing, Products*. 2d ed. Westport, Conn.: Avi Publishing Co., Inc., 1973.

———. *Tree Nuts: Production, Processing, and Products*, 2 vols. Westport, Conn.: Avi Publishing Co., Inc., 1967.

Woolrich, W. R., and E. R. Hallowell. *Cold and Freezer Storage Manual*. Westport, Conn.: Avi Publishing Co., 1970.

Wright, Carlton E. *Food Buying*. New York: Macmillan Co., 1962.

Wrisley, Albert L., Ernest M. Buck, and Charles E. Eshbach. *Purchasing Beef for Food Service Establishments*. Food Management Leaflet 16. Amherst Cooperative Extension, College of Agriculture, University of Massachusetts, 1966.

Young, Fred G. "Convenience Foods: A Dissenting Voice," in *Selected Readings for an Introduction to Hotel and Restaurant Management*. Ed. Douglas C. Keister and Ralph D. Wilson. Berkeley, Calif.: McCutchan Publishing Corp., 1971, pp. 158-60.

"Your Guide to Frozen Convenience Foods," *Institutions/Volume Feeding Management*, 76 (February 1, 1975), 52+; (April 15, 1975), 57+.

"Your Guide to Non-Frozen Convenience Foods," *Institutions/Volume Feeding Management*, 77 (August 15, 1975), 41+.

Index

A & P stores, 9
Acceptance service, 37, 140-141, 257
Accounting, 25-26
Accounting department: buyer's records in, 96-97; controller and, 167; inventories by, 165; receiving by, 126, 137, 139
Additives, food, 36, 219-220
Advertising media, 19, 228. *See also* Labels
Advisory Commission on Food and Fiber, 45
Agents. *See* Middlemen
Agricultural Marketing Services (AMS), 16, 18, 37-42, 44, 271-272
Agricultural Marketing Services Act, 37-42
Airlines: computerized reservations of, 213; and convenience foods, 12
Alcohol, Tobacco, and Firearms Division, 44
American Airlines, 213
American Can Company, 22
American Dietetics Association, 249
American Dry Milk Institute, 46
American Meat Institute, 46, 107
American Mutual Insurance Company, 190
American Public Health Association, 46

Amphorae, 2
AMS. *See* Agricultural Marketing Services
Animal and Plant Health Inspection Service (APHIS), 35
Antimerger (Celler-Kefauver) Act, 34
Apicius, 2
Apples, Canadian grading of, 327
Associated Press reports, 83
Auctions, 89-92, 95
Authority of food buyer, 66-67

Bacon: amounts for 50 servings of (table), 282; specifications for, 110
Bacteria count in dairy products, 196
Bartram, John, 6
Beans, information sources on, 273
Beef: amounts for 50 servings of (table), 281; Canadian grading of, 330-331; dishonesty with, 199-201; ground, 200-201, 259; information sources about, 257-259; portion and yield factors for (table), 277-278; specifications for, 108, 109, 111; standards for grading (table), 288; prices of, 40, 85, 243. *See also* Meats
Beers: Egyptian, 1; information sources on, 276
Bell, Alexander Graham, 9

352   INDEX

Beverages: dishonesty with, 198-199; Egyptian, 1; Greek, 2; information sources on, 273, 274-276; and receiving department, 131-132; regulations of, 22, 42, 44; servings of (tables), 301, 311; storage of, 149, 159, 165. *See also* Milk

Bids: auction, 92; formal written, 88-89

Birdseye, 11

Blind receiving system, 131

Blue Goose, Inc., 114

Bonding, commodity, 22-23

Bookkeepers, 54, 171

Books: food and beverage inventory, 165; log, 140, 171; purchase, 96; quotation, 96

Boutique-type operations, 29-30

Brand names, 20-21; dishonesty with, 202; in specifications, 111-112

Breads: information sources on, 268; turnover rate for, 25

Breakers, defined, 73

Brokers, 16, 28-29, 74

Budget, for food buyer, 112

Building codes for storerooms, 159, 166

Bureau of Standards, 44-45

Butcher shops: in future, 220; in storerooms, 157; testing committee and, 106-107, 116, 124

Butter: Canadian-graded, 325-326; dishonesty with, 196-197; standards for grading (table), 290. *See also* Dairy products

Buy-and-hold system, 83-85

Cadmus, 2

Calcumetric, 319-323

Canada: food information sources in, 262; grading system of, 114, 325-331

Canned foods: information sources on, 272-273; invention of, 7; regulations of, 20-21, 43; servings of (tables), 305-306, 307-309; standards for grading (table), 291, 292; and supply function, 22

Carson, Rachel, 23

Cash payments, 27, 30-31

Catherine de' Medicis, 3-4

Ceilings, storeroom, 159

Cereals, information sources on, 268

Certificates, inspection, 37-38, 41

Chain operations: buying systems of, 17, 83, 85, 87; and convenience foods, 12, 239-240; organization within, 54; specifications of, 114

Character, of food buyer, 63-64

Checklists, 166, 172-190, 209

Cheese: Canadian grading of, 325-326; identity standards for, 42; information sources on, 263-264. *See also* Dairy products

Chefs, 5, 47; duties of, 12, 54, 72; food buyers and, 63; French, 4; Greek, 2; and receiving department, 139

Chicago Hospital Council, 94

Chicken. *See* Poultry

CIF (cost, insurance, and freight), 102

Citations on job-condition violations, 44

Clams, regulation of, 40-41. *See also* Fish; Seafood; Shellfish

Clark's Point Cannery, 20

Clayton Act, 34

Cleaning schedule, storeroom, 166

Coca-Cola Bottling Company, 42

Cocoa, information sources on, 275

Coffee: dishonesty with, 198-199; information sources on, 274-275. *See also* Beverages

Cold storage, defined, 23-24

Commission houses, 28-29, 74, 95

Commissions for auction buying, 92

Committees. *See* Testing committees

Compactors, portable trash, 158

Competitive market buying, 77-82

Computers, 211-219; with convenience foods, 240; purchasing departments and, 214, 218-219; for referral systems, 17; for storerooms, 158, 162, 215; of wholesalers, 30

Consultants, outside, 209; for auditing,

140, 171, 172; for controller checks, 172; for sanitation inspection, 166

Consumer Product Safety Act Commission, 36

Consumers Union publications, 258-259, 260-261, 267-268, 270-271, 273, 275

Containers: servings per (table), 300-303; sizes of (tables), 299, 304; specifications of, 109-110; for storage, 22, 164

Continental Can Company, 22

Contracts, 73, 100, 102-104

Controller's departments, 71, 167-190, 209; in institutions, 48; in motor inns, 53-54; and receiving department, 126, 139-140, 168-169, 201; and storeroom, 143, 144, 145, 160-162, 165, 169-171. *See also* Food and beverage controllers

Convenience foods, 12, 15, 223-240; buying systems for, 83, 92; defined, 223; in future, 220, 239-240; information sources on, 273-274; purchasing departments and, 229-230, 231, 236-239; servings of (table), 315-316

Conventions, 29

Cookbook of Apicius, 2

Cooking loss tests, 124

Cooperage accounts, 164

Cooperative buying, 93-94, 220

Corn varieties, 111, 244

Cornell Hotel and Restaurant Administration Quarterly, 226, 256, 259, 270, 274

Cost-plus buying, 87-88

Costs: of acceptance service, 141; of auction buying, 92; of bonding, 22-23; and buyer's professionalism, 67; per canned food serving (table), 305-306; computer control of, 211, 218; of computers, 212-213, 219; and convenience foods, 230-231, 232-234; with cost-plus buying, 87-88; delivery, 86, 97, 130, 143; with direct buying, 17, 27; of dishonesty, 192-193; and fixed-markup buying, 83; of formal

written bids, 89; future, 220; and ingredient rooms, 158; and make-or-buy decisions, 117-124; of money, 24-25, 97; and one-stop buying, 86-87; of packaging, 164; of payment postponement, 97-98; of purchasing department, 54-55; of quality control, 21; receiving department and, 126; specifications and, 72, 106-107; and speculative buying, 102-103; of storage, 22, 103, 158; of supermarket buying, 76-77; of test marketing, 18; of utility, 27, 28. *See also* Prices, food

Cottam, Howard, 249

Counts, dishonesty with, 201

Covers, defined, 72

Crab meat: dishonesty with, 198; regulation of, 41. *See also* Fish; Seafood; Shellfish

Cream: dishonesty with, 196; information sources on, 262-263. *See also* Dairy products

Creamers, nondairy, 264

Credit, with purveyors, 25, 30, 97, 113

Credit memorandums, 136, 201

Creole cooking, 6

Cultures: and food shortages, 244; and U.S. foods, 8

Curiosity, of food buyer, 64, 66

Cyclamates controversy, 36

Dairy products: Canadian grading of, 325-326; conversion table for, 298; dishonesty with, 196-197; information sources on, 262-264; inspection of, 37; standards for grading (table), 290-291; turnover rate for, 25

Dead stock reports, 169-171

Dealers. *See* Purveyors

Delaney clause, 36

Deliveries: costs of, 86, 97, 130, 143; dishonesty with, 30-31, 93; emergency, 31, 98, 130, 139; receiving department and, 30-31, 130-131, 138-139; responsibilities with, 102-103; and salesmen's attitudes, 98; schedules of, 72-73, 86, 113, 130, 139, 143, 145; and specifications, 113. *See also* Transportation

Delmonico's restaurant, 8

Dessert powder bases, table on, 314

Dietary managers, 47, 48

Dining room manager, 54

Dipper equivalency measures (table), 298

Direct purchasing, 16, 17, 27-28, 220

Discounts, 25-26, 98

Dishonesty. *See* Honesty

Distribution systems: buyer's role in, 56-57; and food shortages, 242-243. *See also* Transportation

Distributors, buyers as, 93

Dog and pony shows, 29

Drainage, storeroom, 159

Drop shipments, 31, 85-86

Dunnage racks, in storeroom, 149

Earnings. *See* Salaries

Ecology, 27, 243, 244

Edison, Thomas, 9

Education, of food buyers, 64-65. *See also* Training

Efficiency experts, 106

Eggs: Canadian grading of, 326; dishonesty with, 197; equivalency table for, 297; information sources on, 261-262; other forms, 262; standards for grading (table), 290; substitutes for, 262; storage of, 23

Egyptian innkeeping, 1

Encyclopedias, food information, 256

Energy: food, 241; fuel, 31, 73, 113, 241, 243

English cuisine, 4-5, 6

Equipment, kitchen: and convenience foods, 229, 230, 231-232, 236-239, 240; Greek, 2

Escoffier, 5

Ethics codes, 193. *See also* Honesty

Exchange: of information, 56; market, 17-18, 24

Experience, of food buyers, 64-66

Extractors, 26-27

Fabricators, 73

Farmers' markets, 73, 76

FAS (free alongside ship), 102

Fast food operations, 12, 83, 220, 239-240

Fats, information sources on, 270-271

FDA. *See* Food and Drug Administration

Federal government. *See* Laws; Regulations, government; United States

Federal Register, 36

Federal Trade Commission, 93, 228

Federal Trade Commission Act, 34

Fertilizers, and world food supply, 243, 246-247

Fidelity bonds, 22-23

Finances. *See* Costs; Prices, food; Salaries

First-in, first-out (FIFO), 31

Fish: in American colonies, 7; buying systems for, 83, 93; dishonesty with, 110, 197-198; imported, 244; information on, 20, 264-268; portion and yield factors for (table), 279-280; regulations for, 36-37, 40-41, 266, 267; servings of (tables), 283, 303, 314-315; specifications for, 108, 110; standards for grading (table), 289-290; world harvest of, 26-27, 245. *See also* Seafood; Shellfish

Fish and Wildlife Service, 40

Fixed-markup buying, 82-83

Floors, storeroom, 158-159

Flours, information sources on, 268

FOB (free on board), 102

Food, Drug, and Cosmetic Act, 36

Food additives, 36, 219-220

Food and beverage controllers, 13; and butcher test card, 124; and controller's department, 168, 209; and receiving department, 139; and specifications, 72; and storeroom, 165, 166

Food and Drug Administration (FDA) regulations, 33, 42-43, 46, 255, 266; of beverages, 42, 44; and crops, 243;

of labels, 45; of seafood, 37, 266

Food and Nutrition Board, 45-46

Food and Nutrition Information and Education Materials Center (FNIC), 255

Food chain, 26-27

Food for Us All (USDA), 45

Foodco, 86

Forms: for bids, 88-89; in controller's department, 168; purchase order, 102, 104, 168; quotation, 77-82; in receiving department, 132-137, 139, 168; requisition, 77, 161-162

Forum of the Twelve Caesars, 24, 25

Freezers, 157, 237

French cuisine, 3-4, 6, 7

Fresh Fruit and Vegetables Market News, 82

Freshness: of eggs, 261; specifications on, 110-111

Frozen desserts. *See* Dairy Products

Frozen foods, 11-12, 15, 72, 224; buy-and-hold systems for, 83; dishonesty with, 110-111, 200; and distributorships, 93; information sources on, 258, 268, 272; standards for grading (table), 291, 292; storage of, 23-24, 72, 156, 157, 160, 165, 237

Fruits: in American colonies, 7; at auctions, 92; Canadian grading of, 327-328; dishonesty with, 203; information sources on, 271-273; inspection of, 21, 37, 41-42; juices of, 273, 301, 311; labels for, 20-21; quantities to purchase of (table), 293-294; servings of (tables), 284-285, 300, 308-309, 310-311; standards for grading (table), 291; storage of, 22, 23-24

Funding, for world food supply, 248-249

Galara, 2

Garbage storage and disposal, 158

Garum sauce, 3

"Gathering short," 94

General Foods, 11-12

Gentlemen's agreements, 65

Gilman, George, 9

Going concern concept, 25

Good Manufacturing Practices (GMP's), 42-43

Goods received without invoice (GRWI) form, 136-137

Government. *See* Canada; Laws; Regulations, government; United States

Grading: by Canadian government, 114, 325-331; dishonesty in, 195-203; information sources on, 108-109, 114, 254-255, 271-273, 288-292; by United States government, 39-42, 108-109, 114, 140-141, 254, 257-258, 260-261, 266, 267, 271-272, 288-292; and world food supply, 220

Grains: information sources on, 268-269; inspection of, 37

Great American Tea Company, 9

Greek cuisine, 2, 3

Hard spot, defined, 125

Hartford, George Huntington, 9

Hartford, John, 9

Headhunters, 63

Health. *See* Occupational Safety and Health Act; Sanitation

Henderson, Ernest, 207-208

Herbs, information sources on, 269-270

Hilton, Conrad, 63-64

Holiday Inns, 115

Honesty, 191-209; in food buyers, 68-69, 204-207; and formal written bid, 89; and receiving department, 30-31, 140, 201, 202, 203; and standing orders, 93

Honey, Canadian grading of, 328-329

Hospitals: cooperative buying by, 94; ingredient rooms in, 158; organization in, 13, 48

Hotels: butcher shops in, 107, 157; buying systems of, 76, 77, 83, 85, 86; dishonesty in, 205-206, 207-208; organization in, 12-13, 48-53, 60, 115;

storerooms in, 153-155, 157-158; testing committees in, 115; and travel increase, 8-9

House accounts, 73

Humor, in food buyer, 64

IBM, 216, 219

Ice cream: dishonesty with, 196; information sources on, 264; standards for grading (table), 291. *See also* Dairy products

Icehouses, 6

Indirect purchasing, 28

Industrial consumers, 19

Industrial espionage, 18

Infant foods, servings per container of (table), 303

Inflation, 94, 97

Information: marketing, 18-21, 68, 94; of purchasing department, 56, 94; on purveyors, 74; sources of, 253-276; in specifications, 107-112, 120-123, 260

Ingredient rooms, 158

Innkeepers, 53-54

Innkeeping, 1

Inspection: Canadian, 325-331; continuous, 41, 266; controller's departments and, 166, 172-190, 209; and dishonesty, 209; in Egypt, 1; of storerooms, 166; U.S. Department of Agriculture, 21, 35, 37-42, 140-141, 257; U.S. Department of Commerce, 36-37, 266, 267; U.S. Department of Labor, 44

Institutions, 9, 11; buying systems of, 54, 76, 77, 86, 87, 93, 94; and convenience foods, 12; ingredient rooms in, 158; and make-or-buy decisions, 117; organization in, 13, 48; vegetable and salad preparation in, 157-158

Internal Revenue Service (IRS), 44, 203

International Agricultural Research Consultative Group, 247

International Association of Milk and Food

Sanitation, 46

Inventories: computerized, 213, 218, 219; drawdowns of, 30; production, 169; storeroom, 72, 144, 160-161, 164, 165, 169, 218, 219; turnover rates of, 25

Israelites, 1-2

Italian cuisine, 3

Jams, table on, 312

Jaspen, Norman, 207

Jefferson, Thomas, 6

Jellies, table on, 313

Job conditions. *See* Occupational Safety and Health Act

Job descriptions, 59-62, 67

Jobbers, 16, 30, 31

Johnson, Lyndon, 45

Journal information, 256

Juices: information about, 273; servings of (tables), 301, 311

Jungle (Sinclair), 35

Keys, storeroom, 159-160, 171

Kitchen: equipment in, 2, 229, 230, 231-232, 236-239, 240; for testing, 115-116

Labels: dishonesty of, 202; regulations for, 20-21, 35, 36, 45, 228; specifications of, 260. *See also* Grading

Lamb: amounts for 50 servings of (table), 281; Canadian grading of, 330; portion and yield factors for (table), 278; standards for grading (table), 289. *See also* Meats

Land resources, 242, 244, 247

Laws, 34-44; antitrust, 33, 34, 94; and contracts, 100, 102, 103-104; ecological, 243; on job conditions, 43-44, 127, 145, 166, 187, 243; sanitation, 11, 35, 45, 145, 166, 187-190; truth-in-menu, 220, 228

Lever Brothers Company, 18

Libby, McNeill, and Libby, 20

Lighting: and eating out, 9; in storerooms,

159
Lincoln, Abraham, 64
Liquor: bonding of, 22; information sources on, 276; inventory of, 165; stewards and, 12; storage of, 22, 149, 159, 165
Lists: check, 166, 172-190, 209; quotation, 77-82. *See also* Specifications
Location: of buyer's office, 95; of markets, 16-17, 72-73; of quality commodities, 111; of receiving department, 126-127; of storeroom, 153
Logbooks, 140, 171
Loma Linda foods, 30
Loose receivers, 30
Louis XIV, 4

McGuire Act, 34
Magazine information, 254
Make-or-buy decisions, 116-124
Management (general): and buyer, 48-57, 62-63, 64, 66-67, 71, 204-205, 228; and computers, 212, 214; and controller's department, 167, 168, 171-172, 187; and convenience foods, 229-233; and dishonesty, 204-205, 207-209; in future, 221; organization of, 13, 47-56, 71, 112, 115, 126; and receiving department, 126, 130, 140; and specifications, 71, 105, 106, 112; and storeroom, 144, 157, 166; and supplier selection, 74-75; and testing committee, 71, 74, 113, 115, 117
Manuals: operations, 209; sanitation, 190
Manufacturer's agents, 16, 29
Maple syrup, Canadian grading of, 329
Margarine information, 264
Market reports, 16, 18, 82, 83, 256
Markets, food, 15-31, 66, 72-73, 75-95, 113, 220
Mayonnaise, information sources on, 271
Meat Buyer's Guides, 108, 216, 218, 257
Meat Inspection Act, 11, 35
Meats: in American colonies, 7; buying systems with, 76, 83, 88, 94-95; dishonesty with, 199-202; information

sources on, 108, 216, 218, 257-260; packing of, 6-7, 73; portion and yield factors for (table), 277-279; portioned, 106, 107, 110, 199-200, 220, 257; prices of, 40, 85, 243; servings of (tables), 281-282, 302-303; specifications for, 108, 109, 110, 111; standards for grading, 35, 109, 114, 140-141, 257-259, 288-289, 329-331; turnover rates for, 25
Menus, and specifications, 71-72, 113
Mercantilism, 30
Merchandising plan, 117-124
Metric system converter, 319-323
Middlemen, 16, 27, 28-31, 74, 220
Milk: Canadian grading of, 325-326; conversion table for, 298; dishonesty with, 196; information sources on, 262-263; standards for grading (table), 290. *See also* Dairy products
Minicomputers for ingredient rooms, 158
Missionary selling, 29, 74
Money, costs of, 24-25, 97
Monopolies, 34
Moore, Robert, 207
Morningstar Farms, 30
Morrill Land Grant Act, 247
Motels, 17, 56, 77, 153-155
Motion economy tradition, 30
Motor inns, 53-54, 56
Mussels, regulation of, 40-41. *See also* Fish; Seafood; Shellfish

Naderism, 23
Names: brand, 20-21, 111-112, 202; for specifications, 108, 111-112
National Association of Meat Purveyors (NAMP), 114, 257
National Canners' Association, 46
National Cash Register Company, 219
National Commission on State Workmen's Compensation Laws, 44
National Institute for Occupational Safety and Health (NIOSH), 43
National Live Stock and Meat Board, 216,

National Oceanographic and Atmosphere Administration (NOAA), 36, 265
Negotiated-price buying, 85
Newspaper information, 83, 253-254
Nolo contendre plea, 34
Notices on job-condition violations, 44
Nutrition programs, international, 247
Nuts: information sources on, 269; vacuum-packed shelled (table), 309

Occupational Safety and Health Act (OSHA), 43-44, 127, 145, 166, 187, 243
Oiling, in egg business, 197
Oils, information sources on, 270-271
Olives, table on, 312
One-stop shopping, 15-16, 30, 86-87, 102, 219
Open market buying, 77-82
Order clerks, 66
Ordering schedules, 145
Orders: purchase, 102, 104, 168; standing, 92-93
Organization, management, 13, 47-56, 71, 112, 115, 126
OSHA. *See* Occupational Safety and Health Act
Ovens, types, 237-238
Oysters, regulation of, 40-41. *See also* Fish; Seafood; Shellfish

Packaging: dishonesty in, 202-203; materials for, 22; regulations on, 20-21, 36; for storage, 22, 164
Packer grade, 20
Packers, meat, 6-7, 73
Pallets, in storeroom, 149
Parks, William, 7
Payment methods, 26, 27, 30-31, 97-98, 102
Payoffs, 12, 205-207
Peaches, canned, 20-21, 22. *See also* Fruits; Canned foods
Pennsylvania Dutch cuisine, 6
Perishable Agricultural Commodities Act, 42
Perishables: and drop shipment method, 86; and formal written bids, 88-89; lists of, 71, 72; quotation buying of, 77; rotation of, 163-164; specifications for, 111
Personality, of food buyer, 59, 63-64
Pesticides, and food shortages, 248
Pickles, table on, 311-312
Pie fillings, table on, 310
Place strategy, 28
Plastic service items, 221
Plaza Hotel, 124
Population growth, 244-245
Pork: amounts for 50 servings of (table), 281, 282; dishonesty with, 199; information sources on, 259; portion and yield factors for (table), 278-279; specifications for, 108, 110; standards for grading (table), 289. *See also* Meats
Portion and yield factors (table), 277-280
Portion-ready purchases, 66, 106, 107, 110, 199-200, 220, 257
Potatoes: Canadian grading of, 327; information sources on, 273. *See also* Vegetables
Poultry: in American colonies, 7; amounts for 50 servings of (table), 282; Canadian grading of, 331; dishonesty with, 197; information sources on, 260-261; portion and yield factors for (table), 279; servings per container of (table), 302-303; specifications for, 110, 111; standards for grading (table), 289
Poultry Products Inspection Act, 35
Poverty class, 45
Preserves, table on, 313-314
Prices, food, 64; in American colonies, 7; and buying systems, 75, 76, 77-82, 83, 85, 86, 87, 89, 93, 168; discount, 25-26, 98; dishonesty with, 202; information sources on, 256; low-ball, 99; sale, 24; stabilization of, 40;

257, 258

National Marine Fisheries Service (NMFS), 36-37, 40, 255, 265-267
storerooms and, 144, 162; and testing, 116, 124; in value analyses, 227-228; and world food supply, 243-244, 245-246. *See also* Costs

Primary markets, 16

Processed foods. *See* Canned foods; Convenience foods; Frozen foods

Processors, food, 73; buying systems of, 77, 83, 85, 92; Canadian, 328; ingredient rooms of, 158; regulations on, 20-21, 41-42, 43

Produce: at auctions, 92; commission men and, 29; dishonesty with, 196, 201. *See also* Fruits; Vegetables

Producers, 16, 26, 83

Producers Price-Current, 82, 83

Product positioning, 18

Production department: and control system, 171; and convenience foods, 230, 231; organization of, 47, 53, 54; and purchasing department, 56

Production inventories, 169

Prohibition era, 12-13

Protein, nonmeat, 30, 250-251, 260

Public markets. *See* Farmers' markets

Purchase books, 96

Purchase orders, 102, 104, 168

Pure Food and Drug Act, 35-36

Purveyors, 73-75; buyer relations with, 98-100; and buying systems, 77, 82, 85, 86, 87-88, 89, 92; and convenience foods, 234-236; and credit buying, 25-26, 97, 113; dishonesty among, 30-31, 195-207; and payment postponements, 26, 97-98; and receiving department, 138-139; specifications with, 105, 107. *See also* Wholesalers

Pynchon, John, 6-7

Quality: of brand names, 20-21, 111-112; and contracts, 104; and convenience foods, 227-228, 230, 231, 235-236,
240; dishonesty about, 195-201; at farmers' markets, 76; of food buyers, 59, 63-64, 68-69, 204-207, 253; and geographical area, 111; and ingredient rooms, 158; of portion-ready meat, 107; receiving department and, 130, 138; standards for, 20-21, 37, 39-40, 41, 230, 253, 257-258; in supermarkets, 77; tests of, 116; in value analyses, 227-228

Quotation books, 96

Quotation buying, 77-82, 83, 168

Quotation lists, 77-82

Railroads, 7-8, 9, 22

Raisins, information sources on, 273

Raw-to-ready scale, 224-226

Receiving department, 125-141; and buyer's office, 96, 139; and computers, 214-215, 218; and controller's department, 126, 139-140, 168-169, 171, 201, 209; and dishonesty, 30-31, 140, 201, 202, 203; records of, 131-137, 168-169

Recommended Daily Allowances (RDA), 45

Records: in buyer's office, 66, 96-97, 168; and convenience foods, 230; in receiving department, 131-137, 168-169; storeroom, 159, 169; testing, 124

Referral systems, 17

Refrigeration, 9; and convenience foods, 237; in specifications, 109; in storeroom, 145, 157; and supply, 21. *See also* Frozen foods

Regulations: of beverages, 22, 42, 44; in Egypt, 1; and food shortages, 243; information sources on, 255; of labeling, 20-21, 35, 36, 45, 228; price, 40, 93. *See also* Laws; Standards

Reputation, of food buyer, 69, 253

Requisitions: buyer's, 77; storeroom, 145, 161-162, 169

Restaurant Associates, 76

Restaurants: buying systems of, 76, 77, 83, 85, 86; convenience foods in, 12;

organization in, 12-13; specialty, 220-221; and travel increase, 8, 9

Rice, information sources on, 268-269

Ripeness, specifications on, 111

Robinson-Patman Act, 34

Roman cuisine, 2, 3

Roquefort Cheese Association, 42

Rotation of stock, in storeroom, 162-165

SABER computer system, 213-214

Safety. *See* Occupational Safety and Health Act

Salad, preparation areas for, 157-158

Salad dressings, information sources on, 271

Salaries: and dishonesty, 209; of food buyers, 63, 65; future, 221

Sales agents, 18, 29-30

Sales departments, 53

Salesmen, 16, 73-74, 85-86; buyer's relations with, 95-100; receiving clerk and, 130

Salmon, information sources on, 20, 265. *See also* Fish; Seafood

Sanitary Engineering Center, 45

Sanitation: and convenience foods, 230; and dairy products, 196; regulations for, 11, 35, 45, 145, 166, 187-190; in storerooms, 145-149, 158-159, 166

Scales: for receiving department, 127, 131, 201; in storeroom, 149

Scallops, dishonesty with, 198. *See also* Fish; Seafood; Shellfish

Scandinavian cuisine, 6

Schedules: delivery, 72-73, 86, 113, 130, 139, 143, 145; and convenience foods, 233; ordering, 145; storeroom, 145

School lunch programs, 40

Score sheets, taste test, 124

Seafood: buying systems for, 83, 93; dishonesty with, 197-198; information sources on, 20, 246-248; regulations of, 36-37, 40-41, 266, 267; servings of (tables), 283, 303, 314-315. *See also* Fish; Shellfish

Seasonings: information sources on, 269-270; in storerooms, 164-165

Secondary markets, 16

Security measures, 159-160, 171, 193, 207

Seeds, information sources on, 269-270

Sexism, 2

Shellfish: dishonesty with, 198; information sources on, 265-268; portion and yield factors for (table), 280; regulation of, 40-41, 266, 267; standards for grading (table), 289-290. *See also* Fish; Seafood

Shelving, in storeroom, 145-149

Sheraton hotels, 207

Sherbets: dishonesty with, 196; information sources on, 264. *See also* Dairy products

Sherman Antitrust Act, 33, 34

Shield, federal grading, 41

Shortages, food, 242-244

Shrimp: dishonesty with, 198; information sources on, 267-268. *See also* Fish; Seafood; Shellfish

Silent Spring (Carson), 23

Sinclair, Upton, 35

Skimming (market), 19

Slacking out, 197, 198

Small Business Administration, 44

Smith, Adam, 30

Soul food, 6

Soups: condensed (table), 316-318; ready-to-serve (table), 318; servings per container of (table), 302

Southern cooking, 6

Soy proteins, 260

Soyer, 5

Specialty restaurants, 220-221

Specifications, 71-72, 105-114, 124, 125; in bids, 89; and computers, 218; controller's departments and, 168; guidebooks for, 253, 260; information in, 107-112, 120-123, 260; for legal defense, 100, 104, 209; on purchase order, 102; receiving department and, 130, 131; with speculative buying,

103; testing committee and, 67, 71, 74, 106-107, 113, 114, 168, 209; and world food supply, 250-251

Specificity of tasks, 31

Speculative buying, 102-103

Spices: information sources on, 269-270; in storerooms, 164-165

Spot checks, 140, 171, 172, 187

Stamps: buyers', 94-95; inspection, 37, 41; pricing, 162; receiving, 132-136, 168-169; in storeroom, 162, 164, 169

Standard operating procedures (SOP), questionable, 195

Standards: of fill, 42; identity, 41-42; information sources on, 108-109, 114, 254-255, 257-258, 271-273, 288-292; microbiological, 46; for quality, 20-21, 37, 39-40, 41, 230, 253, 257-258; for specifications, 106-112, 114; weight and measure, 44-45; and world food supply, 219-220. *See also* Grading; Laws

Standing orders, 92-93

Staples: amounts for 50 servings of (table), 285-287; lists of, 71-72

Steam equipment, 238-239

Steward duties, 5, 12

Stokely-Van Camp Corporation, 20-21

Storage: areas for, 152-155, 156-158; costs of, 22, 103, 158; and shortages, 242; and specifications, 112-113; and supply, 22-25, 73; time limits for, 155-156

Store-at-first-point-of-use concept, 30-31

Storeroom management, 72, 145-166; computers for, 215, 218, 219; controls for, 143, 144, 145, 160-162, 165, 169-171, 218, 219; and purchasing department, 144

Strikes, 98, 231

Supermarket pricing stamps, 162

Supermarkets, 9, 16-17, 76-77

Suppliers. *See* Purveyors

Supplies: crop, 39, 243-244, 249-250; market, 21-22, 65, 73-75, 94, 143; single-service, 221

Syrup, maple, Canadian grading of, 329

Talent scouts, 63

Tea Inspection Act, 42

Teas, information sources on, 274-275. *See also* Beverages

Telephone buying, 75, 82, 95-96

Telephones, invention of, 9

Temperatures, storeroom, 155, 157

Tertiary markets, 16

Test marketing, 18-19

Testing committees, 114-124; food buyer and, 112; specifications approved by, 67, 71, 74, 106-107, 113, 114, 168, 209; and supplier selection, 74

Texturized vegetable protein (TVP), 30

Thawing units, 237

Thievery. *See* Honesty

Time locks, for storerooms, 160

Time savings, with convenience foods, 230, 232

Tomato varieties, 111. *See also* Vegetables

Trade associations, 19-20

Trade puffing, 19, 100

Training: of backup persons, 62; of buyer, 65, 68; of receiving clerk, 130; for use of convenience foods, 231-232

Transfer of ownership, 18, 27

Transportation: and auction buying, 92; and government regulation, 11; and supply, 21-22, 65; and travel increase, 6-9. *See also* Deliveries

Trash, storage and disposal of, 158

Tremont House, 8

Trim, specifications for, 110

Truck hucksters, 27

Trucks, storeroom, 149

Truth-in-menu laws, 220, 228

Tuna: in food chain, 26-27; imported, 244; information sources on, 265, 268. *See also* Fish; Seafood

Turkey: amounts for 50 servings of (table), 282; information sources on, 260-261; specifications on, 111. *See also* Poultry

Turnover: of food buyers, 66; inventory, 25
TVP. *See* Texturized vegetable protein
Tydings-Miller Act, 34

Ultimate consumers, 19
Uniforms, for storeroom personnel, 152
Unions: and convenience foods, 231; and dishonesty, 208; and supply, 65
Unit specifications, 109-110
United Nations, 246-249
United States: food history of, 5-8; and world food supply, 249-250. *See also* Laws; Regulations, government
United States Congress, 23
United States Department of Agriculture (USDA): and dairy products, 37, 262-263, 264, 290-291; and frozen foods, 11, 258, 272, 291, 292; inspections by, 21, 35, 37-42, 140-141, 257; market reports of, 16, 18, 82; and meats, 35, 109, 114, 140-141, 257-259, 288-289; on nuts, 269; and poultry, 260-262, 289; and produce, 21, 37, 41-42, 271-273, 291, 292; on seasonings, 269; standards published by, 108-109, 114, 254-255, 257-258, 261, 271-273, 288-292; trade regulation by, 42; yearbook of, 45
United States Department of Commerce (USDC), 36, 265, 266, 267
United States Department of Health, Education, and Welfare (HEW), 43, 264
United States Department of Labor, 43, 44
United States District Court, 44
United States Public Health Service (USPHS), 40-41, 45, 46
United States Quartermaster Corps, 46
United States Supreme Court, 203-204
United States Treasury Department, 44
Universal Product Code (UPC), 216-219
University of Massachusetts, 158, 261, 262
Upgrading, 195-203
Urner Barry market report, 82, 256

USDA. *See* United States Department of Agriculture
USDC. *See* United States Department of Commerce
USPHS. *See* United States Public Health Service
Utility, time and place, 27, 28

Valuable food, storage, 159-160
Value analyses, 227-228
Vatel, 4
Veal: amounts for 50 servings of (table), 281; dishonesty with, 200; portion and yield factors for (table), 278; standards for grading (table), 288. *See also* Meats
Vegetables: in American colonies, 7; Canadian grading of, 327-328; in future, 220; information sources on, 271-273; inspection of, 37, 41-42; preparation areas for, 157-158; quantities to purchase of (table), 294-296; servings of (tables), 283-284, 301, 307-308; specifications for, 110, 111; standards for grading (table), 292; storage of, 23-24
Ventilation, storeroom, 159
Vestibules, storeroom, 157

Wagon jobbers, 30
Walls, storeroom, 158-159
Warehouse Act, U.S., 42
Water for crops, 244, 247-248
Weather, and food shortages, 244
Weights: dishonesty with, 201; in specifications, 109, 110; standards for, 44-45
Wheat, information sources on, 268
Wheeling-Lea Act, 34
Whiskeys: bonding of, 22; information on, 276
Wholesalers, 16, 25-26, 30-31, 73-74, 95. *See also* Purveyors
Wholesome Meat Act, 35
Wholesome Poultry Products Act, 35